HANDBOOK OF EMPLOYMENT AND SOCIETY

T0313821

Handbook of Employment and Society

Working Space

Edited by

Susan McGrath-Champ

Associate Professor in Work and Organisational Studies, Business School, University of Sydney, Australia

Andrew Herod

Distinguished Research Professor of Geography and Adjunct Professor of International Affairs and of Anthropology, University of Georgia, Athens, GA. He is also an elected official, serving as a member of the government of Athens-Clarke County, Georgia, USA

Al Rainnie

Professor, Graduate School of Business, Curtin University, Western Australia, and formerly at the Centre for Labour Market Studies, University of Leicester, UK

Edward Elgar

Cheltenham, UK • Northampton, MA, USA

Published by
Edward Elgar Publishing Limited
The Lypiatts
15 Lansdown Road
Cheltenham
Glos GL50 2JA
UK

Edward Elgar Publishing, Inc.
William Pratt House
9 Dewey Court
Northampton
Massachusetts 01060
USA

Paperback edition 2011

A catalogue record for this book
is available from the British Library

Library of Congress Control Number: 2009937895

ISBN 978 1 84720 054 9 (cased)
ISBN 978 0 85793 583 0 (paperback)

Typeset by Servis Filmsetting Ltd, Stockport, Cheshire
Printed and bound by MPG Books Group, UK

Contents

v

Figures

Tables and boxes

Contributors

Jeremy Anderson, Head of Strategic Research, International Transport Workers' Federation, and Queen Mary, University of London, UK.

Peter Bain (1941–2007), formerly Senior Lecturer, Department of Human Resource Management, University of Strathclyde, UK.

Chris Baldry, Professor, Institute for Socio-Management, Stirling Management School, University of Stirling, UK.

Christian Berndt, Professor, Department of Human Geography, University of Frankfurt, Germany.

Andries Bezuidenhout, Senior Researcher, Society, Work and Development Institute, University of the Witwatersrand, South Africa.

Noel Castree, Professor, Geography Discipline, School of Environment and Development, Manchester University, UK.

Enrique de la Garza Toledo, Professor, Department of Sociology, Universidad Autónoma Metropolitana, Mexico.

Bradon Ellem, Associate Professor, Work and Organisational Studies, University of Sydney, Australia.

Ian Fitzgerald, Research Associate, School of the Built Environment, Northumbria University, UK.

Michael Gillan, Lecturer, Business School, University of Western Australia, Australia.

Paula Hamilton, Dockers' Assistant Secretary, and Queen Mary, University of London, UK.

Andrew Herod, Professor, Department of Geography, University of Georgia, USA.

Bob Jessop, Distinguished Professor, Department of Sociology, Lancaster University, UK.

Philip F. Kelly, Associate Professor, Department of Geography, York University, Canada.

Rob Lambert, Professor, Business School, University of Western Australia, Australia.

Eric Lee, Founding Editor of LabourStart (a global trade union news and campaigning website).

Susan McGrath-Champ, Associate Professor, Work and Organisational Studies, University of Sydney, Australia.

Robina Mohammad, Research Fellow, Department of Geography, University of Reading, UK.

Ronaldo Munck, Professor, Internationalisation and Social Development, President's Office, Dublin City University, Ireland.

Kathryn J. Oberdeck, Associate Professor, Department of History, University of Illinois at Urbana-Champaign, USA.

Jamie Peck, Professor, Canada Research Chair in Urban and Regional Political Economy, University of British Columbia, Canada.

John Pickles, Distinguished Professor, Department of Geography, University of North Carolina at Chapel Hill, USA.

Ngai Pun, Associate Professor, China Social Work Research Centre, Peking University-Hong Kong Polytechnic University, Hong Kong.

Al Rainnie, Professor, Graduate School of Business, Curtin University, Western Australia, and formerly Centre for Labour Market Studies, University of Leicester, UK.

Michael Samers, Associate Professor, Department of Geography, University of Kentucky, USA.

Adrian Smith, Professor, Department of Geography, Queen Mary, University of London, UK.

Chris Smith, Professor, School of Management, Royal Holloway, University of London, UK.

Alison Stenning, Reader, School of Geography, Politics and Sociology, Newcastle University, UK.

John Stirling, Head, Division of Sociology and Criminology, Northumbria University, UK.

Phil Taylor, Professor, Strathclyde Business School, University of Strathclyde, UK.

Nik Theodore, Associate Professor and Director, Centre for Urban Economic Development, University of Illinois at Chicago, USA.

Peter Turnbull, Professor, Cardiff Business School, Cardiff University, UK.

Peter Waterman, formerly at the Institute of Social Studies, The Hague, Netherlands.

Edward Webster, Professor Emeritus, Society, Work and Development Institute, University of the Witwatersrand, South Africa.

Jane Wills, Professor, Department of Geography, Queen Mary, University of London, UK.

Matthew Zook, Associate Professor, Department of Geography, University of Kentucky, USA.

1 Foundations

Andrew Herod, Susan McGrath-Champ and Al Rainnie

The origins of this book lie in a workshop held by the Department of Work and Organisational Studies at the University of Sydney in 2001. Amongst other things, the workshop was designed to encourage greater engagement on the part of scholars of work and employment with some of the developments that had been taking place within the geographical literature in the previous two decades or so, concerning theorising about how social actors' lives are deeply geographically structured and what that means for how we understand their behaviour. The perceived need for the workshop emerged out of the fact that whilst there had been exceptions, it seemed to the organisers that theoretical advances in conceptualising the role of space in structuring how capitalism works had largely bypassed much of the standard study of work and employment, a bypassing exemplified by a number of key texts then extant in the literature.[1] The workshop represented, in effect, an effort to promote adoption of a spatial sensitivity and awareness that had largely been lacking in much of the mainstream literature concerned with industrial relations, workers, work and employment. Consequently, in the spirit of encouraging interdisciplinary conversation, the workshop's Keynote Address was given by geographer Jamie Peck, who had recently published what has since become one of the foundational texts seeking to spatialise labour market theory (Peck, 1996). For her part, Susan co-convened and presented a paper at the workshop whilst Al, recently arrived in Australia from the UK, acted as discussant on a number of the papers, several of which were subsequently published in a special edition of the Australian journal *Labour and Industry* in 2002, in which Andy, who had been arguing the case for some years that students of labour, work and employment needed to take place and space seriously, was subsequently invited to contribute a review article.

Looking back, we find it somewhat ironic that at the time of the workshop there had been relatively little crossover between scholars interested in matters of space and geography and those interested in issues of work and employment, given how our own work lives and those of many others who focus on such matters speak to the issues concerning 'work and space'. Certainly, for both Andy and Al as Brits living and working in the US and Australia respectively, the question of the geographical mobility of labour in a globalising world was very close to home. So, too, for Susan, a geographer from Western Australia who had been trained partly in Canada yet who was working in the Department of Work and Organisational Studies at the University of Sydney. In terms of our own positionality, although as a geographer Andy had been seeking for several years to engage with scholars of labour and industrial relations effectively from the outside, and Susan, with a heightened sense of place and space due to her disciplinary background yet employed in a department focusing upon work and employment studies, had sought to engage over matters of geography and space with colleagues effectively from within the disciplinary boundary, it was perhaps Al who most accurately reflected the majority position at the time within studies of labour, work and employment, having just begun to realise that this debate was important but not as yet having found the intellectual arsenal necessary to fully engage with it. If Al could have been taken at that time as fairly emblematic of many scholars of work and employment, it is fair to say that on the geographical side many writers, whilst they had a highly developed sense of spatial theory, had engaged little with the rich literature on work, employment, labour history and industrial relations. The result of such disciplinary non-interaction was that, despite attempts by geographers like Jane Wills, Jamie Peck and Don Mitchell and labour scholars such as Bradon Ellem and John Shields (together with, we would like to think, our own efforts) to theorise matters of work and employment from a specifically spatial point of view, in the early part of the new century the engagement between geography and industrial relations was an engagement still largely waiting to happen (Herod et al., 2003, p. 176).

However, writing a scant few years later, the three of us would argue (Herod et al., 2007; Rainnie et al., 2007) that issues of spatiality (by which we mean how social life is organised geographically) appeared now to be squarely 'on' the intellectual agenda within contemporary studies of workers, work and employment. (This and our other two introductory chapters draw upon these 2007 articles in *Work, Employment and Society* and *Industrial Relations Journal*.) Indeed, the commitment of a publisher to publish this current volume of essays addressing the intersection of spatiality and work life, essays written by geographers and by scholars of labour, work and employment, suggests that perhaps a kind of intellectual event horizon may have been crossed. Of course, some might point to the long tradition of comparative research in a slew of disciplines and question whether issues of space were ever really 'off' the intellectual agenda – after all, it is the geographical similarities and differences between conditions and processes in assorted places which give meaning to any form of comparative research. However, what is different about the contemporary '(re)assertion of space in critical social theory' (Soja, 1989) is that it is marked by a very much deeper interrogation of the role of space in structuring social life and how this geographical structuring can enable and/or constrain economic and political praxis. Such interrogations, then, do not merely seek to understand how economic and political processes play out *across* space – a rather naive 'geography is important because everywhere is different' approach. Rather, recent conceptual developments have argued for a more profound appreciation of issues of geography wherein the economic landscape is conceived of not simply as a reflection of the social relations of life or as a passive 'stage' upon which such relations play out but, instead, as *constitutive* of social praxis, as something with which social actors such as workers, unions, employers and the state must actively engage. Such developments, in the words of Doreen Massey (1984a, p. 4), argue that spatial patterns are 'not just an outcome [of social relations but are] part of the explanation' thereof.

From distinctions between space and place (with the former seen as a somewhat abstract product of social forces whilst the latter is used to refer to particular locales within a landscape which are imbued with historical meaning (Taylor, 1999)) to ideas such as the 'spatial division of labour' (how the social division of labour is articulated geographically (Massey, 1984b)) through analyses of how labour markets are geographically structured (Peck, 1996) to the idea that social actors' spatial embeddedness and 'locality dependence' (Cox and Mair, 1988) shape their economic and political praxis in important ways, a vibrant conceptualisation has sought to spatialise the study of work, employment and resistance. Much of this effort has been conducted by economic geographers working within the field of 'labour geography' (Herod, 2001), though such geographers themselves have drawn on a longer tradition within critical geography that contends that space is a constitutive element in how capitalism operates. This idea has perhaps been most forcibly explored by David Harvey in his 1982 book *The Limits to Capital*, wherein he argued that the dynamics of capitalism as a mode of production are predicated on the production and reproduction of a differentiated yet integrated space-economy (see Gregory, 2006, p. 8). Indeed, for Harvey, one of the limits to Marx's work was his failure to more explicitly develop a historical *geographical* materialist understanding of capitalism. The vital importance of Harvey's intervention, then, as Callinicos (2006, p. 49) points out, is that his upgrading of Marx's historical materialism does not consist of a simple addition of independently formed concepts intended to specify social spatiality. It is not, in other words, an additive approach to understanding capitalism, in which we should simply add space as yet another 'factor' to the intellectual mix and then stir vigorously. Rather, Harvey starts from basic analytical principles to develop an investigation of capitalism that sees the geographically uneven economic landscapes it produces as central to – instead of as tangential to – the accumulation process.

Although the engagement with space has been slow – the recent *Oxford Handbook of Work and Organization* (Ackroyd et al., 2005), for instance, exhibits the same blindspots to space and spatiality as did many older texts – all is not forlorn, however, as there have been major studies by, amongst others, Doreen Massey (1984a and b; 1999), Jamie Peck (1996) and Ray Hudson (2001) which have each sought to infuse studies of work, employment, gender and resistance with insights from geography. More recently there have been articles in, amongst other outlets, *Work, Employment and Society* (Herod et al., 2007; Ward, 2007), special editions of *Economic and Industrial Democracy (2005)* and *International Labor and Working-Class History* (2003), together with the previously mentioned *Labour and Industry*, and an important book from Noel Castree and colleagues (Castree et al., 2004) that have attempted to take the engagement further. We ourselves have made a couple of attempts to argue for a more spatially sensitive approach to studying workers, work and employment, with one attempt being more theoretically orientated (Herod et al., 2007) whilst the other sought to demonstrate how some commentators have held within their analysis, apparently unwittingly in some cases, the very approach that we are advocating (Rainnie et al., 2007).

The book
Given that there does appear to be the beginnings of a greater cross-pollination between insights drawn from geography and those drawn from labour studies, industrial relations and work and employment studies, the time appears ripe, we think, for the present volume, one which we hope will both outline where the literature has been, but more importantly, provide a catalyst for the growth of a branch of analysis with much firmer and deeper roots. It is to reflect the multifaceted nature of this debate on work, place and space that we have adopted the sub-title 'Working space'. The ambiguity and versatility of the meaning of these two words when conjoined is quite intentional. We are not simply playing a rather obvious game with words, for, as we hope the essays in this volume make clear, where people work, and the geographical relationships within which they do so, has an intimate relationship with the work that they actually do, as does the ordering of people's lives beyond the workplace. Every working space is a work in progress, a place

of ebbs and flows, absences and presences, power, control and resistance and a node in wider sets of economic and political relationships that have their own specific spatialities, even if those spatialities may, on occasion, be somewhat ephemeral. Thus, if the global economic crisis that began in 2008 teaches us anything, it is that the apparently footloose and hyper-mobile financial capital that is often viewed as leading the charge towards a world in which physical location is no longer important is, actually, far more grounded than many analysts would have had us believe before the crisis began. Further, the rapidity with which the infection spread worldwide, together with its differential impact, highlighted simultaneously the global economy's interconnectedness but also how it is differentially developed, with the crisis spreading to particular parts of the planet before impacting on others. Moreover, the rise and fall of various regional economies based upon the relative overvaluing and subsequent dramatic devaluing of housing stocks has reminded us quite forcefully that uneven development is a dynamic and ever-changing mosaic that lies at the heart of global capitalism, one that people experience and react to in the places where they live and work.

The purpose of the book, then, is to further deepen and extend the engagement between research concerned with work and employment in the widest sense, and some of the basic concepts dealing broadly with the politics of place that human geographers (in the main) have developed in recent years. In planning the book we set out quite deliberately to invite contributions from researchers who, between them, could cover the depth and spread of issues in work and employment. Consequently, we invited contributions from scholars around the world who have been concerned with the questions that arise at the intersection of the worlds of production, reproduction and consumption. Crucially, however, we chose contributors who we believed already, to a greater or lesser degree, had taken up the basic argument we were trying to put forward. So as to make this as much of a two-way intellectual engagement as possible, we deliberately sought authors based both in geography and non-geography academic disciplines, producing a final mix of 14 of the former and 22 of the latter (including history, sociology, labour studies/industrial relations and management/organisational studies).

In terms of the book's layout, the present chapter has four more sections in which we outline a number of concepts, specifically those of the *socio-spatial dialectic*, the *spatial fix*, the *politics of place* and the increasingly contested notion of *geographical scale*. After that is Part 1, 'Work, Space and the State', containing chapters by Bob Jessop and Peter Turnbull which, in the process of addressing issues to do with the state and labour organisation, raise many of the issues that will re-emerge as the book progresses. The remainder of the book is divided into two further major parts and an Afterword. Part 2, 'Working Spaces', deals with workers as objects rather than subjects in socio-spatial relations. This part is divided into two sub-sections: 'Regionalisation, Globalisation and Labour' and 'Building Space'. Part 3 concentrates more overtly on questions of accommodation and resistance, under the title 'Workers in Space'. The part then divides into two sub-sections: 'Labour Institutions in Space and Place' and 'Organising in Space and Place'. Rather than attempting to provide a detailed prologue to issues raised in Parts 2 and 3 in this introduction, we provide an introductory chapter and overview at the beginning of each of them.

Finally, Noel Castree contributes an Afterword in which he reviews the origins of the debate upon which we have been focusing, addressing both how it has developed but, more importantly, some of the gaps and oversights that remain in the literature and where we might go from here.

Why worry about space and place?
When seeking to understand work and employment (W&E) practices, why should we worry about space and place? Perhaps we can begin to answer this question by considering one very simple example, namely the debate over globalisation. Specifically, many of the triumphalist neoliberal claims about processes of globalisation articulated by people such as Kenichi Ohmae (1990; 2005) – and not a few of the fears expressed by left-wing fatalists – rest upon a number of particular claims about geography. First, they assume that capital, as a totality, is inherently more geographically mobile than is labour, as a totality, and that, consequently, the best thing workers can do is to get on the globalisation train to make 'their' communities more attractive to mobile capital vis-à-vis others with whom they are in competition for investment (for example, see Kanter, 1995; Bryan and Farrell, 1996). In this formulation, capital is viewed as capable of transcending space, whilst labour is necessarily confined to place, a confinement which will encourage workers to be quiescent if they hope to secure their economic futures through drawing mobile capital to their community. Second, and relatedly, such a formulation assumes that globalisation is heralding 'the death of distance' (Cairncross, 2001) and leading us towards a 'borderless world' in which 'nothing is overseas any longer' (Ohmae, 1990, p. viii) and the 'world is flat' (Friedman, 2006). In such a world, so the argument goes, the 'friction of distance' (that is, the 'dragging' effect that crossing space has on degrees of interaction between social actors) and geographical location are no longer important – if corporations can ship commodities from one part of the world to any other in little more than 24 or 48 hours, then where they choose to locate production facilities makes little difference (Herod, 2000).

However, not only does this simple example highlight the geographical conundrums associated with theorising a process such as globalisation where, in the same neoliberal account, geography both explains everything (capital's spatial mobility allows it to play workers against each other, whereas labour's immobility encourages quiescence) and yet is seen as completely irrelevant (firms can choose to locate their production pretty much anywhere and still serve a global market), but it also points the way to how a more geographically sensitive approach can reveal important lacunae in such theorising. Thus, understanding how certain segments of capital – public utilities, large industrial plants, mortgage companies who are dependent upon realising loans made in particular places – have significant sunk costs which prevent their ready relocation to greener pastures shows us that place, and being spatially trapped in particular localities, clearly matters not just for workers but also for such forms of capital. Indeed, it is the case that many capitalists are just as fixed in place as are workers (and some are more so, if we consider that workers may migrate elsewhere), such that their spatial immobility encourages them to engage in the kinds of boosterist politics identified by Molotch (1976) thirty years ago as a way to ensure the economic vitality of the communities within which they are located and, thus, their own economic survival.

Equally, as globalisation breaks down spatial barriers of distance *à la* Ohmae, many communities, workers and capitalists are finding themselves competing with those across the globe, such that small differences in the quality of labour on offer (its price, its skill levels, its quiescence) in myriad locations across the planet and the degree of local state supplication take on signal importance. Thus, as globalisation means that mobile capital is increasingly able to roam planetarily for the best investment opportunities, where such capital does in fact choose to locate often hinges upon almost imperceptible differences in conditions between places. The result is that rather than location becoming increasingly irrelevant for mobile capital in a shrinking globe, paradoxically the specificities of place actually become ever more important as globalisation unfolds.

Whatever else it may be, then, globalisation is clearly a geographical process which is transforming the social and spatial relationships between actors located in different parts of the globe. Such transformations suggest that a spatial sensibility can provide important insights into the reworking of W&E relations as various segments of capital and labour come into conflict and/or cooperation as they pursue their interests in particular places. However, as we have already hinted, whereas the exploration of how the changing geography of capitalism structures and is structured by W&E relations is well developed within economic geography, conceptual developments concerning how geography plays a constitutive role in W&E practices have largely passed much W&E research by for three interrelated reasons. These are: i) there has been a tendency in much research on W&E to conceive of economic actors as 'contained' within particular spatial units which are viewed as discrete social and geographical entities; ii) there has been a tendency to view 'geography' as little more than a complicating contextual 'factor'; and iii) much work has conceived of W&E practices as unfolding upon an empty spatial stage called 'place' without evaluating how that stage is itself constructed and how it plays a constitutive role in shaping W&E practices. Put another way, such theorisation has viewed space and place undialectically, with the spatiality of capitalism simply being viewed as the geographical reflections of its social relations (Burgess, 2001).

Locating space and place

How, then, are we to theorise space, place and locality? Ellem and Shields (1999) suggest that the following five issues need to be acknowledged:

1. whilst social relations and processes are constructed over space, space is not a given but is constructed in different ways by different actors;
2. there are tensions between different concepts and constructions of place and space;
3. the scope of any analysis of W&E relations has to move beyond the workplace to include issues of labour reproduction and consumption;
4. labour markets are regulated in place-specific ways;
5. local labour markets are the focal point for the organisation and reproduction of labour.

As a way of providing some greater theoretical heft to these assertions, here we will explore some of the debates over what geographers call 'the production of space' and the 'production of geographical scale', for both are important elements in how W&E practices are structured. Specifically, we will explore the idea of the '*socio-spatial dialectic*', the '*spatial fix*', the '*politics of place*', and the production and discursive representation of '*geographical scale*', amongst others. These concepts take us away from the view that space is merely a reflection of social relations and towards one in which space is understood to be constitutive thereof and in which different discursive representations of space and scale can have significant political and theoretical implications.

On the making of the geography of capitalism
The belief that the spatial relations of social life are important to theorise is deeply inter-twined with the notion of the *'production of space'*, by which is meant how economic and social landscapes are actively struggled over. Central to this idea is the concept of the *'socio-spatial dialectic'* (Soja, 1989), which views spatial relations and social relations as mutually constitutive, such that spatiality is both a material product of social relations and a shaper of them. This approach to understanding the operation of capitalism has been most fleshed out by a number of Marxist geographers. Of particular importance in this regard is David Harvey, who has done much to develop the idea of what he calls the *'spatial fix'*. For Harvey (1982), the key to understanding how capitalism operates is to recognise that, in order for accumulation to proceed, the economic landscape must be structured in particular ways – as a landscape of profitability rather than unprofitability, for instance. This necessitates capitalists ensuring – either individually or collectively – that they have workers on hand who can access a particular workplace, that raw materials can reach factories, that finished commodities can reach consumers and that information and capital can flow to where they are needed. All of these considerations require a certain spatial arrangement of investments in plant, infrastructure and the built environment more generally – what Harvey calls the 'spatial fix'. In pointing out that the geography of capitalism has taken on particular appearances at different historical moments, Harvey has argued (1982, pp. 416–17), then, that 'the territorial and regional coherence that . . . is at least partially discernible within capitalism is actively produced rather than passively received as a concession to "nature" or "history"'. At the same time, though, the way in which the landscape is structured materially shapes how social relations unfold – hence the relocation of jobs from one place to another will impact workplace politics greatly, for instance.

A significant insight provided by Harvey, particularly given the triumphalist 'end of geography' rhetoric coming from neoliberal globalisers, is the proposition that even the most footloose capital can never be entirely free of spatial constraints or considerations because capitalists must always negotiate two contradictory spatial tendencies – the need for sufficient geographical mobility to be able to seek out investment opportunities in new locations, and the need for sufficient geographical fixity so that accumulation may occur. This tension results from the fact that, as Marx pointed out, capital can only ever be in one of two states during the circulation process – motion or fixity – and it can never remain permanently in either state if self-expansion is to occur. Whilst for his part Marx was keen to explore the accumulation process as a temporal one – analysing how money capital was transformed into commodity capital and back again in the course of circulation – Harvey argues that because capital and commodities exist in space as well as in time, fixity in time also implies fixity in space, whilst motion through time usually implies motion through space. Put another way, even the most flighty of capital must come to ground at some point, since for all of their innovative capacities capitalists have not yet found, at least to our knowledge, an ethereal way of accumulating capital. Thus, the trillions of dollars which circle the planet daily can never entirely escape the draw of space, for they must flow from place to place through particular sets of infrastructures (roads, railways, fibre-optic networks, satellite connections and the like). All of these infrastructures have specific spatialities to them, and must, at some point, come to rest in the stock markets and other corners of the global financial system to be managed by brokers and analysts who themselves are fixed in place and who rely upon local business networks within which they are spatially and socially imbricated.

There is, however, a paradox in all this, namely that, as time passes and as new modes of production organisation or commodity distribution come into being, capitalists may find themselves increasingly constrained by the very economic landscapes which previously facilitated accumulation – as when new forms of transportation technology (like the internal combustion engine) require new spatial infrastructures (namely, roads) as they replace older forms (such as railways) and the spatial infrastructures (train tracks) around which the built environment had previously been structured. To escape the constraints of the spatial fixity that was appropriate at one historical moment but may no longer be so, then, capital must construct new forms of the built environment – in this case, a built environment constructed around the internal combustion engine rather than the railroad. The result is that, as Harvey (1978, p. 124) puts it, capital must build 'a physical landscape appropriate to its own condition at a particular moment in time, only to have to destroy it, usually in the course of a crisis, at a subsequent point in time'. The paradox, therefore, is twofold: not only are the spatial configurations which are appropriate at one historical moment not necessarily appropriate at another, but in its effort to escape such spatial configurations capital must create other, different spatial arrangements. Not only, then, is there a dialectic between space and social relations, but there is also one between the past and the present – the landscapes of the past shape how those of the present are made, even as the creation of these new landscapes gradually erases those of the past.

Although Harvey (1978, p. 124) has focused primarily on how 'capital represents itself in the form of a physical landscape created in its own image', this approach has been critiqued for forgetting that workers also seek to shape the landscape in ways they see as beneficial (Herod, 2001). For example, whilst industrialists may wish to relocate to suburban locations, central city workers may prefer that factories remain in urban areas because they are physically unable to access suburban sites. All of this shows that capital and labour can have quite different visions for how they would like to see the economic landscape evolve. Equally, it suggests that different segments within the categories of 'capital' and 'labour' may have quite different visions for the future development of the economic landscape – fearing that labour scarcities may drive up wages, suburban capitalists may not want urban firms to relocate, whilst one group of workers' (central city) loss may be another's (suburban) gain. The point, then, is that different groups of social actors may prefer to see quite different economic landscapes put in place, such that much of the political and economic conflict between them revolves around the matters of whose preferred spatial fix will be implemented and how this will, in turn, be challenged by those with competing visions.

The politics of place

'Place' has typically been conceived of in rather unproblematic terms, simply as the spot in which the W&E action occurs. However, as Agnew (1987) has argued, the term 'place' can be seen to incorporate three related aspects of locality: place as *location* (a distinct point on the Earth's surface), place as *locale* (a physical arena for everyday life) and place as a *locus of identity* (a focus for personal and collective loyalty, affect and commitment). These each have different implications for understanding W&E practices. Thus, a locality's absolute location on the Earth's surface determines the judicial framework within which its inhabitants must operate – communities in South Wales and those in New South Wales must structure their W&E practices according to quite different legal systems, for instance. At the same time, its location relative to other communities will have dramatic implications for political and economic praxis in ways that are not understandable unless one appreciates how the locality fits within a broader socio-spatial organisational schema – is this locality a branch plant community or a centre of R&D, and how 'close' in organisational space is it to the centres of corporate power? Equally, 'place' serves as a physical milieu within which everyday life is played out, one whose boundaries are constantly made and remade by that everyday life – residents' growing reliance upon commodities produced overseas, for instance, will extend a place's economic 'footprint' spatially far beyond its jurisdictionally defined territorial limits. Finally, 'place' can serve as a focal point of emotional attachment, such that what geographers call 'topophilia' ('love of place') can have significant bearing upon how workers or capitalists feel about 'their' places, an allegiance which ties into notions of territoriality and the defence thereof.

This multifaceted nature of 'place' is important to engage with conceptually because it highlights that places' characteristics – what gives them their 'uniqueness', such that Paris, France, is different from Paris, Texas – are derived both from their own internal characteristics and histories and from their dialectical relationships with other places, which may be spatially proximate or spatially quite distant. Thus, as Massey (1999, p. 22, emphasis in original) has put it,

> 'places' may be imagined as particular articulations of . . . social relations, including local relations 'within' the place and those many connections which stretch way beyond it. And all of these embedded in complex, layered, histories. This is place as open, porous, hybrid – this is *place as meeting place* . . . This is a notion of place where specificity (local uniqueness, a sense of place) derives not from some mythical internal roots nor from a history of relative isolation – now to be disrupted by globalisation – but precisely from the absolute particularity of the mixture of influences found together there.

What is significant in all this, then, is that whilst places seem to express a certain uniqueness, this uniqueness is theorisable, traceable to broader social processes such as the circulation of capital, a place's location within a broader spatial division of labour, the articulation of class (and other) conflicts within particular places and so forth. This recognition is important because it forces us to acknowledge that places are not simply idiosyncratic 'boxes' or 'arenas' for social life but are continually reconstituted by the social relations within which they are located and, in turn, constantly shape how such social relations play out as a result of such places' historical 'geographical path-dependence' – that is to say, how what has happened in that place in the past shapes its future characteristics and possibilities.

Such efforts to theorise 'place' in a more sophisticated manner are crucial for understanding W&E practices, we contend, for the places which are constituted by and through the factories, offices, fields or homes in which workers toil and which are themselves set within the broader system of cities, regions and national territories are far more than simply a space in which to work for a wage (or not, in the case of unpaid domestic labour). Rather, they are a 'continuously fashioned mélange of meanings, values, and relationships that are effected by shared and ongoing social practices [which] construct, sustain, and transform the context in which economic, social, and political life is produced and reproduced on a daily basis and into which new members are socialized' (Hudson, 2001, p. 267).

The result of all this, Castree et al. (2004) suggest, is that because people, institutions and things come together in unique (though, again, not untheorisable) ways in different locations, social relationships, regulations and institutions have a high degree of local 'stickiness' and actors are necessarily geographically embedded to greater or lesser degrees in the long-standing structures and relationships of place, an embeddedness which shapes their social praxis. Hence, as Storper and Walker (1989, 157) put it, the day-to-day immobility of both labour and capital, itself the result variously of their embeddedness in local employment relations, kinship ties, market relationships, the spatial drag of sunk investment and the like, 'gives an irreducible role to place-bound homes and communities' in how they interact and behave. The fact that it

> takes time and spatial propinquity for the central institutions of daily life – family, church, clubs, schools, sports teams, union locals, etc. – to take shape [and that, once established,] these outlive individual participants to benefit, and be sustained by, generations of workers [means that there] is a fabric of distinctive, lasting local communities and cultures woven into the landscape of labor [and capital] (Storper and Walker, 1989, p. 157).

Given the dialectical nature of the relationship between social and spatial relations (Soja, 1989), this 'distinctive fabric' both shapes the activities of labour and capital on an ongoing basis and continues to be shaped by them.

To draw back, then, this understanding of place is important because such particularities mean that labour markets operate in different ways in different places, such that relationships of supply and demand which 'work' in one place may not in another (Peck, 1996). Moreover, the fact that both workers and capitalists are anchored geographically not only in the labour market but also in the household, the community and the state – all of which have particular spatial forms and geographical relationships to each other – means that the labour supply is both socially and spatially regulated, a fact which distinctively shapes W&E practices.

The production and representation of geographical scale
Recently, economic life has been seen to have experienced a dramatic rescaling, whether this is through processes of 'globalisation', 'localisation', 'glocalisation', 'decentralisation' and/or 'recentralisation'. The issue of the scalar restructuring and reordering of W&E practices is implicitly a geographical one. However, whereas much writing has theorised such rescaling in rather naive terms – seeing spatial scales such as 'the local' or 'the national' as little more than pre-existing and/or fixed levels between which actors shuffle or 'jump' – the concept of geographical scale is not nearly so simple (Herod and Wright, 2002). Although there are several matters of significance in this regard, space constraints mean we can only focus upon arguably the two most important, those relating to what geographers and others have called the 'politics of the production of scale', and how the relationships between different scales are represented discursively.

Producing scale

A lively body of literature has developed within economic geography which seeks to problematise the question of spatial scale. Whereas some authors had historically tended towards a view of scales such as 'the local', 'the regional', 'the national', and 'the global' as somehow natural geographical 'containers' of particular social practices ('process A occurs at the national level whereas process B occurs at the global level'), others have argued that scales are little more than mental fictions for imposing order onto the landscape – 'subjective artistic devices . . . shaped to fit the hand of the individual user' (Hart, 1982, p. 121). In the mid-1980s, however, authors drawing upon Marxist theory began to explore how such geographical scales are socially produced, rather than simply given or imagined. Thus, Taylor (1981, 1982) contended that particular scales served specific roles within the development of capitalism: the 'global scale' was the 'scale of reality', the scale at which capitalism is organised; the 'urban scale' served as the 'scale of experience', the arena in which everyday life is conducted; and the 'national scale' is the 'scale of ideology', the scale at which the capitalist class promulgates ideologies of nationalism which divide workers. At about the same time, Smith ([1984] 1990) laid out a case for considering geographical scales as being produced out of the internal structure of capital. Accordingly, he saw the 'urban scale' as defined by the spatial coherence of local labour markets, the 'regional scale' as delineated by the particular territorial divisions of labour (here a steel-making region, there a wool-producing one), the 'national scale' as resulting from different capitals' needs to retain political and economic control of markets against overseas competitors, and the 'global scale' as the product of capital's efforts to universalise the wage–labour relation, such that whilst the planet's physical limits are geologically determined, the emergence of a global scale of economic organisation is the outcome of capital's expansionist nature.

Such conceptual developments were important for critically considering how particular scales of the organisation of social life come about, although both were criticised on various grounds – Taylor for his functionalism and Smith for a tendency to see scales as emerging out of the internal logic of capital (Herod, 2001). Subsequently, then, a number of theorists argued that scales should be seen not as emerging out of the internal contradictions of capital or as serving particular functions for capital but should, instead, be understood as the product of conflicts and compromises between capital and labour and various segments thereof to equalise conditions across the economic landscape (e.g., by having national-level collective bargaining agreements) and/or to differentiate it (e.g., by localising bargaining). Others, such as Cox (1998, p. 2), sought to question how relationships between different geographical scales are conceptualised. Hence, Cox argued that theorists had tended to characterise scale in areal terms, such that spatial scales were understood essentially as boundaries demarking particular sets of closed spaces of different sizes ('the local', 'the regional', and so on). This was particularly the case when it came to the notion of social actors 'jumping scales', which has been viewed simply as a process of moving up or down the spatial hierarchy from one areal unit, such as 'the local', to another, such as 'the national'. Such a questioning of the conceptualising of scales as areal units led to a vigorous enquiry into how scales were represented discursively and what this meant for conceptualising the world (and, hence, W&E practices).

Representing scale

Issues of how spatial scales are represented discursively have played an important part in efforts to understand how the world is scaled and how social actors' praxis is structured. For instance, the relationship between scales seen as areal units is frequently represented in terms whereby each scale is considered to be, variously, a rung on a ladder (whereby one moves, say, 'up' the scalar hierarchy from 'the local' to 'the global'), or one of a series of concentric circles (in which one moves 'out' from 'smaller' scales such as 'the local' to 'larger' scales such as 'the global', with the latter 'encircling' the former), or perhaps one of a series of Russian matryoshka nesting dolls (in which 'smaller' scales sit snugly 'inside' 'larger' ones). What is important here is that although these three representations share some similarities – they all conceive of different scales as spatially discrete things, such that 'the local' and 'the global' are separate rungs/circles/dolls – they also have significant differences. Hence, in the ladder metaphor 'the global' appears 'above' the other scales, whereas in the circle metaphor it 'encompasses' them. Likewise, the matryoshka metaphor presents the 'outer' scale of 'the global' as 'larger' than all the others and is the most forceful metaphor suggesting the notion of a nested hierarchy in which scales from the very local to the truly global can only fit together in a strict progression (for pictorial representations of these different ways of viewing scale, see Herod (2003)).

Instead of viewing scale in terms of areal boundaries which circumscribe particular territorial units, though, other writers have proposed that a more useful metaphor views scales in terms of networks. Hence Latour (1996, p. 370) has argued that the world's complexity cannot be captured by 'notions of levels, layers, territories, [and] spheres', and should not be thought of as being made up of discrete levels (that is, scales) of bounded spaces which fit together neatly. Rather than portraying scales as capable of somehow being stacked one above the other (the ladder metaphor), placed within one another (the circle metaphor), or fitted together like matryoshka dolls, Latour maintains that we need to conceptualise the world as 'fibrous, thread-like, wiry, stringy, ropy, [and] capillary'. Clearly, such a characterisation provides yet another way of thinking about the scaled relationships between places, suggesting metaphors in which scales are networked and akin to sets of earthworm burrows or tree roots or spiders' webs. In this approach, geographical scales are seen not as spatially discrete and separate levels or spheres of social life but, rather, as ways of describing 'networks that are by nature neither local or global, but are [instead] more or less long and more or less connected' (Latour, 1993, p. 122). In such a view, then, it is still possible to recognise that different scales exist – following the metaphor, earthworm burrows can be viewed as penetrating different strata of the soil, with some going deeper than others – but it is much more difficult to determine exactly where one scale ends and another begins. Another metaphor which conveys these topological characteristics is that of a 'marble' cake. In contrast to a 'layer' cake (where different colours of cake are layered one upon another – akin to the hierarchical, ladder-like notion of scale), in a marble cake, different colours of cake (different 'scales') are intermingled, interwoven, remaining distinct in colour but blended with other colours (scales).

Such matters of how we think about scale ontologically and discursively transform dramatically how we think about the relationships between different scales and what it might mean to talk about such practices as 'scale jumping', 'rescaling', 'scaling-up'/'scaling-down', 'centralising'/'decentralising', 'going global'/'going local', 'thinking globally' but 'acting locally', and the like. In turn, this impacts on how we theorise W&E practices. Thus, to give one simple example, being able to talk of how there have been recent trends to 'decentralise' industrial relations in many nations requires a view of the world which incorporates a scalar hierarchy of separate scales, with contract bargaining being 'relocated downwards' from the 'national' to the 'local' scale (McGrath-Champ, 2005). If, on the other hand, we were to adopt a Latourian view, then some descriptor of recent changes in industrial relations practices other than 'relocation downwards' would be required, one which might encourage us to think about the relationships within which workers and employers find themselves quite differently. Equally, talking of social actors 'going global' or 'jumping' from 'national' to 'global' actions requires us to think, precisely, what such terminology may mean. Hence, representing the practice of, say, creating a national-level collective bargaining agreement to take the place of myriad local ones as one of 'jumping' from one scale to another implies that such scales already pre-exist the action of jumping. This view tends to naturalise the existence of certain scales rather than to view them as having been actively created through political praxis. Likewise, talk of 'going global' raises questions as to what this actually denotes and whether there is a difference between, say, being 'global' and being 'multi-locational' internationally (see Gibson-Graham, 2002). How such spatial scales are represented, then, clearly has significant implications both for actual W&E practices – for workers, trying to organise against transnational corporations which are perceived to be 'global' is quite a different prospect psychologically than trying to organise against those which are perceived to be 'merely' 'multi-locational' and may lead them to adopt utterly different tactics and strategies – and for theorising what is going on.

One turn too many?

Just as we were drafting this introduction, one of our contributors, Bob Jessop, along with two other colleagues, published an article that appeared to confound our very enterprise. The article was entitled 'Theorizing spatial relations' and in the first paragraph the authors argued that: '[a]s previous advocates of a scalar turn, we now question the privileging, in any form, of a single dimension of sociospatial relations, scalar or otherwise' (Jessop et al., 2008, p. 389). In fact, Jessop et al. detailed several explicit 'spatial turns' in various academic disciplines during the last thirty years or so, and identified four spatial lexicons – territory, place, scale and network – associated with various of these spatial turns. The point of their critique is to argue that advocates of any particular turn have been prone to focus on a single dimension of spatiality, neglecting the role of other forms of socio-spatial relations. One-dimensionalism is evident, they continue, in all four socio-spatial lexicons, with each falling into the trap of conflating a part with the whole. For instance, there has been much discussion in recent years about the importance or not of the concept of scale, with opposing sides taking somewhat either/or positions. Hence, Marston et al. (2005) have argued that the term 'scale' should be expurgated from the geographic vocabulary in favour of what they call a 'flat ontology', whilst Leitner and Miller (2007) have simply responded by asserting the importance of scale and arguing for its non-expurgation and for the dismissal of a 'flat ontology'. Taking a quite different approach, though, Jessop et al. conclude that the relative significance of territory, place, scale and networks as structuring principles for socio-spatial relations varies with different types of spatio-temporal fix, that crises of accumulation can be explored in terms of the growing disjunction among historically specific institutional manifestations of these four socio-spatial dimensions, and that strategies of crisis resolution entail attempts to reorder the relative importance of the four dimensions. Put another way, the question is not about whether scale is important or not as a concept but, rather, how its importance may vary based upon the relative importance in particular contexts of the other dimensions. In contradistinction to such one-dimensional approaches, then, Jessop et al. argue instead for a socio-spatial theory that refers to historically specific geographies of social relations and that explores contextual and historical variation in the structural coupling, strategic coordination and forms of interconnection of those relations. Their argument, then, is not with spatiality per se but with the way that some advocates have developed the debate, often as an either/or proposition.

As it turns out, the argument that Jessop et al. make – that the relative importance of various aspects of the spatiality of social life varies according to specific contexts – is actually very much along the lines of what we are seeking to argue here, namely that rather than prioritising one dimension of socio-spatial relations, we should explore the interconnections between them. This provides for a much richer conceptualisation of spatiality, one that sees spatiality not in unidimensional ways but as a multifaceted set of aspects that are always in dialectical relationship to one another, such that on some occasions in some places the power of, say, place is more significant than that of the spatially extensive network within which particular actors may be imbricated, whereas in others, matters scalar will have more pull over actors than do those of place. This recognition of the multidimensionality both of concepts and of power relations has very practical consequences for questions of control, acquiescence and resistance. Hence, as Castree et al. argue (2004, p. 8), the increasingly stretched nature of social relationships between place-based workers across national and supranational space can take a variety of forms which may vary in time and across space. This fact generates for workers a complex landscape of geographical difference and interdependence, which in turn creates dilemmas of scale – at what level(s) are accommodation or resistance to be organised or imagined? The conclusion to be drawn from all of this is, as Holgate (2007, p. 909) argues, that the scale at which action should be taken to defend working conditions is always relative and contingent. Thus, whilst in most cases worker or union activity is likely to be place-based – focusing on the workplace – the increasing scale(s) of economic activity demands that new spatial structures be developed by labour to counter the power of capital's (often) superior command of space. Moving from the local to the global, then, has to mean more than simply upscaling forms of action, for the process is more dialectical than the phrase suggests. It is not a linear process, nor is it an either/or choice. Instead, it is dependent on the situation in which workers find themselves, and may involve a mix of organising approaches which have quite different spatialities embedded within them.

We will return to this issue and the others we have raised in this introduction in Parts 2 and 3, 'Working Spaces' and 'Workers in Space'. Before then, however, in Part 1, 'Work, Space and the State', Bob Jessop and Peter Turnbull each provide overviews of many of the themes and issues that will arise throughout this volume. For his part, Jessop (Chapter 2) provides a spatially sensitive analysis of the emergence of a Schumpeterian welfare, post-national state to argue that states have played a key role in promoting and resisting globalisation and, further, that states are key to establishing and regulating the spatio-temporal matrices of social life and the impact of uneven development. In related fashion, Turnbull (Chapter 3) examines the relationship between labour, the state and the market. In particular, he confronts a number of myths concerning the powerless state and the omnipotent market – myths made clear by the global economic crisis of the late 2000s and the Bush and Obama governments' bailing out of large sections of the US financial services and manufacturing sectors – to show how labour is responding to the new 'territorial spaces and management systems' which are emerging particularly as a result of the actions of transnational corporations in different sectors of the European transport industries. These two articles are particularly apposite, given how the state appears to be back – really, it was never away, despite neoliberal declarations of its demise (Ohmae, 1995) – in the post-2008 global financial crisis world of myriad bank nationalisations, bailouts of other industries and government-provided economic stimulus packages. The fears of global economic depression that might result from the meltdown of the US housing market have not only exposed weakness in theory and practice, with a retreat from neoliberalism being accompanied by a rediscovery of Keynes (and to a lesser extent Marx), but they have also highlighted the fundamentally geographical nature of markets, the fundamentally geographical nature of how the state is organised and the central role that states play – and have always played, despite neoliberal efforts to claim otherwise – in structuring markets.

Note

1. We are thinking here of books such as the first edited text on labour process theory that emerged from the International Labour Process conference (Knights and Willmott, 1990) and which contained little or no reference to place and space beyond the, at the time, prevalent view of place as a stage or some sort of contextual backdrop to the main social action, or Paul Thompson's ([1983] 1989) highly influential book on labour process theory, which tended to treat the issues in much the same way.

References

Ackroyd, S., R. Batt, P. Thompson and P.S. Tolbert (eds) (2005), *The Oxford Handbook of Work and Organization*, Oxford: Oxford University Press.

Agnew, J. (1987), *Place and Politics: The Geographical Mediation of State and Society*, London: Allen and Unwin.

Bryan, L. and D. Farrell (1996), *Market Unbound: Unleashing Global Capitalism*, New York: John Wiley.

Burgess J. (2001), 'Revisiting the scene of the crime', paper presented to Colloquium on Geography and Industrial Relations, University of Sydney, November.

Cairncross, F. (2001), *The Death of Distance: How the Communications Revolution is Changing Our Lives*, Boston, MA: Harvard Business School Press.

Callinicos, A. (2006), 'David Harvey and Marxism', in N. Castree and D. Gregory (eds), *David Harvey: A Critical Reader*, Oxford: Blackwell, pp. 47–54.

Castree, N., N., Coe, K. Ward and M. Samers (2004), *Spaces of Work: Global Capitalism and Geographies of Labour*, London: Sage.

Cox, K. (1998), 'Spaces of dependence, spaces of engagement and the politics of scale, or: looking for local politics', *Political Geography*, **17** (1), 1–23.

Cox, K. and A. Mair (1988), 'Locality and community in the politics of local economic development', *Annals of the Association of American Geographers*, **78**, 307–25.

Ellem, B. and J. Shields (1999), 'Rethinking "regional industrial relations": space, place and the social relations of work', *Journal of Industrial Relations*, **41** (4), 536–60.

Friedman, T.L. (2006), *The World is Flat: The Globalised World in the Twenty-First Century*, London: Penguin.

Gibson-Graham, J.K. (2002), 'Beyond global vs. local: economic politics outside the binary frame', in A. Herod and M.W. Wright (eds), *Geographies of Power: Placing Scale*, Oxford: Basil Blackwell, pp. 25–60.

Gregory, D. (2006), 'Introduction: troubling geographies', in N. Castree and D. Gregory (eds), *David Harvey: A Critical Reader*, Oxford: Blackwell, pp. 1–25.

Hart J.F. (1982), 'The highest forms of the geographer's art', *Annals of the Association of American Geographers*, **72** (1), 101–31.

Harvey, D. (1978), 'The urban process under capitalism: a framework for analysis', *International Journal of Urban and Regional Research*, **2**, 101–31.

Harvey, D. (1982), *The Limits to Capital*, Oxford: Basil Blackwell.
Herod, A. (2000), 'Workers and workplaces in a neoliberal global economy', *Environment and Planning A*, **32** (10), 1781–90.
Herod, A. (2001), *Labor Geographies: Workers and the Landscapes of Capitalism*, New York: Guilford Press.
Herod, A. (2003), 'Scale: the local and the global', in S. Holloway, S. Rice and G. Valentine (eds), *Key Concepts in Geography*, London; Sage, pp. 229–47.
Herod, A. and M.W. Wright (2002), 'Placing scale: an introduction', in A. Herod and M.W. Wright (eds), *Geographies of Power: Placing Scale*, Oxford: Basil Blackwell, pp. 1–14.
Herod, A., J. Peck and J. Wills (2003), 'Geography and industrial relations', in P. Ackers and A. Wilkinson (eds), *Understanding Work and Employment: Industrial Relations in Transition*, Oxford: Oxford University Press, pp. 176–92.
Herod, A., A. Rainnie and S. McGrath-Champ (2007), 'Working space: why incorporating the geographical is central to theorizing work and employment practices', *Work, Employment and Society*, **21** (2), 247–64.
Holgate, J. (2007), 'Producing: changing patterns of work', in I. Douglas, R. Huggett and C. Perkins (eds), *Companion Encyclopedia of Geography: From Local to Global*, 2nd edn, London: Routledge, pp. 901–12.
Hudson, R. (2001), *Producing Places*, New York: Guilford Press.
Jessop, B., N. Brenner and M. Jones (2008), 'Theorizing spatial relations', *Environment and Planning D: Society and Space*, **26**, 389–401.
Kanter, R.M. (1995), *World Class: Thriving Locally in the Global Economy*, New York: Simon and Schuster.
Knights, D. and H. Willmott (eds) (1990), *Labour Process Theory*, London: Macmillan.
Latour, B. (1993), *We Have Never Been Modern*, Cambridge, MA: Harvard University Press.
Latour, B. (1996), 'On Actor-Network Theory: a few clarifications', *Soziale Welt*, **47**, 369–81.
Leitner, H. and B. Miller (2007), 'Scale and the limitations of ontological debate: a commentary on Martson, Jones and Woodward', *Transactions of the Institute of British Geographers*, **32**, 116–25.
Marston, S., J. Jones and K. Woodward (2005), 'Human geography without scale', *Transactions of the Institute of British Geographers*, **30**, 416-32.
Massey, D. (1984a), 'Introduction: geography matters', in D. Massey and J. Allen (eds), *Geography Matters! A Reader*, New York: Cambridge University Press, pp. 1–11.
Massey, D. (1984b), *Spatial Divisions of Labour: Social Structures and the Geography of Production*, London: Macmillan.
Massey, D. (1999), 'Power-geometries and the politics of space-time', Department of Geography, University of Heidelberg, Hettner Lectures, Number 2.
McGrath-Champ, S. (2005), 'Enterprise bargaining and regional prospects: the effects of rescaling wage regulation in Australia', *Economic and Industrial Democracy*, **26** (3), 413–42.
Molotch, H. (1976), 'The city as growth machine: toward a political economy of place', *American Journal of Sociology*, **82**, 309-32.
Ohmae, K. (1990), *The Borderless World*, New York: HarperBusiness.
Ohmae, K. (1995), *The End of the Nation State: The Rise of Regional Economies*, New York: McKinsey and Company.
Ohmae, K. (2005), *The Next Global Stage: Challenges and Opportunities in Our Borderless World*, Upper Saddle River, NJ: Wharton School Publishing.
Peck, J. (1996), *Work-Place: The Social Regulation of Labor Markets*, New York: Guilford Press.
Rainnie, A., A. Herod and S. McGrath-Champ (2007), 'Spatialising industrial relations', *Industrial Relations Journal*, **38** (2), 102–18.
Smith, N. ([1984] 1990), *Uneven Development: Nature, Capital and the Production of Space*, Oxford: Basil Blackwell.
Soja, E. (1989), *Postmodern Geographies: The Reassertion of Space in Critical Social Theory*, New York: Verso.
Storper, M. and R. Walker (1989), *The Capitalist Imperative: Territory, Technology, and Industrial Growth*, New York: Basil Blackwell.
Taylor, P.J. (1981), 'Geographical scales within the world economy approach', *Review*, **5** (1), 3-11.
Taylor, P.J. (1982), 'A materialist framework for political geography', *Transactions of the Institute of British Geographers*, **7** (1), 15–34.
Taylor, P.J. (1999), 'Places, spaces and Macy's: Place-space tensions in the political geography of modernities', *Progress in Human Geography*, **23** (1), 7–26.
Thompson, P. ([1983] 1989), *The Nature of Work*, 2nd edn, London: Palgrave Macmillan.
Ward, K. (2007), 'Thinking geographically about work, employment and society', *Work, Employment and Society*, **21** (2), 265–76.

PART 1

WORK, SPACE AND THE STATE

2 Globalisation and the state

Bob Jessop

Although the topic of 'globalisation and the state' is common in economic and political debate, in actuality 'globalisation' is too chaotic a concept, and the 'state' too abstract, to support solid, testable arguments. To overcome this problem, this chapter presents globalisation as a complex, incomplete (and incompletable) process and notes its crucial temporal as well as spatial moments and, likewise, explores the complexities of statehood and its variability. It then considers: (a) the implications of economic globalisation for changes in the state and the exercise of state power; and (b) the role of states and state projects in rescaling economic activities in the world market. In particular, rather than assume a generic, ubiquitous relation, it distinguishes forms of globalisation as well as types of state and political regime. While advanced capitalist economies and their associated states in the postwar period provide the key reference point, other economic and political regimes and other periods are also mentioned.

Globalisation*s*

Globalisation is a relatively recent word for a process with a much longer history that, unsurprisingly, has also been described in other terms, such as the rise of the world market, world economy, imperialism, world system, world society and empire. Its origins are also disputed. They have been linked to: the exodus of *Homo sapiens* from Africa around 60 000 years ago (Gamble, 1994); the first world systems some 5000 years ago (Frank, 1990); European expansion in the 1500s (Wallerstein, 1980); late nineteenth-century European imperialism (Hobson, 1902; Lenin, 1917); or only to the late twentieth-century (Scholte, 2000). Yet, whenever global integration (as opposed to global dispersion) may have begun, it is still incomplete, witnessing much resistance and many reversals. Indeed, major objective and subjective limits make it inherently incapable of completion (Hirst and Thompson, 1996; Altvater and Mahnkopf, 2007). Finally, whereas some critics see globalisation as an ideological category that hides the continuities of today's global economy with older forms of imperialism, others regard it as a neutral, scientific concept that can be operationalised, tested, and used to guide research, strategy and policy. Given these complexities, this chapter focuses on economic globalisation, its extra-economic supports, and the state.

Globalisation is not a single process with a universal, unitary logic that affects all institutions and social forces in the same way everywhere. At least five features make it hypercomplex. Specifically, globalisation: (a) emerges from the interaction among activities in many sites around the globe, including peripheral and semi-peripheral locations as well as imperialist metropoles; (b) arises from actions on many scales that co-exist and interpenetrate in complex ways – indeed, what some describe as globalisation may also be viewed, perhaps more fruitfully, as internationalisation, triadisation, regional bloc formation, global city network-building, cross-border region formation, international localisation, glocalisation, transnationalisation, and so on; (c) involves an increasingly dense nexus of temporalities and time horizons, especially due to growing space–time distantiation and/ or compression; (d) emerges from competing strategies and counter-strategies and takes many different forms: world market integration along neoliberal lines is only one form and even this varies in its modalities and degree; and, more generally, (e) is rooted in the contingent interaction of many different causal processes (cf. Jessop, 2002). It follows that the regularisation and governance of globalisation involves many different sites, scales and temporal horizons and the intersection of many causal chains.

The most recent globalisation wave (dating loosely from the 1980s onwards, depending on countries, regions and reference points) is distinctive less for the growing planetary integration of events, processes, institutions, systems, and the lifeworld than for the growing *speed* of these interconnections and the more rapid spread of their nth-order effects due to new material and social technologies (but see Standage 1998 on the telegraph). Space–time distantiation stretches social relations over time and space so that relations can be coordinated over longer periods of time (including the ever more distant future) and longer distances, greater areas, or more scales of activity. This is reflected in the growing complexity of commodity chains based on an extensive global division of labour. Space–time compression intensifies 'discrete' events in real time and/or the increased velocity of material and immaterial flows over a given distance. This creates a 'runaway world' in which major problems arise even more, to the extent that these can be separated analytically, from the *temporal* than the *spatial* qualities of globalisation. The once common, but one-sided, claim that economic integration was greater in 1913 than in the 1990s ignores this acceleration and resulting capacity of the world market to operate in real time, especially in global finance and world money, faster than other key systems (such as law, politics or education).

Finally, as the fifth point emphasises, nothing can be explained in terms of the causal powers of 'globalisation in general'. This does not exclude specific hypotheses about the impact of clearly specifiable processes on particular sets of social relations. Thus one might argue that hypermobile, superfast financial capital challenges the capacity of national states to set real interest rates for their national economies with a view to securing full employment levels of demand; or, again, that the capacity of some industrial capitals to relocate (or plausibly threaten to do so) could enhance their power vis-à-vis organised labour and/or a corporatist state. But at least some national states have been able to pursue other policies for full employment or full employability; high-wage, high-skill, high-productivity corporatist arrangements are not always anathema to industrial capital; and the new state-sponsored global 'war for talents' has enabled some key workers to join the transnational labour aristocracy. Moreover, in so far as hypermobile and superfast capital flows depend on relatively fixed and slow-to-mature infrastructures and socio-cultural practices, they are vulnerable to strategically-targeted state action or other external forms of control. In short, we must specify the conditions and effects of globalisation in particular contexts rather than make blanket claims.

States

Statehood rests on the territorialisation of political power: its key features are state territory, the state apparatus and the state population. The great majority of states today – and all of the most powerful – enjoy mutually recognised formal sovereignty over their respective (large) territories. With rare exceptions, even sovereign city-states and small island states that are economically important (for example, as entrepôts, financial centres, homes to sovereign wealth funds, tax havens, or major tourist spots) lack significant political and military power. While sovereign territorial states are conventionally traced back to the 1648 Treaty of Westphalia, they have developed more slowly and intermittently, peaking in the twentieth-century after two world wars, stepwise decolonisation, and soviet bloc collapse. Of course, sovereign states do not exist in majestic isolation overseeing the rest of society but are closely related to other orders (notably the economy and law) and 'civil society'. In addition, relative control over organised coercion is just one state capacity among many forms of 'hard power' and co-exists with various forms of 'soft power' rooted in socio-cultural relations (Gramsci, 1971; Mann, 1986; Nye, 1990). State strength varies greatly with the configuration of state capacities, state managers' ability to project power beyond the state's multiple boundaries, and current challenges. Moreover, in extreme cases states may even disintegrate or show other signs of 'state failure'.

Given these complexities, globalisation does not (and could not) generate a uniform set of pressures on all states. Indeed, for such a self-evidently geographical process, there is a surprising lack of spatial and scalar as well as temporal differentiation in many accounts of the impact of globalisation. Thus it is important to note that the perspective developed here excludes a zero-sum approach to globalisation and state power – especially when posed in terms of a singular emergent borderless flow-based economy operating in timeless time that is expanding at the expense of a plurality of traditional national territorial states operating as 'power containers' inside fixed territorial boundaries.

This sort of zero-sum account would:

- oversimplify the world market's complexities and contradictory dynamic;
- ignore its dependence on changing economic and extra-economic competitive advantages that are place- and time-bound;
- exaggerate how far a truly global economy has emerged, even in international financial, let alone in the industrial and commercial, fields;
- overlook the complexities of the state as an institutional ensemble and of state power as a social relation;
- neglect how all states are involved in constituting the economy as an object of regulation (this is also true of committed laissez-faire states);
- disregard how more powerful states actively seek to reorganise the world market (or resist these attempts);
- miss the ways and extent to which the logic (and illogic) of globalisation constrain firms as well as political actors.

These reflections invite four conclusions. First, the world market is irreducible to flows – whether of merchandise, productive capital, interest-bearing capital, variable capital (that is, labour-power), non-commodified use values, or people in other capacities. It has important territorial dimensions (reflected in concepts such as industrial districts, agglomeration economies, global cities, and regional or national capitalisms). Second, states are more than 'power containers': they are also power connectors, that is, nodes in a network of states and other political forces. More generally, they have a key role in connecting and organising places, spaces, scales and networks inside and across their respective borders and frontiers. Managing the flow of people is an important illustration of this connective role. Third, world market integration does not put pressure on *the State* (sovereign or otherwise) in general but on particular forms of state or political regime with specific state capacities and liabilities. Different forms of integration affect different forms of state in quite different ways. Fourth, the widening, deepening and intensification of global competition also put pressures on capital and labour.

Despite the formal equivalence among sovereign states in today's nominally post-imperial state system, as signified, for example, in United Nations membership (192 states, ranging from tiny Tuvalu to the USA), they vary significantly in state capacities to exploit, absorb, resist or counteract any pressures from globalisation in all its forms. Some states and populations are seriously disadvantaged by globalisation (notably in its neoliberal form) as state capacities are undermined, some states fail, and spaces are opened for warlordism, trade in 'blood diamonds' and other booty, people-smuggling networks, narco-fiefdoms, or *nomenklatura* asset seizure. But other states and populations may benefit from integration into the world market, pressures for good governance and so on. Moreover, in influencing and constraining state capacities, globalisation also modifies the balance of forces within states, often giving advantage to some economic, political and social forces over others and opening spaces for renewed struggles to reorganise state forms and capacities and seek to influence globalisation.

This said, as the latest globalisation wave has intensified, postwar national states can no longer presume, as they did at the height of Atlantic Fordism, East Asian Exportism, or Latin American import-substitution industrialisation, that their chief economic task is to govern their respective *national* economies and their insertion into the *inter*national economy. They are now increasingly involved in managing various transnational or even planetary processes and creating appropriate spatial and temporal fixes. Crucial here are: (a) the changing relation between economic and extra-economic factors bearing on competitiveness; (b) states' roles in redefining the boundaries between economic and extra-economic factors and forces and/or in reorganising and subordinating the extra-economic to the perceived demands and pressures of economic globalisation; and (c) the effects of global environmental change. Thus, to take a paradoxical example, even as neoliberal states seem to disengage from the market economy, they intervene more in the extra-economic field and subordinate it to the demands of valorisation and realisation. More generally, states (and the social forces they represent) regularly seek to constitute and reconstitute the spatio-temporal matrices that organise economic and political activities, including their international moments (Poulantzas 1975, 1978; Gross 1985). For example, they try to redraw the spatio-temporal matrices in which capital operates with a view to managing the tension between: (a) potentially mobile capital's interests in reducing its place-dependency and/or liberating itself from temporal constraints; and (b) their own interest in fixing (allegedly beneficial) capital in their own territories and rendering capital's temporal horizons and rhythms compatible with their statal and/or political routines, temporalities and crisis-tendencies.

Capital and the wage-relation
The complex mutual implications of economic globalisation and state power are significantly mediated through: (a) the inherent contradictions in the capital relation, especially between use value and exchange value; and (b) the typical separation of the

profit-orientated, market-mediated capitalist economy from its crucial extra-economic preconditions.

First, whereas advocates of globalisation tend to see it as spreading the mutual benefits of free exchange beloved of capitalism's apologists, opponents tend to emphasise how globalisation generalises capitalism's inherent contradictions. These include: (a) the contradiction between the growing socialisation of productive forces through the deepening of the social division of labour on a global scale and the continuing private ownership and control of the forces of production and the appropriation of profit; and (b) the contradiction between the use value and exchange value aspects of the commodity form and its related forms in the capital relation. While more and more economic spaces are being more tightly integrated into the global division of labour and the world market, economic power is increasingly concentrated and centralised. Nonetheless the uneven development entailed in capitalism also reorganises the division of labour, displaces growth poles and zones of instability, and generates new centres of accumulation. This generates many conflicts around the exercise of economic power, the attribution of responsibility for particular effects of globalisation, and the distribution of its costs and benefits. Globalisation also modifies the relative importance of the use- and exchange-value moments of different aspects of the capital relation. Thus productive capital is both abstract value in motion (notably in the form of realised profits available for reinvestment) and a concrete stock of already invested time- and place-specific assets in the course of being valorised. The worker is both an abstract unit of labour power substitutable by other such units (or, indeed, other factors of production) and a concrete individual (or, indeed, part of the collective labourer) with specific skills, knowledge and creativity. The wage is both a cost of production and a source of demand. Money functions both as an international currency exchangeable against other currencies (ideally in stateless space) and as national (or supranational) money circulating within national societies or pluri- or supranational monetary blocs that is subject to some measure of relevant state control. Land functions both as a form of property (based on the private appropriation of nature) deployed in terms of expected revenues in the form of rent and as a natural resource (modified by past actions) that is more or less renewable and recyclable. Knowledge is both the basis of intellectual property rights and a collective resource (the intellectual commons). In each case (neoliberal) globalisation reinforces the exchange-value moment over the use-value moment, thereby benefiting value in motion, the treatment of workers as disposable and substitutable factors of production, the wage as a cost of (international) production, money as international currency (especially due to the increased importance of derivatives), nature as a commodity, and knowledge as intellectual property (cf. Jessop, 2002).

Second, capitalist reproduction cannot be secured exclusively through the profit-orientated, market-mediated logic of accumulation. It also depends, as scholars from left, right and centre acknowledge, on crucial extra-economic mechanisms (for example, Smith, [1776] 1937; Polanyi, 1957; von Hayek, 1960; Weber, 1961; Marx, [1867] 1967). States are heavily involved in this supplementation both directly and through their modulation of other extra-economic modes of regulation. Thus most modern states are involved in securing, directly or indirectly, certain key conditions for the valorisation of capital and the reproduction of labour power as a fictitious commodity. We can illustrate this in terms of the transition in forms of state in advanced capitalist economies.

The Keynesian Welfare National State
The type of state that became dominant in North Western Europe, North America, Australia and New Zealand during the 1950s to 1970s was closely linked with the Fordist growth dynamic based on mass production and mass consumption. It can be described ideal-typically in terms of its broad economic functions as the Keynesian Welfare National State (or KWNS). Other perspectives are possible. But this is well suited to issues of employment and work and enables us to assess changes in the state and their relationship to globalisation.

First, in promoting the conditions for profit-orientated, market-mediated economic expansion, the KWNS was distinctively *Keynesian* in so far as it aimed to secure full employment in a relatively closed national economy and did so mainly through demand-side management and integrated national infrastructural provision. Thus a key feature of the KWNS was managing national labour markets. Second, in contributing to the day-to-day, lifetime, and intergenerational reproduction of the labour force and in managing the state population more generally, its social policy had a distinctive *welfare* orientation in so far as it: (a) instituted economic and social rights for all citizens so that they could share in growing prosperity (and contribute to growing demand) even when not employed in the high-wage, high-growth Fordist economic sectors; and (b) promoted forms of collective consumption favourable to the Fordist growth dynamic based on mass production and mass consumption. Third, the KWNS was *national* in so far as these distinctive economic and social policies were pursued within the historically specific (and socially constructed) matrix of a national economy, a national state, and a society seen as comprising national citizens. For, within this relative isomorphic spatio-temporal matrix, it was the national state that was mainly charged with developing and guiding Keynesian welfare policies. Local and regional states were chiefly relays for policies framed nationally, and the leading international regimes established following the Second World War were mainly intended to restore and maintain national economic and political stability. And, fourth, the KWNS was *statist* in so far as hierarchically organised state institutions (on different levels) and state-led planning and policies were the chief supplement and corrective to the failure of market forces in a 'mixed economy' that was concerned with national economic growth and national social integration.

There was never a pure Keynesian Welfare National State, but various hybrid national forms within the international economic and political framework of Atlantic Fordism. Nor was there a generic economic, political and hegemonic crisis that affected all such forms identically in the 1980s and 1990s. Nonetheless, they have all faced broadly similar pressures associated with the crisis of Atlantic Fordism and its repercussions within the world market as a whole. The first signs of crisis in Fordist growth emerged in the mid-1970s, and matters worsened in the 1980s. The processes behind the current wave of globalisation undermined the effectiveness of the national state (in its postwar forms) because its distinctive powers and capacities became less relevant to the new spatio-temporal matrices as the relative significance of wages as cost of production and source of demand and of money as national money and international currency were reversed relative to how these functioned in Atlantic Fordism, and as the contradictions between states' social welfare-providing functions and their need to compete successfully within a globalizing, knowledge-based economy became greater (Jessop, 2002). Further, the structured coherence (or spatio-temporal congruence) of the national economy–national state–national society configuration was weakened by changes linked to globalisation, internationalisation, the rise of multi-tiered global city networks, the formation of triad economies (such as European economic space), and the re-emergence of regional and local economies. This made it harder to secure the conditions for full employment and expanding welfare states through the normal KWNS apparatuses and policy instruments. An initial response was to attempt to pursue these twin policy commitments through more interventionist measures with a more corporatist and/or dirigiste character; but, as these served to postpone rather than resolve the crises of Atlantic Fordism and the KWNS, a trial-and-error search was initiated to develop a new state form more adequate to the changing conditions of accumulation.

As a result, what is tendentially replacing the KWNS is a Schumpeterian Workfare Post-national Regime (SWPR). First, this is *Schumpeterian* in so far as it tries to promote permanent innovation and flexibility in relatively open economies by intervening on the supply side and by strengthening as far as possible these economies' overall competitiveness. Schumpeter is invoked here, of course, as the theorist of innovation, entrepreneurship and competition. Second, as a *workfare* regime, the SWPR subordinates social policy to the demands of labour market flexibility, employability, and economic competitiveness. This includes putting downward pressure on the social wage *qua* cost of international production but also, given the economic and political limits to austerity, re-functionalising the inherited welfare state to serve economic interests. The entity which has emerged out of these developments is sometimes called the social investment state. However, neoliberalism is only one variant of workfare or social investment policy in this sense – there are also neo-corporatist, neo-statist, and neo-communitarian forms. Part of this workfarist reorientation involves state efforts to create new economic and political subjects as partners in the innovative, knowledge-based, entrepreneurial, flexible economy and its accompanying self-reliant, autonomous, empowered workfare regime.

Third, the SWPR is '*post-national*' in so far as the national territory has become less important as an economic, political and cultural 'power container'. This involves a transfer of economic and social policy-making functions upwards, downwards and sideways. What is emerging is a series of multi-level government and/or governance regimes concerned to manage economic and social policies broadly understood across a growing range of scales of economic and political organisation. These operate above and below the national state, with an expanding role for the local, urban and regional as well as supranational organs, for while policies intended to influence the microeconomic supply-side and social regeneration are said to be designed best close to their sites of implementation, conversely policies concerned with macroeconomic stability should be conducted, it is argued, at international, transnational or supranational levels. Thus policies to promote the global space of flows co-exist with different kinds of *Standortpolitik* (locational policy) concerned to fix capital in place, whether through continuous upgrading or a race to the bottom. In short, economic and social policies are no longer mainly determined at the national level.

Finally, the SWPR relies increasingly on non-hierarchical forms of governance to compensate for market failures and inadequacies, rather than on state command grounded in territorial sovereignty. This shift from govern*ment* towards govern*ance* means that traditional forms of intervention have become less important in economic and social policy. Law and money have not disappeared from the state's armoury, of course; but active economic and social steering now relies on soft regulation, reflexive law, additionality, private–public partnerships, organisational intelligence and information-sharing, and so on. A key role falls here to 'meta-governance', that is, the organisation of the institutional framework and rules for individual modes of governance and the re-balancing of different modes of governance (see below).

Trends and counter-trends in the state

A common failure of discussions of globalisation and the state is taking the 'Anglosphere' and/or Western Europe as their main or only reference point. This reinforces the view that globalisation undermines the national state and ignores the extent to which globalisation could be seen as the 'revenge' of post-imperialist or post-colonial states (plus Japan) as 'Eastern' economies and their developmental states have gained economic and political power in the world market. Only now that they are being affected by economic pressures originating from newly dynamic regions in East Asia and, more recently, India, post-socialist Russia, the Middle East and Brazil, have the states of Western Europe and the United States belatedly discovered how their own expansion and imperialism had previously impacted on the 'South' and/or 'East'. Nonetheless globalisation has very different meanings for, and impacts on, post-colonial states, post-socialist states, export-orientated developmental states, rentier oil states, and so on. The comparative and competitive advantage of economic spaces and the relative capacities of their associated states matter greatly here. Thus oil-rich econo-mies will experience globalisation differently from those whose chief asset is low-waged, low-skilled labour, while strong developmental states will experience it differently from so-called failed states.

Taking the KWNS in advanced capitalist economies as our benchmark, then, the current reorganisation of the institutional architecture and modalities of state power can be summarised in terms of four empirically interrelated, often overlapping trends and countertrends.

1. *Denationalisation of statehood.* Powers are being transferred from the national territo-rial level to supra-regional or international bodies, regional or local states, or cross-national alliances among local, metropolitan or regional states with complementary interests. In addition, new state powers have been allocated to scales other than the national. Sometimes described as the 'hollowing out' of the national state, this descrip-tion makes sense only relative to the postwar period in advanced capitalist societies: in earlier times, local government was more important, and world empires and classical imperialism have also figured significantly. On a global level, this trend is seen in the so-called inter- or trans-nationalisation of the state as ever more international agencies (like the IMF, World Bank, OECD and ILO) and intergovernmental forums (such as the G-8, that is, the world's eight largest economies) seek to steer crucial policy agendas. The European Union is a powerful macro-regional example of the same trend. This is reflected in the tendential Europeanisation of labour market policies, the transforma-tion of national corporatist and bargaining arrangements to allow for greater local and regional differentiation, and the development of 'social pacts' that bundle economic and social policies together to advance worker, business and national interests.

2. *De- and re-statisation* shift boundaries between state and non-state apparatuses and political activities. While the first trend concerns the *territorial* dispersion of the national state's activities, the second redraws 'public–private' divides and re-allocates state-assumed or state-delegated tasks across it. Thus some particular technical-economic, narrowly political (administrative, legislative, fisco-financial, police-military, and so on), and ideological functions performed by states (on any scale) have been transferred entirely to, or shared with, parastatal, non-governmental, private or commercial actors, institutional arrangements or regimes. This is often depicted as a shift from govern*ment* to govern*ance* but there is also traffic in other directions as states gain new responsibilities previously undertaken, if at all, by the market or civil society. This trend sees the increased importance of quite varied forms (and levels) of partnership between official bodies, parastatal organisations and NGOs in managing economic and social relations, such that the state is often only first among equals. This may not reduce the overall power of government, however, as if power were a zero-sum resource. Indeed, it may enhance the state's capacity to project its influence and secure its goals by mobilising knowledge and power resources from key non-governmental partners or stakeholders. Two important, albeit contrasting, examples of this process are the increasing importance of international regimes for the relative stabilisation of a globalising economy and the rise of cybernetworks in an extra-territorial, telematic space that is allegedly beyond state control.

3. Also important is the *re-articulation of the economic and extra-economic*. The boundaries and division of labour between the political and economic systems are being redefined to take account of changed understandings of the economy and the conditions making for sound economic performance. The economy is no longer interpreted narrowly but has been extended to include many additional factors that were deemed 'non-economic' under the KWNS regime and are now regarded as vital to economic performance and competitiveness. Thus an increasing range of previously 'non-economic' factors are now integrated into the search to promote innovation, competitiveness, an entrepreneurial culture, lifelong learning, and so on.

4. *Re-ordering political hierarchies*: nested hierarchies of power within territorially exclusive sovereign states and formal equality among them were never fully realised in the world political system, but this institutional framework did shape the ways in which forces sought to control state power and/or modify the balance of international forces. This framework has become more tangled as different scales of economic and political organisation proliferate and different scale strategies are pursued. This affects local and sub-national regional states as well as supranational state forms and international regimes, and is also reflected in the emerging inter-regional and cross-border linkages connecting local and regional authorities and governance regimes in different national formations.

There are also counter-trends, however. First, if a relative de-nationalisation of state-hood has occurred relative to the respective heydays of Atlantic Fordism, East Asian developmentalism, or Latin American import substitution industrialisation, states nonetheless continue their efforts to control the upward, downward and sideways transfer of powers and also seek to shape interscalar articulation. This can be seen not only in the forms and scope of functional networks and cyberspace(s) and their associated activities but also in the re-articulation of geoeconomic and geopolitical scales. Thus national states have an important role in producing and regulating extra-territorial spaces, such as off-shore financial centres, export processing zones, flagging out, and tax havens. They seek to shape and institutionalise the new *lex mercatoria* governing international economic relations in order to benefit their own economic spaces and firms (regardless of national provenance) that operate within it. The same holds for *lex cybertoria* and the governance of cyberspace. States on other scales also try to engage in interscalar management, of course, but even the European Union, the most advanced supranational political apparatus, still lacks the powers and legitimacy to do this to the same extent as its larger national states.

The dual shift from government to governance in the second and third trends does not make states redundant but offers new roles in meta-governance as states try to manage governance mechanisms and their interconnections in terms of the overall balance of class forces and the demands of social cohesion. Even as states cede formal juridical sovereignty in the face of an increasingly complex world and transfer responsibilities to non-statal bodies, networks and regimes, they also seek to define and steer the self-organisation of these new arrangements and their interrelations in order to promote particular state functions and to ensure political stability and social cohesion. Alongside their organisational roles here, states may also try to promote collective learning about functional linkages and material interdependencies among different sites and spheres of action. Furthermore, politicians at and across different territorial scales often get involved in creating shared visions that guide diverse forms of governance and maximise their complementarity and effectiveness.

These counter-trends highlight the extent to which a restructured national state remains central to the effective management of the emerging spatio-temporal matrices of capitalism, patterns of post- or transnational citizenship, and other challenges. Not all states are equally capable of pursuing these new objectives. Nonetheless, powerful national states have become even more important arbiters of the movement of state powers upwards, downwards and sideways, they have become even more important meta-governors of the increasingly complex multicentric, multiscalar, multitemporal and multiform world of governance, and they are actively involved in shaping the forms of international policy regimes. Given these asymmetries, this involvement can be seen as a political complement to the reorganisation of imperialism – a phenomenon that excludes both arguments about the rise of a neo-medieval political world and the emergence of an ultra-imperialist superstate or a networked transnational form of 'Empire' (Hardt and Negri, 2000).

The expanded definition of the economic at the expense of the extra-economic clearly involves a key role for states (on whatever scale) in mediating this re-articulation, steering the resulting commodification and re-commodification of social relations, and coping with the increasing dominance of capitalist logic in the wider society. Moreover, whereas the promotion of the micro-social conditions for capital accumulation in these changing circumstances may well be better handled at other levels than the national, problems of territorial integration, social cohesion and social exclusion are currently still best handled at the level of the large territorial national state, as the latter is still currently irreplaceable given its fisco-financial powers and its scope for redistributive politics in rearranging spatio-temporal fixes.

Spatio-temporal contradictions in contemporary capitalism
This said, there are few, if any, individual states with an effective global reach and an ability to compress their routines to match the time–space of fast hypermobile capital. Even the more powerful states still encounter external pressures from other states, from other power centres, and from the logic of the world market, as well as from the repercussions of their own policies and the resistance these generate. The multicentric, multiscalar, multitemporal, multiform and multicausal processes associated with globalisation pose real problems for capital accumulation because they both affirm and threaten its inherent spatio-temporal logic.

On the one hand, globalisation enhances capital's capacity to defer and displace its internal contradictions, if not to resolve them, by increasing the scope of its operations on a global scale, by reinforcing its capacities to disembed certain of its operations from local material, social and spatio-temporal constraints, by enabling it to deepen the spatial and scalar divisions of labour, by creating more opportunities for moving up, down and across scales, by commodifying and securitising the future, by deferring past and present material problems into the future, by promoting long-term technology forecasting, organisational learning and trust-building, and by re-articulating different time horizons. Above all, globalisation helps to emancipate the monetary profit-orientated, market-mediated moment of capital accumulation from extra-economic and spatio-temporal constraints, increases the emphasis on speed, acceleration and turnover time, and enhances capital's capacity to escape the control of other systems in so far as these are still territorially differentiated and fragmented. This is linked to globalisation's increased capacity for discounting events (so collapsing the future into the present), its increased capacity for time–space compression, its resort to complex derivative trading to manage risk, and its capacities to jump scale. Globalisation enhances the economic power of capital in so far as it weakens the capacity of national states to guide capital's expansion within a framework of national security (as reflected in the 'national security state'), national welfare (as reflected in social democratic welfare states), or some other national project with a matching spatio-temporal fix. It also increases pressures on national states to adjust to the time horizons and temporalities of mobile capital able to operate beyond their frontiers.

On the other hand, globalisation reinforces uneven spatial development and the continual search for material, social and spatio-temporal fixes to compensate for capitalism's inability to expand through exclusive reliance on profit-orientated, market-mediated economic forces. These fixes are material (based on the built environment), social (rooted in specific economic and extra-economic social relations), and spatio-temporal (time-and-place specific). The latter emerge when an accumulation regime and its modes of regularisation co-evolve to produce a certain structural coherence within a given spatio-temporal framework by displacing and/or deferring conflicts and contradictions beyond its territorial and/or social boundaries. Thus a spatio-temporal fix secures a zone of relative stability by pushing instability elsewhere and/or into the future. The primary scales and temporal horizons for such fixes and their relative coherence and stability obviously vary considerably.

In short, globalising capitalism typically intensifies the spatio-temporal contradictions and tensions inherent in the capital relation and/or its articulation and co-evolution with the spatialities and temporalities of the natural and social world beyond the sphere of value relations. I now discuss five tensions or contradictions that have been aggravated by the increasing organisational and spatio-temporal complexity and flexibility in the circuits of capital associated with globalisation.

1. Globalisation reinforces the contradiction between the complex, many-sided substantive reproduction requirements of real natural, social and cultural processes and the simplified, one-sided, monetised temporalities involved in capital's emphasis on maximising profit, as reinforced by the neoliberal concern with shareholder value and the explosive growth in derivatives, hedge funds and private equity buyouts. Thus capital finds it easier to destroy the local bounties of first and second nature and exit without regard to their long-term reproduction (cf. Brennan, 2000).[1]
2. Globalisation intensifies conflicts between the many and varied substantive temporalities of human existence (biological, sentient, socio-cultural, self-reflexive) and the abstract time inherent in wage labour and the dominance of formal market rationality (Stahel, 1999, p. 108; cf. Polanyi, 1957). This is reflected in the stresses of everyday life and a growing sense of time–space compression.
3. Globalisation intensifies the tension between short-term calculation (especially in financial flows) and the long-term dynamic of 'real competition' rooted in resources (skills, trust, heightened reflexivity, collective mastery of techniques, economies of agglomeration and size, local systems of innovation, learning regions, and so on) that take years to create, stabilise and reproduce. This is reflected in the contrast between the global economy as a space of flows and as an interconnected set of places.
4. Globalisation reinforces the tension between the drive to accelerate the turnover time of capital by shortening the production cycle between design and final consumption and the long-term infrastructural development on which this depends.
5. Finally, this latter tension has a spatial dimension in so far as the extension of markets through the annihilation of space by time also depends on fixed infrastructure to enable rapid movement through space (which must be destroyed in turn as the next round of accumulation develops) (Harvey, 1996, p. 6).

The growing dominance of the logic of capital

Marx and Engels argued that, during the initial development of capitalism,

> [t]he movement of capital, although considerably accelerated, still remained, however, relatively slow. The splitting up of the world market into separate parts, each of which was exploited by a particular nation, the exclusion of competition among themselves on the part of the nations, the clumsiness of production itself and the fact that finance was only evolving from its early stages, greatly impeded circulation ([1845] 1976, 56n).

If the expansion of the world market is inherent in the logic of capital, as they argued, this logic has become more powerful thanks to world market integration. This is because globalisation reduces the frictions associated with 'national power containers' in the global circulation of commodities, industrial capital, labour-power, and finance. This, in turn, reinforces the dominance of exchange value and frees money capital as its most abstract expression to move at will within the world market to maximise opportunities for profit (Jessop, 2002). In particular, through neoliberal globalisation, capital develops its chances of avoiding the structural constraints of other systems and their attempts at control, thereby increasing its 'indifference' to its social environment and the likely costs of neoliberal market failures.

Different degrees of liquidity, flexibility and fungibility mean that capitals vary in their ability to respond to such pressures and competition. International finance capital controls the most liquid, abstract and generalised resource and has become the most integrated fraction of capital. Derivatives have developed as the most generalised form of this capacity and, indeed, have an increasing role in the commensuration of all investment opportunities in the world market, serving thereby as a self-generating, self-referential expression of capital in general on a world scale (cf. Bryan and Rafferty, 2006). This does not mean that finance (let alone the economy more generally) can escape its overall dependence on other functional or, of course, crisis tendencies rooted in its own contradictions and dilemmas. Attempts to escape particular constraints and particular attempts at control can nonetheless occur through its own internal operations in time (discounting, insurance, risk management, futures, derivatives, hedge funds, and so on) or space (capital flight, relocation, outsourcing abroad, claims to extra-territoriality, and so on) and/or through external pressures on other systems via their dependence on revenues generated by market forces (including non-profit activities, borrowing or taxation), by lobbying or forcing them to take account of how their activities impact on 'competitiveness', or by personal corruption through bribery and 'revolving doors'.

One could argue that the overall impact of capitalism on societal dynamics on a global scale is closely related to the extent to which its internal competition, internal complexity and loose coupling, capacity for reflexive self-reorganisation, scope for time–space distantiation and compression, externalisation of problems, and hegemonic capacities can be freed from confinement within limited ecological spaces policed by another system (such as a political system segmented into mutually exclusive sovereign territories). Disembedded from other systems, internal competition to lower socially necessary labour-time and socially necessary turnover time becomes an ever more powerful driving force in accumulation. Liberalisation, de-regulation, privatisation, state-sponsored commodification, internationalisation, and the lowering of direct taxes all boost the scope for internal variation and selection in the profit-orientated, market-mediated economy. Combined with an emphasis on shareholder value, this particularly benefits hypermobile financial capital, reinforcing its competitiveness and ratcheting up its ability to displace and defer problems onto other economic actors and interests, other systems and the natural environment. In contrast with the structured coherence of Fordism and the post-Fordist knowledge-based economy, the post-Fordist neoliberal financial regime militates against the long-term structured coherence of accumulation regimes and their modes of regulation. In particular, it weakens the spatio-temporal fixes with which regimes based on the primacy of productive capital manage the contradictions between fixity and motion in order to produce zones of relative stability by deferring and displacing their effects. This can be seen in the impact of financialisation, not only in Atlantic Fordism but also in the export-orientated economies of East Asia and the viability of import-substitution industrialisation strategies in Latin America and Africa. The destructive impact of financialisation in this regard is reinforced through the neoliberal approach to accumulation through dispossession (especially the politically licensed plundering of public assets and the intellectual commons) and the dynamic of uneven development (enabling financial capital to move on when the disastrous effects of financialisation weaken those productive capitals that have to be valorised in particular times and places). Yet this also enhances the scope for the contradictions and dilemmas of a relatively unfettered (or disembedded) capitalism to shape the operation of other systems and may thereby undermine crucial extra-economic conditions for accumulation.

Temporal sovereign*ties*
States have territorial sovereignty when they exercise exclusive juridico-political control over their territory and population. But this is often severely constrained by state dependence on resources provided by other systems and by material interdependencies among states. All states depend on tax revenues and loans originating in the private sector and on access to strategic resources (such as oil), and superpowers have means of influencing the decisions of client and/or weak states despite their formal sovereignty. The latter also depends in part on the often-neglected issue of temporal sovereignty, that is, the state's ability to make decisions according to its own political routines rather than the rhythms of other systems. States increasingly face temporal pressures in policy making and implementation due to new forms of time–space distantiation, compression and differentiation. As the multiple temporalities of the economy and economic decision making accelerate relative to those of the state and political decision making, the time to determine and coordinate political responses to economic events shrinks – especially regarding hypermobile, superfast capital. This reinforces conflicts between the time(s) of the state and the time(s) of the market, with some states more actively involved in, and/or more vulnerable to, time–space distantiation and compression. More generally, the pressure to comprehend more information and address issues in real time tends to collapse the future into the present, pressuring states to adapt by withdrawing from areas where they are too slow to make a difference, speeding up their routines through fast policy and fast tracking, or seeking to slow down economic movements.

There are four strategies to cope with this:

1. Abandon attempts to control short-term economic activities and movements, even as states still seek to control medium- to long-term economic decisions and movements. This might work if short-term market movements were marginal and self-compensating but, where they are radically destabilising, such efforts could reinforce the impact of deregulated financial markets and economic crises.
2. Compress decision-making cycles to enable more timely and apt state action, as seen in the shortening of policy development cycles, fast-track decision-making, rapid programme roll-out, institutional and policy experimentation, relentless revision of guidelines and benchmarks, and retreat from fixed legal standards towards more flexible, discretionary, reflexive laws. This solution privileges those who can operate within compressed timescales – fast movers, thinkers, talkers and decision makers – and limits room for deliberation, consultation and negotiation. Such fast policy privileges the executive over the legislature and judiciary, finance over industry, consumption over long-term investment. It weakens corporatism, stakeholding, the rule of law, formal bureaucracy, and, indeed, the routines and cycles of democratic politics more generally.

3. Create relative political time by slowing the circuits of 'fast capitalism'. The best known proposal is the Tobin tax, which aims to decelerate the flow of superfast, hypermobile financial capital and limit its distortion of the real economy. Other examples include energy taxes on fossil fuels and nuclear power, a global 'polluter pays' principle, a global prudential principle regarding new technologies, and inclusion of recycling and disposal costs in the price of goods.

4. Establish the institutional framework for economic, political, and social self-regulation based on subsidiarity (dealing with problems at the lowest scale possible compatible with the general interest) and continuous monitoring of such self-regulation in terms of deliberatively agreed criteria (Scheuerman, 2004). This could focus on the nature of the wage relation and spatio-temporal contradictions of global capitalism, prioritise the use value dimensions of these contradictions, and integrate policies to decelerate the 'runaway world' and address environmental problems and global social injustice. The alter-globalisation movement and initiatives from many different social forces at many scales illustrate this approach. It nonetheless poses major problems of institutional and organisational design and of transforming social identities, subjectivities and expectations.

Concluding remarks

A research agenda on globalisation and the state should include a comparison of the relative weight of different state policies involved in promoting and/or resisting globalisation. States have long played a key role in establishing and regulating the spatio-temporal matrices of social life and the impact of uneven development. This remains true of the latest wave of globalisation. Key activities include: deregulating, liberalising and shaping the institutional architecture of finance, facilitating thereby its accelerating internationalisation and its global acceleration; modifying institutional frameworks for international trade and foreign direct investment; planning and subsidising the spatial fixes that support the activities of financial, industrial and commercial capital within and across borders; promoting uneven development through policies for inter-urban and interregional as well as international competition; cooperating in the rebordering and rescaling of state functions – including decentralisation and cross-border region formation, regional bloc formation, and participating in forums for inter-triad negotiation; de-statising current state functions by transferring them to private–public partnerships or place-bound market forces and thereby linking them to market-orientated temporalities; de-territorialising some state functions by transferring them to private forms of functional authority (including international regimes) and/or to mobile market forces; attempting, conversely, to fit some non-territorial problems into an areal structure (for example, requiring states to enforce international compacts on global warming); and, finally, addressing the multiformity of globalisation through state involvement in struggles over the rules to harmonise or standardise diverse technological, economic, juridico-political, socio-cultural and environmental issues.

Note

1. 'First nature' refers to that part of the Earth's natural environment that has not been impacted by humans, whereas 'second nature' refers to humanly produced nature, that is to say 'nature' that has been shaped in some way by human activities (see Smith, 1990).

References

Altvater, E. and B. Mahnkopf (2007), *Die Grenzen der Globalisierung*, 6th edn, Münster: Westfälisches Dampfboot.
Brennan, T. (2000), *Exhausting Modernity: Grounds for a New Economy*, London: Routledge.
Bryan, R. and B. Rafferty (2006), *Capitalism with Derivatives: A Political Economy of Financial Derivatives, Capital and Class*, Basingstoke: Palgrave.
Frank, A.G. (1990), 'A theoretical introduction to 5000 years of world system history', *Review*, **13** (2), 155-248.
Gamble, C. (1994), *Timewalkers: The Prehistory of Global Colonization*, Cambridge, MA: Harvard University Press.
Gramsci, A. (1971), *Selections from the Prison Notebooks*, London: Lawrence and Wishart.
Gross, D. (1985), 'Temporality and the modern state', *Theory and Society*, **14** (1), 53–81.
Hardt, M. and A. Negri (2000), *Empire*, Cambridge, MA: Harvard University Press.
Harvey, D. (1996), 'Globalisation in question', *Rethinking Marxism*, **8** (4), 1–17.
Hayek, F.A. von (1960), *The Constitution of Liberty*, South Bend, IN: Gateway.
Hirst, P.Q. and G. Thompson (1996), *Globalisation in Question*, Cambridge: Polity.
Hobson, J.A. (1902), *Imperialism: A Study*, London: James Nisbett.
Jessop, B. (2002), *The Future of the Capitalist State*, Cambridge: Polity
Lenin, V.I. (1917), *Imperialism*, Moscow: Progress Publishers.
Mann, M. (1986), *The Sources of Social Power*, Vol. 1, Cambridge: Cambridge University Press.
Marx, K. ([1867] 1967), *Capital*, Vol. 1, London: Lawrence and Wishart.
Marx, K. and F. Engels ([1845] 1976), *The German Ideology*, in K. Marx and F. Engels, *Marx-Engels Collected Works*, vol. 5, London: Lawrence and Wishart.
Nye, J.S. (1990), *Bound to Lead: The Changing Nature of American Power*, New York: Basic Books.
Polanyi, K. (1957), *The Great Transformation*, Boston, MA: Beacon Press.
Poulantzas, N. (1975), *Classes in Contemporary Capitalism*, London: Verso.
Poulantzas, N. (1978), *State, Power, Socialism*, London: Verso.
Scheuerman, W.E. (2004), *Liberal Democracy and the Social Acceleration of Time*, Baltimore, MD: Johns Hopkins University Press.
Scholte, J.A. (2000), *Globalisation: a Critical Introduction*, Basingstoke: Palgrave.
Smith, A. ([1776] 1937), *An Inquiry into the Nature and Causes of the Wealth of Nations*, New York: Modern Library.
Smith, N. (1990), *Uneven Development: Nature, Capital and the Production of Space*, 2nd edn, Oxford: Blackwell.
Stahel, A.W. (1999), 'Time contradictions of capitalism', *Culture, Nature, Society*, **10** (1), 101–32.
Standage, T. (1998), *The Victorian Internet: The Remarkable Story of the Telegraph and the 19th Century's Online Pioneers*, London: Weidenfeld and Nicolson.
Wallerstein, I. (1980), *The Modern World System II*, London: Academic Press.
Weber, M. (1961), *General Economic History*, New York: Collier.

3 Creating markets, contesting markets: labour internationalism and the European Common Transport Policy

Peter Turnbull

Introduction

In the textbook world of neoclassical economics, markets appear as 'natural' phenomena. An infinite number of firms compete to produce goods or provide services, prices are determined by the 'invisible hand' of supply and demand, and there are no dominant players in the market. There are certainly no firms or other institutions that can 'make the market'. Deviations from the competitive market are certainly recognised (for example, oligopoly, duopoly, monopoly and monopsony) but it is the ideal world of (perfect) competition that informs the neoliberal agenda and the seeming desire to emancipate the economic sphere in general, and markets in particular, from state control. In reality, of course, markets are neither 'natural' nor 'self-correcting'. Rather, '[m]arkets are created by governments, ordered by institutions, and sustained by regulations . . . markets are social institutions governed by a set of rules, many of which are framed by the public authorities' (Wilks, 1996, pp. 538–9). Social actors 'play by the rules' but also seek to change the rules to their own advantage. In particular, through the 'social production of space', capital, together with the state, seeks to construct material geographies that it can use to facilitate the extraction and realisation of surplus value. As Harvey (1982) demonstrates, capital must create particular 'spatial fixes' in the landscape at particular times to allow accumulation to proceed. Today, these spatial fixes extend well beyond the remit of the nation state.

In days gone by, the ultimate authority of the state over the markets within its borders was widely accepted. In some markets, such as civil aviation, the authority of the state was absolute – state sovereignty was recognised both nationally and internationally within the airspace above the state's geographical territory. As a result, any airline wishing to gain access to the airspace of a foreign country, whether simply to overfly the country in question or to set down and pick up passengers, had to rely on the state to negotiate access on its behalf. In an age of globalisation, however, it appears that capital has now 'outgrown' the state:

> [t]rans-national corporations have gone global and function in near real time, leaving behind the slower moving, state-mediated inter-*national* world of arm's-length economic transactions and traditional international legal mechanisms, even as they depend on that world for their licences to operate and to protect their property rights (Ruggie, 2004, p. 503, emphasis in original).

The creation of these new 'non-territorial spaces and management systems' not only poses a challenge for traditional territorially-based rule-making (Ruggie, 2004, p. 503), but also social democracy:

In an era when the movement of goods, capital, and labor across borders seems to escape the control of the nation state, *laissez-faire* arguments gain heft. And as they do, they weaken the conviction that had made democracy so compelling through the centuries: the idea that if people have influence on the state, they can use that influence to shape the conditions of their own well-being. (Fox Piven, 2006, p. 44)

Those seeking (social) protection from the market through their own 'spatial fix', most notably the working class (Herod, 1997), have tended to 'follow the market' in terms of building their collective organisation and repertoires of contention 'from the ground up'. Thus, workplace trade union organisation and collective bargaining would typically be extended to embrace cooperation between workers in local firms, with regional and national organisation to follow (Commons, 1909). However, this process is by no means automatic (Marginson and Sisson, 2004, p. 312) as the 'politics of scale' intervene (Marston, 2000). Moreover, the contest between 'market making' (economic) policies and 'market correcting' (social) policies has always been uneven, with labour invariably aligned against (domestic) capital and the (nation) state. This is not to deny the success of labour and social reformers in developing extensive welfare systems and employment protection in many countries; rather it is to highlight the deep political roots of the union movement in national political systems (Pasture and Verberckmoes, 1998, p. 20). In contrast, '[i]f workers are to enjoy collective rights in the new world order, they will have to invent new strategies at the scale of international capital' (Tilly, 1995, p. 5). To do this demands what Tarrow (2005, p. 121) defines as a 'scale shift', characterised by a change in the number and level of coordinated contentious actions to a different focal point, involving a new range of actors, different objects and broadened claims. In this respect, geographic scales do not merely express social relations but actively enable and constrain, empower as well as confine (Ward, 2007, p. 273). Thus, '[t]oday's international system offers a special challenge for activists because it both opens conduits for upward shift and can empower national, regional and local contention with international models of collective action' (Tarrow, 2005, p. 121).

The significance of new scales of contention for organised labour is perhaps most evident in the European Union, where economic and social processes are increasingly constituted at the European level and where relationships between the local, regional, national and international have been transformed in recent years (Sadler, 2000, p. 148). For example, around half of all legislation and over three-quarters of all economic legislation passing through EU member state parliaments now bears the 'made in Brussels' stamp (Greenwood, 2003, pp. 9–10). Also, while there has always been a 'political decoupling' of economic integration and social protection (Scharpf, 1999, 2002) – the former residing increasingly with the EU institutions and the latter with the nation state – the interaction between them is one in which contending economic and political philosophies are 'played out' through a multilevel system of 'deliberative governance' (Teague, 2001). To be sure, social (market correcting) policies are 'secondary' and 'subservient' to economic (market making) policies (Sadler, 2000, p. 144), giving rise to (labour cost) competition between member states (Streeck, 1998; Marginson and Sisson, 2004, p. 5), but social protection is now enshrined in the European Treaty (agreed in Amsterdam 1997), which aims to 'promote employment, improved living and working conditions, so as to make possible their harmonization while the improvement is being maintained, proper social protection, dialogue between management and labour, the development of human resources with a view to lasting employment and the combating of exclusion' (European Communities, 1997, Art. 136).[1] This is an important point of leverage for organised labour as the shift of policy making from the local and the national to the supranational level creates information flows and offers both resources and opportunities that trade unions can utilise to form coalitions across borders (Hooghe and Marks, 2001). Neither the institutional framework nor the political commitment to social policy is to be found in other free trade agreements such as NAFTA, APEC or Mercosur (Haworth and Hughes, 2002, p. 66).

While the EU offers unrivalled political opportunities for organised labour to mobilise and influence policy outcomes (Marks and McAdam, 1999), it also presents a major challenge, some would say an 'unstoppable tide for labour interests to contend with' (Greenwood, 2003, p. 149). For most of their history, 'international' trade unions have been overwhelmingly European in inspiration, composition and leadership (Hyman, 2005a, p. 140), but European trade union structures have been weakest at the industry level, where national trade unions are strongest, and strongest at the peak level, where national unions are weakest (Dølvik and Visser, 2001). This serves to reinforce the domestic orientation of national unions while international union organisations focus on routine and bureaucratic functions, with a 'lowest common denominator' approach to more substantial issues. 'Internationalism from above can thus marry efficiency to impotence' (Hyman, 2005a, p. 145) and in a European context the industry-based trade union federations (European Industry Federations [EIFs]) affiliated to the European Trade Union Confederation (ETUC) 'possess extremely restricted capacity either to influence capital or the EU decision-makers, or to communicate with the members whom they in theory represent' (Hyman, 1999, p. 111). However, if national unions can 'shift scale' by mobilising their considerable organisational strength at the industry level, thereby crossing the horizontal spatial divide between different political cultures and the vertical gap between different levels of the international system (Tarrow, 2005, p. 122), then workers might still retain some protection from the vagaries of the (Single European) market.

This is readily demonstrated through the contrasting experience of two sectors of the European transport industry, namely civil aviation and ports. In the now liberalised European civil aviation industry, national carriers have been transformed into 'community airlines' (Mawson, 1997) who enjoy the right of 'cabotage' (that is, the right to carry passengers or cargo between two points in a foreign state), whereas in port transport the European institutions are still struggling to open access to the market. In the former case, unions remained wedded to their immediate place and conventional (national) repertoires of contention. Consequently, aviation unions failed to 'shift scale'. In the latter case, on the other hand, localities were not simply 'places of dependence' but 'spaces of engagement' (Cox, 1998, p. 2) that created multiple opportunities for resistance. Consequently, as dock workers shifted scale, the targets of their new repertoire of contention were global capital and the supranational institutions of the EU. Having defeated two proposed 'Directives On Market Access to Port Services' (CEC, 2001c, 2004), labour's spatial fix has now forced the European Commission to revise both the process of 'market making' and the level of social protection afforded to organised labour as a condition of any future liberalisation of the market. In sum, port workers were able to externalise their conflict with (global) capital and the (supranational) state (that is, project domestic claims onto international institutions and foreign actors), whereas aviation workers were unable to progress much beyond what Tarrow (2005, pp. 32–3) identifies as 'global issue framing' (that is, the mobilisation of international symbols to frame domestic conflicts) and 'internalisation' (that is, responding to foreign or international pressures within domestic politics).

In this context, the account that follows is a 'labour geography' – that is, 'an effort to see the making of the economic geography of capitalism through the eyes of labor by understanding how workers seek to make space in particular ways' (Herod, 1997, p. 3) – which acknowledges that if workers can take advantage of the resources at one scale to overcome the constraints encountered at other scales, in the way that more powerful actors can do, then 'they may have greater potential for pressing their claims' (Staeheli, 1994, p. 388). However, before reviewing how the market has been created and contested in these two industries, it is instructive to explore the role of transport services in the global economy and to establish precisely how, and why, the supranational state has sought to create a single European transport market.

Globalisation, transport and the Single European Market (SEM)

If globalisation is understood to involve processes that are truly global and intercontinental in character – 'a process (or set of processes) which embodies a transformation in the spatial organisation of social relations and transactions . . . generating transcontinental or interregional flows and networks of activity, interaction, and the exercise of power' (Held et al., 1999, p. 16) – then European integration and the creation of a Single European Market (SEM) is hardly evidence of globalisation (Hay, 2006). EU member states trade predominantly with other member states (El-Agraa, 2004, pp. 92–3) and most foreign direct investment originating in member states is destined for other EU member states (Dicken, 2003, p. 59; Rugman, 2003; Hay, 2006, p. 17). In fact, foreign direct investment becomes a substitute for trade over distance, with TNCs from outside the EU investing in Europe to secure access to the SEM (Hay, 2006, p. 17).

Transport is central to the processes of globalisation in general and European economic integration in particular. As transport specialists readily acknowledge, the sector is both a proactive agent of globalisation – as lower transport costs enable TNCs to manufacture or source almost anything, almost anywhere in the world, and then ship it to almost anywhere else, without transport costs being a constraining factor (Lim, 1998, p. 369) – and a principal beneficiary of global trade (which grows at a much faster rate than the rate of global GDP growth) (UNCTAD, 2003, p. 1). In particular, transport 'acts as a catalyst for reduced restrictions on international trade, promotes new technologies and markets them on a global basis, seeks both national and international policy measures to support expanded transport investments, and often discourages regulatory measures to internalize the negative social and environmental costs associated with transport activities' (Janelle and Beuthe, 1997, p. 200). In Europe, the transport industry is recognised as important in its own right, accounting for about 7 per cent of European GDP and around 5 per cent of employment in the EU, but more important is the industry's contribution to the competitiveness of other European industries and services, the integration of member states and the mobility of European citizens (CEC, 2006a).

Although the original member states of the European Economic Community recognised the importance of transport, placing it alongside agriculture and trade as an area that warranted a common policy, the transport Title (IV) of the Treaty of Rome (1957) proved highly contentious, not least because of the different transport systems operated by more (or less) interventionist (liberal) member states. So, even though the original six committed themselves to a common transport policy, they did not commit themselves to a common market for transport services.[2] This was certainly the case for air and sea transport, which were pointedly excluded from Title IV.[3] Article 84(2), which appears almost as an afterthought, does state that '[t]he Council [of European Ministers] may, acting by unanimity, decide whether and to what extent and by what procedure appropriate provisions may be laid down for sea and air transport', but there was no inclination on the part of the original member states to act on this Article. As a result, during the first phase of the common transport policy (CTP) (1957–85), the provision of transport services was principally a matter for individual member states (Schmidt and Giorgi, 2001). The situation only began to change with the accession of more liberal member states, most notably the UK, and as a result of legal proceedings before the European Court of Justice.

The Community's policy-making authority in the maritime (seafaring) industry was confirmed in the early 1970s (Case 167/73) but this had little practical impact on the port transport industry (Turnbull, 2008). Aviation remained the subject of bilateral air service agreements (BASAs) negotiated by nation states, and any attempts by the Commission to liberalise air transport in the late 1970s and early 1980s met with a hostile response from member states (O'Reilly and Stone Sweet, 1998, pp. 167–8). However, the European Parliament (in 1983) brought a case against the Council of Ministers in the European Court of Justice in which the Court (in 1985) found that the Council, in failing to develop a common policy for transport, was in breach of its Treaty obligations. Henceforth, the Council was obliged to adopt measures to liberalise the transport industry 'within a reasonable time'. Concurrently, in its White Paper on 'Completing the Internal Market' (1985), the Commission identified transport as a significant barrier to further economic integration. To expedite reform, the Single European Act (February 1986, effective July 1987) extended qualified majority voting in the Council[4] to air and sea transport, providing both the Commission and more liberally-minded member states in the Council with the leverage they needed to push forward the liberalisation of transport services.

Further impetus was provided by the Treaty of Maastricht (1992) which marked 'the completion date of the Internal Market; for transport it was very much the starting date' (CEC, 2006a, p. 21). In the same year, the Commission published a White Paper on 'The Future Development of the Common Transport Policy', accompanied by subsequent action programmes for 1995–2000 (CEC, 1995) and 1998–2004 (CEC, 1998b), which enlarged the objectives of the CTP (to include sustainability and social cohesion) but retained the emphasis on liberalisation. Indeed, most 'progress' under the CTP has been in respect of 'removing barriers to competition' (Schmidt and Giorgi, 2001, p. 296), although in some sectors (for example, rail and ports), and in several member states, the transport sector is still 'open only on paper' (CEC, 2005, p. 16). The emphasis on 'negative (de)regulation' (for example, opening and/or widening access to the market, insisting on a minimum number of service providers to ensure competition, policing anti-competitive behaviour, controlling mergers and acquisitions, etc) as opposed to 'positive regulation' (that is, setting agreed rules and standards) is a common feature of economic integration in the EU (Hix, 1999). In fact, European integration can be defined as 'a process of *economic liberalization by international means* . . . the opening up of national economies through [an] internationally negotiated expansion of markets beyond national borders' (Streeck, 1998, p. 429, emphasis in original).

The implications of liberalisation for transport workers, and indeed for all European citizens, is a potential 'race-to-the-bottom'. In a multilevel political economy, 'where politics is decentralized in national institutions located in and constrained by integrated *competitive markets extending far beyond their territorial reach*, and where supranationally centralized institutions are primarily dedicated to implementing and maintaining those markets' (Streeck, 1998, p. 431, emphasis added), any international pressures for economic integration are 'mediated by national institutional arrangements and refracted into *divergent struggles over particular national practices*' (Locke and Thelen, 1995, p. 338, emphasis added). This exposes the working class in different member states of the EU to 'regime competition' (Streeck, 1998, p. 432) as both substantive terms and conditions of employment and procedural rules (for example, collective bargaining) are 'adjusted' (in most cases eroded and undermined) in accordance with competitive interdependence. In this context, the problem for (organised) labour is not simply the fact that markets are no longer coterminous with national borders, but that any pressures for the political defence of social cohesion – the desire to prevent the market economy becoming a market society – tend to be deflected to national systems of politics and/or employment regulation where competition and xenophobia, rather than international solidarity, might then prevail (Wills, 1998, p. 118). In essence, this is what happened during the crucial stages of liberalisation in the civil aviation industry (1987–92) but which port workers have been able to avoid when they have faced a similar assault from TNCs and the supranational state (2001 to date).

Creating a single market for air transport
Civil aviation is a highly regulated industry, not only in terms of market access but also health and safety and general working conditions. In fact, it is widely regarded as being subject to greater state regulation than any other mode of transport (Armstrong and Bulmer, 1998, p. 174; O'Reilly and Stone Sweet, 1998, p. 165), the object of what Kassim (1996, p. 106) described as 'restrictive and protectionist policies of patriotic interventionism'. The product market was governed by a system of bilateral air service agreements (BASAs) through which nation states would exchange the first 'five freedoms' of the air (listed in Box 3.1) under the auspices of the International Air Transport Association. As a result, 'in some countries it was difficult to tell where the management of the airline ended and the state began' (Kassim, 1996, p. 114). With a highly regulated product market – BASAs would typically specify which airlines could fly designated routes (usually the two national 'flag' carriers), with capacity sharing (typically 50:50), agreed fares, flight frequency, and even revenue sharing – national trade unions were able to secure a firm foothold in the labour market. Certainly, most European aviation unions identified strongly with their national flag carrier and many took little, or at least far less, interest in organising workers in other carriers (for example, charter airlines and regional carriers). Airline personnel employed at the national flag airline generally enjoyed very favourable terms and conditions of employment, which economists and neoliberals attributed to 'rent sharing' under conditions of 'bilateral monopoly' (Barrett, 1987, p. 11; Windle, 1991).

BOX 3.1   THE FREEDOMS OF THE AIR

Freedoms defined by the International Air Transport Agreement and exchanged in bilateral agreements

First Freedom: the freedom to overfly the territory of another state

Second Freedom: the freedom to land for technical reasons in another state

Third Freedom: the freedom to carry commercial traffic from the home state to the foreign state

Fourth Freedom: the freedom to carry traffic from the foreign state to the home state

Fifth Freedom: the freedom for a carrier to carry commercial traffic between two foreign states on a route to or from the home state

Other Freedoms

Sixth Freedom: the freedom to operate commercial services between two foreign states via the home state

Seventh Freedom: the freedom to operate commercial services directly between two points in a foreign state (also known as 'cabotage')

Source: Based on Doganis (1991, p. 346).

At the inception of the Treaty of Rome, Europe already had a well established system of regulation for air transport, under the auspices of the European Civil Aviation Conference (ECAC),[5] with BASAs between member states providing for both capacity and revenue sharing on most routes. By the mid-1980s, of 988 intra-EU airline routes only 48 had multiple designations and only 88 routes permitted fifth freedom rights (Armstrong and Bulmer, 1998, p. 173). As O'Reilly and Stone Sweet (1998, p. 164) pointed out, 'national governments still guarded virtually unchallenged authority to regulate air transport'. But just a decade later, 'nearly every significant aspect of that authority falls within the competence of the European Community' (1998, p. 164).

The initial step towards supranational regulation of the market – a memorandum issued by the Commission in 1979 (CEC, 1979) – was greeted with an overwhelmingly negative response from member states, the European Parliament, the Association of European Airlines and civil aviation unions, while subsequent measures put forward in the early 1980s were either rejected by the Council or watered down to such an extent that they had little or no impact (for example, attempts to encourage competition on regional air services) (O'Reilly and Stone Sweet, 1998, pp. 167–8). However, the introduction of qualified majority voting for air transport in the Council following the passage of the Single European Act (see note 4), the lobbying of consumer groups and, crucially, the 'pace-setting' (Börzel, 2002) of more liberal member states in the Council, allowed the Commission to apply pressure on the 'foot-dragging' and 'fence-sitting' member states. This was done through a legal strategy that presented itself when the European Court of Justice (ECJ) ruled against national price-fixing in the *Nouvelles Frontières* (1986) case.[6] Based on this decision, the Commission (DG Competition), as the guardian of the Treaty and the body responsible for administering EU competition law, called upon all European airlines to abandon price fixing. More precisely, the Commission could now use its powers under Art. 85 of the Treaty to investigate any 'agreements', 'decisions' or 'concerted practices' in the aviation sector that 'have as their effect the prevention, restriction or distortion of competition within the common market, and in particular those which directly or indirectly fix purchase or selling prices or any other trading conditions'. Just as the price-fixing mechanisms of the French Civil Aviation Code were found to have distorted competition within the EU (see note 6), other member states feared that their BASAs and other arrangements would also fall foul of EU competition law.[7] Thus, member states faced two choices: either develop a new aviation policy for the Community or seek to maintain national authority under the constant threat of legal action from the Commission.[8] While Italy, Greece, Spain, Portugal and Denmark still dragged their feet, the UK and the Netherlands continued to set the pace in the Council.

The UK already had the most liberal civil aviation market in the EU, having pioneered low-cost travel in the 1960s and 1970s and having established an independent regulatory authority for civil aviation. But liberalisation was pursued with renewed vigour by the Thatcher government. The sale of British Airways (BA) was announced early on, although privatisation was delayed until 1987, and the Conservative government removed barriers to entry and regulations on fare-setting in the domestic market in 1984. This was followed by the negotiation of a series of liberal BASAs with other member states, most notably with the Netherlands in 1984 and then Ireland, Belgium and Germany. The Dutch proved to be the UK's strongest ally in the Council, no doubt because both BA and KLM (the Dutch national carrier) were seeking to develop their main airport (Heathrow and Schipol respectively) as European gateways to the rest of the world (that is, freer access to the EU market would enable these airlines to consolidate passengers from all over Europe at their primary 'hub' for onward transcontinental flights – in effect, the EU would become their 'domestic' market).[9] The preferred spatial fix of transnational capital was set out during the UK's presidency of the EU (in the second half of 1986), which was followed immediately by that of the Dutch government. This enabled the pacesetters to 'punch above their weight' in Council negotiations (Armstrong and Bulmer, 1998, p. 190) and press for liberalisation at precisely the time when the Commission's right to enforce competition law in the civil aviation industry had been affirmed by the ECJ in the *Nouvelles Frontières* case (see note 6). At this stage, however, the pacesetters did not have a qualified majority over the 'foot-draggers' (Spain, Portugal, Greece, Italy and Denmark) and the 'fence-sitters' (Germany, France, Belgium, Luxembourg and Ireland), who were only willing, at that time, to entertain a limited form of 'deregulation'. The foot-draggers, in particular, were keen to protect regional air services.[10]

A compromise package of reforms was therefore agreed (in December 1987). Unlike the 'big bang' that marked the liberalisation of the US domestic aviation market in 1978, the EU's approach to liberalisation could best be described as 'evolutionary', with two further packages of reform (agreed in 1990 and 1992) that eventually created an internal air transport market for European civil aviation (from 1 April 1997). The three packages, summarised in Table 3.1, comprised three related elements: market building, market regulating and market strengthening (Kassim, 1996, pp. 115–19). Of the market building measures, the third package was clearly the most significant, lifting restrictions on fifth freedom rights and allowing cabotage. Corresponding measures to regulate the market, most notably to ensure the application of EU competition rules, were also introduced. For example, established (flag) airlines might have to give up landing/take-off slots that made it difficult for new airlines to enter the market, and any payments from a member state to its flag airline were now subject to EU rules on state aid.[11] Measures to strengthen the market included a non-discriminatory and transparent process for allocating landing/take-off slots as well as measures to remove sources of 'market distortion' (for example, codes of conduct on computer reservation systems used by travel agents which originally brought up only the flights of airlines who paid to be on these systems). To many observers, this process represented a paradox:

> On the one hand, regulations have been and continue to be removed to allow more direct and intense airline competition. On the other hand, a host of rigid rules and codes of conduct are being introduced with the twin aim of harmonizing the terms of competition and of consumer protection, but which increasingly constrain airline managers' freedom of action. (Doganis, 1991, p. 95)

Of course, markets can never be completely 'deregulated', if that term is understood to mean a 'free market' without regulations. More importantly, what Doganis and others failed to acknowledge was how the new 'rules of competition' and the geographic reach of the market created opportunities as well as constraints for airline management, especially in relation to the control of labour costs and the revision of work practices.

The relationship between European places had been redefined by liberalisation, enabling capital to level economic space by equalising the rate of exploitation across the internal market. Put differently, all European (flag) carriers would now have to match the costs and efficiency of all other airlines in the market, including low-cost new entrants such as easyJet and Ryanair, as opposed to just the one other airline with whom they previously shared the route and fixed the tariff.[12] While some airlines saw this as a constraint, others welcomed the opportunity to expand their market share at the expense of their rivals (instead of sharing capacity and revenue on a 50:50 basis). This is not, of course, a market in which capital is now capable of simply transcending space, while labour is necessarily confined to place, as 'even the most flighty of capital must come to ground at some point' (Herod et al., 2007, p. 253). But the 'framing processes' that influenced the initial response of European civil aviation unions to liberalisation – that is, 'the way in which unionists perceive and think about changes in their external context' (Frege and Kelly, 2003, p. 14) – were largely parochial. Most unions aligned themselves with 'their' airline and focused their attention on the nation state, seeking to protect their interests through 'conventional' means (that is, institutionalised, elite lobbying within established political channels) via the Council of Ministers. Although the Council is the most important legislative body of the EU, as an intergovernmental institution the path to exerting pressure on its decision-making runs through individual member states (that is, unions lobby their national transport minister to protect their interests in Council negotiations). Thus, once this path is chosen, the logic of political activity, 'indeed political pressure in general, is clear: operate within respective member states rather than at the European level' (Marks and McAdam, 1999, p. 105). As a result, while open access to the product market created

Table 3.1   From bilateral air service agreements to the single market

Policy	BASA	EU First Package	EU Second Package	EU Third Package
Fares:	Agreed by both governments	Zonal system: automatic approval of discount and deep discount fares within defined range	Zonal system extended; conditions on availability of discount fares relaxed	Airlines set own fares; safeguards for excessively high or low fares
Licensing:	National rules	No change	No change	EU criteria for ownership, airworthiness and economic fitness
Access:				
• relations between state and own airlines	Governments' full discretion	No change	No change	Subject to EU regime
• relations with foreign carriers	Negotiated bilaterally	Subject to EC rules	Subject to EC rules	Subject to EU rules
• multiple designation (country to country)	Negotiated bilaterally case by case	Yes under EC rules	Yes under EC rules	Yes under EU rules
• multiple designation (city pairs)	Negotiated bilaterally	Automatic above defined thresholds	Thresholds lowered	Full access allowed
• safeguard provisions			Provisions for regional development	Provisions for regional development
• fifth freedom	Rarely	Permitted for 30% traffic p.a.	Permitted for 50% traffic p.a.	Permitted without quota constraint
• cabotage	Never granted	No change	No change	Full cabotage rights from 1 April 1997
Capacity:	Generally 50:50	55:45 then 60:40	60:40 plus additional 7.5% p.a.	No limits but safeguard can be triggered

Source: Kassim (1996, p. 116).

progressively more intense international competition in the labour market, workers' struggles failed to match the geographic scales at which capital now operated.

To be fair, transport unions probably lacked the organisational capacity and resources to 'shift scale'. The relevant European Industry Federation (EIF), in this case the Comité syndicales des transports dans la Communauté européenne (CSTCE), established in 1958, was staffed by just one full-time and one part-time official (plus a secretary) and the member unions were divided over whether the 'Brussels Committee', as it was commonly known, should simply service the various Joint Committees appointed by the European Commission[13] or whether it should function as a proper international trade union federation that could organise political campaigns and coordinate industrial action. This was indicative of the fact that workers' activities, 'in terms of their desire to create particular spatial fixes appropriate to their own conditions and needs at particular times in particular locations' (Herod, 1997, p. 17), often focus on protecting their local place instead of the defence of wider (international) class interests. Moreover, even the defence of place can be undermined by internal divisions within the labour movement (for example, cabin crew and pilots felt more threatened, at the time, by liberalisation, compared to ground baggage-handling workers, who were targeted much later by capital and the supranational state) and by the alignment of some unions with 'their' national flag carrier (for example, specialist cabin crew and pilot unions versus general aviation or transport unions). These divisions made concerted European action all the more difficult.

Notwithstanding these organisational (structural) constraints, the unions' chosen strategy was always likely to fall short. By focusing on the process of liberalisation – the intergovernmental negotiations in the Council – rather than the purpose of liberalisation, which was to establish a new system of supranational governance beyond the reach of the nation state, aviation unions sought only to protect their respective place instead of looking to the new spaces created by the internal market. In particular, the labour movement failed to appreciate that the growing intensity and value of cross-national transactions was the root cause of the increasing demand for EU-level rules and dispute resolution mechanisms (Stone Sweet and Sandholtz, 1998, p. 14). This is perhaps best illustrated by the fact that the eventual outcome – cabotage – went well beyond what most member states initially feared or hoped for (Armstrong and Bulmer, 1998, p. 189). As Stone Sweet and Sandholtz (1998, p. 12) point out,

> intergovernmental bargaining in the EC more often than not is responsive to the interests of a nascent, always developing, transnational society. Indeed, the demand for EC rules and regulations provides the subject matter for the bargaining . . . [R]ather than being the generator of integration, intergovernmental bargaining is more often its product.

This is where the role of the Commission is vital, as it is much more than just an 'agenda setter' (Schmidt, 2000). By using its legal powers to enforce the Treaty and EU competition law, the Commission can either 'divide and conquer' member states (that is, single out governments that might vote against the Commission's interests in a Council negotiation and request the member state to adapt their national regulations) or work towards change by proposing a comprehensive reform that puts pressure on unwilling member states to propose an alternative, 'lesser evil' position (Woll, 2006). Aviation unions were slow to shift their focus from the nation state to Brussels, unlike the major airlines and consumer/passenger groups (Armstrong and Bulmer, 1998, p. 179; Kassim, 1996, p. 126; O'Reilly and Stone Sweet, 1998, pp. 170–72)[14] and they failed to mount any serious campaign of contentious political or industrial action at the international level. In sum, the labour movement initially failed to appreciate that:

> [t]he EU represents an 'elite pact' between some of the world's most powerful business organisations – the trans-national corporations based and/or active in Western Europe – and the 'political entrepreneurs' of the Brussels centre. As part of this pact the EU provides EU-based trans-nationals with economic space and other kinds of comparative advantage (Böröcz and Sarker, 2005, p. 159).

As a result, although aviation unions framed their interests in a global context, mobilising around 'international symbols' such as the 'internal market' and 'Council negotiations' to frame their domestic conflicts and 'boost' their national airline, they failed to progress beyond 'internalisation' (that is, the migration of international pressures and conflicts into domestic conflicts) (Tarrow, 2005, pp. 79–80). Such forms of contention are commonplace in the EU, but while they might improve the leverage of national governments in Council negotiations (Tarrow, 2005, p. 96) they are unlikely to divert the course of liberalisation unless they are diffused across borders to like-minded groups in other member states (who might then constitute sufficient votes to block a qualified majority). But this is not sufficient to build a transnational movement: 'For that to happen requires sustained work at an international level, the formation of broader networks of trust, and the coordination of collective action beyond the nation state' (Tarrow, 2005, p. 119). In short, unions and other opponents of liberalisation need to 'shift scale', which is 'not simply the reproduction, at a different level, of the claims, targets, and constituencies of the sites where contention begins; they produce new alliances, new targets, and changes in the foci of claims and perhaps even new identities' (Tarrow, 2005, p. 121).

Ultimately, the spatial fixes pursued by national aviation unions, which were certainly beneficial (in the short-term) to certain segments of capital in terms of facilitating a major restructuring of national flag airlines (for example, Bruch and Sattelberger, 2001; Martínez Lucio et al., 2001; Turnbull et al., 2004), served only to create a new form of 'regime competition' at the industry level. Moreover, as Stevis (2002, p. 148) points out, 'regulatory competition at the level of sectors and firms will be a disaster for union politics.' The limitations of this 'boosterist' strategy were subsequently and cruelly exposed as many aviation workers lost their jobs while others suffered a sharp deterioration in their terms and conditions of employment, most notably as a result of 'benchmarking' exercises that led to work intensification and other cost-cutting measures (Blyton et al., 1998a, 1998b; 2001, pp. 452–5).[15] Aviation unions, then, had focused their attention on the terms and timing of the transition to a new internal European market for air transport, rather than opposition to the transfer of competency from the national to the supranational state. Port workers were not to make the same mistake.

Contesting the single market for port transport

Ports have long been the 'Cinderella' of the Community's Common Transport Policy (CTP) (Chlomoudis and Pallis, 2002), but their centrality to the European market, economic integration and the global competitiveness of the EU has never been questioned. The EU is in fact the world's leading maritime power, the maritime regions of the EU account for over 40 per cent of its GDP (CEC, 2006b, p. 3), and ports handle over 40 per cent of intra-EU trade and over 90 per cent of Europe's external trade. However, most EU ports are owned, and many are also operated, by the local rather than the nation state (unlike airlines). The great Hanseatic ports of northern Europe in particular have always fiercely guarded their local autonomy. For these and other great European city-ports, the support of the nation state might be welcome (for example, financial assistance for infrastructure investment such as road and rail links), but any 'interference' by the supranational state has invariably been rejected out of hand. Even after the Community's policy-making authority in the maritime sector was confirmed by the European Court of Justice in the early 1970s, Europe's ports proved adept at side-stepping any attempts by the Commission to extend its regulatory powers (Chlomoudis and Pallis, 2002; Turnbull, 2008).

EU ports policy only gained momentum in the early 1990s, following the Treaty of Maastricht, when transport policy was placed 'in the forefront of moves towards the completion of the internal market' (CEC, 1992, p. 4). In 1997, the Commission published its first Green Paper to deal exclusively with ports, focusing primarily on the funding of port infrastructure (CEC, 1997). However, proposals to fund all future port investment on the 'user pays' principle flew in the face of ports' autonomy to determine their own charges and, more importantly, the right of the local (and national) state to fund port infrastructure. In many European countries, ports are developed as Maritime, Industrial and Distribution AreaS, with 'pump priming' investment by the local and/or nation state intended to create the 'MIDAS touch' by attracting not only more trade but also industrial activities and ancillary services (for example, ship repair, forwarding, insurance, and so on). Opposition to the Green Paper was both vociferous and widespread, forcing the Commission to undertake 'further research' on port pricing before coming forward with any concrete proposals,[16] while the question of infrastructure investment was incorporated into a more wide-ranging, multi-modal policy review of 'Fair Payment for Infrastructure Use' (CEC, 1998a).[17] However, while public port authorities (ESPO, 1998), private port operators (FEPORT, 1998, p. 9) and international shipping lines expressed reservations, if not outright opposition, to the Commission's proposals on pricing and port infrastructure, Community action 'in the form of developing a regulatory framework aiming at the more systematic liberalisation of the port services market' (CEC, 1997, p. 4) garnered enthusiastic support.

International shipping lines were especially keen to see more open access to ports in the Mediterranean, where the state plays a much larger role than in the north European ports (Barton and Turnbull, 1999), as this would allow them to develop intermodal transport services to Central and Eastern Europe (instead of calling at North European ports) when plying the dominant east–west trade routes via the Suez Canal. In particular, if they could invest in their own dedicated facilities, then shipping lines could improve vessel productivity and integrate their services with land-side transport, which many also provide as part of a 'door-to-door' logistics service for TNCs. But access to the product market is only a necessary and not a sufficient condition for capital's spatial fix. Workers' activities can directly and significantly shape the geography of capitalism because any improvement in labour productivity and the utilisation of equipment in port has a particularly beneficial effect for shipping lines in terms of reducing the vessel's waiting time for a berth, as well as reducing the time a vessel spends at the berth (UNCTAD, 1987).

This means that any improvement in port efficiency will have a disproportionate effect on the economics of onward cargo movement in terms of cost and transit time to market (Goss, 1990, pp. 214–15). Put differently, improving labour productivity and the efficiency of port services can significantly extend the market, providing new trading opportunities with new trading partners.[18] *Ipso facto*, opening up the dockland labour market to greater competition, alongside open access to the European port services market, would not only reduce costs and drive up productivity, but redefine the geographic scale of the market.[19]

The proposed 'Directive on Market Access to Port Services' (CEC, 2001c), which incorporated proposals originally put to the Commission in 1998 by the European Community Shipowners' Association (ECSA) and the European Shippers' Council (ESC), was intended to liberalise both the product and the labour market (Turnbull, 2006, p. 311). The Directive stipulated a minimum of two service providers for each category of cargo handling and other port services such as pilotage, stowage, mooring and passenger services, thereby opening access and ensuring competition in the product market. Indirectly, this would create more competition in the labour market as firms seek to cut costs and win business from their rivals. More directly, the labour market would be liberalised through provisions for 'self-handling', defined as 'a situation in which a port user provides for itself one or more categories of port services' (CEC, 2001c, p. 28), a definition which implied 'the right to employ personnel *of his own choice* to carry out the service' (CEC, 2001c, p. 29, emphasis added). This would allow shipping lines, for example, to employ seafarers on cargo handling activities while the ship is in port (for example, to un/lash containers on deep-sea services or un/lash roll-on/roll-off vehicles on short-sea services) or allow shipping lines and terminal operators to hire non-recognized dock workers from employment agencies or other sources of labour supply.[20] In some EU member states there is already competition in the product market, most notably in Northern Europe (Barton and Turnbull, 1999, 2002), and in others there is already competition and casual employment in the labour market, most notably the UK (Turnbull and Weston, 1993; Saundry and Turnbull, 1999). But in the Mediterranean in particular there is still limited or no competition in either market. It was no coincidence that the Transport Commissioner, Loyola de Palacio, was a former minister in the Spanish conservative government and during its presidency of the EU in 2002 the Spanish government managed to broker a political agreement between member states who, at the start of Council discussions, could find little common ground. Any objections from other stakeholders such as ESPO and FEPORT were addressed during the consultation process (Verhoeven, 2007), leaving organised labour as the only serious opponent of the proposed Directive.

Although dock workers have a reputation for militancy (Turnbull and Sapsford, 2001), including international solidarity (Turnbull, 2000), such action has traditionally been focused on the nation state and rarely extends beyond the 'blacking' of cargoes diverted from ports in other countries where a dispute is in progress. European dock workers were certainly better organised than their counterparts in civil aviation a decade earlier, but they were the last major transport group to join the political structures of the Fédération Syndicale des Travailleurs des Transports Européens (FST),[21] and significant divisions exist both within and between the relevant international union federations, divisions which have compounded structural divisions between port unions in several member states. For example, there has always been an uneasy relationship between the FST and the International Transport Workers' Federation (ITF), even after 1999 when the former became the European Transport Workers' Federation (ETF) and joined the regional structure of the ITF. Whereas many affiliates of the ETF have adopted a 'fortress Europe' approach to international affairs, the leadership of the ITF views developments in Europe as part of a wider global strategy by international transport and logistics companies. Furthermore, while most European port unions are affiliated to the ITF/ETF, several major left-wing unions in France, Spain, Sweden and Greece are affiliated to the International Dockworkers' Council (IDC), a rival (grassroots) organisation that emerged during the long-running dispute at the port of Liverpool in the late 1990s (see Castree, 2000 for details).

It is often said that unions need to 'jump scale' if they are to address the challenges of globalisation and liberalisation (Marston, 2000, p. 232), but this assumes that there is something to 'jump to' (Herod, 1997, p. 16). The challenge facing dock workers, like aviation workers before them, was to create new forms of international organisation in order to contest the spatial constitution of capitalism, not only in the port transport industry but beyond (given the industry's centrality to international logistics and the global production and distribution strategies of TNCs). Organising across space is about developing new geographic scales of support (Herod, 1998, p. 18), which dock workers were able to construct on the foundations of high levels of trade union membership, local traditions of solidarity and effective (national) repertoires of industrial and political action, and ultimately a recognition that their future as 'dock workers' in their own country required them to adopt a new identity, or at least a new repertoire of contention, as 'European port workers'.[22] It was on such foundations that dock workers were able to engage with a new 'politics of scale', 'where the territorial requirements of capitalism articulate extensions of power at the same time that these manifold scales provide openings to resist that power' (Marston, 2000, p. 228).

Within the ETF/ITF, union strategy was initially uncertain as some unions, most notably Ver.di (Germany), wanted to engage with the Commission on the wording of the Directive and seek appropriate amendments – what della Porta and Kriesi (1999, p. 20) call the 'information-gathering report-writing lobby resolution-passing game [that] leaves little room for grassroots mobilisation'. However, the ITF was keen to engage in direct action, 'to mobilise big actions against specific issues' (Kees Marges, ITF Dockers' Secretary, quoted by Turnbull, 2006, p. 312). The key issues for the ITF were self-handling and the right of operators to employ labour of their own choice, which the Federation feared would enable shipping lines and global terminal operators to create 'ports of convenience' to service vessels that already fly a 'flag of convenience' and employ a 'crew of convenience' (that is, on the lowest possible international standards) (Lillie, 2004, pp. 49–50). In short, the ITF feared an international 'race-to-the-bottom'. By linking the campaign against the ports Directive to developments in the international shipping industry, the ITF was better able to frame issues in a global context and persuade affiliates to internalise the dispute (that is, respond to international pressures within domestic politics). This was achieved through a series of 'educational stop-work meetings' to explain the Directive to rank-and-file dock workers, as well as the production and dissemination of campaign materials that local affiliates could use to develop a political campaign directed at both national politicians and Members of the European

Parliament. As one might expect, the 'take up' of such (coordinated) activities was more robust in some member states than others, namely those where the Directive posed the greatest threat to national employment arrangements and union organisation, but gradually the battle was extended across the EU, and dock workers were able to 'shift scale'.

The coordination of collective action at the international level was dependent on more effective 'union articulation' (that is, stronger interrelationships between the workplace, national and international levels of union organisation) and new labour networks that emerged during the campaign. Many of the structures to effect the former were already in place, but it was notable that the threat of a 'common enemy' brought unions together at the national level in those countries where dockers' unions had previously been rivals (for example, Spain, France and Sweden), and at the international level (as with ententes both between the ITF and ETF and between the ITF/ETF and IDC) (Turnbull, 2006, pp. 313–15). As others have observed (Herod et al., 2007, pp. 257–8), different scales are often 'networked', rather than representing different (self-contained) 'levels' that workers can simply 'move from' or 'jump to'. The new labour networks that emerged in Europe's ports, then, were both 'relational' – based on strong bonds of kinship, trust and cultural identity within specific port ranges such as the Baltic, northern Europe and the Mediterranean – and non-relational (for example, electronic networks created by union activists).[23] These networks provided both horizontal and vertical connections between dock workers, and in several countries helped to bring together rival unions and connect them with other national and international union organisations. They were also instrumental in developing the new repertoire of (unconventional) action that characterised the dockers' campaign against liberalisation.

The 'war on Europe's waterfront' (2001–03) was marked by the first ever coordinated European dock strikes, targeted at both international shipping lines and/or global terminal operators as well as the supranational state, and mass demonstrations in the streets of Brussels, Strasbourg (the home of the European Parliament), Rotterdam (a stronghold of the ITF/ETF) and Barcelona (a stronghold of the IDC) (Turnbull, 2006, p. 319). These demonstrations were timed to coincide with key stages in the legislative process as the Directive was debated and amended in various committees and in sessions of the European Parliament. Dockers exploited all available 'political opportunities' and successfully combined national and international, conventional and unconventional action, depending on the target in question. For example, as Marks and McAdam (1999, p. 104) point out, the European Parliament only 'occasionally provides a juicy target for a strategy of unconventional political activity' such as mass demonstrations. Consequently, dock workers marched in the streets of Strasbourg whenever key debates or votes on the Directive took place. When faced with a 'choice' between the 'logic of influence', where unions 'adapt their aims and methods to the actual decision-making processes on which they exert an impact', and the 'logic of membership', which 'requires unions to maintain their representative credentials by articulating the wishes and interests of their constituents' (Hyman, 2005b, p. 24), it was the latter that ultimately prevailed (Turnbull, 2007). The war on Europe's waterfront was just that – a series of battles fought mainly through direct action on the streets outside the physical institutions of the EU and on the picket lines outside the port gates, rather than inside the corridors of power in Brussels.

If the narrow rejection of the first ports Directive by the European Parliament in November 2003 was something of a surprise (Turnbull, 2006, p. 320), the resounding rejection of the second ports package in January 2006 was not (Turnbull, 2007). In fact, the second Directive (CEC, 2004) was opposed by a broad spectrum of port interests and several member states (for example, Germany, the Netherlands and the UK), largely because of new provisions for the authorisation of port service providers, the duration of any lease granted to those service providers, compensation for outgoing service providers and a range of other technical issues (van Hooydonk, 2005). This allowed the labour movement to build alliances with the local and national state, national and international port employers,[24] as well as other international interests such as ESPO and FEPORT (Turnbull, 2007, 2008). Crucially, however, having previously demonstrated their ability to shift scale and organise coordinated international action, threatening international supply chains (the life-blood of global capital) and striking at the very heart of the supranational state, other stakeholders, including international shipping lines, were now prepared to see 'self-handling' removed from the Directive. Despite this, the Commission refused to remove these provisions from the proposed Directive, and the Transport Committee of the European Parliament ultimately failed to agree to a revised text that met the interests of dock workers. More importantly, in the Transport Committee's final vote on the Directive (in November 2005), it was agreed to send the Directive to the European Parliament without any compromise amendments.[25] As a result, ESPO and many other stakeholders joined the trade unions in calling for the Directive to be rejected outright by Parliament. While dock workers demonstrated in the streets of Strasbourg, fighting running battles with riot police and smashing windows in the Parliament building, MEPs voted by 532 votes to 120 (with 25 abstentions) to reject the Directive.

The Commission has since embarked on an extensive programme of consultation with the principal stakeholders to determine a future EU ports policy, although it was soon apparent that the Commission's strategy was to 'divide-and-conquer' (Woll, 2006) rather than build a genuine consensus (Turnbull, 2008). This strategy was thwarted, however, by the coalition of stakeholders that endured from the campaign against the second failed Directive. A series of 'non-meetings' that took place between the ETF and other stakeholders in 2005 continued in 2006, with interest groups reaching agreement on key areas of EU ports policy outside the formal process initiated by the Commission. As a result, labour and their allies have effectively wrested control over future EU ports policy from the Commission (Turnbull, 2008). As Jacques Barrot (2007, p. 2), the new Transport Commissioner was forced to admit, the industry has 'taken its own future in hand'. Self-handling is no longer on the agenda and the EFT recently managed to scupper an attempt within the Commission to launch a legal challenge against port labour pools that preclude the employment of non-recognised dock workers (for example, those hired from external employment agencies). An ECJ ruling against labour pools would have given the supranational state similar leverage to that enjoyed by the Commission (DG Competition) in civil aviation following the *Nouvelles Frontières* case, but lobbying by the ETF persuaded the transport Directorate (DG TREN) not to pursue this option. This represents a remarkable transformation in the relationship between organised labour and the supranational state. During the war on Europe's waterfront, any consultation between the Commission and the ETF could at best be described as 'perfunctory', while even during the campaign against the second ports Directive, the Commission steadfastly refused to exclude provisions for self-handling or the right of operators to employ labour of their own choice. These and other employment-related issues will soon come under the remit of a new Sector Social Dialogue Committee for the port transport industry, thereby excluding the Commission from any direct jurisdiction, following an agreement between the ETF and FEPORT.[26]

In sum, while maintaining a strong 'logic of membership', there is a new 'logic of influence' on the European waterfront arising from dock workers' ability to produce and manipulate geographic space to their own advantage. This has proven to be a potent form of social power, enabling port unions to influence the agenda of EU ports policy instead of merely seeking to mitigate the worst excesses of the Single Market. The new agenda is characterised by 'positive regulation' (for example, setting agreed European rules and standards for health and safety and the training of dock workers throughout the EU) instead of 'negative (de)regulation'. Through their influence on the supranational state and their opposition to global capital, dock workers have retained the ability to shape the conditions of their own well-being.

Conclusion

Although it is widely recognised that capital is not simply able to but actually needs to display mobility and thereby fragment labour over space (Sadler, 2000, p. 148), there is still a tendency to overlook the active role of labour in shaping economic landscapes – the economic geography of capitalism is often seen simply to 'evolve *around* workers who themselves are disconnected from the process' (Herod, 1997, p. 3, emphasis in the original). Mainstream accounts of the liberalisation of European civil aviation epitomise this neglect (for example, Kassim, 1996; O'Reilly and Stone Sweet, 1998; Stone Sweet and Sandholtz, 1998), presenting a workerless landscape through their focus on the activities of (global) capital, intergovernmentalism and the role of the supranational state. To be sure, aviation workers were not prominent international opponents of liberalisation, unlike port workers, but their geographical 'solutions' to the problems of ensuring their own self-reproduction – a boosterist strategy that sought to protect regional air services and the viability of 'their' national (flag) airline – had a profound impact on the geography of capitalism. Workers' spatial praxis not only facilitated the ongoing restructuring of major European airlines but ultimately 'permitted' an open market for civil aviation in which regime competition was intensified, most notably via the entry of low-cost airlines. At the time, this appeared to be a viable trade union strategy, especially as many European states were willing and able, at least initially, to facilitate and fund the staged transition to a single aviation market (for example, via state aid, measures to protect regional air services and gradual changes to capacity rules, as detailed in Table 3.1). While many aviation unions recognised the importance of organising across space, they lacked the resources and the necessary solidarity to shift scale. Equally important, they fixed their attention, and focused their contention, on the process of liberalisation (that is, intergovernmental negotiations in the Council) rather than the purpose of supranational (de)regulation (that is, an open market beyond the reach of the nation state). Consequently, they failed to anticipate the market entry of low-cost airlines, despite the success of this business model in the deregulated US domestic market.

The failure of transport unions to 'shift scale' has precipitated an international 'race-to-the-bottom' in the European civil aviation industry, where the bottom is now occupied by low-cost airlines such as Ryanair, a vehemently anti-union company that eats into the market share of established (flag) airlines.[27] When Ryanair recently retrained pilots to convert from Boeing 737-200 to 737-800 aircraft, it sought to impose a condition in pilot contracts that if the company were 'compelled to engage in collective bargaining with any pilot association or trade union within 5 years of your conversion training, then you will repay the full training cost [of €15 000]'. When a subsequent case of bullying and harassment was heard by the courts – brought by Ryanair against pilots who dared to join a union and encouraged others to unionise – the judge described the management of the airline as 'unburdened by integrity', their attitude displaying 'all the hallmarks of action in terrorem' (that is, designed to terrify) (*Irish Times*, 16 October 2006). But while the judge may have found 'without hesitation' against Ryanair in this particular case, in the wider conflicts over whose spatial fix (capitalists' or workers') is actually set in the landscape, which ultimately lies 'at the heart of the dynamism of the geography of capitalism' (Herod, 1997, p. 17), it is global capital that has emerged victorious in the European civil aviation industry.

Dock workers, in contrast, were well aware that an open market for port services might trigger an international 'race-to-the-bottom', especially as they have fought for many years to improve the pay and conditions of 'crews of convenience' onboard 'flag of convenience' shipping (via cooperation with seafaring unions on the Fair Practices Committee of the ITF). By campaigning against the creation of 'ports of convenience', port unions sought explicitly to deny (global) capital access to places (ports) where labour might be poorly paid, casually employed and without the protection of union recognition. Dock workers understood, or were quickly made aware, that open access to the port services market also entailed open access to the dockland labour market. Consequently, they fought to shape the economic landscape in ways that differed substantially from the spatial fix sought by (global) capital and the supranational state. Translocal ties on the waterfront proved to be particularly strong, port unions had the resources to mount a concerted international campaign of opposition to the proposed Directives, and European ports were not just places of dependence but spaces of engagement. By shifting scale, port workers were able to exploit a multitude of new opportunities for resistance, building on their long tradition of militancy and solidarity. Unlike aviation workers, they succeeded in constructing a landscape that augments their social power and undercuts that of capital.

Notes

1. If Art. 136 was fully realised – that is, if social costs did not vary spatially – then it is theoretically possible for labour to play absolutely no role in explanations of the economic geography of a particular industry (Herod, 1997, p. 6). However, as Herod (1997) demonstrates, such arguments are merely descriptive of labour and conceptualise human capital as nothing more than a factor of production and location (a relative variable cost in location decisions), an approach which fails to acknowledge working-class people as 'sentient social beings who both intentionally and unintentionally produce economic geographies through their actions'. In practice, of course, Art. 136 will only come to fruition through labour's spatial fix.

2. Art. 75 of the Treaty of Rome established the legal basis of the common transport policy (CTP), stating that '[the Council shall] lay down: (a) common rules applicable to international transport to or from the territory of a Member State or passing across the territory of one or more Member States; (b) the conditions under which non-resident carriers may operate transport services within a Member State; (c) measures to improve transport safety; and (d) any other appropriate provisions'.

3. Title IV states that 'the provisions of this Title shall apply to transport by rail, road and inland waterways' (Art. 84).

4. Currently a minimum of 255 votes out of 345 (73.9 per cent) is required to reach a qualified majority, with larger member states allocated more votes. In practice, Council decisions on transport policy tend to be unanimous (CEC, 2001b).

5. ECAC was formed in 1954 and had twenty members. The Conference was the principal forum for the discussion of technical and commercial aviation matters while its sister organisation, the Joint Aviation Authorities, brought together national airworthiness authorities for the purpose of devising Joint Aviation Requirements (JARs) for Western Europe.

6. Joined Cases 209-213/84. The decision of the Court annulled a French judgment against a number of private airlines and travel agencies who sold cheap, non-approved tickets. The ECJ argued that Art. 84(2) merely restricted the scope of Title IV and did not bar the application of competition rules to air transport.

7. Whenever member states fail to meet their obligations under European law, the Commission can start an infringement procedure (Art. 227). Under competition law, the Commission can confront both firms and national regulations that are not in conformity with EU law. Non-compliance can result in fines of up to 10 per cent of the worldwide turnover of TNCs.

8. Thirteen airlines were charged by the Commission in 1986/87, which created strong pressure on member states to develop a common, more liberal, civil aviation policy (Schmidt, 2004, p. 115).

9. Around 60 per cent of BA's passengers come from outside the UK. It is important to note that while the UK demanded liberalisation when looking to Europe, it insisted on maintaining a highly regulated market to North America (Dobson, 1995, p. 6). BA earns around a third of its revenue and half its profits on transatlantic routes. Like BA, the majority of KLM's shares were in private hands by the late 1980s.

10. These included services to the Balearics and Canaries, Madeira and the Greek Islands. Denmark's concerns arose out of the 'peripheral' location of the Scandinavian market and were complicated by the non-EU membership of its partners (Sweden and Norway) in Scandinavian Airlines System (SAS).

11. The principle applied by the Commission, in simple terms, is whether the state acts in the same way as a private investor (which is acceptable) or whether it offers the airline preferential terms (which is not acceptable).

12. At the time of these reforms, surveys found that systematic 'benchmarking', with airlines comparing costs and productivity across the industry, had become commonplace (Blyton et al., 2001, pp. 455–6).

13. Joint Committees, with an equal number of union and employer representatives, had been established for road transport in 1965, inland navigation in 1967, railways in 1972, and maritime transport in 1987. The Joint Committee for civil aviation was only established in 1990 (Keller, 2003). The Committees are a forum for joint consultation rather than collective bargaining.

14. TNCs are particularly adept when it comes to lobbying the Commission (Böröcz and Sarker, 2005, p. 159), as are the business associations that represent national and global capital (Greenwood, 2003).

15. The 'fall out' from this process is still evident today, as the recent events at Alitalia (2008) serve to illustrate.

16. Although the Commission had previously undertaken research on pricing and public financing in EU ports, the results had not been published. The proposal for a more transparent review was supported by the European Transport Ministers in the Council in June 1998, but the quality of information received from different ports 'ranged from "scant two-page statements" with virtually no information at all, to substantial documentation in both volume and quality' (CEC, 2001a, p. 4).

17. Ports were incorporated into the second phase (from 2001) of a step-by-step approach to implementing the 'user pays' principle.

18. This a concrete example of the general observation made by Herod et al. (2007, p. 250) that as distance matters less, any difference in labour cost or quality becomes more significant.

19. Short-sea shipping lines were especially keen to see more open access to the labour market as cargo handling charges typically account for 40 to 60 per cent of the total door-to-door costs of transporting goods on these services (compared to around 10 to 25 per cent for deep-sea services) (CEC, 1997, p. 14) and labour costs account for around 60 to 70 per cent of these cargo handling charges.

20. In most European ports, any additional labour over and above the operator's 'core' or permanent workforce is typically hired from a well-established 'labour pool' that only employs recognised dock workers.

21. The CSTCE became the FST in 1996.

22. As other port service providers were also threatened by the Directive (for example, tugboats, mooring and pilotage) dock workers were keen to build alliances with other port unions and defend the interests of all port workers and not just those involved in cargo handling.

23. See http://www.havenarbeiders.be and http://www.havenforum.nl

24. In the UK, this led to the bizarre situation where some port employers paid travel expenses for their shop stewards to attend workers' demonstrations in Brussels. At other times, these same employers have refused shop stewards time off for union duties.

25. Over 300 amendments had been tabled by MEPs and voted on by the Committee, but this left them with a Directive that the majority believed was even worse than the original draft.

26. ESPO initially refused to join the social dialogue, maintaining that it is a business organisation and not an employer's association, but has now relented following an agreement between public (ESPO) and private

(FEPORT) port operators. The one remaining stumbling block is the lack of agreement between the ETF and IDC on the proportion of representatives for each organisation on the proposed Sector Social Dialogue Committee.

27.   Low-cost airlines achieved a market share of 43 per cent of all domestic and intra-European routes in 2008, more than double their share of 17 per cent in 2003.

References

Armstrong, K.A. and S.J. Bulmer (1998), *The Governance of the Single European Market*, Manchester: Manchester University Press.

Barrett, S. (1987), *Flying High: Airline Prices and European Regulation*, Aldershot: Avebury/Adam Smith Institute.

Barrot, J. (2007), 'Keynote speech: "European Port Policy"', presented at the ESPO Annual Conference, Algeciras, Spain, 1 June.

Barton, H. and P. Turnbull (1999), *End of Award Report: Labour Regulation and Economic Performance in the European Port Transport Industry*, ESRC Award R000235425, Boston Spa: Economic and Social Research Council.

Barton, H. and P. Turnbull (2002), 'Labour regulation and competitive performance in the port transport industry: the changing fortunes of three major European seaports', *European Journal of Industrial Relations*, **8** (2), 133–56.

Blyton, P., M. Martínez Lucio, J. McGurk and P. Turnbull (1998a), *Contesting Globalisation: Airline Restructuring, Labour Flexibility and Trade Union Strategies*, London: International Transport Workers' Federation.

Blyton, P., M. Martínez Lucio, J. McGurk and P. Turnbull (1998b), *Globalisation, Deregulation and Flexibility on the Flight Deck*, report prepared for the European Cockpit Association, Cardiff Business School, Cardiff University.

Blyton, P., M. Martínez Lucio, J. McGurk and P. Turnbull (2001), 'Globalisation and trade union strategy: industrial restructuring and human resource management in the international civil aviation industry', *International Journal of Human Resource Management*, **12** (3), 445–63.

Böröcz, J. and M. Sarker (2005), 'What is the EU?', *International Sociology*, **20** (2), 153–73.

Börzel, T.A. (2002), 'Pace-setting, foot-dragging and fence-sitting: member state responses to Europeanization', *Journal of Common Market Studies*, **40** (2), 193–214.

Bruch, H. and T. Sattelberger (2001), 'Lufthansa's transformation marathon: process of liberating and focusing change energy', *Human Resource Management*, **40** (3), 249–59.

Castree, N. (2000), 'Geographical scale and grass-roots internationalism: the Liverpool dock dispute, 1995–1998', *Economic Geography*, **76** (3), 272–92.

CEC (1979), 'Air transport: a community approach', Bulletin of the European Communities, Supplement 5/79, Luxembourg: Office for Official Publications of the European Communities.

CEC (1992), 'The future development of the Common Transport Policy: a global approach to the construction of a Community framework for sustainable mobility', COM(92)494, Brussels: Commission of the European Communities.

CEC (1995), 'Common Transport Policy action programme 1995–2000', COM(95)601, Brussels: Commission of the European Communities.

CEC (1997), 'Green Paper on sea ports and maritime infrastructure', COM(97)678, Brussels: Commission of the European Communities.

CEC (1998a), 'Fair payment for infrastructure use: a phased approach to a common transport infrastructure charging framework for the EU', COM(1998)466 final, Brussels: Commission of the European Communities.

CEC (1998b), 'The Common Transport Policy. Sustainable mobility: perspectives for the future', COM(98)716, Brussels: Commission of the European Communities.

CEC (2001a), 'Commission staff working document on public financing and charging practices in the Community sea port sector', SEC(2001)234, Brussels: Commission of the European Communities.

CEC (2001b), 'European Transport Policy for 2010: time to decide', COM(2001)370, Brussels: Commission of the European Communities.

CEC (2001c), 'Proposal for a Directive of the European Parliament and of the Council on Market Access to Port Services', COM(2001)35, Brussels: Commission of the European Communities.

CEC (2004), 'Proposal for a Directive of the European Parliament and of the Council on Market Access to Port Services', COM(2004)654, Brussels: Commission of the European Communities.

CEC (2005), 'Working together for growth and jobs: a new start for the Lisbon strategy', COM(2005)24, Brussels: Commission of the European Communities.

CEC (2006a), 'Keep Europe moving – sustainable mobility for our continent (mid-term review of the European commission's 2001 Transport White Paper)', COM(2006)314, Brussels: Commission of the European Communities.

CEC (2006b), 'Green Paper – towards a future maritime policy for the Union: European vision for the oceans and seas', COM(2006)275 final, Brussels: Commission of the European Communities.

Chlomoudis, C.I. and A.A. Pallis (2002), *European Union Port Policy: The Movement Towards a Long-Term Strategy*, Cheltenham, UK and Northampton, MA, USA: Edward Elgar.

Commons, J. (1909), 'American shoemakers 1648–1895: a sketch of industrial evolution', *Quarterly Journal of Economics*, **24** (1), 39–84.

Cox, K.R. (1998), 'Spaces of dependence, spaces of engagement and the politics of scale, or: looking for local politics', *Political Geography*, **17** (1), 1–23.

della Porta, D. and H. Kriesi (1999), 'Social movements in a globalizing world: an introduction', in D. della Porta, H. Kriesi and D. Rucht (eds), *Social Movements in a Globalizing World*, Basingstoke: Macmillan, pp. 3–22.

Dicken, P. (2003), *Global Shift: Reshaping the Global Economic Map in the 21st Century*, 4th edn, London: Sage.

Dobson, A.P. (1995), *Flying in the Face of Competition: The Policies and Diplomacy of Airline Regulatory Reform in Britain, the USA and European Community 1968–94*, Aldershot: Avebury Aviation.

Doganis, R. (1991), *Flying off Course: The Economics of International Airlines*, London: Routledge.

Dølvik, J.E. and J. Visser (2001), 'ETUC and European social partnership: a third turning point', in H. Compston and J. Greenwood (eds), *Social Partnership in the EU*, Basingstoke: Palgrave Macmillan, pp. 11–40.

El-Agraa, A.M. (2004), *The European Union: Economics and Policies*, 7th edn, London: Prentice Hall.

European Communities (1997), 'Treaty of Amsterdam amending the Treaty on European Union, the treaties establishing the European Communities and certain related acts', Luxembourg: Office for Official Publications of the European Communities.

European Sea Ports Organisation (ESPO) (1998), 'Response to the Green Paper on Sea Ports and Maritime Infrastructure', Brussels: European Sea Ports Organisation.

Federation of European Private Port Operators (FEPORT) (1998), 'Position of FEPORT on the Commission's Green Paper on Sea Ports and Maritime Infrastructure', Brussels: Federation of European Private Port Operators.

Fox Piven, F. (2006), 'Response to "American Democracy in an Age of Inequality"', *Political Science and Politics*, January, pp. 43–6.

Frege, C. and J. Kelly (2003), 'Union revitalization strategies in comparative perspective', *European Journal of Industrial Relations*, **9** (1), 7–24.

Goss, R.O. (1990), 'Economic policies and seaports: 1. The economic functions of seaports', *Maritime Policy and Management*, **17** (3), 207–19.

Greenwood, J. (2003), *Interest Representation in the European Union*, Basingstoke, UK: Palgrave Macmillan.

Harvey, D. (1982), *The Limits to Capital*, Oxford: Basil Blackwell.

Haworth, N. and S. Hughes (2002), 'Internationalization, industrial relations theory and international relations', in J. Harrod and R. O'Brien (eds), *Global Unions? Theory and Strategies of Organized Labour in the Global Political Economy*, London: Routledge, pp. 64–79.

Hay, C. (2006), 'What's globalization go to do with it? Economic interdependence and the future of European welfare states', *Government and Opposition*, **41** (1), 1–22.

Held, D., A. McGrew, D. Goldblatt and J. Perraton (1999), *Global Transformations: Politics, Economics and Culture*, Cambridge: Polity.

Herod, A. (1997), 'From a geography of labor to a labor geography: labor's spatial fix and the geography of capitalism', *Antipode*, **29** (1), 1–31.

Herod, A. (1998), 'The spatiality of labor unionism: a review essay', in A. Herod (ed.), *Organizing the Landscape: Geographical Perspectives on Labor Unionism*, Minneapolis, MN: University of Minnesota Press, pp. 1–36.

Herod, A., A. Rainnie and S. McGrath-Champ (2007), 'Working space: why incorporating the geographical is central to theorizing work and employment practices', *Work, Employment and Society*, **21** (2), 247–64.

Hix, S. (1999), *The Political System of the European Union*, New York: St Martin's Press.

Hooghe, L. and G. Marks (2001), *Multi-Level Governance and European Integration*, Lanham, MD: Rowman & Littlefield.

Hyman, R. (1999), 'Imagined solidarities: can trade unions resist globalization?', in P. Leisink (ed.), *Globalization and Labour Relations*, Cheltenham, UK and Northampton, MA: Edward Elgar, pp. 94–115.

Hyman, R. (2005a), 'Shifting dynamics in international trade unionism: agitation, organisation, bureaucracy, democracy', *Labour History*, **46** (2), 137–54.

Hyman, R. (2005b), 'Trade unions and the politics of the European social model', *Economic and Industrial Democracy*, **26** (1), 9–40.

Janelle, D.G. and M. Beuthe (1997), 'Globalization and research issues in transport', *Journal of Transport Geography*, **5** (3), 199–206.

Kassim, H. (1996), 'Air transport', in H. Kassim and A. Menon (eds), *The European Union and National Industrial Policy*, London: Routledge, pp. 106–31.

Keller, B. (2003), 'Social dialogues at sectoral level: the neglected ingredient of European industrial relations', in B. Keller and H-P. Platzer (eds), *Industrial Relations and European Integration: Trans- and Supranational Developments and Prospects*, Aldershot: Ashgate, pp. 30–52.

Lillie, N. (2004), 'Global collective bargaining on flag of convenience shipping', *British Journal of Industrial Relations*, **42** (1), 47–67.

Lim, S-M. (1998), 'Economies of scale in container shipping', *Maritime Policy and Management*, **24** (4), 361–73.

Locke, R.M. and K. Thelen (1995), 'Apples and oranges revisited: contextualized comparisons and the study of comparative labor politics', *Politics and Society*, **23** (3), 337–67.

Marginson, P. and K. Sisson (2004), *European Integration and Industrial Relations: Multi-Level Governance in the Making*, Basingstoke, UK: Palgrave Macmillan.

Marks, G. and D. McAdam (1999), 'On the relationship of political opportunities to the form of collective action: the case of the European Union', in D. della Porta, H. Kriesi and D. Rucht (eds), *Social Movements in a Globalizing World*, Basingstoke: Macmillan, pp. 97–111.

Marston, S.A. (2000), 'The social construction of scale', *Progress in Human Geography*, **24** (2), 219–42.

Martínez Lucio, M., P. Turnbull, P. Blyton and J. McGurk (2001), 'Using regulation: an international comparative study of the civil aviation industry in Britain and Spain', *European Journal of Industrial Relations*, **7** (1), 49–70.

Mawson, J. (1997), 'Air transport liberalization in the European Union: an assessment', *Regional Studies*, **31** (8), 807–22.

O'Reilly, D. and A. Stone Sweet (1998), 'The liberalization and European re-regulation of air transport', in W. Sandholtz and A. Stone Sweet (eds), *European Integration and Supranational Governance*, Oxford: Oxford University Press, pp. 164–87.

Pasture, P. and J. Verberckmoes (1998), 'Working-class internationalism and the appeal of national identity: historical dilemmas and current debates in Western Europe', in P. Pasture and J. Verberckmoes (eds), *Working Class Internationalism and the Appeal of National Identity*, Oxford: Berg, pp. 1–41.

Ruggie, J.G. (2004), 'Reconstituting the global public domain – issues, actors and practices', *European Journal of International Relations*, **10** (4), 499–531.

Rugman, A.M. (2003), 'Multinational enterprises are regional, not global', *Multinational Business Review*, **11** (1), 3–12.

Sadler, D. (2000), 'Organizing European labour: governance, production, trade unions and the question of scale', *Transactions of the Institute of British Geographers*, **25** (2), 135–52.

Saundry, R. and P. Turnbull (1999), 'Contractual (in)security, labour regulation and competitive performance in the port transport industry: a contextualised comparison of Britain and Spain', *British Journal of Industrial Relations*, **37** (2), 273–96.

Scharpf, F.W. (1999), *Governing in Europe: Effective and Democratic?* Oxford: Oxford University Press.

Scharpf, F.W. (2002), 'The European social model: coping with the challenges of diversity', *Journal of Common Market Studies*, **40** (4), 645–70.

Schmidt, M. and L. Giorgi (2001), 'Successes, failures and prospects for the common transport policy', *Innovation*, **14** (4), 293–313.

Schmidt, S.K. (2000), 'Only an agenda setter? The European Commission's power over the Council of Ministers', *European Union Politics*, **1** (1), 37–61.

Schmidt, S.K. (2004), 'The European Commission's powers in shaping European policies', in D.G. Dimitrakopoulos (ed.), *The Changing European Commission*, Manchester: Manchester University Press, pp. 105–20.

Staeheli, L. (1994), 'Empowering political struggle: spaces and scales of resistance', *Political Geography*, **13** (5), 387–91.

Stevis, D. (2002), 'Unions, capitals and states: competing (inter)nationals in North American and European integration', in J. Harrod and R. O'Brien (eds), *Global Unions? Theory and Strategies of Organized Labour in the Global Political Economy*, London: Routledge, pp. 130–50.

Stone Sweet, A. and W. Sandholtz (1998), 'Integration, supranational governance, and the institutionalization of the European polity', in W. Sandholtz and A. Stone Sweet (eds), *European Integration and Supranational Governance*, Oxford: Oxford University Press, pp. 1–26.

Streeck, W. (1998), 'The internationalization of industrial relations in Europe: prospects and problems', *Politics and Society*, **26** (4), 429–59.

Tarrow, S. (2005), *The New Transnational Activism*, Cambridge: Cambridge University Press.

Teague, P. (2001), 'Deliberative governance and EU social policy', *European Journal of Industrial Relations*, **7** (1), 7–26.

Tilly, C. (1995), 'Globalization threatens labor's rights', *International Labor and Working-Class History*, **47** (Spring), 1–23.

Turnbull, P. (2000), 'Contesting globalization on the waterfront', *Politics and Society*, **28** (3), 273–97.

Turnbull, P. (2006), 'The war on Europe's waterfront – repertoires of power in the port transport industry', *British Journal of Industrial Relations*, **44** (2), 305–26.

Turnbull, P. (2007), 'Dockers versus the Directives – battling port policy on the European waterfront', in K. Bronfenbrenner (ed.), *Global Unions and Global Companies*, Ithaca, NY: Cornell University Press, pp. 120–49.

Turnbull, P. (2008), 'No lesser evil than divide and conquer: contesting access to the European port services market', mimeo, Cardiff University.

Turnbull, P. and D. Sapsford (2001), 'Hitting the bricks: an international comparative study of conflict on the waterfront', *Industrial Relations*, **40** (2), 231–57.

Turnbull, P. and S. Weston (1993), 'Co-operation or control? Capital restructuring and labour relations on the docks', *British Journal of Industrial Relations*, **31** (1), 115–34.

Turnbull, P., P. Blyton and G. Harvey (2004), 'Cleared for take-off? Management–labour partnership in the European civil aviation industry', *European Journal of Industrial Relations*, **10** (3), 281–301.

United Nations Conference on Trade and Development (UNCTAD) (1987), 'Measuring and evaluating port performance and productivity', UNCTAD Monographs on Port Management, No. 6, Geneva: UNCTAD.

United Nations Conference on Trade and Development (UNCTAD) (2003), 'Review of maritime transport, 2003', Geneva: UNCTAD.

van Hooydonk, E. (2005), 'The European Port Services Directive: the good or the last try?' *Journal of International Maritime Law*, **11** (3), 188–220.

Verhoeven, P. (2007), 'Editorial', *ESPO News*, **9** (10), 1–2.

Ward, K. (2007), 'Thinking geographically about work, employment and society', *Work, Employment and Society*, **21** (2), 265–76.

Wilks, S. (1996), 'Regulatory compliance and capitalist diversity in Europe', *Journal of European Public Policy*, **3** (4), 536–59.

Wills, J. (1998), 'Taking on the CosmoCorps? Experiments in transnational labor organization', *Economic Geography*, **74** (2), 111–30.

Windle, R.J. (1991), 'The world's airlines: a cost and productivity comparison', *Journal of Transport Economics*, **25** (1), 31–49.

Woll, C. (2006), 'The road to external representation: the European Commission's activism in international air transport', *Journal of European Public Policy*, **13** (1), 52–69.

PART 2

WORKING SPACES

4 Working spaces
Al Rainnie, Susan McGrath-Champ and Andrew Herod

Globalization and the new economy encapsulates the transformation of economic and social relations across the globe. People and places are increasingly interlinked through the organization of work, the flow of goods and services and the exchange of ideas. Even so the contemporary world is characterized by difference rather than uniformity and widening rather than narrowing inequality but the spatial pattern is complex; while some people and places are involved in highly interactive global networks others are largely excluded, creating new and reinforcing old patterns of uneven development. Despite the enormous advances in human ingenuity and technology that have created unparalleled wealth and an economically integrated world, social and spatial divisions are widening. (Perrons, 2004, p. 1)

. . . while capital must on the one side strive to tear down every spatial barrier to intercourse i.e., exchange, and conquer the whole earth for its market, it strives on the other to annihilate this space with time. (Marx, [1941] 1973, p. 539)

Introduction

Recently, the world crossed over a significant event horizon as, for the first time in history, its urban population came to exceed its rural population, the consequence primarily of rural dwellers moving to cities in search of work. The most obvious outcome of this migratory process has been the burgeoning of mega cities with populations of more than 8 million people and a more than doubling of the world's urban labour force since 1980. Such trends are likely to continue, with the result that cities will account for virtually all future world population growth, expected to peak at about 10 billion in 2050. Ninety-five per cent of this future growth will occur in the so-called developing countries.

We mention this brief example because it speaks to what we want to argue here, namely that capitalism is a fundamentally spatial phenomenon. Hence, in the case of the millions of rural farmers who are being remade into urban workers as a result of their migrating across space from one socio-spatial context to another, the construction and reconstruction of class, we would suggest, cannot be understood without spatially informed analysis. The process of contemporary proletarianisation occurring across the global South, as peasants become wage labourers, has distinct spatial dimensions to it – classes form differently in different places but also shape various places' material landscapes in different ways, depending upon the specificities of the places in which class actors are located (more on this below). Place, in other words, plays a central role in processes of class formation (Herod, 1991). Furthermore, spatial transformation seems to have been marked by a dramatic social transformation within contemporary capitalism. Hence, whatever may be the complexities of proletarianisation and specific labour markets' restructuring in particular places, one clear price of such a dramatic transformation in the planet's urban, economic and population geographies seems to be that of increasing inequality (both social and spatial), as, by the late 1990s, one billion workers, representing one-third of the world's labour force, were either unemployed or under-employed (Davis, 2006). Significantly, although this phenomenon of increasing inequality has a distinctly unevenly developed geography to it – most of these workers were in the urban global South – it is also a spatially quite widespread one that is not confined just to the global South. Hence, similar social and spatial unevenness has also been exacerbated in countries like the United Kingdom, where the gap between rich and poor is today wider than it has been at any time in the past 40 years, and the poor and the wealthy have become more and more clustered in different geographical areas as many wealthier people have moved to the suburbs and/or countryside whilst the poor have remained in inner cities. The result has been that growing numbers of people are becoming concentrated in enclaves of high poverty and high wealth (Dorling et al., 2007).

Frequently, such social and spatial inequalities are seen as unintended outcomes of capitalist economic development, especially in market-based economic discourses like those associated with supporters of neoliberalism. However, as Davis and Monk (2007, pp. xiii–iv) illustrate, dynamic, ever-growing socio-spatial inequality is, in fact, actively produced at the very heart of the contemporary capitalist economy and is not its inadvertent consequence. The great binge of the super-rich, in other words, has social and spatial consequences:

> [m]odern wealth and luxury consumption are more enwalled and socially enclaved than at any time since the 1890s . . . the spatial logic of neoliberalism (cum plutonomy) revives the most extreme colonial patterns of residential segregation and zoned consumption. Everywhere, the rich and near rich are retreating into sumptuary compounds, leisure cities and gated replicas of imaginary California suburbs . . . The 'Off Worlds' advertised in the apocalyptic skies of Blade Runner's Los Angeles are now open and ready for occupancy from Montana to China. Meanwhile a demonized criminal underclass . . . everywhere stands outside the gate (although sometimes as little more than symbolic lawn jockeys), providing a self-serving justification for the withdrawal and fortification of luxury lifestyles.

As we already substantially outlined in Chapter 1 and shall further see below, the production of an unevenly developed economic landscape, then, is central to how capitalism as a system operates.

Whereas understanding that capitalism is essentially a spatial phenomenon is one thing, accounting for and analysing that phenomenon is another matter entirely. For instance, as we saw in Chapter 1, analysts of globalisation have come up with numerous, often contradictory, explanations for contemporary dynamics of the global economy. Indeed, the globalisation debate highlights quite nicely some of the spatial conundrums with which we must deal as analysts and with which social actors must engage in their praxis. Thus, a well-documented belief in much of this debate – at least that from a neoliberal perspective (Friedman, 2005; Ohmae, 1995, 2005) – is that capital is mobile and labour relatively immobile and that, as a result, the best thing that workers can do is get on the globalisation train or be left at the developmental station. Put another way, capital crosses space whilst labour can only occupy place, the implication being that capital is always more geographically itinerant than is labour, and that the specificities of place are of little interest to capital when the whole world 'is its oyster'. However, in the dog-eat-dog world of regional development, where companies play localities against each other as sites for investment, we see that place clearly does matter to capital. Hence, across the world, regions are competitively marketing themselves and the places they contain as 'open for business' and rushing to reduce financial and social benefits in order to attract the mobile capital that will, they hope, bring vast *quantities* of jobs, even as they may sacrifice the *quality* of jobs along the way. In such place competition, minute differences in the quality of labour on offer – price, skill levels, quiescence and so on – often come to be of central importance to the place marketing that is intimately connected to regional development. Paradoxically, then, as transnationally organised capital's ability to cross space has increased – the result of improvements in transportation and telecommunications technologies – place and space have ever more entered the firmament of industrial relations.

In considering how place matters to capital, though, it is important also to recognise that workers are not necessarily confined to place or incapable of crossing space – through their migration they can physically move from place to place, crossing space much as does capital, whilst through their solidarity activities they have a long history of coming together across space (indeed, Southall (1988, p. 466) has argued that unionisation is actually 'a process of coming together, of organizing over space'). In fact, many forms of capital are actually much more confined to place than are workers. Hence, for instance, utilities like water, gas and electricity companies are usually tied to particular places through the magnitude of their sunk costs in pipes, transmission lines and other types of infrastructure, as are steel mills and other manufacturers with significant investments in particular places, together with small, local newspapers – thus, few people in Sydney, let alone London or Paris or New York, will be interested in reading newspapers published in small central Australian communities, we suspect, with the result that their sales base is reliant on those who live in or nearby the actual communities in which they are published.

These recognitions mean two things. First, although place has long been recognised as a locational factor, a recognition found both in early work on the emergence of a 'new international division of labour' (Fröbel et al., 1980) and in more recent work on, for instance, the offshoring of call centres (Monbiot, 2003), the approaches have tended to be overly simplistic, viewing place passively as merely a location in which things happen. Second, and relatedly, there has been a paucity of theorising and/or recognition in much study of work, employment, capitalists and workers both that different sets of actors not only may have quite different relationships to place but also that the same actors may have different experiences of embeddedness in, and freedom from, particular places at different times (by way of example, younger workers who are without mortgages may more easily leave a place than may older workers who are so encumbered). Thus, rather than a crude dualism of 'capital is free of place whilst labour is stuck to it', we must consider how different fractions of capital and labour are differentially embedded in place. This fact is important to recognise because, at a very basic level, *all* social action must take place somewhere – it does not occur on the head of a pin, after all – and so the changing relationships of social actors to various places are central to understanding the work and employment relationships between such different actors and how these might vary over time.

As one effort to develop an approach to labour market analysis within the context of globalisation that is more sensitive towards, and inclusive of, issues of space and place, Castree et al. (2004, pp. 18–21) have identified what they call six globalisation myths, several of which have quite explicit geographical aspects. The first such myth is that we live in an increasingly borderless world in which distance, geographical boundaries and location are really no longer important. The second is that the forces driving the spatial barrier- and distance-erasing juggernaut of 'globalisation' are unstoppable: TINA (as in There Is No Alternative) rules. Third, globalisation heralds the inevitable end of the nation state as a spatial container of economies (on the nation state's representation as such a container, see Mitchell, 1998, p. 90; Herod, 2007). Fourth, there is the myth of the inevitability of worker vulnerability. On this reading, workers face 'hegemonic despotism' (Burawoy, 1985), a world wherein one group of workers' wages are continually undercut by other workers in different places and all resistance is deemed futile. Connected to the fourth myth, the fifth concerns cheap labour. This suggests that firms will inevitably move to the location that provides the cheapest appropriate source of labour. Finally, the sixth myth argues that if workers are to resist the predations of globally organised capital then the only way to do so is for them to 'upscale' their action, that is to develop a global strategy to match translocal forces.

In this chapter and the introduction to Part 3 ('Workers in Space'), we start to unravel some of these myths and their supposed spatial implications, although as we write in early 2009 global recession is, perhaps serendipitously, already undermining the foundations of many of them for us. The recent nationalisation of various financial institutions suggests that the nation state still has some life in it, whilst high oil prices in 2008 encouraged some manufacturing companies in the US and elsewhere to actually bring back manufacturing operations they had previously offshored to countries like China (Voice of America, 2008). In so doing, we start to apply some of the theory outlined in Chapter 1. We also introduce the chapters in Part 2 which deal with workers in places from dormitory regimes to various types of workplace to specially constructed communities. The chapter is organised as follows. First, we explore some of the ways in which the nation state and markets have been presented within the literature on the restructuring of labour markets, especially as these representations have spatial imaginaries tied up within them. We then briefly delve into some debates concerning regions, given that there has been much made recently about the apparent emergence of a 'New Regionalism' in the face of the alleged break-up of the nation state. The third section contemplates the meaning of 'place' as an analytical category, whilst the fourth investigates the benefits that might accrue from using a value chain analysis to understand some issues related to work and employment and their spatiality. Finally, we provide an outline concerning what the substantive chapters in this portion of the book cover.

Mounting the scales

One of the key issues in discussions of labour market restructuring and globalisation is that of the rescaling of the nation state and what this means for workers. In this regard, Castree et al. (2004, p. 131) provide a fairly familiar diagrammatic representation of how the nation state, which has its own particular labour control mechanisms, is seen to sit within a nexus of other scales of social action and how developments at these other scales within a globalising world can impact upon the nation state's labour control regimes (see Figure 4.1). We have chosen to use this diagram here as a jumping off point for our discussion because it is a very common pictorial representation of how the relations between the national scale and other scales are imagined to exist, and because thinking through how the scales between various levels of labour control are so portrayed can aid us in thinking through some of the spatial matters concerning 'globalisation',

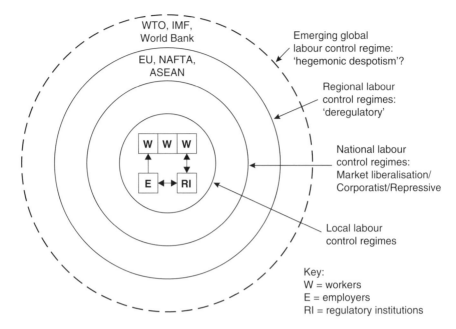

Source: Castree et al. (2004, p. 131).

Figure 4.1 *The 'scaling' of labour control regimes*

'regionalisation' and how space may be used for structuring social relations (the focus of the chapters included in this section of the book).

A useful starting point in all this, then, is a consideration of the role of the nation state in the contemporary political economy. Despite the ubiquity of neoliberal rhetorics concerning the supposed 'end of the nation state' (the phrase is Ohmae's (1995)), the myth of the declining state has been effectively challenged both analytically (see Fairbrother and Rainnie, 2006; Herod, 2009) and materially – when even an Ayn Randian like former US Federal Reserve Board Chairman Alan Greenspan argues, as he did in response to the 2008 financial meltdown, that the US banking system needed to be nationalised, the ridiculousness of bland proclamations that the state is withering away are blindingly clear. In place of such rhetorics of nation state shrivelling have come calls for a more theoretically sophisticated alternative to the dichotomous view that there was more of the state in the past and there is less of it now.

The work of Bob Jessop in particular has been highly influential in providing a more theoretically robust alternative to such 'disappearance of the state' arguments. Interestingly, at the centre of his analysis lies a clear spatial sensitivity (see Chapter 2 in this volume). In particular, Jessop argues that permanent innovation and flexibility lie at the heart of the new state forms that are emerging, with social policy increasingly subordinated to the demands of labour market flexibility, employability and economic competitiveness. Perhaps the most significant issue from our perspective, though, is the decidedly post-national nature of the new Schumpeterian Workfare state, in so far as the national-scale state seems to have become less important as an economic, political and cultural power container. What has emerged instead is a multilevel governance regime with policy-making functions transferred outwards to the supranational scale, inwards to the regional and/or local scale and sideways within the nation state, and in which the shift from government to 'meta-governance' is of fundamental importance.[1]

In terms of Figure 4.1, the transfer to the supranational scale is represented by a move of decision-making capacities to the outer ring of the diagram, wherein organisations like the World Bank, IMF and WTO are increasingly said to be undermining national sovereignty.[2] Such movement is described as facilitating the emergence of a particular type of labour control regime: 'hegemonic despotism'. This concept of 'hegemonic despotism', developed by Michael Burawoy (1985) and further refined by Jonas (1997), has at its core the argument that a new global politics of production is emerging based on the relative mobility of capital and the relative immobility of labour. As myth number four suggested, in these circumstances competition between regions around the world leads to an inevitable ratcheting down of wages and conditions, and the institutions mentioned in the outer ring of Figure 4.1, along with consultancies and other organisations, are seen to actively promote the necessity of this race to the bottom as a way of kick-starting a proto-capitalist economic development (the dominance of this discourse has led to it being called the 'Washington consensus'). These organisations are frequently seen to be aided in this by a nascent 'transnational managerial class' (though see Rainnie and Fairbrother (2006) for a critique of this argument).

There are, however, several issues with such analyses of rescaling and the growing dominance of global-scale organisations like the WTO that are argued to be bringing about an international regime of hegemonic despotism. One is that considerations of complexity and contradiction (never mind resistance) are downplayed in the face of the seemingly unstoppable forces – located at a supranational level – of globalisation. This would appear, then, to be simply a social democratic version (given that entities like the European Union might be seen to be responsive to the voting public) of the TINA mantra. It also appears to be a version of the 'one best way' fallacy in which it is suggested that, at any given time, there can only be one successful resolution to the problems of strategy and structure confronting organisations (see Hyman, 1987). Additionally, it fails to take into account the heterogeneity of TNC structures and dynamics (see Ferner et al., 2004).

Another issue to consider, one which has more spatial overtones, is that in such a formulation the processes of neoliberal globalisation are seen as somewhat supernal. Globalisation is viewed as if it were something imposed from above (if we are using the ladder scalar metaphor) or outside (if we are using the concentric circle metaphor), rather than organically derived from and in various localities. It is as if global forces have arrived within the global economy fully-formed, rather than having been developed in particular locations (like Washington, DC) and then diffused across the economic landscape following certain pathways – that is to say, following certain spatial conduits and courses. At its core, then, this representation lacks a geography – global forces are unconnected to particular localities and are seen to be universal. Finally, when different scales are represented in areal terms like in Figure 4.1 – as circles or as steps on a ladder, for instance – 'the global' is also presented as being a distinctly different realm from that of 'the local' or 'the national', as separate from these other scales. Given how 'the global' is usually portrayed as more powerful than are these other scales (Gibson-Graham,

1996), this representation facilitates discourses which view 'the national' and 'the local' as being subjugated by 'the global', with little recognition that these other scales may, in fact, impact upon 'the global' and/or that national-level or local-level political actions might be capable of defeating 'global' forces (Herod, 2001a).

Returning to the question of the nation state and its regulation of labour (and other) markets (see Turnbull, Chapter 3 in this volume, for more on the social construction of markets), Burnham (2006) views the relationship between states and markets as often having been conceived of in similar ways to those of 'the global' and other scales as outlined in Figure 4.1 (i.e., as external and contingent), for both have tended to be viewed as spatially self-contained entities that simply interact with one another.[3] However, Burnham argues that rather than conceptualising states and markets in such a fashion, the connections between them should be seen as internal and necessary (in a realist sense (Sayer, 1984)), for states are an aspect of social relations of production and their power derives from their ability to reorganise capital–labour relations within, and often beyond, their boundaries to enhance the accumulation of capital. Recent changes in global political economy are therefore predominantly about reorganising rather than bypassing states, and this recomposition is actively undertaken by state managers as part of a broader attempt to restructure and respond to a crisis of labour–capital relations in the market.

For Burnham, the form that this restructuring takes is the so-called 'depoliticisation' of the state, with depoliticisation being a government strategy of placing at one remove the political character of decision making. However, despite claims that depoliticisation is taking the politics out of state restructuring – which is also market restructuring, given how states' regulatory and other activities significantly shape how markets function – such depoliticisation is actually a highly political process. In fact, for Burnham depoliticisation is important precisely because of the highly political pressures that capitalist states are now under. The strength of Burnham's analysis, then, is that it unites the form and function of state restructuring (such as marketisation of the public sector) with analysis of work and workers. More importantly for our purposes, though, depoliticisation through privatisation, outsourcing and decentralisation has significant spatial implications, contributing to the central dynamic behind the process of combined and uneven development (to which we shall return later) because the processes of privatisation, outsourcing and decentralisation – and worker responses to these – are, in fact, highly geographically variable (Painter, 1991).

The importance of such an analysis of the liberal democratic state is that, in addition to destabilising ideas of the state and the market as spatially discrete entities that simply interact, labour becomes both object and subject of policy and analysis. As Dick Bryan (2000, p. 5) has pointed out,

> [i]n a world of international mobility (and pricing) of capital commodities, national costs come down predominantly to labour as the economic factor which, by its relative immobility internationally, is the one most imbued with the characteristics of 'nationality'. Labour costs become the key to national success. They also become the zone of sacrifice in order to achieve that success.

The point to be made here, then, is that even when contradictions or complexities arise for the state in the market at the level of the capital–capital relationship, relief is usually sought at the site of the capital–labour relationship, either directly through job loss or wage cuts or indirectly through attacks on the social wage and welfare state. However, hostility between capitals not only manifests itself within states (in geographically uneven ways), depending on the dominant fractions of capital, but also between states. Consequently, the state's ability to compete depends on the relative size, composition and quality of the sections of capital that fall within its orbit and their geographical structure: to bring Harvey (1982) back in to the analysis, their particular spatial fixes/ geographies of organisation will shape their ability to respond to competition. However, whilst the Burnham analysis is critical it should also be extended, since paradoxically it does not place the state centre stage as a site of contested social relations that play out unevenly across and through space. As a result, it is an analysis that overlooks how state relations are emerging as the site for labour struggle, both within and against the state.

If Burnham argues that capital–capital conflicts are often transformed into capital–labour ones by and through the state, Mooney and Law (2007) argue that one unforeseen consequence for capitalists and state managers of this assault on labour by the state has been that the longstanding division – both analytical and in terms of people's identities – between individuals as producers and as consumers has begun to be broken down in many cases. For instance, in the UK, although uneven and partial, there is a growing merging of the concerns of some public sector workers and their unions and the demands of some service users and their welfare clients. Thus, campaigns against Private Finance Initiatives (PFI – a mechanism to fund public activities in return for their partial privatisation) and Public Private Partnerships (PPP – a proposal to involve the private sector in the operation of public services), as well as Keep Our NHS Public and Defend Council Housing, have been important cases in point. Similar concerns have been expressed elsewhere.

Around the world, then, privatisation – or threats thereof – in all its many forms has worked to re-energise debates around health and other public services. In the UK, New Labour (and the Conservatives before them) have inadvertently repoliticised the whole question of welfare and public sector provision, as did the Bush Administration with its plans – which it had to abandon in response to public outcry – to privatise social security (the state-provided pension system). For their part, PFIs have been adopted in countries such as Canada, France, the Netherlands, the Czech Republic, Norway, India, Australia, Malaysia and the US, but have elicited concerted opposition from organised labour and others. Indeed, the growing hostility on the part of many towards plans for capital-driven and for-profit forms of welfare provision has increasingly led to the emergence – or, rather, re-emergence – of a more energetic political unionism in many parts of the world where, for much of the twentieth century, a rather moribund bread-and-butter unionism had previously dominated as official union movements played their role in the Keynesian-Fordist compromise that emerged in places like the US, the UK, Australia, New Zealand and other parts of the industrialised world after 1945.[4] This process, as we shall see in Chapter 14, raises important scalar and spatial questions.

What is a region?
Returning to Figure 4.1 we can see that it details the existence not just of supranational labour control regimes but also of those existing at the regional and local scales. We will deal with this latter formulation – local labour control regimes – in more detail in

Chapter 14, although for the time being it is worth noting that the existence of local labour control regimes does imply the existence also of a coherent scale and place that can be defined as 'the local'. However, our attention here is upon 'regional labour control regimes'. The issue of regional labour control regimes has become more noteworthy in recent years (see, for instance, *Regional Studies* special edition, vol. **41**(9), Nov/Dec 2007). However, this raises the matter of how we might understand the nature of 'regions', which have become increasingly significant as economic units that are viewed to lie somewhere between 'the local' and 'the global'. Ohmae (1995), for instance, has quite clearly seen such regions as taking over from nation states as the geographical location where the economic 'action' takes place.[5] Such understanding is especially important because much contemporary writing has focused upon the emergence in the past two decades or so of what has been called a 'New Regionalism' in economic development and labour control, in which regions play a more important role than in the recent past when most of the economic development and labour market regulatory capacities were seen to devolve from the national scale.

In essence, much of this debate over the surfacing of a New Regionalism has been spawned by the apparent disintegration of the nation state as an economic and regulatory entity. Interestingly, though, the debate has incorporated specific spatial imaginaries within it. In particular, much of the debate has been over whether to see the emergence of a New Regionalism in territorial or in relational/networked terms – or, putting it slightly differently, in topographical versus topological terms.[6] This territorial versus relational/topographical versus topological distinction has its origins in different intellectual traditions. Thus, on the one hand, MacLeod and Jones (2007) trace the emergence of the New Regionalism in the late twentieth century to a resurgence of the regional science of the mid-century. This is important because regional science was dominated by neoclassical economics and robust statistical techniques and viewed regions very much in terms of them being areal units within which things economic took place. On the other hand, Keating (1998) and Brenner (2004) have identified the emergence of a significant New Regionalism based on a decomposition and recomposition of the territorial framework of economic life and the rescaling of statehood.

For some, then, the emergence of this New Regionalism was driven by a social democratic concern with associational democracy (Cooke and Morgan, 1998; see Rainnie and Grobbelaar, 2005) – that is to say, the belief that the nation state had anti-democratic tendencies and therefore that organisation at the regional scale (whether at the subnational, more 'local' scale, or at the supranational scale as per, say, the European Union) was more democratic. However, for others the transformation of regions was being brought about by the influx and activities of an emergent new creative class (Florida, 2003; see Rainnie, 2005). For yet others, like Ohmae, regionalisation was a product of globalisation, which was making the nation state increasingly irrelevant as an economic container, with the result that this older economic unit was being replaced by a newer one.

However, alongside this (contested) New Regionalism, the relational/networked view also gathered force and was particularly associated with writers like Amin (2004) and Allen and Cochrane (2007). Thus, Amin (2004, p. 33) argued that

[i]n this emerging new order, spatial configurations and spatial boundaries are no longer necessarily or purposively territorial or scalar, since the social, economic, political and cultural

inside and outside are constituted through the topologies of actor networks which are becoming increasingly dynamic and varied in spatial constitution.

He added further that

[i]n a relationally constituted modern world in which it has become normal to conduct business – economic, cultural, political – through everyday trans-territorial organization and flow, local advocacy . . . must be increasingly about exercising nodal power and aligning networks at large in one's own interest, rather than about exercising territorial power. . . . There is no definable regional territory to rule over. (Amin, 2004, p. 36)

Nevertheless, Amin's formulation has come in for some criticism, with MacLeod and Jones arguing that such an approach downplays issues of power within networks. The world, they contend, is neither as flat (cf. Jones et al., 2007) nor as multinodal as such an approach contends (MacLeod and Jones, 2007). Christopherson and Clark (2007) concur, pointing to the importance of power asymmetries between small businesses and transnational corporations in regional/local networks.

A number of other authors, though, have taken a far more bleak view of the operation of new networked forms of organisation like manufacturing clusters, public–private partnerships, multi-client service organisations, multi-employer work sites, franchising models of business operation and the growing use of labour agencies to provide temporary workers who can be readily hired and fired according to the dictates of the economy at any one time. Hence, Marchington et al. (2005) have argued that the blurring of organisational boundaries, driven by the emergence of new managerial forms, does pose challenges for analyses of work and employment. They suggest, then, that a focus simply on the relationship between, on the one hand, the restructured organisation or newly emergent organisation and, on the other, the organisation's workforce is misleading, for such restructuring creates new and highly complex inter- and intra-organisational relationships (networks), which have severe implications for internal labour markets, regimes of training and skill acquisition, career paths, organisational commitment and loyalty and employment stability.

A more critical theme is developed by Noteboom (2004), who argues that collaboration in networks does not always entail creation of a balance of mutual value, dependence and power. Alvesson and Thompson (2005) concur, arguing that, for instance, information technology (IT) systems facilitate, rather than remove, managerial control in post-bureaucratic networks. This point is reinforced by Brown et al. (2003), who suggest that information and communications technology (ICT) plays a more dominant role in networked organisations than in many other types of organisation. They also argue that whereas employees may experience more cooperation through greater consultation by managers courtesy of such ICT, they may also be subject to new forms of managerial control that are facilitated by it (such as greater electronic monitoring of their activities). Overall, Grugulis et al. (2003) have argued, rather than being liberatory organisational structures, networked forms of organisation often diminish employee discretion as workers are subject to increased auditing and a decrease in control.

More brutally, and emphasising the role that the state has to play in determining the path and pattern of networked forms, Hebdon and Kirkpatrick (2005), in an overview of public sector restructuring, suggest that privatisation in the UK and US may be producing a two-tiered labour force – a full-time core workforce surrounded by a temporary one whose members are hired and fired on the basis of management needs for numerical and/or functional flexibility. They also emphasise the uneven pattern of change across developed countries, the result of differing social, political and economic regimes. This network form, then, makes the concept of the spatial fix more complex than ever before. Furthermore, we want to argue that the notion of a network, taken in isolation, may not be particularly helpful, as it covers too many disparate forms. Finally, we also suggest that when it has engaged with the spatial, the network form of analysis has hitherto tended toward a rather simplistic spatial analysis (focusing upon simple clustering). Questions of power and uneven development – and the failure of such network analysis to adequately address them – lead us, then, to prefer a form of analysis based on value chains (see below and Perrons, 2004).

As a final point, it is important to recognise that, in response to the growing popularity in recent years of networked views of the New Regionalism and regions, there has actually been something of a spirited defence mounted of the analytical and political importance of territorialised approaches to the region. Hence Hudson (2007), drawing upon Foucault's notion of governmentality, has argued that in order to govern (at whatever scalar level) it is necessary to render visible the space over which governmental activities are territorially demarcated – in other words, regions need to be defined and represented and their boundaries marked out as both objects and subjects of governing. As he puts it:

> regional economies are constituted via regional statistics, which have a key role in 'making economies visible' and constituting them as objects for policy action. The capability to decide upon these defining statistical measures is clearly a critical issue [within a context in which,] through a process of mobilization, the truth claims of accredited authority figures, under the guise of neutrality and efficiency, set out the norms of conduct that enable distant events and people to be governed at arm's length. (Hudson, 2007, p. 1154)

There are, therefore, political reasons why some groups may seek to define areas in territorial terms. This can have positive and negative outcomes for such groups and those with whom they are in conflict, as we will see in Chapter 14 when we look at local labour control regimes and issues like community unionism and growth coalitions.

Therefore, although we set out an essentially relational approach to space and place in Chapter 1, we perhaps should now refine this somewhat and agree with MacLeod and Jones (2007, p. 1186), who argue that when promoting a (relational) politics of scalar structuration, 'the degree to which one interprets cities or regions as territorial and scalar or topological and networked really ought to remain an open question: a matter to be resolved *ex post* and empirically rather than *a priori* and theoretically.' Hudson (2007, p. 1151) concurs, suggesting that a both/and, rather than an either/or, perspective would be helpful.

Locating place

Putting all of this together, how, then, are we to theorize space, place and locality? For many analysts of work and employment, places have long been seen simply as the rather self-evident and inert locations in which social action unfolds. They have, in other words, been little theorised except in terms of how they might serve as a context for social actors' decision-making processes. However, within the geographic literature there is a rich tradition of theorising place, a tradition which we feel has some pertinence for efforts to study work and employment. Hence, for Hudson (2001, pp. 257, 260), for instance, places are open, discontinuous, relational and internally diverse. Furthermore, localities must be seen as a complex mosaic of mechanisms of growth and decline, a changing mix of flows through place. Hence, place should be thought of as the sphere where local and non-local systems of rules, norms, customs, legal structures and regulatory mechanisms intersect to shape and institutionalize the behaviour of both workers and employers. In addition, it is important to recognise that over time a locality's fortunes depend on its changing role within the broader spatial division of labour: is it a mining community, whose economic health is dependent upon economies in places distant from it booming and so using its products, or is it a community with myriad corporate headquarter offices which are designed to manage the far-flung operations of various TNCs?

What these questions suggest, then, is that local socioeconomic and social structures are the complex and institutionally mediated outcome of the distinctive role played by localities in successive spatial divisions of labour (Herod and Wright, 2002) as local and non-local processes combine with existing differences to produce and reproduce unevenness within and between localities (Castree et al., 2004). Consequently, uneven development is not accidental nor simply an unfortunate by-product of economic development that will be evened out over time but, rather, is fundamental to the nature of capitalism. It is the result of the working out of various spatial tensions faced by different actors. Hence, for Smith (2007, pp. 188–9) the law of value under capitalism is based on a fundamental contradiction between, on the one hand, a constant tendency for differentiation rooted in the division of labour, and an opposite tendency towards universalisation that finds its apotheosis in the tendency towards an equalisation of the general rate of profit. Consequently, the differentiation of places is less and less a question of locational and natural endowment and increasingly the product of a spatial logic as inherent to this mode of production as is Marx's temporal theory of capitalist crisis. The result is that this contradiction simultaneously establishes discrete places differentiated from each other whilst it also presses them all into the same mould. Successive spatial fixes then reinforce the nature of combined and uneven development. Smith (2007, p. 190) concludes that '[u]neven development represents a forced yet contested, momentarily fixed yet always fluid resolution to this central contradiction of capitalism.' Equally, though, it is important to recognise that uneven development is not just produced out of the internal tensions within capital, as workers and others can also play important roles in shaping the uneven development of capitalism's landscapes (Herod, 2001b).

For their part, Castree et al. (2004, p. 66) argue that the permeability of place has two important implications:

1. There is an important paradox with regard to place differences, namely that they persist because of, not despite, heightened place interconnectivity. Hence, although different places may get swept up in similar flows, local differences arise because not all places are connected to the broader world in the same way, as different places are wired into different sets of wider relations and connections. Non-local processes combine with existing local differences, then, to produce unique outcomes.
2. Places are not simply different from one another but are unevenly and causally

related. Networks of social relations are not simply uneven in their reach but work through diversity and difference. Place relations construct unevenness in their wake and operate through the pattern of uneven development already laid down.

For Castree et al., then, everyday life is simultaneously local (placed) and translocal (spaced), and whilst the world is increasingly well connected, most people lead intensely local lives, the implications of which we will explore in Chapter 14.

By way of example, Stenning and colleagues provide a concrete example of the way that uneven development, in this case seen through the lens of ethnic minority enterprise, arises.

> The local neighbourhood – through its formal and informal institutions, and the mix of minority ethnic and 'mainstream' populations – is seen to be absolutely critical to the development of minority ethnic enterprise. Particular sites within minority communities can act as '*hot spots* of information . . . crucial in obtaining a job, a house or a partner' . . . A 'critical mass' of immigrants allows for the 'nurturing of social capital', the development of social networks, and the servicing of a 'captive' market (Kloosterman and Rath, 2001), whilst the wider institutional environment at the urban and regional level shapes markets, entrepreneurial opportunities and development potential. For these reasons, Kloosterman and Rath stress the importance of what they call 'mixed embeddedness' which is the articulation of the migrant entrepreneur with both immigrant social/community networks and the wider economic and institutional context. [Meanwhile,] Barrett et al. (2001, p. 241) stress the importance of spatially-sensitive and locally-variable policies for migrant enterprise support. Their reasoning is [that] 'the uneven geography of migrant and native age and class structures, and the varied legacies of earlier economic cycles in the urban fabric, mean that localities and regions possess differing potential for business development. The number of potential entrepreneurs varies; the availability of co-ethnic labour differs; markets are distinguished along dimensions of culture, prosperity and sector; and the competitive context is rarely the same'. (Stenning et al., 2006, p. 17, emphasis in the original)

Following from this, Holgate (2007) concludes that although the nature of uneven development might have historically been characterised primarily in terms of unequal wealth and class/gender relations, it is also clearly acutely racialised. Drawing upon Smith's ([1984] 1990, p. 155) argument that '[u]neven development is [both] social inequality blazoned into the geographical landscape, and it is simultaneously the exploitation of that geographical unevenness for socially determined ends', Holgate (2007, p. 906) suggests that 'capital and neo-liberal policies have created spatial discontinuities between groups of workers, in the type of work undertaken, [particularly] in areas where black and minority ethnic communities live'.

How, then, are we to analyse the dynamics of a particular region or locality and how and why it differs from other regions or localities? In arguing against a rather traditional 'varieties of capitalism' school of thought (Hall and Soskice, 2001) approach to such questions, Peck and Theodore (2007, pp. 760–61, emphasis in the original) suggest that:[7]

> [w]hat is [really] called for . . . is a nuanced analysis of the temporality *and spatiality* of capitalist development . . . Long skeptical of descriptive labeling and typologizing approaches to capitalist development, and reluctant to sequester causal processes to particular scales or locales, [in this regard] economic geographers might indeed be well-placed to help make sense of the kinds of relationally combined, multiscalar hybrid forms of restructuring that tend to confound formalized, system-centric analyses. This means moving beyond the routine pluralization of capitalism, and the alternating proliferation and pruning of a reified set of 'models,' to probe

the principles, sources and dimensions of *capitalist variegation*, understood as a more explicitly 'relational' conception of variety. In other words, it means coming to terms with the causes and forms of capitalism's polymorphism.

Having explored in various ways the role of the state within contemporary capitalism, the emerging network form of organisation and the nature of regions, in the next section we draw on value chain analysis to suggest a way in which these three elements might be drawn together into a more comprehensive and mutually reinforcing form of analysis.

Towards an analytical framework
Marchington et al. (2005) point to the importance of combinations of value chains in analysing contemporary developments in work and organisations (as does Dicken's ([1988] 2007) earlier work on global value chains). We think that a robust theoretical framework that incorporates value chain analysis, promoted by Rainnie and colleagues (Smith et al., 2001; Smith et al., 2002), is a useful starting place to examine geographical and organisational fragmentation and its implications. This is because it moves us 'away from . . . approach[es] that stres[s] a one best way of organising either firms (learning organization) or region (knowledge economy) towards one that stresses different forms of network/firm organization constituted through value chains' (Smith et al., 2002, p. 43). Such a framework, then, enables a focus on the geographies of the activities of the state (national and sub-national), labour and firms. It also allows us to think about inequalities in the creation and appropriation of value and the value flows between places, since this latter underpins the mosaic of regional inequality. We would argue that by building on the insights of commodity chain analysis (Gereffi and Korzeniewicz, 1994) we can start to identify sites of power and governance within production systems and value networks by identifying the role and importance of various 'economic agents'.

Our approach moves away from a focus on the commodity per se and towards a focus upon the mechanisms by which value in particular sectors of activity is governed by the networks of linkages that comprise the complexity of contemporary economic life (Smith et al., 2002; Waring et al., 2004; Fairbrother and Rainnie, 2006). In this regard it is similar to how Perrons (2004, Chapter 4) examines the feminization of employment in the 'cool chains, the integrated circuit and care chains' sectors (by which she means employment in agribusiness, the electronic circuit and the care chain) to understand how paid employment has affected women's lives. Such an approach, we believe, is appropriate because it is sensitive to a number of crucial issues, the first of which is the importance of seeing workers as both objective and subjective actors in any analysis. This is a significant development because, as Marchington et al. (2005) argue, the network literature largely excludes a consideration of the implications of these networks for workers and employment relationships (cf. Rainnie and Fairbrother (2006) on labour and restructuring of the state).

The second matter to which our approach seeks to be sensitive is that of the linked issues of race, gender and skill. We have already seen how questions of race and gender lie at the heart of the dynamics of uneven development. Hebson and Grugulis (2005) argue that although new organisational forms are usually highly gendered because they build on existing gendered power relations and leave women to experience the brunt of organisational change, the rhetoric of employee choice and equality (in networks, everyone is frequently viewed as an equal member of a 'team', for instance) often makes gender formally invisible. New organisational forms, then, may represent a break with the bureaucracy of the past, but this is usually not because of attempts to redress pervasive inequalities but, rather, because the extant bureaucracy is not seen as able to accommodate new business opportunities and competitive pressures. Hence, the danger here is that new networked forms of organisation simply open the path to new forms of inequalities and exploitation that merely build on existing gender divisions, which are still present, even if they may be less visible. These new networked forms of organisation, then, are not inherently more liberatory than older forms of work structuring.

Perrons (2004, p. 103), for instance, highlights how gender inequality is simply being reformatted, rather than eliminated, when she pulls together value chain analysis with a focus on gender in her analysis of women in the food industry, ICTs and care chains. Hence, as the emerging global division of labour has led to factories, call centres and packing plants being established in or relocated to poorer countries and regions, rural to urban migration as people move in search of work and a better life has emerged on an unprecedented scale, as we outlined in the opening paragraphs of this chapter. Likewise, international migration from the global South to the global North has also increased. What Perrons (2004, p. 89) has found, though, is that structural adjustment programmes in the global South have reduced the amount of paid regular employment, especially for male workers, whilst the feminisation of employment in both rich and poor countries has generated gaps in childcare provision for poor children as their mothers – who are still overwhelmingly responsible for providing such care – are not in the home as much as previously (or may even have migrated overseas, as in the case of, say, Filipina maids). These transformations and structural adjustments, then, are creating a global care chain in which wealthy but time-poor people in the global North and the affluent neighbourhoods of global South countries establish a demand for marketised personal and domestic services, which are generally low paid and in which women are generally over-represented.[8] The end result, though, is that these women care for the children of the wealthy at the expense of their own. For Yeates (2004), however, and echoing a theme in our argument, it is important to highlight the role of the state in all this, as it is the state that governs care chains via labour (de/re) regulation, immigration laws, welfare restructuring and such like. Furthermore, Yeates stresses the importance of the family status of migrant workers as a variable in care chain analysis. Nevertheless, for Perrons (2004, p. 105) it is vitally important to recognise that there is a crucial difference between the care chain and other value chains in that value is not unequally appropriated at different points in the chain; rather, 'care chains take a directly hierarchical form on the basis of gender, race and generation as poorer people, usually women from poor regions of the world, care for the children and elderly relatives of people in richer regions'. Based upon her observations, then, Perrons concludes that 'uneven development within the context of globalization, together with the undervaluation or non-recognition of qualifications from poorer countries can [thus] create a [significant] spatial dislocation by social class' (2004, p. 105).

The third issue our approach can address is the importance of small firms in the process of labour market restructuring, particularly given that such firms are often seen as being key hubs within broader networks of flexible production (as in much of the literature on, for instance, the Third Italy). We do this by incorporating into our value chain analysis the heuristic device developed by Barrett and Rainnie (2002) to analyse the role of small firms in contemporary patterns of restructuring. Rather than relying on simplistic spatial forms of cluster analysis, small firms, we would argue, must be examined in terms of their *particular* relationships to large firms and the state, as well as to each other, for these relationships have signal consequences for how labour relations are played out (see also Christopherson and Clark, 2007). In particular, such an approach allows for consideration of significant heterogeneity with regard to small firms' models of industrial relations (that is, there is no assumption of a 'one-size-fits-all' approach to small firms' management practices as has tended to be the case with the 'small is beautiful' arguments common in much recent writing about small firms' centrality to reinvigorating capitalism (cf. Piore and Sabel, 1984)). It also provides an analytical framework for exploring the effect of a range of factors (and not simply size) on industrial relations and it incorporates at its heart the dialectic between agency and structure. The key question in all of this, though, is that of how labour control is maintained, both as a result of activities within the firm but also those beyond the workplace. What we feel is especially important in all this is to treat firms not as analytical containers that are theorised as if they were somehow hermetically sealed off from the larger world, but instead to adopt an approach that links what occurs in the spaces within the firm's workplaces to those of the broader economic landscape within which these workplaces are located. Again, such an approach stresses the importance of the dynamics of combined and uneven development, as these dynamics outside the workplace can have important impacts on how labour relations are conducted within it, whilst the way in which these labour relations are conducted within the workplace can dramatically impact those broader patterns of combined and uneven development (see Herod, 2001b).

To summarise, in what we have tried to do conceptually so far, it is possible that our account could be accused of failing to address questions of labour as subject. This is fair based on what we have written so far, as in this chapter we have been largely concerned with labour as an object of history and geography and have been intent on placing labour and spatiality at the heart of contemporary analysis. We will, however, turn to the question of labour as a subject in our introductory chapter to Part 3. Before then, though, we preview the contributions to Part 2, which themselves focus upon labour as object.

Preview of Part 2

Section 2.1   Regionalisation, globalisation and labour
Section 2.1 deals with issues that can be broadly grouped under the heading of a spatially aware analysis of the processes of globalisation and their effects on labour. These vary from the impact of ICTs, through the growth of contingent labour and the experience of Filipino migrant workers in Canada. We also bring together the effects of class, race, gender and religion when confronting the labour markets of the twenty-first century.

In the first chapter in this section, Peck and Theodore (Chapter 5) examine the labour market 'from the bottom up', through an analysis of the restructuring of low-wage work in the neoliberal era in Chicago's temporary employment sector. Their focus is on one wave of restructuring cum re-regulation, the rise of contingent work since the 1980s. In particular, they stress the stubbornness of 'localness' in the creation of labour markets, arguing that geography and scale continue to matter even in an era of 'globalisation' but that they matter in different ways than in the past. They conclude that it is now appropriate to declare the 'arrival' of a neoliberal order, at least in the creation of contingent labour markets, though they suggest that although the neoliberal order has constructed 'local labour' in competitive terms, there are important complexities and contradictions in this process. Thus, whereas politically assisted uneven development may have played a role in levering down labour standards, it has also generated new spaces of contradiction and new spaces of resistance.

For their part, Pickles and Smith (Chapter 6) are concerned with a fundamental pivot in patterns of employment and economic life in Central and Eastern Europe after 1989 – a story, initially at least, of geo-political shifts, economic violence and retrenchment alongside the emergence of wild forms of capitalist social relations. Specifically, they focus on the consequences of the post-1989 upheaval for the conditions of work and organising in the clothing industry. Since 1989, the futures of workers and trade unions have remained complex and differentiated, both within the industry and across the region. In this context, the expanded pace and scope of outsourcing, the restructuring of supply chains and questions of ethical sourcing initiatives are all making for complex conditions of work. The chapter stresses the impossibility of operating conceptual models of the global economy that are not attentive to place specificity and locally/historically situated institutional practices.

Zook and Samers (Chapter 7) look at the relationship between labour and information and communication technologies (ICTs), which they argue is an issue that remains startlingly under-researched by human geographers, except in the case of call centres. They focus specifically on ICT-enabled e-commerce (B2B, B2C), abandoning technological determinism and replacing it with a dialectical form of analysis of the relationship between technology and social relations. Despite some apocalyptic predictions, the authors argue that the sectoral complexities of e-commerce mean that jobs are not simply disappearing into the ether of e-commerce, nor is all labour equally accessible (see also Taylor and Bain, Chapter 24 in this volume). Instead, through confronting a series of 'myths', Zook and Samers conclude that whilst new ICTs are facilitating changes in the social and spatial contours of capitalism, they are not leading inevitably to the end of work. Furthermore, ICTs do not lead inevitably to dualistic labour markets or to offshoring, and it is possible, they suggest, for workers to use ICTs to fight for a more equitable economic geography.

Mohammad (Chapter 8) forefronts the question of race and gender in an examination of the significance of space for working-class British Pakistani Muslim women, particularly in relation to their access to the labour market. In particular, she argues that much feminist analysis has focused on white, Western, middle-class women's experiences. Instead, she examines the ways in which the character of space becomes significant for the extent and nature of Pakistani women's access to the formal labour market in the UK. Mohammad concludes that it is the centrality of women's bodies and concepts of heterosexual purity in the making of marriage and the Muslim family which has important effects on women's mobility within the built environment and thus the labour market. This is due to the institutionalisation of a gendered segregation of space wherein ambiguous or opaque spaces outside the home – education or labour-market related – are viewed as dangerous or degrading by fathers and husbands because they do not allow as ready monitoring of women as is the case when spaces are more transparent.

Finally, Kelly (Chapter 9), who focuses on the experience of Filipino migrant workers in Toronto, Canada, seeks an explanation for why Filipinos have come to occupy the least secure, least remunerated and least desirable places in the global labour market. He concludes that the types of jobs occupied by Filipino migrants reflect (*inter alia*) a squeeze on service sector and manufacturing jobs, cuts in public healthcare, a rise in temporary and contract labour and a general bifurcation in the labour market between, on the one hand, well-paid jobs and, on the other, flexible, low-paid work. However, Kelly argues, it is important to realise that the labour markets in which Filipinos work are shaped by sets of spatialities operating at various scales, from that of the global economy to the micro-geography of Toronto itself. Thus, for instance, both home and host states shape the experience of migrant workers in important ways, whilst more locally the geographical relationship between places of work and home (which plays a central role in processes of social reproduction) is also a key shaper of access to labour markets. Lastly, all these factors must be understood in the context of colonialism and global capitalism, particularly the relationship between the Philippines (a former Spanish and US colony) and the global North, which have left a legacy of racialised and gendered hierarchies that have marked certain bodies as more fit for certain types of work. This has resulted in employment and workplace structures being 'colour coded', with the labour market's upper levels being overwhelmingly white, a fact that further structures how labour markets operate geographically. Labour markets, homespaces and workplaces, then, do not necessarily create the inequalities outlined; rather, these must be understood in the context of the structure of spatial power within contemporary global capitalism.

Section 2.2   Building space
In section 2.2 we are more concerned with an analysis of the spaces of labour, whether they be workplaces or places of residence. The first two chapters deal with towns and the relationship between the experience of home and that of work. The remaining two chapters deal more narrowly with workplaces and how they are constructed both as places where work is experienced and also where employment and residence can coincide.

With regard to the issue of how the economic landscape can be manipulated for purposes of trying to shape social relations in the workplace, Oberdeck (Chapter 10) presents a case study of spatial policy induced and provoked by welfare capitalism town planners, in her case in the example of the Kohler Company of Wisconsin (US). These planners hoped to use town planning techniques to channel and shape the scale of employee affiliations and to control workers. In particular, Oberdeck is concerned with conflicts over spatial scale, the gendering and racialisation of space and the mutual reinforcing of spatial perspectives on the part of both workers and employers that grew out of the 'worker-oriented' town planning. Located in a discussion of the experience of town planning as spatial labour control, what Oberdeck demonstrates is that both dynamic and ever-changing processes that underlie a particular spatial fix have the power to destroy as well as to create. The nature of commitment to place, then, is complicated.

Stenning (Chapter 11) looks at the articulation of work and community in both the construction and collapse of 'socialism' in Central Europe, particularly in the case of Solidarity in Poland. Specifically, she argues that the changing nature of the work/

community relationship has been critical to the shape of labour politics and working-class struggle. Furthermore, that same relationship and its changing nature is central to the formation of identities, life chances and the economic practice of working people in the context of repeated and deep change in the post-socialist world. Stenning links these experiences to the new intellectual arena of working class studies, connecting industrial relations to debates on identity, multiculturalism and social justice. This is again a debate about the construction of new communities and worker resistance, analysing how the changing geography of the worker/community nexus has shaped, on a number of scales, both labour politics and the economic and social geography of the region.

Baldry (Chapter 12), in a case study of the 'Hols Travel' call centre in Scotland, is concerned with the way in which a spatial dimension is incorporated into social analysis, in particular with 'assembly points', points in space where capital and labour power are brought together – more commonly referred to as workplaces. His argument is that the built environment cannot be understood without reference to its geo-spatial and political economic context. However, the physical layout of the workplace – its microgeography – is important because it is more than a backdrop to action. Rather, it is locked into a reflexive relationship with the lived experience of the world of those who occupy it. In making such a claim, then, Baldry is arguing against both those who see buildings as neutral shells and those who see them as determinors of worker behaviour. He suggests instead that work buildings must be seen as objects of contest – workers' behaviours are shaped by the spatiality of the built environment within which they find themselves, but such workers also find ways to resist the spatial engineering efforts of managers and architects. Further, he avers that control strategies are taking on a more qualitative and subjective dimension through the manipulation of the interior work environment, in this case the decor of a call centre. Baldry concludes that the built form of the workplace is constituted to encapsulate and reproduce the interests of those in power. However, although employees are still free to exercise their own judgement, this may actually encourage greater dissention, for if workers are told that the workplace is 'fun' but their experience is a target-driven intensification of work that contributes to headaches and sore throats, then their disenchantment may be even more acute than if they had no expectations of having fun at work.

Finally, Pun and Smith (Chapter 13) argue that conceptualising contemporary changes in the nature of work as representing a shift from Taylorism/Fordism to flexible accumulation is problematic. Instead, they suggest that labour control regimes – at least in China, the focus of their study – are arguably little different from the types of practices that might have been found in Europe at the beginning of the Industrial Revolution. Using the example of the emergent semi-proletariat in China, Pun and Smith explore how the state and private capital, both local and transnational, are seeking to control migrant labour through the use of worker dormitories. Specifically, they argue that the 'freedom' of rural migrant workers to seek work in urban industrial settings is both facilitated by, but also constrained by, the operation of dormitory labour regimes. From the perspective of the state and private capital, they suggest, the dormitory regime provides a useful way of controlling the rural labour that migrates to China's industrial zones and upon which the Chinese economic 'miracle' is based. Hence, if workers become too unruly, they can be more easily removed than if they were living in private residences in the cities which are home to the factories in which they work. Equally, the fact that they live close to their place of work – often on the firm's grounds – means they are always on hand to work should last-minute orders require it, whilst they are also more readily monitored on their time away from the shopfloor than would be the case if they lived in non-company residential facilities. The spaces of the dormitories, in other words, are more readily available to the penetrating gaze of the state and the workers' employers than are other living places. Finally, the systemic provision of industrial dormitories facilitating access to fresh labour reserves depresses wage demands and inhibits collective organisation. As a spatial politics of production, then, this labour management regime concentrates labour but also helps to undermine labour organisation.

Notes

1. Given that we are using Figure 4.1, with its concentric circles of state organisation, for purposes of illustrating our points, then we use the language of 'outwards' and 'inwards' when talking about the transfer of powers from the nation state to either supranational or more regional/local entities. Had we chosen a ladder-like figure as our jumping-off point, the analysis we present below would have been equally applicable, except that we would have used the language of 'upwards' and 'downwards'.
2. As an aside, of course, this claim conveniently forgets that such organisations were only created through the actions and consent of various nation states.
3. This representation of 'the market' as a separate entity from 'the state' has a long history. Hence, Poovey (1996, p. 2) argues that the invention of things like double-entry bookkeeping allowed for 'the development of a system for representing commercial transactions [that] permitted early modern English merchants to conceptualize experiences that were heterogeneous by nature as comparable in kind, and then to generalize from these transactions a "market" that appeared to be a separate and law-abiding domain; this conceptual abstraction was eventually institutionalized, in banks and instruments of credit, so that it actually became a domain separate from politics and theology'.
4. This compromise was marked by a situation in which unions increasingly gave up militancy in return for more-or-less guaranteed increases in wages and benefits negotiated on the back of postwar economic expansion facilitated by Keynsian macroeconomic policies.
5. The geographical terminology here is a little imprecise, for regions are sometimes taken to be sub-national entities that exist between the urban and the national scale and they are sometimes taken to be supranational entities which exist between the national and the global scale and/or cross over various national boundaries (as with, for example, the growing San Diego–Tijuana economic region, which exists – in regard to certain economic exchanges – largely as if the US–Mexico border were not there, and the 'growth triangle' of Singapore and some of its neighbouring Indonesian islands). This is not the place for a discourse into matters of how the regional scale is conceptualised (see Herod (2010) for more on this matter). Instead, we merely wish to highlight the fact that 'regions' have come to be seen as more important in recent debates over economic development, as witnessed by the growth of a discourse on 'New Regionalism'.
6. 'Topographical' here refers to views which see regions in areal terms (with regional boundaries serving as containers of regional spaces) whereas 'topological' refers to views which see regions in networked terms (with regions conceptualised as nodes within a scalar network which links the local with the global, and other scales).
7. The 'Varieties of Capitalism' approach is an effort to understand how diversity within economic models under capitalism comes about. Essentially, it explores the relationship between various sub-systems – the financial system, labour market, interfirm relations and so forth – within any particular society and the degree to which these are coordinated. On this basis, it delineates two distinct varieties of capitalism: the Coordinated Market Economy, characterised by a dependence upon non-market relations and collaboration on the part of firms, and the Liberal Market Economy in which arm's-length, competitive relations are dominant, supply and demand operate in response to price signals (as opposed to non-market mechanisms like corporate obligation between firms), and there is formal contracting between firms. Different societies are then seen to sit at various points along the spectrum between these two extremes, depending upon the particularities of their institutional set-ups.
8. These chains are also highly racialised. Hence, Perrons (2004, p. 105) notes that 'Caucasian workers are generally paid more than Asians and Asians more than those of African descent. [Hence, in] Canada, Filipinas are 'housekeepers' and have to combine housework with childcare while Europeans are more likely to be 'nannies' and only required to care for children, even though the Filipina may be a university graduate and the European a qualified nursery nurse but with fewer years of education'.

References

Allen, J. and A. Cochrane (2007), 'Beyond the territorial fix: regional assemblages, politics and power', *Regional Studies*, **41** (9), 1161–75.

Alvesson, M. and P. Thompson (2005), 'Post-bureaucracy?', in S. Ackroyd, R. Batt, P. Thompson and P.S. Tolbert (eds), *The Oxford Handbook of Work and Organization*, Oxford: Oxford University Press, pp. 485–507.

Amin, A. (2004), 'Regions unbound: towards a new politics of place', *Geografiska Annaler*, **86B**, 33–44.

Barrett, G., T. Jones and D. McEvoy (2001), 'Socio-economic and policy dimensions of the mixed embeddedness of ethnic minority enterprise in Britain', *Journal of Ethnic and Migration Studies*, **27** (2), 241–58.

Barrett, R. and A. Rainnie (2002), 'What's so special about small firms? Developing an integrated approach to analysing small firm industrial relations', *Work, Employment and Society*, **16** (3), 415–31.

Brenner, N. (2004), *New State Spaces: Urban Governance and the Rescaling of Statehood*, Oxford: Oxford University Press.

Brown, K., S. Ridge, S. Royer and J. Waterhouse (2003), 'Virtual workforces and the shifting frontier of control', paper presented at the 13th World Congress of the International Industrial Relations Association, Berlin, 8–12 September.

Bryan, D. (2000), 'National competitiveness and the subordination of labour: an Australian policy study', *Labour and Industry*, **11** (2), 1–16.

Burawoy, M. (1985), *The Politics of Production: Factory Regimes Under Capitalism and Socialism*, London: Verso.

Burnham, P. (2006), 'Restructuring state–economy relations', in P. Fairbrother and A. Rainnie (eds), *Globalisation, State and Labour*, Abingdon: Routledge, pp. 12–28.

Castree, N., N. Coe, K. Ward and M. Samers (2004), *Spaces of Work: Global Capitalism and Geographies of Labour*, London: Sage.

Christopherson, S. and J. Clark (2007), 'Power in firm networks: what it means for regional innovation systems', *Regional Studies*, **41** (9), 1223–36.

Cooke, P. and K. Morgan (1998), *The Associational Economy: Firms, Regions, and Innovation*, Oxford: Oxford University Press.

Davis, M. (2006), *Planet of Slums*, London: Verso.

Davis, M. and D.B. Monk (eds) (2007), *Evil Paradises: Dreamworlds of Neoliberalism*, New York and London: The New Press.

Dicken, P. ([1988] 2007), *Global Shift: Mapping the Changing Contours of the World Economy*, 5th edn, New York: Guilford Press.

Dorling, D., J. Rigby, B. Wheeler, D. Ballas, B. Thomas, E. Fahmy, D. Gordon and R. Lupton (2007), *Poverty, Wealth and Place in Britain, 1968 to 2005*, York: Joseph Rowntree Foundation.

Fairbrother, P. and A. Rainnie (eds) (2006), *Globalisation, State and Labour*, Abingdon: Routledge.

Ferner, A., P. Almond, I. Clark, T. Colling, T. Edwards, L. Holden and M. Muller-Camen (2004), 'Dynamics of central control and subsidiary autonomy in the management of human resources: case study evidence from US MNCs in the UK', *Organisation Studies*, **25** (3), 363–91.

Florida, R. (2003), *The Rise of the Creative Class: And How It's Transforming Work, Leisure, Community and Everyday Life*, New York: Pluto Press.

Friedman, T.L. (2005), *The World is Flat: A Brief History of the Twenty-First Century*, New York: Farrar, Straus and Giroux.

Fröbel, F., J. Heinrichs and O. Kreye (1980), *The New International Division of Labour*, Cambridge: Cambridge University Press.

Gereffi, G. and M. Korzeniewicz (eds) (1994), *Commodity Chains and Global Capitalism*, Westport, CT: Praeger.

Gibson-Graham, J.K. (1996), *The End of Capitalism (as we knew it): a Feminist Critique of Political Economy*, Oxford: Blackwell.

Grugulis, I., S. Vincent and G. Hebson (2003), 'The rise of the network firm and the decline of discretion', *Human Resource Management Journal*, **13** (2), 45–59.

Hall, P. and D. Soskice (eds), (2001), *Varieties of Capitalism: The Institutional Foundations of Comparative Advantage*, Oxford: Oxford University Press.

Harvey, D. (1982), *The Limits to Capital*, Oxford: Blackwell.

Hebdon, R. and I. Kirkpatrick (2005), 'Changes in the organization of public services and their effects on employment relations', in S. Ackroyd, R. Batt, P. Thompson and P.S. Tolbert (eds), *The Oxford Handbook of Work and Organization*, Oxford: Oxford University Press, pp. 530–33.

Hebson, G. and I. Grugulis (2005), 'Gender and new organizational forms', in M. Marchington, D. Grimshaw, J. Rubery and H. Willmott (eds), *Fragmenting Work: Blurring Organizational Boundaries and Disordering Hierarchies*, Oxford: Oxford University Press, pp. 217–38.

Herod, A. (1991), 'Local political practice in response to a manufacturing plant closure: how geography complicates class analysis', *Antipode*, **23** (4), 385–402.

Herod, A. (2001a), 'Labor internationalism and the contradictions of globalization: or, why the local is sometimes still important in a global economy', *Antipode*, **33** (3), 407–26.

Herod, A. (2001b), *Labor Geographies: Workers and the Landscapes of Capitalism*, New York: Guilford Press.

Herod, A. (2007), 'The agency of labour in global change: reimagining the spaces and scales of trade union praxis within a global economy', in J.M. Hobson and L. Seabrooke (eds), *Everyday Politics of the World Economy*, Cambridge: Cambridge University Press, pp. 27–44.

Herod, A. (2009), *Geographies of Globalization*, Chichester: Wiley-Blackwell.

Herod, A. (2010), *Scale*, Key Ideas in Geography Series, London: Routledge.

Herod, A. and M.W. Wright (2002), 'Placing scale: an introduction', in A. Herod and M.W. Wright (eds), *Geographies of Power: Placing Scale*, Oxford: Basil Blackwell, pp. 1–14.

Holgate, J. (2007), 'Producing: changing patterns of work', in I. Douglas, R. Huggett and C. Perkins (eds), *Companion Encyclopedia of Geography: From Local to Global*, 2nd edn, London: Routledge, pp. 901–12.

Hudson, R. (2001), *Producing Places*, New York: Guilford Press.

Hudson, R. (2007), 'Regions and regional development forever? Some reflective comments upon theory and practice', *Regional Studies*, **41** (9), 1149–60.

Hyman, R. (1987), 'Strategy and structure? Capital, labour and control', *Work, Employment and Society*, **1** (1), 25–55.

Jonas, A.E.G. (1997), 'Localisation and globalisation tendencies in the social control and regulation of labour', in M. Taylor and S. Conti (eds), *Interdependent and Uneven Development: Global–Local Perspectives*, Aldershot: Ashgate, pp. 253–82.

Jones, J.P. III, K. Woodward and S.A. Marston (2007), 'Situating flatness', *Transactions of the Institute of British Geographers*, New Series, **32** (2), 264–76.

Keating, M. (1998), *The New Regionalism in Western Europe: Territorial Restructuring and Political Change*, Cheltenham, UK and Northampton, MA: Edward Elgar.

Kloosterman, R.C. and J. Rath (2001), 'Immigrant entrepreneurs in advanced economies: mixed embeddedness further explored', *Journal of Ethnic and Migration Studies*, **27** (2), 189–201.

MacLeod, G. and M. Jones (2007), 'Territorial, scalar, networked, connected: in what sense a "regional world"?', *Regional Studies*, **41** (9), 1177–91.

Marchington, M., D. Grimshaw, J. Rubery and H. Willmott (eds) (2005), *Fragmenting Work: Blurring Organizational Boundaries and Disordering Hierarchies*, Oxford: Oxford University Press.

Marx, K. ([1941] 1973), *Grundrisse*, London: Penguin.

Mitchell, T. (1998), 'Fixing the economy', *Cultural Studies*, **12** (1), 82–101.

Monbiot, G. (2003), 'The flight to India', *The Guardian*, 21 October.

Mooney, G. and A. Law (2007), 'New Labour, "modernisation" and welfare worker resistance', in G. Mooney and A. Law (eds), *New Labour/Hard Labour? Restructuring and Resistance inside the Welfare Industry*, Bristol: Policy Press, pp. 1–22.

Noteboom, B. (2004), *Interfirm Collaboration, Learning and Networks: An Integrated Approach*, London: Routledge.

Ohmae, K. (1995), *The End of the Nation State: The Rise of Regional Economies*, New York: McKinsey and Company.

Ohmae, K. (2005), *The Next Global Stage: Challenges and Opportunities in Our Borderless World*, Upper Saddle River, NJ: Wharton School Publishing.

Painter, J. (1991), 'The geography of trade union responses to local government privatization', *Transactions of the Institute of British Geographers*, New Series, **16** (2), 214–26.

Peck, J. and N. Theodore (2007), 'Variegated capitalism', *Progress in Human Geography*, **31** (6), 731–72.

Perrons, D. (2004), *Globalization and Social Change: People and Places in a Divided World*, Abingdon: Routledge.

Piore, M. and C. Sabel (1984), *The Second Industrial Divide: Possibilities for Prosperity*, New York: Basic Books.

Poovey, M. (1996), 'Accommodating merchants: accounting, civility, and the natural laws of gender', *differences: A Journal of Feminist Cultural Studies*, **8** (3), 1–20.

Rainnie, A. (2005), 'Regional development policy and social inclusion', in P. Smyth, T. Reddel and A. Jones (eds), *Community and Local Governance in Australia*, Sydney: UNSW Press, pp. 131–8.

Rainnie, A. and P. Fairbrother (2006), 'The state we are in (and against)', in P. Fairbrother and A. Rainnie (eds), *Globalisation, State and Labour*, Abingdon: Routledge, pp. 29–52.

Rainnie, A. and M. Grobbelaar (eds) (2005), *New Regionalism in Australia*, London: Ashgate.

Sayer, A. (1984), *Method in Social Science: A Realist Approach*, London: Hutchinson.

Smith, A., A. Rainnie and M. Dunford (2001), 'Regional trajectories and uneven development in the "New Europe": rethinking territorial success and inequality', in H. Wallace (ed.), *Interlocking Dimensions of European Integration: One Europe or Several?*, Basingstoke: Palgrave, pp. 122–44.

Smith, A., A. Rainnie, M. Dunford, J. Hardy, R. Hudson and D. Sadler (2002), 'Networks of value, commodities and regions: reworking divisions of labour in macro-regional economies', *Progress in Human Geography*, **26** (1), 41–63.

Smith, N. ([1984] 1990), *Uneven Development: Nature, Capital and the Production of Space*, Oxford: Basil Blackwell.

Smith, N. (2007), 'The geography of uneven development', in B. Dunn and H. Radice (eds), *100 Years of Permanent Revolution: Results and Prospects*, London: Pluto Press, pp. 180–95.

Southall, H. (1988), 'Towards a geography of unionization: the spatial organization and distribution of early British trade unions', *Transactions of the Institute of British Geographers*, New Series, **13** (4), 466–83.

Stenning, A., T. Champion, C. Conway, M. Coombes, S. Dawley, L. Dixon, S. Raybould and R. Richardson (2006), 'Assessing the local and regional impacts of international migration', Final Report for Department of Communities and Local Government, CURDS, University of Newcastle, UK.

Voice of America (2008), 'High oil prices bring back some US jobs' VOA News, 3 August, available at www.voanews.com/english/archive/2008-08/2008-08-13-voa22.cfm?moddate=2008-08-13; accessed 20 March, 2009.

Waring, P., D. Macdonald and J. Burgess (2004), 'Globalization and confrontation: the transformation of the Australian coal industry', in Y.A. Debrah and I.G. Smith (eds), *Work and Employment in a Globalised Era: An Asia Pacific Focus*, London: Frank Cass, pp. 21–45.

Yeates, N. (2004), 'A dialogue with "global care chain" analysis: Nurse migration in the Irish context', *Feminist Review*, **77** (1), 79–95.

Section 2.1

Regionalisation, Globalisation and Labour

5   Labour markets from the bottom up
Jamie Peck and Nik Theodore

Introduction

This chapter examines labour markets from the bottom up, conceptually and substantively, by way of a critical commentary on the restructuring of low-wage work in the neoliberal era. In contrast to pervasive, orthodox understandings of labour markets qua markets, the conceptual bedrock for one-size-fits-all labour 'flexibility' programmes, the chapter is grounded in a heterodox vision of the labour market – as a site of conflicting power relations, enduring regulatory dilemmas, necessary (but problematic) forms of institutionalisation, embedded path dependencies and systematic uneven development. This is not the labour market of demand-and-supply schedules and parsimonious theorising, but an institutionally cluttered zone marked by successive waves of restructuring and re-regulation. In fact, we take one such wave of restructuring cum re-regulation – the rise of 'contingent work' in the period since the 1980s – as the focus of our commentary. As a signifier of the fragmentation and 'desecuritisation' of jobs, contingent work has not only been a bearer of new labour-market practices, it has also been a site of intensive regulatory reinvention. And in an era characterised by various forms of devolved governance, decentralised control and deferred risk, the street-level regulation of contingent work reveals a lot about new sources of downward gravitational pull in the labour market.

The issue of contingent work exposes in hypertrophied form the contradictory character of 'localised' forms of labour regulation, in the context of deepening economic globalisation and neoliberal downloading: even as labour and capital flows selectively transnationalise and even as market-complementing and market-reinforcing modes of governance increasingly represent the international 'standard', there is a stubborn 'localness' in the functioning of labour markets and in the dynamics of labour politics. Geography, and geographical scale, continue to matter in this context, but they are coming to matter in new ways, reflecting new configurations of labour–capital relations and new landscapes of labour regulation. Many of the contingent workers in the low-wage economies of US cities, for example, are themselves transnational migrants; many of them are even employed – directly or indirectly – by transnational corporations – but the terms on which they enter and re-enter the job market, often on a daily basis, are also powerfully shaped at the local level. Driven by business models based on the wholesaling of 'flexible' workers on employers' terms, temp agencies and labour contractors target specific neighbourhoods and specific segments of the job market in their search for pliable and elastic labour supplies. Meanwhile, undocumented workers' lack of employment papers translates into radical deficits in workplace rights, social entitlements and bargaining power. In this nexus, localised enclaves of economic exploitation have been established, though these most flexible of flexible labour markets are not the anomalies that they once were. Increasingly, they reflect and shape the terms of a reworked, if unstable, labour-market settlement, systematically skewed against the interests of labour – a downscaling and atomisation of employment relations.

Contingent work can be regarded as a neoliberal keyword. It was coined, appropriately, in the United States in the 1980s, as a signifier for an unattractive bundle of part-time, short-term and insecure jobs. These had three shared characteristics: first, they were growing remarkably fast; second, employers seemed to like them about as much as workers disliked them; and third, as labour-market 'others', they all deviated from the Fordist norm of relatively secure, year-round and often unionised employment. The continued proliferation of contingent work in the ensuing decades has been driven by a range of supply-side, demand-side and regulatory forces. On the regulatory front, the cumulative 'deregulation' (or regressive re-regulation) of the job market, through the erosion both of worker protections and the value of the minimum wage, has been accompanied by the promotion of competition, both internationally and within national and local employment regimes. On the supply side, the state-assisted crowding of low-wage labour markets by way of employability measures, and the forcing of labour supplies through workfare programmes and undocumented immigration, has intensified shoulder-to-shoulder competition for jobs. And last, but by no means least, on the demand side, there has been a marked ascendancy of lean-and-mean corporate 'flexibility' strategies, designed to deflect risk and uncertainty to the workforce, by way of de-unionisation, contracting out and the proliferation of 'no strings attached' employment strategies. These forces have combined to define contingent labour markets as fundamental pressure points in the contemporary US labour market (Peck, 2001; Pollin, 2003; Prashad, 2003).

Characteristic of the geographer's take on the labour market, the following commentary is not only a view from below – looking 'up' into the labour market from the swelling contingent economy – but it is also a view from somewhere. In this case, somewhere is the contemporary United States in general and the city of Chicago in particular. Since the Reagan era, the United States has been the primary platform for the generation and dissemination of contingent labour norms, while cities like Chicago have experienced this destabilising 'transition' with particular intensity. Chicago has also been a key location for the generation of regulatory norms and organisational innovations in the contingent economy, particularly in relation to the upstart temporary work 'industry'. The site, a century ago, of Upton Sinclair's ([1906] 2003) damning indictment of employment conditions in the meatpacking industry, *The Jungle*, post-New Deal Chicago may be on the way to reclaiming a place at the frontier of labour-market regression. Since geographers, too, tend to privilege place-specific and context-rich accounts of local labour-market restructuring, their work necessarily raises the methodological question of how, most appropriately, to 'read out' from local circumstances to more general understandings of structural conditions and tendential processes. Understanding labour markets from the bottom up, in this sense, must extend beyond idiographic storytelling, to explore ways of placing local labour markets, both conceptually and politically. Local labour markets and constitutive scales of labour regulation do not simply exist, as it were, 'out there'; they are *social* constructions, made and remade by contending social forces and agents. Labour markets, in this sense, are not merely the 'containers' of universal economic processes; they represent terrains of struggle and spaces of regulatory reinvention.

Labour markets, from above and below

Geographers have always had a distinctive take on the labour market. From early concerns with commuting behaviour, the kinds of questions geographers pose tend to be concerned with the daily grind – the lived experience of labour markets. At one level, the issue of the journey to work might seem a mundane one, no more profound than the challenge of getting from A to B, and in truth much of the associated literature is preoccupied with 'technical' questions like boundary delimitation and degrees of self-containment for travel-to-work areas. But lurking behind these questions – with employment access and the integrity of local labour markets – lies a much deeper set of concerns, concerns that more recently have come to the fore. Daily commuting fields are foundational to the constitution of urban and regional economies, defining the zone in which labour can be substituted on a short-term basis, shaping the scope and terms of competition for and between workers, and framing the contradictory relationship between the labour market and those relatively autonomous systems of social reproduction on which it depends (Storper and Walker, 1983; Scott, 1988; Harvey, 1989). Geographical divisions of labour position localities within shifting hierarchies and networks of production, spawning distinctive local cultures of production and reproduction, and reflecting the ever-changing ways in which capital–labour relations are refracted through and stretched across space (Clark, 1981; Massey, 1984; Lovering, 1989). The spatial separation of home and work is a structuring condition of hegemonic forms of gender relations, with far-reaching consequences for domestic divisions of labour, the social structure of the waged workforce and the social relations of 'caring economies' (McDowell, 1991; England, 1993; Hanson and Pratt, 1995). Local cultures of working-class politics, themselves co-produced with the uneven development of employment patterns and relations, configure the terrain of labour-union capacities and potentialities, in turn shaping emerging geographies of work (Jonas, 1996; Wills, 1996; Herod, 2001).

Correspondingly, geographers' conceptions of the local labour market are richly textured. The key to the more-than-contingent geographical distinctiveness of local labour markets, what is *local* about them, lies in the conjuncturally unique embedding of employment regimes within both spatial divisions of labour and modes of regulation, reinforced by locally mediated processes of institutionalisation, reproduction and socialisation (Warde, 1985; Peck, 1996; Martin, 2000). The distinctive character and functioning of employment regimes in, say, Silicon Valley, Shanghai or Sunderland, is not merely transitory 'noise' around some singular labour-market form; it reflects unique historical trajectories, particular positions within spatial divisions of labour, and peculiarly local intersections of labour supply, labour demand and social regulation. Labour markets are not simply aggregate outcomes of atomised, competitive behaviour, neither are they monologically governed through the price mechanism. They are inescapably social spaces, profoundly (if unevenly) institutionalised, destabilised as well as driven by competitive pressures, imperfectly regulated through various 'hard' and 'soft' regimes of governance, fissured by contradiction, but also marked by creativity. They are not trending toward some equilibrium point, but as social forms are always emergent and incomplete.

Hence the critical importance of labour regulation is as an enduring institutional problematic, in both theoretical and political terms. In a neo-Polanyian sense, the fact of labour-market regulation might be considered to be overdetermined (in the sense that labour markets qua markets are not, and cannot be, self-regulating), but the variegated forms of social regulation are radically underdetermined – they are not only politically, institutionally and historically, but also, geographically contingent. In other words, 'local' forms of labour regulation can be seen as institutionally-patterned responses to relatively enduring contradictions and regulatory dilemmas in the labour market, though as institutional forms they are socially shaped, path dependent and unevenly developed, rather than functionally predetermined. Moreover, regulatory functions are not transcendentally fixed at one geographical scale or another. Their scaling (and re-scaling) reflects the balance of social forces in general and the outcomes of regulatory struggles in particular (see Swyngedouw, 1997). National 'systems' of social protection and employment rights, redistributive taxation and welfare provision, such as the New Deal in the United States, for example, do not naturally 'belong' at this scale; they were consolidated there as a result of political responses to the Great Depression, and they were defended and augmented not only by labour unions and progressive forces, but also by governmental elites and certain fractions of capital (see Gordon et al., 1982; Cohen, 1990). By the same token, the accelerating institutional dissolution of this system in the period since the early 1980s has been no less a political act: redistributive tendencies have been reversed, federal protections and programmes have been dismantled, new forms of social and spatial competition in the labour market have been institutionalised. This downscaling of labour regulation has, in the context of a generalised movement towards neoliberal forms of governance, tipped the balance of power in favour of capital, while exposing labour at the local level to the whip of economic competition. Not all forms of regulatory downscaling and localised governance are regressive, of course; political content and context really matter. In this historical instance, the neoliberal form of re-scaling was regressive in both intent and effect. It was about 'restoring the right to manage'; it was about dismantling the social contract embedded in the New Deal, progressive taxation and welfare systems and Fordist employment relations; and it was about making flexible labour markets.

Local labour markets, in this sense, are more than data-reporting units; they define zones of political contestation and institutional transformation. They are, in other words, 'meaningfully local'. In analytical terms, the 'localness' of local labour markets can be revealed in at least two ways. First, there is the issue of intersectionality. Both labour demand and supply are internally differentiated and socially structured in relatively autonomous ways. Since the local scale is that at which labour is mobilised on a daily basis, the meshing of labour demand and supply tends to be variable at this scale. And this nexus is an important one for the generation of labour market norms and practices. For example, processes of ethnic succession in urban labour supplies tend to be associated with shifts in prevailing employment practices, including the deployment of recruitment channels, degrees of externalisation or outsourcing, reward systems and so forth (see Peck, 1996; Hiebert, 1999). Next, there is the problematic of social regulation. Since labour does not take a commodity form, but a 'pseudo-commodity' form, the labour market does not behave like a self-regulating commodity market (Offe, 1985). This means, in turn, that processes of *social* regulation are endemic to the labour market, just one manifestation of which is the continuous – but continuously problematic – involvement of the state in issues like the management and manipulation of the labour supply (for instance, through child labour laws, retirement pensions policies, mandatory schooling, disability and sickness benefits, job training, welfare provision and so on). These interventions, too, tend to be geographically variable, most explicitly between nation states, but also at the local level. And even the 'same' policies have been shown to be associated with quite different outcomes at the local level, by virtue of implementation politics, interactions with local labour markets, the capacities and orientations of street-level bureaucracies and so on (see Jones, 1998; Peck, 2002). So, processes of social regulation are locally mediated, often in finely grained ways; the institutional 'fabric' of the labour market is geographically differentiated.

The geographer's take on the labour market consequently begins with the recognition of spatial complexity, conjunctural distinctiveness, uneven development and institutional embeddedness, in sharp contrast to the austere, orthodox conception of the labour market qua commodity market – as an idealised space of exchange relations and equilibrating forces, the pristine isotropy of which is only disrupted and distorted, after the fact, by 'imperfections' like unionisation, legal regulation, employer cartels, imperfect knowledge and so on. The orthodox economist's view of the labour market, one might say, is a view from above – the dispassionate and distant gaze of the Walrasian auctioneer; visualising the labour market as a zone of impersonal forces, engaging through the parsimonious analysis of demand and supply. In contrast, if the geographer's view of the labour market can likewise be typified, the vantage point is much closer to the ground, a view from below – reading the landscape through the eyes of actors and protagonists, visualising the labour market as a contradictory space of social struggle and asymmetrical power relations, engaging through contingent analyses of inherently messy socioeconomic relations and cluttered institutional environments.

And there are pronounced normative differences too. If orthodox economists are primarily concerned with issues of efficiency and market adjustment, economic geographers tend to be more focused on equity and social justice. While the former will invariably praise, if not pine for, 'flexible' labour markets, the latter will be inclined to deconstruct the regressive politics of the 'flexibility offensive'. If orthodox economists are liable to legitimate and recycle conservative arguments about the solutions to labour-market problems like unemployment and low pay (invest in human capital, work harder, be prepared to accept lower wages if that's what the market deems you are worth), economic geographers will typically rail against the injustices and inequities of the job market, advocating social and governmental strategies for living wages, social equity and employment security. For the orthodox economist, regulatory incursions into the labour market, like minimum wages or entitlement benefits, tend to be viewed as aberrations or interferences, the 'cost' of which should be minimised. Here, neoliberal 'deregulation' tends to be seen as a step in the (preferred) direction of freer labour markets. For economic geographers, regulation is typically understood as a contradictory necessity or fact of life, the notion of a self-regulating labour market having practically no currency. Here, progressive re-regulation tends to be seen as a step in the (preferred) direction of fairer labour markets. In this sense, the rise of 'labour geography' since the 1980s has been something of a counter-cultural movement – a political and analytical reaction to historically specific processes like de-industrialisation and de-unionisation, and a reaction against the joint (re)ascendancy of orthodox economics and neoliberal governance.

The rise of contingent work
The unloved neologism 'contingent work' entered the labour-market lexicon in the mid-1980s as a shorthand description for a variegated set of 'non-standard' jobs. The term first appeared in a 1985 Conference Board report by labour economist Audrey Freeman,

who used it to 'connote conditionality' in employment relationships (quoted in Polivka and Nardone, 1989, p.10). For Freeman, contingent work described those 'conditional and transitory employment arrangements as initiated by a need for labour – usually because a company has increased demand for a particular service or product or technology, at a particular place, at a specific time'. Despite being initially invoked in the positive context of economic competitiveness and 'labour market flexibility', contingent work quickly became a critics' term during the Reagan years, since beyond the benign language of efficiency and flexibility it evoked a telling connection between strategic shifts in governmental policies and corporate practices and the production of not only non-standard but substandard jobs. It pointed, in other words, to some of the ways in which the very structures of the labour market were changing. The growth of contingent employment did not simply represent a lifestyle choice for workers seeking more flexible employment arrangements, nor was it simply a short-term fix for businesses in a tight spot; instead, its rise reflected a deeper set of changes in the regulatory organisation and normative orientation of American labour markets.

In this vein, Harrison and Bluestone (1988) pointedly associated the growth of contingent employment with the erosion of internal labour markets and employment protections during the 1970s and 1980s. Here, contingent employment strategies were conceived alongside union busting and wage freezes as part of a wider attack on labour. And it was employers that were constructing and pursuing these strategies, aided and abetted by a federal government intent on establishing a more 'pro-business' industrial relations regime.

When the threat of contingent work first emerged in the 1980s, the more alarming estimates put the size of the flexible workforce at 8 million in 1980, rising to 18 million by 1985, and then to between 30 and 36 million by the end of the decade – approaching one-third of the total workforce (see Pollock, 1986, p. 52; Belous, 1989). Not surprisingly, researchers at the Bureau of Labor Statistics (BLS) were sceptical of these broad – and somewhat loose – measures, based as they seemed to be on an 'operational definition of a contingent job [as] any arrangement which differs from full-time, permanent, wage and salary employment' (Polivka and Nardone, 1989, p. 10).

Yet even if the distinguishing, common feature of the motley collection of jobs that comprise the 'contingent economy' could only really be defined negatively – as irregular, non-standard, substandard forms of employment – this hardly represents a trivial characteristic, either theoretically or politically. In many ways, it is an appropriate metaphor for the kinds of labour market regression implied by the ascendancy of contingent work. Here, the absence of a continuing contract of employment means that these jobs deviate – admittedly in a range of ways – from what were previously normalised and institutionalised as conventional, typical forms of work. This may not lead to crisp and unambiguous statistical outcomes, but the trends are no less real or significant for that. Although BLS researchers concede that job insecurity is '[p]robably the most salient characteristic of contingent work' (Polivka and Nardone, 1989, p. 10), their formal and narrow definition speaks more to the need for statistical tractability than it does to any understanding of the normative implications of unstable work, or of the underlying causal processes involved.

While it is necessary to be sensitive to the differentiated nature of contingent employment conditions, at the same time it is important to recognise that, even on average, contingent work continues to differ markedly from 'non-contingent' employment. Taken as a group, contingent jobs are disproportionately found in the personal services, agri-culture and construction industries, though there have recently been significant inroads into manufacturing; they are significantly more likely to be organised on a part-time basis than non-contingent jobs; they are much less likely to have health or pension ben-efits; they pay substantially less, even for the same hours of work – contingent workers experience an earnings penalty of between one quarter and one third, while remunera-tion levels tend to rise more slowly over time, if at all; and they are less likely to fall within the ambit of union agreements (see GAO, 2000; EPI, 2007). It would be wrong to claim that contingent jobs, so defined, are uniformly 'bad' jobs, though in the aggregate their characteristics are broadly consistent with those traditionally associated with the periph-eral, unstable or 'secondary' sector of the labour market. As one careful assessment of the evidence on both sides of this debate concluded,

> the picture that emerges is that employment arrangements clearly are changing and that at least some 'standard' work arrangements may be both becoming relatively less pervasive and tending to more closely resemble nonstandard jobs. In addition, the evolving nature of firms and labor markets, as well as the labor force, in the late 20th century may have given rise to new employment arrangements that may come to resemble those of the pre-New Deal era but for the most part they are likely to be new. Virtually all of the emerging forms of nonstandard arrangements, however, compare unfavorably with standard employment and internal labor markets in meeting the needs of workers for security and rising living standards. (Carré et al., 2000, p. 15)

Compared to the non-contingent workforce, contingent workers are more likely to be female and young; they are disproportionately drawn from minority populations and they are considerably more likely to be foreign born and non-citizens; they are much less likely to be union members and slightly more likely to be multiple job-holders; and – crucially – they are less likely to be satisfied with their present employment arrange-ments, which they probably accepted either because they could get nothing else or because they faced some sort of constraint that limited their job options. In other words, those typically understood to be 'disadvantaged workers' in the labour market are dis-proportionately crowded into contingent jobs. In fact, it is a labour-market strategy fashioned around this vulnerable labour supply.

Chicago's 'temp' sector
Our work on the Chicago temp sector underlines this point. The city has been an organi-sational centre for the fledgling temporary employment industry since the 1920s, where modern forms of temping had first emerged as an adjunct to the office equipment business (Moore, 1965). Initially focused on the clerical sector, the temp business generated good returns for a handful of pioneer companies, though in labour-market terms it had been no more than a marginal presence until the late 1970s. But prevailing norms in the labour market were about to change, dramatically. The advent of de-industrialisation, which hit Chicago especially hard, destabilised large parts of the manufacturing employment base, accelerating what has been a pattern of long-run decline. The city lost one-third of its factory employment base in the 1980s, then an additional quarter in the 1990s; real wages in the city's manufacturing sector fell by 17 per cent over this two-decade period, approaching twice the national average rate of decline (Moberg, 2006; Doussard et al.,

2009). As businesses sought to restrain costs on an ongoing basis, while also confronting a more uncertain competitive environment, they turned increasingly to outsourcing and contracting out as a means of managing the bottom line. What is more, the truncated and one-sided social contract around temp work – 'at will' employment – is distinctly favourable to employers, being especially attractive to those unwilling or unable to commit to stable employment contracts.

A conspicuous beneficiary of these developments, the temp sector began its transition from a specialist service to a de facto industry during this period, registering explosive revenue and employment growth during the 1980s. In Chicago, the size of the temp sector doubled during this decade. Initially, most of the growth came through clerical staffing, the industrial unions having been successful – for a time at least – in resisting the placement of temps on the shop floor. By the 1990s, however, when temporary employment surged again, it was new business opportunities in the blue-collar sector that led the way (Theodore and Peck, 2002; Doussard et al., 2009). During this period, storefront temp agencies became a common feature of the marginal commercial strips in Chicago's low-income neighbourhoods – their boarded-up windows symbolising the industry's contemptuous attitude toward regulatory surveillance (Peck and Theodore, 2001).

By the end of the 1990s, an estimated 100000 temps were employed on an average day in Chicago. This was equivalent to 3 to 4 per cent of the overall workforce, with much higher shares in casualised occupations like assembly work, materials moving, hand-packaging and other manual-labour assignments right across the manufacturing and warehousing sectors. In Illinois, it was estimated that as much as half of all vacancies in manufacturing at the peak of the late 1990s' economic cycle were for temporary workers (Gunset, 1998), while a third or more of all those leaving welfare in Chicago – following the institutionalisation of a workfare system after 1996 – were 'transitioning' into temp jobs. The flow of employment opportunities – particularly for low-income/disadvantaged workers and those trapped in unstable, 'secondary sector' jobs – had become disproportionately dominated by temporary jobs. For their part, the temp agencies that service the bottom end of the manufacturing sector tended also to seek out neighbourhoods with an oversupply of underemployed workers – the labour-market 'slack' which they sell on to the factories as a commoditised form of flexible staffing. As the manager of a temp service in one of Chicago's low-income neighbourhoods characterised the situation, 'The only reason we're here is for the people. Obviously, this is not the nicest neighbourhood. . . . That's the only reason we're [here] – to access the people' (quoted in Peck and Theodore, 2001, p. 483).

The growth of the temporary staffing business in Chicago was remarkable in part for the precocious challenge it registered to prevailing employment norms in this relatively highly unionised, blue-collar city. But in comparison with many other parts of the country, the temporary employment boom was actually somewhat impeded here. National data reveal that, during the 1980s and 1990s, temporary staffing grew at approximately twice the rate in sunbelt cities, like Houston and Miami, compared to rustbelt cities like Chicago and Detroit. Similarly, relative to high union-density cities like Chicago, temp employment expanded almost three times faster in cities where state-level 'right to work' laws impeded union organisation (Theodore and Peck, 2002). The long-term, concerted nature of the push towards more contingent labour-market forms is, however, revealed in the fact that the previously 'protected' manufacturing sector has been the most important 'new market' for the Chicago temp industry since the early 1990s: restructuring through growth, followed by a second wave of de-industrialisation, was associated with a more than fivefold surge in the penetration rate of temp work (Doussard et al., 2009).

It must be acknowledged that the temp sector, like the wider contingent economy which envelopes it, is a heterogeneous one. High-end temping, in occupations like accounting and information technology, where highly qualified workers could earn wage premiums, also expanded during the 1990s (Peck and Theodore, 1998). But the general pattern is for temps to be crowded into low-wage occupations. In Chicago, agencies find the volume business that enables them to grow around the minimum-wage level. Some 'backstreet' agencies even operate below this point, targeting vulnerable groups like the homeless and undocumented workers, and placing them in dirty and often dangerous jobs (Oehlsen, 1997). The repugnant industry practice of 'bodyslamming' refers to the placement of drunks and vagrants in some of the lousiest jobs in the city.

In orthodox analyses, those workers who earn low wages do so because they are inherently less productive than other workers, or if we can update Hicks's (1932, p. 82) famously blunt statement of this position, contingent labour is 'often badly paid, not because it gets less than it is worth, but because it is worth so appallingly little'. In fact, the case against the regulation of contingent work continues to be made in similar terms. Hylton (1995, pp. 856–7), for example, argues that the lower wages paid to contingent workers can be explained by the fact that this is what they *earn* – these discounted wages are the 'functional equivalent of a subminimum wage', an insight that Hylton attributes, not to a flashback to Economics 101, but to 'discussions with personnel managers at various temporary agencies'.

Our own discussions with temp agency managers, in Chicago and elsewhere, have revealed a rather different picture. We know from national statistical analyses that a significant wage gap exists between contingent and non-contingent jobs, even after controlling for personal characteristics or 'human capital' endowments (see Lester, 1998; Kilcoyne, 2005; EPI, 2007). This presents a real problem for orthodox, supply-side accounts of contingent work. Contingent workers face a wage penalty not simply because their human-capital endowments indicate that this is what they deserve; they are paid less because employers *can* pay them less – and employers can pay them less by virtue of the combination of a permissive regulatory 'settlement', socioeconomic vulnerability and local labour-market crowding. As Gottfried (1992) has explained, tri-angular employment relations of the temp labour process, which designates the agency as the 'employer of record', effectively shields worksite employers of temp labour from regulatory responsibilities and obligations (including unemployment insurance, pension rights and health and safety provisions) (see also Vosko, 2000). Furthermore, the fact that worksite employers only pay for temporary labour if and when they actually need it means that not only do they never pay for slack time, they are off the hook for vacation and sickness pay too. As any temp-agency sales operative will explain, this adds up to substantial savings on the hourly and annual 'cost' of temporary workers, relative to their full-time counterparts. Temp workers can be employed both cheaply and flexibly, and their deliberately ambiguous regulatory status reduces the exposure of worksite employers on other fronts. As the manager of a Chicago agency, specialising in blue-collar placements, explained:

[i]f there's a company with an assembly line that uses day-to-day people, odds are they're using temps or they're going to use temps. If they haven't heard about them, they're crazy, because the money they save is astronomical . . . They (normally) have to pay somebody $8–9 an hour, for instance, where they can pay us $6.50, and everything's out of their hands. . . . And we're flexible. They can call us and they can have an order for 20 people in the morning and all of a sudden a shipment comes in and they need 20 more, they can call us any time of the day and we'll get 20 people out to them. It's *that* easy. Imagine if they were trying to call 20 people and trying to hire them that day. It would never happen. It wouldn't be possible. (quoted in Peck and Theodore, 2001, p. 478)

Working around the constraints of the traditional, Fordist-era employment relationship – based on a continuing contract, and a range of rights and entitlements – is not, therefore, an incidental feature of temporary-agency work, but central to its very rationale. Agencies turn a profit by 'making markets' under a very particular set of socio-spatial conditions. In Chicago, following the exodus of manufacturing plants from the urban core, this entailed the construction of connections between various under-utilised, inner-city labour pools on the one hand, and suburban employers' apparently insatiable demand for low-cost flexibility on the other. In those Chicago neighbourhoods that accommodate large numbers of recent immigrants, there is a plentiful supply of workers willing, indeed needing, to work under almost any circumstances. Many are undocumented. Agencies have fashioned strategies for reaching deep into under-employed, inner-urban labour pools, primarily in Latino communities, subsequently marketing this labour supply to suburban employers.

Even though this is clearly a highly commodified job market – agencies are, on the face of it, selling disembodied labour by the hour – it is also a socially structured and institutionalised one, saturated by asymmetrical power relations. Only in the most superficial sense does the temp labour market resemble the kind of 'spot market' for labour envisaged in orthodox economics: price factors strongly shape the terms of trade, but the valuation, allocation and management of labour are all inescapably social processes. Wages are low in temp jobs because agencies actively seek out crowded (local) segments of the labour market. As the largest local 'employer' in many low-income neighbourhoods, they are in a position to dictate wages. The agencies' placement systems favour 'reliably contingent' workers who are available every day and whose work attitudes, job capabilities and personal attributes render them acceptable to employers. The temp job queue is also socially structured according to race, gender and physical appearance, responding as much to such ascribed characteristics of workers as their human-capital attributes. By anticipating and delivering what employers want, temp agencies harden and institutionalise processes of labour segmentation at the point(s) of entry into the job market, with wide-ranging and long-term consequences for occupational mobility, employment security and wage prospects. At one level, temp agencies are simply businesses, and they will do what they need to do to turn a profit on their core activity: the sale of (generally) low-wage labour, with a mark-up for administrative costs, in the context of price-sensitive markets with low entry barriers, conditions which exert powerful pressures to hold down prices, margins, and, therefore, wages, across the industry (Theodore and Peck, 2002). But in a wider sense, temp agencies also perform a range of 'regulatory' functions – setting wages, allocating workers to jobs, bringing vacancies to the market, connecting with jobseekers, renegotiating the costs of employment, shaping the design of jobs at worksites and so forth. In other words, they are centres of rule-making and rule enforcement in contingent labour markets.

Regulating contingent labour markets

The motivation for using the term, contingent work, Spalter-Roth and Hartmann (1998) observe, is usually to draw attention to one or more of the following labour-market features. First, in terms of labour-market categories, contingent employment represents the 'other' of the full-time, full-year, 'standard' job, the rise to prominence of which has disrupted the conventional methods of enumerating labour-market phenomena since these were all designed around the norm of the 'regular job'. Second, contingent employment tends to be associated with low pay and inadequate benefits, at least relative to this established norm, with the consequence that its characteristic problems invariably overlap with those traditionally associated with underemployment, working poverty and 'secondary sector' conditions. Third, contingent work relations connote a relative lack of attachment, on the part of both employers and employees, to the job, a tenuous employment relationship, *sans* strings, of the sort that is likely to provide flexibility for businesses at the price of vulnerability for workers. Adding a fourth dimension, duRivage et al. (1998, pp. 264–5) point out that contingent work occupies a very particular place within the overall pattern of labour-market regulation:

> Part-time and contingent workers stand outside the traditional permanent, full-time employment relationship upon which the framework of employment and labor law was built in the 1930s and 1940s and thus lack basic protections. Partly as a result, part-time and contingent workers suffer from a series of problems: few or no benefits; low wages; reduced employment security and barriers to advancement; low productivity, due in part to employer and employee's diminished commitment to each other; and the possibility of being trapped in these arrangements involuntarily. . . .Very low rates of union representation leave part-time and contingent workers ill-equipped to address these problems. (duRivage et al., 1998, p. 264)

Framed in new ways, these concerns echo those that surfaced around the dual labour market debates of the 1960s. The dualist thesis was initially developed to explain the exclusion of African-Americans – particularly those living in central-city areas – from stable, good-quality jobs with promotion prospects in the 'primary' segment of the labour market. These workers, along with other disadvantaged workers such as women, young people, ex-offenders, recent immigrants and the disabled, were likely to become trapped in the unstable, 'secondary' sector of the labour market, in jobs with low pay and poor prospects (Doeringer and Piore, 1971). The forces that trapped these workers included employer discrimination plain-and-simple, a reluctance to expend training dollars on workers who might be expected to be only marginally attached to the job, and a desire amongst employers to constrain unionisation. Those excluded from primary jobs would often, through socialisation, subsequently contribute to their own marginalisation by adopting 'street corner lifestyles', along with an indifferent attitude towards work and managerial authority. In a circular fashion, these traits would themselves become markers of impaired 'employability' in the eyes of potential employers. Yet it was a characteristic of the dual labour market thesis that 'street corner lifestyles' were generally regarded as a consequence rather than a cause of underemployment, explanatory arrows that would later be reversed in neoliberal arguments around welfare dependency (Peck,

2001; Schram, 2006). Rather than some failure of will, character, or raw human capital on the part of the poor, the dualists' explanation for the causes of ghetto poverty was located in the structure of the labour market itself.

In the United States, labour segmentation strategies accompanied, and helped secure, the Fordist economic expansion after World War II, having their origins in the 1920s and reaching their institutional limits by the 1970s:

> [l]arge corporations initiated the period of segmentation in the 1920s and early 1930s when they began to explore new mechanisms for more effective and reliable labor control. In the mid-1930s workers in mass-production industries revolted on an unprecedented scale, high-lighted by the massive sitdown strikes of 1936–1937, and succeeded in gaining recognition for industrial unions. The consolidation of the segmentation process was achieved only after this extended industrial conflict in the 1930s had been moderated by the labor peace constructed in the late 1940s and early 1950s. This capital–labor accord required a set of social and govern-mental arrangements; a crucial part of these arrangements included employer recognition of unions, grievance procedures, and seniority rules for layoffs and promotions; in return, employ-ers gained discretion over changes in the organization of work, provided that increases in wages were granted in return for increases in productivity. (Gordon et al., 1982, pp. 15–16)

The internal labour market lay at the symbolic, institutional and material centre of this prevailing pattern of work relations, shaping employment norms across the corpo-rate sector of the labour market, even amongst large, non-union firms (see Pfeffer and Baron, 1988; Stone, 2001). The secondary segment, in marked contrast, existed in the shadows of the internal labour market, absorbing both the costs of economic fluctua-tions and those workers denied access to primary-sector jobs (see Sengenberger, 1981; Rubery et al., 1987). These inherited conditions, as Gordon et al. (1982, p. 16) explain, 'established the context within which corporations and workers began to respond to and seek leverage over the economic crisis of the 1970s and early 1980s'.

The emergence of contingent work during the 1980s represented more than a continu-ation of secondary labour-market conditions, for it can be seen as a strategic response to the deepening problems associated with the extant – but then dissolving – pattern of labour segmentation and regulation. The previous regime – which was modelled around the institutional practices of the internal labour market at the enterprise level and the regulatory framework of the New Deal at the systemic level – depended indirectly on the secondary sector as a 'buffer zone' for economic fluctuations. However, during the 1970s and 1980s, market conditions began to fluctuate on a much more generalised basis, while incipient processes of globalisation exposed even 'core' workers to wage and job compe-tition, and to the political realities of concession bargaining. All of the vital indicators of economic growth – profit rates, productivity levels, real incomes – started to flatten. This established the context for US corporations' increasingly insistent search for new forms of 'flexibility', especially in labour relations.

Contingent labour strategies have been playing a key role in this wider process of restructuring. Again, the explosive growth of the temp industry is a case in point. As Gonos (1998, p. 174) explains, the attractiveness of the 'temporary solution' for employ-ers is that it enhances managerial control over job tasks and the pace of work, it desta-bilises collective structures in the workplace, it pushes wages back out into competition and it holds 'the potential for significantly increasing both the numerical and functional flexibility of the firm's workforce [constituting] an effective means of relocating work out of primary (or 'core') labour markets and into secondary (or 'competitive') ones'. As temp industry advocates would pointedly ask, why relocate production to Mexico when the same conditions of employment can be recreated right here at home?

Technically, what defines 'temporary work' is not the duration of work assignments per se, but the formal relations of precariousness that have become enshrined in legal, business and social conventions. The deliberate regulatory ambiguity of the triangulated employment relationship means that many of the provisions and protections which typically apply to employee–employer relations under New Deal legislation are effectively voided, evaded, or at the very least obfuscated. What Gonos (1998, p. 173) terms the 'temporary help formula' is therefore a specific legal construction that permits the business clients of agencies 'to utilize labor without taking on the specific social, legal and contractual obligations that have increasingly been attached to employer status since the New Deal'. As staffing industry insiders Lewis and Molloy (1991, p. 27) concede, this division of managerial and legal responsibilities is the crux of the temporary employment relationship, because temp workers 'are employed by the temporary help service, the client company is relieved of the burdens and costs associated with hiring [permanent employees]'.

The growth of contingent work is intricately and causally related to the now well-established managerial strategy for evading, avoiding and eroding New Deal-style employment relations (see Kochan et al., 1986; Cappelli et al., 1997; Stone, 2001). The significance of contingent work strategies like temping, beyond the facilitation of workforce restructuring in the short term, is that they are becoming norm-making sites in a reorganised labour market. The telling historical parallel is with the institution of the internal labour market, which, though certainly never dominant in pure numerical terms at the point at which it began to exert a normative influence on the framing of regulatory legislation (and practice), did have significant impact upon the fashioning of, for example, the Wagner Act of 1935 (which legalised the right of workers to join independent unions); the Employment Security Act of 1946 (which committed the federal government to employment maximisation policies and counter-cyclical initiatives); the Social Security Act of 1935 (which established the basic structure of the welfare state, like unemployment compensation and old-age assistance, while linking key benefits to employment status); and the Taft–Hartley Act of 1947 (which curbed militant elements in the union movement and established a relatively conservative and restrictive legal framework around union activities).

During the Fordist expansion, this regulatory framework – together with the constellation of political forces that first constituted and then defended it – played a fundamental role in establishing a kind of anti-gravitational pull in the labour market. Thus, it was a period in which minimum-wage legislation and welfare provisions constituted a 'floor' in the job market, which was then gradually ratcheted up; core workers achieved significant employment security, expanded the legitimate scope of union activities and secured an institutionalised system of cost-of-living raises; real incomes rose across the class distribution, doubling for the typical worker during the decades of the Fordist expansion, and rising more sharply at the bottom than the top; and a muted dynamic of social and spatial redistribution developed (Bluestone and Harrison, 2000). These 'Golden Age' labour markets also exhibited high levels of racial, ethnic and gender discrimination, though this too was part of their 'logic', since labour segmentation played a major role in countering tendencies toward workforce homogenisation, while restricting access to primary jobs (Gordon et al., 1982).

This institutional complex has been gradually pulled apart over the past three decades, a process actively assisted by a plethora of corporate and government initiatives, such that these Fordist anti-gravitational forces were at first stalled and then subsequently reversed. In the regressive regulatory climate established in Fordism's wake, then, the (admittedly partial) upward pull of progressive labour and welfare standards has been overcome by a downward gravitational drag. This has been associated with distinctive forms of 'scale politics', as regulatory protections and social rights previously anchored in federal legislation have been deliberately eroded, and as various forms of regime competition at the state and local level have been encouraged, if not actively orchestrated. The geographically uneven unpicking of the welfare safety net – a process effectively 'managed' by successive federal governments since the 1980s through (auto)critiques of welfarism and self-administered forms of institutional hollowing out – is a case in point (Peck, 2002; Schram, 2006).

The New Deal configuration, in which marginalised workers were excluded from primary-sector jobs on the basis of a set of institutionalised rules related, in one way or another, to their ascribed characteristics and reflected in stable patterns of segmentation and segregation, is being progressively and unevenly displaced by a neoliberal, post-welfare configuration in which the contingent workforce is located at the sharp end of a systemically insecure and turbulent employment regime, based on the principles of (enforced) market inclusion and individualised 'employability'. Segmentation and segregation, of course, are hardly things of the past in this more fiercely competitive labour-market order, but their contours and foundations have been reorganised under an employment regime predicated on the goals of extending managerial discretion over labour, while increasing the substitutability, interchangeability and disposability of workers.

This neoliberal mode of labour regulation has its origins in the deregulations and rollbacks of the 1980s, which extended and intensified market discipline within the employment system, forcing and flexibilising the labour supply through measures like workfare programmes, employability initiatives and welfare cutbacks. Crucially, for many of those workers located on the edges of the labour market, this involved an inversion of the New-Deal logic of labour-market exclusion (extending basic welfare supports to those whose wage-labour is only required on a discontinuous basis), replacing this with a neoliberal emphasis on labour-market inclusion. Labour-market inclusion involves the maximisation of wage-labour participation through the curtailment of benefit eligibility, forced job search and the development of measures to improve individual 'employability' (see Peck and Theodore, 2000; Standing, 2002). All such strategies, of course, are predicated on the assumption that the labour market's absorptive capacity is sufficiently elastic to accommodate those, such as former welfare recipients, rendered newly 'dependent' (to borrow a term) on low-wage jobs. While New Deal labour markets were typically slow to respond to such pressures, emanating from excess labour supplies 'from below', post-welfare labour markets are substantially defined by this adaptability and porosity. The result is that locally calibrated and enforced forms of flexibility are highly significant – symbolically and strategically – in the era of neoliberal labour regulation. Moreover, it is in this context that the structural significance of contingent work should be understood, the growth of which has entailed a series of demand-side reforms designed creatively to capitalise on the availability of persistently under-employed labour. There is, then, an ugly logic to the manner in which the generation of short-term, insecure, high-turnover jobs (a.k.a. contingent work) meshes with the desperate need for work amongst under-employed workers with few, if any, alternative sources of subsistence, such as former welfare recipients and undocumented workers.

Contingent work, then, is not just a new label for 'secondary labour market', since the context in which it is embedded has changed markedly. The secondary sector always represented something of a residual theoretical category in dualist models of the labour market, which associated the primary sector with most of the advanced, dynamic, modern and positive features of the (Fordist) employment system (Peck, 1996). While the secondary sector provided much-needed flexibility for the production system as a whole, and a kind of repository for undervalued labour, it did so as a backward and anachronistic zone of outmoded employment practices, suboptimal business strategies and rigid balkanisation from the 'mainstream' labour market, in accordance with the sharp lines of racial, ethnic and gender discrimination. By way of contrast, the con-tingent economy, while it echoes and re-works many of these features, emerged under quite different structural conditions. The rupturing of the New Deal social contract had dissipated and disrupted the upward pull on pay and conditions that had been such a strong feature of the Fordist expansion. In its place, a concerted downward drag on pay and conditions was being constituted, partly as an opportunistic response to the new labour-market conditions of underemployment and job insecurity, and partly as an outcome of deliberate corporate and governmental policies. Consequently, in a signifi-cant volte-face, today the zone of the labour market that is represented as anachronistic and outdated is the primary sector, with its unionised practices, its 'jobs for life' ethos, its bureaucratic hierarchies, its blue-collar work cultures and 'organisation man' styles of management. Meanwhile, the contingent labour market is celebrated as a font of flexibil-ity – the shape of things to come. Two amongst many recent developments illustrate this trend: the recent redrawing of European employment regulations removing legal restric-tions on the use of agency labour in order to recognise the 'positive role' of temp agencies as 'human capital managers' (Employment Taskforce, 2004, p. 32), and International Labour Organisation (ILO) directives and provisions increasingly favouring the spread of contingent work (Peck et al., 2005).

Conclusion: contingent politics?

The troubled history of contingent work as a labour-market keyword can be read as a narrative on America's post-welfare economy. Since entering the employment policy lexicon 20 years ago, contingent work has passed from being a provocative term, favoured by Reagan-era critics during debates around 'McJobs' and contract-ing out, through its orthodox absorption as a relatively benign statistical category of the labour-market census during the Clinton years, to what may be an incipient process of re-politicisation in the present context of anaemic jobs and wage growth, continuing polarisation and unabashed trickle-up economics. Beyond these specific translations of the term, contingent work also has been characterised here as a potent signifier for an entrenched pattern of labour market restructuring, couched in terms of an increasingly hegemonic form of neoliberal rationality. Analytically imprecise and empirically ambiguous, contingent work retains a measure of salience as a rough-and-ready umbrella term for a heterogeneous bundle of labour market practices that deviate decisively, in both material and ideological terms, from the prevailing norms of the Fordist–Keynesian economy. In contrast to the conceptual and political humility of its predecessor, the secondary labour market, contingent work occupies a much more precocious position within the neoliberal reform agenda, as a symbol of a flexible future rather than a residue of the past.

The regulation of contingent work represents a moment of strategic, analytical and political significance in the wider process of neoliberalisation. While there has been understandable squeamishness about proclaiming the arrival of a neoliberal order – since many of the arguments used to sustain such claims are often associated with functionalism, fatalism, faddishness, or all three – in the context of contingent labour markets, such a declaration is now surely warranted. But, by the same token, the manner in which contingent labour markets have been neoliberalised reveals a great deal about the complex, contradictory and contested realities of 'marketisation', since contingent work is one of the most intensively institutionalised sites of the contemporary economy. It may also speak to the wider macro-regulatory dynamics of the neoliberal period: if neoliberalism's initial impetus was in part a reactionary response to the way in which Keynesianism politicised the economy during the era of stagflation, profound consequences may also follow from the ways in which neoliberalism has re-politicised economic relations, especially at the 'bottom' of the labour market.

The historically combined processes of downscaling labour regulation, displacing and downloading socioeconomic risks, and dismantling welfare-state institutions, in this sense, clearly do not mark the end of the story. New kinds of scale politics are being made all of the time, though they must now be constructed on an entirely different institutional terrain and in the context of a transformed configuration of labour–capital relations. The neoliberal offensive constructed 'local labour' in competitive terms – amplifying job and wage competition both within and between local labour markets – while opening up new spaces for regressive institutional experimentation, notably in strategically important fields like employment relations and social entitlements (for a different example of how such spaces of experimentation are being formed, see De la Garza, Chapter 18 in this volume). In macro-political terms, this had the (desired) effect of positioning labour in a defensive, and strategically vulnerable, posture. But the neoliberal utopia of infinitely mobile capital and infinitely flexible labour could never be fully realised. In recent decades, politically-assisted forms of uneven spatial development may have played a role in levering down labour standards, but they have also generated new spaces of contradiction, and new terrains of resistance. The distinctively neoliberal form of competitive downloading, regulatory decentralisation and individualisation, in this sense, should not be mistaken for some one-way, terminal or end-stage process; it must be understood as part of a wider, political dialectic of spatial and scalar transformation.

However, in fitful, but perhaps also telling, ways contingent labour strategies are beginning to be met by (new kinds of) resistance, including strikes against employment casualisation, living-wage campaigns, organising drives amongst day-labourers and contract workers and so forth. In Chicago, for example, grassroots labour organisations, including immigrant worker centres, community–labour coalitions and networks of workers' rights activists, have sought to confront substandard conditions in contingent labour markets through a two-pronged strategy of legislative action and reinvigorated labour-law enforcement. On the legislative front, these organisations have successfully pressed for state- and local-level regulation of day labour temp agencies as a way to curtail predatory surcharges (for transportation, cheque cashing and the like) that had often pushed hourly wage rates below the state-mandated minimum. In the area of labour-law enforcement, workers' rights organisations are counteracting the tendency for contingent workers to endure substandard employment conditions privately and individually, by actively organising workers and giving voice, by aggregating multiple grievances against abusive employers and by presenting state enforcement agencies with extensive records of employment law violations. These grassroots efforts have been effective in collectivising workers' experiences in what was rolled out as a highly atomised job market. As a result, the balance of power relations in contingent labour markets, which have been tilted so decisively in the direction of employers, are rebalanced somewhat, offering contingent workers recourse against the most abusive employers.

Cumulatively, these efforts reflect an increasing politicisation of contingent labour and they seem also to signify intensifying pressure to visualise and realise more humane and sustainable alternatives. At the very least, they represent a shot across the bows; more ambitiously, they may be the first indications of labour markets being re-regulated from the bottom. Whether or not it is yet appropriate to think in terms of potentially transformative contingent-class consciousness, as Prashad (2003) does quite explicitly, these developments lend further credence to the claims that the contingent labour market is both a zone of structural stress and a space of political possibility. These are not simply spaces of infinite Darwinian regression, or unfettered commodification. Just as their construction was a political project, they may now be encountering a political pushback . . . from below.

References

Belous, R.S. (1989), *The Contingent Economy*, NPA Report 239, Washington, DC: National Planning Association.

Bluestone, B. and B. Harrison (2000), *Growing Prosperity*, Boston, MA: Houghton Mifflin.

Cappelli, P., L. Bassi, H. Katz, D. Knoke, P. Osterman and M. Useem (1997), *Change at Work*, New York: Oxford University Press.

Carré, F., M.A. Ferber, L. Golden and S.A. Herzenberg (2000), 'Nonstandard work: the nature and challenges of changing employment arrangements', in F. Carré, M.A. Ferber, L. Golden and S.A. Herzenberg (eds), *Nonstandard Work: The Nature and Challenges of Changing Employment Arrangements*, Champaign, IL: Industrial Relations Research Association, pp. 1–20.

Clark, G.L. (1981), 'The employment relation and spatial division of labor: a hypothesis', *Annals of the Association of American Geographers*, **71**, 412–24.

Cohen, L. (1990), *Making a New Deal: Industrial Workers in Chicago, 1919–1939*, New York: Cambridge University Press.

Doeringer, P.B. and M.J. Piore (1971), *Internal Labor Markets and Manpower Analysis*, Lexington, MA: D.C. Heath.

Doussard, M., J. Peck and N. Theodore (2009), 'After deindustrialization: uneven growth and economic inequality in "postindustrial" Chicago', *Economic Geography*, **85** (2), 183–207.

duRivage, V.L., F. Carré and C. Tilly (1998), 'Making labor law work for part-time and contingent workers', in K. Barker and K Christensen (eds), *Contingent Work: American Employment Relations in Transition*, Ithaca, NY: ILR Press, pp. 263–80.

Economic Policy Institute (EPI) (2007), *The State of Working America, 2006–2007*, Ithaca, NY: Cornell University Press.

Employment Taskforce (2004), *Jobs, Jobs, Jobs: Creating More Employment in Europe*, Luxembourg: European Commission.

England, K. (1993), 'Suburban pink collar ghettos: the spatial entrapment of women?', *Annals of the Association of American Geographers*, **83**, 225–42.

General Accounting Office (GAO) (2000), *Contingent Workers*, GAO/HEHS-00-76, Washington, DC: US General Accounting Office.

Gonos, G. (1998), 'The interaction between market incentives and government actions', in K. Barker and K. Christensen (eds), *Contingent Work: American Employment Relations in Transition*, Ithaca, NY: Cornell University Press, pp. 170–91.

Gordon, D.M., R. Edwards and M. Reich (1982), *Segmented Work, Divided Workers*, Cambridge: Cambridge University Press.

Gottfried, H. (1992), 'In the margins: flexibility as a mode of regulation in the temporary help service industry', *Work, Employment and Society*, **6**, 443–60.

Gunset, G. (1998), 'Factory jobs not extinct', *Chicago Tribune*, 15 October, p. B1.

Hanson, S. and G. Pratt (1995), *Gender, Work and Space*, London: Routledge.

Harrison, B. and B. Bluestone (1988), *The Great U-turn*, New York: Basic Books.

Harvey, D. (1989), *The Urban Experience*, Baltimore, MD: Johns Hopkins University Press.

Herod, A. (2001), *Labor Geographies: Workers and the Landscapes of Capitalism*, New York: Guilford Press.

Hicks, J.R. (1932), *A Theory of Wages*, London: Macmillan.

Hiebert, D. (1999), 'Local geographies of labor market segmentation: Montreal, Toronto, and Vancouver, 1991', *Economic Geography*, **75**, 339–69.

Hylton, M.O. (1995), 'The case against regulating the market for contingent employment', *Washington and Lee Law Review*, **52**, 849–60.

Jonas, A.E.G. (1996), 'Local labour control regimes: uneven development and the social regulation of production', *Regional Studies*, **30**, 323–38.

Jones, M.R. (1998), *New Institutional Spaces*, London: Jessica Kingley.

Kilcoyne, P. (2005), 'Occupations in the temporary help services industry', in *Occupational Employment and Wages*, May 2004, Washington, DC: US Department of Labor, pp. 6–9.

Kochan, T.A., H.C. Katz and R.B. McKersie (1986), *The Transformation of American Industrial Relations*, New York: Basic Books.

Lester, G. (1998), 'Careers and contingency', *Stanford Law Review*, **51**, 73–145.

Lewis, W.M. and N.H. Molloy (1991), *How to Choose and Use Temporary Services*, New York: Amacom.

Lovering, J. (1989), 'The restructuring debate', in R. Peet and N. Thrift (eds), *New Models in Geography*, vol. 1, London: Unwin Hyman, pp. 198–223.

Martin, R.L. (2000), 'Local labour markets: their nature, performance and regulation', in G.L. Clark, M.S. Gertler and M.P. Feldman (eds), *The Oxford Handbook of Economic Geography*, Oxford: Oxford University Press, pp. 455–76.

Massey, D. (1984), *Spatial Divisions of Labour*, London: Macmillan.

McDowell, L. (1991), 'Life without father and Ford: the new gender order of post-Fordism', *Transactions of the Institute of British Geographers*, **16**, 400–19.

Moberg, D. (2006), 'Economic restructuring: Chicago's precarious balance', in J.P. Koval, L. Bennett, M.I.J. Bennett, F. Demissie, R. Garner and K. Kim (eds), *The New Chicago*, Philadelphia, PA: Temple University Press, pp. 32–43.

Moore, M.A. (1965), 'The temporary help service industry: historical development, operation, and scope', *Industrial and Labor Relations Review*, **18**, 554–69.

Oehlsen, N. (1997), 'Caught in the machinery', *Chicago Reader*, **26**, 1–25.

Offe, C. (1985), *Disorganized Capitalism*, Cambridge: Polity.

Peck, J. (1996), *Work-Place: The Social Regulation of Labor Markets*, New York: Guilford Press.

Peck, J. (2001), *Workfare States*, New York: Guilford Press.

Peck, J. (2002), 'Political economies of scale: fast policy, interscalar relations, and neoliberal workfare', *Economic Geography*, **78**, 331–60.

Peck, J. and N. Theodore (1998), 'The business of contingent work: growth and restructuring in Chicago's temporary employment industry', *Work, Employment and Society*, **12**, 655–74.

Peck, J. and N. Theodore (2000), 'Beyond "employability"', *Cambridge Journal of Economics*, **24**, 729–50.

Peck, J. and N. Theodore (2001), 'Contingent Chicago: restructuring the spaces of temporary labor', *International Journal of Urban and Regional Research*, **25**, 471–96.

Peck, J., N. Theodore and K. Ward (2005), 'Constructing markets for temporary labour: employment liberalization and the internationalization of the staffing industry', *Global Networks*, **5**, 3–26.

Pfeffer, J. and J. Baron (1988), 'Taking the workers back out: recent trends in the structuring of employment', in B. Straw and L.L. Cummins (eds), *Research in Organizational Behavior*, Greenwich, CT: JAI Press, pp. 257–303.

Polivka, A.E. and T. Nardone (1989), 'On the definition of "contingent work"', *Monthly Labor Review*, December, pp. 9–16.

Pollin, R. (2003), *Contours of Descent*, London: Verso.

Pollock, M.A. (1986), 'The disposable employee is becoming a fact of corporate life', *Business Week*, 15 December, 52–6.

Prashad, V. (2003), *Keeping Up with the Dow Joneses*, Cambridge, MA: South End Press.

Rubery, J., R. Tarling and F. Wilkinson (1987), 'Flexibility, marketing and the organisation of production', *Labour and Society*, **12**, 131–51.

Schram, S. (2006), *Welfare Discipline*, Philadelphia, PA: Temple University Press.

Scott, A.J. (1988), *Metropolis: From Division of Labor to Urban Form*, Berkeley, CA: University of California Press.

Sengenberger, W. (1981), Labour market segmentation and the business cycle', in F. Wilkinson (ed.), *The Dynamics of Labour Market Segmentation*, London: Academic Press, pp. 243–59.

Sinclair, U. ([1906] 2003), *The Jungle*, Tucson, AZ: See Sharp Press.

Spalter-Roth, R. and H. Hartmann (1998), 'Gauging the consequences for gender relations, pay equity and the public purse', in K. Barker and K Christensen (eds), *Contingent Work: American Employment Relations in Transition*, Ithaca, NY: Cornell University Press, pp. 69–100.

Standing, G. (2002), *Beyond the New Paternalism*, London: Verso.

Stone, K.V.W. (2001), 'The new psychological contract: implications of the changing workplace for labor and employment law', *UCLA Law Review*, **48**, 519–661.

Storper, M. and R.A. Walker (1983), 'The theory of labor and the theory of location', *International Journal of Urban and Regional Research*, **7**, 1–41.

Swyngedouw, E. (1997), 'Excluding the other: the production of scale and scaled politics', in R. Lee and J. Wills (eds), *Geographies of Economies*, London: Arnold, pp. 167–76.

Theodore, N. and J. Peck (2002), 'The temporary staffing industry: growth imperatives and limits to contingency', *Economic Geography*, **78**, 463–93.

Vosko, L. (2000), *Temporary Work*, Toronto: University of Toronto Press.

Warde, A. (1985), 'Spatial change, politics, and the division of labour', in D. Gregory and J. Urry (eds), *Social Relations and Spatial Structures*, London: Macmillan, pp. 190–212.

Wills, J. (1996), 'Geographies of trade unionism: translating traditions across space and time', *Antipode*, **28**, 352–78.

6 Clothing workers after worker states: the consequences for work and labour of outsourcing, nearshoring and delocalisation in postsocialist Europe

John Pickles and Adrian Smith

Introduction

The year 1989 signalled not only a shift in the geopolitical structure of Europe, but a fundamental pivot around which patterns of employment and economic life were reorganised throughout Central and Eastern Europe (CEE). The integrated supply chains of state socialism with their regional divisions of labour and tightly interwoven networks of full-package producers were – almost overnight – stripped of their primary markets and the planning system that generated materials and wage inputs. Most industrial branches experienced budgetary crises, and decades of infrastructure and know-how were consigned to obsolescence in a matter of months. Hidden and open unemployment burgeoned as state-owned and newly privatised enterprises struggled to retain one of their primary roles under the Soviet system – the reproduction of the labour collective (Clarke, 1993). What Kornai (1992) had called the soft budget constraints of state socialism, with their associated coordination of manager and worker interests to meet quotas and maintain wage bills and input supplies, were transformed overnight into hard budget constraints and intense inter-factional competition to control state assets, re-direct machinery and wages, and either cash-out or leverage control over resources to maintain economic power and viability (Pickles, 1995; Begg and Pickles, 1998; Smith, 1998). The story – one of dramatic geopolitical shifts, economic violence and retrenchment, alongside the emergence of 'wild' forms of capitalist social relations – is by now a familiar one (Burawoy and Krotov, 1993; Burawoy, 1996; Herod, 1998, 2001; Ost, 2002, 2005; Pavlínek, 2002).

After 1989, the trilateralism in which organised labour was embedded (state, business and unions) gave trade unions a short-term place in industrial policy formation, but compromised efforts at union organising on the shop-floor and among the unemployed, and produced little more than a weak corporatism (Ost, 2002). Their formerly compromised position as political unions – the transmission belts of the party state – was, as a result, compounded first by anti-communist purges and subsequently by scandals surrounding the *nomenklatura* and plant managers and the voucher privatisations in which they usually participated. Over time, the position of trade unions was further weakened as policies that favoured the rapid privatisation of state enterprises were pursued by national governments across the region (Herod, 1998; Kubicek, 1999; Pollert, 1999).

New democratic unions (like *Podkrepa* in Bulgaria) were generally weak and poorly positioned in workplaces, while older national unions struggled in conditions in which unemployment was deepening and industrial activity was becoming increasingly precarious.[1]

This weakness was compounded by the suspicion and active exclusion of trade unions by leading institutions of structural reform (the World Bank, International Monetary Fund, Economic Bank for Reconstruction and Development) which created what Standing (2002, p. 51) called the first revolution to be led by international financial institutions.

More recently, the pursuit of vigorous policies of neo-liberalisation has resulted in a further erosion of the position of organised labour as industrial retrenchment continued alongside an increasing segmentation of labour markets (Ost, 2002; Rainnie et al., 2002; Smith et al., 2008a). The initial hope that large-scale foreign direct investment (FDI) would re-capitalise at least some regional industries initially failed to materialise, perhaps with the single exception of food processing (Pickles and Smith, 2005). By the mid-1990s, FDI levels were picking up but the resulting regional and sectoral concentration had created a dual economy of isolated 'cathedrals in the desert' (Grabher, 1994; Pavlínek and Smith, 1998). Only a few branches of industry (for example, automobiles) developed real 'spread effects', although there too there have been uneven impacts (Pavlínek, 2002).

The great losers were the workers in the industries that experienced large-scale retrenchment. In many industrial regions, unemployment soared, forced withdrawal from the labour market became common, and many took early retirement or were effectively written out of labour market participation figures by changes in unemployment benefit eligibility regulations (Rainnie et al., 2002; Smith et al., 2008a). As a result, average family incomes declined and informal economies flourished as unregistered employment, international labour migration (especially since EU enlargement in 2004), an economy of jars (in which agricultural products are reciprocally exchanged through systems of gift giving, such that each household is thus situated in a network of mutualistic interactions), informal natural resource extraction (as with scavenging for coal), and corruption became important means of sustaining minimal livelihoods (Smollet, 1989; Ledeneva, 1998; Staddon, 2001; Pickles, 2002; Cellarius, 2004; Smith and Stenning, 2006; Smith et al., 2008a).

In this chapter we focus on the consequences of this political economy of postsocialist transformation for the conditions of work and labour organising in CEE. We use the example of the clothing industry to show how the changing geographies of regional integration and trade liberalisation, outsourcing and delocalisation from Western Europe have shaped the fortunes of workers in CEE. In particular, we focus on how, in such a geographically mobile sector, the place-based nature of social relations creates conditions for partially enhancing the positional power of workers in the former workers' states. The account we provide is not a straightforward one of either gains or losses for labour. Work conditions and the positional power of organised labour were themselves already conflicted under state socialism, and since 1989 the fortunes of workers and of their representative organs have remained complex and highly differentiated, even within this one industry and across the region. With the expanded pace and scope of outsourcing and nearshoring, along with supply chain consolidation and ethical sourcing initiatives, the current conditions of work and opportunities for organised labour are far from straightforward.

From full package to export processing: outward processing and the European project of regional economic integration
The textiles and clothing industry was one of the hardest hit by the collapse of Council of Mutual Economic Assistance (CMEA) export markets and declines in domestic

consumption in the early 1990s. Employment collapsed across the region with only core workers and regions sustaining any production and employment at all. Between 1980 and 1993, employment in Western and Central European textile, clothing and footwear industries more generally had declined precipitously as sourcing moved to lower-cost locations (ILO, 1996). As a result, after 1989 policy makers in reform countries of CEE quickly wrote off entire industries, with state authorities in Bulgaria, for example, going as far as to declare the clothing industry moribund (Pickles and Begg, 2000). Policy makers throughout the region adopted similar 'common sense' understandings that these were 'footloose', 'sunset' industries whose likely demise should be reflected in state policies.

In fact, industry analysts were largely misinterpreting employment declines in Western Europe and intense intra-enterprise struggles for capital and power in Eastern Europe as industrial decline. As Gereffi and his colleagues have shown, production systems in the US and Europe rapidly re-organised their supply chains in the 1990s, shedding low-value work to increase productivity and upgrading to higher value-added activities (Gereffi, 1999, 2006; Gereffi et al., 2002; Gereffi and Memedovic, 2003). In Europe, productivity gains and enhanced value creation came at the expense of employment, delocalisation of assembly operations and the expansion of regional production networks into Eastern Europe and the Euro-Mediterranean region. As a result, at the very time the state-run clothing industry was experiencing significant difficulties, factories and workshops were being rapidly integrated into supply chains of European buyers as the nearest export processing zone for the West European clothing industry (Begg and Pickles, 1998). In Eastern Europe, integration into international production networks coincided with economic reform at home. Together these stimulated intense wars of position over control of the industry. The book value of enterprises was run down as prospective new owners sought to acquire enterprise assets at below their actual value, while the same owners simultaneously cultivated their international contracts. Thus, as private enterprises emerged from the parent state enterprises and as greenfield operations were opened, drawing on plant and personnel from the state enterprises, managers of small- and medium-sized enterprises found that they could embed their production in outsourcing networks supported by state and European Union nearshoring policies (Graziani, 1998; Pellegrin, 2001; Smith et al., 2005). Except in Ukraine, Russia and Poland, clothing employment first stabilised and then grew (see Figure 6.1), and soon accounted for almost one quarter of manufacturing employment in countries like Bulgaria and Macedonia, and almost one fifth of total manufacturing employment in Romania.

The incorporation of proximate assembly producers in low-wage countries on the margins of the European Union was part of a broader EU strategy of labour market reform orchestrated under pressure from large industry and retailer associations. The principal instrument of this strategy was a customs arrangement that allowed the temporary export of fabrics and trim for outward processing in CEE countries and the re-import of manufactured clothing with duties being paid only on the value-added, that is the cost of labour for stitching-up – a system of outward processing trade or OPT (Pellegrin, 2001; Begg et al., 2003; Smith, 2003). The re-emergence of clothing manufacture across CEE was, thus, mirrored by a downsizing and 'delocalisation' in the European Union and loss of employment in the EU clothing industry between 1985 and 1995 of 40 per cent (Stengg, 2001, p. 3).

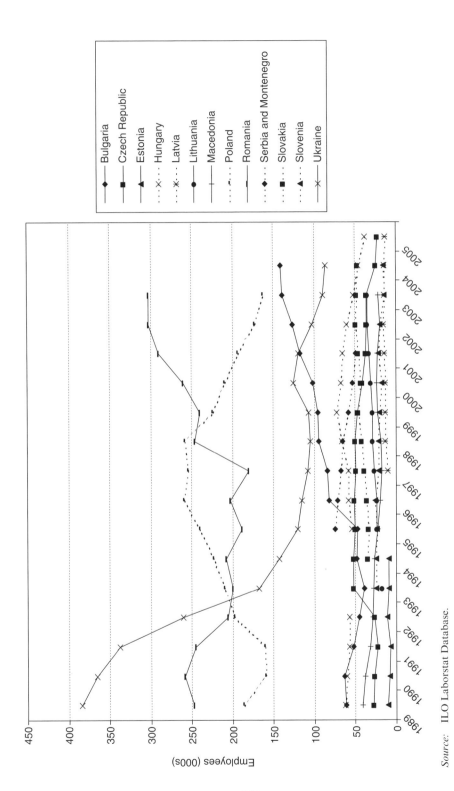

Legend:
—◆— Bulgaria
—■— Czech Republic
—▲— Estonia
·····×···· Hungary
·····✳···· Latvia
—●— Lithuania
—+— Macedonia
·········· Poland
—|— Romania
·····✦···· Serbia and Montenegro
·····■···· Slovakia
·····▲···· Slovenia
—×— Ukraine

450
400
350
300
250
200
150
100
50
0

Employees (000s)

1989 1990 1991 1992 1993 1994 1995 1996 1997 1998 1999 2000 2001 2002 2003 2004 2005

Source: ILO Laborstat Database.

Figure 6.1 Clothing employment in selected CEE countries (000s employees)

Trade liberalisation, unionism and workers

In fact, the delocalisation of the West European clothing industry and the offshoring and nearshoring of assembly production to CEE began as early as the 1960s and 1970s (Fröbel et al., 1980; Gereffi, 2006, p. 1). The process intensified after the 1980s as a result of EU outward processing trade policies and, more recently, with the end to quota-constrained trade in textiles and clothing under the World Trade Organisation's Agreement on Textiles and Clothing (ATC). Under the ATC, member states of the World Trade Organisation (WTO) agreed to phase out the system of quantitative quotas established under the Multi-Fibre Arrangement (MFA) in four phases over ten years, with the final quota ending by 1 January 2005. International buyers were free to source clothing in any amount from any country and suppliers could compete for contracts without quota restraint, subject only to a system of national and regional trade agreement tariffs, non-tariff barriers and WTO-sanctioned safeguards.

At the same time, global apparel supply chains were also undergoing intense consolidation, particularly with the emergence of large network organisers such as Li and Fung, and full package producers (Gereffi, 2006, pp. 33–8). The size of orders required by buyers increased, unit prices decreased and demands on quality and delivery time rose. At the same time, buyers increased pressure on manufacturers to take on more functions (such as input sourcing, quality control, packing, labelling, warehousing, and logistics), shoulder more of the burden of financial risk and accept lower contract prices.

The consequences for labour are by now well known: the internationalising of post-socialist European, Indian and Chinese labour markets in the same decade effectively doubled the global labour force and intensified downward pressure on contract prices and wages while simultaneously allowing buyers to leverage tighter delivery schedules, increased flexibility, and higher penalties for non-compliance (see Oxfam, 2004; Hale and Wills, 2005). In some cases, these adjustments led to a rapid increase in imports from more 'cost-effective' locations (especially from China and India) (see Gereffi, 2003). As production shifted to these regions, other locations lost contracts, shed employment and intensified pressure on workers. There is, as a result, a deepening sense of uncertainty and threat among officials, managers and workers and a growing consensus that the geography of 'winners' and 'losers' in the global clothing industry will change even more rapidly in the coming years, with a 'race to the bottom' seemingly the most likely outcome (see OECD, 2003; EU High Level Working Group, 2004; Mayer, 2004; Nordås, 2004; Oxfam, 2004; US-ITC, 2004; UNCTAD, 2005; Conway, 2006).

The consequences for Central and East European apparel producers and workers are potentially devastating. Having only recently rebuilt their industry, inserted themselves into international supply chains, and upgraded technology and workforce capacities, CEE producers are again seeing their contracts threatened by competition from lower-cost producers in south-eastern Europe, the Euro-Mediterranean, and Asia (Smith et al., 2008b). The consequences for low-wage workers have been particularly devastating in higher-cost locations in Central Europe (such as Poland, Hungary, the Czech and Slovak Republics). These marginally higher cost production sites in Central Europe had initiated the drive to outward processing export production in the 1980s and 1990s, but they soon began to see job loss as cost differentials ate into their competitiveness and as clothing employment continued to expand in south-eastern Europe in the late 1990s and the first years of the twenty-first century (see Figure 6.1).

Hale (2005) has already suggested that continued liberalisation and geographical instabilities in the industry will result in the emergence of greater deregulation in labour markets, with correspondingly difficult challenges for workers: production jobs will continue to be lost in high-cost locations and in countries of the global South that were reliant on quota-based trade (such as Bangladesh); labour standards will be lowered as firms compete to undercut the price of other suppliers; and informalisation and flexibilisation of production will increase, notably through the increased use of home-workers. Such unstable, locationally mobile and organisationally flexible and precarious working conditions have now become widely generalised in many parts of the clothing industry, leading to a global sweatshop economy and the further immiseration of labour (Hale and Wills, 2005).

Postsocialist enterprises and their workers offered West European manufacturers and retailers an opportunity to recapture some competitive advantage by extending their production systems into low-wage labour markets (Fröbel et al., 1980; Graziani, 1998; Coe et al., 2004; Smith et al., 2005). At the cost of relatively small (and rapidly diminishing) increases in logistical and transaction costs, regionally extended supply chains were able to tap into large, low-cost (yet skilled) labour pools. This labour was in settings in which industrial infrastructures, laws and norms were well established and in which existing product capabilities – high quality men's and women's suits, for example – fed into niche markets in EU countries requiring regionalised production, stock replenishment and tighter control over logistics and quality control (Abernathy et al., 2006; Pickles, 2006; Pickles et al., 2006; Smith et al., 2008b).

Perhaps surprisingly in these circumstances, however, workers in the CEE clothing industry have been able to achieve marginal gains in real wages. These gains were partly driven by expectations of potential wage gains around EU enlargement and were partly the result of enterprise adjustments to the paradoxical situation of skilled worker shortages in conditions of chronic regional unemployment and large-scale outmigration following EU accession (Pickles, 2002; Pickles et al., 2006). As some workers suffered the consequences of downgrading, these pressures simultaneously encouraged workforce upgrading. With increasing competition, concentration in the supply chain and punitive quality requirements and delivery deadlines, place-based workforce capacities have increasingly become an important determinant of success in international markets. Pickles (2002) had already noted the emergence of tightening labour markets among export assembly producers in south-eastern Bulgaria as early as the late 1990s, a labour market tightening that seemed to have been generated by growing competition for skilled workers in conditions of surplus unskilled unemployed workers. More recently, Gospodinova (2006) has similarly highlighted the problems of worker training in Bulgaria, where low levels of training and increasing demand for skilled workers generally (turners, millers, welders and builders, as well as managerial-level employees) have become more important as other parts of the economy have grown and as EU accession allows for greater levels of labour outmigration. Employers, however, remain wary of making such investments in training and working conditions because of the widespread practice of inter-enterprise poaching of qualified workers whose training has been financed by another employer.

In the next section we turn to how we might think about work and labour in the clothing industry in ways that further question the model of clothing as an unproblematically flexible and footloose industry. We consider the role of lean retailing and the management of capital at risk in supply chains to suggest alternative spatial logics for the management of 'factor' (especially labour), logistical and policy costs in the industry. These alternative logics draw on a well-developed body of literature in economic geography, economic sociology and postsocialist studies that suggests that models of footloose industries shifting in 'slippery space' need to be more carefully articulated with the 'sticky logics' of locally embedded practices and their sustaining social networks. The point we wish to make in all this is that highlighting the continuing embeddedness of export production may mean – at least, in some circumstances – that workers have more resources at their disposal than models of mobile and footloose capital might suggest. We then turn to the historical legacies of regionally-based garment export capacity that continue to shape sourcing decisions and the conditions of work they generate. We highlight some of the ways in which the place-specific state socialist commitment to the social reproduction of the labour collective (for example, the social wage) continue to matter in important and strategic ways. Finally, we conclude with consideration of emerging new forms of industrial governance spurred in part by EU policies governing codes, standards and labour mobility in an enlarged Europe. We assess the potential role of these forms of industrial governance for understanding improvements in the position of labour in pan-regional production.

From export processing to industrial upgrading: place and the embeddedness and changing positionalities of labour in regional production networks

Lean retailing and the challenges of regionalisation
The turn to lean retailing in many parts of the clothing supply chain has led to corresponding changes in the ways in which manufacturers and retailers juggle costs, quality, time-to-delivery, and capital at risk in their decision making, in turn placing greater emphasis on supply chain management (see also Abernathy et al., 1999; Abernathy et al., 2006). This, then, is a story of sourcing strategies in which policy and logistical costs at times outweigh the advantages of lower 'factor' costs (such as low labour costs) and result in sourcing decisions that privilege and sustain production in regions close to major markets. Hence, as pressures on retailers and buyers in major markets increase, the challenge of managing capital at risk in the supply chain (money invested in fabric, machines, 'surplus' production and labour) has emerged as even more important, especially because the longer and more geographically distant the supply chain, the longer the replenishment period in retail markets and the longer it takes retailers to respond to shifts in market demands and tastes. Moreover, the longer the supply chain, the more capital is in circulation and at risk at any one time, and the longer is its turnover time, which delays its realisation as surplus value and potential profit (Harvey, 1982). This is significant, for the greater the amount and forms of capital that are at risk, the tighter are the demands of contractors on suppliers and the more likely are contractors to adopt more diverse production and geographical sourcing strategies.

What is important to bear in mind in all this, too, is that regional trade agreements such as CAFTA and EU enlargement policies influence these costings and also drive post-MFA responses of firms in supplier countries. As Neidik and Gereffi (2006) show for Turkey, and Bair (2006) demonstrates for Mexico, large and mid-sized firms with sufficient financial depth and global connections were already positioning themselves along the European rim and in Latin America to supply EU and US markets long before the ending of quotas under the ATC in 2005. Perhaps more surprisingly, some large Indian clothing firms have been preparing for the post-quota era by buying up small and medium-sized European distribution houses (in Italy and the UK) to access the EU market via domestically rooted legal entities that they own or control (Tewari, 2001). Similar adjustments have occurred in south-eastern Europe where some major domestic producers in Bulgaria, for example, have been approached by Chinese apparel firms seeking strategic corporate alignment as a way of closer market access to the EU. As Bair suggests, changes in these 'regional trading blocs' depend on the specific conditions and timings under which the local textile and clothing industries have been inserted into international commodity chains (see also Gereffi, 1999; Bair and Gereffi, 2001, 2002, 2003; Gereffi et al., 2002). The combined effect, however, is to suggest that the complete hollowing out of production and employment in the apparel sector in higher-cost locations is unlikely (Smith et al., 2008b). Consequently, workers and labour organisations need to be attentive to these supply chain dynamics if they are to shape the conditions of work that can emerge in those enterprises that remain viable. Regional production arrangements of these kinds may indeed sustain locational stability in some product areas over a period of time for workers in the industry. These, in turn, create limits to the global 'race to the bottom' for low-wage labour and renewed opportunities for direct worker action as international buyer and local producers increasingly agree on the need for corporate social responsibility.

We have shown elsewhere how EU buyers and Central and East European producers are experimenting with a wide range of strategies to sustain production within a context of increasing competition (Pickles et al., 2006; Smith et al., 2008b). Some producers have adapted to the demands of lean retailing, some have established extensive networks of regional and transborder subcontracting, and yet others have opted for, or been forced to accept, low-price assembly contracts, more reminiscent of a 'race to the bottom'. Some producers are experimenting with legal and illegal subcontracting to meet the demands for larger contracts and tighter production deadlines, some are cooperating with other small and medium enterprises to bid on the larger contracts available, and others are adding capacities, investing heavily in new technologies, enhanced training for workers, and local sourcing strategies to capture higher value contracts and larger rents in the supply chain. Industrial upgrading, reworking management–labour relations and worker-training programmes, technical and labour upgrading articulated with international corporate social responsibility and ethical workplace concerns to protect (and attract) future contracting have all become a central element of such restructuring. The result is a much more complex landscape of sourcing arrangements than simply competing on the basis of 'factor' costs – such as the price of labour – would imply.

Given that the cost of labour is generally around 8 to 12 per cent of total full-on-board (FOB) price for a garment, compared to around 60 per cent for fabric and trim, it is not surprising that buyers and producers have increasingly focused their attention on the sourcing of fabric and trim as a source of cost reduction and increased profit, rather than simply a search for cheaper labour. In some cases, this involves import substitution of more expensive inputs in favour of cheaper imports or domestically sourced materials. In other cases, producers have switched some or all of their production to domestic markets where sales volumes and prices may be lower but profit margins may be higher, particularly if producers can create local brands or access guaranteed markets like those to manufacture government uniforms or specialised outdoor clothing (Knappe, 2003; Pickles et al., 2006). The result in both cases may be a geographical shift towards more local supplier and buyer networks, with corresponding implications for the organisation of production and the organisational opportunities for workers. Significantly for the story we tell here, both phenomena (local sourcing and sales to the domestic market) have become important in Central and Eastern Europe and are even clearer in China and India (Berger et al., 1997; Berger and Lester, 1997; Tewari, 1999). What is important in all this, then, and notwithstanding the continual emergence of reports on poor working conditions and the use of child labour in international supply chains in the clothing industry, is for workers and their organisations to recognise the diverse trajectories local sourcing and domestic markets produce in each region and to interrogate the different opportunities and constraints they produce. Even in China, where arguably one of the world's most controlled labour forces operates, increasing levels of labour unrest and difficulties with large numbers of young migrant workers in low-wage assembly industries have led to growing enterprise and state commitment to improved working conditions, product and process upgrading, and corporatist strategies for enhancing enterprise responsibility (see Pun and Smith, Chapter 13 in this volume, on how the Chinese state has sought to control migrant workers in various manufacturing zones).

The importance of state socialist legacies
Export assembly production in CEE is almost exclusively for EU markets. Paradoxically, the structure and practices of organised labour under state socialism produced the very conditions for success in such forms of assembly industrialisation (see Herod et al., Chapter 1 in this volume, for a similar argument about geographical path dependence). With the shift from forms of 'full-package' soviet production to globalised assembly production, wages dropped significantly, stable work contracts were replaced by increasingly flexible working arrangements, and standardised socialist norms gave way to deregulated, and at times predatory, capitalist practices. This occurred at the very time that embedded party unionism had become largely de-legitimised, with the mass of state and former state workers disaffected with trade unions after 1989 and little pressure from workers for unionisation in new private firms. In important large former state-owned factories, trade unions continue to cooperate with managers, and health and labour inspectorates continue to regulate work conditions as they had before 1989. However, while trade unions and labour, health and environmental inspectorates were often ignored under state socialism, the integration of postsocialist enterprises into international value chains has provided important, albeit occasional, opportunities for worker mobilisation and for managers to garner contracts from buyers who are concerned about their compliance with the codes of conduct demanded by their customers.

While there may be a bifurcation of experience between non-unionised new firms and former state-owned factories, in those factories where unionisation remains significant, workers may benefit from wage and non-wage conditions that have their roots in state socialism. For example, in one former state-owned factory in a major garment-producing region in central Slovakia, the now privatised enterprises employ 2600 workers, of whom 70 per cent are unionised. Management has maintained a commitment to continuing worker supplements – what used to be called the 'social wage' of state socialism – above individual wage payments. These include enterprise contributions to a social fund to provide subsidised recreational facilities and financial assistance (low-cost credit and loans) to employees, the continued provision of onsite health services and medical care, and a series of wage subsidies averaging an addition of about 14 per cent to average monthly salary payments (monthly food subsidies, annual salary bonus payments, Mother's Day payments, cash payments to purchase factory-made clothing and transport subsidies). Management has retained the social wage partly because of continuing trade union presence and partly because of the increasingly tight labour markets as skilled stitchers are recruited away to other factories or leave the industry for higher-paying jobs. While such commitments enable management to maintain some workforce stability and thereby guarantee in-factory skill capacities, they also create pressures on factory cost structures at a time when contract prices are being squeezed downwards. One way in which some of the larger clothing enterprises are dealing with these pressures is to provide extra support to sustain core workers while engaging in secondary outsourcing to lower-cost producers in countries like the Ukraine (Pickles et al., 2006; Smith et al., 2008b). The implications these pressures and responses may have for the longer-term position of garment workers in countries like Slovakia is not yet clear. However, the terrain on which management and workers now have to act and the continuing role that the geographically and place-specific legacies of 'worker states' provide in shaping the landscape of production and the experience of workers is made particularly difficult by both the perceived and the real fragility of contracting relations in a fully liberalised trade environment. These difficulties are compounded by conceptual models of 'global industries' (such as textiles and clothing) that do not pay sufficient attention to the ways in which locally contingent labour and employment practices create a 'friction' to models of 'slippery space' and de-localisation.

Labour, work and the rise of ethical sourcing
In response to the deepening of competition in global production networks in the 1990s, largely stimulated by the opening of India and China and the liberalising of the system of quota constraints on access to the EU and US markets, Corporate Social Responsibility (CSR), ethical sourcing, fair work and monitoring of codes and standards have become much more important in the regulation of working conditions and employment practices. Indeed, labour unions and the ILO have increasingly supported 'fair work' programmes, corporate interests have focused to a greater extent on CSR and consumer organisations, and worker rights NGOs have focused more on ethical trading initiatives, ecological labelling, international standards, compliance monitoring and/or direct action campaigns. Here we identify three key aspects of this emerging global system of workplace governance. First, there is a set of internationally agreed-upon norms for workplace standards, such as the ILO's Core Labour Standards, which have provided the basis for the establishment of codes adopted by organisations such as the UK Ethical Trading Initiative (ETI). Second, there is a group of largely NGO and multi-organisational initiatives attempting to provide the basis for the negotiation and establishment of workplace Codes of Conduct and their monitoring and implementation. The most important are probably the Fair Labor Association (FLA) and Workers' Rights Consortium (WRC) initiatives in the USA and the ETI in the UK (see Hughes, 2001, 2005). Third, there are

individual corporate codes of conduct established and implemented by global corporations themselves, although increasingly with some of the multilateral and NGO institutions. In this section we highlight how the rolling out of such institutionalised practices
has transformed the regulation of workplaces in the CEE clothing sector, in some cases
creating improved conditions of work and new forms of (always partial) positional
power for workers to improve conditions in global supply chains, while in other cases
creating a kind of corporatist-gloss that demobilises direct action by workers either at
the level of the shopfloor or in broader terms.

In Central and Eastern European clothing factories there are real concerns about
freedom of association, harassment, health and safety violations, overtime and unpaid
wages, especially in smaller *de novo* firms (Musiolek, 2004; Hale and Wills, 2005).[2] There
have been notable instances of harassment and abuse, as the Clean Clothes Campaign
rightly highlights (see also Hale and Wills, 2005). For example, the case of four women in
Roska's cooperative in southern Bulgaria illustrated the tenuous and exploited position
of small-scale garment production for cross-border Greek contractors. Hence,

> [t]he four women tried to negotiate with the buyer [a Bulgarian intermediary for Greek
> contractors], but the buyer would not accept their price. Roska reports that another coop-
> erative of 20 women got orders but then were not paid for their work. They had finished
> the order, but as they became a source of competition for the client, the client did not pay
> them, citing a frivolous quality excuse. This is the way Roska believes the Greek employers
> control the sweatshop industry and prevent serious competition. (Clean Clothes Campaign,
> 2001, p. 3)

Poor working conditions, workplace abuses, instances of child labour, forced labour and
debt bondage occur throughout the region.

These kinds of abuses are, however, at times ameliorated by the existence of national
Labour Codes with their roots in state socialist ideologies concerning the protection of
the socialist worker. These legacies of institutional practices and discourses of worker
protection mean that the generally close relationship between the clothing industry and
sweatshops has been mediated through these institutions and discourses in different ways
in CEE than has been the case in other parts of the world. Part of their growing effectiveness (if indeed that is the case) derives from a change in the ways in which industry
and trade associations, multilateral institutions, and citizen interest groups have become
more actively engaged in major markets to ensure that imported clothing meets basic
labour and environmental standards.

New coalitions and associations of interest have emerged and new legislative practices
are being implemented, ranging from investment programmes for technical upgrading
and training to the deployment of non-tariff barriers (which themselves range from anti-
dumping clauses to protect local industries and experiments in collegiate licensed apparel
with designated factory programmes to rewarding with higher prices and guaranteed
contracts those producers who improve labour standards). One core element of such
emerging forms of governance, impacting directly on workplace practices and working
conditions, is CSR.

There is an extensive debate over the relative merits of corporate social responsibility,
codes of conduct and multi-stakeholder approaches to ethical trade (Hale, 2000; Hughes,
2001, 2005; Jenkins et al., 2002; Hale and Wills, 2005). While some dismiss codes of

conduct outright, largely because they fail to deal with the critical issue of unequal power relations in apparel supply chains, Hughes (2001, 2005) has highlighted the complexity of potential effects of codes of conduct established through the UK's ETI and the limits set by corporate imperatives of cost competition and divergent strategic positions of buyer departments and ethical monitoring departments, even within the same corporate organisation. In the CEE apparel industry the increasing adoption of such codes in some production locations is having real, yet uneven, effects. For example, in one firm in southern Bulgaria with two production locations and a 'show factory' producing for the clothing retailer GAP contracted through a Turkish buyer, the implementation of codes of conduct (checked regularly through buyer and contractor inspections) was a critical part of the firm's strategy for gaining and retaining orders. Moreover, in a competitive local labour market, managers believe that the presence of such codes and the improvements that have resulted from their implementation have enabled the factory to attract workers more easily. The codes also have the further advantage of inducing the Turkish intermediary to maintain a regular payment schedule, which in turn results in regular wage payments to workers. Interviews with trade union representatives in Bulgaria also suggest that codes provide important, yet always partial, positional power for workers in the industry in a way that they did not have in the past, although these are not without their problems. Thus,

> [c]odes tend to improve working conditions in factories, because otherwise management would lose their contract if they didn't implement them. The problem is that buyers only negotiate with management. Social auditors do talk with workers and trade unions when they visit the factory. Workers are interviewed separately (not with the trade union). They often focus on the payment of overtime. But in Kurdjali it is only the firms with contracts with large US and EU buyers (for example, Adidas) that have social audits. (KNCB interview, KNCB Kurdjali, 2004)

Equally, the legacies of a continuing and extensive factory inspectorate system enable certain working conditions to be monitored carefully. For example, interviews in Bulgaria at the Plovdiv Labour Inspectorate suggest that factories are receiving increased support from buyers for the improvement of labour and work conditions, especially through factory visits and code enforcement. Buyers such as Puma and Adidas, both large contractors in the Plovdiv region, have visited the Labour Inspectorate even though much of their contracting is carried out through Greek middlemen. Puma visits often involve teams with staff responsible for different parts of factory monitoring, such as working time, work conditions, health and safety and garment quality control. Indeed, codes of conduct are used explicitly by buyers to identify factories to which they are able to contract production. In Bulgaria, codes of conduct often resemble the national labour code, although in addition they focus on ILO core standards relating to age, sex and ethnic discrimination. As a consequence, the Labour Inspectorate is actually reducing its monitoring schedule in factories that have enforced codes of conduct with Western buyers, particularly where the inspectorates are satisfied that firms apply such codes across their entire supply chain and among all their subcontractors in the region. They are then able to redirect their efforts to less regulated workplaces.

In this sense, codes of conduct play a dual role as a disciplining and an enabling 'technology' to retain workers by improving work conditions in factories and to enable contractors to retain orders with Western buyers. In these cases, they also seem to have the indirect function of expanding the range and effectiveness of state monitoring across a broader range of regional producers. Hurley (2005) has suggested that the implementation of the labour code and factory inspections are more problematic in smaller firms in Bulgaria, but it remains unclear whether this will continue to be the case if inspectorates continue to upgrade their capacities and are able to work in more targeted ways.

Not surprisingly, the codes and the inspectorates have, at times, come under threat, particularly when they have figured as flashpoints over struggles to deregulate the industry and reduce state expenditures. For example, in Slovakia in the early 2000s the neoliberal state was fully committed to the widespread liberalisation of the labour code; hiring and firing of workers was made much easier and short-term contract work became effectively deregularised, with such workers no longer able to access the protection accorded to those on more permanent contracts (Smith et al., 2008a). For the apparel industry such changes have immediate effects – not least the way in which unprotected short-term work is often used to deal with seasonal fluctuations in the contracting system. These forms of liberalisation have more limited impacts on larger firms and the former state-owned sector, where longer-term employment contracts are more common.

The resulting picture is of a highly differentiated landscape of working conditions across the region in which the legacies of state socialism and embedded institutional practices of labour regulation continue to matter to the experience of factory work and labour organising. But these institutional and discursive legacies are not mere 'residues' of that prior period, but are the specific sites and terrain on which struggle continues to occur. Thus, for example, the collapse of the neoliberal Slovak government in 2006 and the election of a left-nationalist bloc with strong trade union support have already led to the rewriting of the liberalised labour code, with important and potentially positive implications for conditions of work in the clothing sector.

Conclusion

The worker states of Central and Eastern Europe were anything but worker democracies and the socialist impulses of individuals were typically overridden by the strong bureaucratic powers of party cadres and *nomenklatura* power. State accumulation of power and wealth came at the expense of incipient worker movements and democratic workplaces, although paradoxically it did lead to new forms of negotiated workplace politics, as managers struggled to sustain worker support for hoarding and storing labour and raw materials to meet the demands of centrally set planning targets. Lacking political power, workers nonetheless were able to sustain some influence over the allocation of wage bills and ensure that social services and community infrastructures were underwritten by state enterprises.

Workers quickly lost even these 'negotiated' tools after 1989 and their nominal voices of organisation, the party unions, struggled initially to rearticulate their political role in more liberalised contexts. Enterprise closure and unemployment in the early 1990s further weakened trade union structures, and as new private enterprises began to emerge in the 1990s they did so largely hostile to trade union organisation. In the clothing industry, the result of decline in the integrated textile and clothing state firms was loss of employment for all but core workers in key enterprises, and this was quickly followed by the re-employment of former stitchers at low wages in the smaller workshops in the towns and villages. Working conditions deteriorated, fly-by-night operators took advantage of (mostly female) workers, and long working hours and abusive work became the norm in many workshops and factories through the region.

By the mid-1990s, however, heightened interregional competition itself faced further competition from large global producing regions like Turkey, India and China. The result was a rapid 'sorting out' of the industry and a desperate search for long-term contracts, product upgrading, and the addition of higher-value services. By the early 2000s, the pace of change in the postsocialist clothing industry was creating intense uncertainties among manufacturers and great concern among workers. Centre-right governments throughout the region had systematically undermined labour legislation and the effectiveness of state agencies, such as labour inspectorates and health and safety inspectorates, while trade unions – now restructured and better positioned in the economy, partly as a result of their participation in privatisation programmes and partly because of enhanced organisational support from their international bodies – still had been unable to re-establish any strong positions in other than a few former state enterprises.

The current situation seems to be one in which parts of postsocialist Europe are seeing a return to power of centre-left governments, often supported directly by organised labour, and they are already opening negotiations about renewing their commitment to mechanisms of trilateralism and strengthening the instruments of state regulation in workplaces. To some extent these interests coincide with those of enterprise managers now desperate to re-position their companies in the rapidly changing international value chains. Under threat of a 'drift to China' and demands by buyers for larger orders, tighter deadlines and higher quality goods, manager–worker relations in Central and East European clothing firms are changing quickly. Some enterprises have reintroduced the former state enterprise model of onsite social provision (daycare for children, cafeterias and bus services), others are experimenting with the incorporation of higher-value production and tasks (with the corresponding investment in worker training and higher wages), and yet others are developing innovative cooperative ventures or investment in upstream and downstream parts of the production cycle (through joint ventures, cooperative bids for larger contracts, or regional and cross-border subcontracting). The role of international trade unions, ethical production and trading campaigns, consumer-led pressure, environmental movement calls for ecologically sound production and corporate responsibility and monitoring efforts are all becoming important elements in the calculus of contracting and production. In particular, at the enterprise level, while these function as barriers to entry for some producers, for many others they provide opportunities to capitalise on market strengths, workforce capacities, position in the region and firms' ability to mobilise once again the legacies from prior periods of export production.

In each of these settings, there remains an unsteady balance between downward pressure on wages and working conditions wrought by intense price competition for export contracts on the one hand, and the necessity of adopting strategies of industrial and product upgrading to meet enhanced contracting demands on the part of buyers on the other hand. But each of the dynamics we have explored in this chapter highlights the impossibility of operating with conceptual models of work in the global economy that are *not* attentive to place specificity and locally/historically situated institutional practices. Each structures the positional power of workers in the former workers' states in important, yet contradictory, ways. Worker states may not have delivered their promise to workers, but the legacies of worker states, the local organisation of export platforms and the responses of local actors to broader struggles over the shape of globalisation may provide important, if fragile, capacities for shaping and sustaining future clothing work and the conditions of that work in this region.

Acknowledgements
Support for this research was provided by the National Science Foundation Award No. BCS/SBE/GRS 0225088 and BCS-0551085. The authors would like to thank our close collaborators Poli Roukova, Milan Buček, and Robert Begg, as well as Stelian Dimitrov and Katya Mileva (Department of Geography, University of Sofia), Mariana Nikolova, Maxi Emilova, Christa Petkova, Angel Sharenkov (Institute of Geography, Bulgarian Academy of Sciences), Aneta Spendzhatova (Political Science, UNC-CH) and Rudolf Pástor (Economics University, Bratislava) for their research assistance in Bulgaria and Slovakia. We would also like to thank Gary Gereffi, Meenu Tewari, Annelies Goger and Dennis Arnold for their input. A previous version of the chapter was presented at the 'Seminars of the Aegean' on the theme of 'Changing European Spaces: Winners and Losers', Chania, Crete, Greece, 2007. We alone are responsible for the interpretations we give in this chapter to the findings of our collaborative research efforts.

Notes

1. Perhaps the one main exception was Solidarity in Poland which retained – largely as a result of its position against the party state before 1989 – a strong base of support among workers and has spent periods of time in government.
2. Interviews conducted at the Trade Union Confederation of Slovakia in Bratislava also confirm such reports.

References

Abernathy, F.H., A. Volpe and D. Weil (2006), 'The future of the apparel and textile industries: prospects and choices for public and private actors', special issue on Trade liberalization, industrial upgrading and region-alization in the global clothing industry, *Environment and Planning A*, **38** (12), 2207–32.

Abernathy, F., J. Dunlop, J. Hammond and D. Weil (1999), *A Stitch in Time: Lean Retailing and the Transformation of Manufacturing – Lessons from the Apparel and Textile Industries*, New York: Oxford University Press.

Bair, J. (2006), 'Regional trade and production blocs in a global industry: towards a comparative framework for research,' *Environment and Planning A*, **38** (12), 2233–52.

Bair, J. and G. Gereffi (2001), 'Local clusters in global chains: the causes and consequences of export dynamism in Torreon's blue jeans industry', *World Development*, **29** (11) (November), 1885–903.

Bair, J. and G. Gereffi (2002), 'NAFTA and the apparel commodity chain: corporate strategies, inter-firm networks, and industrial upgrading', in G. Gereffi, D. Spener and J. Bair (eds), *Free Trade and Uneven Development: The North American Apparel Industry After NAFTA*, Philadelphia, PA: Temple University Press, pp. 23–50.

Bair, J. and G. Gereffi (2003), 'Upgrading, uneven development, and jobs in the North America apparel industry', *Global Networks*, **3** (2), 143–69.

Begg, R. and J. Pickles (1998), 'Institutions, social networks, and ethnicity in the cultures of transition: industrial change, mass unemployment and regional transformation in Bulgaria', in J. Pickles and A. Smith (eds), *Theorising Transition: The Political Economy of Post-Communist Transformations*, London: Routledge, pp. 115–46.

Begg, R., J. Pickles and A. Smith (2003), 'Cutting it: European integration, trade regimes and the reconfiguration of East-Central European apparel production', *Environment and Planning A*, **35**, 2191–207.

Berger, S. and R. Lester (1997), *Made by Hong Kong*, New York: Oxford University Press.

Berger, S., D. Gartner and K. Karty (1997), 'Textiles and clothing in Hong Kong', in S. Berger and R. Lester (eds), *Made by Hong Kong*, New York: Oxford University Press, pp. 139–85.

Burawoy, M. (1996), 'The state and economic involution: Russia through a China lens', *World Development*, **24** (6), 1105–17.

Burawoy, M. and P. Krotov (1993), 'The economic basis of Russia's political crisis', *New Left Review*, **198**, 49–69.

Cellarius, B.A. (2004), *In the Land of Orpheus: Rural Livelihoods and Nature Conservation in Postsocialist Bulgaria*, Madison, WI: University of Wisconsin Press.

Clarke, S. (1993), 'The contradictions of "state socialism"', in S. Clarke, P. Fairbrother, M. Burawoy and P. Krotov (eds), *What about the Workers? Workers and the Transition to Capitalism in Russia*, London: Verso, pp. 5–29.

Clean Clothes Campaign (2001), 'Inside Roska's cooperative', *Newsletter* 14, available at: www.cleanclothes. org/news/newsletter14-bulgaria.htm, Last accessed November 2007.

Coe, N.M., M. Hess, H.W.-C. Yeung, P. Dicken and J. Henderson (2004), '"Globalizing" regional development: a global production networks perspective', *Transactions of the Institute of British Geographers*, **29** (4) (December), 468–84.

Conway, P. (2006), 'Global implications of unraveling textile and apparel quotas', paper presented at the 'Industrial upgrading, off-shore production and labor' conference, Center on Globalization, Governance and Competitiveness, Duke University, USA, November.

EU High Level Working Group (2004), 'The challenge of 2005: European textiles and clothing in a quota free environment', available at http://ec.europa.eu/enterprise/textile/documents/hlg_report_30_06_04.pdf, last accessed March 2009.

Fröbel, F., J. Heinrichs and O. Kreye (1980), *The New International Division of Labour: Structural Unemployment in Industrialised Countries and Industrialisation in Developing Countries*, Cambridge: Cambridge University Press.

Gereffi, G. (1999), 'International trade and industrial upgrading in the apparel commodity chain', *Journal of International Economics*, **48** (1), 37–70.

Gereffi, G. (2003), 'The international competitiveness of Asian economies in the global apparel commodity chain', *International Journal of Business and Society*, **4** (2) (July), 71–110.

Gereffi, G. (2006), 'The new offshoring of jobs and global development', ILO Social Policy Lectures, Jamaica, December 2005, Geneva: International Labour Organization, International Institute for Labour Studies.

Gereffi, G. and O. Memedovic (2003), *The Global Apparel Value Chain: What Prospects for Upgrading by Developing Countries?*, Vienna: United Nations Industrial Development Organization, Sectoral Studies Series.

Gereffi, G., D. Spener and J. Bair (eds) (2002), *Free Trade and Uneven Development: The North American Apparel Industry after NAFTA*, Philadelphia, PA: Temple University Press.

Gospodinova, Z. (2006), 'Low qualification levels an obstacle to economic competitiveness,' Balkan Institute for Labour and Social Policy (BILSP), 12 December, available at: http://www.eurofound.europa. eu.eiro/2006/10/articles/bg0610049i.html (last accessed 1 August 2009).

Grabher, G. (1994), 'The disembedded regional economy: the transformation of East German industrial complexes into Western enclaves', in A. Amin and N. Thrift (eds), *Globalization, Institutions and Regional Development in Europe*, Oxford: Oxford University Press, pp. 177–95.

Graziani, G. (1998), 'Globalization of production in the textile and clothing industries: the case of Italian foreign direct investment and outward processing in Eastern Europe', *BRIE Working Paper 128* (May), Berkeley, CA: University of California.

Hale, A. (2000), 'What hope for "ethical" trade in the globalised garment industry?', *Antipode*, **32** (4), 349–56.

Hale, A. (2005), 'The phase-out of the Multi-Fibre Arrangement from the perspective of workers', in A. Hale and J. Wills (eds), *Threads of Labour: Garment Industry Supply Chains from the Workers' Perspective*, Oxford: Blackwell, pp. 210–33.

Hale, A. and Wills, J. (2005) (eds), *Threads of Labour: Garment Industry Supply Chains from the Workers' Perspective*, Oxford: Blackwell.

Harvey, D. (1982), *The Limits to Capital*, Oxford: Blackwell.

Herod, A. (1998), 'Theorising trade unions in transition,' in J. Pickles and A. Smith (eds), *Theorising Transition: The Political Economy of Post-Communist Transformations*, London and New York: Routledge, pp. 197–217.

Herod, A. (2001), *Labor Geographies: Workers and the Landscapes of Capitalism*, New York: Guilford Press.

Hughes, A. (2001), 'Multi-stakeholder approaches to ethical trade: towards a reorganisation of UK retailers' global supply chains?', *Journal of Economic Geography*, **1**, 421–37.

Hughes, A. (2005), 'Corporate strategy and the management of ethical trade: the case of the UK food and clothing sectors', *Environment and Planning A*, **37**, 1145–63.

Hurley, J. (2005), 'Unravelling the web: supply chains and workers' lives in the garment industry', in A. Hale and J. Wills (eds), *Threads of Labour: Garment Industry Supply Chains from the Workers' Perspective*, Oxford: Blackwell, pp. 95–132.

International Labour Organization (ILO) (1996), 'Globalization changes the face of textile, clothing, and footwear industries', Monday 28 October, available at: www.ilo.org/public/english/bureau/inf/pr/1996/33. htm; last accessed 12 March 2006.

Jenkins, R., R. Pearson and G. Seyfang (eds) (2002), *Corporate Responsibility and Labour Rights: Codes of Conduct in the Global Economy*, London: Earthscan.

Knappe, M. (2003), 'Textiles and clothing: What happens after 2005?', *International Trade Forum*, International Trade Centre, available at: http://www.tradeforum.org/news/fullstory.php/aid/611/Reaching_Out_to_Garmout_Manufacturers.html (last accessed 1 August 2009).

KNCB Kurdjali (2004), Interview with KNCB representatives, Kurdjali, Bulgaria, May.

Kornai, J. (1992), *The Socialist System: The Political Economy of State Socialism*, Oxford: Clarendon.

Kubicek, P. (1999), 'Organized labour in postcommunist states: will the Western sun set on it, too?', *Comparative Politics*, **32** (1), 83–102.

Ledeneva, A.V. (1998), *Russia's Economy of Favours: Blat, Networking and Informal Exchange*, Cambridge: Cambridge University Press.

Mayer, G. (2004), 'Not totally naked: textiles and clothing trade in a quota free environment', Geneva: UNCTAD.

Musiolek, B. (2004), *Made in . . . Eastern Europe: The New 'Fashion Colonies'*, Berlin: Clean Clothes Campaign.

Neidik, B. and G. Gereffi (2006), 'Explaining Turkey's emergence and sustained competitiveness as a full-package supplier of apparel', *Environment and Planning A*, **39** (12), 2285–303.

Nordås, H.K. (2004), 'The global textile and clothing industry post the agreement on textiles and clothing', Discussion Paper No. 5, World Trade Organisation, Geneva, Switzerland.

Organisation for Economic Cooperation and Development (OECD) (2003), *Liberalising Trade in Textiles and Clothing: A Survey of Quantitative Studies*, Paris: OECD Trade Directorate.

Ost, D. (2002), 'The weakness of strong social movements: models of unionism in the East European context', *European Journal of Industrial Relations*, **8**, 33–51.

Ost, D. (2005), *The Defeat of Solidarity: Anger and Politics in Postcommunist Europe*, Ithaca, NY: Cornell University Press.

Oxfam (2004), *Trading Away Our Rights: Women Working in Global Supply Chains*, Oxford: Oxfam International.

Pavlínek, P. (2002), 'Transformation of the Central and East European passenger car industry: selective peripheral integration through foreign direct investment', *Environment and Planning A*, **34**, 1685–709.

Pavlínek, P. and A. Smith (1998), 'Internationalization and embeddedness in East-Central European transition: the contrasting geographies of inward investment in the Czech and Slovak Republics', *Regional Studies*, **32** (7), 619–38.

Pellegrin, J. (2001), *The Political Economy of Competitiveness in an Enlarged Europe*, New York: Palgrave.

Pickles, J. (1995), 'Restructuring state enterprises: industrial geography and Eastern European transitions', *Geographische Zeitschrift*, **2**, 114–31.

Pickles, J. (2002), 'Gulag Europe? Mass unemployment, new firm creation, and tight labour markets in the Bulgarian apparel industry', in A. Rainnie, A. Smith and A. Swain (eds), *Work, Employment and Transition: Restructuring Livelihoods in Post-Communism*, London: Routledge, pp. 246–72.

Pickles, J. (2006), 'Trade liberalization, upgrading and regionalization in the global apparel industry', *Environment and Planning A*, **38** (12), 2201–06.

Pickles, J. and R. Begg (2000), 'Ethnicity, state violence, and neo-liberal transitions in post-communist Bulgaria', *Growth and Change*, **31** (2), 179–210.

Pickles, J. and A. Smith (2005), 'Technologies of transition: foreign investment and the (re-) articulation of East Central Europe into the global economy', in D. Turnock (ed.), *Foreign Direct Investment and Regional Development in East Central Europe and the Former Soviet Union*, Aldershot: Ashgate, pp. 21–37.

Pickles, J., A. Smith, M. Buček, P. Roukova and B. Begg (2006), 'Upgrading, changing competitive pressures and diverse practices in the East European apparel industry', *Environment and Planning A*, **38** (12), 2305–24.

Pollert, A. (1999), 'Trade unionism in transition in Central and Eastern Europe', *European Journal of Industrial Relations*, **5** (2), 209–34.

Rainnie, A., A. Smith and A. Swain (2002), 'Employment and work restructuring in "transition"', in A. Rainnie, A. Smith and A. Swain (eds), *Work, Employment and Transition: Restructuring Livelihoods in Post-Communism*, London: Routledge, pp. 9–34.

Smith, A. (1998), *Reconstructing the Regional Economy: Industrial Transformation and Regional Development in Slovakia*, Cheltenham, UK and Northampton, MA: Edward Elgar.

Smith, A. (2003), 'Power relations, industrial clusters and regional transformations: pan-European integration and outward processing in the Slovak clothing industry', *Economic Geography*, **79**, 17–40.

Smith, A. and A. Stenning (2006), 'Beyond household economies: articulations and spaces of economic practice in post-socialism', *Progress in Human Geography*, **30** (2), 190–213.

Smith, A., A. Stenning, A. Rochovská and D. Świątek (2008a), 'The emergence of a working poor: labour markets, neoliberalisation and diverse economies in postsocialist cities', *Antipode*, **40** (2), 283–311.

Smith, A., J. Pickles, M. Buček, B. Begg and P. Roukova (2008b), 'Reconfiguring "post-socialist regions": trans-border networks and regional competition in the Slovak and Ukrainian clothing industry', *Global Networks*, **8**(3), 281–307.

Smith, A., J. Pickles, B. Begg, P. Roukova and M. Buček (2005), 'Outward processing, EU enlargement and regional relocation in the European textiles and clothing industry: reflections on the European Commission's Communication on "The future of the textiles and clothing sector in the enlarged European Union"', *European Urban and Regional Studies*, **12** (1), 83–91.

Smollet, E. (1989), 'The economy of jars', *Ethnologie Europa*, **19** (2), 125–40.

Staddon, C. (2001), 'Restructuring the Bulgarian wood processing sector: linkages between resource exploitation, capital accumulation and transition in a post-communist locality', *Environment and Planning A*, **33** (4), 607–28.

Standing, G. (2002), 'The babble of euphemisms: re-embedding social protection in "transformed" labour markets', in A. Rainnie, A. Smith and A. Swain (eds), *Work, Employment and Transition: Restructuring Livelihoods in Post-Communism*, London: Routledge, pp. 35–54.

Stengg, W. (2001), 'The textile and clothing industry in the EU: a survey', Enterprise Papers No. 2, Enterprise Directorate General, European Commission.

Tewari, M. (1999), 'Successful adjustment in Indian industry: the case of Ludhiana's woollen knitwear industry', *World Development*, **27** (9), 1651–71.

Tewari, M. (2001), 'The challenge of reform: how Tamil Nadu's textile and apparel sector is facing the pressures of liberalization', India Program, Center for International Development, Harvard University, available at: http://www.cid.harvard.edu/archive/india/pdfs/challenge_textile_lib_tewari0101.pdf, accessed March 2009.

UNCTAD (2005), *TNCs and the Removal of Textiles and Clothing Quotas*, New York and Geneva: UNCTAD.

US-ITC (2004), 'Textiles and apparel: assessment of the competitiveness of certain foreign suppliers to the US market', Washington DC, report declassified in January 2004.

7 Tele-mediated servants and self-servants of the global economy: labour in the era of ICT-enabled e-commerce
Matthew Zook and Michael Samers

Introduction
The relationship between labour and information and communication technologies (ICTs) has remained startlingly understudied by economic geographers,[1] and beyond the large body of work on call centres, this dearth is equally prevalent across the social sciences more generally (Downey, 2001).[2] Notable contributions by geographers and related thinkers on the role of technology, such as Brunn et al.'s (2004) edited collection *Geography and Technology*, Leinbach and Brunn's (2001) *Worlds of E-Commerce*, Wheeler et al.'s (2000) *Cities in the Telecommunications Age*, and the otherwise comprehensive *Cybercities Reader* (Graham, 2004), say very little about this relationship. And while economists have for a long time tackled these connections, their analyses are often limited to sectoral studies whose geographies may be implied rather than explicit. It is in this sense, then, that our chapter explores the explicit relationship between labour and ICTs (or, more specifically, information and communication technology-enabled e-commerce – henceforth ICT-EC).[3] We view the use of ICT-EC between firms (so-called B2B) or firms and consumers (B2C), as a key element in the transformation of work and labour relations, and it is ICT-enabled e-commerce that forms the core (though not exclusive domain) of our analysis.[4] Our argument weaves a story that involves both the temporal and spatial dimensions of this relationship. A focus on its spatial dimensions is vital as a corrective to the dominance of the temporal or historical emphasis so dear to other – especially popular – analyses of the subject. Though we mainly draw on research from richer countries (or regions), at least some of our discussion is relevant to labour issues in poorer countries (or regions) as well. Moreover, like most sophisticated and nuanced discussions of the relationship between ICTs and economic geographies (for example, Leamer and Storper, 2001), we wish to abandon technological determinism, and rather explore the dialectical relationship between technology and social relations.[5]

With these caveats and explanations in hand, we do three things in this chapter. First, we review the growth of e-commerce in the US context, paying particular attention to dismissing simplistic ideas that the 'Internet is everywhere'; second, we critically assess the broad relationship between ICT-EC and labour within the space–time of capitalism by dispelling certain myths or common arguments about this relationship; and third, we deepen the analysis by discussing the implications of ICT-EC for the welfare of workers.

The expansion and composition of ICT-enabled e-commerce: an overview
E-commerce, that is the application of ICTs to market-based transactions, can be conceptualised in a number of ways, ranging from simple email-based orders between

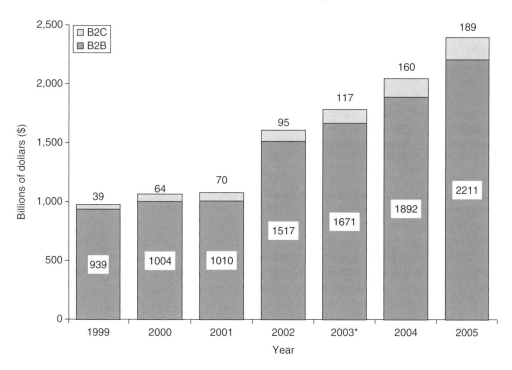

Note: * Beginning in 2003 sales by manufacturers' sales branches and offices are included in B2B: US Census E-stats.

Source: E-commerce figures are based on data from the US Census E-stats Program (http://www.census. gov/eos/www/ebusiness614.htm); B2B E-commerce consists of Manufacturing and Merchant Whole Trade and B2C consists of Retail Trade and Selected Services.

Figure 7.1 *Share of Business-to-Business (B2B) and Business-to-Consumer (B2C) e-commerce (US data), 1998–2005*

firms, to individuals shopping at online stores, to integrated and automated supply chain management tied to sophisticated logistics systems (OECD, 2001; Urbaczewski et al., 2002). Common to all these definitions is the use of electronic technology to transmit information, although the use and integration of the transmitted data varies widely. Due to this heterogeneity, the US Census (2007) defines e-commerce quite broadly as 'goods and services sold online' via 'the use of the internet, intranet, extranet, as well as proprietary networks that run systems such as Electronic Data Interchange (EDI)'.[6] This definition provides a consistent data source over time that charts the expansion of ICT-enabled e-commerce between a variety of actors and within a number of sectors.

For example, Figure 7.1 illustrates the size and growth of the two principal forms of e-commerce, that is business-to-business (B2B) and business-to-consumer (B2C).[7] It shows that e-commerce activity has steadily expanded since the late 1990s and represented US$2.4 trillion of transactions in 2005. More significantly, it illustrates that the bulk of e-commerce activity is between businesses (B2B), as B2C e-commerce represents only 7.9 per cent of this activity. Therefore, contrary to the rhetoric of Internet

Table 7.1   Top sectors with e-commerce as a percentage of total shipments (US data), 2004

NAICS Code*	Description	Value of e-commerce shipments, 2004, billions of dollars ($)	e-commerce as % of total shipments
4242	Drugs, drug proprietaries and druggists' sundries (wholesale)	246 028	53.0
336	Transportation equipment manufacturing	346 473	52.2
312	Beverage and tobacco product manufacturing	52 783	47.2
315	Apparel manufacturing	8694	26.1
314	Textile product mills	8472	25.4
324	Petroleum and coal products manufacturing	77 527	24.8
335	Electrical equipment, appliance, and components	25 177	24.2
454	Non-store retailers (retail)	53 630	23.9
5615	Travel arrangement and reservation services (services)	6268	22.2
334	Computer and electronic product manufacturing	76 197	21.0
325	Chemical manufacturing	102 967	19.5
333	Machinery manufacturing	52 292	19.4
331	Primary metal manufacturing	33 410	18.6
326	Plastics and rubber products manufacturing	33 220	18.2
4232	Furniture and home furnishings (wholesale)	11 250	14.7
4244	Groceries and related products (wholesale)	77 791	14.1

Note: * North American Industry Classification System.

Source: E-commerce figures are based on data from the US Census E-stats Program (http://www.census. gov/eos/www/ebusiness614.htm); some sectors (for example, wholesale apparel or motor vehicles) do not appear in this table due to data restrictions based on confidentiality.

ubiquity and despite the mass-market visibility of online retailers like Amazon.com, most e-commerce activity takes place 'behind the scenes' in transactions between businesses (B2B). This has serious implications for where and how workers will be impacted by the use of e-commerce. Retail jobs are arguably the least impacted by e-commerce, which accounted for only 2.5 per cent of retail sales in the US in 2005. This contrasts sharply with manufacturing and wholesaling, in which 26.7 and 18.3 per cent respectively of all sales were conducted via e-commerce systems (US Census, 2007).

This variation between the level of adoption of e-commerce extends to the sectoral level. Table 7.1 illustrates the top sectors in terms of percentage of sales that utilise e-commerce and the value of these sales.[8] Not surprisingly, given our observation above, the table is dominated by manufacturing and wholesaling sectors with particularly high levels of e-commerce adoption within oligopsonistic sectors. Firm size has been repeatedly identified as a factor in e-commerce implementation. While e-commerce is arguably a boon to small and medium-sized enterprises, since it provides a low-cost means to compete globally (Auger and Gallaugher, 1997; OECD, 2001), smaller firms (particularly from non-technology sectors) often find it difficult to implement e-commerce (Fillis et al., 2004) or find themselves pushed into adopting systems desired by the powerhouses of an industry. For example, transportation equipment manufacturing is dominated by a few big firms that introduced e-commerce systems, such as Covisint (Kandampully, 2003), which redistribute power away from suppliers and to assemblers (Rutherford and Holmes, 2007). This suggests for labour that, in addition to the nature of one's work, one's place within the commodity or value chain is increasingly important in determining job security and wages. The 2005 bankruptcy filing of auto parts manufacturer Delphi Corporation highlights the difficult position that faces suppliers to dominant players in a commodity chain. Moreover, the appearance of a number of 'low-tech' sectors such as beverage and tobacco manufacturing, apparel manufacturing and textile mills in Table 7.1 highlights that e-commerce adoption is a potential concern for labour in industries seemingly far removed from ICTs.

The US Census data on e-commerce is limited to the United States and unfortunately does not provide spatial information. It is clear, however, that ICT-enabled e-commerce has become a global, rather than simply a US, phenomenon (OECD, 2006), even if many people, businesses and parts of the world are only marginal participants or are even non-participants. While there is no comparable dataset on e-commerce at the global level, a simple, albeit rough, proxy is the growing number of Internet users. As Figure 7.2 illustrates, the number of Internet users has been steadily expanding since the 1990s, and by 2007 there were close to 1.1. billion people with Internet access at home, work or public facilities. Moreover, the make-up of the user population has evolved from largely US-centric in 1997 to an increasingly global population, albeit one that continues to be unevenly distributed (for example, it is clustered within urbanised areas) (Zook, 2005). Emblematic of this change is China's increased share of Internet users, growing from 0.4 per cent in 1997 to 12.1 per cent in 2007. This expansion of Internet use (and, by implication, the reach of e-commerce) represents a widening of accessible labour.

Although capital has long sought sources of lower-cost labour, the essential element of e-commerce (that is, the use of electronic technology to share information) has greatly reduced the cost and difficulty in accessing and controlling distant labour. This, however, does not imply a simple technologically determined 'race to the bottom'. Our brief review highlights some of the sectoral and geographical complexities of e-commerce use and argues that jobs are not simply disappearing into the ether of e-commerce, nor is all labour equally accessible. For example, despite the expansion of online retailers and service providers, retail purchases continue to be made largely offline, and many personal services such as hairdressers and house cleaners simply require that labour be physically present (Drezner, 2004). On the other hand, ICT-EC has allowed for significant changes for labour within a number of sectors and jobs. Powerful point of sale (POS) technologies within large retailers such as Wal-Mart increase distribution and stocking efficiency, and self-checkout kiosks have lowered the number of needed cashiers. Moreover, it is clear that for some service occupations, such as call centre operators, ICTs will have a significant effect in shaping the form and geography of the industry, not to mention call centre operators' lives, even if the transactions involved do not often involve a 'sale'. In short, it is not e-commerce per se that changes conditions for labour; ICT-EC is not 'everywhere' nor does it change 'everything'. Instead, it is the way in which ICT-EC is

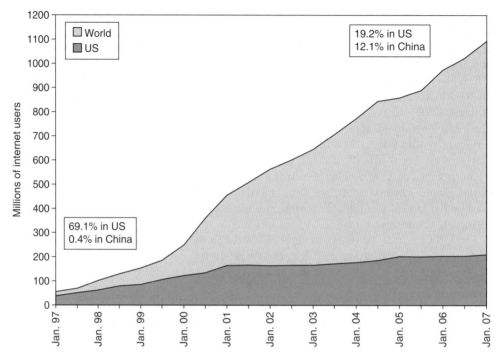

Source: Longitudinal data assembled by authors from NUA (2000), ClickZ Stats (2005), and InternetWorldStats.com (2007).

Figure 7.2   Growth of Internet users worldwide, 1997–2007

used to change the accessibility of labour that reshapes the spatial organisation of labour practices (Wynarczyk, 2005; Wright and Lund, 2006).

ICT-EC and labour under capitalism: a critical assessment
Despite the complexity of ICT-EC, some 'vulgar' readings of the relationship between technology and labour within capitalism continue to reproduce some general myths about the relationship between ICT-EC, labour and space. Below, we briefly discuss some of these overly simplistic (and sometimes alarmist) arguments.

Does ICT-EC lead to deskilling and the end of human labour?
A common refrain – indeed a well-rehearsed idea – is that technology leads ineluctably to either the 'deskilling' of labour (Braverman, 1974), poor 'job quality' (Rubery and Grimshaw, 2001), or redundancy. While these are certainly tendencies within capitalism, such tendencies are temporally provisional and spatially uneven. For example, while ICTs have allowed police officers to access data remotely and directly when 'in the field' (thus eliminating much of the work of clerical intermediaries such as dispatchers), the use of the Internet and official police webpages for crime and related services has created a demand for the new skills of 'webmasters' among police forces (O'Mahoney and Barley, 1999). Being a 'webmaster' involves at least a certain degree of computer

literacy and related communication skills. Similarly, while the technology associated with twenty-first century capitalism has created millions of entry-level, data-entry jobs that have replaced skilled manufacturing positions in the 'higher wage' economies (for example, Reich, 1991), it has also enabled the creation of semi-skilled jobs in call centres (for example, in India), which require quite sophisticated English and other 'cultural' skills (Poster, 2007; Taylor and Bain, Chapter 24 in this volume). Finally, ICT-EC has also accompanied the development of skilled positions (symbolic-analytic jobs) in cities from Dubai to São Paolo.

With regard to the argument that ICT-EC simply reduces the aggregate (global) number of jobs, science fiction films and popular accounts have done their part to reinforce this misperception. To be sure, deskilling and job losses are certainly facilitated by ICT-EC, but the destruction and creation of jobs is a geographically differentiated affair that owes as much to a host of other processes as it does directly to ICT-EC (for example, Rubery and Grimshaw, 2001). Let us consider some of the evidence in this respect. In the US retail sector, census data show that only 2 per cent of retail sales are conducted online, yet grocery retailing, for example, relies upon ICT-EC for an assortment of other tasks ranging from inventory to checkout (Mohtadi and Kinsey, 2005, p. 582). Until the 1970s, pricing at grocery stores was accomplished via hand labelling. The advent of both the Universal Product Code (UPC) and related scanners rendered these jobs obsolete and greatly reduced the labour costs for grocery stores (Kinsey and Ashman, 2000). They describe the effects of ICT-EC on inventory and ordering:

> [c]omputerized ordering, based on the UPC, was soon developed to simplify one of the most difficult and time-consuming jobs in the store [replenishment ordering] . . . After computerized ordering, the ordering process was reduced to entering or scanning the UPC and the amount to be ordered for each product into a hand held computer-ordering machine. The machine was then plugged into a modem to transfer the data to the main office. (Kinsey and Ashman, 2000, p. 86)

Likewise, the self-checkout lanes at grocery stores that ICT-EC has allowed can result in fewer cashier positions. In fast food restaurants, too, firms continue to experiment with new ways to telemediate work that previously had required physical co-presence. For example, some fast food restaurants have centralised drive-through ordering at remote call centres hundreds of miles away in an effort to increase productivity and reduce error rates (Ruth, 2007). Although there remains a need for labour onsite to prepare and distribute the ordered food, this example highlights that even some jobs that appear to be firmly tied to specific locations are potentially open to telemediation.

However, the process of job loss through ICT-EC can be cyclical (or at least temporally uneven) and ICT-EC can also create jobs, rather than simply destroy them – a fact that may provide some cold comfort to those workers who lose their jobs. Consider the case of banking in the US. Here, Fung (2006) found that while aggregate output in the banking industry in the US grew by 45 per cent between 1992 and 2002, employment stagnated during the same period. This reduction in demand for banking staff constituted a 'first round' of effects by innovations in ICT-EC, including ATMs (Automatic Teller Machines), credit scoring and home banking, among others. But this 'first round of effects' has been followed by a 'second round' which has reduced wage costs, in turn increasing output, and increasing the number of 'labour hours' in the banking industry, especially in the number of telephone-banking jobs (in call centres). In short, what Fung found is that 'labour-saving' technologies actually expanded, rather than reduced, employment over more than a decade of restructuring.

It is important to recognise in all of this, of course, that ICT-EC facilitates rather than determines job losses, or at least a reduction in labour demand. For instance, the lockout of longshoremen at the Long Beach port in Los Angeles during 2002 created an enormous log-jam of ships, with the media focused on the cost of the shutdown (Hall, 2004). Many claimed that the implementation of ICT-EC figured at the centre of debate, and that the negotiation of the introduction of ICT-EC in port facilities between labour and management caused the problems. But, as Olney (2003) argues, it was not the introduction of information technologies per se that was the primary axis of dispute between labour and management. Instead, the dispute centred on an expanding workforce in cargo-handling which management increasingly shifted to distribution centres many miles inland from the docks that drew on non-union labour and cheaper real estate. In short, jobs that were once necessarily restricted to the confines of the port have increasingly shifted both geographically and institutionally through ICT-EC. The point is that ICT-EC enabled the geographical restructuring of jobs through reshaping the relationship between labour, management and governmental actors, but ICT-EC did not determine the contours of this process.

Does ICT-EC lead to the dualisation or polarisation of labour markets?
If, by now, we can agree that ICT-EC does not lead teleologically to either widespread deskilling or the redundancy of human labour, then a second and related claim associated with ICT-EC and the 'information or knowledge economy' is the creation of a dualism in, or polarisation of, labour markets. These processes are, in part, associated with the very 'deskilling' discussed above (Rubery and Grimshaw, 2001; Egger and Grossmann, 2005). Castells (1996) seems to typify such an analysis. For him, ICTs have brought about an 'epochal change', such that the prevailing model for labour in the new, information-based, economy is now that of a core labour force, formed by information-based managers and by '"symbolic analysts"', and a disposable labour force that can be automated and/or hired/fired/off-shored, depending upon market demand and labor costs' (Castells, 1996, p. 272).

While, again, there is some evidence of a dualisation of labour markets into the 'information haves' and the 'information have-nots' (the so-called 'digital divide') at a variety of 'scales' (global South–North, inter-national, intra-national, intra-city and so on), Castells has been criticised for his overly deterministic and historically myopic analysis (Blok, 2003). Indeed, in later research in China, Cartier et al. (2005, p. 11) explored the use of information technologies by the 'information have-less' who, for them, consisted of low-income groups, retirees, state employees, laid-off workers and millions of rural-to-urban migrants who desire wireless services but are limited to Internet cafes, pagers and prepaid phone cards. This enormous amalgam of varied workers represents 'a middle ground between the information haves and have-nots' and 'shows that the actual pattern of differentiation can be more refined than the idea of the digital divide' (Cartier et al., 2005, p. 28). In short, as recent literature has suggested, one should speak of digital divides among workers (for example, Wagner et al., 2002) stratified by gender, ethnicity, class and so forth, rather than simply a digital divide. In any case, as Guy (2000) writes, '[w]hat produces a new class of low-paid workers in the information economy is not a lack of skill in the new information technologies. The low-paid jobs use just those technologies, but are on the wrong end of it [*sic*]' (Guy, 2000, p. 15, cited in Rubery and Grimshaw, 2001, p. 184).

In other words, even if there is evidence that labour markets in, for example, the United States have become increasingly polarised since the 1970s (for example, Hudson, 2007), it is not simply the case that ICT-EC is the main culprit, even though it may be intimately involved in this process of dualisation. This point may seem more obvious if we consider the relationship between ICT-EC and economic development at a global level – only a die-hard technological determinist would suggest that workers in the poorest countries of the global South exist on below-subsistence wage levels solely because of the lack of ICT-EC.

ICT-EC, 'off-shoring', 'home-shoring' and their implications for labour

'Off-shoring' A final generalisation postulates that ICT-EC has precipitated the use of both 'off-shoring' and 'home-shoring', which in turn has enhanced the mobility of capital to the disadvantage of immobile labour. These are separate but related issues, and we take each of these in turn. Let us begin by defining 'off-shoring' before we continue. For our purposes, we understand it as the international trade in services (see for example, Bhagwati et al., 2004), but also manufactured goods,[9] as mediated through ICT-EC.[10] In fact, while the most commonly noted form of off-shoring seems to be services such as call centre work that are located in, or relocated to, 'lower wage countries',[11] off-shoring also occurs in many other types of work, ranging from processing X-rays and other medical diagnostics to handling routine banking services and architectural drafting in countries outside the 'triad' of east and south-east Asia, Europe and North America. Furthermore, ICT-EC is involved in the international restructuring of manufacturing by fostering various kinds of flexibilities and facilitating the development of global production chains (Luthje, 2002; Bruun and Mefford, 2004). Thus, it is not incorrect to argue that ICT-EC has facilitated off-shoring, but it certainly does not determine it.

Indeed, the growth of ICT-EC should not imply an unequivocal trend towards off-shoring. While recognising that the geography of global economic activity is exceedingly complex, below we outline some reasons why off-shoring is not always inevitable with respect more directly to ICT-EC and labour. To begin with, ICT-EC allows for some routine or unskilled operations and jobs to be off-shored relatively easily, but this owes as much to the standardisation of these products or services (such as accounting, data entry and IT support) as it does to technological innovation itself (Drezner, 2004). Thus, the parts of firms' production processes that are more complex, interactive or innovative – including, but not limited to, marketing, research and development – are much more difficult to shift to low-wage countries because of the kinds of highly-skilled labour that are required. Highly-skilled labour is not ubiquitous, nor are the legal (for example, data privacy), educational, vocational and technological institutions that support it (for example, Farrell, 2006; OECD, 2006, pp. 122–5). Second, and by the same token, many jobs (from retail and restaurants to marketing and personal care) require geographic proximity. In other words, such work needs to be produced and consumed locally, rather than telemediated. While the percentage of jobs that this entails is highly debatable, Drezner (2004, p. 27) estimates that this accounts for about 90 per cent of the jobs in the United States. Third, capital remains tied to, or attracted to, more affluent urban areas because of the presence of fibre-optic infrastructure (often created by firms themselves). This dissuades capital from moving to places that are 'off the grid' or less connected (Graham and Marvin, 2001). Fourth, many business functions still seem to require face-to-face interaction (Gertler, 2003; Zook, 2004), although Leamer and Storper (2001) note that this may be challenged increasingly by innovations in Internet-enabled video links. Fifth, because of firm policies or manager behaviour (such as the desire among managers to maintain a certain surveillance over their workforce), many jobs are not telemediated, whether this maximises profit or not.

Sixth, 'off-shoring' harbours both risks and rewards for firms. As Ante (2004) writes, '[s]hoddy quality, security snafus, and poor customer service often wipe out any benefits'. Indeed, firms based in high-wage countries have also encountered a rejection of out-sourced services. This has been the case of the UK-based Lloyds TSB Bank. British bank customers called for the return of customer services to the UK from India because of what they perceived as the poor quality of telemediated services in India (see Taylor and Bain, Chapter 24 in this volume). Lloyds responded by returning some of its service operations back to the UK (Treanor, 2007). This phenomenon of 'on-shoring' – in other words, firm strategies of not exporting work to lower-wage countries or of returning work to the high-wage countries – is often overlooked in the haze of popular media focus on off-shoring. For example, the OECD (2006, p. 234) notes that in the UK, employment growth in 'ICT-related' and call centre occupations that could be potentially affected by off-shoring over the period 2001–2005 was 8.8 per cent compared to 3.2 per cent for total employ-ment, in spite of the numerous media reports that such jobs were being 'outsourced'. While this is only a very partial picture of this phenomenon (below, we examine how one element of 'on-shoring', 'home-shoring', forms a central feature of ICT-EC work), it does suggest that the off-shoring of jobs because of ICT-EC may be exaggerated.

Yet despite all of these caveats, off-shoring is a significant feature of the economic geography of capitalism today. Indeed, in 2006, the OECD (2006, p. 231) reported that 'around 20% of all people employed (in selected OECD countries) carry out the kinds of tasks and functions that could potentially be carried out from any geographic location owing to technological advances in ICTs and the increased tradability of services'. This certainly does not mean that all these service jobs will necessarily be relocated, but simply that the technological potential is there. Nonetheless, some low-wage countries, such as India, have become the location of skilled off-shored jobs, particularly in computer programming.

What general implications does the material reality of off-shoring have for workers? All of this has greatly increased the ability of firms to use space strategically as a means to extract concessions from particular localities and their workers (LeRoy, 2005), not least through the rhetorical power of ICTs to enable capital mobility. As McGrath-Champ et al. (2006, p. 13) insist:

> [w]hether all call centres will go to India is not the point. The widely held belief that this is the case and the promotion in certain quarters that this is inevitable and unstoppable is used as a disciplining device to defuse any opposition to such moves, and causes enormous problems for trade unions in particular.

Thus, the ability of ICT-enabled e-commerce to facilitate capital mobility and off-shoring – by whatever means – has led to the rapid expansion of telemediated work aided by trade liberalisation policies developed over the past several decades.

'Home-shoring'   While politicians have a stake in keeping jobs in the high-wage countries, and will not fail to advertise the extent to which this has been achieved, critics claim that much of these on-shored jobs involve 'home-shoring'. In fact, it may be that ICT-EC allows the practice of on-shoring jobs to continue, precisely because of the cost savings allowed for by facilitating 'home-shoring'. Consider, for example, that America On-Line (AOL) offered free accounts in exchange for volunteer labour to monitor AOL message boards in the early 1990s. In the US many Jet-Blue Airlines reservations agents work out of their homes, while in the UK the Co-op Travel agency employs a workforce of some 600 people operating out of their homes (Conlin, 2006). To what extent are the critics correct – in other words, is 'home-shoring' growing relative to aggregate job creation in high-wage countries, and what are the implications of ICT-EC-enabled 'home-shoring' for workers? The first of these questions we will attempt to answer in this section, and we elaborate on some of the consequences for workers of this 'home-shoring' of jobs in the following section.

For its part, then, so-called 'home-shoring' is hardly novel to the geography of capitalism, but it does seem to be the latest term for the active strategy by firms to create 'teleworking', 'telecommuting'[12] or simply home-working. In seeking to understand this phenomenon, though, it is important, we feel, to contrast this active strategy by firms (home-shoring) with its effect (the phenomenon of home-working). This is because the latter can involve not only those who are forced to work from home but also those who choose to do so, such as self-employed individuals like consultants. In fact, in a study of telemediated work in Europe, Bates and Huws (2002) found that self-employed workers constituted over 60 per cent of those working from home – in other words, most workers who worked from home did so on their own volition.

In any case, as we understand it, home-shoring refers to the phenomenon whereby a firm will employ an individual to perform the bulk of their work responsibilities from the home through the mediation of ICT-EC. This may be formally written into a job contract, or such practices may evolve over time informally (Clear and Dickson, 2005). However, as with many things, actual practices of home-shoring and home-working are, in fact, more complicated than what is provided for by the fairly simple definition above. In this respect, it may be useful to distinguish between remote work and telecommuting. Remote work (such as that performed by sales representatives or truckers) refers to 'jobs whose duties require employees to work away from their employer's location' (O'Mahoney and Barley, 1999, p. 128). These jobs have traditionally always been 'remote'. In contrast, telecommuting 'is typically defined as doing work that was previously performed in the office away from the office using digital telecommunications' (O'Mahoney and Barley, 1999, p. 129). This distinction is useful but we substitute the term 'telemediated' for 'telecommuting' because we think the former captures the complexity of more hybrid forms that combine physical co-presence 'in the office', home and other locations using ICTs (or ICT-EC) as the primary means of communication (Hislop and Axtell, 2007).

Whatever the quality of the distinction above, however, data concerning telemediated

Table 7.2　Estimates of tele-homeworkers, e-enabled workers and e-enhanced workers in Europe, 2000

Type of telemediated work	Estimated number in 2000
1. Home-based employees who use a computer and telecommunications link to conduct their work (person equivalent)	810 000
2. Multilocational employees who use a computer and telecommunications link to conduct their work (person equivalent)	3 700 000
3. e-lancers providing business and related industries who use a computer and telecommunications link to conduct their work	1 450 000
4. Number of person equivalent e-workers: sum of 1–3 above (EMERGENCE narrow definition)	5 960 000
5. Number of e-enabled self-employed workers who require a computer and telecommunications link to conduct their work not working in business-related industries	3 080 000
6. Number of person equivalent e-workers: sum of 1–3 and row 5 above (EMERGENCE broad definition)	9 040,000
7. Estimated number of e-workers based on Continuous Labour Force Survey (CLFS) and UK Labour Force Survey (LFS) (including irregular e-workers)	9 830 000

Source:　Bates and Huws (2002).

work are not disaggregated along these lines. In fact, 'telemediation', like the other nouns above, is notoriously difficult to measure (Potter, 2003; Clear and Dickson, 2005). Nonetheless, a number of studies provide reasonable data (at least from the US and Europe) to gauge the extent of this phenomenon. A study of the US found that 'telecommuting' has been growing rapidly since the 1990s, and in particular jumped by 17 per cent between 2000 and 2001, involving approximately 20 per cent of the US labour force, or 29 million people. Similarly, data from the Office of National Statistics in the UK point to a doubling of the labour force involved in home-working (or, more accurately, telemediated working involving considerable work at home) from 4 per cent in 1997 to 8 per cent in 2005 (Ruiz and Walling, 2005; see also Felstead et al., 2005). Lastly, Table 7.2 indicates the estimated number of workers in various categories of 'home-working'/ telemediated jobs in the European Union (EU = 15) in 2000.

The data presented above suggest that telemediated work in its various forms certainly is or will be a widespread phenomenon in the EU, at least. However, its extent falls short of Toffler's (1980) vision of 'electronic cottages'. Indeed, there are limits to home-shoring through ICT-EC, some of which, ironically, mirror the problems of 'off-shoring', especially data security concerns. Among the most important impediments to home-shoring are, first, that 'low-skilled' workers may not be able to engage in home-work if they are not provided with the necessary technical and other 'soft' skills to take advantage of ICT-EC. This makes the generalisation of home-shoring for all workers problematic. Second, home-based work is viewed by many employers as detrimental to intra-firm social networking, knowledge-transfer, cooperation, innovation and ultimately productivity and profitability (Clear and Dickson, 2005). Third, home-working requires a rather sophisti-cated balancing of work and home life, which many individuals and families find difficult to manage (Salaff, 2002; Halford, 2006). Thus, as the geographical literature on ICTs has demonstrated abundantly, it may be theoretically possible for people to work from anywhere with a laptop computer, a source of electricity, and access to the Internet, but in practice the reality of workers' lives is more complicated.

To very briefly summarise this relationship between ICT-EC, labour and the various kinds of 'shoring', then, we have maintained that ICT-EC does not lead ineluctably to off-shoring but that it has allowed firms to pursue (and switch between) a variety of 'shoring' strategies that are sometimes contradictory, sometimes complementary and whose logics vary across space.

ICT-EC and workers' lives
Counter-arguments such as those presented above have now become as common as the myths that they (and we) seek to dispel. But even the counter-arguments may appear emollient in their abstract proclamations about the consequences of ICT-EC for workers' lives. Thus, beyond abstract arguments about 'deskilling' or 're-skilling', job destruction or job creation, dualisation or digital divides, off-shoring or home-shoring, are real workers shaping and shaped by technical and organisational innovation, in which whole occupations and jobs are destroyed, moved or reconfigured to involve new temporalities (changing work schedules) and new spatialities (job relocations within urban regions, requirements to telecommute and so forth)? It is far too easy to lose sight of some of the consequences of ICT-EC for actual people. Indeed, ICT-EC does not just alleviate routine and monotonous labour, but it also creates new forms of stresses and pressures that may mirror 'old economy' jobs. In this sense, below we discuss three consequences of ICT-EC for workers' experiences.

ICT-EC, workers and unions   It is now well known that at least 'conventional' trade unions have declined – in terms of union density – across the high-wage economies (for example, Checchi and Visser, 2005; Monastiriotis, 2007; Slaughter, 2007; Ellem, Chapter 19 in this volume). What is less clear is whether ICT-EC can facilitate a rebalancing of the employment relation in favour of workers. There are two issues here – one is whether it matters that 'conventional' or 'traditional' unions are in decline, as new 'social move-ment unionisms' (Moody, 1997) fostered through ICTs (if not ICT-EC) have to some extent filled the void (see Lee, Chapter 23 in this volume). The second is whether, in fact, ICTs (or ICT-EC) have served to improve the lives of workers through these new forms of worker organisation. Since an answer to the first question requires an entirely different chapter, we will comment only on the second question.

For many observers, the outlook for unions is bleak. Unions in the United States, for example, have arguably suffered under the weight of ICT-EC, regardless of whether cyber-unions (Shostak, 2002), cyber-organisers and cyber-strikes have punctuated the negotiating landscape as a response (Chaison, 2002). For example, evidence from GM shows that the use of ICT-EC to 'outsource' or 'off-shore' production has damaged the ability of once-large units to bargain for worker-friendly policies, whether this concerns wages or other working conditions, even if unions such as the US-based United Auto Workers retain a strong presence on the Internet with a comprehensive website that offers a range of services to members (Townsend et al., 2001). For others, 'IT' or 'ICTs' provide the means by which unions can respond to changes in business organisations that ICT-EC has facilitated. Certainly, ICTs have allowed unions to internationalise communication, to reduce communication costs (such as providing answers to frequently asked questions on websites) and reduce fixed costs (for example, by having a website rather than an office), to improve marketing of the unions and appeal especially to younger workers, and to instigate campaigns more rapidly in response to employer mandates (Fiorito et al., 2002). The consequence, it seems, is that as capital has gained advantage through ICT-EC, unions and their varied social movements aligned with them have used ICTs as an instrument in return. And yet again, it would be foolish to argue that ICTs (as a response to ICT-EC and new types of business organisation and strategies) can alone serve to address workers' needs and demands. At the same time, ICTs do allow unions to nationalise and internationalise their strategies with an ease and rapidity hitherto unavailable (Chaison, 2002). Whether it is useful for unions and workers to use such national and international 'scalar' strategies to win battles against capital (Castree, 2000) and produce their own 'spatial fix' (Herod, 2001) is quite another story.

The workplace as digital panopticon?   A final myth concerning ICT-EC is that it is leading to increasingly stressful workplaces with more intense regulatory and work regimens. In addition to the ever-present concern that ICT-EC leads to outsourcing and/or off-shoring, these technologies have forced workers to conform more closely to management-designed protocols with little worker autonomy. An often-cited example of this increased stress is the growing ease with which managers can deploy 'input' controls (Depickere, 1999), that is the ability of firms to, *inter alia*, log employee hours, automatically log calls, and use key stroke counters to continuously monitor workers' performance and productivity in the 'office', the home, or other remote sites (see Sewell and Wilkinson, 1992; Lyon, 1994). Although the effort to extract more from workers has been a constant refrain in economic relations, ICT-EC provides managers with a granularity and completeness of observations that is theoretically a panopticon. Workers can be monitored in real time with rewards, and rebukes meted out accordingly. Although time management studies of workers hark back to Taylorism's management of the factory floor, scrutiny of workers by ICT-EC is particularly well suited to white collar and office jobs (see Baldry, Chapter 12 in this volume).

Such surveillance technologies have generally been viewed in dystopian terms – especially in the context of call centres – as a reduction of privacy, dignity and autonomy that provides workers with little choice but to conform in the new 'sweatshops' of the information age (Richardson et al., 2000; Fernie and Metcalf, 1998). In effect, ICT-EC is enabling a piece-rate put-out system for manipulating data in the twenty-first century 'knowledge economy' – at least in the high-wage countries. Through home-shoring and 'telemediated work', firms can reduce labour costs by reducing the cost of housing and transportation to workers, they can avoid 'social wage' costs by employing workers (not only women) who work part-time to balance other domestic work, and they can reduce real estate and related costs such as insurance and equipment (Downey, 2001; Halford, 2006). Firms can achieve these cost savings by leveraging residential broadband connections, wireless connectivity and other software systems in the home or between the home, office and other remote sites. While for many workers, work at home liberates them from the constraints of a fixed 'office' location and allows them the time and space to balance domestic responsibilities with other work responsibilities via the flexibility to work 15-minute shifts (Conlin, 2006), it is doubtful whether any workers are free from the disciplining effects of profit-driven (or, for that matter, non-profit) enterprises, and there are other psychological, social and economic implications that dampen the benefits that the flexibilities of home-work may offer.

In contrast, Bain and Taylor (2000) argue that much of the discussion on workplace surveillance is empirically thin, and show how workers are able to subvert and resist ICT-based controls. Using an ongoing study of a call centre, they highlight the cost of surveillance and the 'massive commitment of supervisory time and energy' required to monitor workers who are engaged in 'acting collectively and creating oppositional structures' as part of a 'conscious and purposeful dimension [of] resistance' (Bain and Taylor, 2000, p. 15). It is clear, however, that the dichotomy of total management control or strident worker resistance does not capture the complexities and contradictions inherent in these systems. Critiquing this dichotomy as reductionist, Button et al. (2003, p. 60) use a case study within the printing industry to illustrate the complexity of control in the everyday workplace in which 'employees may simultaneously resist some aspects of management control of their activities and nevertheless seek to perform their allocated tasks to the best of their abilities'. Yet it is not simply in the call centres, back offices and company headquarters where workers are experiencing increased stress through ICT-EC. For example, workers aboard ships have experienced drastic changes in the daily geographies of their work. Hence, Sampson and Wu (2003) note that ICT-based systems which allow for faster turnaround time in ports have made it more difficult for ship workers to access onshore facilities and generally give them less time off ship. They argue, then, that, '[p]aradoxically, for a workforce engaged in an occupation driving the process of time–space compression, the lives of today's seafarers are becoming more inwardly focused, as they are increasingly trapped in the hyperspace characteristic of the internal territory of their vessels' (Sampson and Wu, 2003, p. 147).

Another potential point of stress for workers involved in ICT-enabled e-commerce is the increased interaction with an array of individuals and institutions whose cultural and linguistic practices are unfamiliar. While increased exposure to diversity can be seen as something worthwhile in itself, it nevertheless can render daily interactions more difficult for some workers. This has led to 'national identity management' in which call centre employees in countries such as India adopt different 'national identities', depending upon the customer with whom they are speaking. Since these strategies are designed for customer comfort rather than worker comfort, many Indian call centre workers are hesitant about conforming to management's wishes and find various ways to resist these demands (Poster, 2007).

ICT-EC and a new 'spatial equity' for workers?   The relationship between ICT-EC, spatial equity and workers is fraught with contradictions that should come as no surprise to observers of the historical geography of capitalism. On the one hand, there is now a substantial body of theoretical and empirical work on the centralising tendencies of ICT-EC, which has resulted in a dismissal of the 'cybertopia/cyberhyperbole' literature of the mid-1990s. In other words, ICT-EC seems to be strengthening the affluence of certain metropolitan regions to the detriment of others (Graham and Marvin, 2001). While this may or may not represent the inevitable uneven capitalist development posited by some geographers (for example, Harvey, 1982; Smith, 1984), what the empirical evidence shows is certainly not that there is more spatial equity at any 'scale' (from the international to the local). Rather, some countries, some areas of countries and some areas of cities have created or attracted disproportionate levels of capital investment, aided by a nexus of endowments that include 'hard' infrastructure (anything from fibre-optic networks and superior bandwidth capacity to internationally-connected airports), 'soft' infrastructure (highly-educated/skilled individuals), and, lest it be forgotten, a huge pool of low-paid workers to perform all of the 'dirty jobs' and 'supporting roles' (Graham and Marvin, 2001). The disparities in economic development exacerbate existing digital and offline divides, while capital (and governments) have to cope with the contradictions of this centralisation (congestion, higher real estate prices, electronic traffic and breakdown and so on). The result is a tension between the centralisation of economic activity and its decentralisation (from off-shoring to relocating to 'greenfield sites') or increasingly deploying telemediated workers to offset the problems of the high cost of socially reproducing workers (from high commuting costs to skyrocketing housing prices).

Some observers might argue that ICT-ECs allow for spatial equity on an 'international scale' (and especially between the high-wage and low-wage countries), pointing out that countries such as India and China are rapidly increasing their share of Internet use (see above) and the commercial uptake of ICT-EC. But this, too, deserves not a little bit of critical scrutiny. For one, there are huge disparities in the integration of ICT-EC within China (consider the differences between, let us say, Shanghai and remote villages in western China) and differences within India (such as between Bangalore and Bhopal). Moreover, the growth of such internationally connected nodes in the global economy may not be unrelated to the uneven development in the richer countries. Indeed, cities which have experienced long-term industrial decline in Europe and North America over the last 30 years continue to be somewhat 'off the map' (despite a barrage of remedial ICT-oriented policies) in terms of the 'hard' and 'soft' infrastructure that is attractive for capital investment. Those workers unfortunate enough to live in areas that have been abandoned by economic investment when capital has fled to more profitable 'shores' are thus left to the ravages of unemployment or are forced to migrate to those (urban) areas of the world well integrated into the worlds of ICT-EC. In the context of 'development' on a world scale, Wilson reminds us of David Harvey's telling point: '[t]he problem of space is not eliminated but intensified by the crumbling of spatial barriers' (Harvey, 1989, p. 124, cited in Wilson 2001, p. 292).

Conclusions

The opening years of the twenty-first century represent a transition from the overblown rhetoric of the dot.com boom on how 'the internet changes everything' to a quieter, albeit steady, adoption of ICT-EC by firms. Although less flashy than the spectacle of the venture capital-fuelled excess of the previous decade, the adoption of these technologies promises to have a much more fundamental role in shaping the complexity of the spaces of labour. Ironically, as ICT-EC becomes less of a visible novelty and simply a 'taken for granted' business standard, its power to shape the structure and geography of work and labour increases. Although the use of ICT-EC is far from ubiquitous and exhibits the clusters and marginalisations associated with any new innovation, these technologies do wield great power in shaping daily lives. This, however, is not to argue that somehow ICT-EC singly determines the character of work, labour and labouring in the twenty-first century, nor are we arguing that the Internet and related technologies have yielded a more socially just world for labour. Instead, we simply suggest that ICT-EC opens up new forms of work and capital–labour relations that demand our attention.

In this chapter we detailed and critically assessed three myths often associated with the relationships between ICT-EC, space and labour. Firstly, we argued that whilst ICT-EC may serve in part to deskill some jobs and be involved in the elimination of other jobs, this is clearly not a linear or ineluctable process. While there is no doubt that new ICTs are facilitating changes in the social and spatial contours of capitalism at the beginning of the twenty-first century, they are not inevitably leading to the end of work. The nature, location and scale at which jobs are deskilled, destroyed or created depend upon ongoing negotiations between labour and management. ICT-EC creates the potential for new structures and processes of work but their implementation depends on the power to put these changes into effect. Secondly, in a similar manner we argue that ICT-EC does not lead inevitably to the dualisation of labour markets, even though this may be a feature of labour markets across the advanced economies. To be sure, the use of ICT-EC and high wages are often correlated but there are a number of examples where jobs are purely information processing but remain poorly paid. Finally, we argue that ICT-EC does not necessarily lead inevitably to off-shoring, given that the mobility and power of capital has increased tremendously vis-à-vis labour. Instead, we note that the situation is significantly more complicated as off-shoring (and the related processes of near-shoring or home-shoring) is tempered by a number of issues ranging from the use of tacit knowledge in production to concerns about privacy and the ability to access skilled labour. To illustrate the inaccuracies of these myths we sketched out some of the social and spatial consequences of ICT-EC for workers' lives, from the problem of reorganising unions to cope with the new forms of business organisations facilitated by the very development of ICT-EC, to the new stresses created by call centres and similar 'sweatshops' of the twenty-first century, to questioning whether ICT-EC can lead to a spatially equitable landscape for workers.

Our main point is that it is not simply ICT-EC which alone shapes the labour geographies of the twenty-first century. Clearly, other processes figure in this calculus, and in disavowing some 'magic technological bullet' to resolve workers' often dreadful lot, it helps us to recognise that a more equitable economic geography for workers has to be fought for by other means as well.

Notes

1. For some exceptions of work by economic geographers, see Benner (2001) and Niles and Hanson (2003).
2. In the social sciences more broadly, Fountain (2005) and Chapple (2006) note that the more recent 'digital divide' literature focuses more on technological skills than employment and upward job mobility.
3. We avoid discussing, for example, the explicit relationship between wireless technologies like mobile phones and work or labour. We also prefer the term 'ICT' rather than 'IT', because we think it better captures the range of technologies involved in e-commerce.
4. Over the last five years or so, a key development in ICTs has been the movement from fixed (wired) to untethered (or wireless) connections. Though the implications of wireless technologies have attracted some attention from academics and other observers (for example, Shankar and O'Driscoll, 2002), we think it too premature to offer any substantial claims as to their impacts at this stage.

5. By this we mean the mutually constitutive, but also contradictory, relationship between ICT-EC and labour. In this relationship, it is assumed that technology and labour are distinguishable. We recognise the limits of such an analysis, particularly the notion that labour is becoming more 'cyborg-like' and that ICT-EC and labour are mutually transformative (as in the socio-technical systems so dear to Michel Callon and actor-network theory – Callon and Latour, 1981).
6. While straightforward, this definition masks the much more profound changes in organisational or industry structure that are engendered through the incorporation of ICT-EC (Castells, 1996; Schiller, 1999).
7. It should be noted that the census figures are not inclusive of e-commerce activities in the entire US economy (namely agriculture, mining, construction, utilities and non-merchant wholesalers), but instead leverage existing annual surveys, such as the Annual Survey of Manufacturers (US Census, 2007).
8. A number of NAICS codes for wholesale sectors which are likely to have high e-commerce use (for example, Motor vehicles and automotive equipment (4231)) are not listed in Table 7.1 due to census reporting restrictions resulting from confidentiality issues.
9. Bhagwati et al. (2004) restrict their definition to the international trade in services, pointing out that 'off-shoring' is nothing new, but that it has come to imply such international trade. We concur with Bhagwati et al.'s point but, as noted above, we add manufacturing to this understanding. In any case, off-shoring is in some sense the latest word to describe the international restructuring of capital encapsulated by Harvey's 'spatial fix'.
10. We see 'off-shoring' as one element of 'outsourcing' more generally, but we focus on 'off-shoring' specifically because we are concerned about its international dimensions.
11. We use this term rather than 'developing countries', 'global South' or poorer countries.
12. The term 'telecommuting' seems to be more widely used in the US while 'teleworking' is more widely used in the UK and elsewhere (Clear and Dickson, 2005). Yet, as we note below, we prefer to use the term 'telemediated' jobs or work.

References

Ante, S. (2004), Commentary: 'Shifting work offshore? Outsourcer beware: quality and security woes can eat expected savings', *Business Week*, 12 January, available at www.businessweek.com/magazine/content/04_02/b3865028.htm.

Auger, P. and J. Gallaugher (1997), 'Factors affecting the adoption of an internet-based sales presence for small businesses', *The Information Society*, **13** (1), 55–74.

Bain, P. and P. Taylor (2000), 'Entrapped by the "electronic panopticon"? Worker resistance in the call centre', *New Technology, Work and Employment*, **15** (1), 2–18.

Bates, P. and U. Huws (2002), 'Modelling ework in Europe: estimates, models and forecasts from the EMERGENCE project', Institute for Employment Studies (IES) Report 388, Brighton: IES.

Benner, C. (2001), *Work in the New Economy: The Flexible Labor Markets in the Silicon Valley*, Oxford and Malden, MA: Blackwell.

Bhagwati, J., A. Panagariya and T.N. Srinivasan (2004), 'The muddles over outsourcing', *Journal of Economic Perspectives*, **18** (4), 93–114.

Blok, A. (2003), 'Introduction', *Internationaal Instituut voor Sociale Geschiedenis Supplement*, **48**, 1–11.

Braverman, H. (1974), *Labor and Monopoly Capital: The Degradation of Work in the Twentieth Century*, London and New York: Monthly Review Press.

Brunn, S.D., S.L. Cutter and J.W. Harrington (eds) (2004), *Geography and Technology*, Dordrecht, The Netherlands and Boston, MA: Kluwer Academic Publishers.

Bruun, P. and R.N. Mefford (2004), 'Lean production and the internet', *International Journal of Production Economics*, **89** (3), 247–60.

Button, G., D. Mason and W. Sharrock (2003), 'Disempowerment and resistance in the print industry? Reactions to surveillance-capable technology', *New Technology, Work and Employment*, **18** (1), 50–61.

Callon, M. and B. Latour (1981), 'Unscrewing the Big Leviathan: how actors macrostructure reality and how sociologists help them to do so', in K. Knorr-Cetina and A.V. Cicourel (eds), *Advances in Social Theory and Methodology: Toward an Integration of Micro- and Macro-Sociologies*, London and Boston, MA: Routledge and Kegan Paul, pp. 277–303.

Cartier, C., M. Castells and J.L. Qiu (2005), 'The information have-less: inequality, mobility, and translocal networks in Chinese cities', *Studies in Comparative International Development*, **40** (2), 9–34.

Castells, M. (1996), *Rise of the Network Society*, Oxford and Malden, MA: Blackwell.

Castree, N. (2000), 'Geographic scale and grass-roots internationalism: the Liverpool Dock dispute, 1995–1998', *Economic Geography*, **76** (3), 272–92.

Chaison, G. (2002), 'Information technology: the threat to the unions', *Journal of Labor Research*, **23** (2), 249–59.

Chapple, K. (2006), 'Networks to nerdistan: the role of labor market intermediaries in the entry-level IT labor market', *International Journal of Urban and Regional Research*, **30** (3), 548–63.

Checchi, D. and J. Visser (2005), 'Pattern persistence in European trade union density: a longitudinal analysis 1950–1996', *European Sociological Review*, **21** (1), 1–21.

Clear, F. and K. Dickson (2005), 'Teleworking practice in small and medium-sized firms: management style and worker autonomy', *New Technology, Work and Employment*, **20** (3), 218–33.

ClickZ Stats (2005), 'Stats – Web Worldwide', www.clickz.com/stats/web_worldwide.

Conlin, M. (2006), 'Call centers in the rec room: "Homeshoring" takes off as moms and others provide an alternative to offshoring', *Business Week*, 23 January, available at www.businessweek.com/magazine/content/06_04/b3968103.htm?chan=search.

Depickere, A. (1999), 'Managing virtual working: between commitment and control?', in P.J. Jackson (ed.), *Virtual Working: Social and Organisational Dynamics*, London and New York: Routledge, pp. 99–120.

Downey, G. (2001), 'Virtual webs, physical technologies, and hidden workers: the spaces of labor in information internetworks', *Technology and Culture*, **42** (2), 209–35.

Drezner, D. (2004), 'The outsourcing bogeyman', *Foreign Affairs*, **83** (3), 22–34.

Egger, H. and V. Grossmann (2005), 'Non-routine tasks, restructuring of firms, and wage inequality within and between skill-groups', *Journal of Economics*, **86** (3), 197–228.

Farrell, D. (2006), 'Don't be afraid of offshoring', *Business Week*, 22 March, available at www.businessweek.com/globalbiz/content/mar2006/gb20060322_649013.htm?chan=search.

Felstead, A., N. Newson and S. Walters (2005), *Changing Places of Work*, Basingstoke: Palgrave.

Fernie, S. and D. Metcalf (1998), '(Not) hanging on the telephone: payment systems in the new sweatshops', Discussion Paper No. 390, Centre of Economic Performance (CEP), London School of Economics, London.

Fillis, I., U. Johannson and B. Wagner (2004), 'Factors impacting on e-business adoption and development in the smaller firm', *International Journal of Entrepreneurial Behaviour and Research*, **10** (3), 178–91.

Fiorito, J., P. Jarley and J.T. Delaney (2002), 'Information technology, US union organizing and union effectiveness', *British Journal of Industrial Relations*, **40** (4), 627–58.

Fountain, C. (2005), 'Finding a job in the internet age', *Social Forces*, **83** (3), 1235–62.

Fung, M.K. (2006), 'Are labor-saving technologies lowering employment in the banking industry?', *Journal of Banking and Finance*, **30** (1), 179–98.

Gertler, M.S. (2003), 'Tacit knowledge and the economic geography of context, or the undefinable tacitness of being (there)', *Journal of Economic Geography*, **3** (1), 75–99.

Graham, S. (ed.) (2004), *The Cybercities Reader*, London and New York: Routledge.

Graham, S. and S. Marvin (2001), *Splintering Urbanism: Networked Infrastructures, Technological Mobilities and the Urban Condition*, London and New York: Routledge.

Guy, F. (2000), 'Technology, planning, bargaining and the growth of inequality since 1980', Department of Management, Birkbeck College, London, mimeo.

Halford, S. (2006), 'Collapsing the boundaries? Fatherhood, organization and home-working', *Gender, Work and Organization*, **13** (4), 383–402.

Hall, P.V. (2004), '"We'd have to sink the ships": impact studies and the 2002 West Coast Port lockout', *Economic Development Quarterly*, **18** (4), 354–67.

Harvey, D. (1989), *The Condition of Postmodernity: An Enquiry into the Origins of Cultural Change*, New York: Blackwell.

Harvey, D. (1982), *The Limits to Capital*, Oxford: Blackwell.

Herod, A. (2001), *Labor Geographies: Workers and the Landscapes of Capitalism*, New York: Guilford Press.

Hislop, D. and C. Axtell (2007), 'The neglect of spatial mobility in contemporary studies of work: the case of telework', *New Technology, Work and Employment*, **22** (1), 34–51.

Hudson, K. (2007), 'The new labor market segmentation: labor market dualism in the new economy', *Social Science Research*, **36** (1), 286–312.

InternetWorldStats.com (2007), 'Internet usage statistics – The big picture: World internet users and population stats', available at http://internetworldstats.com/stats.htm

Kandampully, J. (2003), 'B2B relationships and networks in the internet age', *Management Decision*, **41** (5), 443–51.

Kinsey, J. and S. Ashman (2000), 'Information technology in the retail food industry', *Technology in Society*, **22** (1), 83–96.

Leamer, E. and M. Storper (2001), 'The economic geography of the internet age', *Journal of International Business Studies*, **32** (4), 641–65.

Leinbach, T.R. and S.D. Brunn (eds) (2001), *Worlds of E-Commerce: Economic, Geographical and Social Dimensions*, Chichester and New York: Wiley.

LeRoy, G. (2005), *The Great American Jobs Scam: Corporate Tax Dodging and the Myth of Job Creation*, San Francisco: Berrett-Koehler Publishers.

Lyon, D. (1994), *The Electronic Eye: The Rise of the Surveillance Society*, Minneapolis, MN: University of Minnesota Press.

Luthje, B. (2002), 'Electronics contract manufacturing: global production and the international division of labor in the age of the internet', *Industry and Innovation*, **9** (3), 227–47.

McGrath-Champ, S., A. Rainnie and A. Herod (2006), 'Here come the space cadets: industrial relations and space', International Sociological Association, World Congress Research Committee 44, Labour Movements, 29 July, Durban, South Africa.

Mohtadi, H. and J.D. Kinsey (2005), 'Information exchange and strategic behavior in supply chains: application to the food sector', *American Journal of Agricultural Economics*, **87** (3), 582–99.

Monastiriotis, V. (2007), 'Union retreat and regional economic performance: the UK experience', *Regional Studies*, **41** (2), 143–56

Moody, K. (1997), *Workers in a Lean World: Unions in the International Economy*, London: Verso.

Niles, S. and S. Hanson (2003), 'The geographies of online job search: preliminary findings from Worcester, MA', *Environment and Planning A*, **35** (7), 1223–43.

NUA (2000), 'NUA: How many online', available at www.nua.ie.

OECD (Organisation for Economic Cooperation and Development) (2001), *The Internet and Business Performance, Business and Industry Policy Forum Series*, Paris: OECD.

OECD (Organisation for Economic Cooperation and Development) (2006), *Information Technology Outlook*, Paris: OECD.

Olney, P. (2003), 'On the waterfront: analysis of ILWU lockout', *New Labor Forum*, **12** (2), 33–41.

O'Mahony, S. and S.R. Barley (1999), 'Do digital telecommunications affect work and organization? The state of our knowledge', *Research in Organizational Behavior*, **21**, 125–61.

Poster, W.R. (2007), 'Who's on the line? Indian call center agents pose as Americans for US-outsourced firms', *Industrial Relations*, **46** (2), 271–304.

Potter, E.E. (2003), 'Telecommuting: the future of work, corporate culture, and American Society', *Journal of Labor Research*, **24** (1), 73–84.

Reich, R.B. (1991), *The Work of Nations: Preparing Ourselves for 21st-Century Capitalism*, New York: A.A. Knopf.

Richardson, R., V. Belt and N. Marshal (2000), 'Taking calls to Newcastle: the regional implications of the growth in call centres', *Regional Studies*, **43** (4), 357–69.

Rubery, J. and D. Grimshaw (2001), 'ICTs and employment: the problem of job quality', *International Labour Review*, **140** (2), 165–92.

Ruiz, Y. and A. Walling (2005), 'Home-based working using communication technologies', *labour Market Trends*, **113** (10), 417–26.

Ruth, E. (2007), '"Want fries with that?" could be coming from Delaware', *USA Today*, 14 May, available at www.usatoday.com/money/companies/management/2007-05-14-drive-through_N.htm.

Rutherford, T. and J. Holmes (2007), '"We simply have to do that stuff for our survival": labour, firm innovation and cluster governance in the Canadian automotive parts industry', *Antipode*, **39** (1), 194–221.

Salaff, J.W. (2002), 'Where home is the office: the new form of flexible work', in B. Wellman and C. Haythornthwaite (eds), *The Internet in Everyday Life*, Oxford and Malden, MA: Blackwell, pp. 464–95.

Sampson, H. and B. Wu (2003), 'Compressing time and constraining space: the contradictory effects of ICT and containerization on international shipping labour', *International Review of Social History*, **48** (11), 123–52.

Schiller, D. (1999), *Digital Capitalism: Networking the Global Market System*, London and Cambridge, MA: MIT Press.

Sewell, G. and B. Wilkinson (1992), 'Someone to watch over me: surveillance, discipline and the just-in-time labour process', *Sociology*, **26** (2), 271–89.

Shankar, V. and T. O'Driscoll (2002), 'How wireless networks are reshaping the supply chain', *Supply Chain Management Review*, **6** (4), 44–51.

Shostak, A.B. (2002), *CyberUnion: Empowering Labor through Computer Technology*, London and Armonk, NY: M.E. Sharpe.

Slaughter, M.J. (2007), 'Globalization and declining unionization in the United States', *Industrial Relations*, **46** (2), 329–46.

Smith, N. (1984), *Uneven Development: Nature, Capital and the Production of Space*, Oxford: Blackwell.

Toffler, A. (1980), *The Third Wave*, New York: Bantam.

Townsend, A., S.M. Denmarie and A.R. Hendrickson (2001), 'Information technology, unions, and the new organization: challenges and opportunities for union survival', *Journal of Labor Research*, **22** (2), 275–86.

Treanor, J. (2007), 'Lloyds closes Indian call centres', *The Guardian*, 2 March, available at www.guardian.co.uk/money/2007/mar/02/business.india.

Urbaczewski, A., M.J. Leonard and B. Wheeler (2002), 'Electronic commerce research: a taxonomy and synthesis', *Journal of Organizational Computing and Electronic Commerce*, **12** (4), 263–305.

US Census (2007), 'E-stats – Frequently asked questions', available at www.census.gov/eos/www/faq.html.

Wagner, G.G., R. Pischner and J.P. Haisken-DeNew (2002), 'The changing digital divide in Germany', in B. Wellman and C. Haythornthwaite (eds), *The Internet in Everyday Life*, Oxford and Malden, MA: Blackwell, pp. 164–85.

Wheeler, J., Y. Aoyama and B. Warf (eds) (2000), *Cities in the Telecommunications Age: The Fracturing of Geographies*, London and New York: Routledge.

Wilson, M. (2001), 'Dot com development: are IT lines better than tractors?', in T.R. Leinbach and S.D. Brunn (eds), *Worlds of E-Commerce: Economic, Geographical and Social Dimensions*, Chichester and New York: Wiley, pp. 277–92.

Wright, C., and J. Lund (2006), 'Variations on a lean theme: work restructuring in retail distribution', *New Technology, Work and Employment*, **21** (1), 59–74.

Wynarczyk, P. (2005), 'The impact of connectivity technologies on e-flexible working practices of small and medium-sized enterprises in the North East of England', *New Technology, Work and Employment*, **20** (3), 234–47.

Zook, M.A. (2004), 'The knowledge brokers: venture capitalists, tacit knowledge and regional development', *International Journal of Urban and Regional Research*, **28** (3), 621–41.

Zook, M.A. (2005), 'The geographies of the internet', *Review of Information Science and Technology (ARIST)*, **40**, 53–78.

8 Gender, space and labour market participation: the experiences of British Pakistani women
Robina Mohammad

In this chapter I examine the significance of space for working-class British Pakistani Muslim women's access to the formal labour market.

Space and power: geography, feminism and labour

> ... [j]ust as none of us is outside or beyond geography, none of us is completely free from the struggle over geography. (Said, 1994, p.7)

According to Foucault, space is key to disciplinary technologies: 'discipline proceeds from an organization of individuals in space, and it requires a specific enclosure of space' (cited in Rabinow, 1991, p. 17), a particular spatial ordering, spanning the body, the local, the global, public and private. Put another way, power proceeds from the control and regulation of space. Thus, the struggle for power and equality is necessarily a struggle over space.

The struggle over geography was most obviously central to the decolonisation movements of the post-World War II period but it is also significant for other social movements, most notably postwar Anglo-American feminism. Then in its second wave, this movement foregrounded geography in the struggle for gender equality by calling into question the taken-for-grantedness of women's location within the private domestic sphere and the gender division of labour by which they were allocated non-paid work. One strand of feminist thought argued that women's exclusion from power was underpinned by their exclusion from the public sphere, from participation in the formal economy and politics. For Betty Friedan, regarded as the midwife of second-wave feminism, the site of the home was not only politically and economically disempowering but also physically isolating, emotionally and mentally stifling and lay at the heart of the issue (Friedan, 1963).

Indeed, for white, Anglo-American middle-class feminists, women's liberation at times was often regarded as a simple journey from the home to the paid workplace, for the workplace offers women not only economic independence but also greater visibility in the public sphere, an opportunity to be 'counted'. The achievements of Anglo-American feminism, then, are evident in the transformations of the gender of the labour force at all levels which have taken place in the context of social, economic and cultural transformations, including the decline of old industries, the growth of service-sector jobs and the feminisation of the labour market. In this chapter, by way of contrast, I want to specifically examine working-class British Pakistani Muslim women's experiences of the labour market to think about broader questions of the community's social position and level of social mobility in Britain. I have organised the chapter as follows: I begin with a discussion of methodology followed by a section on South Asian migration to Britain and the socioeconomic profile of the UK's Pakistani community. I then consider the ways in which the character of space becomes significant for the extent and nature of working-class British Pakistani women's access to the formal labour market.

Methodology

The data used in this chapter are drawn from research that was carried out between 1995 and 1996 for a two-part project in Reading, UK, a university town and commercial centre some 40 miles west of London. The project was funded by the Department of Employment (via the local council) on an exploration of barriers to Pakistani women's access to the formal labour market. Initiated by 'community leaders' at the Pakistani Community Centre, and undertaken in collaboration with Sophie Bowlby and Sally Lloyd-Evans, this research included 50 in-depth interviews in total, breaking down into 25 interviews with women in the under-30 age group and 25 in the over-30 age group. As age is a key factor in explaining the extent and form of women's participation in the formal labour market, in this chapter I will restrict my analysis to the under-30 age group. The respondents were recruited using the snowball method where initial respondents were encouraged to recommend others for interview. The names of initial respondents were put forward by the Pakistani Community Centre. The interviews were based on semi-structured questionnaires and typically lasted between one to two hours. This provided considerable opportunity for respondents to raise issues that concerned them within the remit of the research. I also circulated in key community sites, such as the Muslim Women's Association, the Milan group (an alternative to the Muslim Women's Association) and the Pakistani Women's Mother and Toddler Group to gain broader understandings of the community. Before proceeding with a discussion and analysis of the findings, however, it is necessary to reflect a little on the context of postwar South Asian migration to the UK and the broader socioeconomic position of British Pakistanis, which provides context for understanding the Reading-based community.

South Asian migration to Britain

Migration from the sub-continent was facilitated by the existence of colonial links. Anwar (1979) notes four main 'push' factors influencing outward migration: chain migration opportunities opened up by early settlers; the partition of the sub-continent in 1947 instituted by the British prior to granting independence; the conflict in Kashmir, which remains ongoing; and the construction of the Mangla Dam in Mirpur (in the early 1960s), which displaced a large percentage of the population. This latter is important because Mirpur, in Pakistan, had a predominantly agricultural economy with little industrialisation, and the rocky and largely infertile character of the land encouraged young men to leave the region (Anwar, 1979; Hiro, 1971). This perhaps explains why a large percentage of Mirpuris were recruited by the British army and navy, opening up possibilities to settle in Britain. Thus, prior to and in the immediate post-World War II period early migrants from Mirpur were largely seamen settlers, whereas the majority of other early migrants were from professional classes. These early settlers opened up the possibilities for others to leave for the UK, as they became the first link in a process of chain migration. Subsequent migrants, however, were largely from working-class, rural origins. The partition of India and the subsequent conflict with Kashmir saw the displacement of millions, many of whom migrated overseas.

Simultaneously, the availability of work and British policies for the recruitment of

SCOTLAND
4.25

NORTH EAST
1.88

NORTHERN IRELAND
0.09

NORTH WEST
15.65

YORKSHIRE & HUMBERSIDE
19.58

EAST MIDLANDS 3.72

WEST MIDLANDS
20.68

EAST
5.19

WALES
1.11

GREATER LONDON
19.10

SOUTH WEST
0.90

SOUTH EAST
7.83

Source: Office for National Statistics, April 2001 Census (http://www.bl.uk/popups/apkdemog.html).

Figure 8.1   Percentage distribution of the Pakistani population UK-wide

cheap labour provided a significant pull factor to migrants. In the pre-1960 period the Pakistani government, like the Indian government, had placed stringent controls on intercontinental travel, controls which kept outward migration to a minimum. However, in 1960 the Indian Supreme Court ruled that it was unconstitutional for the Indian government to deny passports to Indian nationals, a decision that led to a relaxation of these restrictions. In turn, this promoted parallel developments in Pakistan. These developments, together with immigration restrictions imposed by the British government in the form of the 1962 Commonwealth Immigration Act, led to a massive acceleration in the number of immigrants. The majority of Pakistani arrivals in the early 1960s were males who saw their residence in Britain purely in economic terms, as a means of making money. Given their motivations, the majority migrated to industrial regions where they could find work in factories (Figure 8.1 shows the geographic distribution of the Pakistani population in the UK). Many saw their stay in Britain as a temporary sojourn away from home. The 1962 Act's restrictions on entry, though, prompted a reconsideration of the nature of their residence in the UK, which led to more permanent arrangements. Thus, the arrival of women and children to join husbands and fathers in Britain began in earnest. This was significant, because it was only when women and children arrived that something of a 'community' began to emerge amongst Pakistanis in British localities (Hiro, 1971). These historical considerations explain why the socioeconomic character of South Asian and Pakistani migration to the UK differs considerably from subsequent migrations to the United States, which primarily attracts urban-based, highly skilled professionals. Having examined how this migration stream was initiated, in the next section I will examine the socioeconomic profile of the Pakistani population in Britain, thereby situating the Reading-based population.

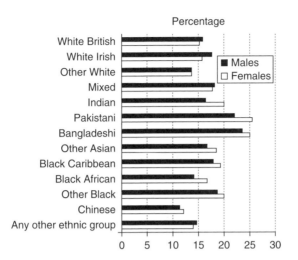

Source: Office for National Statistics (http://www.statistics.gov.uk/cci/nugget.asp?id=464).

Figure 8.2 Age standardised limiting long-term illness, by ethnic group and sex: England and Wales (April 2001)

Socioeconomic profile of the UK-based Pakistani community

A glance at the socioeconomic profile of Pakistanis across the UK confirms their marginal status within ethnic minority groups. The 2001 census data show that Pakistani men and women have the highest rate of limiting long-term illness, with this rate being directly related to social class (see Figure 8.2). This is confirmed by other economic indicators; for example, Figure 8.3 shows that Pakistani men and women have the second-highest rate of those who leave school with no formal educational qualification. The rate of unemployment is also high amongst both men and women. Standing at 11 per cent, Pakistani men's unemployment rate is twice that of white British or white Irish men, while women's unemployment is almost double again (see Figure 8.4). While women in all groups are more likely to be economically 'inactive', ethnic minority women have the highest rates of economic 'inactivity' (see Figure 8.5). The rate for Pakistani women stands at 69 per cent, with only the 75 per cent for Bangladeshi women being higher. However, it is important to remember that this measure neglects economic activity that is informally undertaken from home, for example, as many Pakistani women undertake informal economic activity from home such as piecework or supplying local shops with home-cooked food stuffs.

Another explanation for the high level of inactivity may be the higher levels of fertility amongst Pakistani women, so that many are at home raising families (see Figure 8.6). Nevertheless, a question on the 1991 census revealed that Pakistani women had a higher-than-expected rate of entry into the professions, standing at 11 per cent, higher than British white women although lagging in comparison with other white groups (21 per cent), Indians (16 per cent) and Chinese (15 per cent). On the other hand, at 9 per cent, Pakistani men's entry into professional occupations is lower than Pakistani women's and is the lowest of the ethnic groups. This suggests that there is a preference by Pakistani

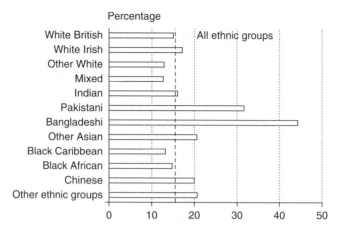

Source: Office for National Statistics (http://www.statistics.gov.uk/cci/nugget.asp?id=461).

Figure 8.3   People of working age with no qualification by ethnic group: Great Britain (2004)

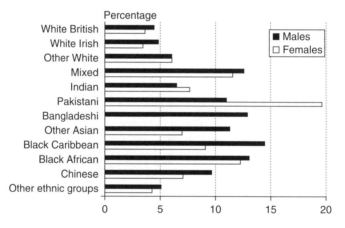

Source: Office for National Statistics (http://www.statistics.gov.uk/cci/nugget.asp?id=462).

Figure 8.4   Unemployment by ethnicity and gender: Great Britain (2004)

women for professional occupations that is encouraged and supported by their parents, as I will discuss later.

The Reading community

Census 2001 suggests that there were 3828 Pakistanis in Reading, making up 2.7 per cent of the population. The population of the group is geographically concentrated in a few clusters around the town (see Figure 8.7). The largest cluster can be found on the east side and two smaller clusters in the south and west side. My circulation in 'community' sites located in different parts of the town enabled a recruitment of respondents from a

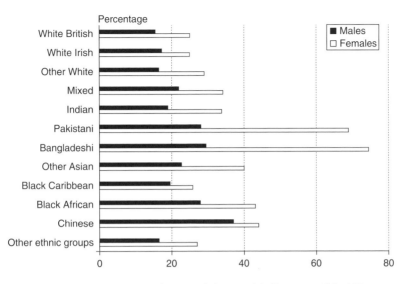

Source: Office for National Statistics (http://www.statistics.gov.uk/cci/nugget.asp?id=462).

Figure 8.5   *Economic inactivity by ethnicity and gender: Great Britain*

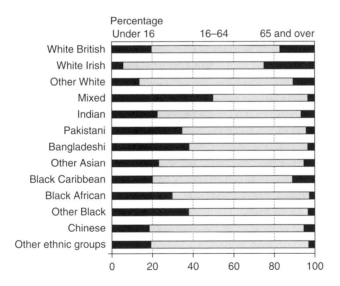

Source: Office for National Statistics (http://www.statistics.gov.uk/cci/nugget.asp?id=456).

Figure 8.6   *Demography and ethnicity: Great Britain*

variety of areas. In keeping with the characteristics of the wider Pakistani 'community', my respondents were all working class of Mirpuri origin.

Nineteen of the respondents were aged between 15 and 19. Two respondents were aged 20 and four were aged 25 and above. Of the 19 respondents aged 15 to 19, all but two

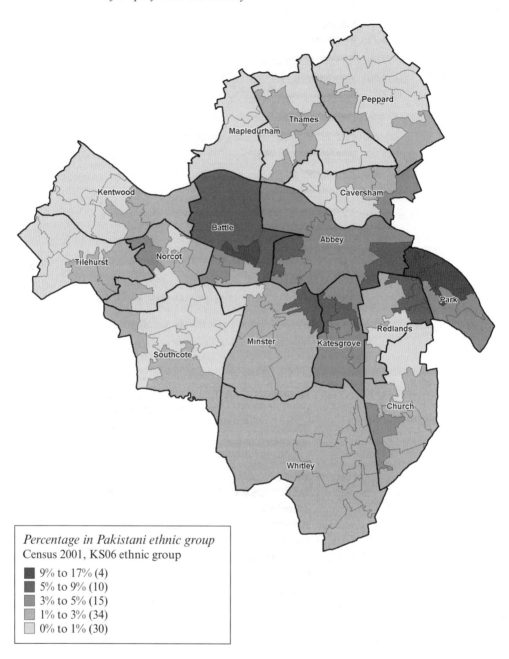

Percentage in Pakistani ethnic group
Census 2001, KS06 ethnic group

- 9% to 17% (4)
- 5% to 9% (10)
- 3% to 5% (15)
- 1% to 3% (34)
- 0% to 1% (30)

Source: Reading Borough Council.

Figure 8.7   Distribution of Pakistani population in Reading

(who were aged 16) were students. Only three respondents (at the time of interview) were in paid work: Selina (aged 20), Sharon (aged 20) and Nina (aged 25).[1] Selina had done a variety of jobs and at the time of research was working on the shop floor of a major supermarket. Sharon was also working on the shop floor of a high street department store. Nina, who took a YTS (youth training scheme) placement after leaving school, was working as an administrator but had gone part-time after having a baby. Zarina had just had a baby and was on maternity leave and unsure about when or if she would return to paid work. The majority of the younger women in post-16 education were in school. Only three respondents (Zara, Tara and Reena) had been, or were, attending college. Only two respondents were aiming to attend university (to study law and medicine respectively). Only two respondents were university graduates. The majority of women had achieved at least six passes in the national General Certificate of Secondary Education (GCSE) examinations upon completion of a two-year course of study. Five were studying for General National Vocational Qualifications (GNVQ) and six were either studying for or had achieved three A-levels (pre-university course).[2] Nonetheless, the path from school to university and then the labour market, for the majority of respondents, was neither smooth nor direct. The issue of space–time constraints dominated all the interviews with the respondents.

In and outside the closet

> Pakistani girls and women have a lot to offer. Unfortunately we are denied our right to go further and to pursue our goals, dreams and ambitions. Our families are still living in the dark ages and instead of encouraging . . . us to blossom, attempt to stifle any growth they feel threatens their control over us and place unjustified obstacles in our paths to keep us isolated and trapped. (Seema, aged 25)

British Pakistani women's motivation, direction and achievements in education and the labour market are shaped not only by their membership of a marginal ethnic community but also by their economic class and, within this, the educational levels of their parents. The lower the economic class and parental educational levels, generally the lower the value placed on education and social mobility and, in turn, the greater the parental barriers to their daughters' achievements in these areas. This is significant, because multiple marginalisations that combine class and ethnicity with the experiences of displacement and dislocation frequently support a retreat into difference. Indeed, as sociologist Tariq Modood (1992, p. 261) has pointed out, this 'semi-industrialized, newly urbanized, working class community that is only one generation away from rural peasantry' is so marginalized in British society that it may be referred to as an underclass.

In response, identification with Islam promotes a sense of empowerment as it transforms a marginal 'community' within the heart of the West into a member of an imagined global community. It is in this context that the family has become particularly significant. As Taraki (1995, p. 645) has argued, radical Islam 'created an area of [Muslim] cultural resistance around women and the family which came to represent the inviolable repository of Muslim identity'. Thus, the family offers working-class British Pakistanis a refuge from marginalisation and a means of resistance through the marking and maintenance of a collective Muslim and/or Pakistani identity that centres on women, which legitimates the control and regulation of women.

Marginalisation, collective identity and womanhood

The Muslim family is the foundation of Muslim collectivity (Afshar, 1998). Foucault (1979) points out that the family is a key site for the production of subjectivity. In this sense, it is a unit for the reproduction of the collectivity both biologically and culturally. Only marriage is seen to ensure that children who are born to 'women are not only biologically but also symbolically within the boundaries of the collectivity' (Yuval-Davies, 1992, p. 285). Heterosexual purity is posited as a requirement for making a good marriage (Rozario, 2002) and the formation of Muslim families. Mothers not only bear responsibility for the reproduction of the collectivity in biological terms but also in ideological terms: they are the ones seen as principally responsible for the transmission of culture to future generations. Thus women are posited as the guardians of collective identity, which in turn makes them the guarded (Afshar, 1994), legitimating the ordering of women's bodies in space and time. As one 'community' elder with whom I spoke argued, 'women must be protected. They must be shielded from corruption, because they are in charge of our future generations'. It is in this context that their bodily presence and visibility in fields defined as masculine become subject to varying, and often highly restrictive, regulations. Family and/or male honour is perceived to reside in women's bodies and their heterosexual purity (Afshar, 1989). Women's heterosexual purity is scripted as being endangered by unrelated or *na-muharram* men, but it is women's own bodies that are held responsible for they are regarded as *fitna* (Badran, 1995), that is 'naturally' provocative, exuding sexuality, enticing men and thereby undermining the family and threatening social chaos.

At the same time, though, patriarchal discourses, both secular and religious, posit male sexuality as 'naturally' 'rampant and unfettered' (see McDowell and Court, 1994, p. 730). Consequently, the concern for women's (hetero)sexual purity, and through this for the Muslim family and identity, becomes heightened within spatial contexts that enable or foster their encounters with *na-muharram* men. In order to counter the possibilities for the loss of sexual control, the sexes must be spatially segregated to reduce the risk of sexual tensions. This segregation of the sexes is referred to as the system of *purdah* (literally meaning curtain) that is instituted in many Muslim states. *Purdah* also refers to veiling. Since male sexuality is constructed as rampant by nature, it is women who are held responsible for maintaining control thus they, rather than men, endure spatial containment, being ideologically, discursively and physically restricted when and where possible to the private sphere and the veil. The veil forms an enclosure, a barrier, to counter the threat from the sexualised feminine body. Accordingly, as feminist theologian Riffat Hassan (quoted in Rahman, 1996, p. 92) notes, Islamist ideologies relegate 'women . . . [to] a sphere and the rest of the world belongs to men'. As a result, from an early age Pakistani girls learn that their access to public spaces is restricted. Hence, Reena recalled how, from as far back as she could remember, 'we were not even allowed to visit the corner shop or friends', while for her part Hina commented how 'girls are not allowed out even to town for personal shopping, for longer than say a couple of hours. Boys are allowed to be out all day'.

In discussing such ideological constructions of the family and, especially, women's bodies, however, it is important to recognise that in the diasporic context in Britain, working-class Pakistanis faced with the need to maintain and strengthen collective identity negotiate a very different kind of space compared to those living in Islamist states.

In many such states, for example in the large cities of Pakistan, there exists a feminine public sphere (albeit one which is very unevenly developed) allowing women some presence in the public sphere without challenging the gender boundaries. In Britain, however, Pakistani Muslim women must contend with liberal, Western urban landscapes that not only enable mixed-sex encounters but, at times, might also require them. As Rhea points out, 'parents say that you can't work with boys but this is an English country; you can't change that'. Given this reality, the 'community' therefore seeks to address and limit the impact of these landscapes on women's (hetero)sexual purity through the imposition of many contradictions and paradoxes. Hence, families and 'community' members actively seek, for instance, to police women's dress, behaviour and presence in British public spaces.

It is perhaps worth remembering, in this context, that Foucault (1980, p. 153) talked about the fear of dark spaces that haunted the eighteenth century because darkness prevented the 'visibility of things of men and truths'. These spaces, then, were the dark, shadowy nooks and crannies of the landscape where disease, social and political unrest could grow and fester without being detected and countered, and it is appropriate to remind ourselves that the century of Enlightenment was a project to eliminate areas of darkness. Significantly, though, 'dark', or as I prefer to call them 'opaque', spaces do more than simply block the light; they also block the gaze, they block visibility. Hence, crowded urban streets are opaque spaces, for as many social theorists have commented, urban streets allow anonymity and the freedom to disappear into the crowd of city life and escape the gaze of the community. Thus, in Reading it is not so much Pakistani Muslim women's visible presence in transparent public spaces that provides cause for concern, but their presence in insufficiently regulated opaque spaces. As a result, there is a constant tension between permitting young women to take up opportunities and progress in the education system and concern for the family honour and for the daughter's marriage, which remains the main goal for the majority of parents. As one of my respondents, aged 17, lamented: 'marriage, I feel, is something that is emphasized too much in our religion; everybody has to get married'.

The importance of marriage was reflected in the lives of my respondents, as the four aged 25 and over were all married, and five aged between 16 and 20 were engaged to be married. However, marriage is often a major point of discontinuity in the lives of young women. Thus, while educating daughters to secondary school-level is compulsory and acceptable, when marriage is the main goal higher education and paid work are not seen as worthwhile, particularly if their pursuit threatens family honour and future marriage. This attitude draws from longstanding cultural mores in South Asia, where a daughter is historically regarded as *praya dhan* or wealth that belongs to another – that is, wealth that belongs not to the parents but to the in-laws, the family into which the daughter will marry. Within this context, once the daughter is married and safely transferred into the hands of her husband and in-laws she is held responsible for their honour and it is they who have the authority over her to safeguard it. The result is that, as interview respondent Quaida observed, 'there is life before marriage and life after marriage and the two are very different'. The impact upon these young women's lives of such practices is evident in the case of 16-year-old Farah, whose future mother-in-law called for the date of the marriage to be brought forward so that, as a daughter-in-law, Farah could take over the household duties. This meant that Farah had to abandon her dream of post-16 education and teacher training because 'they expect you to cook and clean [and this gives you] no chance to work outside the home'.

Such mores are reflected in labour market data. As I noted earlier, census 2001 data for the UK as a whole show that the number of Pakistani women participating in the formal labour market is the second lowest for all women, including ethnic minority women. One of my respondents pointed out to me that in Reading, until recently, young Pakistani women were expected to leave school and remain in the parental home awaiting marriage. However, changes in immigration laws in the 1980s, affecting British nationals seeking overseas marriages, have forced more young Pakistani women into the formal labour market. The tight-knit kinship structure of Pakistani families and the preference given to cousin marriages has meant that, as second generation British-born Pakistanis began reaching marriageable age, the number of marriages to partners in Pakistan rose rapidly (Ballard, 1991; Berrington, 1991). Home Office figures suggest that more Pakistani fiancés and husbands are accepted for settlement in Britain than is the case for any other ethnic group (Berrington, 1991). In order for overseas fiancés/husbands to gain entry into the UK, though, British nationals must be able to demonstrate that they are able to provide them with financial support. While this requirement offers some women who become engaged to overseas fiancés opportunities to pursue formal employment, for others, though, it signals the end of opportunities for further/higher education. For instance, once Seema's marriage was arranged to a man in Pakistan she came under pressure from her family to leave school and to abandon her goal of completing A-levels and undertake a degree course at university so that she could work and thereby ensure that her fiancé gained entry to Britain for marriage. Seema took up employment, but against great pressure from her family enrolled in evening-based A-level courses. As her fiancé's visa was delayed she enrolled in a degree course to study law, in spite of her father's opposition (he would not speak to her for six months). Finally, after Seema graduated, her fiancé was able to gain a visa and they were married. After marriage, Seema's new husband would not permit her to gain employment.

Significantly, many of the younger respondents had negotiated parental permission to work very locally during the school holidays (for a discussion of the ways in which young women negotiate parental constraints, see Mohammad, 1999). The majority were required to be home by early evening, a requirement which restricted them to employment in jobs that were 9 am to 5 pm and in the proximity of their locality. They did not see this situation changing when, or rather if, they were able to seek and gain permanent employment. What is noteworthy in this is that these spatial and temporal constraints prohibit women from entering many occupations or professions and not only those that involve evening or night shifts – they can even prevent women taking jobs which require attendance on training courses away from home. This happened to Sharon (aged 20), who was working at that time as a sales assistant in the cosmetics department at a high street store and who recalled how she had to turn down a number of work opportunities which required her to do evening hours on a regular basis.[3] She also had to turn down opportunities for promotion within her present work, such as a move from general sales to become a representative for a cosmetic house, because this involved spending a week away from home on a training course. Tara noted how, when travel away from home was required as part of paid work or for educational purposes, places which are familiar – that is, those that have a cultural proximity to the parental everyday environment – are much more likely to see an easing of parental restrictions than those places which seem foreign. Thus, a school or work trip to Edinburgh, for example, would be more likely to find parental approval than one to Paris, despite the geographical proximity of Paris. Tara told me that it is very difficult for Pakistani women to embark on careers that might involve regular travel away from home. She suggested that the most she could expect to negotiate is a few, occasional nights away from home during the week. Weekends, she argued, were a different matter for, like particular spaces, they are seen to be more conducive to immoral activity 'because of all the stuff you can get up to. The weekend is free time for you to do what you want'. The weekend is, then, a space–time that offers greater opportunity to socialise with the opposite sex and hence nurture office romances.

One respondent, Sharon, was pressured by her father to leave an office job with prospects. Although her employers permitted her to wear *salwar/khameez* (Pakistani dress) in the office (one of her father's earlier conditions for her entry into the labour market), her father would not entertain his daughter's continued employment in the mixed-gender environment of the office. Soon after her appointment he became aware that the office environment contrasted with school environment in that office discipline was related to work efficiency with little or no control on office relationships. For him, a mixed-gender environment that blocks the policing gaze of the parents was perceived to foster romantic liaisons. Although Sharon later took the position of shop assistant in a town-centre store, it is notable that here, in contrast to the office space, on the shop floor she is made immobile, both socially (there are fewer possibilities for promotion) and spatially. For her father, then, the shop floor is a transparent and panoptic space. In this space Sharon performs her duties as shop assistant wearing a modified uniform that identifies her as a member of staff, engaged with the customers. Sharon's body is disciplined and self-regulated at all times by the public gaze and by the presence of closed-circuit TV cameras monitoring the activities of the shoppers and the staff. Moreover, while in the office Sharon could often slip in and out for half an hour or even a whole day away without her father becoming aware of it. In contrast, on the shop floor she may only leave for lunch and her two daily breaks at set, pre-established times. Moreover, Sharon's father, who lives close by, is able to call in to the store any time during the day on the pretext of browsing the merchandise and ensure that his daughter is exactly where she claims to be.

A final issue involves the matter of clothing, particularly adoption of the headscarf, and its impact upon women's position in the labour market. At the time of research only one of my respondents had adopted a headscarf and none of the women were veiled. Veiling has grown noticeably amongst second- and even third-generation Pakistanis, particularly in the larger cities such as Birmingham. The issue of the veil in the public arena in the context of the classroom and in the labour market is a highly controversial topic, exciting much debate around the world. The demands in France of Moroccan/Algerian students and in Singapore of Malay students for permission to wear the veil in school have been met with great resistance. In Britain the issue has also surfaced with respect to the labour market, with two recent cases opening up a wider debate on the integration of immigrant minorities. In the first, Shabnam Mughal, an immigration lawyer who refused to remove her full face veil, was taken off a case when the judge adjourned the hearing.[4] Both Ms Mughal and the judge were later replaced. In the second, Aishah Azmi, a 23-year-old assistant teacher, was hired to provide language support to children for whom English is a second language.[5] Although she attended her interview unveiled,

Aisha insisted on being veiled in the classroom. Aisha was dismissed from her job when the children complained that they had difficulty understanding her English lessons. In October 2006, Jack Straw, a senior British Cabinet Minister, courted controversy with his statement that the veil is a 'visible symbol of separation and difference' and that it makes community relations more difficult.

In considering the issue of veiling, though, it is important to understand that the current resurgence of the veil has to be viewed in its historical context, for it is often a radically modern, rather than a traditional, phenomenon. Indeed, the veil has become a politically charged symbol of Islam. With the decline of secularism and rise of Islamic fundamentalism, as a response to Western imperialism or 'Westoxification', the veil has become a symbol of resistance. In Britain the rise in the veil's significance for second- and third-generation young Muslim women relates to growing centrality of Islam as a mode of identity, in response to persistent and enduring alienation. After 9/11, as Islamic identity has become racialised and racial tensions have increased, the sense of alienation has intensified and it is in this context that veiled Muslim women have become more visible in the public sphere, in part due to increased numbers, but also because of the spotlight they are under. It is important to remember that whilst many Muslim women insist on wearing the veil, there are many professional Muslim women who reject it. Moreover, many Muslim feminists argue that the veil is not mandatory in Islam and that historically it was part of Christian dress (Badran, 1995). Nevertheless, the veil serves at least three functions.

First, it acts as a marker of Islamic identity, thus in a diasporic context it is about marking a difference and separation. Secondly, it is a way to declare a commitment to heterosexual purity and, by desexualising the female body, it is a means of maintaining heterosexual purity. Thus the veil can be seen as a strategic move for young women who are able to negotiate greater spatial and cultural freedoms by adopting the headscarf or veil. However, there is also a third function that the veil enables: it produces an opaque space, that is, the full-face veil, or *burqa*, blocks the gaze, including the policing gaze, by hiding the identity of the wearer (see Goodwin, 1995). The veil, then, creates a microgeography of separation, allowing complete anonymity by blocking, and therefore offering protection from, the sexual gazes of unrelated men. At the same time, this seclusion and anonymity offered by the veil is enabling of alternative lives/lifestyles, sexualities that might contravene Islam under its cover. (It is notable, for instance, that a suspect in the hunt for an alleged terrorist in Britain was reported to have made his escape under the cover of a veil by disguising himself as a Muslim woman (O'Neill and Browne, 2006).) However, despite the veil's growing popularity for the reasons just outlined and its, perhaps paradoxical, ability to provide some women a degree of opacity in public spaces, the presence of veiled women in spaces of the labour market is being challenged, both for practical reasons (that it does or is perceived to interfere with the job) but also because of the discrimination that ethnic minority women continue to experience in the labour market and to which the veil is seen by many to contribute.

In response to some of the issues addressed above, a 2005 report on ethnic minority populations of Reading made several recommendations to increase Pakistani women's participation in the labour market at the level of training and employment (Rhamie, 2005). These include the setting up of women-only courses within the community; offering degrees within the community for women who are not permitted to attend universities;

and offering women-only residential courses in an academic environment. The report also suggested that employers be culturally sensitive and ensure that not only are women permitted to wear Islamic dress in the workplace but, also, that they are made to feel comfortable with it. Employers were also encouraged to ensure that Pakistani women do not have to work in close contact with men. The report, then, sought to promote the development of human capital amongst the community and to change the nature and perceptions of the workplace amongst Pakistani parents. What the report specifically did not address, however, is the ways in which the focus on marriage affects women's motivation for achievement. Hence, while the labour market can adapt to accommodate Muslim women's requirements, what of parental concerns over those women who do not wish to regulate themselves in accordance with Islam? Paradoxically, then, the more the labour market offers women opportunities to achieve and succeed, to become upwardly mobile, the more it is going to be perceived by many traditionalists as dangerous to the social order within the working-class community. Without making more fundamental changes, working-class women's participation in the labour market can be improved, but for the majority of women it will remain very restricted.

Conclusion

In this chapter I have examined the role of space as a significant factor in the gender politics of the working-class Pakistani community in Reading, with consequences for Pakistani women's participation and success in the labour market and opportunities for upward mobility. I have argued that the centrality of women's bodies and their heterosexual purity to the making of marriage and the Muslim family, which are integral to the production of group identity, affects women's spatial mobility. In order to 'protect' women's heterosexual purity, ideological and, where possible, physical gender segregation of space is instituted. This system is known as *purdah* (literally: 'curtain') and implies a form of enclosure. It is also the term used for the veiling which reduces the sexual tension produced by the presence of women's bodies in the space of the masculine public arena. In societies where gender segregation is in place within the public arena, the concern is to ensure that when women step outside their homes they maintain a very discreet presence. In the UK, however, opaque spaces outside the home that are mixed-gender and not regulated to prevent the development of male–female intimacy are viewed as dangerous. These may be spaces of school, the university campus or the labour market. Given that marriage and family are largely regarded as the main orientation for the lives of daughters, the pursuit of opportunities in the education system and labour market that carry a threat to young women's heterosexual purity and to the family honour, with all the consequences this brings for their marriage prospects, is thus not deemed worthwhile. To improve the employment prospects for diasporic working-class Pakistani women, then, requires attention to the status of British Pakistani men, whose sense of marginality translates into the social and spatial control and regulation of women.

Notes

1. All of the names of respondents in this chapter are pseudonyms.
2. GNVQs are vocational qualifications which prepare students who have left secondary school for employment. They are generally undertaken at colleges of further education, which are distinct from universities in that the former rarely, if ever, offer degree courses.

3. The pseudonym Sharon was chosen to reflect this young woman's vision of her own position within the Pakistani 'community'.
4. www.telegraph.co.uk/news/main.jhtml?xml=/news/2006/11/08/nmuslim08.xml.
5. http://news.bbc.co.uk/2/hi/uk_news/6068408.stm.

References

Afshar, H. (1989), 'Gender roles and the "moral economy of kin" among Pakistani women in West Yorkshire', *New Community*, **15** (2), 211–25.
Afshar, H. (1994), 'Muslim women in West Yorkshire: growing up with real and imaginary values amidst conflicting views of self and society in feminist thought', in H. Afshar and M. Maynard (eds), *The Dynamics of 'Race' and Gender – Some Feminist Interventions*, London: Taylor and Francis, pp. 127–47.
Afshar, H. (1998), *Islam and Feminisms: An Iranian Case Study*, Basingstoke: Palgrave.
Anwar, M. (1979), *The Myth of Return Pakistanis in Britain*, London: Heinemann Educational Books.
Badran, M. (1995), *Feminists, Islam, and Nation: Gender and the Making of Modern Egypt*, Princeton, NJ: Princeton University Press.
Ballard, R. (1991), 'The Pakistanis: stability and introspection', in C. Peach (ed.), *The Ethnic Minority Populations of Great Britain*, Vol. 2, London, HMSO, pp. 121–49.
Berrington, A. (1991), 'Marriage patterns and inter-ethnic unions', in David Coleman and John Salt (eds), *Ethnicity in the 1991 Census*, London: HMSO, pp. 178–212.
Foucault, M. (1979), 'On governmentality', *Ideology and Consciousness*, **6**, 5–22.
Foucault, M. (1980), *Power/Knowledge: Selected Interviews and Other Writings 1972–1977*, New York: Pantheon Books.
Friedan, B. (1963), *The Feminine Mystique*, London: Gollancz; Harmondsworth: Penguin.
Goodwin, J. (1995), *Price of Honour: Muslim Women Lift the Veil of Silence on the Islamic World*, London: Warner.
Hiro, D. (1971), *Black British, White British: A History of Race Relations in Britain*, London: Paladin.
McDowell, L. and G. Court (1994), 'Performing work: bodily representations in merchant banks', *Environment and Planning D: Society and Space*, **12** (6), 727–50.
Modood, T. (1992), 'British Asian Muslims and the Rushdie Affair', in J. Donald and A. Rattansi (eds), *'Race', Culture and Difference*, London: Sage in conjunction with Open University, pp. 260–77.
Mohammad, R. (1999), 'Marginalisation, Islamism and the production of the "other's" "other"', *Gender, Place and Culture*, **6** (3), 221–40.
O'Neill, S. and A. Browne (2006), 'Suspect in terror hunt used veil to evade arrest', *The Times* (London), 9 October, available at: http://www.freerepublic.com/focus/f-news/1716055/posts.
Rabinow, P. (1991), *The Foucault Reader*, London: Penguin.
Rahman, F.N. (1996), 'A feminist theologian on women, Islam and feminism', *Women's Own Karachi*, Riaz Ahmed Mansuri, August, pp. 91–3.
Rhamie, J. (2005), 'Reading Testbed Learning Community: a mapping exercise of research on ethnic minority groups in Reading', Reading Learning Partnership, Reading, available at www.readingllp.co.uk.
Rozario, S. (2002) 'Poor and "dark": what is my future? Identity construction and adolescent women in Bangladesh', in L. Manderson and P. Liamputtong (eds), *Coming of Age in South and Southeast Asia: Youth, Courtship and Sexuality*, Richmond, Surrey: Curzon, pp. 42–57.
Said, E. (1994), *Culture and Imperialism*, New York: Vintage Books.
Taraki, L. (1995), 'Islam is the solution: Jordanian Islamists and the dilemma of the "modern woman"', *British Journal of Sociology*, **46** (4), 643–61.
Yuval-Davies, N. (1992), 'Fundamentalism, multiculturalism and women in Britain', in J. Donald and A. Rattansi (eds), *'Race', Culture and Difference*, London: Sage in conjunction with Open University, pp. 278–91.

9 Filipino migration and the spatialities of labour market subordination

Philip F. Kelly

In 1987 a national controversy erupted in the Philippines when it was revealed that the new edition of the Oxford English Dictionary would include the word 'Filipino', and that one of the associated usages of the word would refer to 'domestic help'. A few years later, a Greek dictionary similarly defined the word as a generic term for a maid or nanny – as in, 'my Filipina is Mexican'. These incidents epitomised a nagging malaise afflicting Filipino national self-esteem. By the late 1980s, for many countries around the world, the Philippines had become a major supplier of subordinate working-class labour. As engine hands on ships, as construction workers in the Middle East, as production line operators in Taiwanese factories, or as domestic workers in Canada and Europe, expatriate Filipinos have come to occupy the least secure, least remunerative and least desirable places in the global labour market.

Why is it that Filipinos appear to have been incorporated into the global labour market in this way? This is essentially two questions, rather than one: why Filipinos, and why the concentration in subordinate occupations? An orthodox approach to these questions would focus upon the education and skills that an employee brings to the labour market and the motivations and rationalities that a migrant acts upon in deciding to work and live overseas. But such approaches devolve all explanation to the scale of the individual migrant worker and are entirely inadequate to explain why migrant workers from a particular place appear to be over-represented in particular segments of the work-force somewhere else. This chapter focuses instead on the multiple spatialities that shape, contain, regulate, discipline and construct migrants, and through which they move. In this way, a more complete explanation for Filipino segmentation and subordination in the labour market can be constructed.

Labour market outcomes demand locally contextualised explanations – and in the case of immigrant workers, this means attention to both specific sending areas and specific host cities. This chapter will therefore focus on the experiences of Filipino immigrant workers in Toronto, Canada. This allows the dimensions of the issue to be empirically defined (through data on Filipino labour market integration in the city) but it also allows a variety of geographical processes to be identified. The empirical puzzle in the Toronto case involves a recent Filipino immigrant population with high levels of education, language skills and other forms of human capital being over-concentrated in low-paying, precarious jobs in the service sector or manufacturing. In attempting to explain this anomaly, I identify four spatialities involved in the process of migration and labour market integration. The first relates to the territorial regulatory spaces in which administrative structures of both labour export and labour import are established in the Philippines and Canada – these include labour export strategies, immigration programmes and rules governing access to professional accreditation. The second concerns the spaces of home or social reproduction that are intimately linked to immigrants' experiences of the workplace and labour market – either in the spatiality of home–work relationships in Toronto, or the transnational relations that exist between migrants and family members left behind in the Philippines. The third spatiality is within the micro-scale of the workplace – where hierarchies are established and enforced, often based upon access to certain workplaces or spaces within workplaces. Finally, the elephant in the room that underpins all of these spatialities is global capitalism in both its contemporary and historical forms. Past forms have left a legacy of racialised and gendered hierarchies, which mark certain bodies as 'naturally' subordinate and others as superior (Espiritu, 2003). Contemporary and past processes of uneven development under capitalism have defined the unequal relationship between Canada and the Philippines, such that labour flows move in one direction and not the other.

Together these spatialities provide an explanatory framework for understanding Filipino labour market subordination. While some of the issues that arise are necessarily specific to the Canadian or Philippine contexts, many are also generically applicable to migrant workers the world over. They illustrate the productions of space that convert skilled professionals from one place into the underclass of another.

Defining the problem: Filipino labour market subordination

The Canadian economy, like many others around the world, has become increasingly dependent on a steady flow of temporary and permanent migrant workers to replenish its dwindling native-born labour force (Hiebert, 2000). In the 1990s 70 per cent of all net labour force growth in Canada came from immigration, and by 2011 it is estimated that this figure will be 100 per cent (Statistics Canada, 2003). And yet it has been increasingly recognised that while immigrants are being selected on the basis of academic and professional credentials, the occupations they end up finding leave them deskilled and deprofessionalised. As this section will show, the Filipino experience of labour market integration provides a particularly aggravated example of this process (for further details, see Kelly, 2006).

In the 2001 census just over 223000 people in Canada (out of a national population of around 30 million) were recorded as immigrants with Filipino[1] ethnic identities. This was a large increase over previous censuses, reflecting the fact that the Philippines had been Canada's third most important source of immigrants in the 1990s (after China and India) – indeed, over half of all Filipinos recorded in the 2001 census had arrived since 1990.

Canada has a variety of immigration programmes, including independent skilled worker categories, family reunification and business/investor categories. Filipinos have used all of these categories but have also dominated a much smaller programme for 'live-in caregivers'. During the 1990s, the Live-in Caregiver Programme accounted for around one-quarter of all Filipinos gaining immigrant status in Canada. As I will explain later, this has had a major influence on the experiences of Filipinos in the Canadian labour market and on the gender composition of the Filipino community – overall, women comprised almost 60 per cent of immigrants from the Philippines in the period 1980–2001.

The geography of Filipino settlement is decidedly urban, and is concentrated in just a handful of gateway cities. Of the 308575 people who declared their 'visible minority'[2] status to be Filipino in the 2001 census (including both immigrants and Canadian-born),

133 675 were in the Toronto Census Metropolitan Area (CMA). Many of the rest were in the Vancouver, Winnipeg and Montreal areas. Filipinos have, therefore, tended to settle in Canada's urban centres, with Toronto the single largest destination. Within Toronto and Vancouver, however, Filipinos are remarkably dispersed. Research has shown that statistically, Filipinos exhibit among the lowest levels of residential segregation of any visible minority group in Canada (Bauder and Sharpe, 2002). This is important, as it speaks to the integration of Filipino immigrants into the Canadian urban fabric.

Almost 57 per cent of Filipino immigrants residing in Toronto in 2001 had some university-level education. This compared with 33 per cent for all immigrant groups, and just under 35 per cent for all residents of Canada. Moreover, most Filipinos arrive with a strong command of English. This is reflected in the 'Canadian Language Capability' recorded by immigration officials. Proficiency in neither English nor French was recorded for 44 per cent of all immigrants between 1980–2001, but this applied to only 21 per cent of Philippine-born immigrants. Furthermore, arriving from a society in which educational and governmental institutions, and many cultural practices, were largely shaped by US colonialism, Filipinos come with a high degree of familiarity with North American culture and institutions.

However, a distinctive feature of Filipino integration is the concentration of immigrants in relatively few labour market niches. Healthcare and manufacturing, in particular, are prime destinations for working Filipinos, and Filipinos have been shown to have among the highest relative levels of segmentation when compared with other groups. Of even more significance, however, is that within these sectors there is a tendency towards concentration in lower status occupations. Despite their high levels of human capital, then, as a group Filipinos occupy marginal socioeconomic positions after arrival in Canada.

A numerical way of representing concentration in the labour market using the 2001 census is to calculate the ratio (or location quotient) between the percentage of Filipinos in a job category and the percentage of the population as a whole in a job category (see Table 9.1). In healthcare, for example, Filipino men and women are respectively 5.3 and 3.3 times as likely to be working in 'assisting occupations' than are the male and female populations as a whole. But in occupations such as physician, dentist or surgeon, Filipinos are greatly under-represented – using a similar calculation, there are about one quarter as many Filipino men and about one half as many Filipina women as there 'should be' in such occupations. (Table 9.1 shows the jobs in which Filipinos are most over- and under-represented. It illustrates both the pattern of concentration in healthcare and manufacturing sectors, and in the lower occupational echelons within these sectors.)

The over-representation of Filipinos in lower-end jobs is also reflected in aggregate income data. Census data from 2001 show Filipino men and women earning less than any other comparison group – indeed, only gender is a more significant predictor of earnings than is being Filipino (see Table 9.2).

The picture of labour market outcomes for Filipino immigrants is not, therefore, a positive one. To summarise, Filipinos tend to have high levels of education as well as other less tangible forms of cultural preparedness, including high levels of English language competency. These assets result in a relatively successful integration, both into the social fabric of Canadian cities and into formal employment – overall, Filipinos have very

Table 9.1   Selected occupational location quotients (LQ)* for Filipino immigrants in Toronto, 2001

LQ	MALE Filipino immigrants	LQ	FEMALE Filipina immigrants
5.4	Nurse supervisors and registered nurses	4.1	Childcare and home support workers
5.3	Assisting occupations in support of health services	3.3	Assisting occupations in support of health services
3.6	Childcare and home support workers	2.7	Nurse supervisors and registered nurses
3.0	Assemblers in manufacturing	2.2	Technical and related occupations in health
2.9	Technical and related occupations in health	1.8	Assemblers in manufacturing
2.5	Machine operators in manufacturing	1.7	Mechanics
2.1	Labourers in processing, manufacturing and utilities	1.4	Machinists, metal forming, shaping and erecting occupations
0.4	Judges, lawyers, psychologists, social workers, ministers of religion, and policy and programme officers	0.3	Senior management occupations
0.4	Construction trades	0.3	Technical occupations in art, culture, recreation and sport
0.3	Professional occupations in art and culture	0.3	Professional occupations in art and culture
0.2	Professional occupations in health	0.2	Teachers and professors
0.2	Teachers and professors	0.0	Construction trades
0.2	Senior management occupations	0.0	Heavy equipment and crane operators, including drillers

Note: * Calculated as a ratio of per cent Filipino Immigrants in Occupational Category to per cent of Total Population (by gender) in Occupational Category. Hence a figure of 1.0 means no relative over- or under-concentration in a particular job.

Source: Calculated from Statistics Canada (2001).

Table 9.2   Employment earnings ($CAD) of Filipinos and others in Toronto CMA, 2000

	Filipino immigrants	All visible minority immigrants	All visible minority non-immigrants	All immigrants	All non-immigrants	Entire population
Male income	39 295	43 162	46 746	50 748	66 133	58 789
Female income	31 846	33 273	39 088	36 198	45 395	40 984

Note: These figures refer to average employment incomes in Canadian dollars from full-year full-time employment in 2000 for the Toronto Census Metropolitan Area.

Source: Calculated from Statistics Canada (2001).

high levels of participation in the labour force, low levels of unemployment and welfare claims and a low incidence of self-employment. Nevertheless, integration has tended to be in subordinated places and roles – in Toronto, for instance, Filipinos generally live in poorer neighbourhoods and are heavily concentrated in certain occupational roles.

In the context of real lives and immigration experiences, what these data imply is a process of deprofessionalisation and subordination in the workforce for Filipinos. Even where they are employed in the sectors or industries for which they are trained, Filipinos are frequently found in lower-paid, lower-status and less-professionally recognised jobs. Thus, production engineers become machine operators, accountants become data-entry clerks, and registered nurses become nursing assistants. While Filipino immigrants appear to endure a particularly accentuated process of deprofessionalisation, it is a pattern that is repeated across many visible minority immigrant groups, as research has consistently demonstrated the mismatch that exists between immigrant human capital and labour market outcomes (see, for example, Bauder, 2003; Galabuzi, 2006).

A narrow labour market analysis of this situation would argue that immigrants are not bringing the right kinds of skills and experiences to the labour market and are being evaluated against what the market requires (Li (2003) provides a summary of this view, while Becker ([1964] 1993) provides a definitive statement of human capital theory; see also Peck and Theodore, Chapter 5 in this volume, for how these arguments are articulated in slightly different contexts). It has been argued, for example, that demand in the Canadian labour market is for tradespersons and low-skilled occupations, rather than the degree-holding professionals favoured by current immigration programmes (Reitz, 2001). Thus, deskilling and deprofessionalisation in the labour market is taken to be a reflection of the fact that immigrants are not coming with the skills for which there is demand in the labour market. The emphasis of studies that focus solely on market supply and demand, therefore, is upon the inadequacies of the immigrant rather than upon the operation of the labour market.

Similar conclusions can be reached when the immigrant is individualised and treated as the agent of his or her own professional demise. In Statistics Canada's Longitudinal Survey of Immigrants to Canada, for example, immigrants are asked to explain the difficulties they face in the labour market. The respondents cite the lack of Canadian work experience, their lack of contacts in the relevant labour market, the lack of recognition of foreign experience or credentials and their lack of language skills (Schellenberg and Maheux, 2007). In each case it is some dimension of 'lacking' on the part of the immigrant that explains labour market subordination. A further economic approach emphasises labour market conditions at the time of immigration, noting that weak demand in the labour market will often leave even well-qualified immigrants without appropriate employment (McDonald and Worswick, 1998).

While there is some evidence to support such human capital approaches to immigrant labour market integration, data also suggest that the market evaluation of credentials is an incomplete explanation for disparities in immigrant earnings and occupational segmentation (Li, 2003). What all have in common is that they locate explanations for subordination outside of the market, which is seen simply as an impartial sorting mechanism. Furthermore, the market is rendered as aspatial – a process usually conceptualised and contained at either urban or national scales, but neglectful of geographical processes that might be at work within or beyond those scales. The rest of this chapter explores these geographical processes and argues that they represent an important part of any explanation for immigrant labour market subordination.

Territorial regulatory spaces

The first spatiality to be explored concerns the territorial regulatory regimes that shape migrants and shape the opportunities that exist for mobility. The first of these regulatory spaces is found in the Philippines, where various branches of the national government oversee the training, marketing and deployment of overseas Filipino workers. The second is constituted by the Canadian federal government, which determines work visa programmes and immigration categories, along with the conditions that are attached to each. A third regulatory space is provided by Canadian provincial authorities, which are responsible for labour market regulation in general and access to professional accreditation in particular.

Any analysis that reads Filipino migration as the outcome of individual decisions misses the structures that shape and constrain such decisions within the Philippines. Various branches of the Philippine government have played a significant role in training, promoting and deploying Filipinos working overseas. While this apparatus is geared largely towards temporary contract work in places such as East Asia, the Middle East and Europe, the outcome of these deployments is often a subsequent application for permanent migration to immigrant-receiving countries such as Canada, the US, Australia and the UK.

Although Filipinos have been working overseas in significant numbers for at least a century, the Philippine state's active promotion of overseas work is generally dated from 1974, when the administration of Ferdinand Marcos (then ruling through martial law) enacted the Labour Code of the Philippines. The Code, and subsequent legislation, established an infrastructure that would promote the recruitment of Filipino workers overseas (Gonzalez, 1998; Tyner, 2004). It did this in several ways. First, the government established state bureaucracies that effectively acted as recruitment agencies for overseas workers. Later, as a private sector recruitment industry developed, state agencies turned to its regulation rather than active participation in the recruitment process. Second, the Philippine government actively promoted Filipino workers, for example through marketing missions to major destination countries and through monitoring of potential new demand for overseas contract workers around the world (Ball, 1997). Third, the state promulgated a discourse that represents overseas workers as heroic figures, working for the betterment of their families and homeland (Rodriguez, 2002). Hence, returning overseas workers are afforded special (though superficial) privileges upon arrival back in the Philippines (dedicated customs/immigration desks, duty free allowances, special foreign currency transactions and so on).

In addition to the promotion and regulation of overseas contract workers, the Philippine state has also overseen the creation of a training infrastructure that is, in many cases, explicitly aimed at preparing workers for employment around the globe. By 2003 there were, for example, nearly 300 licensed nursing colleges in the Philippines (up from about 120 in 1990) (Tan, 2003). Of the 354 154 nurses who passed the qualifying board exam in the Philippines between 1970 and 2004, fewer than 30 000 were actually employed as nurses in the Philippines. Thus, over 300 000 nurses trained in the Philippines had either left the profession or left the country.

The orientation of a nursing education to overseas work is explicit in a number of ways. Several colleges market themselves as preparing students for the global labour market. One university, for example, tags itself in brochures and other material as 'Your link to a global career'. Curricula are often explicitly designed for overseas employment. In an article in the *Philippine Journal of Nursing*, such a 'global approach' to nursing education was strongly endorsed:

> I think instead of lamenting the fact we are losing our graduates to foreign employee [*sic*], we should look at the positive side of it. The global market for our nurses demands that our nursing students should be educated not only [in] our local health systems, practices, and problems. . . . Our students should be taught about various cultures, health practices and beliefs they will be exposed to . . . (Barcelo, 2001, p. 16)

Paradoxically, however, while the country has a huge infrastructure for training nurses, local hospitals face a shortage of qualified personnel, and nursing schools have difficulty in retaining faculty (PCIJ, 2005). The expanding training infrastructure that exists is clearly geared towards the export of nursing labour. At least a part of the puzzle concerning Filipino labour market segmentation in healthcare, then, is that the Philippines has established itself as a training ground for a global workforce in this sector. Similar points could be made in relation to other occupations, such as domestic workers, childcare providers, and seamen, all of which are represented by an extensive training infrastructure in the Philippines.

The strategic creation of Philippine regulatory space as a training ground for certain kinds of globalised workers is only part of the story, however. The Canadian state is also implicated in labour market experiences of its Filipino immigrants. There are a variety of ways in which this argument could be substantiated, but the most directly relevant concerns the Live-in Caregiver Programme (LCP), which has been mentioned several times already. The LCP was established in 1992 as a successor to a previous visa programme for domestic workers. The LCP requires that enrollees live in the home of their employer for at least two years, as caregivers for children, the elderly or the disabled. At the end of that period the caregiver can apply for permanent residency (PR) status (which eventually leads to citizenship). PR status releases the caregiver from various restrictions placed upon them while under the LCP. As well as being required to live in the homes of their employers, caregivers may not do any work outside the home, may not be joined by their families, and may not avail themselves of educational and training programmes directed towards residents of Canada. These, though, are just the formal restrictions. Thus, even where educational opportunities might exist, the ability of a live-in caregiver to find either the time or the money to take advantage of them is very limited.

The result is that after their 'graduation' from the programme, caregivers have no Canadian work experience except domestic labour, they have been separated from their previous occupations or professions for several years, and very few have been able to engage in further training or education. With around 20 per cent of Filipinos entering Canada under the LCP in the 1980s and 1990s, these restrictions shape the subsequent labour market experiences for a great many immigrants. Regardless of their previous occupations or professions, many end up in precisely the kinds of jobs highlighted in Table 9.1 – low-level, insecure employment in healthcare, childcare and various other kinds of domestic work (McKay, 2002).

The effects of the LCP extend further, however, as immigrants arriving under other immigration categories are often joining relatives who had come earlier as caregivers. It is common practice for new immigrants to rely upon earlier immigrants for help and advice on settlement and job search issues. The contacts that caregivers provide will inevitably reflect their own occupational positions – thus childcare workers, hospital porters and personal support workers guide new immigrants into precisely these kinds of occupations. Furthermore, the period of separation enforced upon caregivers is not simply from their previous professions but also often from their own families. Evidence suggests that the children of caregivers who are eventually reunited with their parents in Canada undergo a severe psychological rupture, and high school dropout rates are high among such children – leading to a continuation of economic marginalisation into the second generation (Pratt, 2003).

In a less tangible way, the concentration of Filipinos in low-status occupations leads to stereotyping and racialisation processes in which Filipinos become constructed as 'naturally' suited to caring work – 'good with children', 'compassionate for the elderly', having 'a pleasant bedside manner'. Thus Filipino bodies become imbued with certain connotations, which further encourage their concentration in certain kinds of front-line care work (and which explicitly do not reference the Filipino body as managerial, supervisory or technically skilled) (England and Stiell, 1997; Pratt, 1999).

A quite different form of regulatory space is constructed at a sub-national scale in Canada, where provincial governments have jurisdiction over the regulation of labour markets. In the case of licensed professions (of which there are over 40, including engineering, accountancy and nursing), this jurisdiction has largely been devolved to independent professional regulatory bodies (the Professional Engineers of Ontario and the College of Nurses of Ontario, for example). Such regulatory bodies work at arm's length from government oversight, and while recent legislation in Ontario has attempted to enforce greater transparency in their adjudications over the equivalency of foreign credentials, they remain essentially autonomous. This autonomy empowers regulatory bodies to decide who will be granted access to practise a profession in the province, how foreign credentials and experience will be assessed, and what retraining or upgrading is needed before immigrant professionals can be licensed. Essentially, the professional regulatory bodies are the gatekeepers for professional accreditation, which also means that they police the barriers that immigrant professionals must clear (Girard and Bauder, 2007).

For many Filipino immigrants, the barriers to professional accreditation have been insurmountable. Many arrive with a debt load created by the costs of immigration, or an obligation to financially support family members left behind in the Philippines. As a result, the costs of retraining or upgrading skills are often unaffordable. Furthermore, many also complain that their credentials are not fairly assessed by regulatory bodies, which are not always well-informed about the nature and standards of curricula followed in the Philippines. Such ignorance often also leads to arbitrary assessments of Philippine credentials, so that graduates from the country's most prestigious schools (with rigorous English language instruction and North American curriculum materials) are treated more harshly than those from institutions with more impressive-sounding names. For Filipino professionals, then, the barriers erected and policed by regulatory bodies create a territorial exclusion from using their skills in Ontario. The explicit territoriality of this framework is emphasised by the relative ease with which foreign-trained professionals can practise in the United States. Indeed, significant numbers of Filipino immigrants to Canada subsequently move south of the border in order to practise their professions. For those that remain, the result is often an enforced deprofessionalisation and consignment to employment that does not require formal accreditation or which requires shorter periods of retraining. Thus, registered nurses will convert themselves into personal support workers, and accountants will become clerical workers or retail cashiers.

Spaces of home
Thus far, the explanation for Filipino deprofessionalisation and economic marginalisation has focused upon the territorial state (and quasi-state) apparatuses that shape and regulate migrants and their employment opportunities. However, the spatialities of immigrant economic experiences go far beyond this formulation of space as a territorial container for state power. A second form of spatiality in relation to the labour market has been widely recognised by economic geographers and takes the form of relationships between workplaces and homeplaces (Hanson and Pratt, 1995; McDowell, 1999). Decisions such as whether to participate in the waged workforce, whether to apply for a new job or a promotion, whether to take on an extra job or sideline activity and whether to seek additional training are not generally made by individuals in isolation but in the context of household responsibilities and relationships (Creese et al., 2006). In this case, however, 'homeplace' has a double meaning – it may refer either to the ways in which decisions in relation to waged work are shaped by unwaged responsibilities, obligations and divisions of labour in the immigrant household in Toronto, or it might relate to ongoing ties and relationships to family members back 'home' in the Philippines.

The economic marginalisation of immigrant households is a key starting point for understanding how families organise their engagement with the waged labour market. In a city such as Toronto, economic survival means, first of all, that all adults in a household are likely to be involved in waged work – even more so when individuals are working in the low-paid occupations where Filipinos are concentrated. Financial imperatives may also prevent Filipino immigrants from waiting to find work in an appropriate field, or from engaging in further training, or from applying for promotions that would decrease job security (for example, by taking a worker out of a union collective bargaining agreement). It would also not be uncommon to find people holding down two or more jobs in order to make ends meet and provide for dependents. A Filipina immigrant in Toronto might, for example, be working as a retail clerk during the day, as a babysitter in the evening and holding down another job at the weekend.

But there are inevitably spatial limits on job searches. These limits might relate to where social networks exist and thus how information about job opportunities circulates (Hanson and Pratt, 1995). They might also relate to how far individuals are able to commute in order to get to work. This in turn is related to how domestic responsibilities are divided within the household – who has to be home to meet children after school, who takes care of shopping, who does the cooking in the evening and so on (Dowling et al., 1999). Households may also find themselves juggling schedules so that the shift patterns of parents are coordinated in order to provide for childcare needs. In all of these ways, the home as a space in which divisions of labour are negotiated (and contested) has direct implications for the engagement of individuals with the waged labour force

(McDowell et al., 2005). The spatial ties between workplace and homeplace, then, dictate how these outcomes are configured.

Another set of homeplace ties concerns transnational linkages with family members in the Philippines. For some, the expenses of migration will have resulted in debts that need to be repaid – land might be mortgaged, or relatives might have loaned money to finance the application, the air ticket or the immigration consultant's fees. Over the longer-term, transnational obligations consist of responsibilities to support relatives: by subsidising their daily economic needs (usually in the case of immediate family members); by paying for specific expenses such as college fees or home improvements; or by assisting with occasional costs, such as the applications of other family members to work abroad. Whatever the nature of these transnational obligations, they are shouldered by many Filipino immigrants, and where they are financially onerous they will have material effects on the labour market decisions made by immigrants. Just as household financial needs in Toronto may necessitate holding down multiple jobs, or preclude engaging in further training, transnational obligations may have the same kinds of effects. In both cases, the demands of 'home' may create a set of financial obligations that lock immigrants into a pattern of deprofessionalised work and upward immobility.

The transnational linkages between the Philippines and Toronto may also go beyond the financial responsibilities and take the form of information networks. Even before an immigrant arrives, then, social networks are mobilised to glean information about job prospects and other practicalities of settlement. For many new arrivals, it is the network of friends, relatives, classmates and so forth already in Toronto who provide them with labour market intelligence that will facilitate their absorption into the workforce. However, there are two implications that arise from this widespread dependence on social networks, as noted earlier in relation to the Live-in Caregiver Programme. First, only certain types of jobs are filled through personal referrals or internal recommendations. Typically, these would be at the lower end of the occupational hierarchy, with relatively few professional and managerial jobs being filled in this way. Second, the process can clearly lead to a self-perpetuating occupational segmentation – if Filipinos are relying heavily upon other Filipinos in their job searches, then there will naturally be a reproduction of existing occupational niches. Hospital janitors recruit more hospital janitors, data entry clerks recruit more of the same and so forth. Labour market subordination can therefore be perpetuated through the use of transnational information networks (see also Waldinger and Lichter, 2003).

Spatialities of the workplace

The processes discussed so far have focused upon the spatialities that shape and constrain immigrants' engagement with the labour force, but all have drawn attention to processes working at scales beyond the workplace itself. An important element to add to the explanatory mix, then, involves processes inside shops, offices, factories, hotels and hospitals. In many cases, Filipino immigrants are in fact working in the professions for which they are trained (for example, nursing) or they are working in occupations for which official accreditation is not necessary (for example, retail, hotels or manufacturing). In these instances, the subordinate status of Filipino workers, and their failure to move upwards into more secure work or into managerial and supervisory roles, may

Table 9.3   Nurses in Toronto, place of employment in 2005, by place of initial education

Place	% of Ontario trained	% of internationally trained (not including US)
Acute care hospital	62.67	56.95
Public health unit	3.72	0.88
Long-term care facility	3.71	12.97
Rehabilitation hospital	3.74	7.91

Source: Table generated using data from College of Nurses of Ontario (2006).

have less to do with regulations or responsibilities at scales beyond the workplace and more to do with intra-workplace micro-politics.

There are several ways in which a spatiality of workplaces may operate to shape and constrain the upward mobility of Filipino immigrants. The example of the healthcare sector is especially instructive because of the variety of practice settings that it incorporates and because it is a sector, as noted earlier, with a heavy concentration of Filipino workers.

First, there is a clear spatial segmentation of the nursing workforce according to differentiated places of work. These relate both to different types of nursing practice (that is, different wards and healthcare settings) but also to an intra-urban geography of healthcare facilities. We find that Filipino nurses, and internationally educated nurses more generally, are heavily concentrated in what are generally seen as the less desirable types of nursing practice and less prestigious settings. Thus, Filipino and other visible minority immigrant nurses tend to be highly concentrated in suburban general hospitals, long-term care facilities, home care and rehabilitation units. White and locally trained nurses, meanwhile, are more likely to be found in prestigious downtown teaching hospitals and in acute care settings. Hence, although the College of Nurses of Ontario does not release data based on visible minority status, Table 9.3 gives some indication of the settings in which internationally trained nurses are over- and under-represented (although this undoubtedly understates the phenomenon in relation to visible minorities, as the data for internationally trained nurses include many immigrants from the UK). The disparity in the figures for each employment setting points to the patterns of segmentation that exist for different types of healthcare. This pattern of spatial segmentation may also be repeated inside hospitals, with certain 'desirable' wards (such as emergency, maternity and teaching facilities) having a lower percentage of immigrant nurses, while less desirable ones (for example, geriatric care, palliative care, psychiatric) are predominantly staffed by visible minorities.

A second form of workplace spatiality concerns the separation of management spaces from the spaces occupied by rank-and-file workers, and the (quite literal) colouring of these spaces. For example, in one focus group I conducted with clerical workers in Toronto in 2006, a Filipina employee of a major accountancy firm described the way in which the four floors of the downtown office building that the firm occupies became progressively whiter with each storey. Thus the lower floors, housing receptionists, mail room staff, data entry clerks and so on, were dominated by visible minorities, while the top floor, occupied by partners, managers and other executives, was overwhelmingly white. The employee felt 'out of place' on the upper floors, in terms of both class and race, and there was a clear sense, in her mind at least (if not in the official position or policies of the firm), that she would not 'fit' with positions above a certain rank. This individual example illustrates the way in which workplace spaces can be coded in specifically 'classed' and 'raced' ways.

A third form of workplace micro-politics with a quite different spatial dimension involves the actual practice of a job and/or specific pivotal episodes associated with it, such as job interviews or promotion panels. Conceptual and empirical work by Bourdieu, as well as other research focused more specifically on workplace practices, has shown that 'doing' a job, or demonstrating an aptitude for a job, is based upon far more than the technical 'hard' skills that might be formally required. In addition, there are a great many culturally learned 'rules of the game' that are learned 'in practice' – what Bourdieu terms 'habitus' (Bauder, 2005). These 'rules' may, however, differ across various cultural settings and so the barriers to workplace promotion and advancement that immigrants face are often not related to technical competence but, rather, to their perceived soft skills and the extent to which they are, as a result, viewed as 'management material'. In many cases the soft skills of practical engagement with the workplace and with co-workers are learned in the cultural settings from which immigrants have come and it is this different habitus (for example, one in which not complaining, or not self-aggrandising, are valued types of behaviour) that may leave them overlooked in their new situations.

A fourth, but closely related, form of workplace spatiality concerns the ways in which being 'from' a certain place leaves immigrant bodies labelled, coded and racialised in particular ways. As noted at the beginning of this chapter, to be from the Philippines means, in many contexts, being stereotyped as having certain aptitudes and 'fitting' into a certain class and occupational category. In many instances this stereotyping involves assuming a strong aptitude for caring work, but excludes an aptitude for managerial and supervisory roles. There is thus both a sectoral and a hierarchical element to these characterisations (McDowell et al., 2007).

In a variety of ways, then, the micro-politics of workplace advancement is constituted through a range of spatialities. As McDowell et al. (2007) argue, these processes play an important part, not just in specific incidences of blocked mobility in the workplace but also in understanding the connections that exist between actual experiences of labour markets and workplaces, on the one hand, and the larger global contexts that they collectively constitute on the other. It is to this much larger context that we now turn.

Spatialities of colonialism and global capitalism

The spatialities described to this point have primarily related to those regulations, relationships and representations that constrain individuals from achieving their full potential in the Canadian labour market. However, an account of this sort would be incomplete without a consideration of the structural context for these contingent processes. Consequently, the wider spatialities of colonialism, neo-colonialism and global capitalism are the backdrop to all of the other processes of labour market subordination discussed below.

In seeking to explore issues of how the wider spatiality of the global economy affects Filipinos' places in local labour markets in Canada, the structural necessity of spatially uneven development under capitalism is an important starting point. Hence, as Harvey (1982), Smith (1984) and others have pointed out, a system of global capitalist relations contains internal logics that require the constant intensification of labour and production processes, an ever-decreasing turnover time for capital to generate profit and an incessant restructuring that finds new technological, regulatory and spatial arrangements for production. These internal dynamics lead necessarily to uneven spatial development, and it is this unevenness that provides an ultimate explanation for the lack of economic security in the Philippines, which has, in turn, driven so many to seek work elsewhere. Whether such work is in Singapore, Saudi Arabia or Canada, the fact that migration is largely predicated on unevenness in opportunities, wage levels, and standards of living is unavoidable. This has long been recognised in traditional migration studies, which have seen migrants as driven from areas of low prosperity to higher prosperity. Such accounts have, however, tended not to recognise the structural causes of such unevenness. In the case of the Philippines, in particular, the country's peripheral and less-developed status in the global economy was established early through its incorporation as a Spanish then American and then a Japanese colony (Kelly, 2000). With military, political and spiritual domination came a resource-based economy servicing the needs of the industrialising global core.

At a more concrete and contemporary level, there is another set of processes of restructuring that shape the flows of migration between countries like the Philippines and global cities like Toronto. These processes have been the basis for urban economic restructuring over the last 30 years. First, competitive pressures in a global city system, and constant squeezes on public sector spending (both driven by a neoliberal ideological and regulatory framework), create the demand for a skilled but low-cost workforce in a wide range of occupations – from retail, to personal services, to manufacturing, to healthcare (Bauder, 2006). Second, a process of wealth concentration, particularly in global cities, has seen the creation of greater disparities and an increase in demand for personal services such as childcare and elderly care (Sassen, [1991] 2001). Third, and intimately connected with the first two processes, a global shift has occurred in global manufacturing industries so that the secure jobs of the Fordist-Keynesian era are no longer as readily available to support the single income, patriarchal families of that era (Harvey, 1989; McDowell, 1991; Dicken, [1986] 2007). This same global shift has seen massive increases in manufacturing investment and production in certain sites in the developing world. Paradoxically (but not inexplicably), though, it has frequently been these very sites of rapid industrial growth and employment generation, in China, Mexico, the Philippines and so on, that have generated the largest numbers of transnational migrants and contract workers (Sassen, 1988).

Alongside the inherent spatial unevenness of capitalism, these processes of economic restructuring provide the context for global migrations. The Philippines and Canada represent places situated unequally in the global economic order, and Canada benefits from the use of labour from the global South to replenish its labour force and maintain its competitiveness. In the process, the costs of social reproduction are borne in the Philippines, but the benefits of skilled labour are reaped in Canada.

Global capitalism, whether in an earlier phase of colonial extraction or a more recent round of restructuring, does not, however, operate solely in an economic register. The ways in which racialised and gendered bodies from the global South are evaluated in the global North are intimately connected with the continuing legacies of colonial cultural hierarchies. In her work on Filipino-Americans, Yen Le Espiritu makes this point clearly: 'The history of US colonialism in the Philippines reminds us that immigrant lives are shaped not only by the social locations of their group within the host country but also by the position of their home country within the global racial order' (Espiritu, 2003, p. 6).

While legacies of colonialism, such as a North American educational system and English as a lingua franca, have left Filipinos with certain advantages in the global labour market, they are inevitably integrated into this market with the cultural baggage of a colonised people weighing heavily upon them. In particular, gendered, racialised and classed identities in relation to white societies (an extrapolation of Spanish and US colonists) shape their economic integration in immigrant societies. This is true for caregivers and other Filipino workers today, just as it was true of Filipino 'stoop labour' in US agriculture in the mid-twentieth century and the menial stewards of the US Navy in the postwar years (Espiritu, 2003). All are transnationalised carriers of racialised, classed and gendered identities partly forged in European and American colonialism. Thus, the ways in which 'Filipino-ness' is read, especially in white-settler societies like Canada, are inseparable from the racial hierarchies established by colonialism. It is important to note the ways in which this racialised subjectivity is also deeply gendered, as it is generally Filipina working bodies that are stereotyped into subordinate caring roles.

The cultural legacies of colonialism are not just found in the attitudes of white societies towards colonised peoples, but also in the reverse direction as well. Just as the denigration of the Filipino and Filipina body was cultivated by colonialism, the valorisation and exultation of the Western, that which lies 'abroad', became deeply seated in Filipino culture. Overseas contract work and migration is therefore about more than the promise of economic survival or success. It is also about the dream of reaching the 'promised land' – the sense that to 'get ahead' in the Philippines inevitably requires 'getting out', and that migrating overseas is to achieve something (somewhere) that really matters. A further cultural legacy of colonialism, then, readily identified by scholars and laypersons alike in the Philippines as being a 'colonial mentality', is that migration is a necessary path to success for those who can afford to take it (Aguilar, 1999).

While the economic consequences of colonialism and contemporary global capitalism are evident in much of the global South, it is the cultural dimensions that are especially apparent in the Philippines and in the place of Filipinos in what Espiritu calls the global racial order. In the reading of Filipino immigrant bodies as suited to certain occupational and class positions in host societies, and in the attitudes towards the cultural significance of migration in the Philippines itself, then, important explanations are to be found for the scale of Filipino migrations and the subordination of Filipinos in the labour market. No account of such subordination would be complete without its contextualisation in the spatialities of colonialism and capitalism.

Conclusions

Filipinos in global cities such as Toronto have generally been incorporated into the labour force in marginal, precarious and low-paid occupations. The types of jobs being occupied by Filipino immigrants reflect a variety of processes: a squeeze on many service sector and manufacturing wages under pressure from global competition; a neoliberal tightening of budgets in public healthcare and the increasing use of temporary and contractual employees; and a general bifurcation of the labour market into well-paid work on the one hand and precarious 'flexible' work on the other. There are various economic geographies at work in creating the structural characteristics of this new global city labour market, but the question addressed in this chapter has been why Filipinos, in particular, are disproportionately represented in specific marginalised niches.

In answering this question, I have explored a set of interconnected spatialities. In some cases they are necessarily contingent and relate specifically to the case of Toronto or Canada. In other cases, they apply to the experiences of Filipinos elsewhere in the world as well. Although they operate at a variety of scales – workplaces, nations and so on – they cannot be readily categorised in this way. All of them operate across scales and, in the process, they produce scales (Herod and Wright, 2002). They are, in short, spatialities – ways in which geographical relationships in space and place affect the operation of social processes.

The construction of territorial regulatory regimes is a necessary starting point in seeking an explanation for Filipino labour market subordination. Both Canadian and Philippine states shape the experiences of migrants in important ways. The Canadian government imposes significant restrictions on Filipinos immigrating through the Live-in Caregiver Programme and, at a different scale, provincial regulatory bodies police access to professional accreditations. Meanwhile, the Philippine state actively promotes the marketing of its citizens as a flexible, hardworking, malleable workforce for the global economy and fosters a training infrastructure to create such workers.

Labour market subordination is also a product of the immediate pressure and obligations upon migrant workers. These obligations might exist in the nexus between home and work, for example as working parents cobble together childcare arrangements in Toronto and attempt to eke out a living wage from low-waged employment. Immigrants' responsibilities to 'home' may also be transnational, as relatives back in the Philippines become dependent upon remittances, and those sending them need to intensify their participation, and minimise their risks, in the Toronto labour market. In both cases, labour market subordination may be forged not in the job interview, the workplace, or the professional board exam, but in the sphere of social reproduction.

Opening up the space of the workplace to scrutiny also reveals a great deal more than 'market forces' at work in the allocation of people to particular kinds of jobs. Assumptions concerning aptitudes based on gender, race and various other kinds of embodied characteristics all shape the opportunities that are available to immigrants. In some cases, workplaces are themselves 'colour-coded', with upper-level job (and spaces) overwhelmingly white. In other cases, it is bodily dispositions (conferred by the cultural context of Philippine workplaces) that are read as connoting a certain level in a hierarchical workplace.

Finally, all of these processes cannot be understood outside the larger context of colonialism and global capitalism. Labour markets, homeplaces and workplaces do not create the inequalities between Canada and the Philippines that make subordinated labour market positions in Canada preferable, in some respects, to professional middle class standing in the Philippines. Rather, the economic disparities between Canada and the Philippines must be understood in relation to the structures of spatial power within contemporary global capitalism. In turn, these have to be understood in relation to the historical construction of a Philippine place in the world through colonialism. Finally, alongside the economic legacies of colonialism must be placed the cultural readings of Filipino otherness that it has bequeathed. Labour market subordination, then, is as much about 'where you are from' – who you are, in the very broadest sense – as it is about 'what you know'.

All of these spatialities of labour market subordination may give an air of uncontestable inevitability to the deskilling of Filipino immigrants. In fact, at least some of them can be addressed through specific policy changes and are being pursued through political mobilisation in the Filipino-Canadian community. The Live-in Caregiver Programme has been a source of consistent advocacy activities by groups in Toronto and Vancouver in particular (Arat-Koc, 2001; Diocson, 2003; Kelly, 2007). Specific demands have included that the federal government grant full permanent resident status to those working as live-in caregivers in order to allow for job mobility and family reunification and that provincial governments apply employment standards legislation to caregivers' workplaces (Pajadura, 2007). These demands have yet to be acted upon, but they have been presented with increasing vigour during policy review processes. Aside from improved working conditions and mobility for those employed as caregivers, such changes would also allow for continued education and training and more rapid integration into other parts of the labour force.

A second focus of mobilisation has been the access of Philippine-educated immigrants to professional accreditation and practice. On this issue, mobilisation across many immigrant communities has attracted a great deal of public attention. In Ontario, the provincial government responded in 2006 by enacting legislation that required greater transparency from professional regulatory bodies and established a 'Fairness Commissioner' to oversee their activities. Nevertheless, licensed professions remain largely autonomous in their gate-keeping activities and are thus immune to demands that they recognise more readily credentials earned outside Canada. This therefore remains an area of policy in which advocacy by immigrant groups continues.

A final area of activism, or rather self-help, has been in the emergence of mentoring and networking organisations to assist immigrants in navigating the labour market and finding opportunities in their field. Within the Filipino community, these have emerged among groups of professionals or university alumni clubs. The University of the Philippines Alumni Association in Toronto, for example, operates a mentoring programme that seeks to link Filipino professionals with those already practising in their fields. The purpose is to provide insights into Canadian workplace and labour market culture, networks for job searches and information about licensing requirements. In this way, professionally qualified Filipino immigrants have sought to overcome the limitations imposed by familial and social networks and the workplace habitus learned in the Philippines. Nevertheless, barriers based on discrimination, regulatory frameworks and poverty remain.

Notes

1. In this chapter I conform to the common usage of 'Filipino' as both a noun and an adjective that refers either to men alone, or to men and women, who identify in this way, while 'Filipina' refers specifically to women. This is not unproblematic, as it reproduces a linguistic device that conflates both sexes into the masculine form. It is, however, the way in which the word is universally used in both English and various

languages spoken in the Philippines. It will therefore be used in this chapter to refer to men and women, while 'Filipina' will be used when specifically discussing women's experiences.

2. The term 'visible minority' is an official designation used by the government of Canada to denote persons who are 'non-Caucasian in race or non-white in colour'. It is used in employment equity programmes as well as census enumeration and other data collection. Respondents can select from the following list: Chinese, Black, South Asian, Filipino, Latin American, Southeast Asian, Arab, West Asian, Korean, Japanese or Other. 'Visible minority' status differs from 'ethnic origin' because it relates to physical appearance rather than cultural background. It is a category that has caused some controversy – for example, the word 'visible' belies the usual invisibility of marginalised groups, and the word 'minority' obscures the fact that such groups are actually majorities in certain parts of cities like Toronto. Nevertheless, the term will be used in this chapter as it allows consistency with the data used, which are based on self-declared visible minority status as 'Filipino'.

References

Aguilar, F.V. (1999), 'Ritual passage and the reconstruction of selfhood in international labor migration', *Sojourn: Journal of Social Issues in Southeast Asia*, **14** (1), 98–139.

Arat-Koc, S. (2001), *Caregivers Break the Silence: A Participatory Action Research on the Abuse and Violence*, Toronto: Intercede.

Ball, R. (1997), 'The role of the state in the globalisation of labour markets: the case of the Philippines', *Environment and Planning A*, **29** (9), 1603–28.

Barcelo, T.I. (2001), 'Internationalisation of nursing education', *Philippine Journal of Nursing*, **71** (3–4), 16–18.

Bauder, H. (2003), '"Brain Abuse", or the devaluation of immigrant labour in Canada', *Antipode*, **35** (4), 699–717.

Bauder, H. (2005), 'Habitus, rules of the labour market and employment strategies of immigrants in Vancouver, Canada', *Social and Cultural Geography*, **6** (1), 81–97.

Bauder, H. (2006), *Labor Movement: How Migration Regulates Labor Markets*, Oxford: Oxford University Press.

Bauder, H. and B. Sharpe (2002), 'Residential segregation of visible minorities in Canada's gateway cities', *The Canadian Geographer*, **46** (3), 204–22.

Becker, G.S. ([1964] 1993), *Human Capital: A Theoretical and Empirical Analysis, with Special Reference to Education*, 3rd edn, Chicago, IL: University of Chicago Press.

College of Nurses of Ontario (CNO) (2006), CNO data query tool (online), Toronto, Canada, available at https://remote.cnomail.org/approot/cno/data_query_tool.htm.

Creese, G., I. Dyck and A.T. McLaren (2006), 'The 'flexible' immigrant: household strategies and the labour market', Research on Immigration and Integration in the Metropolis (RIIM) Working Paper Series, No. 06–19, Vancouver, Canada: RIIM.

Dicken, P. ([1986] 2007), *Global Shift: Mapping the Changing Contours of the World Economy*, 5th edn, Thousand Oaks, CA: Sage.

Diocson, C. (2003), 'Organizing and mobilizing Filipino migrant women in Canada', paper presented at the Asia Pacific Research Network Conference on Globalization and its Impact on Women's Labour, 18–20 June, Bangkok, Thailand, available at www.aprnet.org, accessed 13 February 2008.

Dowling, R., A. Gollner and B. O'Dwyer (1999), 'A gender perspective on urban car use: a qualitative case study', *Urban Policy and Research*, **17** (2), 101–10.

England, K. and B. Stiell (1997), '"They think you're as stupid as your English is". Constructing foreign domestic workers in Toronto', *Environment and Planning A*, **29** (2), 195–215.

Espiritu, Y.L. (2003), *Home Bound: Filipino American Lives across Cultures, Communities, and Countries*, Berkeley, CA: University of California Press.

Galabuzi, G.-E. (2006), *Canada's Economic Apartheid: The Social Exclusion of Racialized Groups in the New Century*, Toronto: Canadian Scholars Press.

Girard, E.R. and H. Bauder (2007), 'Assimilation and exclusion of foreign trained engineers in Canada: inside a professional regulatory organization', *Antipode*, **39** (1), 35–53.

Gonzalez, J.L. (1998), *Philippine Labour Migration: Critical Dimensions of Public Policy*, Singapore: Institute of Southeast Asian Studies.

Hanson, S. and G. Pratt (1995), *Gender, Work and Space*, New York: Routledge.

Harvey, D. (1982), *The Limits to Capital*, Oxford: Blackwell.

Harvey, D. (1989), *The Condition of Postmodernity: An Enquiry into the Origins of Cultural Change*, Oxford: Blackwell.

Herod, A. and M.W. Wright (2002), 'Placing scale: an introduction', in A. Herod and M.W. Wright (eds), *Geographies of Power: Placing Scale*, Oxford: Blackwell, pp. 1–14.

Hiebert, D. (2000), 'Immigration and the changing Canadian city', *Canadian Geographer*, **44** (1), 25–43.
Kelly, P.F. (2000), *Landscapes of Globalization: Human Geographies of Economic Change in the Philippines*, New York: Routledge.
Kelly, P.F. (2006), 'Filipinos in Canada: economic dimensions of immigration and settlement', Centre of Excellence for Research on Immigration and Settlement (CERIS), Working Paper 48, Toronto: CERIS.
Kelly, P.F. (2007), 'Pathways to politics: integration and activism among Filipinos in Canada', in L. Goldring and S. Krishnamurti (eds), *Organizing the Transnational: The Experience of Asian, Caribbean and Latin American Migrants in Canada*, Vancouver: UBC Press, pp. 215–31.
Li, P.S. (2003), *Destination Canada: Immigration Debates and Issues*, Toronto: Oxford University Press.
McDonald, J.T. and C. Worswick (1998), 'The earnings of immigrant men in Canada: job tenure, cohort, and macroeconomic conditions', *Industrial and Labor Relations Review*, **51** (3), 465–82.
McDowell, L. (1991), 'Life without Father and Ford: the new gender order of Post-Fordism', *Transactions of the Institute of British Geographers*, **16** (4), 400–19.
McDowell, L. (1999), *Gender, Identity and Place: Understanding Feminist Geographies*, Minneapolis, MN: University of Minnesota Press.
McDowell, L., A. Batnizky and S. Dyer (2007), 'Division, segmentation, and interpellation: the embodied labors of migrant workers in a Greater London hotel', *Economic Geography*, **83** (1), 1–25.
McDowell, L., D. Perrons, C. Fagan, K. Ray and K. Ward (2005), 'The contradictions and intersections of class and gender in a global city: placing working women's lives on the research agenda', *Environment and Planning A*, **37** (3), 441–61.
McKay, D. (2002), 'Filipina identities: geographies of social integration/exclusion in the Canadian metropolis', Research on Immigration and Integration in the Metropolis (RIIM) Working Paper Series, No. 02–18, Vancouver: RIIM.
Pajadura, S. (2007), 'Our few just demands for caregivers', statement on the Asia Pacific Mission for Migrants website, 4 November, www.apmigrants.org/statements/24.html, accessed 13 February 2008.
PCIJ (Philippine Centre for Investigative Journalism) (2005), 'Nursing the world: Filipinas in the global care industry', Quezon City: PCIJ.
Pratt, G. (1999), 'From registered nurse to registered nanny: discursive geographies of Filipina domestic workers in Vancouver, BC', *Economic Geography*, **75** (3), 215–36.
Pratt, G. (2003), 'Between homes: displacement and belonging for second-generation Filipino-Canadian youth', *BC Studies*, **140** (Winter), 41–68.
Reitz, J.G. (2001), 'Immigrant skill utilization in the Canadian labour market: implications of human capital research', *Journal of International Migration and Integration*, **2** (3), 347–78.
Rodriguez, R. (2002), 'Migrant heroes: nationalism, citizenship and the politics of Filipino migrant labor', *Citizenship Studies*, **6** (3), 341–56.
Sassen, S. (1988), *The Mobility of Labor and Capital: A Study in International Investment and Labor Flows*, Cambridge: Cambridge University Press.
Sassen, S. ([1991] 2001), *The Global City: New York, London, Tokyo*, 2nd edn, Princeton, NJ: Princeton University Press.
Schellenberg, G. and H. Maheux (2007), 'Immigrants' perspectives on their first four years in Canada: highlights from three waves of the Longitudinal Survey of Immigrants to Canada', *Canadian Social Trends*, special edn, April 2007, Ottawa: Statistics Canada.
Smith, N. (1984), *Uneven Development: Nature, Capital and the Production of Space*, Oxford: Blackwell.
Statistics Canada (2001), *2001 Census*, Metropolis Project Core Data Set Tabulations, Ottawa.
Statistics Canada (2003), 'Census of population: labour force activity, occupation, industry, class of worker, place of work, mode of transportation, language of work and unpaid work', *The Daily*, 11 February, Ottawa: Statistics Canada, available at http://www.statcan.ca/Daily/English/030211/td030211.htm, accessed 19 September 2008.
Tan, J.Z.G. (2003), 'Realities and challenges for the global nursing community', *Philippine Journal of Nursing*, **73** (1–2), 8–10
Tyner, J.A. (2004), *Made in the Philippines: Gendered Discourses and the Making of Migrants*, London and New York: RoutledgeCurzon.
Waldinger, R.D. and M.I. Lichter (2003), *How the Other Half Works: Immigration and the Social Organization of Labor*, Berkeley, CA: University of California Press.

Section 2.2

Building Space

10 Competing geographies of welfare capitalism and its workers: Kohler Village and the spatial politics of planned company towns

Kathryn J. Oberdeck

This chapter offers a case study of spatial politics produced by welfare-capitalist company town planning. Focusing on the town planning efforts of the Kohler Company of Wisconsin, it sets Kohler's case in the context of diverse objectives that guided company town planning across the globe in the nineteenth and twentieth centuries. Its aim is to illustrate key conflicts over spatial scale, the gendering and racialisation of space and the mutual refashioning of spatial perspectives on the part of employers and workers that grew out of global currents in garden-industrial town planning visible in Kohler Village.

The culture of company town planning in which Kohler participated located labour conflict in workers' daily navigation of neighbourhoods and homes. However, workers challenged the boundaries such plans drew around the scale of 'home', how they distinguished industrial from domestic space and how they connected the 'local' to wider spatial scales. In Kohler and other welfare-capitalist towns, such conflicts could lead to complex politics of scale, as connections between the local, the national and the global articulated with spatial divisions of private and public, domestic and industrial, along with class, gender, ethnic and racial affiliations. Recognising company town planning in Kohler and elsewhere as an integrated geographical project intertwining strategies of labour control, company publicity and marketing, this chapter examines how wider maps in which company publicity situated the town for marketing purposes helped to provoke particular spatial strategies of labour unrest, as well as shifting geographies of labour–management conflict. When Depression-era wages and house foreclosures threatened satisfactions associated with the Village's spatial design, frustrated workers attempting to organise a union at the plant challenged company efforts to assign local identities to workers whose homes and products it mobilised in global networks of manufacture and marketing. To use Andrew Herod's terminology, they refigured the company's geography of labour into an alternative labour geography that approximated but also redefined the global scale on which the company operated (Herod, 2001).[1] A spatial understanding of the planned company town involves analyses of how the scales invoked in such conflict were configured and contested in various circumstances by company officials, planners, workers, residents and consumers.

Town planning as spatial labour control: a global survey

Starting in the nineteenth century, town planning techniques were addressed to a range of labour-control imperatives, in North America and beyond, producing new geographies of labour power. The garden-industrial town planning model visible in Kohler was deployed by a variety of firms to attract stable, skilled workforces to remote areas, to reward anti-union actions, to both cultivate and placate status and racial divisions, and to instil styles of life deemed appropriate to a company's public image. Moreover, corporations and employers mixed and matched such goals as they employed planners and architects to design company towns and then questioned the design visions their planning professionals offered. The results varied with regard to how social relations were organised spatially, and how residents embraced, lived with and resisted such organisation.

Company town planning efforts shared a general goal of engineering workers' daily environment so as to attract specific sorts of labourers, offset industrial degradation, and control worker behaviour on the job. Early applications of such environmentalist approaches to worker control can be seen in textile manufacturing towns established in the mid-nineteenth century in the north-eastern United States. New England textile magnates sought mainly to preserve long-term family investments in established manufacturing concerns that were spatially fixed by the requirements of water power and so had to attract workers to them (rather than being able to move to where the labour was) by providing company-owned housing, along with cultural amenities like libraries and churches (Garner, 1984; Crawford, 1995).

Though some of these projects reflected the influence of planning experts, they were not professionally shaped to the degree apparent in later model industrial housing ventures such as those at Port Sunlight, developed by Lord Leverhume of the Lever Brothers soap company, or Bournville, the company town developed by chocolate manufacturer William Cadbury outside Birmingham, England. Somewhat similar to the earlier example of Saltaire, the textile town established by Sir Titus Salt in Yorkshire, these efforts were self-consciously designed to avoid the degrading environments of 'dark satanic mills' or urban industry. Whereas Salt had sought a new urban style, however, Lever and Cadbury combated urban industrial evils through a studied pastoralism connected with transnational ideas of 'garden city' developments. Lever and Cadbury both became affiliated with the Garden City Association founded by Ebenezer Howard, a social reformer who sought to cure the ills of industrial life by displacing factories to green-belted 'garden cities' owned by resident stockholders and rendered in the picturesque groupings developed by architects Barry Parker and Raymond Unwin. These ideas, combined with the concepts of neighbourhood house placement developed by Austrian architect Camillo Sitte, had wide-ranging impact on landscape planners and architects who sought to alleviate 'slum' conditions by relocating industrial landscapes in villages with scenic neighbourhoods defined by imaginatively grouped homes (Crawford, 1995, pp. 70–74, 107–08; Creese, 1966; Day, 1981).

The spatial planning of an uplifting environment, whatever its motivation, was widely connected with elements of paternalistic control over workers' personal lives that became the focus of growing controversy after the catastrophic strike they fuelled in the US town of Pullman, Illinois in the early 1890s. The object of widespread admiration in the mid-1880s, the design of Pullman reflected the faith of its founder – George Pullman, head of the Pullman Palace Car Company – in what he called the 'commercial value of beauty'. Believing that his lavish sleeping cars inspired good behaviour on trains, Pullman applied a similar philosophy in building a town for workers south of Chicago. Here, cultural facilities like a respectable theatre and uplifting library replaced 'baneful' influences of urban saloons and brothels, while access to aesthetically designed rental housing encouraged 'habits of respectability' such as good manners, cleanliness, industriousness, sobriety, self-improvement and savings. The vision, realised in attractively ornamented brick row houses that were provided for the skilled labour force Pullman wanted to secure for his new plant, was more one of improving working-class urban life than of reorganising urban residential space as in the model Kohler would follow (Bruder, 1967, pp. 43, 61).

Its combination of profit-motive and tight control over amenities soon transformed Pullman from model experiment in urban design to a paternalist example demonstrating what employers interested in town planning should avoid. Pullman's proprietary care of the town's rented dwellings included painting and upkeep routines over which tenants had little control. Combined with the town's high-priced cultural amenities, such intrusions raised questions as to whether his town provided worker 'homes' or merely attractive way stations on the way to communities where workers could purchase property and control culture. Pullman's intransigent insistence on the business basis of his community, even when declining wages in the 1890s stretched the budgets of renters, aggravated the workplace demands that brought Pullman and his enterprise into violent confrontation with the American Railway Union in 1894. A strike commission appointed by President Cleveland to investigate the event scoffed at high-priced aesthetic amenities that 'have little money value to employees, especially when they lack bread' (Crawford, 1995, p. 42; see also Bruder, 1967; Gilbert, 1991).

Pullman shared his objective of controlling the everyday spaces of workers' lives with less aesthetically engineered versions of company housing that were also coming under fire by advocates of housing and land planners who helped popularise Kohler-style 'garden industrial villages'. As a series of government-sponsored housing reports from the late nineteenth century to the early twentieth century pointed out, the provision of housing and town amenities to workers was often governed by a bottom-line that produced little in the way of beauty or comfort. In southern mill towns and northern and western extractive industries, the provision of housing was necessary to bring people to out-of-the-way or new industrial environments, but also became bound up in the profit-orientation of firms themselves. Houses were laid out on unimaginatively grid-like streets and workers were compelled to patronise retail and entertainment facilities dominated by companies that ran them as profit-making concerns.

Though the beauty of working-class homes was more a concern in Pullman than in other profit-orientated company towns, Pullman nevertheless shared with them a rigid mapping of class and racial social distinction. In Pullman, spatialisation of class difference took form in distinctive housing types: barrack-like hostels or 'model' tenements for unskilled workers, small row houses for skilled workers, and detached single family dwellings for foremen and managers, all on separate streets. All of the residents in these housing types were white, distinguished racially from the company's African American porters until the 1920s, when the car works began hiring African Americans ostracised from the community by the now home-owning residents (Reiff, 2000). In many other company towns, differentiation of housing and neighbourhood by skill paralleled racial distinctions. Copper mining towns in the south-western United States, bauxite mining towns in Arkansas, and mill towns throughout the south implemented town plans that segregated racialised and ethnic groups. Mine and mill owners began providing relatively substantial, electrified houses sometimes supplied with modern sanitation to skilled white workers whom they sought to attract to remote areas or rural populations whom they tried to transform into reliable industrial labour. However, they relegated African Americans, Mexicans and Mexican-Americans, and Native Americans to smaller homes or tents in segregated camps, and often left them to build their own shelters. Such arrangements supported prevailing patterns of segregation in the US South and redlining in the North, while also mapping onto residential arrangements the relatively casual and impermanent position of non-white workers within company town industries (Allen, 1966; Baker, 1995; Crawford, 1995; Gordon, 1999; Keltner, 2001).

Industries with more elaborately planned model villages also made the amenities provided for residents into exclusionary boundaries of racial or ethnic identity. Bertram Goodhue, architect of the copper town of Tyrone, New Mexico, designed two-room houses for Mexican labourers who had been left to provide their own houses in other Phelps-Dodge company towns, but they were smaller than houses for white workers and located in a segregated canyon (Crawford, 1995, pp. 136–43). At Vandergrift, Pennsylvania, the Apollo Iron and Steel company commissioned Frederick Law Olmsted to develop middle-class suburban landscaping and amenities to ensure the loyalty of skilled, non-union employees who also enjoyed the distinction of 'American' standards, which were quite different from those experienced by increasingly immigrant and unskilled workers in less picturesque settlements nearby (Mosher, 2004, chapter 4). Similarly, on Canada's resource frontiers in the 1920s, efforts to attract qualified workers through garden industrial projects like Corner Brook, a town designed for Newfoundland Pulp and Paper Company, Ltd, limited such comforts to skilled workers, leaving unskilled 'transient' workers to find their own housing, while excluding Jews, Lebanese and Chinese emigrants from employment – and thus company housing schemes – entirely (White, 2004; Saarinen, 1986). In such arrangements, the racialised bodies of the workers themselves etched distinctions of residential 'standards' and occupational skill onto company town streetscapes.

These North American arrangements found echoes in model company towns built worldwide, with further ramifications for the social identifications mapped by industrial town planning efforts. Company towns, in fact, were widespread US exports in the late nineteenth and early twentieth centuries, sometimes on the part of the very companies famous for model industrial town planning within the US. This was the case of the plantations developed by Milton Hershey in Cuba to ensure a steady supply of sugar to his chocolate factory in Pennsylvania. Like his rural Pennsylvanian facility, Hershey's Cuban installations provided garden-city style company towns, complete with company-supplied trees, flowers and maintenance, as well as a philanthropic school. However, these facilities also inscribed on the ground the social distance between North American and European managers and the local, as well as imported, labour they oversaw, with the officials of Central Hershey, for instance, enjoying privileged access to a golf course and country club from which locals were largely excluded (Wilkins, 1974; O'Brien, 1993; Winpenny, 1995). Certainly, company town amenities did often improve the lives of the local labour force, but only in the context of apartheid-like divisions that mapped American and European convictions of racial and commercial superiority, as well as visions of appropriate domestic gender relations and household decor, onto colonised spaces. Moreover, participation in such improvements could actually produce profound conflicts over the meaning of place when companies, beset by losses, sometimes abruptly reversed their 'civilising' efforts and turned houseproud workers off their land; in the case of United Fruit's Ecuadorian installations, for instance, such actions led to a brief worker takeover (Striffler, 2004).

These arrangements had diverse ramifications across the globe, but contests over the implications of company-organised local space and place for ethnic, racial, gender and national identities were common. Combined with the capacity for North American and European enterprises to generate dynamic mobility among racially diverse labourers in Latin American and other colonial contexts, company town provisions could help fuel and spatialise complexly racialised conceptions of anti-imperialist nationalism. Conflicts over the provisions made for imported Haitian and West Indian labour in Cuba's sugar industry and Costa Rica's banana plantations, for instance, sparked racist claims on such improved domestic spaces for self-identified 'white' members of those countries' nationalising working classes. In the Guyanese bauxite towns of Christianburg–Wismar–Mackenzie, the spatial legacy that segregated white, North American from black, Guyanese settlements made company spaces of managerial sociability anathema to post-colonial Guyanese white collar workers. Thus, racialised space in colonial company towns shaped both inter-racial relations mobilised by international enterprise and the ways space could be inhabited in post-colonial societies (Grant, 1971; Harpelle, 1994; Chomsky, 1996).

In South Africa, varied claims of white, coloured and African labourers to national projects of urban development, housing 'improvement', or, alternatively, 'native' affairs similarly shaped and circumscribed company town spatial strategies of labour control. Thus, at Pilgrim's Rest, a white company town established by the Transvaal Gold Mining Estates in the early twentieth century, white workers were able to mobilise their claims on South African citizenship to effect modest improvements in sanitation and park facilities within a profit-driven company town. Meanwhile, African workers settled as rent-paying farm tenants who were also obligated to provide mine labour found it possible to leverage the company's trade of land for labour into relatively advantageous flows of household labour between farm and mine. However, such flexibility was always underlain by brutal methods of enforcing labour agreements that became even more draconian when African labour supplies tightened, although they could also become the object of appeal on the part of organisations such as the Transvaal Native Congress or the Industrial and Commercial Workers' Union (Bonner and Shapiro, 1993).

To the south-west, the coast town of Velddrift gradually transformed from a feudal estate funded by rents and fishing rights income paid by informally housed tenants to an increasingly sanitary, planned community. Here the pressure for change came partly from public health authorities and the interests of new industrial concerns seeking to turn independent fishermen into satisfied industrial workers, often through reliance on state-supplied infrastructural development. But racial distinctions in this process produced pressures from below that also shaped company town amenities. Thus, the enduring focus on providing housing and infrastructural improvements for white workers meant that African and coloured workers were obliged to seek housing from the rentier paternalists who, supported by modernising industrialists, regularly blocked moves toward local municipal control. This situation was ultimately addressed only by easing up the restrictions on company-supplied housing for non-white workers, a move broadening the 'sanitation syndrome' which usually mobilised state housing efforts to prevent black urban settlement from 'endangering' white health. Here, cleanliness was supervised among new white and coloured homeowners as well as African tenement dwellers. Though largely engineered from above, in other words, the pressures produced by racialised space at

Velddrift enlarged the scope of the civilising and modernising project of town planning on the South African urban periphery (Swanson, 1977; Van Sittert, 2001).

The rapid urbanisation of Persian Gulf oil-producing regions beginning in the early twentieth century illuminates further the complex politics ensuing from the use of town planning to modernise worker behaviour. Two of the largest oil cities, Masjed-Soleyman and Abadan, perpetually challenged the plans and programmes of the Anglo-Persian Oil Company (APOC) that constructed them. The spatial organisation of these towns was intended to satisfy the housing needs of a segregated European management while redesigning customary local domestic space to produce environments that encouraged dependence on modern amenities, the segregation of nuclear from extended families and the reliance on a male breadwinner rather than a gendered mix of household crafts. These ends were achieved through rigidly separated neighbourhoods for different classes and ethnicities and the rejection of local urban residential patterns in favour of controllable neighbourhood spaces. In place of the spatial pattern of rural Khuzestan's historic towns – where high walls lining winding streets defended neighbourhoods against wind, dust, heat and military attack while also facilitating public interaction – company towns featured short, straight streets to enable quick detection of suspicious gatherings and focus sociability on domestic consumption. However, the perpetual lag between company housing produced for local labourers and the national demand on APOC to increase its hiring of local employees constantly disrupted this pattern of development. 'Informal' settlements produced autonomous public spaces and institutions that the company – and its international and nationalised successors – struggled to control. Such spatial hybridity would eventually produce a cosmopolitan urban population whose civil institutions participated in efforts to nationalise the oil industry at mid-century but then questioned the 'Islamisation' of national identity in the 1970s and 1980s (Seccombe and Lawless, 1987; Ehsani, 2003).

Efforts to control labour through planned urban space, then, provoked a number of labour geographies mobilised to challenge scales of local, national and global affiliation proposed by company town design, as well as the differentiations of class, race, ethnicity and gender that figured within such politics of scale. Though no particular case can comprehensively represent the variety of such spatial contests, the history of spatial organisation and conflict at Kohler demonstrates a number of dynamics that connect the global variety of company strategy and worker/resident agency in organising and conceptualising company town space. Kohler officials and town planners reacted to the conflicts produced by spatial class differentiation and paternalism in examples like Pullman by organising Kohler Village to promote broad-ranging participation in common 'American' standards sought by 'independent' homeowners in a company-orientated community. Class and occupational distinctions in residence were elided in favour of gendered zones within the town and a global range of living standards to which Kohler homes were favourably compared. While the company sought to filter Village residents' connection to such wider spatial scales through localised preoccupations with home products that were supposedly civilising the globe and 'national' hygienic standards that were realised in Village dwellings, however, Kohler workers themselves produced competing affiliations with the scales of the local, the national and the global in the course of their contests with the company. The following section reviews Kohler's history, with an emphasis on these spatial politics as they linked to wider trends in company town designs and disputes.

Kohler's welfare-capitalist politics of space and scale

Contests over Kohler's geography of labour took shape out of the diverse purposes that motivated the town's design. Developed in the wake of the Kohler Company's late nineteenth-century move from Sheboygan – a small city bordering Lake Michigan and 50 miles north of Milwaukee – to the rural village of Riverside four miles west, Kohler Village's location was itself the result of the kind of spatial fix that economic geographers have identified with changing strategies of capital accumulation. The company had begun as a Sheboygan agricultural implements factory owned by its founder, John-Michael Kohler, in a series of partnerships with skilled craftsmen. By the 1890s Kohler had reshaped it into a growing plumbingware firm of his own and engineered the move to what became Kohler Village in the midst of consolidating control, expanding production and weathering a strike of moulders who avidly used city space in parades and marches designed to make their case to strikebreakers and the general public (Uphoff, 1966, pp. 3–7).

However, while the company's move west represented a spatial fix in relation to capital expansion and labour relations, its founder carried with him wider civic and culture-building practices that shaped the Village's development. A patron of theatre and the arts in Sheboygan, as well as urban developments associated with the city's harbour and welfare institutions, John-Michael Kohler set an example of civic-mindedness that his son, Walter Jodok Kohler, the company executive primarily responsible for developing the town, would carry on in the planning and administration of Kohler Village after his father's death in 1900. Concerned lest the unplanned development of workers' housing produce a slum around the expanding factory, Walter toured European garden industrial villages in the 1910s. On his return he employed German planning expert Walter Hegemann, a champion of planning to produce 'civic' beauty. Steeped in vital cross-currents of garden city and town planning discourses, Hegemann developed an initial plan featuring homes interspersed with monuments and museums. Though Walter Kohler ultimately implemented only portions of this plan and later turned town planning over to the more established Olmsted Brothers firm of Massachusetts, its influence helped to shape a village steeped as much in culture provision as labour control (*Sheboygan City News*, 1899, 8 March; Alanen and Peltin, 1978; Oberdeck, 2005).

Central to Kohler Village's town plan was a vision of 'American' standards of domestic life that became key to the contested geographies connecting the Village to the company's markets. The 'American' virtues that Walter Kohler and other leaders of this largely family-run company made a point of emphasising had features that made Kohler Village a distinctive version of welfare-capitalist town planning. While borrowing from models such as those developed in Britain and Germany for Port Sunlight, Bournville, the Krupps firm and the Garden Cities movement, Walter Kohler was eager to dissociate his town from what he regarded as old-world styles of paternalism. He linked its 'American' character to the independence of home ownership that also distinguished it from company-owned towns such as Pullman, Illinois. Incorporated as a village under state statutes in 1912, Kohler Village was governed by an elected Village Board that provided further evidence of its independence. While usually friendly to company interests, the board and the planning commission that eventually emerged to support it would sometimes question company-instigated plans (Uphoff, 1966, pp. 8–9).

Kohler Village's 'American' character also had an assimilationist dimension aimed particularly at the many foreign-born single men for whom the Village's 'American Club' was intended as an ideal residence. Here immigrant men could begin to adopt the 'American' style of independent domestic life inculcated in Kohler Village homes without interfering as boarders with the domestic economies and cultures for which those homes were designed. It was expected, and often happened, that such men would graduate to owning Kohler-built homes where a cross-class ideal of 'American' home life was available on attractive, sanitary streets inhabited by company officials side-by-side with factory operatives (Oberdeck, 2001). This inclusive culture set Kohler off from towns with plans designed to distinguish spatially a hierarchy separating 'American' workers from immigrant and non-white labourers (Kohler Co., 1925; *Kohler of Kohler News*, June, 1917) (see Figure 10.1).

While the 'American' ideals associated with the town implied an inclusive classlessness, Kohler Village was arranged into distinct gender-specific spaces. Highlighted in company publicity that touted 'zoning' divisions between the Village's industrial, residential and commercial areas, this gendering of Village space also had important implications for the way that Village life figured in the company's wider marketing geographies. The residential zone became the realm of distinctively female domestic concerns celebrated in the Village's Woman's Club, overseen by Walter Kohler's sisters. With an extensive programme of domestic self-improvement and, eventually, contribution to the US government-sponsored Better Homes Week, the Woman's Club focused pre-eminently on the perpetuation of 'the idea of the home'. The industrial zone occupied by the factory was distinctively male, as emphasised by the depiction of 'manly' energies being concentrated on 'formidable' industrial tasks in the murals of Kohler production featured in the foyer to the company offices. In between the male industrial and female residential zones was the ambiguous commercial zone occupied by the American Club, a carefully managed meeting and eating place for men and women that also prepared single men for home and factory life (Oberdeck, 2001). Idealised in advertisements that featured women happily presiding over Kohler-produced bathroom hygiene while men bent to the work of Kohler production, this gender zoning also figures importantly in contests over space at Kohler.

The company's newspaper, *Kohler of Kohler News*, provides crucial purchase on the model village's complicated geographies and their intertwining of town planning and marketing agendas. A house organ intended for employees and Kohler Village residents, as well as sales representatives and consumers, the *News* was one of many publications whereby welfare capitalist-orientated companies attempted at once to generate employee loyalty and to broadcast the company's concern for employees to a wider world. In Kohler's case, this dual project placed Kohler workers and residents in particular relations to the widening markets they served. Advertisements in the *News*, which reproduced ads used in national popular magazines, encouraged Village dwellers and consumers to see the Village as a community of home-proud workers whose concern for domestic comfort on the job and off resulted in high-quality fixtures for the 'modern' sanitary bathroom: the 'bathroom as we in America know it today' for which there was 'no precedent in the lives and customs of other peoples' (Kohler Co. 1928, 1934).[2] This bathroom was, in turn, situated in a progressively more efficient and sanitary home that Kohler Company claimed to be spreading from urban to rural and Euro-American to the global South and non-West through its plumbing and electrical products. Advertisements

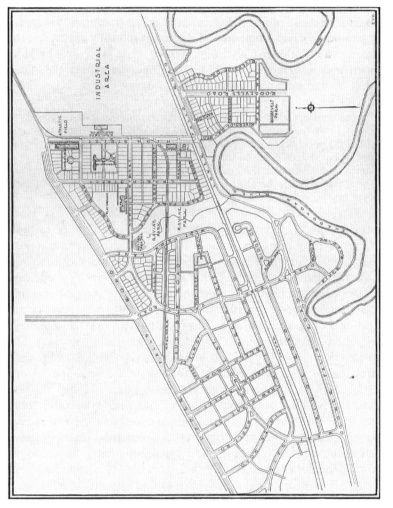

Note: The map shows the streets, parks, and other prominent features of those portions of Kohler Village which have been built up or are at present being developed. The Kohler Co. factory and office are situated in the industrial area east of High Street, indicated in the upper right corner of the map. Influenced by the contours of the ground or the course of the river, many of the streets are winding. The area within the corporate limits of the Village is much larger than the section included in this map, embracing approximately 2100 acres.

Source: Kohler Co. (1928). Courtesy of Kohler Company.

Figure 10.1   Kohler Village

for these products, highlighting Kohler-outfitted bathrooms as 'shrines of cleanliness' exemplifying modern hygienic standards, also featured drawings of Kohler houses where workers who made these products reputedly lived up to modern standards of hygiene in their own homes.[3]

Early on, the *Kohler of Kohler News* located this model of hygiene in a widening map of modern sanitation delineated through the growing markets for Kohler products. By the 1920s the *News* was documenting Kohler plumbing and electrical installations across an ever-wider global market, which also produced a rising tide of hygienic modernisation (*Kohler of Kohler News*, November 1916, pp. 4, 7; February 1917, p. 9; March 1917, p. 17; July 1917, p. 17). This growing reach of Kohler plumbing was graphically depicted at the 1933–34 Century of Progress Exposition in Chicago. A mural outside the Kohler building underlined this reach with images from Greenland, Mexico, China, Indochina, the Malay States, Africa and Turkey. As the accompanying text described:

> [t]he tireless search for materials of a definitely high standard for Kohler products leads to strange places of the earth. From the hinterland of Greenland comes Kryolith – from the mines of Chile, salt-peter – from the open pits of the Malay States, tin oxide – from China, antimony oxide – from England, ball clay, China clay and Cornwall stone. . . .
>
> Just as Kohler of Kohler finds raw materials in many parts of the earth, so likewise are the finished products sent everywhere. There is scarcely a country in the world where Kohler plumbing fixtures, electric plants or heating equipment have not been installed. (Kohler Co., 1934)

Kohler Village was also featured in detail at the exhibition. According to the company's exposition brochure, the enjoyment of numerous amenities that 'contribute to healthful living' in a community where 'industrial workers own substantial homes, with modern conveniences' helped to make the Village the hub of a widening network of modernity carried outward by Kohler products through 'an intangible, improving quality passing into every product which bears the Kohler mark' (Kohler Co., 1934).

As events in Kohler itself would show, however, this triumphal geography of modern sanitation contained significant fractures soon to be prised open by Kohler workers. The labour strife that erupted in Kohler during the two summers of the Century of Progress exposition demonstrated these fractures. Spurred by diminishing Depression-era work hours and shrinking pay cheques, unionisation efforts had begun at Kohler in 1933 following the passage of the National Industrial Recovery Act with its union-friendly Section 7(a). By August 1933 Kohler's unionists had gained enough support to receive a charter from the American Federation of Labor (AFL) designating their organisation as Federal Labor Union No. 18545. Though the company countered by forming a company union called the Kohler Workers' Association, Local 18545's leadership continued to meet with company representatives to try to negotiate a contract. When little progress had been made on the union's main demands a strike was called, effective 16 July, 1934 (Uphoff, 1966; Oberdeck, 2001).[4]

Though the 1934 strike was about many issues that were not spatial in nature, issues of Village space and the ways the company situated the Village in various scales of geographical identity loomed large. Company publicity represented strikers as 'outsiders' threatening the home-centred lives of Villagers. In public statements and company publicity, Walter Kohler complained that the strike had surrounded his plant and invaded the town with 'hundreds of pickets, the mass of whom had never worked for the Company and fewer than a dozen of whom are residents of Kohler Village' (*Kohler of Kohler News*, August 1934, p. 3; *The New Deal*, 1934, July 20). Such statements reasserted workers' identification with company-defined 'home interests' enacted in the Village, obscuring the fact that most employees still lived in the city of Sheboygan and nearby towns. By picturing the Village as a home-centred space invaded by 'outsiders', the company thereby sought to enhance its identity as a bounded place, obscuring the grievances of Village residents who were union members, including Local 18545 president Arthur Kuhn and sometime financial secretary Guy Burbey (*New Deal*, 1934, 3 August, 7 August).[5]

According to the company, this self-contained identity was accentuated by the strike's most dramatic altercations. A violent exchange between rock-wielding strike supporters and gun-toting Village deputies on 27 July 1934 resulted in the deaths of two strikers, the arrival of the National Guard to keep the peace in the Village and an escalation in the strike's national visibility. Reflecting on this 'riot', it was remarked in the *Kohler of Kohler News* that:

> [h]undreds of men and women have made sacrifices and faced perils in repulsing a vicious attack upon their homes and upon their freedom as citizens and workers. . . .
>
> These many years the Kohler Co. organization has been actuated by a vital spirit of purpose and achievement which even outside observers remarked. That spirit is stronger than ever before. . . . [T]he fabric of common purposes and aspirations that has made it possible for the Village of Kohler to achieve the unusual, in beauty and practicality, is far more closely knit than at any previous time. . . .
>
> With a unanimity so thorough that the handful of exceptions only emphasized it, the people of the Village have rallied under the leadership of their elected officials to protect their freedom and their homes. (*Kohler of Kohler News*, August 1934, p. 3)

According to this rendition, rioting unionist 'outsiders' threatened 'American' freedoms that Walter Kohler had always associated with life in Kohler Village. In the process, the company reaffirmed the boundaries that made the Village a sanctuary for such freedoms and the home-centred lives that they required and encouraged.

Such representations of the town, however, contradicted the extensive web of materials and markets that the company emphasised in its ongoing exhibit at the Century of Progress Exposition and, before it, decades of reporting in the *Kohler of Kohler News*. Union spokespeople were quick to pick up on this as they elaborated an alternative geography of Kohler worker interests. These labourite spatial politics found especially clear expression in *The New Deal*, a labour weekly launched in May 1934 on the eve of the Kohler strike in the nearby city of Sheboygan. Here workers asserted the claims to networks of influence and common interest as far-reaching as the sources of materials and markets Kohler claimed for its products. 'For Mr Kohler, who goes to the far corners of the earth to sell his product . . . to cry out against active "outside" interest in the strike', the paper complained, 'is to ask for rights for himself that he would deny to his employees' (*The New Deal*, 1934, July 20). It was also to restrict workers to relating to the rest of the world only through the white and lavender bathtubs the company produced. Through the advances of Section 7(a) of the National Recovery Act, *The New Deal* claimed, Kohler workers had established a different kind of identification with the producers of the materials Walter Kohler and his company reached across the world to procure. For Walter Kohler to deny such identification in his defence of the Kohler factory and Village from 'outsiders' was to forget, *The New Deal* writers argued, the labour that went into the worldwide resources upon which his manufacture relied:

[h]e forgets that workers, brothers in the working class of his employees, have slaved to produce these materials. He forgets that the coal that fires the furnaces that burn the faces of his employees and the sand that eats their lungs were dug out of the earth in the world outside of Kohler.

   Of all the 'outsiders' who have a right to be concerned in the welfare of the Kohler workers, the members of the organized labor movement the world over are in the foreground . . . Through the gloss of the tubs it sees the misery of workers frustrated in their efforts to be free men. (*The New Deal*, 3 August 1934)

According to this labour geography, Kohler workers were more interested in the workday perils of their labouring counterparts on the map of Kohler's widening global interests than in the resources they produced or the bathtubs they bought. For these workers, the map of modern hygiene had to be charted through global worksites as well as the homes, bathrooms and public buildings where Kohler ware was installed.

As Kohler strikers extended their affiliations beyond the Village and home-centred interests the company had delineated for them, they also challenged the company's gendered renditions of Village industrial and domestic space. Indeed, according to the company, its fiercest altercations with workers developed in large part out of defiance of the Village's gendered zones. Hence, the company justified the Village deputies' use of arms as a defence of the women and children of the Village's residential section. The deputies had made their first assaults with tear gas when 'the mob . . . was about to rush the entrance to the office, where girl telephone operators were working'. But, 'it was not until the mob was threatening the village that the police resorted to their guns. Only by doing so were they able to drive the rioters from the Village and protect the lives of women and children'. Within the micro-geography of the Village, though, the business zone between the 'residential area', where women and children resided, and the predominantly male 'industrial area' posed an especially precarious problem for company control of gendered space. In the aftermath of the riot Walter Kohler expressed regret that women and children who had joined the crowd in this zone had not 'heeded the warning' of Village President Anton Brotz, who had commanded that they 'stay away from the vicinity of all unlawful assemblage'. Their presence in the business zone, Kohler complained, 'hampered the activities of the law-enforcing officers' (*Kohler of Kohler News*, August 1934, p. 3).

Significantly, though, unionist publicity, especially that devised by some of the predominantly male strikers' own womenfolk, responded with very different conceptions of the geographical range of women's domestic interests. Often expressed in the 'Woman's Page' of *The New Deal*, such rescaling of domestic labour mobilised concerns that accorded superficially with those that the spatial and cultural organisation of Kohler Village allocated to women. Like the Village's women's organisations, *The New Deal* Woman's Page featured suggestions on cooking, economical home decoration, and child-rearing. But such contributors as Eva Burbey, wife of Local 18545 financial secretary Guy Burbey, included in their suggestions pointers on the link between the home and union struggles for economic justice. Child-rearing columns included tips on raising generous and egalitarian children and offered guidance on family life which implied that good motherhood cultivated children whose character expressed their respect for working-class labour. In general, Burbey's columns reminded working-class mothers that their interests went beyond the Kohler ideal of producing well-appointed domiciles. She enlarged the scale of their concerns by connecting them not just to other consumers of domestic products but also to wider social struggles for economic justice (*The New Deal*, 1935, 1 February, 22 February, 15 March).

Ultimately, the Kohler strikers of the 1930s lost their battle and the company union – the Kohler Workers' Association – represented Kohler employees into the 1940s. Nevertheless, Local 18545 did bequeath to later Kohler workers their alternative geography of labour interest. A longer and fiercer strike in the 1950s produced even more substantial links between Kohler workers and plumbingware producers elsewhere in the country through the agency of an industrial union. Formed out of the increasingly disgruntled KWA membership, UAW-CIO Local 833 struck the Kohler plant in 1954 when negotiations on their second annual contract with the company ground to a halt. Once again, a battle over issues not entirely spatial took on geographical significance: the company designated unionists as 'outside agitators' assailing satisfied Village residents/workers, and unionists again replied that few industrial workers actually enjoyed arrangements in the model village that the company was trying to protect. Both company and union also charged one another with threatening and 'manhandling' women within the ambiguous zone that separated the male area of the factory from the female, residential section of the Village (*Kohler of Kohler News*, April 1955, pp. 10, 31; UAW-CIO, 1954, p. 12; UAW-CIO, 1955, p. 19).

Through its affiliation with an industrial union seeking industry-wide contracts, however, UAW Local 833 also reshaped the geography of labour disputes at Kohler. To refute the company's image of the Village's home-centred life as a primary link between Kohler's worker-residents and the outside world, UAW-CIO publicity pictured Kohler workers in cross-regional relations to other producers of kitchen and bathroom fixtures. Local 833 members compared pay and benefits among widely dispersed plumbingware workers to show that Kohler's wages and welfare programmes did not measure up. Such comparisons provided more direct cross-regional links of working-class sympathy than Local 18545 had asserted. Connected to other bathtub and toilet makers through an industrial union, Kohler workers could make direct contrasts between their pay and that received by plumbingware workers who enjoyed UAW representation. This explicit refiguration of Kohler workers' geographical affiliations had ramifications in the way the union, as compared to the company, identified 'outsiders' and distinguished 'private' and 'public' space. Thus, to the union, the 'outsiders' whom Kohler officials labelled 'UAW thugs from Detroit' instead identified as members of a national union community connected in a cross-regional pursuit of improved wages and benefits (Kohler Local 833, UAW-CIO, 1954a). In the discursive struggles over geographic labelling, the 'outsiders' who had invaded Kohler were not, according to Local 833, their UAW supporters. They were, instead, the company-imported strikebreakers who could not stand the rigours of labour at Kohler or construct far-reaching solidarities. As pictured in Local 833's *Daily Strike Bulletin*, strikebreakers who came to Kohler from California, Texas and Florida complained about the heat and difficulty of labour in the plant. Instead of establishing cross-regional alliances, as UAW-CIO members did, strikebreakers vied with one another in their efforts to keep up with the company's pace (Kohler Local 833, UAW-CIO, 1954b).

Local 833, however, also posed new challenges to the company's design and interpretation of space within the Village. Hence, the union cited the lack of public spaces such as taverns and coffee shops in which pickets could congregate as a hindrance posed by the Village plan to strikers' activities. Union literature also highlighted uses to which union workers put Sheboygan homes and gardens that were free from the Village's company-dominated aesthetic standards. Insisting that front yards were proper venues for the expression of union sentiments, the daily strike bulletin supported demonstrations by strike supporters in front of the homes of workers who crossed picket lines at Kohler. It also endorsed the use of a union member's lawn to rebuke his strike-breaking neighbour with a sign reading 'SCAB' and sporting an arrow pointing next door. Such uses of domestic space for the purposes of union struggle revised the arrangement of 'zones' through which Kohler Village expressed the company's vision of spatial relations between home, community and business life. The company pictured the residential sections of the Village as restricted domains where women and children enjoyed the fruits of industry and were protected from its conflicts. In contrast, the union regarded such spaces as contiguous with shopfloor struggles, challenging the company's designations of public and private, industrial and domestic space (Kohler Local 833, UAW-CIO, 1954c; UAW-CIO, 1955, p. 19; see also Uphoff, 1966).

As their strike dragged on through the 1950s, Local 833 and the national UAW organisation that supported it eventually challenged the company on the very terrain of commerce and marketing it had abrogated to itself, while relegating workers and their families to local and home-based concerns. The union pursued a nationwide boycott of Kohler products that often involved strikers following Kohler delivery trucks to distant destinations to picket their recipients. Rather than being represented to such markets as contented Village residents producing attractive domestic fixtures, boycott teams struck out on the company's retail networks to assert their alternative identification with unionists across the nation (UAW Local 833, n.d.).[6]

Though tactics like the boycott challenged intertwined geographies of labour control and publicity the company had long maintained, Local 833's strategies left some elements of these geographies notably intact. This was particularly the case with regard to the Local Union's mapping of gender. Though nationally the UAW reimagined the nexus of domestic and industrial space by taking up issues such as maternity leave and childcare, Local 833 tended to reproduce gendered spatial imaginaries of home and work that conformed to the company's organisation of space in Kohler Village. Images of female strikebreakers' homes implied that chaos prevailed in domestic spaces when women were too busy keeping the Kohler factory clean. At the same time that Local 833 refigured the company's calibration of local and national space, its national appeals reproduced prevailing images of female domestic and male industrial space that earlier union men and women at Kohler had challenged.

Local 833's eventual success in the longest US strike of the twentieth century thus bears out complex shifts in the geography of labour power. Like other unions of its time, it prevailed by challenging the spatial scale according to which the Kohler company had figured its employees' concerns, laying claim, like its predecessor Local 18545, to the company's own broader national and global networks of marketing and publicity. Won ultimately in the courts, its victory turned on its ability to assert the primacy of National Labor Relations Board decisions over the rulings of the more anti-union Wisconsin Economic Relations Board favoured by the company (Uphoff, 1966, pp. 300–319). On the road to that court victory, Local 833 and its predecessors had persistently refuted the company's spatial ordering of worker allegiances on a number of fronts, from the front

yard to the global marketplace. Though Local 833's success signalled company acceptance of the union's national mapping of Kohler worker identifications, this national
fixing of worker identifications did, however, sacrifice challenges to local and global
renderings of gendered space that had loomed larger in the context of Local 18545's
conception of labour solidarity.

Late twentieth-century transformations of company-town space

Kohler workers' reassertion of the national scale of their labourite identifications in
the 1950s occurred on the eve of shifts to a global production and assembly system
that altered the place of Kohler Village and its factory in the worldwide network of the
company's concerns. In the midst of the 1950s strike Kohler established its first plant
outside Wisconsin – a facility for producing vitreous china and fibreglass reinforced
plastic bathtubs and showers – in Spartanburg, South Carolina. This began an ongoing
extension of the company's production south and eventually east to regions with lower
labour costs and fewer unions. By the 1970s the company had opened another china and
fibreglass plastic facility in Brownwood, Texas, and by the 1990s had a string of plumbing, furniture and engine plants across the US and Canada, in addition to a *maquiladora*
in Monterrey, Mexico. Recently, the company has opened a second *maquiladora* in
Reynosa, Mexico, more factories in China, and is developing a plant in Gujarat, India.[7]

In the Village itself a new 50-year master plan conceived in the 1970s under the leadership of current company head Herbert V. Kohler Jr. (Walter J. Kohler's nephew) in
consultation with the Frank Lloyd Wright Foundation transformed the American Club
into a luxury resort hotel and convention centre, complete with high priced restaurants, a
shopping mall nearby, several championship golf courses, a sports club and a private wild-
life preserve. Kohler Village now operates as a magnet for regional and global holiday-
makers who can integrate the 'gracious living' of the company's hospitality industries into
their homes through Kohler fixtures. Intriguingly, labour unions also advertise Kohler
Village as a recreation spot for union members, where they can tour one of the declining
numbers of factories that still enjoy the benefits of union representation.[8]

Kohler's transformation is part of a wider shift in the geography of production that
has altered the nature of company towns in many places and the company's pattern of
industrial expansion and local transformation expresses general trends among firms that
had produced welfare-capitalist garden-industrial villages, as well as more paternalisti-
cally and less imaginatively designed company towns, but that subsequently sought to
shed or reorient them. Much of this transformation in the nature of company towns was
associated with broader mid-century restructurings in the spatiality of life in the US and
elsewhere. Hence, in the 1930s and 1940s, the spread of automobiles among the relatively
skilled workers that company towns had sought to attract diminished the appeal of
localised housing schemes for both workers and employers. Moreover, Kohler was not
alone in discovering that such appeals were not reliable protections against alternative
geographical affiliations offered by national and international unions. Other planned
company towns, like Hershey, Pennsylvania, and the multi-industry settlement designed
by John Nolen in Kingsport, Tennessee, unionised in the 1930s (Crawford, 1995, pp.
200–207; Bussel and Bischof, 2004).

At the same time, along with supporting workers' rights to organise, the New Deal
committed the federal government to aid in providing the access to housing and home

loans, old age security, outdoor recreation resources and other amenities that corporate welfare programmes had provided to workers as employees. Though often charged with government 'paternalism' and, in the case of federal loan programmes, productive of the same racialised spatial divisions that company towns had often realised, such federal programmes had the self-proclaimed virtues of providing benefits for citizens who could, at least theoretically, use their votes to influence decisions about their localities and their relations to wider scales of civic engagement. In this climate, manufacturing concerns that had developed company towns found the burdens of multiple identities as employers, municipal leaders and landlords untenable. Many gratefully sold out to enterprising real estate developers like John Galbreath, who made a career out of marketing company-owned housing to workers (Allen, 1966, p. 141; Crawford, 1995, pp. 202–203; Blank, 1958).

These transformations found parallels in company towns worldwide, where the politics of nationalism and decolonisation also challenged the paternalistic politics of social control (Grant, 1971). The politics of localising control was even apparent in regions where company town development had come relatively late to resource frontiers requiring new supplies of skilled labour. In the Pilbara mining region of Western Australia, for example, suburb-like housing facilities were set up by transnational joint-venture companies to mine iron ore for sale to the expanding Japanese steel industry in the early 1960s (for more on the Pilbara, see Ellem, Chapter 19 in this volume). By the early 1970s these towns experienced labour unrest focused, in part, on the provision of 'town amenities'. As a result, by the mid-1970s these towns had become the objects of various 'normalisation' schemes designed to shift their administration to local government authority – schemes presented as opportunities for worker governance though they derived from secretive government-business deals jealously guarded by company representatives (Thompson, 1981).

What these developments all demonstrate, of course, is the vastly changed geography of capital that has reshaped the landscapes of industrial villages and former company towns, with diverse implications for their residents and workers. By the 1970s, capitalists were abandoning the spatial fixes that underlay the welfare-capitalist company town – the effort to attract stable, materially ambitious non-union workforces to garden villages where they would identify with a company-defined local culture. Firms were on the global move seeking ever-cheaper sources of labour, and it was unions and local governments that were often making the investments, in the form of benefit sacrifices and tax breaks, to keep their employers or attract new ones. This had somewhat ironic implications for company town residents who had once contested the localising scalar politics of welfare capitalism by constructing wider spaces of union affiliation. Now, it is resident workers who, through strikes, protests and political action, seek to remind companies that their erstwhile insistence on local ties is betrayed by ambitions to save labour costs, move factories, or dedicate residents' communities to new purposes. Thus, at Pullman residents faced with a Chamber of Commerce-sponsored plan to raze the dying town in favour of a new industrial park rallied around the preservation of a company town whose local boundaries its original inhabitants had rarely respected (Reiff, 2000). Residents and workers at Hershey, Pennsylvania, battled in 2002 to save a classic welfare-capitalist health plan and prevent the charitable trust that owned Hershey foods from selling out and compromising local ties (Bussel and Bischof, 2004). And in Kohler, Village planning commissioners and trustees wondered why housing for the elderly needed by long-term Village residents was postponed in favour of sports and hospitality facilities (*Sheboygan Press*, 1977, 20 May, 6 June, 19 August). For company towns, like other locations of labour contest, then, spatial politics are ever shifting, as workers/residents adjust to company-generated renovations of the landscapes both groups once helped to define.

Notes

1. This analysis is also informed by the analytical perspectives of a number of critical economic geographers, including Soja (1989), Massey (1994) and Smith (1992).
2. On the role of the *News*, see Uphoff (1966, pp. 3–4). On the link between welfare capitalism and 'Americanisation', see Cohen (1990, chapter 4).
3. For further publicity on Kohler Village as a model of modern living, see Kohler Co. (1933, p. 21). For other examples of town publicity, see Kohler Co. (n.d., 1920, 1925, 1931).
4. The demands included collective bargaining, seniority rights, protection against peremptory discharge, a 30-hour work week and reinstatement of laid-off workers.
5. For another example of the designation of local union activists as spatial 'outsiders' in the 1930s, see Mitchell (1998).
6. The boycott also relied on the geographically expanded labour support available through the recent AFL–CIO merger.
7. See Kohler History Timeline, available at www.kohler.com/corp/timeline/time_frame.html; *India Daily*, 11 May 2006, available at www.indiadaily.com/editorial/8766.asp; China Labor Watch, 'The Kohler Company's Factory in Foshan, China', New York, June, 2005, available at www.chinalaborwatch.org/upload/kohlerreport.pdf?article_id=50264.
8. *AFSCME Public Employee Magazine*, 'Union fun in the summer sun', May/June 1997, available at www.afscme.org/publications/8466.cfm (last accessed 29 March 2009); *The Wisconsin Laborer*, 'Odds and ends: Local #1086 retirees find ways to stay active', available at www.solidarity.com/oddsn.htm, Fall 1997 (last accessed 29 March 2009).

References

Alanen, A.R. and T.J. Peltin (1978), 'Kohler, Wisconsin: planning and paternalism in a model industrial village', *Journal of the American Institute of Planners*, **44** (2), 145–59.

Allen, J. (1966), *The Company Town in the American West*, Norman, OK: The University of Oklahoma Press.

Baker, S.L. (1995), 'Jackson Fibre Co.: welfare capitalism and public work in a southern textile village, 1900–1926', *The West Tennessee Historical Society Papers*, **49**, 46–65.

Blank, J.P. (1958), 'He turned company towns into home towns,' *American Business*, **28** (9), 12–14.

Bonner, P. and K.A. Shapiro (1993), 'Company town, company estate: pilgrim's rest, 1910–1932', *Journal of Southern African Studies*, **19** (2), 171–200.

Bruder, S. (1967), *Pullman: An Experiment in Industrial Order and Community Planning, 1880–1930*, New York: Oxford University Press.

Bussel, R. and A. Bischof (2004), '"Everybody's town": defending the social contract in Hershey, Pennsylvania', *Labor*, **1** (2), 27–39.

Chomsky, A. (1996), *West Indian Workers and the United Fruit Company in Costa Rica, 1870–1940*, Baton Rouge, LA: Louisiana State University Press.

Cohen, L. (1990), *Making a New Deal: Industrial Workers in Chicago, 1919–1939*, New York: Cambridge University Press.

Crawford, M. (1995), *Building the Workingman's Paradise: The Design of American Company Towns*, London: Verso.

Creese, W.L. (1966), *The Search for Environment – The Garden City: Before and After*, New Haven, CT: Yale University Press.

Day, M.G. (1981), 'The contribution of Sir Raymond Unwin (1863–1940) and R. Barry Parker (1867–1947) to the development of site planning theory and practice c. 1890–1918', in A. Sutcliffe (ed.), *British Town Planning: The Formative Years*, New York: St Martin's Press, pp. 156–93.

Ehsani, K. (2003), 'Social engineering and the contradictions of modernization in Khuzestan's company towns: a look at Abadan and Masjed Soleyman', *International Review of Social History*, **48** (3), 361–99.

Garner, J. (1984), *The Model Company Town: Urban Design through Private Enterprise in Nineteenth-Century New England*, Amherst, MA: University of Massachusetts Press.

Gilbert, J. (1991), *Perfect Cities: Chicago's Utopias of 1893*, Chicago, IL: University of Chicago Press.

Gordon, L. (1999), *The Great Arizona Orphan Abduction*, Cambridge, MA: Harvard University Press.

Grant, C.H. (1971), 'Company towns in the Caribbean: a preliminary analysis of Christianburg-Wismar-Mackenzie', *Caribbean Studies*, **11** (1), 46–72.

Harpelle, R.N. (1994), 'Ethnicity, religion, and repression: the denial of African heritage in Costa Rica,' *Canadian Journal of History*, **29** (1), 95–113.

Herod, A. (2001), *Labor Geographies: Workers and the Landscapes of Capitalism*, New York: Guilford Press.

Keltner, R. (2001), 'Tar paper shacks in Arcadia: housing for ethnic minority groups in the company town of Bauxite, Arkansas', *The Arkansas Historical Quarterly*, **LX** (4), 341–59.

Kohler Co. (n.d., c. 1930s), 'An organization and a community contribute to healthful living', Kohler, WI: Kohler Co.

Kohler Co. (1920), 'Kohler: a place to work and live', Kohler, WI: Kohler Co.

Kohler Co. (1925), 'Kohler Village: a hopeful and stimulating example of American community life', Kohler, WI: Kohler Co.

Kohler Co. (1928), 'Kohler Village: a town-planned Wisconsin industrial community, American in spirit and government', Kohler, WI: Kohler Co.

Kohler Co. (1931), 'Kohler Village', Kohler, WI: Kohler Co.

Kohler Co. (1933), 'Kohler of Kohler: sixty years of progress', Kohler, WI: Kohler Co.

Kohler Co. (1934), *Kohler of Kohler: A Century of Progress, 1934*, Kohler, WI: Kohler Co., pp. 7–9.

Kohler Local 833, UAW-CIO (1954a), *Daily Strike Bulletin*, 2 July.

Kohler Local 833, UAW-CIO (1954b), *Daily Strike Bulletin*, 2 September.

Kohler Local 833, UAW-CIO (1954c), *Daily Strike Bulletin*, 6 April, 21 August, 25 August, 26 August, 6 September, 6 October.

Massey, D. (1994), *Space, Place, and Gender*, Minneapolis, MN: University of Minnesota Press.

Mitchell, D. (1998), 'The scales of justice: localist ideology, large scale production, and agricultural labor's geography of resistance in 1930s California', in A. Herod (ed.), *Organizing the Landscape: Geographical Perspectives on Labor Unionism*, Minneapolis, MN: University of Minnesota Press, pp. 159–94.

Mosher, A.E. (2004), *Capital's Utopia: Vandergrift, Pennsylvania, 1855–1916*, Baltimore, MD: Johns Hopkins.

Oberdeck, K.J. (2001), 'Class, place, and gender: contested industrial and domestic space in Kohler, Wisconsin, USA, 1920–1960', *Gender and History*, **13** (1), 97–137.

Oberdeck, K.J. (2005), 'Archives of the unbuilt environment: documents and discourses of imagined space in twentieth-century Kohler, Wisconsin', in A. Burton (ed.), *Archive Stories: Facts, Fictions, and the Writing of History*, Durham, NC: Duke University Press, pp. 251–73.

O'Brien, T.F. (1993), 'The revolutionary mission: American enterprise in Cuba', *American Historical Review*, **98** (3), 765–85.

Reiff, J.L. (2000), 'Rethinking Pullman: urban space and working-class activism', *Social Science History*, **24** (1), 7–32.

Saarinen, O.W. (1986), 'Single-sector communities in Northern Ontario: the creation and planning of dependent towns,' in G.A. Stelter and A.F.J. Artibise (eds), *Power and Place: Canadian Urban Development in the North American Context*, Vancouver: UBC Press, pp. 219–64.

Seccombe, I. and R. Lawless (1987), *Work Camps and Company Towns: Settlement Patterns and the Gulf Oil Industry*, Durham, NC: Center for Middle Eastern and Islamic Studies.

Smith, N. (1992), 'Contours of a spatialized politics: homeless vehicles and the production of geographic scale', *Social Text*, **33**, 53–81.

Soja, E. (1989), *Postmodern Geographies: The Reassertion of Space in Critical Social Theory*, London: Verso.

Striffler, S. (2004), 'Class formation in Latin America: one family's enduring journey between country and city', *International Labor and Working-Class History*, **65**, 11–25.

Swanson, M.W. (1977), 'The Sanitation syndrome: bubonic plague and urban native policy in the Cape Colony', *Journal of African History*, **18**, 387–410.

Thompson, H. (1981), '"Normalisation": industrial relations and community control in the Pilbara', *The Australian Quarterly*, **53** (3), 301–24.

UAW-CIO (1954), *For These We Fight: A Report about People Who Will Not Be Denied*, Detroit: UAW-CIO.

UAW-CIO (1955), *The Kohler Workers' Story*, Detroit, MI: UAW-CIO.

UAW Local 833 (n.d.), 'The Kohler boycott' UAW Local 833 Collection, Box 30, Folder 12, Wayne State University Archives of Labor and Urban Affairs.

Uphoff, W. (1966), *Kohler on Strike: Thirty Years of Conflict*, Boston, MA: Beacon Press.

Van Sittert, L. (2001), '"Velddrift": the making of a South African company town', *Urban History*, **28** (2), 194–217.

White, N. (2004), 'Creating community: industrial paternalism and town planning in Corner Brook, Newfoundland, 1923–1955', *Urban History Review*, **32** (2), 45–59.

Wilkins, M. (1974), *The Maturing of Multinational Enterprise: American Business Abroad, 1914–1970*, Cambridge, MA: Harvard University Press.

Winpenny, T.R. (1995), 'Milton S. Hersey ventures into Cuban sugar', *Pennsylvania History*, **62** (4), 491–502.

11 Work, place and community in socialism and postsocialism
Alison Stenning

Introduction

One of the most important and best known features of postwar labour history in East Central Europe was the emergence of Solidarity (Solidarność) in Poland in the early 1980s. Solidarity eventually emerged as a trade union, but a union rooted not only in workplaces but also in communities. This geographical connection between work and community was critical to Solidarity's creation and development – and testifies to the central importance of spatial practices and spatial identities in worker activism (Herod, 1997; Rainnie et al., 2007). Yet, as I and others have argued elsewhere, the tight labour–community connection which Solidarity used so well in its development and survival was a legacy of an earlier policy, that which tied workplaces to communities in the construction of postwar Poland (Bivand, 1983; Stenning, 2003). Thus, in both the construction of socialism and in its collapse, the spatial articulations between work and community were key.

The focus of this chapter is the changing nature of the work–community relationship in the socialist and postsocialist world, exploring the ways in which this spatial relationship has been critical not only to the shape of labour politics and working class struggles but also to the formation of identities, life chances and economic practices amongst working people in the context of repeated and deep social change in the now postsocialist world. In the postwar period, these states were constructed, at least in theory, as workers' states (Haraszti, 1977; Crowley and Ost, 2001). For this reason, the work–community nexus is of particular importance in this part of the world, all the more so as new postsocialist worlds of work shape new communities of interest and new spaces of everyday life. This chapter begins by exploring this connection within socialism, focusing primarily but not exclusively on the experiences of Poland, before moving on to consider the articulation of the work–community nexus with the collapse of socialism and the ways in which the relationship is transformed in – and transforms – the contemporary postsocialist world.

Work, class and community

The connection between work/community and labour politics, identities and life chances is one which has attracted considerable attention from geographers and sociologists. Building on earlier work (such as Williamson, 1982), researchers turned their attention in the mid- to late 1980s to the ways in which the processes of deindustrialisation were contested and lived in working class communities, and thus the ways in which workers shaped economic life (Robinson and Sadler, 1985; Hudson and Sadler, 1986; Beynon et al., 1989). As Strangleman (2001) has suggested, work is intertwined with family, kin, friendship, locality and class in complex social networks, which connect to the formation of both economies and identities. The material and discursive connections between work and community flow not only through employment and pay, but also through myriad other relationships between employer and community. Employers finance and manage a range of local infrastructures and services, including housing, heating, water, schools and health facilities and facilities for leisure and recreation, and engage, formally or informally, in local politics.

The work–community relationship, however, extends beyond the employer. Through trade unions, community spaces and a variety of other institutions and practices, communities of workers create 'shared meanings' (Williamson, 1982; Hudson and Sadler, 1986). As Richard Hyman suggested, acknowledging that his depiction was somewhat caricatured, there

> is a stereotype of the traditional proletarian status which emphasises a common work situation, an integrated and homogenous local community, and a limited repertoire of shared cultural and social pursuits. Though exaggerated, this stereotype does identify a core of historical reality, particularly in . . . single-industry manual working-class milieux (Hyman, 1999, p. 3).

In such communities, the intertwining of spheres of production, consumption and reproduction grounded workers and their families in particular places and supported the development of dense social networks.

Of course it has long been acknowledged, following Young (1990; see also Panelli and Welch, 2005), that community has the potential to be oppressive and exclusionary. As identities and practices are constituted every day, so too are gender contracts, racialisations and other exclusions. Communities are rarely, if ever, homogeneous, and are much more likely to be formed through more than one constellation of institutional and social relationships (Stacey, 1969). And as Massey and McDowell (1984), amongst others, have argued, the traditionally-conceived working class community was marked by its very clear gender geographies, and by other fault lines. Such communities are also dynamic, despite their often nostalgic construction as places of stability. Not only do internal differentiations and contestations constantly reshape communities, but wider economic shifts also lead to the 'internal recomposition of communities' (Rees, 1985).

Notwithstanding these important limits, numerous authors have drawn attention to the strategic employment of community in the face of, often external, threats. For working class communities, such threats are often closure and downsizing, driven by the wider restructuring of industry, which stimulate trade union, company and community campaigns for survival and further investment (Rees, 1985; Hudson and Sadler, 1986). Whilst raising questions about the occasional alliance of capital and labour in these campaigns, it is also possible to highlight the 'common cause' of community cultivated by the experience of living and working together. The recent renaissance of community unionism, which works to unite disparate interests in place-based campaigns, echoes this harnessing of common cause (Wills, 2001).

These more exceptional experiences of industrial action and political activism connect to the everyday routines of life and work to reinforce the construction of community identities, both within and beyond the community itself. In this way, community and worker activism became part of the characterisation of places, as just one more factor of production; militancy, compliance and the shape of the community were seen as features of the local labour market to be factored into investment decisions and analyses of the spatial divisions of labour (Massey, [1984] 1995).

Recent years have seen a shift in the study of work/non-work relationships towards a focus on home–work connections and the work–life balance (see, for example, McDowell, 2004), which has perhaps eroded the focus on community as championed by the locality and community studies of the 1980s. The turn away from work and community has been reinforced by recent writing which claims that rising short-termism and demands for flexibility in the 'new worlds of work' result in individualism and a consequent diminishment of community (Sennett, 1998; Beck, 2000). Sennett (1998) thus relates a tendency for redundant workers to withdraw from civic life and turn inward to find meaning.

The shift away from the formal spaces of workplaces and unions calls for new ways of documenting and analysing working class lives. In this context, a new working class studies has emerged (Linkon and Russo, 2002; Russo and Linkon, 2005) which attempts to connect longer-standing accounts of working class life, in labour history, industrial relations and industrial sociology, for example, to contemporary debates around identity, multiculturalism, social justice and redistribution/recognition. Research written in the context of the new working class studies counters the 'end of work' debates by pointing to the continued importance of older forms of work through both their material legacies, in the shape of networks, institutions and relationships built at work, and the community memories of work. These meanings and practices, whilst rooted in the institutions of work, must be seen as at least partially autonomous, such that, despite the erosion of industrial work, the destruction of community need not be inevitable. This insistence is not only empirical but also political; in many old industrial communities, the dominant tropes are ones of loss, decline and failure, to the detriment of a more constructive consideration of alternative stories of community change which might ease the process of economic and political restructuring (Gibson et al., 1999; Byrne, 2002).

Work, community and the construction of socialism

Whilst Herod (1997, 2001) has noted the persistent exclusion of workers from the geographies of capitalism, it is perhaps still more surprising that the anglophone geographies of socialism in East Central Europe and the Soviet Union paid so little attention to the place of workers. The worker was central in the spaces of socialism, as both the subject and the object of the socialist drive to industrialise and urbanise. Workers were expected to build and work in the new districts, towns, cities and workplaces and to be remade within them (Siemieńska, 1969). Yet the embodied worker seemed to get lost both in the mythical representations of the 'worker hero' within the region and in the dominant totalitarian framework invoked in the West to describe and analyse the socialist regimes of the region (Stenning, 2005a). Neither perspective allowed the multiple and contested practices of workers and their communities to be fully considered in accounts of the construction of socialism, though recent research in history is beginning to fill this lacuna (Kenney, 1997; Kotkin, 1997; Fitzpatrick, 2001; Pittaway, 2002, 2005a; Horváth, 2005).

On the other hand, what has been thoroughly documented is the massive growth of the industrial workforce and of industrial workplaces in the early socialist years (after the revolution in the Soviet Union and after World War II in East Central Europe). In Poland, a 'transfer of workers both from country to town and from east to west' (Pounds, 1960) was driven by a conscious attempt to redevelop town life around industry and encourage a 'movement to work' in small towns (Pounds, 1960). In the three years to 1949, one million new workers entered industry (North, 1958) and between 1946 and 1960, 2.5 million Poles moved to urban areas from the countryside (Nowakowski, 1967, p. 7), increasing the urban share of the population from 31.8 per cent to 48.1 per cent (Pounds, 1960, p. 239). Similar transformations were witnessed in other countries – French and Hamilton estimate that over 1000 new towns were built across the Soviet Union from the 1920s (French and Hamilton, 1979, p. 6) and some 60 in the smaller territories of East Central Europe (Hamilton 1979, p. 183) – and in the countryside, in part as an attempt to collectivise, urbanise and industrialise rural space (Lampland, 1995; Buchowski, 2001). Perhaps as important as the material transformation of the landscape, though, was the symbolic value of these new spaces in the construction of socialism. Hence, as Horváth argues in his historical account of everyday life in Hungary's Sztálinváros, we should see 'early state socialism as a project of cultural transformation' (2005, p. 24) as much as an attempt to build new economies.

Within these new spaces, the workplace was to become 'the main axis of organisation of social life' (Ciechocińska, 1993, p. 32), such that 'collective survival and individual status' (Offe, 1996, p. 235) were founded almost entirely on the relationship to production. Despite clear comparisons between the practices of paternalism in East and West (Domański, 1992, 1997), Offe (1996) stresses that under the socialist regimes of East Central Europe there were rarely alternative providers of income or welfare. As a result, unless they ventured into informal and illegal spheres (Smith and Stenning, 2006), workers had little choice but to accept the centrality of work in their lives (Rainnie et al., 2002; but see Stenning 2007). At the same time, however, for reasons that were not only ideological but also 'rational responses or adaptations to the operation of the central planning system' (Clark and Soulsby, 1998, p. 25), enterprises took on a range of activities well beyond the core production focus. These included education and training, childcare, housing, recreation and leisure, health facilities, retail and consumption, and heating and energy. Clark and Soulsby (1998, p. 36) estimate that in their case study enterprises in the Czech Republic (then Czechoslovakia) this 'social wage' accounted for an additional 17–20 per cent of the average money wage but stress that 'benefits to the community', though more intangible, contributed still further to both the standard and pattern of everyday life. Yet, not only did the community benefit from this enterprise 'benevolence' but so, too, was the enterprise 'reliant on the local economy' (Clark and Soulsby, 1998, p. 37) for labour and skills. These relationships, then, 'wove the enterprises into the fabric of the community' (Clark and Soulsby, 1998, p. 37). The result was that through these interconnections, workers were tied not only to the enterprise but also to each other. Social lives were constructed through the workplace and domestic lives were shaped in large part by relations of production and work status (Kotkin, 1997; Kideckel, 2004; Stenning, 2005b). Through shopping patterns, traffic flows and schedules of work and leisure, the rhythm of life was linked to the rhythm of production.

Since so many of the people settling in these new spaces were migrants, on the move from rural areas or from borderlands, these new communities were intended to provide an opportunity for workers and their families to establish roots (Horváth, 2005) and to create a working class community which would support, with their labour and their votes, the new regimes (Hardy and Rainnie, 1996; Pittaway, 2005b). Yet such optimistic visions of these new socialist spaces failed to take account of both divisions within the new communities and the persistence of old habits and practices. Not only were these new migrants' 'rural attitudes and mores . . . incorporated into the newly constructed urban environment' (Fisher, 1962, p. 262; see also, Kotkin, 1997) but so, too, were pre-socialist prejudices and hierarchies (Kotkin, 1997; Pittaway, 2002; Horváth, 2005). Attempts to construct harmonious and productive working class communities often faltered on inherited and clashing attitudes towards gender and work, skill, education and experience, workers' places of origin and much more. As Pittaway (2005b, p. 5) argues, '[b]oth myths of the "working class" and hegemonic working-class cultures privileged specific worker identities – mostly the skilled, urban, male elite – and marginalised others: women, rural commuters, and the young'. Such myths and cultures were reinforced by processes of regulation and self-regulation (Fitzpatrick, 1993; Kotkin, 1997) such that, as elsewhere, the economic and political construction of the working class was always already a moral process too (Skeggs, 2004). However, the tight connection between worker status and welfare meant that notions of respectable and deserving workers became critical in shaping access to the tenets of security and social mobility.

Work, community and the contestation of socialism

The period of 'high Stalinism' was short-lived. From the death of Stalin in 1953, the region was marked by growing disillusionment in both the material and ideological offerings of the socialist regimes, and in the clear distinction between the promises and realities of working class life. In an irony of history, East Central European socialism was built and died in many of the same places (Harloe, 1996). Many of the places which were bastions of support for socialism (in particular, key industrial centres) were also the ones in which the challenges to socialism were strongest. Indeed, in these places those who fought hardest for socialism, and who were later disenchanted, are often represented as a critical force in the dismantling of socialism and the construction of market economies (see, for example, Bideleux and Jeffries, 1998). Whilst some continued to celebrate the region's working class communities as the vanguard of the revolution, opposition activists were already beginning to identify in the disillusioned worker and the disillusioned spaces of socialism the hopes of undermining communism from within.

In adjusting to their new worlds, though, workers also adapted, resisted and subverted the plans of the new regimes. Their behaviour – collective and individual – 'placed real limits on state action' (Pittaway, 2002, p. 741) both in the workplace and beyond. Pittaway (2002, 2005b) documents the ways in which workers contested the labour process and pay structures, such that 'conflict in the workplace frustrated many of the attempts of the state to mobilise the workforce behind its own economic policy goals' (2005b, p. 2). Horváth (2005), amongst others, has highlighted many of the ways in which workers, beyond the workplace, challenged state attempts to construct them as an ideal proletariat. In these ways, historians of this period have represented the actions of workers as a 'degree of countervailing power' (Pittaway, 2002, p. 740) which delineated the 'limits to dictatorship' (Pittaway, 2002, p. 739).

Yet, in addition to these everyday contestations, in 1956, 1968, 1970 and 1976 communities of workers, often in alliance with students and the intelligentsia, rose up in more marked moments of protest, frequently sparked less by formal political actions than by fairly mundane concerns over food shortages and overnight price hikes. In Poland these events culminated in the strikes of 1980, which were from the very beginning deeply connected to particular industrial communities which became the focus of organising, unrest and occasionally violence. These communities, however, were not simply the sites of, or arenas for, strikes and protests. Rather, the emergence of Poland's Solidarity (Solidarność) was fundamentally shaped by the particular work–community relationship which had developed in these places.[1]

In a paper on Solidarity's geography, Roy Bivand notes that the nascent union, through its inter-factory strike committees, was an explicitly local organisation which reflected 'local abilities, including knowledge of local informal contact networks (for example, parishes) which could be harnessed by local people taking initiatives in their own interests' (Bivand, 1983, p. 399). When Solidarity was legally constituted after the Gdańsk Agreement of August 1980, it took its organisational structure from the units which had emerged during earlier months. It remained a union based on regional and local units, rather than branch or occupational structures (although the latter did exist). As MacShane (1981, p. 67) notes, then, 'from the very beginning, Solidarity was organised on a geographical basis. Workers drew strength from the sense of unity and mutual solidarity provided by organising all workers within a town or region, irrespective of industry or profession'.

Though national leaders repeatedly stressed that Solidarity was a workplace union, many of its activities were focused on satisfying workers' demands at a local scale, from local transport to environmental issues. Solidarity was regarded by the people 'as an agency to whom they could turn in pursuit of their rights in any kind of conflict with the State and its officials' (Bivand, 1983, p. 402; see also, MacShane, 1981; MacDonald 1983). Much of the time and energy of local Solidarity activists in the early months, then, was taken up with responding to mundane and everyday requests from members, relating to issues such as access to healthcare and children's holidays which had previously been facilitated by employers and the official union. During the difficult years of martial law and its aftermath, when economic crisis and political stalemate led to shortages in even the most basic goods, Solidarity's underground incarnation came to play a critical role in daily life, often working in cooperation with local churches and other community organisations (see Kenney, 2002). Yet these local connections were complemented by a more international community, as Solidarity's network of activists and overseas supporters became a vital resource for everyday survival.

Solidarity's extra-workplace role developed out of a number of key features. The union's spatial structure and commitment to a bottom-up, inter-factory constitution was opposed to a branch-based structure which would have been oriented out of the locality. In many communities, the founding committees were very clearly associated with the dominant enterprise but, through kinship and friendship networks, support for them stretched well beyond individual plants. This local orientation and the tight connections between workplace and community also rested on the nature of the construction of socialism in Poland (and East Central Europe more widely) and the role of unions in official structures. The centrality of the workplace in communities under socialism and the expectation that unions provide access to everyday services and facilities was maintained as Solidarity grew and, in this new political context, this connection served the free trade union rather than the regime. Thus, the construction of communities such as Nowa Huta, with one central enterprise, gave Solidarity a set of very strong bases for community action.

Solidarity, then, was a union built on its community alliances. It fed on these coalitions to maintain its strength, especially at times of particular threat, and it acted for the wider community, representing community concerns in dialogue with the state and providing for everyday needs within the community. In the face of official intransigence, Solidarity identified and built on 'common cause' within the locality, beyond the workplace, fostering a network of horizontal connections not only to strengthen the union, but also to sustain the wider community.

New worlds of work

Changes in the sphere of work have been one of the clearest markers of the transformation of the East Central European economies. Millions of jobs were lost in East Central Europe during the first decade of transition, a process accompanied by a 'massive dislocation of the labor force' (Surdej, 2004, p. 6) as employees moved out of employment, into unemployment, retirement or inactivity, or moved to new and expanding sectors. The pace of turnover in the labour market is also perceived to have changed dramatically as job security has plummeted and flexibility has become the watchword of labour market policy. As Cazes and Nesporova (2004, p. 24) suggest, 'introducing employment flexibility and lowering social protection were in most cases offered as the sole means with which to transform labour markets in the new market conditions', conditions shaped not only by the marketisation and globalisation of these economies, but also by the rigorous conditionalities of EU accession and the *acquis communautaire*.

Perhaps most marked has been the emergence and persistence of unemployment, not previously a feature of East Central European labour markets. In most countries of the region, a process of 'transitional recession' (Bradshaw and Stenning, 2001) drove the loss of jobs in the early 1990s, causing unemployment to leap from practically zero to double figures in many countries (see Table 11.1). Hopes that this was a short-lived phenomenon were reinforced as unemployment rates dropped in the mid- to late 1990s in countries like Bulgaria, Lithuania, Poland, Romania and Slovenia, but they were later dashed as the turn of the century saw a dramatic rise.

The persistence of unemployment in many of these countries is exacerbated by the dominance within the ranks of the unemployed of those out of work for more than 12, or

Table 11.1   Unemployment rates in new and candidate EU member states, 1992–2005

	1992	1994	1996	1998	2000	2002	2004	2005 estimate
Bulgaria	15.0	18.6	13.0	16.0	16.4	16.8	12.0	10.1
Czech Republic	2.6	4.3	3.9	6.5	8.8	7.3	8.2	7.8
Estonia	3.7	7.6	10.0	9.8	13.6	10.3	9.7	7.9
Hungary	9.3	10.7	9.9	7.8	6.4	5.8	6.3	7.3
Latvia	3.9	16.7	20.6	14.1	14.4	12.4	10.4	9.9
Lithuania	1.3	3.8	16.4	13.2	16.4	13.8	11.4	8.3
Poland	14.3	16.0	13.2	10.4	15.1	20.0	19.0	17.6
Romania	8.2	10.9	6.6	6.3	7.1	8.4	6.3	5.9
Slovakia	10.4	14.6	12.8	15.6	17.9	17.9	17.1	15.3
Slovenia	8.3	9.1	7.3	7.6	7.6	6.4	6.8	na

Source: Table compiled by the author using data from EBRD (2005).

even 24 months. In 2005, in Poland, Hungary, the Czech Republic and Slovakia between 63 and 81 per cent of the registered unemployed had been out of work for more than six months, and between 46 and 68 per cent for more than 12 months (OECD, 2006, p. 269). This has a number of implications for the health of the labour market, but also clearly for the welfare of individuals, households and communities. Alongside this persistent unemployment, there has also been a marked growth in people leaving the workforce altogether, primarily through early retirement or the receipt of incapacity benefit. This process has perhaps been most marked in Poland, where the employment/population ratio has dropped from 59.9 in 1990 to just 53 in 2004 and fell to a low of 51.4 in 2003, against an OECD average of 65.5 (OECD, 2006, p. 248). Amongst the 50–64 age group, approximately two-fifths of the economically inactive are out of the labour market for reasons of ill-health or disability. A further third of this group – in a pre-retirement age group – are retired (Surdej, 2004, p. 9). However, these trends towards early retirement, often encouraged by generous financial packages offered by restructuring firms, and the growth in the numbers of people claiming benefits for incapacity actually mask higher levels of unemployment amongst this age cohort and what a former minister for labour and social affairs has identified as a 'professional deactivation of the older generation' (Tokarska-Biernacik, 2002).

Alongside these processes of job loss, though, there have been processes of job creation, particularly in new economic spheres. One of the most notable transformations has been the shift to the private sector. Across the region, the share of employment in the private sector has risen to over 70 per cent in almost all cases (EBRD, 2005), and this shift has been accompanied by a declining share of industrial employment and a growth – both relative and absolute – in the share of employment in services. This growth in the service sector has been complex, however, with the creation of employment in both the primary and secondary labour markets. Thus, whilst a number of jobs have been created in high-status, well-paid and secure sectors, such as financial and producer services, the region's labour markets have also seen the expansion of insecure, poorly paid and low-status service jobs in, for example, retail and personal services (Smith et al., 2008). There has also been a decrease in the size of employer. Hence, in contrast to the vast, embedded enterprises of the socialist era, the archetypal firm of postsocialism has been the small or medium enterprise (SME); in the 1990s in Poland, for instance, over 80 per cent of new jobs were created in enterprises with fewer than 100 employees (Kwiatowski et al., 2001).

The postsocialist period has also been marked by the emergence of more atypical work, in part driven by the desire for employment flexibility but also simply by the increasing diversity of the labour market. Cazes and Nesporova (2004) identify a growing trend towards flexible forms of employment, including part-time work, short-term contracts, agency work and 'multiple job-holding'. Yet, in all of these spheres, indicators are considerably lower than in Western European or other OECD countries. There has been a modest growth in part-time employment, though nowhere in the region do part-time employment rates approach OECD averages (OECD, 2006). Indeed, Cazes and Nesporova (2004, p. 27) suggest that 'anecdotal evidence shows very limited use of agency work to date in any transition country', though the increasing involvement of international agencies may mark a clear change (Coe et al., 2006). However, the recorded level of short-term and temporary contracts remains considerably lower than in other EU states (Cazes and Nesporova, 2004).

Equally, Cazes and Nesporova (2004, p. 29) point out striking levels of multiple job-holding. Because much of this secondary work takes place in the informal or even illegal economy, it is notoriously difficult to gauge the scale of such activities, a difficulty that may also account for the counter-intuitively low levels of recorded atypical work more generally. Qualitative research suggests that much of this type of work takes place in the informal or semi-informal economies (Smith et al., 2008) and so escapes measurement. Nevertheless, the growing importance of these insecure and sometimes informal forms of work in the lives of poorer households is critical. In recent research, one of the clearest labour market patterns in poorer households was a process of moving in and out of the formal labour market, into unemployment or casual and short-term employment, and the need to work in more than one workplace to secure a sufficient income (Smith et al., 2008). This evidence raises important questions about the ability of some work in the 'new economy' to offer a living wage. In particular, the high levels of unemployment at the national scale have encouraged governments in the region to focus their attentions on job creation without giving much consideration to the quality of employment, in an echo of Western 'work first' labour market policies (Peck and Theodore, 2000).

As the issue of quality work begins to suggest, these labour market shifts are connected to wider questions of work, its meanings and its geographies, both in people's everyday lives and in their communities. The changing shape of the labour market connects to the place of work but also to the expectations of what work counts and what work is supposed to do. For working class communities, in the East as in the West, recent labour market restructurings are associated with the so-called 'end of work', discussed above, in which neoliberal discourses of enterprise, consumption and individualism are seen to displace the centrality – materially and discursively – of work in people's lives. In postsocialism, the 'end of work' is coupled with the 'end of socialism' to reinforce the dominance of new forms of subjectivity which rest on individualised discourses of the self, most especially the enterprising self (see, for example, Du Gay, 1996). In particular, in its postsocialist version, old socialist subjectivities are reduced to 'dependence, passivity and irresponsibility for self-reliance' (Weiner, 2005, p. 577) and the postsocialist subject is goaded into 'drastic change in order to overcome a debilitating legacy' (Junghans, 2001, p. 390). Within this discursive narrative, working class communities are identified for particular derision and condescension. The value of physical work in old industrial sectors is depreciated (Kideckel, 2002; Buchowski, 2003) and those no longer able to work in these sectors are seen to lack any 'innate' entrepreneurialism (Podgórska, 2004, p. 5). Meanwhile, the aspirations of postsocialist capitalism are seen to pass these spaces by (Stenning, 2005a) in a process of uneven geographical development, and sites of working class employment (or, increasingly, unemployment) are seen to be antithetical to revived capitalism – for Podgórska (2004, p. 6), for instance, working class neighbourhoods are 'anti-entrepreneurial cages'. Within these communities, the erosion of the bonds of collegiality and imposition of a narrative of passivity and opposition work against other notions of community and collective action.

These new worlds of work have had reverberations through the communities built on labour which were at the heart of the old socialist project. In line with the narratives of endings – of work and of socialism – for many commentators, the key motif has been one of loss. Kideckel's work on the miners of Romania's Jiu Valley, in which he argues that 'the economic basis of family life, the unambiguous but ultimately supportive local division of labour, and Valley social networks have become undone . . . [and p]eople have lost work, income, friends, homes, and even life purposes' (Kideckel, 2004, p. 42) is typical of this. Others have similarly drawn attention to injuries of postsocialism, documenting the very real increase in levels of poverty, the erosion of family and kinship connections and the marginalisation of many households and individuals in working class communities. A number of writers have documented the 'retreat to the home' (Ashwin, 1999; Burawoy et al., 2000; Pine, 2002; Stenning, 2005b), a spatial shift and a withdrawal from community, as material and cultural pressures encourage people to socialise less and focus on life within the home. Attention is drawn back to the home in part because the gendering of employment change renders significant dislocations in domestic divisions of labour, emotional and material, and the work–life balance (van Hoven, 2001; Hardy and Stenning, 2002; Rudd, 2006). Within the communities themselves, people identify a listlessness and loss of direction, and a material impoverishment which stretches through the community as more and more households see their incomes fall and the economic health of local shops and services similarly suffers (Stenning, 2005b). The 'dark side' of individualisation is shown in the ways in which job loss and poverty tend to be lived alone, as community spaces are eroded and poorer households are excluded, both socially and geographically, from remaining spaces. Yet, as will be documented in more detail below, communities do struggle to experience these dislocations together. Indeed, Buchowski (2003, p. 55), in his study of one rapidly changing rural community in Poland, explores how 'the self-perception and the reality of being the losers in the new system create an ideological community and fortify resignation'.

These shifts are exacerbated by the divestiture of social assets by privatising, downsizing or closing enterprises. As firms become capitalist and are either privatised or restructured, a common trend, then, has been to focus on core productive activities and to close or sell auxiliary functions, such as health centres, sports clubs, catering facilities and housing (Domański, 1997; Ashwin, 1999). These spheres have either been commodified or transferred to the municipality, such that enterprises no longer command control over such extensive spaces of community life. Although there is some potential for these enterprise assets to be taken into community ownership, the financial obstacles, however, to such a move are usually high and they generally do not remain publicly owned.

Whilst these processes of loss and withdrawal reflect an important aspect of the changing work/community relationship in postsocialism, they are not the whole picture. As was noted in this chapter's introduction, the tendency to tell stories of loss is common across deindustrialising communities, but it is increasingly being acknowledged that loss is not the only story to tell. Even with respect to the withdrawal of enterprise social assets, Domański (2004) finds, in his study of FDI and local embeddedness in Poland, that even large multinationals continue to make significant investments in their host communities. Hence, Domański notes that around one third of foreign investors in Poland invested in infrastructure – including roads, sewage networks and water supply – and in a range of educational, sports and cultural facilities and events. These kinds of social investments were particularly noticeable in smaller towns, where the relationship with local authorities is more direct. Whilst there are a number of questions that could be asked of this modern-day paternalism, it is indicative of a high level of engagement with host communities. Likewise, within domestic firms in the Czech Republic, Clark and Soulsby (1998) note how the level of enterprise embeddedness has had a marked impact on the actions of managers and the nature of restructuring – the more managers perceive their enterprise to be 'entangled' in the community and the more their own daily lives are articulated with those of other employees, the more difficult they find it to impose a 'pure economic logic'. As Clark and Soulsby (1998, p. 45) note, in the case of a particularly embedded enterprise in a small town, 'middle managers were reticent about enacting internal changes that could have resulted in redundancy for people who lived in the same apartment blocks, and shopped in the same stores as they did'. Nevertheless, for all the bonds that such investments build, there is no doubt that capitalist firms are much more likely to fail or withdraw than enterprises commanded by the state.

Within trade unions, too, research has shown that social welfare functions continue to be identified as the most important benefit they can provide for workers (Frege, 2000). Indeed, some (for example, Ost, 2002) have argued that this extensive social role has been a factor in union weakness in the region. However, in working class communities, as we have seen, the population is increasingly likely to be characterised by workers employed casually in small, dispersed workplaces, the geography of which creates challenges of labour organising, and by an increasing number of unemployed and retired workers. These people's needs and interests are not likely to be met by a traditional servicing model and would be incorporated much more successfully by a model that develops new spatial strategies to extend the union's role into the community (Stenning, 2003) and to maintain a broader connection between workplace institutions and the community.

As it happens, it is this kind of broader role which is being fulfilled by the trade unions in, for instance, Nowa Huta, a steel town in southern Poland. Whilst also negotiating and contesting the processes of restructuring and privatisation within the workplace, each of the trade unions – there are half a dozen – focuses considerable energy and funds on the welfare of its members in the community. Social funds offer assistance to both current and former employees for the purchase of medicines, holidays and housing renovations, whilst subsidiary organisations fulfil particular welfare roles. Thus the Towarzystwo Solidarnej Pomocy (TSP, or Mutual Assistance Association) distributes donated medicines to the community through a free chemist, subsidises school meals, provides Christmas and Easter dinners and other hot meals for those in need in the winter, donates Christmas presents, clothing and food packages and pays the utility bills of those in desperate need. Equally, the Centre for Old Age and Disability Pensioners, funded by the steelworks through its Social Fund but managed jointly by the three largest unions, distributes funds to pensioners in need, acts as a collection and redistribution point for in-kind benefits and as an advocate and social centre for pensioners. One union has established a network of assistance and support, visiting the union's pensioners to offer assistance and advice, to provide feedback to the union board on the living conditions of pensioners and their families and to coordinate a kind of second-hand exchange market of goods collected, repaired and reconditioned by workers. In all these ways, the institutions of the workplace continue to play a critical role in the everyday life of the community, even after retirement, redundancy and downsizing.

The formalisation of the network of support for pensioners is indicative of a wider set of resources which persist within communities and derive from the tight work–community relationship of old. To echo Linkon and Russo (2002, pp. 245–6), these communities were not 'always a victim or a place of loss but also home to robust social organisation and community life', much of which was founded on the dense networks of social relationships built at work and in the spaces which connected home and work. In the context of economic insecurity, these networks continue to serve as a taken-for-granted source of advice, support and mutual labour, amongst other things (Stenning, 2005b; Smith and Stenning, 2006), and contain within them the potential for a range of community futures.

Indeed, in a growing number of cases, there are signs that communities are working together to respond to the changing worlds of work, often through new forms of social activism and organisation founded on trade union or other work-related activities. In Ełk, a town in north-east Poland which has been hit hard by restructuring in the agricultural and food processing industries, local activists have formed the All-Poland Union of the Unemployed (Ogólnopolski Związek Bezrobotnych) to offer a range of community development activities. Whilst the centre developed initially as an information exchange for jobs in Poland and abroad, as a meeting place (with a daycare centre) and as a legal advice centre, its activities have grown to include campaigns on benefits, housing, community cohesion, anti-racism and the social economy (Hardy et al., 2008). The Union itself has expanded nationally to incorporate twelve local branches and has built collaborative relationships with a range of social and political groupings, including anti-war, anti-racist and green movements, anti-poverty organisations and pensioner associations to develop local and national campaigns and initiatives around issues such as a minimum guaranteed income and the social economy. In Nowa Huta, EU Equal funding has enabled the creation of a local partnership (www.pin.nowa-huta.net) which brings together community cultural centres, education providers, local NGOs and local government actors to build a social economy and create new workplaces and a 'new chance for Nowa Huta'.

In east Germany, Jancius (2006, p. 229) documents local attempts to respond to deindustrialisation and unemployment with 'economic models that "strengthened communities rather than wearing them down"', models which draw both on the experience of socialism and on the emergence of market economies to build an explicitly 'localised and ethical framework', rooted in the particular spatiality of working class communities. In contrast to Buchowski's ideological communities of resignation, all these groups are working, in the context of job loss, insecurity and poverty, to build active communities of hope and potential which seek to create better forms of work and to recognise and validate the diversity of economic practices important to those in the community. They are using community as 'a strategic form of social collective' (Panelli and Welch, 2005, p. 1592), building on their common geographies to develop an alternative politics. These may not be examples of workers out on the barricades, striking against job loss or closure in a traditional model of labour activism (Siegelbaum and Walkowitz, 1995; Ferguson, 1998; Kideckel, 2002, 2004) but they are spaces of agency which run counter to the tales of labour (ac)quiescence and passivity (see, for example, Crowley, 1997; Ashwin, 1999; Crowley and Ost, 2001; Ost, 2001) which dominate accounts of the postsocialist working class. In part, this passivity is explained through the particular interconnection between the worker and enterprise under socialism, such that the postsocialist worker, it is argued, is, in the face of social and economic strife, reluctant to antagonise their employer for fear of even greater losses. Yet, in an echo of the spaces of everyday life documented by historians who identify the 'limits of dictatorship', these community activities are an indication of the ways in which people are identifying the limits of capitalism and looking to create alternatives within it.

Conclusions

This chapter has documented the changing geography of the work–community nexus in the socialist and postsocialist world, highlighting the ways in which this relationship has shaped, on a number of scales, both labour politics and economic and social geographies in the region. As the construction of capitalism creates new worlds of work, then, so the work–community relationship is transformed. Consequently, the emergence of new economic spaces remakes the spaces of both work and community, creating new inclusions and exclusions, even as pre-existing connections persist and, in growing numbers of communities, act as resources for renewed and new forms of action which are working to reshape capitalism, if not wholesale, then its everyday incarnations.

One new challenge, however, to communities of work in East Central Europe is the recent and rapid migrations to Western Europe. These migrations transnationalise work on a scale unprecedented within Europe – but with echoes through historical migrations (Jacobson, 1995) – and, some have argued, threaten community in both a quantitative and qualitative sense, as out-migrations empty towns and villages and transform local and domestic divisions of labour (Hirszfeld and Kaczmarczyk, 2000; Reynolds, 2006). Yet these migrations also enable the forging and re-creation of communities of work elsewhere, both in destination localities and in transnational spaces (Garapich, 2006), communities shaped in similar ways by relationships of both cooperation and conflict, within and between workers of different generations, different backgrounds and different subjectivities (Jordan, 2002; Grzymala-Kazlowska, 2005). It is too early to tell how these migrations will permanently reshape the geography of work–community relationships in the postsocialist world, but it already appears almost certain that they will, bringing challenges not only for individuals and their families and communities but also for trade unions, employers, and other labour market institutions, east and west.

Note

1. This section is derived from Stenning (2003). For more general material on Solidarity's growth, see, for example, MacShane (1981); Touraine et al., (1983); Misztal (1985); and Mason (1989).

References

Ashwin, S. (1999), *Russian Workers: The Anatomy of Patience*, Manchester: Manchester University Press.

Beck, U. (2000), *The Brave New World of Work*, Cambridge: Polity Press.

Beynon, H., R. Hudson, J. Lewis, D. Sadler and A. Townsend (1989), '"It's all falling apart here": coming to terms with the future in Teesside', in P. Cooke (ed.), *Localities: The Changing Face of Urban Britain*, London: Unwin Hyman, pp. 267–95.

Bideleux, R. and I. Jeffries (1998), *A History of Eastern Europe: Crisis and Change*, London: Routledge.

Bivand, R. (1983), 'Towards a geography of "Solidarność"', *Environment and Planning D*, **1** (4), 397–404.

Bradshaw, M. and A. Stenning (2001), 'The progress of transition in East Central Europe', in J. Bachtler, R. Downes and G. Gorzelak (eds), *Transition, Cohesion and Regional Policy in Central and Eastern Europe*, Aldershot, UK: Ashgate, pp. 11–31.

Buchowski, M. (2001), *Rethinking Transformation: An Anthropological Perspective on Post-socialism*, Poznan: Humaniora.

Buchowski, M. (2003), 'Coming to terms with capitalism: an example of a rural community in Poland', *Dialectical Anthropology*, **27** (1), 47–68.

Burawoy, M., P. Krotov and T. Lytkina (2000), 'Involution and destitution in capitalist Russia', *Ethnography*, **1** (1), 43–65.

Byrne, D. (2002), 'Industrial culture in a post-industrial world: the case of the north east of England', *City*, **6** (3), 279–89.

Cazes, S. and A. Nesporova (2004), 'Labour markets in transition: balancing flexibility and security in Central and Eastern Europe', *Revue de l'OFCE*, April (Special Issue), pp. 23–54, available at www.ofce.sciences-po. fr/pdf/revue/03-89bis.pdf.

Ciechocińska, M. (1993), 'Gender aspects of dismantling the command economy in Eastern Europe: the Polish case', *Geoforum*, **24** (1), 31–44.

Clark, E. and A. Soulsby (1998), 'Organization–community embeddedness: the social impact of enterprise restructuring in the post-communist Czech Republic', *Human Relations*, **51** (1), 25–50.

Coe, N., J. Johns and K. Ward (2006), 'Flexibility in action: the temporary staffing industry and labour market restructuring in the Czech Republic and Poland', The Globalization of the Temporary Staffing Industry Working Paper Series, Manchester, UK: University of Manchester, available at www.sed.manchester.ac.uk/ geography/research/tempingindustry/download/wp_1.pdf.

Crowley, S. (1997), *Hot Coal, Cold Steel: Russian and Ukrainian Workers From the End of the Soviet Union to the Postcommunist Transformation*, Ann Arbor, MI: Michigan University Press.

Crowley, S. and D. Ost (2001), *Workers after Workers' States: Labor and Politics in Postcommunist Eastern Europe*, Lanham, MD: Rowman and Littlefield Publishers.

Domański, B. (1992), 'Social control over the milltown: industrial paternalism under socialism and capitalism', *Tijdschrift Voor Economische en Sociale Geografie*, **83** (5), 353–60.

Domański, B. (1997), *Industrial Control over the Socialist Town: Benevolence or Exploitation?*, London: Praeger.

Domański, B. (2004), 'Local and regional embeddedness of foreign industrial investors in Poland', *Prace Geograficzne*, **114**, 37–54.

Du Gay, P. (1996), *Consumption and Identity at Work*, London: Sage.

EBRD (European Bank for Reconstruction and Development) (2005) *Transition Report 2005: Business in Transition*, London: EBRD, available at www.ebrd.com/pubs/econo/6520.htm

Ferguson, R. (1998), 'Will democracy strike back? Workers and politics in the Kuzbass', *Europe-Asia Studies*, **50** (3), 445–68.

Fisher, J. (1962), 'Planning the city of socialist man', *Journal of the American Institute of Planners*, **28**, 251–65.

Fitzpatrick, S. (1993), 'Ascribing class: the construction of social identity in Soviet Russia', *Journal of Modern History*, **65** (4), 745–70.

Fitzpatrick, S. (2001), *Everyday Stalinism: Ordinary Life of Extraordinary Times – Soviet Russia in the 1930s*, Oxford: Oxford University Press.

Frege, C. (2000), 'Post-communist workplace relations in Hungary: case studies from the clothing industry', *Work, Employment and Society*, **14** (4), 743–55.

French, R.A. and F.E.I. Hamilton (1979), 'Is there a socialist city?' in R.A. French and F.E.I. Hamilton (eds), *The Socialist City: Spatial Structure and Urban Policy*, Chichester: Wiley, pp. 1–21.

Garapich, M. (2006), *London's Polish Borders: Class and Ethnicity among Global City Migrants*, Guildford, UK: Centre for Research on Nationalism Ethnicity and Multiculturalism (CRONEM), University of Surrey, available at www.surrey.ac.uk/Arts/CRONEM/LONDON-Polish-Borders-interim-report.pdf.

Gibson, K., J. Cameron and A. Veno (1999), 'Negotiating restructuring: a study of regional communities experiencing rapid social and economic change', Australian Housing and Urban Research Institute (AHURI) Working Paper 11, Monash, Australia: Monash University, available at www.communityeconomies.org/ papers/comecon/comeconp4.pdf.

Grzymala-Kazlowska, A. (2005), 'From ethnic cooperation to in-group competition: undocumented Polish workers in Brussels', *Journal of Ethnic and Migration Studies*, **31** (4), 675–97.

Hamilton, F. (1979), 'Urbanization in socialist Eastern Europe: the macro-environment of internal city structure', in R.A. French and F.E.I. Hamilton (eds), *The Socialist City: Spatial Structure and Urban Policy*, Chichester: Wiley, pp. 167–93.

Haraszti, M. (1977), *A Worker in a Worker's State: Piece-rates in Hungary*, Harmondsworth: Penguin.

Hardy, J. and A. Rainnie (1996), *Restructuring Krakow: Desperately Seeking Capitalism*, London: Mansell.

Hardy, J. and A. Stenning (2002), 'Out with the old, in with the new? The changing experience of work for Polish women', in A. Smith, A. Rainnie and A. Swain (eds), *Work, Employment and Transition: Restructuring Livelihoods in Post-Communism*, London: Routledge, pp. 99–116.

Hardy, J., W. Kozek and A. Stenning (2008), 'In the front line: women, work and new spaces of labour politics in Poland', *Gender, Place and Culture*, **15** (2), 99–117.

Harloe, M. (1996), 'Cities in the transition', in G. Andrusz, M. Harloe and I. Szelenyi (eds), *Cities after Socialism: Urban and Regional Change and Conflict in Post-Socialist Societies*, Oxford: Blackwell, pp. 1–29.

Herod, A. (1997), 'From a geography of labor to a labor geography: labor's spatial fix and the geography of capitalism', *Antipode*, **29** (1), 1–31.

Herod, A. (2001), *Labor Geographies: Workers and the Landscapes of Capitalism*, New York: Guilford Press.

Hirszfeld, Z. and P. Kaczmarczyk (2000), 'Współczesne migracje zagraniczne ludności Podlasia [Contemporary overseas migrations of the population of Podlasie]', *Prace Migracyjne* no. 30, January, Warsaw, Poland:

Ośrodek Badań nad Migracjami Instytut Studiów Społecznych, available at www.migracje.uw.edu.pl/obm/pix/030.pdf.

Horváth, S. (2005), 'Everyday life in the first Hungarian socialist city', *International Labor and Working-Class History*, **68**, 24–46.

Hudson, R. and D. Sadler (1986), 'Contesting works closures in Western Europe's old industrial regions: defending place or betraying class?', in A.J. Scott and M. Storper (eds), *Production, Work, Territory: The Geographical Anatomy of Industrial Capitalism*, London: Allen and Unwin, pp. 172–93.

Hyman, R. (1999), 'An emerging agenda for Trade Unions?', *ILO – Labour and Society Programme* DP/98/1999, Geneva, Switzerland: International Labour Organization (ILO), available at www.ilo.org/public/english/bureau/inst/download/dp9899.pdf.

Jacobson, M.F. (1995), *Special Sorrows: The Diasporic Imagination of Irish, Polish and Jewish Immigrants in the United States*, Cambridge, MA: Harvard University Press.

Jancius, A. (2006), 'Unemployment, deindustrialization, and "community economy" in eastern Germany', *Ethnos*, **71** (2), 213–32.

Jordan, B. (2002), 'Polish migrant workers in London: mobility, labor markets and the prospects for democratic development', paper presented at Beyond Transition: Development Perspectives and Dilemmas conference, Warsaw, Poland, 12–13 April.

Junghans, T. (2001), 'Marketing selves: constructing civil society and self-hood in post-socialist Hungary', *Critique of Anthropology*, **21** (4), 383–400.

Kenney, P. (1997), *Rebuilding Poland: Workers and Communists, 1945–1950*, Ithaca, NY: Cornell University Press.

Kenney, P. (2002), *A Carnival of Revolution: Central Europe 1989*, Princeton, NJ: Princeton University Press.

Kideckel, D. (2002), 'The unmaking of an East-Central European working class', in C.M. Hann (ed.), *Postsocialism: Ideals, Ideologies and Practices in Eurasia*, London: Routledge, pp. 114–32.

Kideckel, D. (2004), 'Miners and wives in Romania's Jiu Valley: perspectives on postsocialist class, gender, and social change', *Identities*, **11** (1), 39–63.

Kotkin, S. (1997), *Magnetic Mountain*, Berkeley, CA: University of California Press.

Kwiatowski, E., M. Socha and U. Sztanderska (2001), 'Labour market flexibility and employment security: Poland', *ILO – Employment Paper 2001/28*, Geneva: Employment Section, International Labour Organisation (ILO).

Lampland, M. (1995), *The Object of Labor: Commodification in Socialist Hungary*, Chicago, IL: University of Chicago Press.

Linkon, S.L. and J. Russo (2002), *Steeltown USA: Work and Memory in Youngstown*, Lawrence, KS: University of Kansas Press.

MacDonald, O. (1983), 'The Polish vortex: solidarity and socialism', *New Left Review*, **139**, 5–48.

MacShane, D. (1981), *Solidarity: Poland's Independent Trade Union*, Nottingham: Spokesman.

Mason, D. (1989), 'Solidarity as a new social movement', *Political Science Quarterly*, **104** (1), 41–58.

Massey, D. ([1984] 1995), *Spatial Divisions of Labour: Social Structures and the Geography of Production*, 2nd edn, London: Macmillan.

Massey, D. and L. McDowell (1984), 'A woman's place?', in D. Massey and J. Allen (eds), *Geography Matters! A Reader*, Cambridge: Cambridge University Press, pp. 128–47.

McDowell, L. (2004), 'Work, workfare, work/life balance and an ethic of care', *Progress in Human Geography*, **28** (2), 145–63.

Misztal, B. (ed.) (1985), *Poland after Solidarity*, New Brunswick, NJ: Transaction.

North, G. (1958), 'Poland's population and changing economy', *Geographical Journal*, **124** (4), 517–27.

Nowakowski, S. (1967), 'Procesy urbanizacyjne w powojennej Polsce' [Urbanisation processes in post-war Poland], in S. Nowakowski (ed.), *Procesy Urbanizacyjne w Powojennej Polsce*, Warsaw: PWN, pp. 5–31.

OECD (Organisation for Economic Cooperation and Development) (2006), *OECD Employment Outlook 2006: Boosting Jobs and Incomes*, Paris: OECD.

Offe, C. (1996), *Modernity and the State: East, West*, Cambridge: Polity Press.

Ost, D. (2001), 'The weakness of symbolic strength: labor and union identity in Poland, 1989–2000', in S. Crowley and D. Ost (eds), *Workers after Workers' States: Labor and Politics in Postcommunist Eastern Europe*, Lanham, MD: Rowman and Littlefield Publishers, pp. 79–96.

Ost, D. (2002), 'The weakness of strong social movements: models of unionism in the East European context', *European Journal of Industrial Relations*, **8** (1), 33-51.

Panelli, R. and R. Welch (2005), 'Why community? Reading difference and singularity with community', *Environment and Planning A*, **37** (9), 1589–611.

Peck, J. and N. Theodore (2000), '"Work first": workfare and the regulation of contingent labour markets', *Cambridge Journal of Economics*, **24**, 119–38.

Pine, F. (2002), 'Retreat to the household? Gendered domains in post-socialist Poland', in C.M. Hann (ed.), *Postsocialism: Ideals, Ideologies and Practices in Eurasia*, London: Routledge, pp. 95–113.

Pittaway, M. (2002), 'The reproduction of hierarchy: skill, working-class culture, and the state in early socialist Hungary', *The Journal of Modern History*, **74** (4), 737–69.

Pittaway, M. (2005a), 'Creating and domesticating Hungary's socialist industrial landscape: from Dunapentele to Sztálinváros, 1950–1958', *Historical Archaeology*, **39** (3), 75–93.

Pittaway, M. (2005b), 'Introduction: workers and socialist states in postwar central and eastern Europe', *International Labor and Working-Class History*, **68**, 1–8.

Podgórska, J. (2004), 'Nie robim, bo się narobim [We don't work, because we may overwork]', *Polityka*, 8 May, pp. 3–10.

Pounds, N. (1960), 'The industrial geography of modern Poland', *Economic Geography*, **36** (3), 231–53.

Rainnie, A., A. Herod and S. McGrath-Champ (2007), 'Spatialising industrial relations', *Industrial Relations Journal*, 38 (2), 102–18.

Rainnie, A., A. Smith and A. Swain (eds) (2002), *Work, Employment and Transition: Restructuring Livelihoods in Post-Communism*, London: Routledge.

Rees, G. (1985), 'Regional restructuring, class change and political action', *Environment and Planning D*, **3** (4), 389–406.

Reynolds, M. (2006), 'Rush west leaves Polish families in tatters', *Reuters*, 20 September, available at http://go.reuters.com/newsArticle.jhtml?type=ourWorldNews&storyID=13546731&src=rss/lifeAnd LeisureNews.

Robinson, F. and D. Sadler (1985), 'Routine action, reproduction of social relations, and the place market: Consett after the closure', *Environment and Planning D*, **3** (1), 109–20.

Rudd, E. (2006), 'Gendering unemployment in postsocialist Germany: "What I do is work, even if it's not paid"', *Ethnos*, **71** (2), 191–212.

Russo, J. and S.L. Linkon (eds) (2005), *New Working-Class Studies*, Ithaca, NY: Cornell University Press.

Sennett, R. (1998), *The Corrosion of Character: Personal Consequences of Work in the New Capitalism*, London: Norton.

Siegelbaum, L.H. and D.J. Walkowitz (eds) (1995), *Workers of the Donbass Speak: Survival and Identity in the New Ukraine, 1989–1992*, New York: SUNY Press.

Siemieńska, R. (1969), *Nowe Życie w Nowym Mieście*, [New Life in a New City], Warsaw: Wiedza Powszechna.

Skeggs, B. (2004), *Class, Self and Culture,* London: Routledge.

Smith, A. and A. Stenning (2006), 'Beyond household economies: articulations and spaces of economic practice in post-socialism', *Progress in Human Geography*, **30** (2), 190–213.

Smith, A., A. Stenning, A. Rochovská and D. Świątek (2008), 'The emergence of a working poor: labour markets, neoliberalisation and diverse economies in post-socialist cities', *Antipode*, **40** (2), 283–311.

Stacey, M. (1969), 'The myth of community studies', *British Journal of Sociology*, **20** (2), 134–47.

Stenning, A. (2003), 'Shaping the economic landscapes of post-socialism? Labour, workplace and community in Nowa Huta, Poland', *Antipode*, **35** (4), 761–80.

Stenning, A. (2005a), 'Where is the post-socialist working class? Working class lives in the spaces of (post-) socialism', *Sociology*, **39** (5), 983–99.

Stenning, A. (2005b), 'Re-placing work: economic transformations and the shape of a community in post-socialist Poland', *Work, Employment and Society*, **19** (2), 235–59.

Stenning, A. (2007), 'Displacing steel: rethinking Poland's "New Steelworks" beyond the steelworks', in K. Szreder and E. Majewska (eds), *Futuryzm Miast Przemysłowych [Futurism of Industrial Cities]*, Cracow: HaArt.

Strangleman, T. (2001), 'Networks, place and identities in post-industrial mining communities', *International Journal of Urban and Regional Research*, **25** (2), 253–67.

Surdej, A. (2004), 'Managing labor market reforms: case study of Poland', World Bank, 20 February, Washington, DC, available at http://siteresources.worldbank.org/INTWDR2005/Resources/bp_poland_labor_market_reform.pdf.

Tokarska-Biernacik, K. (2002), 'Poland: statement', Statement given at the Second World Assembly on Ageing, Madrid, Spain, 8–12 April.

Touraine, A., F. Dubet, M. Wieviorka and J. Strzelecki (1983), *Solidarity*, Cambridge: Cambridge University Press.

van Hoven, B. (2001), 'Women at work: experiences and identity in rural East Germany', *Area*, **33** (1), 38–46.

Weiner, E. (2005), 'No (wo)man's land: the post-socialist purgatory of Czech female factory workers', *Social Problems*, **52** (4), 572–92.

Williamson, B. (1982), *Class, Culture and Community: A Biographical Study of Social Change in Mining*, London: Routledge and Kegan Paul.

Wills, J. (2001), 'Community unionism and trade union renewal in the UK: moving beyond the fragments at last?', *Transactions of the Institute of British Geographers*, **26** (4), 465–83.

Young, I.M. (1990), 'The ideal of community and the politics of difference', in L.J. Nicholson (ed.), *Feminism/ Postmodernism*, London: Routledge, pp. 300–23.

12 Plastic palm trees and blue pumpkins: synthetic fun and real control in contemporary workspace
Chris Baldry

Spaces and places

The comparatively recent coming together of social geographers, labour process analysts, organisational theorists and researchers of the built environment has resulted from a common desire to see the spatial dimension reincorporated into social analysis. However, as this book demonstrates, this has been marked by a wide variety of ways in which the term 'space' is used in the context of understanding the capitalist organisation. This chapter is concerned specifically with what Harvey (1985) calls 'assembly points' (and what are more conventionally referred to as 'workplaces'), particular points in space where capital and labour power are brought together in order for production to proceed – factories, mills, hospitals, hotels and, particularly, offices.

This built working environment cannot be understood without reference to its geospatial and political-economic context for there are, as Halford (2004) puts it, 'multiple, interlocking spatial scales' in which every workplace is at the intersection of networks of capital and communication and is sited, usually quite deliberately, in a specific socioeconomic locational context. The workplace, however, differs in one fundamental respect from the other spatial dimensions of capitalism in that it forms the immediate context for the extraction of surplus value and the social action associated with this and can thus be said to be directly experienced. On this subjective level, then, the concept of inhabiting or 'dwelling' sums up the way humans relate to places and the fact that our relationship to the built environment is essentially experiential and reflexive: 'The constructed environment is more than a backdrop to action [but] is locked in a reflexive relationship with lived experience of the world' (Parker Pearson and Richards, 1994, p. xi). In other words, buildings are both the outcome and the medium of social existence.

How buildings work

Management writers have repeatedly been guilty of managerial determinism: the idea that there is an ideal management or organisational model – whether Scientific Management, Human Relations, Human Resource Management (HRM), Total Quality Management or whatever the latest school of management thought happens to be – that will mould employee behaviour and raise performance to an optimum level. In this model, particularly given the consistent misinterpretation of the Hawthorne experiments in management textbooks (for a discussion see Baldry et al., 1998), the work building is usually taken as a given or a neutral shell. Conversely, architects are frequently guilty of architectural determinism: the belief that certain structures will 'make things happen' or create desired social and personal satisfactions. Each of these views ignores the existence of the other and thus the possibility that environmental and social structures may not always precisely articulate with each other. More crucially, such a structural functional approach ignores the reality of agency on the part of the building's inhabitants.

Buildings are social as much as physical constructs and thus represent the cultural values and priorities of those responsible for their creation. As is now well recognised, their interface with social action or agency, and the way they mediate that action, occurs both at a functional and at a symbolic level (Berg and Kreiner, 1990; Gagliardi, 1990; Barley, 1991; Strati, 1992; Gieryn, 2002; Dale and Burrell, 2003; Kersten and Gilardi, 2003). When we enter any building, what is it that tells us which kind of behaviour is appropriate to the surroundings? Even when the building is empty and there is no visible activity to give us a clue, why does a church or other faith structure look and 'feel' like a church and an office look and feel like an office?

At the functional level, the building will have been configured to facilitate the relevant kind of social activity, whether that be manufacturing, worship, education, healing or domestic recreation. Our behaviour in buildings is, however, not simply structured by the configuration of walls, corridors and open space, like rats in a maze. We also absorb a wide range of signals given to us by the building, a typological code (Eco, 1980), which indicates, almost without our realising it, the kind of building it is and what kind of social activity is appropriate within it (Stimson, 1986). In other words, the way any human society artificially re-orders its environment will invariably involve not only constructing material containers for social action but also incorporating signs and symbols relating to that action; the design of buildings, then, is partly about encoding information which users then decode. These signs and signals are not just directed at the building's occupants but also at other social groups who may experience the building externally as non-inhabitants. Therefore, there may be quite different sets of signs intended for different audiences.

Rapoport (1982), in an early attempt to analyse how this works, argued that many behavioural cues will derive from two components of the built environment: fixed factors, such as the actual physical structure, appearance and layout of a building; and semi-fixed factors, such as furniture or decor. What is important to understand is that all of these, while they may appear to the inhabitants to be fixed or given, represent sets of social choices and encapsulate social priorities and cultural values, and all of them potentially inform social action both functionally and in terms of their non-verbal communication. Without denying the role of agency, which we will come back to, we can say that, while social structures (power, authority, gender relationships) will provide a mould for behaviour, the environmental cues reinforce what has been socially defined as appropriate or inappropriate.

If the relationship between spatial form and human activity is thus mediated by meaning, it should be understood that the meanings we attribute to places may well change over time as they are interpreted and re-interpreted in the context of how such places are used. Nevertheless, these meanings do come to form a pre-existing social code for understanding any new structures we may encounter (Parker Pearson and Richards, 1994, p. 5). In this context, several recent works on space (for example, Fleming and Spicer, 2004; Halford, 2004) have commented on Lefebvre's (1991) distinction between the imagined, the experienced and the perceived dimensions to space. At the risk of oversimplifying, the first of these may be represented by the design, plan or picture of the building, the second by inhabiting the space and the third by the codes and symbolism conveyed. This, however, seems a needless and not very convincing distinction, as the constant and often unwitting decoding of the building's signage is *part* of the inhabiting; the signs and symbols have no meaning outside the social action and its organisation which the building hosts and is part of.

Therefore, just as we cannot understand a building unless we understand what goes on inside it, we similarly cannot understand the totality of that social action, its structure and its meaning, unless the surrounding built environment is included as part of the picture. It is therefore potentially misleading to continue to talk, as we have done so far, about the 'meaning' of buildings or of built space in general, as if all buildings are used and function in the same way or have the same story to tell. Work buildings differ from domestic or religious buildings in that they are primarily structures of and for control, encompassing both physical control over the production process and social control over the utilisation of labour power (Markus, 1993). Given this, this chapter will summarise the ways in which the work building has been used as a tool of management control and, through a recent case study, will discuss how such control strategies are taking on a more qualitative and subjective dimension through manipulation of the interior working environment.

Going to work

The development of the concept of the workplace as a specific location separate from other structures with social significance, such as domestic dwellings, coincides with the emergence of capitalism and the appearance of a much wider variety of specifically constructed and socially recognisable building types (Markus, 1993). In addition to domestic, religious, military and mercantile structures, there emerged in the late eighteenth century prisons, hospitals, mills and factories, later to be joined by offices. These were the new locations for housing the new social relations of capitalist production and marked the functional separation of domestic and economic life.

As the anthropologist Parker Pearson argues, a socially significant place such as a workplace is usually designated by the cultural artefact of a name (such as Black Dyke Mills, Canary Wharf or the University of Stirling) and the naming of a place gives it recognisable boundaries (Parker Pearson and Richards, 1994, p. 4). Fleming and Spicer (2004) point out that these boundaries between the place of work and the outside world are commonly physically emphasised by walls and fences, and we could add that these are now usually complemented by a security desk and CCTV cameras. These barriers symbolise the transition to a very different environmental regime for those occupying the buildings. Perhaps the most noticeable and immediate difference is the sharp reduction in environmental control. Hence, in the domestic dwelling the occupant has a very high degree of control over decor, spatial arrangements of furniture, heating, lighting and ventilation, the way space is used, and the degree of aural and spatial privacy; in contrast, for the majority of a workplace's occupants, there is virtually no control over any of the above environmental variables. Just as the wage earner gives up control over his or her labour power in return for the wage, so s/he accepts the surrender of any expectation or right to control the physical environment in which that labour power is put to work.

If lack of control over one's work environment is one characteristic of work buildings, a second is the way in which occupants' behaviour is modified as the built workplace environment itself is enlisted in the control of employees, an issue to which I now turn.

Buildings and control

The whole post-Foucault discussion of Bentham's Panopticon has been a reminder of the fact that work buildings have historically been constructed to facilitate control. Much of the symbolic architecture which we now associate with the concepts 'factory' or 'office' derived from attempts to solve the problems of housing and controlling the labour processes of mass production and mass administration in structures which, at first, hampered optimal organisational development through inadequate lighting and ventilation. In the development of the office, early twentieth-century technological improvements in deep space ventilation and artificial lighting went in parallel with the Taylorisation of the white collar clerical function and the creation of the US pre-war 'bull-pen' open office with its serried ranks of desks (Baldry, 1997a, 1997b). The fact that this relationship, between buildings as societal artefacts and the social and historical processes in which they are located, is by no means uni-directional is highlighted in the debate over Guillén's argument that the leading figures of the Internationalist school of architecture were influenced in their visual conceptions of modernity by the organisational regimentation and standardisation arising from Taylorism and Fordism in the USA (Guillén, 1997). While Burrell and Dale (2003) have argued against this view, claiming that Gropius and Le Corbusier were only able to interpret what they felt the new organisational forms represented from the study of a few photographs of Ford's production line, Kersten and Gilardi (2003) see Guillén's suggested connection as a significant identification of the linkage between cultural mode and a particular organisational paradigm.

While the physical structures of our workplaces are the result of an iterative process of articulation between organisational and technological thinking, the interior space can be used either to emphasise or to conceal organisational hierarchy and power structures (Baldry, 1999). The apportioning of the amount of space, the furnishings and aesthetics of movable artefacts such as chairs and pictures (Strati, 1992), the amount of privacy and environmental control available to different groups of inhabitants, the very entrances through which the workplace is entered, may all give daily and recurrent reminders of the location and distribution of organisational power and status. Within this spatial configuration there will be similar hierarchical differences in the degrees of freedom accorded to individuals to enter spaces other than their designated work area.

As I have suggested elsewhere (Baldry, 1999), these daily status distinctions remind us that the work building is often quite literally a 'contested terrain', containing as it does the latent conflict of interests inherent in all capitalist employment relationships. For the employee, as the context in which he or she daily expends their labour power, the work building should be pleasant, healthy and therefore preferably controllable by its occupants; it should afford a degree of privacy and should support the work they do rather than act as an obstacle to meeting production or service targets (Vischer, 2005). For the employer, the building is another cost of production, which is ideally to be minimised. The costs of construction are amortised through rents and leases, and the daily running costs of heating, lighting, ventilation and maintenance will induce a desire in management to increase control over these variables as much as possible. Something as basic and apparently trivial as who has the ability to turn on the office light switch encapsulates this inherent conflict of interests.

This has consequences for any organisation's HRM policy. Thus, an unpleasant working environment becomes translated by workers into the effort-bargain as part of the 'price' of doing the job. Hence Baldamus's definition of effort as 'the sum total of physical and mental exertion, tedium, fatigue or any other disagreeable aspect of work' (Baldamus, 1961, p. 29) would certainly encompass environmental conditions. In Baldamus's original conception, though, effort (for which remuneration is expected) is not a measurable quantity but a subjective evaluation, a combination of past experience and expectations. It might be, then, that those entering and working in a manufacturing work environment have expectations which involve a degree of noise, dirt, even safety hazards, while the expectations of those entering an office may incorporate images of a safe, healthy and well-appointed location. If the experienced reality compares unfavourably to such expectations, the reaction to the environment may be more pronounced.

This inherent conflict may also be reflected in the way in which the work building is 'read' and experienced by different groups of social actors. Hence, for the architect and the owner or main occupier, the exterior of the building has traditionally been the focus of attention and of discussion about what the building symbolises or portrays. For its part, as Kersten and Gilardi (2003) comment, the preferred public portrayal of corporate buildings is that they are 'clean, organized, impersonal, silent and, above all, empty'. Generally, though, less attention has been paid to the responses to the building by its occupants, even though a building's design can have significant implications for those who work in it. Thus, Richard Rogers's building for Lloyds of London, for example, which achieved huge and enthusiastic coverage in the architectural press, was a disaster to work in, hated by the employees, and had to be totally refitted internally within the first year (Baldry, 1999). A further vivid example of the unintended consequences of daring design on the inhabitants' real experience of the workplace is given in Kersten and Gilardi's account of the Pittsburgh Plate Glass Industries building which, as one might expect, prominently features glass, and in which office workers on the 38th floor look out over the city at a height of 600 ft, through sheet glass walls that are barely visible. Many of the workers they interviewed described the experience as so frightening that they placed furniture and other devices to screen the view, and the preferred location for meetings was a huddle in the middle of the room (Kersten and Gilardi, 2003).

HRM and the working environment
There are today emerging wide differences and disparities in the treatment of office work space, which mirror the confusions within contemporary management. While the architectural press still focuses on landmark constructions for a handful of large corporations, white collar work in the average company is moving away from the prestige high-rise city centre office block. Partly a result of the decentralisation to cheaper locations made possible by ICT, such offices are now more likely to be found housed in anonymous buildings or customer service centres at the edge of town, often without even a sign outside to indicate what goes on there or even who occupies them. This may be because, as the customer no longer passes through the door but interacts via phone or Internet, there is no need to impress non-members of the organisation with the power, size, or modernity of the organisation by representing these values architecturally except at head office. If the exteriors and interiors of call centres speak to anyone, then, it is to the employee alone. This serves to illustrate a current ambiguity over the role and nature of the working environment, particularly in offices, which mirrors the contradiction at the heart of HRM (see for example, Legge, [1995] 2004).

For the past two decades such HRM catechisms as 'people are our greatest asset' have been dutifully recited as an essential component of a new management orthodoxy and, whether formally pursued or not, the HRM model has become incorporated into a hegemonic discourse about the relationship between workers and the organisation. Prior (1988) has usefully applied Foucault's idea that discourse is never restricted to spoken and written language but unfolds in specific technical and material settings, to include the way we look at spatial organisation. We can adopt a similar approach to identifying the environmental consequences of the post-1970s' abrupt about-turn in espoused Western management practice, from the low-trust command and control approach of the first three-quarters of the twentieth century to an approach which proclaims itself to be based on involvement, high trust and a raised level of commitment to shared values. If the first approach was mirrored in the Fordist factory and the regimented bull-pen office, how has the new orthodoxy been translated within the built working environment, given that any ideology which stresses that people are the company's strongest asset would presumably have to back this up by provision of quality working surroundings?

Although it is fair to say that the sheer anonymity of many current office buildings does seem to send quite the opposite message to workers (namely, that they are nothing special), in numerous cases transformation in management ideology has resulted in a re-evaluation of the way internal work space is used in offices. Many organisations have revised their view of work buildings as neutral containers and have started to view them as a means of encapsulating organisational values (Berg and Kreiner, 1990). For example, the new HRM message of empowerment or commitment could not be conveyed by Taylorised linear arrangements of desks, as such arrangements are consciously 'sociofugal' (Hall, 1966), directing workers away from each other. Likewise, the fetish of the team requires a more 'sociopetal' use of space, a need reflected in open-plan groupings of 'pods' or islands of workstations. Similarly, the unitarist underpinning of HRM has resulted in a reduction in separate offices for managers (for middle managers, at least).

However, despite the ubiquity of workstation clustering, developments in office space design can currently be observed to be running in two opposite directions, both, ironically, reflecting the realisation that interior design can actively assist in the promotion of corporate values. In the first model, perhaps corresponding to Storey's 'hard' model of HRM (Storey, 1992), the mantra of flexibility, the professionalisation of knowledge work and the reality of cost reduction are used to justify innovations in which the concept of a personal work space is coming close to being eradicated altogether through practices such as hot-desking or hotelling. 'Clean desk' policies are now common, in which no employee is to have any paper on the desk at the end of the day – it is either filed electronically or binned. Usually, in such locations, there are ancillary instructions that there are also to be no pin-ups, postcards or fuzzy toys on the PC, nothing which suggests any vestige of personalisation and locational identity.

However, the considerable research evidence on contemporary office work (for example, Kerfoot, 1995; Baldry et al., 1998; Bunting, 2004) and the extensive literature on call centres (for example, Bain and Taylor, 2000, see also Taylor and Bain, Chapter 24 in this volume; Callaghan and Thompson, 2001; Belt et al. 2002) repeatedly suggests that the daily experience of routine office workers is a long way from being polyvalent and semi-professional. The contemporary 'white collar factories' are more likely to be characterised by performance standards based on time targets and error rates, measurement and costing devices, 'Team Taylorism' (Baldry et al., 1998), and a near universal use of electronic and auditory monitoring.

The consequence of the above development in space planning is therefore problematic for HRM: because such developments strip the workplace of some of those little concessions that might have made these intensified task cycles slightly more bearable, they further strip the employment relationship right down to the cash nexus, skewing the effort-bargain and undermining any rhetoric of commitment. The result, in the absence of the opportunity for collective action, has been increasing levels of labour turnover and voluntary absence.

In a contrasting development, though, where employee/customer rapport is part of the service delivery product, such that the job involves a high degree of emotional work, and where the very feelings of the employee have to be captured and moulded (Flecker and Hofbauer, 1998; Taylor, 1998), we get a closer approximation to the 'soft' model of HRM. Here there have to be physical expressions of team ethos, both through management-stimulated collective activity and through manipulation of the internal working environment as a direct reflection of organisational values. This second model will be demonstrated in the following case study of how a particular call centre-based organisation consciously used the interior environment of its work building to support a 'fun' culture. This was one of eight locations studied over three years as part of a project funded under the ESRC's 'Future of Work' programme.[1] The account in this chapter is based on fieldwork observations, and interviews with management and staff made during the research period 1998–2002.

HolsTravel, Midtown

'HolsTravel' is sited in an anonymous low-rise modern building, indistinguishable from its neighbours, on a small industrial estate at 'Midtown' in central Scotland, an area of deindustrialisation in a community formerly dominated by iron foundries. It had been opened in 1997, and was part of a major travel agent chain processing callers' holiday reservations. With the company's three other centres in the UK, it provided the UK's first major 24-hour, seven-days-a-week telephone travel service. However, unlike the majority of call centre locations, this building had won a Building and Innovation Award from the British Institute of Facilities Management. These awards go to companies who buy the shell of a building and then build it up to the company's own requirements. In the case of HolsTravel, the requirement was to outfit the interior design in a conscious attempt to suggest the concept of 'holiday'.

From the outside, there is minimal signage to indicate who actually occupies the building and the only clue to the organisational culture within is a parking bay next to the front door with the sign 'Reserved for the Employee of the Month'. Entry to the building is through a small conventional corporate foyer, past a reception desk and the displayed Investors in People award and an award for the building itself but then, to reach the main work area, the visitor suddenly enters 'holiday space'. This was excitedly described in the trade press when the building first opened:

> [t]he design of the building is detailed and can only be described as 'out of this world'. From the moment you walk into the tropical atmosphere you can feel the fun, hardworking and motivated atmosphere. Walking up the Innovation Award-winning 'Sensorama', you are met with

the sounds of the jungle; aeroplanes taking off; the smell of a tropical rain forest and lighting which acts as sunrise, high sun and sunset. The walkway platform of this 'Sensorama' crosses a river, the source of which is a 30 ft high waterfall. (*Commerce Business Magazine*, 1999, p.5)

Crossing the walkway over this interior stream, while these holiday sounds play from speakers in the wall, you reach the main open-plan work floor. The ceiling is a dark sky blue with walls painted in bright 'tropical' colours, with murals of exotic red and orange, and plastic palm trees are dotted about the floor amid the workstations. The staff restaurant, accessed from the main floor by re-crossing the stream, is called 'The Shoreline' and has a wavy line of blue-green tiles along one wall, parallel to the artificial stream running in its concrete channel.

Other aspects of the layout of the work area, not mentioned at all by the business property journalists, are concave fronted workstations grouped in clusters of three or four. The floor is zoned into the different functional areas of the company's operations (telephone bookings, teletext bookings, customer service). This zoning is accomplished by workstation grouping rather than physical barriers. The theme is open-plan throughout, with no separate offices for management – the centre manager's desk is prominently located on the work floor. In the middle of each zone is a small circular area below floor level, reached by descending a few steps, within which is a circle of padded bench seats. These are the 'dugouts', where a team leader can take her team off the phones and down into one of these mini wombs for a 'huddle', or take individual members for a one-to-one. However, the most conspicuous structure on the work floor is 'Mission Control', a circle of outward facing desks in the middle of the work floor with, in its centre, a strange conical tower with ascending columns of lights. These were illuminated to mark the achievement of a given percentage of that month's targets (10 per cent, 20 per cent, 30 per cent and so on); when the target was reached, a siren sounded.

Along two walls are a small number of offices and store rooms which the manager refers to as the 'back stage' areas. There is a mezzanine viewing gallery (we are told that the design is supposed to represent a ship, with this being the 'bridge'). Large television monitors hang from all the roof support pillars so as to be visible from anywhere on the floor. Most unusually, pop music is played all day from a PA system – sometimes so loud that agents cannot hear the customer properly.

How do we get to understand this work interior? Is it simply management altruism to provide a brightly coloured environment, or the result of giving space designers a free hand? Organisationally, it has to be said that handling holiday bookings is in every sense 'emotional work'. As potential customers place a lot of importance on getting the right holiday and often spend considerable sums, the consequences of mistakes can be quite traumatic for customers and their families. Obviously, the company, then, is keen that customers return to this company for their next holiday, rather than to one of the increasingly fierce competitors. As a result, the agents have to convey a mixture of friendly efficiency with a foretaste of the holiday spirit. After only a few days' observation it is clear that, to engender this mindset, there is a continuous attempt by management to promote a cultural climate of 'fun' through the pop music, the frequent award of small prizes, dressing up days, and social nights out which culminate in an annual awards evening. As an additional part of this, the TV screens show promotional videos of different types of holidays, or details of coming themed 'fun days', such as James Bond Day or French Day.

An increasing amount of work looking at the promotion of workplace 'fun' cultures (Kinnie et al., 2000; Redman and Mathews, 2002; Alferoff and Knights, 2003) has concluded that the phenomenon can be seen as a compromise reconciliation of the twin goals of, on the one hand, maximising employee commitment and, on the other, of controlling employee behaviour, and this was certainly the case here. Indeed, the call centre frequently presented the paradox of tight and surveillant control structures existing alongside a continuous promotion of frequent spot prizes and social activities for employees. In seeking to understand such management practices, Fleming and Spicer (2004) have commented on the role of decor and brightly coloured surroundings in supporting a 'fun environment' and party atmosphere. In particular, in observing that we can see the sorts of 'fun' behaviours encouraged by management as more usually associated with non-work situations, Fleming and Spicer argue that such management strategies attempt to blur the traditional work/home divide. Hence, they saw in their own case study of an organisation's layout of its workspaces that the personalisation of team cubicles by bringing in adornments and items from home was actively encouraged, a stance quite different from the kinds of 'clean desk' policies often found in 'hard' HRM situations.

At HolsTravel both the company and the building's developers were very clear in their press releases that the built environment had been specifically designed to promote the sense of 'fun' and of 'holiday'. As reported in the *Guardian* (Dhingra, 2000, p. 2):

> [f]or [HolsTravel's] call centre in [Midtown,] Bentley and his team designed a stream running through the office, complete with real palm trees, tropical sounds and smells. 'Everyone says that it always rains in Midtown and it's very difficult to go into an office environment where it's raining all day and sell holidays. So, what we tried to do was make the staff feel different. Using all these designs and using bright colours, we managed to make them feel up, and up for selling holidays', says Bentley.

As the HolsTravel centre manager admitted in our interview, when describing the ideas behind the interior design:

> [w]hen they come to work we want to promote a happy atmosphere, where people are friendly, so that staff are then happy with the customer . . . So the idea was, get people in the holiday mood and then they can talk to the customers . . . It's designed to change people's minds. If people are coming in at 8 a.m. on a dull day we want to change their mind-set so that they are thinking, 'I am now ready to sell dreams' (HolsTravel, male Centre Manager).

These quotations, then, give a clear indication that the interior work space was consciously designed to support the organisational culture, with the hoped-for consequence of raised motivation, satisfaction and performance.

How motivational was it?
In their review of the impacts of 'fun initiatives' upon the workplace, Redman and Mathews (2002, p. 60) conclude by commenting that, at a time when 'work has never been so un-fun-like', with long hours, intensified workloads, employment insecurity, and so on, fun cultures can 'diffuse the high employee stress associated with exceptional levels of customer service' and make such workplaces relatively attractive places to work for the majority of staff. Certainly, it is true that many of the HolsTravel agents liked the

working environment. Thus, Louise[2] in Main Reservations ('Main Res'), liked the fun days and the trees because 'they make things a bit different . . . the layout is informal and open', while Karen, on teletext and in her first ever job, thought the place bright, nice, a fun environment, friendly where 'everyone is up for a laugh, which is what it's all about isn't it?' In assessing the success of such work environment engineering, though, it should be noted that the workforce was very young, even by call centre standards: in 2001 when we surveyed the location, 57 per cent of the workforce were under 30. This may have had some important impacts upon how workers viewed their workplace, as we found that older workers were slightly less enthusiastic and more cynical about some of the 'fun'. Thus, Mairi, with two years' service, responded:

> The sensorama, palm trees . . . It doesn't motivate me. It didn't make me feel as though I wanted to sell a holiday. It's nice . . .
> Q: But it doesn't actually help?
> A: The sensorama, when it's working, doesn't make me feel as though I am in Turkey or somewhere.

Equally, Tracy in Main Res who, in her late twenties, had a longer work history with other employers and had been at Midtown for two years felt that the various stunts like the James Bond Day and Kissogram Day were demeaning and insulting to her and other women colleagues. Such attitudes were probably not in the majority, however, as most workers we interviewed seem to feel that, like Sandra, the surroundings made some impression – 'not that much, but enough to add a little bit of fun'. This, in turn, may have been related to what Redman and Mathews have observed in other situations, namely that employees often feel the constant, management-inspired barrage of 'fun' to be an imposition. This feeling was certainly not absent in HolsTravel – as one agent commented on the expectation to dress up on theme days: 'it's sort of frowned on if you don't'.

The ambivalent feelings towards the job, the culture and the surroundings were probably best summed up, though, by Andrea who, after three years in the place, felt:

> I like it, although I do suppose you become quite complacent [about] it when you have been here for so long, you just take it for granted, you don't notice it any more and it only hits home if perhaps . . . someone externally is coming in, or, you know, you are seeing someone that has never been in the call centre before and they are totally wild by it, and it brings it back to you and you think this a real funky place to work. And having fun days as well, I think is really good because who would sit and do their job, normally in an office, and have games going on round about them and have someone giving them a stick of rock?
> Q: Do you find anyone finds this patronising?
> A: I think probably a lot of people do, but then those that do feel like that I think should be thinking whether this is the right environment for them.

Controlled by fun?

If the building had been consciously designed to support the management goal of fun, what of the twin goal of control? Gieryn (2002) makes the point that buildings not only reveal power and hierarchical relationships but, perhaps more importantly, can serve to conceal them. Thus, at HolsTravel, beneath the plastic palm trees, the tropical coloured walls and the jungle noises, lay a tight management control function. Technological control was exercised through the regular recording and silent monitoring of calls. However, more conspicuous were the TV screens with their ever-present reminders of the current targets – typically, big letter messages saying things like 'We need £0.5 million per day' (to meet the monthly target). Even more prominent was the part played by Mission Control. Mission Control was the source of fun, the source of the pop music and of the frequent broadcast exhortations and announcements, such as the reporting of a big sale made by some team member in response to which everyone was encouraged to cheer. It was also the de facto administrative hub where team members would go to get a shift changed. However, the real function of Mission Control was less concerned with Mission and more with Control: it was where waiting times, call answering times and team performances were constantly monitored on-screen and general performance could be visually monitored as well. This function was reinforced visually by the fact that if you stood up in Mission Control you could see virtually all the open plan work floor. It was, then, the closest thing to a Panopticon the researchers encountered anywhere, and team members who were felt to be underperforming were often moved to a team located closer to the gaze from Mission Control.

I indicated in the earlier part of this chapter that we need to understand work buildings processually, as an integral part of how work processes develop. This assertion may be clarified by recounting what happened to the work process in HolsTravel during our six-week period of observation. The setting and meeting of quantitative and qualitative targets are the universal fact of life in any call centre (Bain et al., 2002) and target levels within a given organisation are the interior reflection of the state of the external competitive market. During our observation period, as the holiday market slumped, targets were constantly revised upwards or made more complex. This labour intensification was compounded by the introduction in early 2000 of 'Blue Pumpkin', a software system that allocated shifts and break-times automatically, thus eliminating what little control workers had had over working time. Previously, although start times could vary, it was usual and expected for an individual's start time to be kept for the week. Under Blue Pumpkin, however, start times could vary by 15 minutes on a random daily basis and Saturday was treated as a normal working day. The ability of agents to take lunch breaks in pairs and at times that allowed breaks to be fitted around call patterns now ended. Complaints abounded that, because hours were allocated to individuals regardless of team membership, team spirit was being undermined as team members might not be working the same days together.

A fun place to work?
At first glance HolsTravel did not appear to be a bad workplace, as such things go. For this observer, it certainly had a more pleasant atmosphere than many other call centres. However, if we start to put together the building, the organisation and the technology, a more complex composite picture emerges of the misfit between organisational culture and the combined socio-technical-environmental system (Baldry et al., 1997; Taylor et al., 2003) which enables us to re-read how the HolsTravel building is experienced. This is illuminated by clues from our interviewees which suggest limitations to the effectiveness of the building's function as a supportive context for work. This is particularly so, given that the work pattern is 24/7 in a building that probably was not designed for continuous occupation and contains a lot of people and a lot of technology, both of which contribute to a significant heat load and strain on the ability to deliver consistent air quality. In this physical context, the inhabitants work long hours as unpaid overtime is common, with 40 per cent of employees doing up to 10 extra hours a week.

Such conditions, we believe, partially explain why, despite practices like a friends and family recruitment policy that aimed at improving employment retention, both staff and management were aware that labour turnover remained high (39 per cent at the time of observation[3]) and the average length of service was only 15 months. Management were also concerned about high rates of sickness absence, which clearly could play havoc with team staffing schedules and, during our observation period, they changed the absence policy to one based on a cumulative penalty points system in an attempt to penalise voluntary absence. However, without denying the incidence of voluntary absence as an individual response to a disliked work situation, these all-too-common kinds of sickness absence policies assumed sickness to be always a voluntary condition, an assumption that both denies legitimacy to genuine illness and also denies the possibility that sickness may be caused by the way work is structured within an unforgiving built environment (Baldry et al., 1997). A few examples from our interviews, then, may illustrate the reality of workplace sickness in an otherwise apparently pleasant environment.

Janette in Main Res regularly uses Strepsils (antiseptic throat lozenges), the need for which she relates to her work environment: 'I drink gallons of water. It's very dry in here, your lips hurt – they should offer lip salve and eye-drops; you get sore eyes'. For her part, Jackie regularly feels her eyes are itchy and that her eyesight has deteriorated over the past year. She tells the interviewer all the things in the centre that she cannot see clearly now compared to when she began there. Meanwhile, Patricia in Main Res frequently bursts into fits of coughing and at one stage had to interrupt her call as she could not control her dry cough:

> My throat is dry and I've got this irritating cough which I've had for a couple of weeks. I can't get rid of it. I find that in here you have to drink water constantly to stop your throat drying up. If you have a cold, it's very difficult to get rid of it here.
>   Q: What about the temperature and AC?
>   A: It's freezing. One of the reasons is that we are close to the window and it can get very cold. My lips dry up all the time and it's obvious that it's because of the air conditioning.

This experience was verified by Lynn, at the adjacent workstation, who declared that

> [w]hen you have a cold and you start a shift you can hardly speak. It's difficult to get the words out.

It is significant in this context that, prominently displayed on the Shoreline restaurant counter, right next to the cash desk, was a large box of Nurofen (a well-known pain relief). The apparent need for this is exemplified in Jack's account of how the work organisation (targets), the technology and the environment (lighting) were all implicated in his experience of regular headaches. However, because of the difficulty of separating these out, he declared, headaches are 'just one of these things':

> [t]here's nothing better than getting told how much money you are getting because you get all your targets. I mean that is great. But knowing the pressure that puts you under to get it in the first place, you know, kind of balances it out sometimes. Me, for one, I know I get a lot of headaches and I don't know whether it's the pressure or not, or if it's the computers or not. But it's just one of those things.
>   Q: Have you looked into it?

A: Yes. I have got painkillers that I take if it gets too bad . . . There is nothing wrong with my eyes to say I need glasses. Whether it is the lights, you know, because a lot of people think it is these UV light things. Or whether it is the pressure, you just don't know.

Finally, the replacement of direct team manager control over working and shift patterns by impersonal computer control stripped bare the last illusions of the holiday workplace. At the end of the day, the barrier between the work floor and The Shoreline restaurant, or 'work and relaxation', was not really the spatial one of the internal stream running through the workplace: rather, it was a barrier imposed by an organisational control system that did not allow staff to choose when to have a break. Unlike the decision to drop into a holiday taverna, it was Blue Pumpkin (not even a named manager but a de-personalised software system) that told the employee when she could refresh herself.

Despite the efforts to use the physical layout of the workplace as a means to engender a sense of loyalty and to encourage the employees to engage in a degree of self-control (such as pushing themselves to higher outputs because of the 'fun' they have at work), if we combine the above physical consequences of a poor environment/technology/work fit with the constant noise from the music, the announcements, the 'games', the exhortations to meet targets, the videos showing holiday movies, the silent monitoring of conversations and the constant necessity to be pleasant to even the rudest customer, then the experience of working in the HolsTravel building can often seem, instead of 'fun', like acute sensory overload. Consequently, it is perhaps hardly surprising when Jackie in Main Res stated that:

[a] friend of mine regularly goes home and just cries. She herself can't bear to use the phone any more. I used to be phoning people all the time but just can't any more; I just want to sit and do nothing at home.

Conclusion

The above example is the basis for yet another plea for a holistic approach to understanding work and work buildings. The experience of working in the HolsTravel building was clearly only marginally improved by the organisational culture, as expressed through officially encouraged behaviours and spatial decor and configuration. This reminds us that the limits to which employees may be treated as a tabula rasa, on which management or architects can write the script for appropriate levels of behaviour and performance, will be set by the employees themselves. In the case of HolsTravel, the employees demonstrated that they were able to distance themselves from the rhetoric, accepting it at face value only as 'a bit of a laugh'. Although seen as a management construction, they were not going to 'resist' a decor which made the workplace that bit different but were clear that it in no way concealed or compensated for the realities of the job. Neither could the palm trees nor the Sensorama prevent the negative aspects of the building function – poor air quality, thermal stability and acoustic quality – from adding to the existing, and increasing, stressors of the work organisation.

The built workplace, then, is constructed to encapsulate and represent the prevailing social values of those with economic power, and will be used by them in an attempt to evangelise those values to the building's occupants, the employees. Those employees, however, are free – indeed, likely – to exercise their own powers of judgement and evaluation resulting from the way in which the building is experienced day by day. As indicated earlier, that evaluation itself may be consequent upon the expectations raised by management rhetoric. If you are told that the workplace is a fun location and work activities within it are a 'bit of a laugh', then the experience of target-driven intensified work, within a built environment which may contribute to regular headaches or voice loss, may make the relative disenchantment all the more acute. The result is that although those who manage workers may have in mind one particular response to the spatiality of the workplace that they design, workers may respond in quite different ways, with the result that the spatialities of workplaces are always contested.

Notes

1. This case study is derived from the ESRC 'Future of Work' project 'Employment and Working Life Beyond the Year 2000: Two Emerging Employment Sectors', ESRC Award No. L212252006.
2. All names are pseudonyms to preserve the anonymity of respondents.
3. This was marginally higher than the other three case studies. Mean turnover was 37 per cent (see Baldry et al., 2007).

References

Alferoff, C. and D. Knights (2003), 'We're all partying here: targets and games, or targets as games in call centre management', in A. Carr and P. Hancock (eds), *Art and Aesthetics at Work*, Basingstoke: Palgrave Macmillan, pp. 70–92.

Bain, P. and P. Taylor (2000), 'Entrapped by the "electronic panopticon"? Worker resistance in the call centre', *New Technology, Work and Employment*, **15** (1), 2–18.

Bain, P., A. Watson, G. Mulvey, P. Taylor and G. Gall (2002), 'Taylorism, targets and the pursuit of quantity and quality by call centre management', *New Technology, Work and Employment*, **17** (3), 170–85.

Baldamus, W. (1961), *Efficiency and Effort: An Analysis of Industrial Administration*, London: Tavistock Publications.

Baldry, C. (1997a), 'Hard day at the office: the social construction of workspace', Department of Human Resource Management Occasional Paper 9, Glasgow: University of Strathclyde.

Baldry, C. (1997b), 'The social construction of office space', *International Labour Review*, **136** (3), 365–78.

Baldry, C. (1999), 'Space – the final frontier', *Sociology*, **33** (3), 535–53.

Baldry C., P. Bain and P. Taylor (1997), 'Sick and tired? Working in the modern office', *Work, Employment and Society*, **11** (3), 519–39.

Baldry, C., P. Bain and P. Taylor (1998), '"Bright satanic offices": intensification, control and team Taylorism', in P. Thompson and C. Warhurst (eds), *Workplaces of the Future*, Basingstoke: Macmillan Business, pp. 163–83.

Baldry, C., P. Bain, P. Taylor, J. Hyman, D. Scholarios, A. Marks, A. Watson, K. Gilbert, G. Gall and D. Bunzel (2007), *The Meaning of Work in the New Economy*, Basingstoke: Palgrave Macmillan.

Barley, S.R. (1991), 'Semiotics and the study of occupational and organizational culture', in P.J. Frost, L.F. Moore, M. Reis Louis, C.C. Lundberg and J. Martin (eds), *Reframing Organizational Culture*, London: Sage, pp. 39–53.

Belt, V., R. Richardson and J. Webster (2002), 'Women, social skill and interactive service work in telephone call centres', *New Technology, Work and Employment*, **17** (1), 20–34.

Berg, P.-O. and K. Kreiner (1990), 'Corporate architecture: turning physical settings into symbolic resources', in P. Gagliardi (ed.), *Symbols and Artifacts: Views of the Corporate Landscape*, Berlin: W. De Gruyter, pp. 41–67.

Bunting, M. (2004), *Willing Slaves: How the Overwork Culture is Ruling Our Lives*, London: Harper Perennial.

Burrell, G. and K. Dale (2003), 'Building better worlds?: Architecture and critical management studies', in M. Alvesson and H. Willmott (eds), *Studying Management Critically*, London: Sage, pp. 177–96.

Callaghan, G. and P. Thompson (2001), 'Edwards revisited: technical control and call centres', *Economic and Industrial Democracy*, **22** (1), 13–37.

Commerce Business Magazine (1999), 'Tropical atmosphere for call centre', *Commerce Business Magazine*, 1 July, p. 5.

Dale, K. and G. Burrell (2003), 'An-aesthetics and architecture', in A. Carr and P. Hancock (eds), *Art and Aesthetics at Work*, Basingstoke: Palgrave Macmillan, pp. 155–73.

Dhingra, D. (2000), 'Screen on the green', *The Guardian*, Office Hours Section, 20 March, p. 2.

Eco, U. (1980), 'Function and sign: the semiotics of architecture', in G. Broadbent, R. Bunt and C. Jencks (eds), *Signs, Symbols and Architecture*, Chichester: John Wiley, pp. 11–69.

Flecker, J. and J. Hofbauer (1998), 'Capitalising on subjectivity: the "new model worker" and the importance of being useful', in P. Thompson and C. Warhurst (eds), *Workplaces of the Future*, Basingstoke: Macmillan Business, pp. 104–23.

Fleming, P. and A. Spicer (2004), '"You can check out any time, but you can never leave": spatial boundaries in a high commitment organization', *Human Relations*, **57** (1), 75–94.

Gagliardi, P. (1990), 'Artifacts as pathways and remains of organizational life', in P. Gagliardi (ed.), *Symbols and Artifacts: Views of the Corporate Landscape*, Berlin: W. De Gruyter, pp. 3–38.

Gieryn, T.F. (2002), 'What buildings do', *Theory and Society*, **31** (1), 35–74.

Guillén, M. (1997), 'Scientific management's lost aesthetic: architecture, organization, and the Taylorized beauty of the mechanical', *Administrative Science Quarterly*, **42** (4), 682–715.

Halford, S. (2004), 'Towards a sociology of organizational space', *Sociological Research Online*, **9** (1).

Hall, E.T. (1966), *The Hidden Dimension*, New York: Doubleday.

Harvey, D. (1985), 'The geopolitics of capitalism', in D. Gregory and J. Urry (eds), *Social Relations and Spatial Structures*, Basingstoke: Macmillan, pp. 128–63.

Kerfoot, D. (1995), 'The "value" of social skills? A case from centralised administration in a UK bank', paper presented at the 13th International Labour Process Conference, Blackpool, April 1995.

Kersten, A. and R. Gilardi (2003), 'The barren landscape: reading US corporate architecture', in A. Carr and P. Hancock (eds), *Art and Aesthetics at Work*, Basingstoke: Palgrave Macmillan, pp. 138–54.

Kinnie, N., S. Hutchinson and J. Purcell (2000), '"Fun and surveillance": the paradox of high commitment management in call centres', *International Journal of Human Resource Management*, **11** (5), 967–85.

Lefebvre, H. (1991), *The Production of Space*, Oxford: Blackwell.

Legge, K. ([1995] 2004), *Human Resource Management: Rhetorics and Realities*, anniversary edn, Basingstoke: Palgrave Macmillan.

Markus, T.A. (1993), *Buildings and Power: Freedom and Control in the Origins of Modern Building Types*, London: Routledge.

Parker Pearson, M. and C. Richards (1994), 'Ordering the world: perceptions of architecture, space and time', in M. Parker Pearson and C. Richards (eds), *Architecture and Order: Approaches to Social Space*, London: Routledge, pp. 1–37.

Prior, L. (1988), 'The architecture of the hospital: a study of spatial organization and medical knowledge', *British Journal of Sociology*, **39** (1), 86–113.

Rapoport, A. (1982), *The Meaning of the Built Environment: A Non-verbal Communication*, London: Sage.

Redman, T. and B.P. Mathews (2002), 'Managing services: should we be having fun?', *The Service Industries Journal*, **22** (3), 51–62.

Stimson, G. (1986), 'Place and space in sociological fieldwork', *The Sociological Review*, **34** (iii), 641–56.

Storey, J. (1992), *Developments in the Management of Human Resources: An Analytical Review*, Oxford: Blackwell Business.

Strati, A. (1992), 'Aesthetic understanding of organizational life', *Academy of Management Review*, **17** (3), 568–81.

Taylor, P., C. Baldry, P. Bain and V. Ellis (2003), '"A unique working environment": health, sickness and absence management in UK call centres', *Work, Employment and Society*, **17** (3), 435–58.

Taylor, S. (1998), 'Emotional labour and the new workplace', in P. Thompson and C. Warhurst (eds), *Workplaces of the Future*, Basingstoke: Macmillan Business, pp. 84–103.

Vischer, J.C. (2005), *Space Meets Status: Designing Workplace Performance*, Abingdon: Routledge.

13 Dormitory labour regimes and the labour process in China: new workers in old factory forms[1]

Ngai Pun and Chris Smith

Introduction

Drawing upon the experience of restructuring in the advanced industrial economies, a number of authors, such as Piore and Sabel (1984), have suggested that there is an epoch shift taking place within capitalism from a system of production organised along Taylorist and Fordist lines (mass assembly line, mass political organisation and welfare-state interventions) to one organised according to the principles of flexible accumulation (flexible production, casual labour, deregulation and privatisation through withdrawal of state interventions) (for more on contemporary transformations of the state, see Jessop, Chapter 2 in this volume). However, whereas such a shift may be occurring within the advanced industrial economies (though, for a counterview, see Hudson (1989)), the evidence from many parts of the 'developing world' in which industrial production is expanding suggests that efforts to characterise capitalist production as a whole as undergoing such a historical transition are problematic. In particular, the idea that we are moving towards an era of flexible production within the global capitalist mode of production does not seem to match the realities of many of the developing countries that are becoming ever more tightly incorporated into the capitalist world economy. Consequently, understanding contemporary changes in the capitalist labour process requires, we would argue, a geographical sensitivity, one that is open to how labour process practices are constituted in time and space (Harvey, 2000, 2001).

For labour process theory, Burawoy's (1985) concept of the 'politics of production' was critical for bringing back the political and ideological effects of production regimes, in which the state was seen to play a central part in shaping the nature of production and labour politics. However, what was largely missing from Burawoy's analysis was a consideration of the *spatial* aspect of production, something that Harvey (1982) had explored through his critique of Marx's theory of capital accumulation. Although Burawoy did not explicitly take on board in 1985 the kinds of ideas about spatiality explored by Harvey, the tremendous transnational reorganisation of world production that has occurred in the past two decades since Burawoy wrote his book, though, makes it even harder today than it was previously to neglect this missing dimension – the spatial politics of production. Hence, growing transnational capital flows, labour migration, and the diffusion of technology, together with the growth of international subcontracting chains and information networks, and the spread of just-in-time production are processes that not only require an intensive reconfiguration of time but also a significant (and often rapid) reorganisation of space. Thus, the time–space compression that is often argued to be characteristic of the global age is not so much bringing an annihilation of space (Hutton and Giddens, 2000) but is, rather, a process whereby new spatial arrangements of social relations (especially those associated with paid work) are being brought about through the creation of a new international division of labour (Fröbel et al., 1980; Henderson, 1989), courtesy of the investment activities of transnational corporations and the international capitalist class (Sklair, 2001), the mobility of labour (Sassen, 1988; Ong, 1998), the transfer of technology from one place to another, and – our focus here – the growth of new factory towns in Latin America, Asia, and, especially, in China (Nash and Fernandez-Kelly, 1983; Deyo, 1989; Eng, 1997; Yeung, 2000). The creation of these new spatial arrangements requires a deep and nuanced consideration of how this geographical reconfiguration of production influences workplace politics, where the macro field of the global economy meets the micro field of local political and labour market institutions and workplace relations (Frenkel, 2003).

How the transnational reorganisation of world production, which draws upon, and brings together, global, national and local factors and social relations, gives birth to new forms of labour regime and workplace relations is our main focus in this chapter. Most specifically, our analysis explores how capital seeks to address a fundamental paradox central to its own existence: although it is imperative that capital be free to relocate to new locales in search of better investment opportunities, it must also embed itself within specific locales and create particular 'spatial fixes' (Harvey, 1982, p. 416) to ensure that surpluses are expropriated within a given timeframe (Massey, 1993). Despite the fact that 'globalisation' may be presenting capital with worldwide investment opportunities, production must always take place *somewhere*. Thus, whilst space may be increasingly seen as irrelevant by some commentators because capital can now flow more rapidly across it, specific classes of employers, managers and workers must still come together in particular localities if production is to occur. As a result, strategies through which mobile capital seeks to localise production processes and gain influence over local communities and control over labour are central elements in the political economy of global capitalism (Peck, 1996; Frenkel, 2003).

Given the above, this chapter focuses specifically upon the character of a 'dormitory labour regime' within China as an example wherein both capital and the state have colluded to facilitate the control of local labour by transnational investors. Specifically, we compare two contrasting case studies of emergent transnational labour regimes and how they are adopting different geographical strategies through which to better control the labour process. The first case, China Golden Garments, represents a local subcontracting strategy, where working and dormitory conditions are of a poor standard but production is maintained through inter-firm networks to first- and second-tier supplier companies that win orders yet must use the subcontracting network of firms to fulfil orders. The second, China Diamond Garments, signifies a new management vision of a model factory using international quality standards and labour codes in order to gain Western-buyer approval for production to overseas markets.[2] The chapter concludes by considering how the dormitory labour regime in China serves as a particular form of labour control by which workers can be fixed in place, such that they are on hand to serve Chinese and international capital.

Mobility and labour: the 'where' and 'which' questions?
In our country case study of China, the mobility of capital (mostly transnational) and labour (mostly national) colludes and condenses in a complicated cartography of production and labour control. Industrial labourers are generally not from the local area

where workplaces are based, but come as inter-provincial migrants for a temporary sojourn in a factory and are usually housed in dormitories that are tied to their employment. Their mobility is framed through a double social conditioning: on the one hand, peasant-workers are 'free' to sell their labour to global and private capital in postsocialist China, whereas on the other hand state laws on population and mobility control (*hukou*)[3] try to contain their freedom of mobility so as to make sure they are both available in particular places to meet the demands of transnational capital and that they conform to the politics of urban development, under which self-determination of residence is tightly controlled. Because of this double social conditioning, labour mobility in China reveals a spatial aspect of production that is fundamentally political – the freedom of the rural migrants to work in the industrial urban settings is checked by the social constraint preventing their free settlement in the cities. Thus, as a way to ensure that the Chinese state's larger economic and urban development objectives, as well as its political aims, are met, migrant workers are housed in industrial dormitories that are extensively used in every industrialised city and town, especially in special economic zones or export-processing regions. On finishing their labour contracts, the migrant workers must return to their place of birth or find another temporary employment contract, when they are again confined within what we are here calling the dormitory labour regime (Lee, 1998; Solinger, 1999). The young semi-proletariat class's spatial mobility, then, is highly constrained.

Labour in capitalism, unlike feudalism or slavery, is not owned directly by the employing agent. Rather, workers possess a capacity (mental, physical, emotional, aesthetic) to work, which they then seek to 'freely' dispose of to their own advantage. Ownership, then, is of workers' labour-time not of actual workers, and, once paid for, utilising this time productively is the responsibility of capital. Within this nexus, both workers and employers seek to manage 'effort power' (which refers to demands made upon capital's and labour's energies within the production process, with capital generally seeking more effort from labour than labour may be willing to give for a certain wage) and 'mobility power' (by which we mean the ability of either capital or labour to relocate elsewhere) (Smith, 2006).

For its part, effort power within the production process is more likely to depend on internalised, voluntary bargaining, as both labour and capital seek to negotiate work effort for particular tasks. However, organised labour and capital will often appeal to the state to limit or extend hours, wages, duties of care and other issues for labour and employment law, which indirectly impact the bargaining arena and agenda. In general, though, what level of productivity is achievable with what quality of labour is a local or internalised matter for actors within the firm to determine.

Mobility power, on the other hand, has a stronger political dimension, as employers use various mechanisms – such as contracts that stipulate length of service and/or that require notice periods for mutual separation – to limit the freedom of workers to move employment at will. Within the firm the uncertainties over mobility (will the employer dismiss? will the worker quit?) create what Mann (1973) calls a 'mutual dependency' obligation, in which workers reduce job searching in exchange for internal promotion opportunities and employers give up seeking external labour and focus, instead, on the utilisation of existing labour. To utilise workers' time to the maximum degree, then, capitalists usually need adequate control over workers' mobility, since the farther away workers live, the less time in any given day they have to spend working – that is, capitalists must control geographical space and the building of the urban landscape to ensure propinquity between workers' residences and places of employment.

In some economies (Japan and Korea, for example) and in some companies, a *paternalist* practice is widely espoused that reinforces mutual obligations beyond the naked cash nexus and keeps labour turnover fairly low. In China, however, there is movement in the opposite direction, towards mobility, high labour turnover (on the order of 30 to 90 per cent per year in China – Smith, 2003) and change. Thus, in contrast with two or three decades ago when the economy was dominated by state-operated enterprises, recent labour reforms allowing greater labour mobility have limited 'mutual obligations' and have led to fairly weak reciprocal dependency relations between *particular* workers and *particular* employers. Indeed, employment relations have become ever more impersonal and short-term, as high labour turnover has been increasingly structurally encouraged by corporations through the widespread use of one- to two-year employment contracts (Nichols et al., 2004).

Although in neoclassical economic theory the market functions best without political (state) intervention – competition between capitals and between workers acts to distribute workers to employers and employment to workers – in practice both labour and capital often appeal to the state to expand their 'realm of freedom' through establishing, variously, controls over the mobility power of labour and controls over the mobility power of capital. In the case of postsocialist China, the emergence of market forces, labour contracts, freedom of employment from a single employer and freedom from state allocation of labour (for the firm and the worker) have all given workers greater freedom of geographical mobility. However, continuation of the *hukou* system of population control, of tying housing to employment and the persistence of securing labour through use of networks of family, kin and localised village relationships rather than through rationalised and formalised markets constrain such freedom of mobility from place to place and job to job. In this way, the question of *which* employer the worker selects is usually a social or institutionalised issue and not an individual question – typically, the migrant worker simply follows others from his or her village to the factory they have selected (Lee, 1998; Pun, 1999). The 'where', or location, question, then, concerning workers' place of employment is shaped through these networks, and generally labour flows to areas of known economic activity, such as the two industrialised areas studied here. Therefore, both indeterminacies are kept checked through collective and institutionalised social networks. However, labour mobility is a top concern not only for management but also for the Chinese state, which has had to deal with 120 million rural migrants flocking to the cities seeking job opportunities each year since the mid-1990s (see Cook, 2000). Consequently, the state has sought to place controls on migration. As we will show, these controls on mobility – a legacy of China's 'socialist development model' – greatly influence labour relations between capital and labour, and are especially evident in the emergence of a widespread dormitory labour regime during the recent period of globalisation in China.

China's dormitory labour regime: case studies
Foreign manufacturing plants in China *systematically* house migrant workers in dormitories attached to, or close to, the factory compound (Smith, 2003). Such dormitories are communal, multi-storey buildings, housing several hundred workers. Rooms are

shared, with between 8 to 20 workers per room. Washing and toilet facilities are communal between rooms, floors or whole units, such that living space is intensely collective, with no area, except within the closed curtains of the worker's bunk, for private space. Workers are typically single, migrant, young and disproportionately female (Andors, 1988; Lee, 1995, 1998; Pun, 1999). Migrant workers in dormitories are separated from families (especially parents), customary locale (and perhaps familiar food, language and surroundings) and concentrated in a factory and workspace as homogenised, same-age labour of migrant genesis.

The connection to the firm is invariably short-term and contractual, in that migrants are not expected to mature their working lives within the firm. Wages can be held down through the linking of the firm to a pool of labour in distant provinces of China, and the availability of accommodation at work creates opportunities for considerable inter-provincial mobility that the *hukou* system would otherwise make impossible. This inhibits the development of local labour markets around the factories, as well as the social and political institutions of industrial relations that typically emerge when workers identify their economic fate with particular employers or a local labour market (Eng, 1997, p. 563). The Chinese situation, then, greatly contrasts, say, with nineteenth-century Britain, where industrialisation facilitated unionisation by bringing workers together geographically and for long periods of time (Thompson, 1963). Alienation of labour, therefore, consists of significantly more than the lack of ownership of product, tools and control of skills sufficient to support independent production. Rather, workers in dorms are alienated from their hometown and parents, and by working within factories dominated by unfamiliar others, languages, food, production methods and products. These objects and subjects confront the new worker virtually 24 hours per day, seven days a week throughout the year.

The structural features of the dormitory labour regime described above, however, do have different articulations in particular firms. There is, in fact, great variety along a 'continuum of control' based on established institutional, organisational and spatial contingencies, with these latter including the management preferences of different national capitals, the size of the firm, the market segment occupied by the firm, whether or not production is geared towards the sale of own-branded goods, the capitalisation of the firm and the resources it can legitimately access within China and abroad. Our two case studies present workers' lives along this continuum. In highlighting the contrasts between our two cases, we do not wish to ascribe a developmental logic here, with one being seen as backward and the other more advanced. Nevertheless, the first case, China Golden, we characterise as having a traditional or neo-paternalist strategy. In this case, the company had a different position in the supply chain to the second firm (China Diamond), with no branded goods, no access to the Chinese market, and the firm playing more of a third-tier subcontractor role, with less pressure from international markets to move up a supply chain and accept more interventions in the management and housing of its workers. In the case of China Diamond, on the other hand, the firm's strategy was to accept the rationalisation logic of international capital by embracing codes of conduct and international quality marks in order to access global markets more directly. This strategy we declare to be a 'modernist' strategy. As a result of these two firms' quite different positions within the market and goals, though, they had quite different practices of dormitory provision. Hence, the former depends entirely on the local state for its dormitory, whereas in the case of China Diamond, the firm intends to build its own dormitory to meet international, not local, standards. We bring out the contrasts between these cases below.[4]

China Golden Garments: practising a neo-paternalistic dormitory labour regime
We initially outline the context and business strategy of China Golden. This is followed by consideration of labour recruitment, accommodation and labour turnover.

Ownership, market position and business strategy   China Golden is a relatively small subcontracting garment factory set up in Dongguan, South China, in 1997, after having moved from its original location, Shenzhen, the first Special Economic Zone in China, across the border from Hong Kong. Situated between Shenzhen and Guangzhou, the two most important cities in Guangdong Province, Dongguan has become one of the most favoured investment sites for Hong Kong capital since the late 1980s because of its geographical proximity to Hong Kong. Like many other firms, China Golden moved to Dongguan because of lower production costs, cheaper land and labour and a better local state-provided investment contract package.

With a workforce of 600, China Golden is a typical Hong Kong-owned enterprise under control of a Hong Kong director with sole authority over the factory's operation and management. It can be characterised as having a quasi-paternalistic style of management. The firm lies in the mid-node of a global subcontracting chain, producing garments for Hong Kong buyers who hold the production orders from American and European corporations. The total production is for export, and no exploration of the domestic market in China has been attempted. This makes capital more dependent on the Hong Kong business networks and has prohibited China Golden from transforming into a modern company directly linked to global production. Nevertheless, in terms of the spatiality of production, transborder movements and connections are intensive, especially between Hong Kong and South China. China Golden has an office base in Hong Kong, which coordinates marketing, production orders, and materials provision, shipping and other activities for facilitating the whole production process in China.

Establishing a reputation for on-time delivery was repeatedly mentioned in our interviews with company representatives as the best strategy for securing business. Also, like many small/medium enterprises, close business relations were used to manage a competitive environment. For example, establishing a close personal relationship with Hong Kong buyers who circulated within the same sector meant that information and business exchanges, along the lines of *Guanxi* ties, were strong and persistent. In addition, establishing a good reputation within the locality, and having close personal relationships with other entrepreneurs in the sector, together with informal sharing of work, kept production going. This personal network-building, instead of expansion of the company profile or living up to international standards for working conditions, was China Golden's main business strategy and is quite typical of Hong Kong-based companies who are invested in China (Lin, 1997).

Labour recruitment, accommodation and turnover   China Golden employed rural migrant workers from the provinces of Guangdong, Hunan, Hubei, Jiangxi, Anhui and Sichuan. The only workers local to Dongguan, where the factory was based, were the accountant and the company's facilities manager. Upon commencing employment, China Golden retains workers' identity cards (a widespread practice considered necessary for constraining workers' mobility power – see Chan, 2001), as well as enforcing a system of deposits (for uniforms, dormitory accommodation and so on) up to a total of RMB 120. In addition to the token 'Disney's Code' (established by the Walt Disney Company for manufacturers of Disney-branded merchandise with which it contracts),[5] China Golden had its own code, the real one, which was far more detailed and disciplinary. Thus, after joining the company every worker received a handbook that contained more than 50 work-related rules and other provisions, examples of which include fines for late arrival at work (ranging from RMB 5 for 10 minutes' lateness to a whole day's pay for being more than one hour late), the doubling of sanctions for more than three instances of late arrival, and termination of a worker's employment contract if they are absent for more than three days.

Working hours were also very long (commonly 8 am to 10 pm) and overtime work on Sundays and every night was expected (see Chan, 2001). If there were rush orders, the workers could be requested to work until midnight. Twelve working hours per day was normal; a rest day would only be provided if there was a break in production orders or during the low season. This meant that the workers worked between 72 hours and 77 hours each week, far more than the working hours allowed by Chinese law (40 hours each week, and 36 hours of overtime work per month). It openly violated the Chinese Law and Disney's Code (see Table 13.1, column 2 for a summary of China Golden.)

The average wage for production workers was RMB 950 per month, inclusive of overtime work, and the highest a person could earn was up to RMB 2000 in the high season. The level of wages for production workers was high when compared to other foreign-invested companies in China (see Chan, 2001) but this was due to the excessive hours of work.

According to the facilities manager, housing these migrant workers was difficult and expensive, though only very basic housing was provided. The three-storey dormitory building was adjacent to the production building, thus facilitating a just-in-time labour system for just-in-time production. Each dormitory room housed 12 to 16 workers, was very crowded, lacked ventilation and adequate lighting, and had absolutely no private or individual space. Workers on each floor had to share common toilets and bathrooms. Managerial, technical and supervisory staff members shared rooms (two per room), but these rooms were also very basic. The management admitted that the living conditions were very poor, but blamed the local government for not providing enough space for adequate dormitory facilities. The dormitory building was built to accommodate 500 workers only, but always had more than 600 workers. In one of the dormitory rooms, the toilet walls were blackened with moisture and covered all over with plastic sheets. The broken window panels had been replaced by plastic, preventing air from entering the room. The general state of both the bathrooms and the toilets was extremely bad, and in some places filthy, indicating long-term neglect.

In China the dormitory system not only constitutes a space of poor working conditions, but at the same time it facilitates a geography of social control over labour in the workplace. The political economy of providing accommodation close to the factory is the linkage of support between the state and capital. Since the migrant working class is deprived of citizenship rights to stay in the city, the state – through residency controls – allows labour mobility, but workers must have employment to support temporary

Table 13.1   Summary of China Diamond and China Golden case studies

Categories	Golden Neo-Paternalist Regime	Diamond Modernist Regime
Ownership	100% HK	JV Chinese/Taiwanese
Location	Guangdong HK	Hi-Tech Zone Shanghai
Business position	Middle	High-end
Sales	100% export	70% export 30% local
No. of workers	600	1000
Percentage in dorms	90%	45% (45% private rented)
Hierarchy in dorms	By position only	By position not skill
Ownership of dorms	Local Authority	Building their own
Migrants as % of workers	95%	90%
Use of labour codes	No	Yes
International standards	No	Yes
Labour turnover	20–30% p.a.	30–40% p.a.
Age of workers	16–40	22–24
Type of worker	Single but 50 married	Single
Composition	70% female	85% female
Hours worked	70–77	60
Compulsory overtime	Yes	Yes
Recruitment channel	90% WoM	90% WoM
Retention devices:		
Delayed wages	No	No
Retain ID cards	Yes	No
Payment in arrears	Yes	Yes
Take deposit	Yes	Yes
Debts	No	No
Use of fines	Yes	Yes
Control system	Familial	Modern
Modern mgt practices	No	Yes

Note: WoM = word of mouth; HK = Hong Kong; JV = joint venture.

residence. Dormitories facilitate the temporary attachment or capture of labour by the companies, but also the massive circulation of labour, and hence the holding down of wages and the extensive lengthening of the working day, as working space and living space are integrated by the employer and state. The result is that a hybrid, transient workforce is created, circulating between factory and countryside, dominated by employers' control over housing needs and state controls over residency permits.

Because both workers and managers lived within this dormitory space, management of China Golden appeared to have exceptional controls over the workforce. With no access to a home space independent of the enterprise, working days are easily extended to suit production needs. This permitted a flexible utilisation of labour time, and meant employers could respond to product demand more readily than in situations where workers' time is regulated by the state or workers. If, as Marx noted, the 'length of the working day fluctuate[s] within boundaries that are physical and social' (quoted in

Harvey, 2000, p. 108), then employers within this dormitory labour form appear to have massive control over both the physical and the social realm of workers' lives, with their command over workers' living spaces allowing them to lengthen their working times at very short notice. Indeed, compared to the 'normal' separation between work and home that usual factory arrangements entail, the spatial propinquity between factory and residence evident under the dormitory labour regime allows a much greater degree of control over both the working and the non-working parts of workers' days.

Neo-paternalism in this workplace reflected not only the managerial style, which was almost a copy from the family-based enterprises in Hong Kong, but also the way the company relied heavily on family networks to recruit workers. For example, a supervisor in charge of 60 workers in the finishing unit who had been with the company for 6 years had 12 relatives in the factory. With 600 workers in the factory, it only took about 50 or fewer extended families to be responsible for recruiting all the workers. From the management side, we saw a few families controlling access to work. For the workers, this system meant access to the factory was totally network-dependent, and strangers could not gain access. This system formed an 'extended internal labour market' (Manwaring, 1984) in which job information was passed to those linked to insiders, usually kin or same-place individuals. In other words, if a family member or same-village member obtained work in a clothing factory, this determined the fate of others that had to follow the flow into this clothing factory, or follow the significant individual around as they moved.

Importantly, this extended internal labour market had the potential to form a dormitory labour 'honeycomb' pattern, one started by one or two core family members but then spiralling out over time to create a network linked to more than ten to fifteen workers in the same company (Pun, 2001). Hence, the finishing unit supervisor took six years to weave his family network connecting individuals to different work positions. Acting as a paternalistic patron, he needed not only to take care of his relatives and co-villagers' daily lives and accommodation, but also was responsible for their work behaviour on the shop floor. All the family members recruited needed to be responsible, and this might act to police the performance of the individual worker; if they let the family down, they let the team down, and payment, which was strongly performance-based, would suffer (Grieco, 1996; Smith, 2006). This created one piece in the cartography of dormitory labour control, encouraging mutual obligations as well as mutual control and group discipline in the workplace. Thus, labour mobility was balanced by these self-regulated, job-hopping networks that served as a stabiliser for ensuring a fairly constant labour force for the dormitory labour regime by reducing levels of labour turnover (at least when compared with China Diamond: see below).

Therefore, for their part, individual workers did not make 'job choices', as these were decided through connections and 'structured' through networks – a system that runs counter to neoclassical economic theory. At the same time, for management this system was one significant way through which to shelter from the high labour turnover rate in the locality. As a result, one frequently-used strategy to ensure a continued labour supply was to poach skilled workers from other firms and retain them through kin and family networks. Consequently, China Golden seldom trained fresh and unskilled labourers, and when newcomers did gain admittance, they typically entered as skilled or experienced workers as their family members or co-villagers, who had work experience in the company, had already trained most of the workers from their villages.

Promotion from within (a quasi-internal labour market) was actively practised – all of the workers in the design/pattern-making department (the most skilled section), for instance, had been promoted internally. Thus, service and loyalty were rewarded with 'career' progression and better pay. This reflected the fact that China Golden favoured a paternalistic management style of rewarding loyal staff and a desire to retain company-specific skills and knowledge within the enterprise. Internal job ladders were used as retention devices and were also an indicator of the relative stability of the workforce, with workers exhibiting a longer tenure, higher age profile and lower quit rate than at China Diamond and other factories (see Zhao and Nichols, 1996; Warner, 2000). As with other features of this case, growing labour skill internally was a rational strategy in a skill shortage environment. However, the structural characteristics of the dormitory labour regime are based on high-circulation of young labour and this acts against skill formation. It was only via this neo-paternalist adaptation, with family labour, a higher age profile for workers, comprehensive network-based recruitment and a Hong Kong family-based business ethic, that internal labour markets of a sort operated.

To summarise, the paternalistic dormitory labour regime enables absolute lengthening of working hours and double extraction of labour power through absolute control of labour time and living space. China Golden was deeply entrenched within its existing paternalistic setting and the forces of inertia to maintain its dormitory labour system were stronger than those favouring change. However, profit margins were low and getting progressively lower. This meant that the Managing Director was considering a number of new business strategies. One of these was to move further into China or south-east Asia to secure lower wages or tax-free advantages, a common strategy for Hong Kong capital (see Yeung, 2000). An alternative strategy, arising from the manager's perception that the company's competitive advantage was its quickness of delivery time, was to get more from the labour process of the existing factory by lengthening the working day. However, there were physical limitations to this as working hours were already long, and any moves to increase hours might upset the relationship between the company and 'loyal' staff within the internal labour market. Competition therefore limited the freedom to change the existing factory, and in 2006 the owner moved production to a cheaper location within China. The spatial politics of production and capital accumulation, then, were important to China Golden, both within the factory (through their ability to control worker out-migration) and through their ultimate decision to move their facility elsewhere to further capitalise on low wages.

China Diamond Garments: imagining a modern dormitory regime
In many ways, China Diamond stands in direct contrast to China Golden in terms of ownership, business 'position', sales outlets, observance of international standards and implementation of labour codes, labour retention strategies and workers' freedom of movement. Nevertheless, there are significant similarities, including the deployment of rural villagers, use of dormitories to provide an 'on tap' labour force to enable just-in-time production and the poor condition of current dormitory accommodation. Unlike China Golden, however, at the time of our research China Diamond had tangible plans to construct a modern, 'quality' dormitory intended to meet international expectations and improve labour retention.

Ownership, market position and business strategy   China Diamond Garments is a joint-venture company owned by a Chinese manager (70 per cent) and a Taiwanese family entrepreneur (30 per cent, down from 50 per cent) in the Shanghai region. The company produces garments and underwear, using cloth bought and dyed in China. Established in 1995, China Diamond was mostly under the control of the Mainland Chinese manager, who was in charge of daily management and production. For his part, the Taiwanese entrepreneur served to provide and secure production orders from a big European corporation and Japanese buyers, although the company also produces its own undergarment brand for the Chinese market. According to management, some 30 per cent of China Diamond's production went to this single European corporation, which enforced very strict company codes of conduct in the factory. China Diamond has a high-end position along the global subcontracting chain and the company possessed direct contacts with the European buyer. It subcontracted some of its orders, in particular the woven process and some knitting activities to local and smaller factories (see Table 13.1).

While the management team was basically Mainland Chinese, China Diamond Garments fostered an ambition of building up the most advanced and modern enterprise in the Shanghai region which could live up to perceived international standards. Using local idiom, the Chinese manager (in his mid-thirties and previously a medical doctor) said the goal was to enable the company to 'get connected to the global rail'. This was thought to ensure that the company would be able to survive and expand in severe global competition by introducing modern management methods and international labour standards. Bright and ambitious, the Chinese manager was keen to imagine a new paradigm of management for the Chinese workplace, which has long been associated with a 'sweatshop' image, internationally and locally.

The spatial politics of production in capital accumulation was crucially important to China Diamond Garments, concerned as it was to tap into the circulation of global production. In March 2001, the company moved into new premises close to Shanghai, built in a high-tech development zone, one newly planned as an export-processing zone for foreign companies, joint-venture companies and private companies. The new compound appeared modern and sophisticated. The vast, 18 000 square metre compound had a substantial unoccupied area, where management planned to erect a modern dormitory with advanced facilities. The compound was walled, as is usual with companies in China (Lee, 1998; Hsing, 1998), and had security guards stationed at the entrance gate. Other guards were also present in the dormitory building, but workers were free to go in and out as they pleased. The dormitory building's gate was closed at 12 am unless a management order was received from above because of overtime work after midnight.

To maintain its niche in the high-end production chain, China Diamond Garments had been certified ISO 9000 in 2000 and ISO 14000 in 2002. The management was proud of their achievements in meeting these international standards on production quality, human resources and environmental issues. Management were planning for SA 8000 in 2003, and a task force of five (the Chinese manager, one Taiwanese consultant, the trade union chair, and two personnel secretaries) was formed to create an assessment and procedure system for promoting labour and human rights standards according to the ILO conventions.[6]

Labour recruitment, accommodation and turnover   Similar to China Golden, 90 per cent of the workforce in China Diamond Garments were rural workers coming from villages or towns in Zhejiang and Jiangsu, two nearby hinterland provinces of the Shanghai region. The remaining 10 per cent were local workers who lived at home. About 85 per cent of the workers employed in China Diamond were women. Most were 22 to 24 years old. The process of recruiting migrant villagers in China Diamond was similar to that in China Golden, including the prominence of using word-of-mouth and family networks. Unlike China Golden, though, China Diamond did not keep the identity cards of workers (only photocopies). The management was proud that they did not adopt this 'inhuman' practice. However, as at China Golden, and contrary to the Code, a system of deposits was adopted. The personnel secretary stated that this deposit was returned to the worker upon termination of employment. Workers were free to leave their workplace at the end of their shift and free to resign.

Working hours were more regular and shorter at China Diamond (an average of 10 per day), except when production was pressed to meet rush orders and a rest day on Sunday would be cancelled. Most workers were remunerated on a piece-rate basis and were paid in cash monthly, with an average wage of RMB 600–700, inclusive of overtime work. This was lower than at China Golden, in part due to shorter hours. Supervisors, technical, managerial and office staff were paid on monthly rates, with a higher average of RMB 800–1500.

Fines were widely used for control purposes. Two different systems of salary deductions for disciplinary reasons were in place: one concerned production workers, and the other concerned supervisory and managerial staff. Fines for the production workers were roughly similar to those at China Golden. For line supervisors, a quite complex system of 'rewards', called '5 S',[7] amounting actually to a system of salary deductions for disciplinary measures, was applied.

Workers at China Diamond seemed to have greater freedom of movement when compared to China Golden or other companies studied by field researchers (Chan, 2001; Hsing, 1998). The company provided a contract for every worker who had passed the probationary period, the latter varying in length from a few days to up to two months. Provision of a contract demonstrated the company's commitment to the workers because many companies in China do not provide contracts (Chan, 2001). The factory used a contract of its own format, which was much simpler than the one required by Chinese labour law[8] and listed fewer clauses.[9]

While the workers had signed a contract for one to two years following their probationary period, when interviewed none of them had received a copy of their contract, and thus had no clear idea of its provisions. Nevertheless, most of them knew they could leave the company before the end of the contract period and wages could still be received by themselves or by their relatives in the company in the subsequent month.

While China Diamond Garments already had an advanced company compound, what was lacking was a modern dormitory building that could meet SA 8000 and the corporate code of the European buyer. Frequent inspections by the European corporation had hastened initiatives concerned with building modern accommodation facilities for the company's workforce. Maintaining the number of employees at around 1000, a suitable size for retaining quality workers, the company hoped that building the onsite dormitory would both improve workforce stability and enhance the just-in-time labour system. Hence, as the task force explained: '[t]he first priority is to build our dormitory as soon as possible. We need to meet the international requirements, but we also need to confine our workers in better living conditions so that they can be more accessible to work.'

From the above quote, having workers 'on tap' and ready for production as and when required seems the priority of management. The 'confinement' of the workforce in relatively good living conditions under stricter management control was deemed a company strategy to retain workers who were often mobile and unstable. Mirroring the high labour turnover rate typical in foreign or private-owned enterprises, China Diamond's turnover was 30 to 40 per cent per year, higher than at China Golden (see Table 13.1).

Accommodating its workers was a sensitive problem for the company, since the new dormitory was still not ready. At the time of visits in December 2002, some 45 per cent of the workers (approximately 500) lived in rented factory dormitories, 15 minutes' walk from the factory compound, and another 45 per cent lived in rooms rented by themselves in suburban areas. Some workers had a half-hour bicycle journey to the factory. The geography of workers' residences, then, reflected a workplace hierarchy in terms of wages, work position, and status (Rofel, 1999), while the huge difference in accommodation provisions between production and non-production staff served to reinforce segmentation of the labour force. The dormitories, rented from the government and housing 8–16 workers per room, were those the company rented when it was operating from the previous premises. Two-bedroom flats were rented for managerial staff, forepersons or office clerical staff whose living conditions were far better than those of production workers. A shared dining room, kitchen, toilet and bathroom with hot water facilities were provided in the flats. Living conditions in the dormitories were generally poor and far from meeting the corporate code's requirements concerning minimum housing standards (see Box 13.1). No kitchen and bathroom were provided, and clauses 5, 6, 9, 10, 12 and 13 were only partially, or not at all, met.

Under pressure to adopt the European corporation's code, the management showed us a very sophisticated dormitory plan, drawn by a construction and design company based on the code's requirements. From the plans, it appeared the new dormitory would provide improved living conditions, including smaller dormitories (maximum six people) and individual and shared facilities, together with communal spaces such as a library, recreational room and clinic.

With improved accommodation facilities, the company expected to benefit by retaining a better quality workforce with more experience and skills for a longer period (in 2002, the average length of tenure at China Diamond was two years). This aim of labour retention, however, was somewhat contradictory, given the very young age profile of the workforce and the relatively low wages reinforced by migrant labour circulation. 'Longer-term' attachment was, therefore, only for a few additional years, and the migrant composition of labour was not expected to change.

Central to the dormitory form is the grouping together of, typically, single, young, female workers. Women and men are highly segregated in order to control sexual behaviour. Separated from family, home and rural life, these women workers concentrate in a workspace and submit to a process of both homogenisation and individuation, since they are taken as 'individual workers' by the management, untying communal bonds and making them responsible for their own behaviour. In so far as their connection to the firm is short-term and contractual, the alienation of labour derives from significantly more than either labour's separation from ownership of the product or labour's lack

---

BOX 13.1   SUMMARY OF EUROPEAN CORPORATIONS' CODE ON HOUSING FACILITIES

1. Dormitory facilities meet all applicable laws and regulations related to health and safety, including fire safety, sanitation, risk protection, and electrical, mechanical and structural safety.
2. Sleeping quarters are segregated by sex.
3. The living space per worker in the sleeping quarters meets both the minimum legal requirement and the local industry standard.
4. Workers are provided with their own individual mats or beds.
5. Dormitory facilities are well ventilated. There are windows to the outside or fans and/or air conditioners and/or heaters in all sleeping areas for adequate ventilation and temperature control.
6. Workers are provided their own storage space for their clothes and personal possessions.
7. There are at least two clearly marked exits on each floor, and emergency lighting is installed in halls, stairwells and above each exit.
8. Halls and exits are kept clear of obstructions for safe and rapid evacuation in case of fire or other emergencies. Fire drills are conducted at least every six months.
9. Directions for evacuation in case of fire or other emergencies are posted in all sleeping quarters. Fire extinguishers are placed in, or accessible to, all sleeping quarters.
10. Hazardous and combustible materials used in the production process are not stored in the dormitory or buildings connected to sleeping quarters.
11. Sleeping quarters have adequate lighting.
12. Sufficient toilets and showers are segregated by sex and provided in safe, sanitary, accessible and private areas.
13. Potable water or facilities to boil water are available to dormitory residents.
14. Dormitory residents are free to come and go during their off-hours under reasonable limitations imposed for their safety and comfort.

---

of production skills. However, more fully controlling the social, non-working lives of workers was envisioned as being possible through a modern dormitory. Hence, as the facilities manager explained: '[m]ore supervisions and inspections can be enforced in the new dormitory building, and women workers can be better protected', with 'protected' being a euphemism frequently used by managers to imply control and/or punishment of women. Significantly, then, such paternalistic concern over female workers' private time – the management's feeling that it needed to 'protect' its female workers through housing them in a dormitory – prolonged management control in a way not possible where there is a geographical separation between home and work.

The regimes of labour control exerted through the construction of dormitories, then, were not supplementary but central to the extraction of surplus labour from workers.

Only those who were able to put up with the strict discipline of the dormitory and, by implication, the workplace too, were able to retain their jobs. The entire ethic of the dormitory regime was not just to impose severe discipline and punishment, but also to create a discourse on self-discipline, which was often emphasised at the workplace. Self-management of dormitory rooms was also expected, so that the workers could learn how to behave themselves as proper, 'modern' workers. Put another way, the modern dormitory regime deployed a series of hard disciplines as well as subtle surveillance and meticulous self-supervision of everyday lives (Foucault, 1977). In short, creating a well-trained female workforce with discipline and fitted to the maximisation of production is the political technology of the dormitory labour regime. Consequently, a more modern dormitory labour regime and replacement of the system of fines for disciplinary reasons by a more positive system of rewards programme were imagined by the managing director as a way to live up to the age of globalising production in a transnational context but also to better secure a workforce capable of so doing.

In sum, it is evident from these two case studies that the dormitory labour regime operates according to the following strategies of control and domination:

1. An absolute lengthening of the workday and a compression of 'work–life': ten years compresses into five years, owing to excessive working weeks, with production based chiefly on deployment of young women workers;
2. A suppression of demands for wage increases: the elevated circulation of labour caused by temporary labour contracts makes it more difficult for workers to demand wage increases through collective pressure;
3. Easy access to labour power during the workday: dormitories provide a just-in-time labour system for just-in-time production, quick-delivery orders, distribution systems and higher profits;
4. Daily labour reproduction: dormitories allow for more direct control of the reproduction of labour power within the factory (accommodation, food, travel, social and leisure pursuits within a production unit);
5. Direct control over the labour process: dormitories provide for a system of labour discipline that imposes penalties on workers;
6. State and non-market interventions: state policies restrict labour mobility, thereby affecting the overall labour process, while there is little genuine implementation of legal labour regulations over the dormitory labour regime.

Conclusion

This chapter has examined the construction of export-orientated factories in China and the role of the Chinese state, transnational capital and internal migrant labour in creating an exceptionally productive labour regime. It analysed the linkages between the production and reproduction of labour power in this transnational labour process space. We sought to characterise a new form of labour regime, the dormitory labour regime in China, as providing production conditions that out-compete other systems, especially flexible production and traditional Fordism in the current period.[10] This is because within this system labour costs are low, the productivity of workers is high and there is access to extensive low-cost labour reserves institutionalised within a political economy that links the state and the market. Further, the form of labour capture allows access to cheap labour *without* a longer-term build-up of labour institutions that would inevitably lead to higher wage pressures and possible militancy, for unlike traditional labour markets in the West, wages and working conditions within the dormitory labour regime are not circumscribed by the operation of geographically rooted norms, trade union institutions and localised practices that normally emerge under geographically bounded social conditions, and which serve to increase wages and workers' living standards (Storper and Walker, 1989: p. 157; Herod et al., 2003). Instead, the *systemic* provision of industrial dormitories for internal migrant labour within or around factories facilitates continuous access to fresh labour reserves from the countryside and depresses wage demands and inhibits collective organisation by workers in a particular industrial space. In terms of the spatial politics of production, dormitories concentrate labour, but not labour organisation, because the high circulation of workers as a transitory, semi-proletarianised class means they are often not sufficiently embedded within one place or space to form working-class community or to 'build institutions, such as trade unions, to articulate their claims' (Harvey, 2001, p. 374). The dormitory labour regime, in concentrating and yet circulating labour between capitals, therefore represents a powerful labour management regime, which China is currently using to fuel its integration with the world economy.

The dormitory labour regime is structured through the high circulation of labour. This is a 'flexible labour force' of a different order from Western economies (Nichols et al., 2004). Task flexibility has not developed; rather an extensive decomposition of tasks appears necessary within this regime to accommodate the high turnover of labour and to prevent job hopping as workers trade skills within a context where skill formation is poorly institutionalised. There is limited incentive for firms to train migrants, because their mobility is spatially fixed by the system, and opportunism based on strong inter-firm competition creates disincentives to move beyond limited task training for fear of fuelling labour turnover; firms fear that workers would quit more readily for small increases in wages if skills were extended. Requirements of deposits or bonds, retention of internal documents or passports, and delayed payments are sanctions considered justifiable, as they inhibit voluntary turnover.

However, there are contradictions within this system, wherein worker-controlled institutions – such as kin, village and localised networks – mediate relations between work and dormitory. These intensive forms of socialising and solidarity construct worker bonds that impede the unfettered management control of labour on the shopfloor (Pun, 1999, 2001). Workers have intensive information exchanges about external job opportunities through dormitory networks and thereby may build a degree of 'mobility power', even as capital attempts to seal in contact within the boundaries of the firm. Equally, although migrant labour is used to try to minimise opportunities for workplace organising that might be easier if such workers were from the local community, workers housed together nevertheless do often build strong social bonds, which spill over into the shopfloor and can create problems for management during industrial disputes (Smith and Pun, 2006).

Although dormitory regimes have been explored in other countries undergoing rapid industrialisation, ultimately the dormitory labour regime may not travel well beyond

China, for it is a production regime with a specific spatiality of global production, national legacies and local reconfiguration. Thus, whereas historically Korea and Japan have both used dormitories, though not as extensively as in China (Smith, 2003; Smith and Pun, 2006), current provision in these countries is sector-limited, and with the growth of private and public housing, company dormitories have to be of a comparable standard to function as a labour retention or reward technique. By way of contrast, Smith (2003) suggests that the movement up the value chain in China has not seen the emergence of independent worker housing but, rather, the reinforcing of dormitories, albeit upgraded through the firm as illustrated in the second case study, for the housing market in the manufacturing towns of the coastal areas in Southern China has not appeared for the benefit of migrant labour but, instead, for foreign managers, Hong Kong residents or local cadres enriched through converting land into industrial use (Eng, 1997). It currently seems that the economic effects of dormitories on wages appear to reinforce their utility, and independent housing is not appearing separately from the enterprise. From our two case studies, though, there is evident variability in the use of dorms, and one would perhaps predict the future development of new hierarchies of housing provision to capture and retain skilled workers beyond those found in the local labour market. This witnesses the making of a new spatialised political economy of the labour regime, and hence a novel form of transnational labour process in China.

Notes

1. A shorter version of this chapter appeared as Ngai and Smith (2007).
2. The company names are pseudonyms.
3. The *hukou* system requires every Chinese citizen to be recorded with the registration authority at birth, and to have his/her residential categorisation (either urban or rural) fixed. Location is decided by the mother's *hukou* rather than birthplace, so a mother with a rural *hukou* can only give her children a rural *hukou*, even if the children were born in the city and their father is an urban resident. Citizenship benefits are tied to one's *hukou*. Only through government authorisation can the *hukou* be changed. The system is designed to control population movement, and especially to keep peasant farmers in rural areas, or cut off from citizenship rights as migrant worker-peasants in urban areas (Solinger, 1999). The system is designed to prevent unplanned urbanisation and overcrowding, which is typical of developing countries that lack statutory internal 'passport' or 'citizenship' controls. Such a statutory, restrictive form of population control, however, is in contradiction with the market reforms in China (Woon, 1999) and the *hukou* is in decay.
4. The material presented was gathered through two different processes. Both cases are from the clothing or garments sector, which has expanded dramatically in the reform period, representing the major part of the labour-intensive export sectors, and 12 per cent of China's GDP. The first case, China Golden Garments, in Dongguan, was visited during summer 2002 and an interview was conducted with the Managing Director and supervisors, as were casual conversations with production workers and supervisors in the dormitories. The second case, China Diamond Garments, in Changzhou, was studied over two weeks during Easter and Christmas 2002, with group interviews with workers and individual interviews with management. Documentation on labour management policies and plans for the development of the firm were also examined. In both cases, all parts of the production process were directly observed, as were the dormitories for male and female workers and supervisors.
5. See http://corporate.disney.go.com/corporate/intl_labor_standards.html.
6. In 2002 China Diamond Garments was required to sign the European corporation's code, which is a statement about the ethical standards that a transnational company claims to uphold and ensure are implemented by its production suppliers or trade partners. The principles of the corporate code are measured against the ILO conventions, in particular those concerning the respect of human rights at work. Key clauses include seven major areas: (no) forced or bonded labour; (no) child labour; (no) discrimination in employment; payment of living wages and benefits; establishment of normal working hours; (no) hazards to safety and health; and ensuring a decent working environment.
7. The 5 S stood for the Chinese words meaning: orderliness; 'fixing' of machines and equipment; cleaning

things and putting away tools; ensuring an adequate workplace environment (that is, clean floors); and practising family-like behaviour with workers.

8. According to Sec. 19 of the Chinese Labour Act, a labour contract should at least contain terms relating to labour protections and working conditions, labour remuneration, labour discipline, conditions for the termination of a labour contract and responsibility for the violation of a labour contract.

9. The contract contained the following provisions: start date; name of the work unit/department and position; need for the worker to abide by the factory regulations; need for the worker to follow the work arrangements concerning a change of position without arguing against it; ensuring and respecting a safe company environment; dismissal of a worker in cases when s/he does not follow the company regulations and causes loss of production; and a guarantee that the company would pay wages, insurance and overtime in accordance with state labour regulations.

10. Other production systems might have provided accommodation or certain forms of housing for labour in certain periods. But, as an extensive and systemic labour-use form, the dormitory labour regime in China is remarkably dominant and deserves distinction and further study.

References

Andors, P. (1988), 'Women and work in Shenzhen', *Bulletin of Concerned Asian Scholars*, **20** (3), 22–41.

Burawoy, M. (1985), *The Politics of Production*, London: Verso.

Chan, A. (2001), *China's Workers under Assault: The Exploitation of Labor in a Globalizing Economy*, London and New York: M.E. Sharpe.

Cook, S. (2000), 'Readjusting labour: enterprise restructuring, social consequences and policy responses in urban China', in M. Warner (ed.), *Changing Workplace Relations in the Chinese Economy*, Basingstoke: Macmillan, pp. 227–46.

Deyo, F.C. (1989), *Beneath the Miracle: Labor Subordination in the New Asian Industrialism*, London and Berkeley, CA: University of California Press.

Eng, I. (1997), 'The rise of manufacturing towns: externally driven industrialization and urban development in the Pearl River Delta of China', *International Journal of Urban and Regional Research*, **21** (4), 554–68.

Foucault, M. (1977), *Discipline and Punish: The Birth of the Prison*, New York: Vintage Books.

Frenkel, S. (2003), 'The embedded character of workplace relations', *Work and Occupations*, **30** (2), 135–54.

Fröbel, F., J. Heinrichs and O. Kreye (1980), *The New International Division of Labour*, Cambridge: Cambridge University Press.

Grieco, M. (1996), *Workers' Dilemmas: Recruitment, Reliability and Repeated Exchange: An Analysis of Urban Social Networks and Labour Circulation*, London: Routledge.

Harvey, D. (1982), *The Limits to Capital*, Oxford: Blackwell.

Harvey, D. (2000), *Spaces of Hope*, Edinburgh: Edinburgh University Press.

Harvey, D. (2001), *Spaces of Capital*, New York: Routledge.

Henderson, J.W. (1989), *The Globalisation of High Technology Production*, London: Routledge.

Herod, A., J. Peck and J. Wills (2003), 'Geography and industrial relations', in P. Ackers and A. Wilkinson (eds), *Understanding Work and Employment: Industrial Relations in Transition*, Oxford: Oxford University Press, pp. 176–92.

Hsing, You-Tien (1998), *Making Capitalism in China: The Taiwan Connection*, New York and Hong Kong: Oxford University Press.

Hudson, R. (1989), 'Labour-market changes and new forms of work in old industrial regions: maybe flexibility for some but not flexible accumulation', *Environment and Planning D: Society and Space*, **7** (1), 5–30.

Hutton, W. and A. Giddens (eds) (2000), *Global Capitalism*, New York: New Press.

Lee, C.K. (1995), 'Engendering the worlds of labor: women workers, labor markets, and production politics in the South China Economic Miracle', *American Sociological Review*, **60** (3), 378–96.

Lee, C.K. (1998), *Gender and the South China Miracle: Two Worlds of Factory Women*, London and Berkeley, CA: University of California Press.

Lin, G.C.S. (1997), *Red Capitalism in South China: Growth and Development of the Pearl River Delta*, Vancouver: UBC Press.

Mann, M. (1973), *Workers on the Move*, Cambridge: Cambridge University Press.

Manwaring, T. (1984), 'The extended internal labour market', *Cambridge Journal of Economics*, **8** (2), 161–87.

Massey, D. (1993), 'Power-geometry and a progressive sense of place', in J. Bird, B. Curtis, T. Putnam, G. Robertson and L. Tickner (eds), *Mapping the Futures: Local Cultures, Global Change*, London and New York: Routledge, pp. 60–70.

Nash, J. and M.P. Fernandez-Kelly (eds) (1983), *Women, Men and the International Division of Labor*, Albany, NY: State University of New York Press.

Ngai, P. and C. Smith (2007), 'Putting transnational labour process in its place: the dormitory labour regime in post-socialist China', *Work, Employment and Society*, **21** (1), 27–45.

Nichols, T., S. Cam, W.G. Chou, S. Chun, W. Zhao and T. Feng (2004), 'Factory regimes and the dismantling of established labour in Asia: a review of cases from large manufacturing plants in China, South Korea and Taiwan', *Work, Employment and Society*, **18** (4), 663–85.

Ong, A. (1998), *Flexible Citizenship: The Cultural Logics of Transnationality*, Durham, NC: Duke University Press.

Peck, J. (1996), *Work*-Place: *The Social Regulation of Labor Markets*, London and New York: Guilford Press.

Piore, M.J. and C.F. Sabel (1984), *The Second Industrial Divide: Possibilities for Prosperity*, New York: Basic Books.

Pun, N. (1999), 'Becoming *dagongmei* (working girls): the politics of identity and difference in reform China', *The China Journal*, **42**, 1–18.

Pun, N. (2001) 'Cultural construction of labor politics: gender, kinship, and ethnicity in a Shenzhen workplace', in A.Y. So, N. Lin and D. Poston (eds), *The Chinese Triangle of Mainland China, Taiwan and Hong Kong: Comparative Institutional Analysis*, London and Westport, CT: Greenwood, pp. 103–116.

Rofel, L. (1999), *Other Modernities: Gendered Yearnings in China After Socialism*, Durham: Duke University Press.

Sassen, S. (1988), *The Mobility of Labor and Capital: A Study in International Investment and Labor Flow*, London: Cambridge University Press.

Sklair, L. (2001), *The Transnational Capitalist Class*, Oxford: Blackwell.

Smith, C. (2003), 'Living at work: management control and the dormitory labour system in China', *Asia Pacific Journal of Management*, **20** (3), 333–58.

Smith, C. (2006), 'The double indeterminacy of labour power: labour effort and labour mobility', *Work, Employment and Society*, **20** (2), 389–402.

Smith, C. and N. Pun (2006), 'The dormitory labour regime in China as a site for control and resistance', *International Journal of Human Resource Management*, **17** (8), 1456–70.

Solinger, D.J. (1999), 'Citizenship issues in China's internal migration: comparisons with Germany and Japan', *Political Science Quarterly*, **114** (3), 455–79.

Storper, M. and R. Walker (1989), *The Capitalist Imperative*, Oxford: Blackwell.

Thompson, E.P. (1963), *The Making of the English Working Class*, London: Victor Gollancz.

Warner, M. (ed.) (2000), *Changing Workplace Relations in the Chinese Economy*, New York: St Martin's Press.

Woon, Y.-F. (1999), 'Labor migration in the 1990s: homeward orientation of migrants in the Pearl River Delta region and its implications for interior China', *Modern China*, **25** (4), 475–513.

Yeung, H.W.-C. (2000), 'Embedding foreign affiliates in transnational business networks: the case of Hong Kong firms in Southeast Asia', *Environment and Planning A*, **32** (2), 201–22.

Zhao, M. and T. Nichols (1996), 'Management control of labour in state-owned enterprises: cases from the textile industry', *The China Journal*, **36**, 1–21.

PART 3

WORKERS IN SPACE

14 Workers in space

Al Rainnie, Andrew Herod and Susan McGrath-Champ

[U]nionism can still stake a claim to constitute a popular movement, by imaginative engagement in a *battle of ideas*. Trade unions have to discover a language which can express aspirations, projects, even utopias which are consistent with the principles which inspired the movement in the past but which address the very different world in which we live today. And as part of this process they have to recognize – as many unions indeed have done, often painfully – that there are other social movements which have captured the enthusiasm, particularly among the young, that unions have largely lost; and that it is necessary to seek common ground with these. (Hyman, 2002, pp. 14–15)

In this part of the book we turn to questions of how our form of spatially informed analysis seeks to incorporate workers and communities as active agents in determining the shape and location(s) of their lives. In particular, we concentrate on questions of union organisation and scales of resistance in the last section of this chapter. Before doing so, however, we start with a more general analysis of globalisation and work, for globalisation appears to be fundamentally reworking the parameters within which workers must live and in which labour markets function.

Globalising work?

We have already seen that work is becoming increasingly urbanised and that the gap between rich and poor is becoming wider, both socially and in terms of the spatial worlds that rich and poor seem to inhabit – gated communities versus inner-city neighbourhoods, for instance. Other accounts, such as that by Huws (2008), point to the increasing informalisation of economies, with precariousness outside the formal economy being paralleled by growing precariousness within it. Much of this precariousness is seen to emanate from the pressures for employer flexibility brought about by globalisation and the need for firms, in a world of global instantaneous communication and the almost-immediate transmission across the planet of the consequences of economic and other decisions and events, to be able to respond in fairly short order to events occurring in myriad places across the globe.[1] If measured by the proliferation of popular and academic articles, job precariousness, then, would appear to be a fairly widespread consequence of the emergence of a world of 'fast capitalism' (Agger, 1989) wherein we live in an 'era of simultaneity' (Foucault, 1986). However, a word of caution is required. Thus, Stirling (2007) argues that although some reports claim that one in five UK workers now qualify as vulnerable and that the full-time job is under threat, reality is more complex. He suggests instead that although the idea of the end of the full-time job has become increasingly engrained in our culture through, for instance, constant news stories about firm downsizing, offshoring and the growing use of temporary workers, there is actually little evidence in the UK, at least, to support it as, at the end of the twentieth century, over 94 per cent of male workers and more than 91 per cent of female workers had permanent contracts.[2] If, in some cases, the reality of precariousness seems perhaps to be somewhat overblown, one important aspect of vulnerability that cannot be ignored is the fear (warranted or not) that 'permanency' may not last for long, since it is on the basis of such fears that workers may often be disciplined within the labour market. Furthermore, if we look at temporary and agency work, then the picture becomes even more complicated as, in the early years of the twenty-first century, it would appear that vulnerable jobs are declining in the form of temporary work but expanding in the form of agency work.

Bearing in mind what processes of globalisation may be doing to the nature of work and how labour markets function, then, in a recent article Jones (2008) suggests that there have been three dominant geographical approaches to analysing the relationship between labour, work and globalisation. In the first, labour is seen as a sticky factor of production, with resulting analysis focusing on TNCs and local labour markets. The second places greater emphasis on an understanding of place itself, and the third sees workers existing in a complex landscape of geographical difference and interdependence. Putting these together, Jones concludes that the very character of work itself is changing in response to processes of globalisation and that this has profound implications for people employed in all sorts of sectors. In making his argument, Jones suggests that much recent research suffers from four epistemological limitations and he draws on actor network theory (ANT) to outline what he considers to be a more productive way of thinking about work in the era of globalisation:

1. Work has typically been understood as a practice undertaken by individuals or groups in physically proximate material space. In contrast, Jones argues, today work is increasingly constituted through distanciated relations.
2. To the extent that research considers the scales at which work takes place, it tends to be on a mono-scalar conception. Instead, Jones suggests, work is better understood as constituted through many scales by associational linkages.
3. Labour is usually conceived of as a social factor of production that undertakes work. Drawing on ANT, though, Jones contends that the human contribution needs to be conceptualised alongside non-human props that are increasingly scattered through globally extensive associational networks.
4. Work is commonly viewed atemporally or as taking place in a linear chronology. In contrast, Jones insists that we understand the sporadic and temporally disjunctive nature of spatialised practices in a globalised world.

There are a number of important transformations in how the nature of work is understood that flow from this argument. First, physical places of work are now only viewed as simply one space within which work is being done, for work is seen as occurring in all sorts of social, technological and informational spaces (such as 'cyberspace') that have a different form to physical workplaces. Second, workplaces can be seen as existing across multiple spatialities. This means that growing numbers of workers are seeing an increase in work-related personal movements on a daily basis in terms of commuting, homeworking and travel to/from new spaces of work activities, movements which, of course, have implications for how various parts of the economic landscape are connected together. Third, the experience of work is changing as everyday working life is increasingly being affected by the globalisation of production itself – for example, workers in different parts of the globe are more and more tied to one another through the production process, as workers in, say, Mexico make components that ultimately end up being used on cars assembled in the US or Canada, with the result that work rhythms in Mexican and US and Canadian plants must increasingly be synchronised. Fourth, the fact that increasing numbers of people are being employed by TNCs produces new and complex sets of power relations in the workplace, with these power relations being multi-scalar and taking complex inter- and intra-organisational – and, hence, spatial – forms. Finally, work exists across a variety of spaces and networks.

Although not relying on an explanation based in ANT, Mittelman (2000), too, explores how the nature of work may be changing in response to globalisation and how this requires an approach to understanding that is geographically sensitive. Hence, he analyses the emergence of new regional divisions of labour, tethered to global structures, each one in unequal transactions with world centres of production and finance and presented with quite distinctive developmental possibilities. For Mittelman, then, globalisation is not a unified phenomenon. Rather, it is 'a syndrome' or reflection of processes and activities that are deeply spatially and culturally varied, which operate at different spatial scales that interconnect various local, regional and global arenas and which mark policy frameworks with geographically specific characteristics. This approach has similarities with that of Smith (2006; see also Pun and Smith, Chapter 13 in this volume), who argues for a transnational labour process perspective on the changing nature of work, one that analyses work relations within concrete or spatially embedded production processes and one which is locked into transnational capital flows, labour flows and work organisation practices that are not nationally bounded but transnational and global in their structure. Here, then, are echoes of the framework of analysis we put forward in Chapter 4.

Workers in place

Having considered how the nature of work and workplaces may be changing in the contemporary economy, we now turn to the issue of how we consider the places within which workers and workplaces are located. This is particularly important, for as we intimated at the end of Chapter 4, it is not possible to understand what goes on within the workplace without understanding how that workplace is embedded within the locality within which it sits – and, given that such localities are linked to other places near and far to themselves via economic, demographic, technological and other means, how it is also embedded within the broader regional, national and global landscapes produced under capitalism. In this regard, then, Hudson (2001, p. 256) has argued that although production occurs in and through the workplace of the factory, office or home it is firmly set within the spaces of cities, regions and national territories. This recognition is important, because places are, for workers, far more than simply spaces in which to work for a wage. Rather, with regard to the places within which workers live and work,

> [o]ne can speak of a place specific culture, a continuously fashioned mélange of meanings, values, and relationships that are effected by shared and ongoing social practices. These practices construct, sustain, and transform the context in which economic, social, and political life is produced and reproduced on a daily basis and into which new members are socialized. Such a culture is born of a lived unity of experience that generated particular 'structures of feeling'. (Hudson, 2001, p. 267)

For their part, Castree et al. (2004) suggest that places give meaning to people just as people give meaning to places. Thus, people, institutions and material objects (like commodities) come together in unique – though not untheorisable – ways in different locations. Moreover, though, because this is the case, social relationships, regulations and institutions have a high degree of local embeddedness. As a result, for workers, employers, state officials and others, class – and thus the labour market, amongst other things – is experienced as a series of place-specific relationships. Significantly, Castree et al.'s formulation has echoes of Bourdieu's notion of '*habitus*', which emphasises the everyday, taken-for-granted elements of social action. Thus habitus represents the cognitive, affective and evaluative internalisation by actors of past experience on the basis of shared experience in particular places. As a result of such common histories and geographies, members of class fractions often share regularities of thought, aspirations, dispositions and patterns of action. Indeed, Robertson et al.'s (2008) research on neighbourhood identities not only shows how neighbourhood identity is established very early on in a neighbourhood's history and proves resilient to change, but also how social class and status underpin such identities. Equally, external perceptions of a neighbourhood's identity are often stronger and more of a caricature than those held by people who live there, a fact which serves to reinforce the neighbourhood's geographical identity from the outside.

Certainly, the notion of habitus has been criticised for being too all-encompassing, something that is seemingly impossible to break out of or to transcend (Callinicos, 1999). Nevertheless, we do believe that it can be helpful in examining the character of places and how such place-based character can shape worker activity, as in the case of Darlington's (2005) account of labour militancy in Merseyside. Thus, although he himself makes no explicit attempt to theorise critically place and space, Darlington nevertheless develops an argument which is deeply geographical. Specifically, in seeking to understand the region's long-standing militancy, Darlington takes issue with analysts who have attributed Merseyside's militancy simply to an over-preponderance of strike-prone industries (of the three most strike-prone industries in Britain during the 1970s and early 1980s, two of them, cars and dock work, were heavily concentrated in Merseyside). He argues that such explanations are overly structuralist and deny the importance of human agency. Most particularly, he suggests, if militancy were to be explained largely by industrial structure, then it would not be unreasonable to imagine that the virtual destruction of the region's car and dock industries would have led to the eradication of militancy. This, however, has not happened. To explain why, Darlington details the relationship between workplace organisation, the particularities of local politics and the nature of political leadership.

Taking issue with Beynon's (1973) notion of 'factory consciousness', Darlington shows how, over time, waves of political organisation within workplaces and beyond created a political habitus, one which has outlived its initial creators (see Storper and Walker, 1989, p. 157, quoted above, p. 10) and has been nourished by the resources of place. This started in the 1930s with the Communist Party and evolved through the influence of Militant, the Socialist Workers Party and other left groups. The region's distinctive (though not exceptional) form of trade union organisation and political struggle emerged over a 40-year period, then, and continues, albeit in a much less dramatic fashion, to the present. What has been key in creating such a habitus, though, has been the connections – social and spatial – between workplaces and the broader community within which they sit. Only by evaluating how the resources of place have coalesced to create such a habitus is it possible to understand how such traditions of militancy have endured. Thus, Darlington (2005, pp. 151–2) concludes, given the right resources of place it might be possible for industrial and political traditions and patterns of behaviour predisposed to adversarialism, which have been initiated and sustained within certain spatially bounded communities, to be reproduced through time and continue to have a long-term influence on industrial relations – even in the context of dramatic changes in the structure and pattern of employment overall.

What is central in all of this, we would suggest, is to understand how contemporary political practice intertwines with previous actions and activities – themselves structured by the way in which the economic landscape has been made – as part of a locale's spatial path-dependency (Chapter 1, p. 9).

Darlington's study, then, raises broader questions of how traditions of militancy or quiescence are generated in particular places, how individuals from those places become socialised within them and how such traditions may be transmitted spatially from place to place. One way for the latter to quite literally 'take place' is through the geographical mobility of workers who bring to new locations traditions of militancy developed elsewhere, such that their arrival can serve as the catalyst of radical change in formerly quiescent and/or non-unionised labour forces and lead to the 'invention' (Hobsbawm and Ranger, 1983) of new traditions. In other cases traditions may be transmitted through what Wills (1998) calls a 'demonstration effect', as workers in one place are inspired by learning about those in more distant places. This latter is a process which does not require the physical movement of workers themselves but does necessitate the spatial diffusion across the economic landscape of information about disputes elsewhere – a fact which raises interesting questions about how the economic landscape's spatial structure may help or hinder the transfer of knowledge from place to place. Certainly, what this all highlights is that the invention and sustenance of tradition is itself spatially embedded and structured. But it also underscores the fact that migrating militants need a supportive milieu of local institutions and ways of living within which to become embedded if they are to be successful, as do local militants who may either be inventing their own traditions *ex nihilo* or drawing inspiration from those they see being articulated elsewhere (we will return to the question of labour migration a little later).

Finally, another way in which to contemplate the meaning of place as a social construction that has real impacts upon workers (and other social actors) and labour markets is that outlined by Strangleman (2001, p. 264), who uses the concept of networks to stress the dynamics of place. He identifies four sets of networks that help shape a place's character (and, so, the nature of labour relations within it): networks based upon occupation/ work; networks that are based on place (such as a sense of loyalty to particular places built up through familiarity with them); networks as shapers of, and as shaped by, class relations; and networks as relationships of family, kin and generation. Although these four networks are often identified and analysed as separate entities, for Strangleman it is their combination and how they are situated in embedded historic events that is seen to be important, for this allows a greater analytical role for agency to shape networks than has typically been allowed by analysts who study networks. Strangleman, then, avers that what is needed is to understand how these networks intersect and how these intersections develop historically. We would add, of course, that it is also crucial to see how these diverse networks intersect differently in various spatial contexts, based upon how places have developed in historico-geographical terms, and what this means for how work and social life more broadly are structured in different places and times. This is important, because such networks help give places a 'structured coherence', that is to say they generate spaces 'within which a relatively coherent labor market prevails' (Harvey, 2001, p. 328–9). Significantly, the spaces of such labour markets can be formally enscripted into the landscape territorially by the state (for instance, through its bureaucratic delineation of, say, Travel-To-Work Areas) or more informally by the creation of, for instance, national, regional or local cultures and consciousness 'that give deeper psychic meaning to territorial perspectives' (p. 329). Part of the way in which such structured coherence comes about, then, is through the intersection of these networks and the fact that community institutions (family, schools, workplaces, neighbourhoods and so forth) became inscribed on the socio-economic-cultural landscape in a lasting but also gradually erasable manner, such that they usually outlive individual members but are not unchangeable (see Chapter 1).

Local labour control regimes

The notion of habitus, then, provides some significant insights into understanding how local labour markets operate. However, theorists have also explored the concept of local labour control regimes (what Jonas (1996, p. 325) has called 'historically contingent and territorially embedded set[s] of mechanisms which co-ordinate the time–space reciprocities between production, work, consumption and labour reproduction within a local labour market'), how these are implicated in the concept of habitus and how they might be used to account for the particularity of place. In this regard, Peck (1996) argues that all local labour markets are spatially specific because they are established at the intersection of 'space' and 'place', the point at which community structures collide with the logics of business organisation. Crucially, Peck suggests, the operation of labour markets can really only be fully understood by looking outside the workplace, into the sphere of reproduction, which extends from production of the next generation of workers to media, education, training, housing and health. This is because workers are anchored not only in the labour market but also in the household, the community and the state, such that both labour supply and labour markets are both socially and spatially regulated. Given that workers, workplaces, households, the community and the state are all spatially fixed in various ways, then to understand the nature of work we must examine the social and spatial relationships between production, labour, labour supply and social reproduction (Ellem and McGrath-Champ, 2002).

It is important to recognise, though, that whilst there are distinctive regulatory milieux in localities, this does not mean that regulation of local labour markets is necessarily solely conducted at the local level. Thus Castree et al. (2004, pp. 115–16) show how the domains of the workplace are fundamentally connected to those of consumption and reproduction, such that the full range of worker, household, firm, civil society, state and quasi-state institutions from the very local to the truly global are involved in shaping the local labour control regime. In this regard, Yeung (2002) emphasises the importance of questions of power, gender and ethnicity in understanding how such local regimes are constructed and operate – hence, for instance, social ties between Taiwanese engineers in both Silicon Valley and Taiwan have contributed to the emergence of a transnational technical community linking both sides of the Pacific, but one with very localised consequences for both California and Taiwan. Therefore, although a local regime constitutes unique, place-specific relations between firms, workers, unions and regulatory institutions that enable labour to be integrated into production, it is defined and shaped by multi-scalar, extra-local processes. Again, like the notion of habitus, the notion of a local regime could be criticised for being too totalising and too all-encompassing, although it is certainly possible to introduce notions of conflict and contradiction within it. However, the key point we want to address here is that place and space not only structure social action but they can also act as a source of conflict. When discussing such conflict, though, it is important to recognise that not only are material geographies a source of, and a focus for, conflict, but so, too, are the ways in which such geographies are represented discursively contested. Thus, as Paasi (2003, p. 481) has put it regions – though we could substitute localities here – are:

> historically contingent processes, related in different ways to political, governmental, economic and cultural practices and discourses. These processes are in a sense unique and this must also be the case with the always contested narratives concerned with regional [local] identities. Whatever their motives and morals may be, social actors are in different positions when producing and reproducing spatial representations and boundaries/social distinctions between 'us' and 'the Other' – for narratives on regional [local] identities are inevitably expressions of 'power geometries'.

More pointedly, he suggests that 'it is important to ask not what regional [local] identities are but what people mean when they talk or write about regional [local] identities' (Paasi, 2003, p. 481).

Drawing all of this together, Hudson argues that the insights outlined above mean, quite bluntly, that there can be no essential nature to 'place', because capital and labour have very different, and largely mutually exclusive, interests in, and commitments to, place. Different social groups within a place, then, may have different and even highly contested readings of its character and different stakes or interests in that place (Hudson, 2002, p. 263; for an examination of the way that these contradictions can result in both contested images of place and also local boosterist cultures, see Rainnie and Paulet, 2003 and Herod, 2006). Within this context, Castree et al. (2004, p. 117) argue that hegemonic discourses within the local regime can augment power structures in three ways. First, influential discourses (for example, those associated with 'globalisation') can have a scalar element, displacing responsibility for important processes either upwards or downwards, whichever is seen to be most useful by certain power groups. Second, these displacing discourses may be used to justify particular forms of action within the locality, such as holding down wages and moderating union action to make the locality competitive. Third, these discourses and representations can be used to validate and prioritise certain segments of the local (and external) labour markets, as with the case of 'creative class' workers explored in the immensely influential, if fatally flawed, work of Richard Florida (Florida, 2002).

Having explored the issue of local labour control regimes, we want now to turn more overtly to questions of worker organisation and resistance. However, before doing so we focus briefly on the issue of labour migration, since the idea that workers are immobile but that capital is mobile is one of the central myths of globalisation outlined by Castree et al. (2004) that helps shape how local labour markets function (by making it easier for capitalists to use the threat of relocating to brow beat workers (Herod, 1991)), even though it is one that bears some examination in the context of understanding labour markets and worker embeddedness. Issues of labour migration are important, then, both theoretically and empirically. With regard to the magnitude of international labour migration, Shelley (2007) suggests that in the early twenty-first century there were around 3 million migrants entering the OECD countries legally every year, with many more entering illegally, many of whom are readily 'tolerated' by various national governments, if not, on occasion, actually encouraged by them. The ILO has suggested that there are several reasons for this secular rise in migration, including the disappearance of livelihoods in sending countries through the loss of public sector jobs, the decline of traditional industries, a loss of agricultural competitiveness and the elimination of job protection as a result of World Bank Structural Adjustment Programmes (Shelley, 2007, p. 19), all of which have created an ever-growing pool of people desperate to improve their circumstances by relocating to somewhere new. Barrientos (2007, p. 8) connects this argument with our focus on value chains, through arguing that the increasing feminisation of global production systems has led to an increase in female migration. (As we have already discussed in Chapter 4, female labour migration has significant implications for how value chains operate in the global economy (see also Kelly, Chapter 9 in this volume).) On the other hand, focusing upon the demand side of the labour equation, Bartram (2005) has argued that there is, in fact, no real imperative in capitalist development that demands cheap migrants. Rather, he argues, developing an institutionalist thread, it is the nature of the state (clientist versus developmental) that influences the tendency to seek out cheap migrant labour. What this means, then, is that there are important geographical variations between states in their degree of dependence upon migrant labour and the degree to which workers will decide to migrate elsewhere (given that the loss of public sector jobs, the decline of traditional industries, the loss of agricultural competitiveness and the elimination of job protection will vary considerably geographically), both of which have significant implications for how local labour markets function.

Focusing upon a particular case study, May et al. (2006) provide a spatially sensitive analysis of how migrant labour in London is shaping the manner in which local labour markets are operating. In particular, they present evidence of a growing occupational polarisation and the emergence of a new migrant division of labour, the emergence of which the British state has had a significant role in shaping. Thus, they suggest, policies of labour market deregulation, welfare 'reform' and of 'managed migration' have helped create a new reserve army of labour in London, one consisting mainly of low-paid, migrant workers. This has been reinforced by the practice of labour recruitment through personal contact, which encourages a tendency towards ethnic segregation at the bottom end of the labour market – a phenomenon that has echoes of our earlier argument regarding uneven development and its roots in class, gender and race divisions.

If May et al. (2006) have explored empirically how labour migration is shaping the unfolding geography of the labour market in one particular locality, Kelly (Chapter 9 in this volume) has provided a more theoretically orientated argument which suggests that there are (at least) four separate spatialities involved in the process of international migration and local labour market integration. The first of these relates to the territorial regulatory spaces in which labour import and export are established – including immigration controls and so on. The second concerns the spaces of home and/or social reproduction that are intimately linked to immigrants' experiences of the workplace and the labour market. The third spatiality is that delineated by the workplace itself and concerns the hierarchies which are established and enforced within it, which are often based on access to certain space within such workplaces (in other words, how is the workplace laid out spatially and how does this micro-geography play a role in shaping how the labour market and labour control function?). Finally, global capitalism, in both its contemporary and historical forms, underpins all these spatialities, as past forms of capitalism have left a legacy of racialised and gendered hierarchies as processes of uneven development have defined the unequal relationship between places, such that labour flows move in one direction rather than another.

Resistance

We start this section on resistance by concurring with Leitner et al. (2008, p. 169) who, in an examination of the spatialities of contentious politics, conclude that

> a variety of spatialities (place, scale, networks, positionality and mobility) matter for the imaginaries, material practices and trajectories of contentious politics. Scale is one of these, particularly given the scaled nature of political and economic structures, but the spatialities of contentious politics cannot be reduced to scale or any other spatial 'master concept'. No single spatiality should be privileged since they are co-implicated in complex ways, often with unexpected consequences for contentious politics.

This recognition is important, for as we shall outline below, the contemporary restructuring of the global economy and the transnationalisation of investments have frequently led both analysts and activists to argue for a rather knee-jerk response on the part of labour to the actions of capital within a globalising world: if capital is becoming global, then so, too, must labour become so.[3] However, whilst we do not want to be seen as arguing that matching the scale of organisation of capital is never appropriate, at the same time we do want to suggest that the spatial complexities of the economic landscape mean that the spatial strategies appropriate to confronting capital in one context may not be the most suitable in another – indeed, it may sometimes be the case that a more locally orientated campaign is more apposite, as when a transnationally organised corporation adopts, say, just-in-time production technologies that make it highly vulnerable to local disruptions in its supply chain (see Herod, 2000 for an example).

In this context, then, we have already seen that contemporary restructuring has been based on a neoliberal agenda which has important spatial assumptions and implications, not least of which has been the simultaneous decentralisation and supranationalisation of many institutions of control. Thus, Turnbull (2006, p. 309) argues that European integration represents economic liberalisation by transnational means, and illustrates how many European unions have sought to challenge this by Europeanising themselves. However, a geographical conundrum that is potentially unleashed by this strategy is that unions based on national arenas may now be faced with the possibility of losing touch with their rank-and-file if they engage too closely with supranational agencies. Upscaling might then lead to a suppression of political alternatives and mobilisation capacity. A similar point is made by MacShane (2008) who, in commenting on the formation of a transatlantic union (from a merger of Amicus and the United Steelworkers of America), argues that it has the potential to make a difference only if it brings together more than simply the union leaderships. At the same time, though, as Hyman (2001, p. 479) argues, if they are to remain significant agents of social and economic mobilisation, unions need new utopias, and these are unlikely to have much purchase if their focus is solely at the national level. Hence, he argues (p. 468), what is needed is, first, a way to generate 'effective articulation between European-level trade union action and the day-to-day realities of national and workplace trade unionism, and second, a struggle to create a European civil society within which the protection of workers' rights can win popular support and which can sustain effective collective mobilisation'. The issue of day-to-day realities, of course, takes us back to the matter of habitus and how workers' embeddedness in particular spatial networks and localities might serve as the basis for the emergence of such a civil society.

In the UK context, Upchurch et al. (2004) argue that 'neoliberal restructuring' has led to the demise of the traditional, highly centralised and bureaucratised system of union organisation. However, drawing on Jessop's arguments concerning the restructuring of the Keynesian welfare state and Hyman's contention that unions need to rediscover and/or refocus their role as protagonists in civil society, Upchurch et al. argue that such demise, though, may actually provide some new opportunities for unions. Hence, as they put it (2004, pp. 3–4), neoliberal restructuring

> liberates organized labour from the institutional and ideological fetters of the KWS [Keynesian Welfare State] and provides the basis for trade unions to regain their autonomy and to rebuild themselves as 'movements' in civil society. This implies an oppositional politics in civil society between 'class' and 'society' in which unions rebuild an autonomous power base in civil society in order to articulate a renewed vision capable of mobilizing critical and oppositional movements.

Rather than a general crisis of trade unionism, then, they aver that what has occurred is a crisis of a specific, narrowly based type of unionism and that restructuring affords new opportunities for mobilising opposition in new and different ways. Hence, the decentralisation and fragmentation of work and organisations can open up different avenues for greater involvement and participation of workers, whilst the internationalisation of work and employment, in the state sector as well as elsewhere, reinforces the relevance and salience of international awareness and the necessity of links and concerted action. There are several spatial considerations and conclusions which flow from this analysis, one of which is that because the nation state no longer seems to be the spatial container of economic and political life that it may have been during the era of the Keynesian Welfare State, increasing numbers of unions appear to be thinking about transnational mergers into single entities (as with Nautilus UK and Nautilus Netherlands, two maritime unions whose members voted to form a new Anglo-Dutch union in 2009, and members of firefighters' unions in Australia, the UK, the US, Canada and New Zealand, who are exploring merging into a single transnational entity: see Herod, 2009, Chapter 8 for more details).

In considering new models being developed by unions in response to contemporary events, it could be argued that the union movement in the US, the UK and Australia, at least, has already begun confronting the new realities they face through the medium of adopting 'Organising' as a strategy and setting up variations on the idea of an Organising Academy. Thus, this, on one reading, represents a refocusing from the national and international levels to a more local, workplace-based focus. However, this apparent refocusing is not at all straightforward. Reviewing the experience of ten years of the UK's TUC Academy, Simms and Holgate (2007) conclude that although the academy has been largely successful in training graduates in basic organising skills, some of the more strategic skills are more tentative. Furthermore, many organisers still reported tensions between organising and servicing within their unions and identified a disappointment that they perceived to be a lack of broader cultural change within them.

Another response has been to look to supranational agencies, specifically global union federations, as a means by which to reinvigorate union movements and come to terms with the new spatial realities of the global economy (see Munck and Waterman, Chapter 15 in this volume). Thus, as we have already seen, confronting global value chains requires a coordinated response and there have indeed been attempts to set up global union structures. However, significant questions remain as to the effectiveness to date of efforts to develop global labour organisations with sufficient power to effect real change. Hence, a number of activists from the International Union of Foodworkers have concluded that, despite the rhetoric of internationalism, the actual practice of global labour organising remains sparse and unsystematic (Garver et al., 2007). Drawing upon a review of their experience of the IUF's Nestlé/ Coca-Cola Global Organizing Project, Garver et al. argued for a new approach to connecting the global with the local, calling for fewer international meetings and urging instead that resources be used to hire 'boots on the ground' in the form of full-time, regional coordinators. This strategy also urges moving away from the signing of International Framework Agreements, which are designed to address issues ranging from union rights to child labour to health and safety rules to a company's environmental practices but which do not depend necessarily upon workers being unionised, and towards more directly securing union recognition.

Finally, one other tactic designed to connect the global and the local and which requires negotiating the spatialities of place is that of 'Community Unionism'.

Community unionism

Building solidarity with community groups and social movements is central to a new form of unionism which has been variously labelled 'social movement unionism' or 'community unionism' (although we would suggest that there are significant differences between the two forms). In particular, an emerging body of literature recognises the growing importance of unions moving beyond the workplace and engaging with communities, and there are numerous studies, mostly from the US, which explore the linkages being developed between unions and community groups. In examining such efforts critically, Wills (2001, p. 466) argues that there are four gains that unions can make by forging common cause with community groups and political campaigns:

- community initiatives are able to tackle issues of justice that stretch beyond any particular workplace;
- unions are able to reach non-union workers who have been traditionally marginalised from trade unions;
- unions are able to reach low-paid, contingent manufacturing and service workers who are often located in small workplaces and who have been difficult to reach with traditional organising methods (see also Yates, 2003; Crawford and Ladd 2003); and
- the community can be invaluable in defending traditional workplace trade union organisation.

It is important to recognise, however, that social movement/ community unionism has also been criticised for having serious weaknesses, including that examples of such campaigns are few and far between, that they have tended to be limited to an 'agonised liberalism' that seeks to appeal to the moral conscience of business and political elites though rarely has much political power to enforce its aims, that they tend to involve single issue campaigns and that there are questions as to whether North American models of organising (where much of the idealised models of community organising originate) are applicable in other countries with quite different histories, regulatory agencies and social institutions and spatialities of work and residence (Taylor and Mathers, 2008). As a result of such alleged weaknesses, and in contrast to the community unionism model, Taylor and Mathers (p. 29) suggest that trade union councils might provide a more organic link to workplace organisations and link trade unionists across a range of sectors and industries, so 'connecting workers and unions across a diverse range of problems and issues'. However, here, too, there are issues to address – such councils often have a narrow and ageing demographic profile, have low levels of affiliation by constituent unions and lack resources. In similar vein, Clawson (2003, p. 23) cautions against neglecting too readily traditional union tactics in favour of social movement tactics, suggesting that

> [i]f unions substitute law suits and press conferences for their greatest source of power – the participation and solidarity of millions of members able to disrupt the economic functioning of the system – it will further undercut the unique promise of the labor movement. But if unions are able to combine the new style and tactics with the mass mobilization characteristic of unions at their best, this would create an awesome political force whose potential is only now being explored.

One example of a union seeking to make links between unions and the community and, perhaps, beginning to think somewhat spatially about how the global and the local are interconnected, is that of the GMB in the UK. Hence, Martin Smith, GMB Head of Organising, has argued that if unions cannot support migrant workers in their communities and end their exploitation whilst simultaneously building solidarity with UK workers, then such unions must ask themselves what their role will be in the globalising economy of the twenty-first century where transnational flows of information, goods *and people* will no doubt only continue to grow. At the same time, though, workplace-based organising, as an end in itself, is still important, for strength in the workplace is probably necessary if strong workplace–community linkages are to be developed. In the case of the GMB, then, although the union itself is based on workplaces, organisers have been founding new branches where workers are contacted through bars, churches and Internet cafes in particular communities as a starting point for augmenting worker strength and adapting to the new spatialities of the contemporary economy (see No Sweat, n.d.; see also Shelley, 2007).

Whilst old occupational communities may, then, be breaking down, it is perhaps too crude, though, to argue simply that 'the community' may now be the 'new workplace', especially given how workers are increasingly living lives that are fragmented and geographically isolated from each other – a phenomenon that raises the question of what, exactly, 'community' means in such a context. Nevertheless, community unionism does seem to be a way to confront the new spatialities of the built environment that processes such as work reorganisation, telecommuting, chain migration and the resulting concentrations of immigrant communities are creating. Although community unionism seems to be an organisational response to the new geography of urbanisation that is being recognised by some unions, Lopez (2004, p. 12), however, goes further. He argues that in distinguishing community unionism from the organising model it is important to realise that community unionism involves not simply a shopping list of tactics but is, rather, a process of change within the labour movement itself, one that is about developing a vision of powerful participatory unions that is very different from the old 'member servicing' varieties of unionism common in many of the industrialised countries during the past half century. Taking a slightly different perspective, for Clawson (2003, p. 92) social movement/ community unionism may really be not so much a new form of organising but a rebirth of old forms that would have been familiar to activists 100 or so years ago (see also Cobble, 1991). However, it does represent a paradigmatic break with the recent past.

For Schenk (2003), too, community unionism is about more than securing a few tactical victories. Rather, for him the central issue facing unions today, if they are to be effective counterweights to transnationally organised capital and to help workers to exert a greater degree of control over their lives, both in and out of the workplace, is the necessity of connecting the democratic basis of the organising model to an alternative vision of society based on equality strategies, the reaffirmation of class-based identities and a celebration of the primacy of rank-and-file trade unionism. The task that awaits, then, is to articulate union and worker issues in a framework of community needs and thereby to overcome the sectional self-interests that have so often plagued various labour movements. Significantly, this vision is highly spatial, for it extends worker praxis beyond the workplace to the labour movement and society as a whole. Lopez (2004, p. 19) argues that such a commitment to social justice, where campaigns are more than simply a union matter, can help overcome internal union organisational blocks and help overcome members' servicing expectations. Meanwhile, Crawford and Ladd (2003, p. 55) suggest that bringing the community development philosophy into debates on union renewal, combined with an examination of working across worksites, elevates an understanding of community unionism as working-class resistance that is simultaneously anti-racist, socialist and feminist.

Logistics, value chains and resistance

In this final section, we seek to bring together our arguments concerning regionality, value chains, worker organisation and resistance through a brief look at one industry, that of the rapidly growing logistics sector. This is a sector that has dramatically grown in importance globally in recent years. In some way, the sector epitomises the transformation of the economic landscape which seems to be at the heart of contemporary processes of globalisation, as the interconnectedness of the new economy, changing relationships between customers and suppliers, just-in-time systems, flexible production and extensive production and service networks demand sophisticated circulation and distribution processes. The global logistics industries themselves are now huge, worth over $4 billion per year. Major organisations include transportation companies, logistics providers, wholesalers, trading companies, retailers and e-tailers. By 2003 major companies such as Deutsche Post and UPS employed more than a third of a million workers each, whilst by 2005 Deutsche Post World Net (owner of DHL) had acquired Excel and was employing around 500 000 people worldwide (Dicken, [1998] 2007). Such growth has implications for the nature of work far beyond simple numerical considerations. Hence, when DHL won the logistics contract for Britain's National Health Service in October 2005, it was reported that they wished to move to a model of 30 per cent employed staff and 70 per cent self-employed or temporary staff, a significant transformation in the workforce's characteristics (Stirling, 2007).

For trade unions, the logistics sector is vital, not just as a new(ish) sector to be organised but also in terms of the global value chain. Hence, if workers and their advocates are to analyse the strengths and weaknesses of the new international systems of production that characterise much of the contemporary global economy so that they might develop appropriate strategies to challenge them, then they must locate individual units within the global value chain. This is because the logistics systems of companies like Wal-Mart, which has a system claimed to be the most efficient in the world, affect not only such companies' own employees but also those of their suppliers, producers, transportation companies and many more indirectly. These companies criss-cross the planet in a net of uneven contractual relationships in which Wal-Mart has secured the power effectively to tell its suppliers how to manufacture their goods, with which other companies such suppliers will and will not themselves trade and myriad other sets of conditions that are placed on suppliers who wish 'the honour' of supplying the merchandising behemoth. In dealing with changes in the organisation and labour markets of companies such as the UK supermarkets, and what this means for workers' abilities to organise, therefore, we have to look at the whole integrated circuit from production through distribution to point-of-sale (nationally and internationally) (Bonacich and Wilson, 2005).

Nevertheless, despite the image of Wal-Mart and other such large globally organised firms as unchallengeable, we can see weaknesses in these companies' system of distribution. Thus, just-in-time distribution is highly vulnerable to disruption by relatively small groups of strategically placed workers, a fact that General Motors discovered (again) in 2008 when a strike of 3600 United Auto Workers members at American Axle forced the idling of more than 40 000 workers in 30 GM plants and shut down a number of parts plants throughout North America (Feeley, 2008).[4] The key for the workers, of course, is to know something about the geography of the supply chain so that they may identify 'choke points' which can be easily struck to great effect.[5] As the 2008 GM dispute illustrated, any such disruption is not only highly visible but can also be very costly for the company so targeted. As Bonacich and Wilson (2005) argue, then, although global logistics may be a point of strength, allowing firms to network various places across the planet into a highly integrated production and distribution system, they can also be the weak point of such global production systems. However, to be fully sensitive to the strengths and weaknesses of global value chains for car workers or migrant care workers (see Yeates, 2004) or anyone else, we have to employ spatial concepts like those of the spatial fix and the politics of place, as we have argued above. Understanding the geographical role of a particular node in a global value chain is thus crucial if we are to understand, for instance, the labour process or how the state operates. As Turnbull (2007, pp. 117–18) has demonstrated in his analysis of port labour (a group of workers that are central players in the logistics sector), such an approach results in a much more sophisticated form of analysis, particularly as it can show how workers and unions may generate unintended geographical outcomes by their actions, outcomes which themselves then serve as the focal points for new rounds of struggle and compromise. Hence, he suggests,

[t]he major concern for port labor in the global era is that by redefining the scale and scope of their operations, global transport companies have effectively reconstituted the geography of social relations among capital, labor and the state, considerably strengthening their own power and control while disempowering others. This is not to suggest that trade unions in the transport sector are now powerless in the face of globalization. On the contrary, a combination of associational power, arising from well-established collective organizations, and structural power, arising from the strategic location of transport workers in the economic system, . . . has led to a robust defense of transport workers' interests. . . . Moreover, the immobility of infrastructure capital and the strategic localization of global companies . . . mean that capital must be sufficiently embedded to exploit labor as a factor of location and not just a factor of production. As a result, transport companies are less likely to use relocation as a strategy to reduce cost in response to declining profitability. For transport workers, however, this can lead to a defense of their local place over the defense of wider, international, class interests. Transport unions, for example, have often cooperated with, or conceded to, the demands of capital and the nation state to restructure their port in order to make it more competitive in the international market for port services, which has typically involved a combination of job losses, greater flexibility, and a deterioration in dockworkers' terms and conditions of employment. . . . Even if transport unions think globally, they invariably act locally.

The point to be made here, then, is that firms like Wal-Mart and others clearly think in geographical terms. We would venture to suggest that workers and their advocates need to do likewise.

Summary

Neither workers nor capital are mere passive elements in the geographies of social relations, for both actively construct the world around them. The control of space and place is thus crucial to the way that jobs are exported, created, lost and fought over. As Hudson (2001) puts it, capital can be thought of as trying to disorganise labour by means of segmenting the labour market (by place, gender, ethnicity and so on), whereas labour seeks to organise (through trade unions and other worker organisations) in order to improve conditions in the labour market. It is therefore impossible, we would aver, to fully understand the dynamics of such struggles without consideration of how, on the one hand, capital seeks its 'spatial fix' as it must embed itself in particular places for the production of surplus value to occur and, on the other, how workers' lives are also deeply spatially contextualised and embedded. However, whereas both capital and labour are always spatially embedded to a degree – after all, social life does not occur on the head of a pin – both must also seek to maintain a degree of geographical mobility: capital to look for new arenas of investment where profits can be secured, and labour for greener fields where wages or working conditions may be better.

For both capital and labour, negotiating the tensions between these contradictory needs for fixity and mobility is, then, a fundamental part of their social activity. Nonetheless, it is important to recognise that different factions within capital and labour may view these tensions quite differently, depending upon their own embeddedness. Hence, some firms may wish to see other firms stay embedded in local places (perhaps if the former are suppliers of a local manufacturer who might lose business if the manufacturer relocates) whilst others may prefer to see them go (perhaps competitors who are now left as monopoly employers in the local community and can use this position to secure concessions from workers). Likewise, some segments of labour may like to see some groups of workers leave the community (thereby reducing the ability of employers to pick and choose amongst them, which gives them power to reduce wages) whereas other segments may prefer to see workers migrate into the community (perhaps if there is too little labour to attract circulating investment). However, the economic, social and political landscapes that ensue from these contradictory and contested relationships have repercussions long after the social relationships that initially produced them have changed. These landscapes can, to coin a phrase, weigh like a nightmare on the minds of the living.

Lest we forget about agency right at the end of this summary, though, in this context it is perhaps appropriate to reflect on Katz's (2004) distinction between resistance, reworking and resilience and to consider how these might have bearing for understanding how the landscapes made in the past, which so weigh on the minds of the living, are themselves subsequently transformed. Thus Katz distinguishes between: a) resistance, which, she suggests, requires oppositional consciousness but seeks to secure emancipatory change; b) other forms of reworking spatialities, which alter the organisation but not the polarisation of power relations; and c) forms of resilience that enable people to survive without really changing the circumstances that make such survival so hard (see Sparke, 2008, p. 424). Of course, these options are shaped differently in different sites, depending upon the institutions and social structures in place in them, and also have an uneven impact on the extant economic landscape.

Having explored issues of spatial embeddedness, place, how local labour markets are regulated geographically and how workers' strategies must be explored through a spatial lens, we now turn to introducing the chapters that comprise Parts 3 and 4 of the book.

Preview of Parts 3 and 4

Section 3.1   Labour institutions in space and place
Section 3.1 deals with workers and institutions, the spatial contexts within which they must act, and the geographical implications of such actions. Several sets of issues are addressed. One of these is the matter of how territoriality shapes unions' activities and possibilities for action. Thus, both German and Mexican unions, for instance, have had to come to terms with a significant reworking of their national space-economies. In the German case, the unions have had to engage with the emergence of a post-Westphalian state in which national boundaries have become much more porous than was the case when the extant model of German labour relations was developed in the early post-WWII era, whilst in the Mexican case traditionally non-industrialised regions (like the northern border region) have come to serve as laboratories within which neoliberal models of work have been developed and from which they have been diffused to other parts of the country. Another set of geographical concerns relates to the geographical rescaling of various labour organisations and what this means for how they function and for how the economic and political landscapes of capitalism are being remade. A third set of issues considers how the geographical organisation of capital in places as divergent as Western Australia and South Africa shapes unions' organisational strategies and how these strategies, in turn, mould how the economic landscape is produced. Finally, there is the matter of the shrinking of distance that modern telecommunications technologies have facilitated and how this has been a double-edged sword for unions – on the one hand, it has allowed firms in, for instance, the telemarketing industry to relocate to

places like India whereas on the other it has enabled workers to connect more easily with fellow workers across the planet through the use of cyber-campaigns.

With regard to individual chapters, Munck and Waterman (Chapter 15) explore how workers might move beyond local, regional and national scales of social contestation to take on capital at a global scale. The authors aver that we need to delve into the historical and structural context of transnational labour practices before examining current dilemmas, combining Polanyian analysis with insights drawn from the spatial turn in labour relations. Having done so, Munck and Waterman argue for a multiscalar labour politics that struggles at all levels simultaneously, and is capable of 'jumping scale' where necessary. However, whilst emphasising that this is not a message of hopelessness, the authors do stress the complexity and difficulty of operationalising this multiscalar international project.

Berndt (Chapter 16) examines the role that territory played in the creation of the institutions that have been central to the development of the 'German Model' of labour relations. Specifically, Berndt argues that this model was based upon a fairly geographically circumscribed, nationally organised space-economy with limited cross-border mobility of both capital and labour. However, whereas this model allowed for relatively high standards of living for a core of the workforce, a new model – one which privileges mobility over stability – has now emerged. Specifically, the growing presence of 'low skilled' transnational migrant labour, much of it now coming from Eastern Europe, and imports of cheap goods have undermined the postwar national compromise. Paradoxically, though, Berndt concludes that the belief that the German space-economy ever could be territorially contained behind fairly impermeable national borders was actually always somewhat illusory, remaining plausible only as long as the underlying contradictions within it remained invisible. Nevertheless, this spatial image of territorial enclosure was central to how German labour–management relations functioned for the half century since the end of WWII.

Fitzgerald and Stirling (Chapter 17), meanwhile, contemplate European Works Councils (EWCs) which, they argue, have established an infrastructure through which multinational trade union solidarities can develop, whilst at the same time they seek to confront territorial competition for jobs and work. As Fitzgerald and Stirling point out, EWCs must walk a geographical tightrope, being sensitive to local conditions in particular plants whilst also looking at conditions across much wider swaths of territory and corporate structure. This spatial tension can cause problems, though. Hence, the contradictions of place and space, solidarity and fragmentation must be worked out by the real activities of worker representatives in an institutional framework imposed by government (the European Union Commission), generally unwelcomed by employers and often unknown to the participants. Despite their limitations, though, the authors suggest that EWCs do, in fact, offer some opportunity to influence working and other conditions, in spite of severe constraints imposed by employers and organisational structures, and that this opportunity is greatly shaped by the relationship between the EWC and local representatives.

Finally, De la Garza (Chapter 18) focuses upon the role that the *maquila* sector and the new assembly plants for the automobile industry are playing as prototypes for a new labour relations model in Mexico. In particular, although this model, characterised by low wages, high quit rates, and weak unionism, was developed in a region of the country which stood outside the traditional industrial heartland in which corporatist unions had long held sway, it is now being diffused to other regions in Mexico. Effectively, neoliberal work practices have been developed in the largely non-union geographical laboratory of northern Mexico for perfecting before being unleashed on the rest of the country's space-economy. Put another way, capital is seeking to produce a fresh spatial fix, one based on a territorialisation of what De la Garza calls 'precarious Toyotaism'. However, whilst the goal of industrialists has been to spread this new model across Mexico's national space-economy, there is emerging evidence that, just like Fordism before it, this new model and attempts to diffuse it geographically has problems and contradictions for capital also.

Section 3.2   Organising in space and place

Section 3.2 focuses more pointedly on questions of worker organisation and resistance. The chapters deal with issues that range from the need for a New Labour Internationalism to the practicalities of organising in cyberspace. However, a conclusion to be drawn from all the chapters is the importance for worker organisation, in both theory and practice, of operationalising the sort of spatial analysis we advocate in this book. Based upon these analyses, it is clear that any call for new (often, multiscalar) forms of organisation needs a level-headed and nuanced scrutiny both of how workers' spatial embeddedness shapes their political praxis and of the spatial implications of current patterns of restructuring and worker response.

Given the above, in his chapter on the Australian mining industry, Ellem's central contention (Chapter 19) is that in the plentiful literature seeking to explain union membership decline across many countries there has been a paucity of detailed considerations of the geography of that decline, whilst even the few studies that have considered union decline geographically have, paradoxically, frequently been rather spatially simplistic – for example, they tend to look at the phenomenon from a national or, less frequently, a regional basis to compare patterns between countries/regions without really examining how local complexities, processes and cultural traditions shape the landscape of unionism at sub-regional scales. However, unionism, Ellem contends, is constructed and challenged not at a national scale alone, but at many scales, including the local, a fact which means that we must focus on the multiscalar nature of the geography of union decline if we are to understand it and, perhaps, help to develop strategies to counter it. In response to his critique of more traditional approaches to understanding union decline, and using an examination of iron ore mining in the Pilbara region of Western Australia, Ellem demonstrates clearly why geography matters, in that the spatial and the social cannot be separated from each other. The processes shaping unions do literally 'take place' and the meanings of, and power over, space change in mutually constitutive ways. Based upon his analysis of the spatial strategies of mining companies who have sought to deunionise their labour forces, Ellem concludes that lack of spatial awareness is not just an element in an academic debate. Rather, capital, the state and labour constantly argue over, use and remake space in efforts to outmanoeuvre each other and to secure political and economic power. How these actors make space, then, is as important as how they make history, even if it has hitherto been less recognised.

Following from this, Bezuidenhout and Webster (Chapter 20) draw on the experience of workers in the white goods (household durables) industry in South Africa to provide an important spatial dimension to Beverly Silver's (2003) Polanyian analysis of crises of legitimacy and profitability within capitalism. Silver explored the process of 'boundary drawing' wherein particular groups of workers are 'cut in' or 'cut out' of partial and temporary attempts by capital to ease the tensions of these interrelated crises. As Silver pointed out, boundary drawing can take the form of the creation of segmented labour markets, the provision through citizenship of certain rights that others (non-citizens) do not enjoy or, indeed, workers forming boundaries themselves (as when certain types of workers might be excluded from unions on the basis of, say, race). The authors argue, however, that these boundaries are not just social but are invariably spatial and subject to contestation and negotiation. Boundary drawing, then, leads to a series of spatial fixes – social, technological and product – all of which have geographical tensions incorporated within them. Through their exploration of social boundaries' spatial constitution and how corporations have engaged in strategies of geographical restructuring (and how unions, in turn, have developed new spatial and scalar strategies to confront the fresh corporate spatial fixes which have been enacted in the post-apartheid period), then, Bezuidenhout and Webster extend Silver's analysis by considering capital, the state and labour implicitly as spatial agents. Thus, central to labour's power in the South African case were workplace-based shop steward committees, which were able to build linkages from the local to the national level and to draw on international solidarity – that is, they were able to 'jump' scales of organisation from the very local to the global.

For their part, Anderson, Hamilton and Wills (Chapter 21) suggest that globalisation has altered the scalar architecture of capitalism and that this is having important implications for trade unions. The emergence of transnational corporations (TNCs), global cities and new transportation nodes challenges the limitations of contemporary trade union organisation, which typically focuses upon workplaces and national trade union structures. Although the chapter draws on a number of examples of current union response to changing patterns of work and organisation, the main focus is on the ways in which the US Service Employees' International Union (SEIU) has led efforts to target TNCs in contract cleaning, catering and security industries. This is followed by an examination of living wage campaigns in low-waged urban labour markets. The examples detailed highlight the need to develop multiscalar approaches to organising workers that include the strategic targeting of corporate power centres, organising across geographical zones rather than in just workplaces, and the development of extra-workplace networks.

Lambert and Gillan (Chapter 22), meanwhile, are concerned with what they describe as the New Labour Internationalism (NLI), which they contrast with long-standing models of existing labour internationalism that they see as being uninspiring, fixated on lobbying and dominated by an ideology of social partnership. For them, one of the things that is different is that the NLI has a much more developed sense of space and spatiality and how matters geographical must be addressed by workers and unions seeking to challenge an increasingly globally organised capital than does the more traditional approach to transnational organising. However, they suggest too that the NLI is not yet fully formed and is very much still in the process of 'becoming'. Drawing upon a number of cases, including the Southern Initiative on Globalisation and Trade Union Rights (SIGTUR) and the creation of the Mining and Maritime Global Initiative (MAMGI), Lambert and Gillan show how unions and civil society movements actively structure spatial and scalar relations to re-empower labour but also caution that efforts to develop new spatialities and scales of organisation invariably spawn political struggles as the NLI model runs up against the institutional inertia of the existing model of labour internationalism.

Whereas much analysis of contemporary capitalism has suggested that it has rescaled itself as many segments of capital have become increasingly globally organised, another central aspect of contemporary discourses of globalisation has been that of the shrinking of our globe facilitated by the annihilation of space by time, of which Marx and others have spoken. Indeed, the geographical consequences for interaction across space occasioned by telecommunications technologies has been quite remarkable. This transformation in the geographical relationships between different parts of the world, uneven as it has been (some places are much more highly interconnected and the distances between them have shrunk to a much greater extent than is the case between other places), has posed both challenges and opportunities for workers and unions. In light of these geographical restructurings, more than ten years ago Eric Lee (Chapter 23) launched LabourStart, a portal for trade union members around the world through which they could keep in contact and, more importantly, organise for change. In his chapter, then, Lee details the history of LabourStart and looks at the way that cyberspace can help overcome the problems that distance can create for union organisation. The chapter deals in particular with how LabourStart spreads information to trade union activists across the globe and how online campaigning has developed. Lee confronts the issue of campaign fatigue but argues that the new communication technologies can amplify the effect of tried and tested techniques, such as solidarity fund-raising, boycotts and traditional real world mobilisation.

Finally, for Taylor and Bain (Chapter 24) business process offshoring is now a core, if not uncontradictory, corporate strategy, with India (because of its relatively high educational levels and the fact that competence in the English language is quite widespread) seen as a significant site for relocation. Thus, an image that emerges in much of the neoliberal rhetoric about the need for capital to have no national loyalties and to be sufficiently mobile as to take advantage of new opportunities that arise elsewhere is that companies, particularly in the financial services, will inevitably migrate from countries such as the UK to India, with the related loss of union membership and wider influence in the country just abandoned. Related to this is the image of English-speaking graduates in India welcoming new employment possibilities. In confronting these images (which are often more myth than reality, as capital is neither as mobile, and Indian workers are not always as happy about working in places like call centres, as the rhetoric portrays), Taylor and Bain argue that the uneven geographical development of global servicing brings parallel and intertwined (although contrasting and asymmetrical) challenges and opportunities for trade unions in both the UK and India. In particular, such relocation from the UK to India links workers in these two places in ways that they had not previously been connected, thereby opening possibilities for transnational labour activities. In this light, the authors examine the nature and effectiveness of some UK-based initiatives to prevent or mitigate redundancies caused by relocation, following this with an examination of the potential for union organisation in India. In particular, they spotlight the formation in India amongst call centre workers of UNITES (the Union of Information Technology-Enabled Services Professionals) under the aegis of the UNI, the Global Union Federation for service-sector workers. The creation of UNITES illustrates that, for all its efforts to escape unions through strategies of geographical relocation, capital can always expect to find workers who are willing to band together to defend what they perceive to be their interests.

Part 4

The book concludes with an Afterword in Part 4. Given the terrain which this *Handbook* embraces, and its dual purpose of both documenting the status quo of the dialogue between geography and the study of work and employment, and forging new frontiers in this engagement, it is appropriate to reflect briefly in order to consider how this informs future directions. Castree (Chapter 25) concludes by considering from whence labour geography has come and highlighting where it might go from here on. Noting the 'spatial turn' and the quite rapid maturation of geographers' study of labour, he observes, first, that labour geography is no longer the preserve of professional geographers and, secondly, that this is celebrated and welcomed by geographers. Castree presents several areas in which he considers that labour geography, as currently constituted, requires further development and undertakes a 'stock take' of the subdiscipline's 'fundamentals' (assumptions, aims, normative values) with a view to ensuring they are appropriately robust for the task of understanding and interpreting the world. From this review, Castree identifies seven aspects that he proposes warrant strengthening. These include: aspects of agency; the phenomenon of labour migration; the 'blind spot' of the state; the need for greater synthesis of geographical concepts; the necessity of putting working people at the centre of analysis; the importance of making explicit embedded implicit 'moral geographies' (the values relating to modes of conduct); and the need to further strengthen labour geography's evaluative and policy contributions/impact. Castree follows this by showing the value of systematic thinking about the geographies of labour. Labour geography, he proposes, is never about labour alone but about working people in a more-than-capitalist world. He challenges those who undertake labour geography (from within and beyond the formal boundaries of the professional or academic discipline) to engage in what he refers to as 'joined-up analysis' – connected, integrated, synthetic analysis – of how economies, forms of work and their geographies co-constitute one another.

Notes

1. To give but one brief example of such instantaneity, within minutes of the first hijacked plane hitting the World Trade Center in New York City on 11 September 2001, stock markets in London, Germany and Brazil had begun to respond negatively, whilst by the end of the trading day on London's FTSE 100 index, British Airways's stock had dropped some 20 per cent in value on fears that oil prices would spike and fewer people would fly (Herod, 2009, p. 5).

2. This appears to be different from the case of the US, though, a fact which simply reinforces the geographical complexities which we seek to highlight here. Thus, in 2000 some 29 600 000 workers (22 per cent of the labour force) worked fewer than 35 hours a week, whilst 27 per cent of workers had worked for their current employer for fewer than 12 months, 8 per cent had worked for their current employer for 12–23 months, 5 per cent had worked for their current employer for 24–35 months, and 16 per cent had worked for their current employer for 3–4 yrs: in other words, 56 per cent of workers had worked for their current employer for fewer than 4 years (Herod, 2007).

3. To pick just one example of this sentiment, we might turn to Richard Trumka (1991, p. 4), Secretary-Treasurer, AFL-CIO, who has stated that 'If we're going to be able to effectively challenge companies like Shell or Exxon or DuPont and other corporations which operate without regard to national boundaries, we have to redefine solidarity in global terms'. Myriad other such examples exist.

4. We say 'again' because GM had had a similar experience in 1998 (Herod, 2000).

5. This does not mean that there are not also weaknesses to such a strategy. For instance, relying on striking those plants that are choke-hold sites may win a strike but may not do much for broader solidarity across

all the worksites represented by the union. The point, then, is not to suggest that this is always the best strategy nor that it would work in all situations. Rather, we suggest that workers and their advocates must be sensitive to how a particular firm is organised economically and geographically and what openings this organisation might present workers. We echo, again, then, the words of Leitner et al. (2008), that different elements of spatiality may need to be emphasised at different times in different places, depending on the spatial specificities of any given dispute.

References

Agger, B. (1989), *Fast Capitalism*, Urbana, IL: University of Illinois Press.
Barrientos, S. (2007), 'Migrant and contract labour in global production systems', paper presented at the 'Living on the Margins' conference, Stellenbosch, South Africa, 26–28 March.
Bartram, D. (2005), *International Labour Migration: Foreign Workers and Public Policy*, Basingstoke: Palgrave Macmillan.
Beynon, H. (1973), *Working for Ford*, Harmondsworth: Penguin.
Bonacich, E. and J.B. Wilson (2005), 'Hoisted by its own petard: organizing Wal-Mart's logistic workers', *New Labor Forum*, **14** (2), 67–75.
Callinicos, A. (1999), *Social Theory: A Historical Introduction*, Cambridge: Polity.
Castree, N., N. Coe, K. Ward and M. Samers (2004), *Spaces of Work: Global Capitalism and Geographies of Labour*, London: Sage.
Clawson, D. (2003), *The Next Upsurge: Labor and the New Social Movements*, Ithaca, NY: Cornell University Press.
Cobble, D.S. (1991), 'Organizing the postindustrial work force: lessons from the history of waitress unionism', *Industrial and Labor Relations Review*, **44**, 419–36.
Crawford, C. and D. Ladd (2003), 'Community unionism: organizing for fair employment in Canada', *Just Labour*, **3**, 46–59.
Darlington, R. (2005), 'Workplace union militancy on Merseyside since the 1960s: extent, nature, causes and decline', *Historical Studies in Industrial Relations*, **19**, 123–52.
Dicken, P. ([1998] 2007), *Global Shift: Mapping the Changing Contours of the World Economy*, 5th edn, New York: Guilford Press.
Ellem, B. and S. McGrath-Champ (2002), 'Industrial relations meets human geography: spatialising the social relations of work', *Labour & Industry*, **13** (2), 1–4.
Feeley, D. (2008), 'Everything's on the line at AAM', *Against the Current*, **134** (May/June), available at www.solidarity-us.org/atc/archives; last accessed 4 April 2009.
Florida, R.L. (2002), *The Rise of the Creative Class: And How it's Transforming Work, Leisure, Community and Everyday Life*, New York: Basic Books.
Foucault, M. (1986), 'Of other spaces', *Diacritics*, **16** (1), 22–7.
Garver, P., K. Buketov, H. Chong and B.S. Martinez (2007), 'Global labor organizing in theory and practice', *Labor Studies Journal*, **32** (3), 237–56.
Harvey, D. (2001), *Spaces of Capital*, New York: Routledge.
Herod, A. (1991), 'Local political practice in response to a manufacturing plant closure: how geography complicates class analysis', *Antipode*, **23** (4), 385–402.
Herod, A. (2000), 'Implications of just-in-time production for union strategy: lessons from the 1998 General Motors-United Auto Workers dispute', *Annals of the Association of American Geographers*, **90** (3), 521–47. [Publisher's erratum for figures published *Annals of the Association of American Geographers*, (2001) **91** (1), 200–02.]
Herod, A. (2006), 'Trotsky's omission: labour's role in combined and uneven development', in B. Dunn and H. Radice (eds), *100 Years of Permanent Revolution: Results and Prospects*, London: Pluto Press, pp. 152–65.
Herod, A. (2007), 'Labour organizing in the New Economy: examples from the USA and beyond', in P. Daniels, A. Leyshon, M. Bradshaw and J. Beaverstock (eds), *Geographies of the New Economy: Critical Reflections*, London: Routledge, pp. 132–50.
Herod, A. (2009), *Geographies of Globalization: A Critical Introduction*, Oxford: Wiley-Blackwell.
Hobsbawm, E. and T. Ranger (1983), *The Invention of Tradition*, Cambridge: Cambridge University Press.
Hudson, R. (2001), *Producing Places*, New York: Guilford Press.
Hudson, R. (2002), 'Changing industrial production systems and regional development in the New Europe', *Transactions of the Institute of British Geographers*, New Series, **27** (3), 262–81.
Huws, U. (2008), 'Break or weld?: Trade union responses to global value chain restructuring', *Work Organisation, Labour and Globalisation*, **2** (1), 1–10.
Hyman, R. (2001), 'European integration and industrial relations: a case of variable geometry?', *Antipode*, **33** (3), 468–83.
Hyman, R. (2002), 'The future of unions', *Just Labour*, **1** (Winter), 7–15.

Jonas, A.E.G. (1996), 'Local labour control regimes: uneven development and the social regulation of production', *Regional Studies*, **30** (4), 323–38.

Jones, A. (2008), 'The rise of global work', *Transactions of the Institute of British Geographers*, New Series, **33** (1), 12–26.

Katz, C. (2004), *Growing up Global: Economic Restructuring and Children's Everyday Lives*, Minneapolis, MN: University of Minnesota Press.

Leitner, H., E. Sheppard and K. Sziarto (2008), 'The spatialities of contentious politics', *Transactions of the Institute of British Geographers*, New Series, **33**, 157–72.

Lopez, S.H. (2004), *Reorganizing the Rustbelt: An Inside Study of the American Labor Movement*, Berkeley, CA: University of California Press.

MacShane, D. (2008), 'What the transatlantic trade unions can do', *The Guardian*, 2 July, available at www.guardian.co.uk/commentisfree/2008/jul/02/tradeunions.usa; accessed 22 April, 2009.

May, J., J. Wills, K. Datta, Y. Evans, J. Herbert and C. McIlwaine (2006), 'The British state and London's migrant division of labour', working paper, Department of Geography, Queen Mary, University of London.

Mittelman, J.H. (2000), *The Globalization Syndrome: Transformation and Resistance*, Princeton, NJ: Princeton University Press.

No Sweat (n.d.), 'Solidarity with migrant workers', London: No Sweat Publication.

Paasi, A. (2003), 'Region and place: regional identity in question', *Progress in Human Geography*, **27** (4), 475–85.

Peck, J. (1996), *Work-Place: The Social Regulation of Labor Markets*, New York: Guilford Press.

Rainnie, A. and R. Paulet (2003), 'Images of community, industrial relations and regional development', *Australasian Journal of Regional Studies*, **9** (2), 151–68.

Robertson, D., J. Smyth and I. McIntosh (2008), *Neighborhood Identity*, York: Joseph Rowntree Foundation.

Schenk, C. (2003), 'Social movement unionism: beyond the organizing model', in P. Fairbrother and C.A.B. Yates (eds), *Trade Unions in Renewal: A Comparative Study*, London: Routledge, pp. 244–63.

Shelley, T. (2007), *Exploited: Immigrant Labour in the New Global Economy*, London: Zed Books.

Silver, B. (2003), *Forces of Labor: Workers' Movements and Globlization since 1870*, Cambridge: Cambridge University Press.

Simms, M. and J. Holgate (2007), 'TUC Academy ten years on', paper presented at the Work, Employment and Society conference, Aberdeen, September.

Smith, C. (2006), 'The double indeterminacy of labour power', *Work, Employment and Society*, **20** (2), 389–402.

Sparke, M. (2008), 'Political geography – political geographies of globalization III: resistance', *Progress in Human Geography*, **32** (3), 423–40.

Stirling, J. (2007), 'Temporary, agency and vulnerable working', report prepared for the Northern Region TUC, Newcastle-Upon-Tyne.

Storper, M. and R. Walker (1989), *The Capitalist Imperative: Territory, Technology, and Industrial Growth*, New York: Basil Blackwell.

Strangleman, T. (2001), 'Networks, place and identities in post-industrial mining communities', *International Journal of Urban and Regional Research*, **25** (2), 253–67.

Taylor, G. and A. Mathers (2008), 'Organising unions, organising communities: trades union councils and Community Union Politics in England and Wales', working paper, Department of Sociology and Criminology, University of West of England.

Trumka, R. (1991), Statement by Richard Trumka, Secretary-Treasurer, AFL-CIO, in *Labor Notes*, November, p. 4.

Turnbull, P. (2006), 'The war on Europe's waterfront: repertoires of power in the port transport industry', *British Journal of Industrial Relations*, **44** (2), 305–26.

Turnbull, P. (2007), 'Dockers versus the directives: battling port policy on the European waterfront', in K. Bronfenbrenner (ed.), *Global Unions: Challenging Transnational Capital through Cross-Border Campaigns*, Ithaca, NY: Cornell University Press, pp. 117–36.

Upchurch, M., A. Mathers and G. Taylor (2004), 'New strategies of UK unions', mimeo, University of West of England.

Wills, J. (1998), 'Space, place and tradition in working-class organization', in A. Herod (ed.), *Organizing the Landscape: Geographical Perspectives on Labor Unionism*, Minneapolis, MN: University of Minnesota Press, pp. 129–58.

Wills, J. (2001), 'Community unionism and trade union renewal in the UK: moving beyond the fragments at last?', *Transactions of the Institute of British Geographers*, New Series, **26** (4), 465–83.

Yates, C.A.B. (2003), 'The revival of industrial unions in Canada: the extension and adaptation of industrial union practices to the new economy', in P. Fairbrother and C. Yates (eds), *Trade Unions in Renewal: A Comparative Study*, London: Routledge, pp. 221–43.

Yeates, N. (2004), 'Global care chains', *International Feminist Journal of Politics*, **6** (3), 369–91.

Yeung, H.W.-C. (2002), 'Industrial geography: industrial restructuring and labour markets', *Progress in Human Geography*, **26** (3), 367–79.

Section 3.1

Labour Institutions in Space and Place

15 Global unions versus global capital: or, the complexity of transnational labour relations
Ronaldo Munck and Peter Waterman

Introduction

The international trade union movement is now confronting the challenges that globalisation poses to workers across the world. Has labour thus 'gone global' to confront the new model of (global) capitalism? Should workers simply move beyond the local, regional and national scales of social contestation to take on global capitalism? To answer these fundamental questions, we need to delve into the historical and structural context of transnational labour practices before examining current dilemmas and strategic responses. Whilst the symmetry and apparently inexorable logic of global unions defending labour against global capital seems appealing, we argue instead for an approach focused on the spatial complexity of transnational labour relations. A crucial element in any understanding of this complex domain must be a sustained focus on the geographical moment of labour organising and contestation of the rule of capital. We argue for a multiscalar labour politics that struggles at all levels simultaneously and is capable of 'jumping scales' where necessary. In addressing these issues we initially set out a possible conceptual framework and consider, in turn, histories, structures, divisions, dilemmas and strategies in the realm of international labour relations.

Frameworks

A decade ago, the International Confederation of Free Trade Unions (ICFTU) declared that globalisation posed 'the greatest challenge for unions in the 21st Century' (ICFTU, 1997). Since then, there has been a growing mood that labour needs to 'go global' to confront the new more internationalised capitalist order we live under. If the global economy is producing a global workforce, then, so the argument goes, global unions seem a logical development. Global economic power might be seen to inexorably produce a global social counter-power. Or, in Polanyian terms, the expansion of the market that lies at the heart of what we call globalisation generates a social counter-movement by which society (and social forces therein) protect themselves from the ravages of the free or unregulated market. That this social process has a spatial dimension is clear enough, even if we just take our references to the 'global' as an indicator of space.

There is now a growing body of literature taking up the Karl Polanyi-inspired focus on the expansion of the free market and the social counter-movement it creates (see Munck, 2002; Silver, 2003; Webster et al., 2008). There has also been a separate, somewhat unrelated, spatial turn in international labour studies (see Herod, 2001; Castree et al., 2004) which stresses how labour relations are embedded in space as much as they are embedded socially. Debates around the 'political economy of scale' (Taylor, 1982) and the underlying notion that 'space is a social construct' (Lefebvre, 1991) have drawn our attention towards a hitherto neglected (except within geography) domain. Social relations simply cannot be conceived without understanding how they are grounded in particular places. Thus the spatial dimensions of transnational labour relations and transnational labour solidarity are crucial to their understanding. Furthermore, contending political projects inevitably contain a particular spatial vision. The forces of capital have their range of spatial fixes, to maintain accumulation and healthy profit rates. Labour likewise has, or needs to have, its own – and often quite different – spatial vision and politics of place. As Neil Smith put it somewhat cryptically, 'The scale of struggle and the struggle over scale are two sides of the same coin' (1993, p. 101).

We would argue that there is now a need to bring together and synthesise the Polanyi and the spatial turns to shape a new transnational, trans-scalar labour studies. In this regard, if we were to construct a basic social–spatial matrix to set our own narrative of labour's varied and multidimensional responses to globalisation in context, it would look something like that shown in Figure 15.1. In this diagram, the horizontal element sets up a basic Polanyian tension between labour organisations that primarily represent workers in the labour market defending the price for their labour power (the left-hand side) and those labour organisations which are more socially embedded (the right-hand side) and take workers to be part of a broader society and community. Trade union strategies might thus be categorised in terms of whether they lean more towards market discipline or take social need as a priority. However, they are also pulled in different spatial ways, from the global (at the top) to the local (at the bottom), reflecting the different scales of human activity. Neither the Polanyian horizontal tension nor the scalar or vertical element can be seen as self-sufficient; rather, they act in a combined, if uneven, manner.

Certainly, the spatial dimension has always been with us, but it is probably fair to say that it has been insufficiently theorised. Anyone who has been involved in labour activities in the South and East, as we have, must be conscious of geography, to put things at their most basic. Indeed, our own engagement with globalisation at 'global', regional, national and local levels has heightened that awareness. Nevertheless, we now need to bring to the fore much more explicitly that labour relations and labour movements are always spatially specific. Our social place in society is also a geographical space. We must understand, however, that the vertical element in our diamond is not a ladder, but a fluid network or spider's web. This is significant, for as the editors of this collection put it, in using the metaphor of a network or a spider's web, rather than, say, that of a ladder, to describe the relationship between the local and the global, 'it is still possible to recognise that different scales exist . . . but it is much more difficult to determine exactly where one scale ends and another begins' (p. 12).

Our rather basic diamond, then, might be taken as a set of force fields pulling labour organisations in various directions. These organisations are pulled in different spatial ways, from the global (at the top) to the local (at the bottom), reflecting the different scales of human activity. But neither the Polanyian horizontal tension nor the politics of scale or vertical element can be seen as self-sufficient; rather, they act in a combined, if uneven, manner. A holistic labour studies and labour strategy must perforce be fully cognisant of the complex combinations of the horizontal and vertical force fields. Hence, just as capital has always operated on the basis of 'spatial fixes' (Harvey, 1999) to deal with crises of profitability through geographical relocation, so does labour also need its own spatial strategy based on a careful analysis of the politics of scale in the era of globalisation.

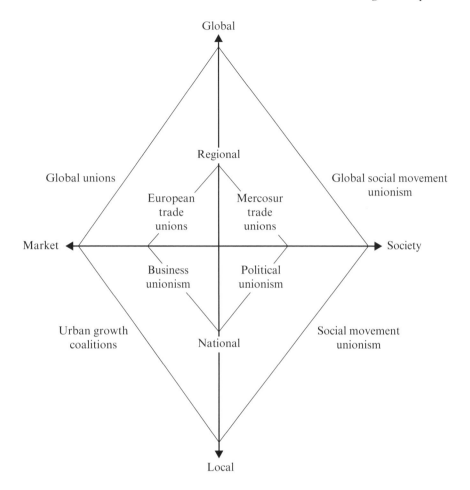

Figure 15.1   Socio-spatial representation of labour's responses to globalisation

Whilst purely illustrative, the diamond diagram (Figure 15.1) does allow us to operate some fairly basic distinctions. Thus, US traditional 'business unionism' operates at a national level and orients almost exclusively to the market where labour power is sold as any other commodity. In Latin America, on the other hand, there has been a prevalence in the past of a 'political unionism', also operating at nation-state level but much more cognisant of labour as a social actor. Locally, unions can engage in the boosterism of urban growth coalitions or take on a more social movement unionism character. At the global level the new Global Unions represent categories of workers as defined by their role in the production process as given by capital and thus can be seen as market orientated, as against the new global social movement unionism emerging in the South in particular. Finally, there is the somewhat neglected in-between space of the regional, where we have rather staid organisations such as the European TUC (see Wills, 2004) but also somewhat more socially orientated labour organisations like those contesting the MERCOSUR in the southern cone of Latin America (see Munck, 2001).

Histories

The history of trade union internationalism that might lead to global unions is a long, if uneven, one. The rise of industrial capitalism in nineteenth-century Europe led to waves of labour and socialist internationalism. Associated with *The Communist Manifesto* of Karl Marx and Friedrich Engels ([1848] 2008) and with the International Working Men's Association (or First International), which lasted from 1864 to 1872/73, labour and socialist internationalism came to be almost synonymous with the word 'internationalism'. After the 1890s, by allying with (or creating their own) women's, peace, and anti-colonial affiliates, labour and socialist internationalism largely hegemonised the word. Trade union internationalism, as the most direct international expression of the working-class movement, was seen as the heart of labour and socialist internationalism. From the 1890s to the 1960s, it was also the most resilient and best-organised part, and, through its representation in the International Labour Organization (ILO, founded 1919), the only one with a recognised place within the new interstate sphere.

The history of international unionism could be seen in terms of a heroic/charismatic earlier period, then a routine/bureaucratic period, and finally a slow death. But early labour internationalism had its limitations, and there were achievements in its second phase. Labour particularisms have been in tension with labour universalisms throughout (Forman, 1998; Silverman, 2000). The heroic earlier period was often marked by craft corporatism, nationalism, racism, militarism and imperialism (van Holthoon and van der Linden, 1988). This history is also marked by geographical discontinuities in so far as the early phase is most clearly centred around Europe whilst the second phase sees the emergence of a new international division of labour entailing the industrialisation of what was once Europe's colonial other world. As a result, in today's globalised, networked world there is no clear centre for either capitalism or for labour's contestation.

The achievements of twentieth-century labour internationalism need to be seen in terms of the quasi-universal geographical spread of trade unionism and continuing international demands for labour and democratic rights. Union internationalism made a significant contribution to the spread of liberal-democratic ideals and practices worldwide. This is no mean achievement compared with past or existing alternatives, and one has to credit the international union movement for its contribution to the establishment, in at least some parts of the capitalist world and for a limited period, of that utopia of social democracy, the capitalist welfare state (see Jessop, Chapter 2 in this volume).

What seemed to have constrained union internationalism throughout the twentieth century, though, was the rise of political, and even financial, dependence, for 'regional integration' or 'development cooperation', on states, state-oriented political parties, interstate organisations (the ILO, European Union, Mercosur) and ideologies of international social partnership with capital and/or the state. This was a worldwide process in the second half of the century, in the liberal-capitalist West, the state-socialist East and the national-developmentalist South. Operating within the ideological parameters of capital and/or the state not only led to the narrowing of traditional notions of international solidarity, but also implied the attrition of any autonomous labour 'worldview' – not to mention any project looking beyond the parameters of capitalism. With the rise of neoliberalism, globalisation and computerisation, however, this model of trade union internationalism is in crisis, and its existence is widely recognised as being under threat (Waterman, 2001; Munck, 2002; van der Linden, 2003a; Hyman, 2005; Wahl, 2004).

What is clear in terms of the spatial dimension is that '[f]or most of its history, "international" trade unionism has been overwhelmingly European in inspiration, composition and leadership' (Hyman, 2005, p. 140). Even whilst the reach of the international movement stretched beyond Europe (and later North America), its resource and organisational base was firmly European. The long postwar confrontation with the Soviet-aligned WFTU (World Federation of Trade Unions) also gave the dominant ICFTU a specific and far-reaching geo-strategic orientation, in defence of 'free' or pro-Western trade union models. The very notion of what a normal or normative labour relation was has always been thoroughly Eurocentric. Yet, globalisation, through its geographical extension and social intensification of market relations, has, in practice, undermined this Eurocentric paradigm and has thus created a crisis in the dominant models of transnational trade union activity. Equally, in the 1970s and 1980s there was a resurgence of Third World or South-based labour organising in countries such as Brazil, South Africa and South Korea. Capital's attempt to modify the spatial fix by relocating production to those countries only led to a relocation and recrudescence of labour struggles. In today's polycentric and networked capitalist order, then, there is no clear priority for any geographical area as locus of struggle, although China cannot be anything other than the next stage for classic labour vs. capital struggles.

Structures

The contemporary structure of the international trade union movement was set in the aftermath of the Second World War. The coincidence of the creation of the ICFTU in 1949 with a peaking of the Cold War has often led commentators to reduce the organisation to this fact alone. The split in the World Federation of Trade Unions (ostensibly over acceptance/rejection of the US Marshall Aid offer to a war-devastated Europe) must, however, also be understood in terms of working-class nationalism/internationalism, of competing labour/socialist ideologies (within the West itself), and of the universal state-dependence of trade unionism during most of the twentieth century. To this must be added the old conflict between international unionism as a relation between national union centres and as industrial/occupational ones. Given that the International Trade Secretariats were the oldest internationals, that they were closer to the unions and workers represented, and that they had a higher practical and lower 'political' or 'ideological' profile, the foundation of the ICFTU (which recognised the autonomy of the ITSs) had labour motives enough.

On the other hand, the split in the WFTU and the creation of the ICFTU was also, inevitably, an effect of the Cold War between the liberal-democratic and capitalist West (dominated in many ways by a USA vastly strengthened by the war), and an economically-devastated Communist bloc. The relative weakness of the latter was compensated for by an authoritarian and militaristic Party-State – to which the unions were subordinate – and an ideology of proletarian rule and internationalism, which, because of wartime success, still proved attractive to anti-imperialist movements.

The major tension in the creation of the ICFTU was between the US and the West European unions. (ICFTU member unions in the colonies or newly-independent countries long remained in a marginal and dependent position.) A US culture of unfettered freedom of enterprise, of military interventionism, of hostility to Communism, to Social Democracy and even 'liberalism', had, by 1949, deeply impacted on its trade union movement. In Europe, the devastated capitalist economies were mostly prepared for a settlement with Social Democracy and the trade union movements and for the creation of the so-called welfare state, thus providing the labour movement with feelings of both protection and power.

During the later twentieth century the international trade union movement was dominated by a small number of organisations, not all of them international. The best known are or were: (a) the Communist-controlled World Federation of Trade Unions (WFTU) in Prague, largely denuded of members and influence by the collapse of the Communist world in 1989; (b) the social-reformist International Confederation of Free Trade Unions (ICFTU) in Brussels, which has grown as a result of the same process; and (c) the (ex-) Social Christian World Confederation of Labour (WCL), also in Brussels, that has had certain membership in Latin America but a marginal one elsewhere.

Throughout the twentieth century and beyond, the (now combined) American Federation of Labor-Congress of Industrial Organizations (AFL-CIO) has played a major international role. It has been inspired more by the American variant of social reformism, known as 'business unionism', than by social democracy. The AFL-CIO has been a major influence within the ICFTU and also a major independent operator. It has acted through corporate and/or state-funded agencies for Asia, Africa and South America, and also engaged in activities in Europe and the Third World in a clandestine, or at least low-profile, manner (Clarke, 1994; Carew, 1996; Ruiz, 2004). Its work was, for a decade or so, carried forward by its Solidarity Centre. In recent years, however, the international activities of the AFL-CIO have been under increasing internal attack (Hirsch, 2004; Scipes, 2006; Worker to Worker Solidarity Committee, 2006): in 2006, for instance, the AFL-CIO's International Affairs Department was closed down. This is in contrast to Europe, where no such significant critique has been launched by solidarity activists where analogous state-dependency is the rule for at least union solidarity activities in the South.

Then there are the oldest international union organisations, those originally related to specific trades or industries. These were once called International Trade Secretariats (ITSs), now reduced in number by mergers (as a consequence of industrial transformation and/or falling union membership) and renamed Global Union Federations. These have long considered themselves more 'unionist' and less 'political' than the ICFTU. They have, however, been similarly associated with social reformism and the ICFTU, and are now literally linked to it through the Global Unions (GU) website. Their industrial specificity nonetheless requires them to address themselves more directly to the workers they claim to represent. Also allied to GU is the Trade Union Advisory Committee of the OECD. A formal structure of regional organisations, this is dependent on the international confederations and their related industry-specific federations. Within Europe there is also the independent, but also social-reformist, European Trade Union Confederation, simultaneously addressed to and dependent on the European Union. Something similar may be emerging in the Common Market of the Southern Cone of Latin America (Mercosur). However, the challenge to neoliberal regionalism by the left-populist regimes in the region may undermine this. Significant regional union structures also exist in Asia, particularly those of the ICFTU (Greenfield, 1999). Finally, there are the 'autonomous' regional internationals, dependent on intergovernmental structures, in the Arab world and Africa. Certainly, efforts have been made to coordinate the policies and activities of European/international federations and those of Latin America. But this project may be dependent on the problematic notion that the European Union represents some kind of 'promised land' for Latin America.

Within this context, towards the end of 2006 there occurred a merger between the ICFTU, the World Confederation of Labour (WCL) and the Global Union Federations (GUFs), that is the old trade secretariats. The jury is still out on the long-term significance of this merger but it certainly represents a significant move towards a global union presence on the world scene. Whether the 176 million members (as claimed) will actually become a global social force, of course, is another matter. To date the founding documents seem to signal no more than a human rights-type global policy and not a radical global social movement or social justice one. The new grouping, then, seems ultimately a Western, top-down initiative owing more to the sclerotic European TUC than the spirit of Seattle 1999; a global Keynesianism rather than a global alternative to the neoliberal order. Even the exclusion of the once-communist WFTU will serve to exclude at national and regional level some significant parts of the global workforce. At a time when a unifying and radicalising initiative might well have taken root, this might have been a good start but it is not really as much as was necessary in the circumstances.

Divisions

Formally speaking, most of the world's trade unions are representative-democratic organisations, are controlled by their members, and advance the interests of the working class generally. They act either defensively for particular categories of workers or more assertively, often by becoming partners or leaders in movements for national liberation, for political and social democracy or for general movements of the poor. However, as critical observers have repeatedly noted, they are also subject to the 'iron law of oligarchy' (Michels, [1915] 1999), have themselves become 'managers of discontent' (Mills, [1948] 2001; Catalano, 1999) and have become involved in forms of 'neo-corporatism' at the risk of making themselves irrelevant (Gorz, 1999). Moreover, throughout the twentieth century, at the regional and global levels, these threats to the unions' social presence and impact increased. Union organisations' greater distance from their base increases such dangers.

Despite their considerable differences – involving ideology, industry/occupation, worker constituency, or geographical reach – the international organisations share a number of common characteristics. They are remote from workers on the shop floor, in the office, or in the community, who, indeed, are usually unaware of their existence. (It would be an interesting experiment, perhaps, to find out whether union members or shop floor activists even know the name of 'their' international, or what it does, or whether they feel they in any way 'own' their international; to the best of our knowledge, no international union or international labour researcher has ever tried.) They were and are marked by their past participation in the Cold War. They tend to reproduce the structure and behaviour of interstate agencies. They were and are largely Northern-based, -led and -staffed. They have tended to reduce the complex reality of working people worldwide to a Western model of the unionised (or unionisable) male worker in lifetime employment in large-scale capitalist or state enterprise. Where they have adapted Western unionism and ILO tripartism in response to the problematic Third World, they have generally adopted the developmentalist ideologies dominant in the North. The 'free' Western internationals have become increasingly dependent on state funding for their 'regional' or 'development' activities, thus taking on the role of state or interstate development agencies. Whilst critical of development NGOs, the unions nevertheless commonly reproduce their top-down, North–South, patron–client relations (Waterman, 2004).

Where independent Southern regional organisations have been set up, such as the International Confederation of Arab Trade Unions or the Organisation of African Trade Union Unity, this has – as suggested above – often been on the initiative of such states or groups. And such new organisations have, like the Southern states and interstate agencies themselves, tended to reproduce rather than challenge the traditional model and relationships. Various projects of South–South collaboration between unions or workers have so far shown limited results, although such may be better developed amongst the specialised new international networks for fishing communities, small farmers, street and homeworkers, or slumdwellers as these lack, perhaps, the state-national assumptions of the national unions, their dependency on the state locally and the Northern unions internationally.

For its part, the International Labour Organisation (ILO), the interstate body for labour questions, was founded in 1919 and became part of the UN in 1945/46. The ILO was established in an attempt to provide the growing international labour movement with an alternative perspective to that of insurrection (developed by the Russian Revolution of 1917, armed uprisings in Germany and Hungary, and labour uprisings in Scotland and elsewhere). The influence of Social Christian doctrine (such as Pope Leo XIII's 1891 encyclical) and other such ideologies of reform-from-above also cannot be ruled out in considering the ILO's origins. Although described as 'tripartite', the ILO is, of course, an interstate organisation, in which power is divided between national governments (50 per cent), employers, (25 per cent) and labour (25 per cent). From a liberal-pluralist view, the ILO is an international reflection of the liberal-democratic nation state, with government(s) holding the scales between labour and capital in order to further economic development, social justice and the general interest. A political economy view, though, might be that the ILO embodied an early twentieth-century settlement between capital and the state (75 per cent), on the one hand, and labour (25 per cent), on the other. At the same time, however, the ILO, as an interstate bureaucracy, has enjoyed relative autonomy from national and international capital and the nation state, and has created both 'texts and pretexts' (as feminists said about the 1995 World Conference on Women) for unions to lean on or make use of.

Dilemmas
It is now widely believed amongst labour specialists that the international trade union movement in general, and the ICFTU (or its successor organisation) in particular, is at a crossroads in terms of how they might meet the challenge of globalisation. For Marcel van der Linden (2003b, p. 20), 'it remains very likely that the coming of transnational internationalism will be a difficult process interspersed with failed experiments and moments of deep crisis'. In this regard, in terms of the overarching spatial and social divide between workers in the affluent North and those in the dominated South, a major dilemma has been the issue of international labour standards. Should the international labour movement argue, on the basis of fairness and legitimacy, that core labour standards should be incorporated into the remit of the WTO? Or are these labour standards

a covert form of Northern protectionism vis-à-vis developing countries? Certainly, as Gumbrell-McCormick (2004, p. 526) puts it, '[t]he ICFTU believes that there is a danger of a "global race to the bottom" and that it must be prevented by binding rules to establish minimum standards for workers in the global economy'. The problem, though, is that for workers in the majority world, the 'social dialogue' approach and social economy model upon which this is premised, are not available.

At the same time we increasingly find the regional moment of labour activity coming to the fore. Whether it is at the level of the EU, NAFTA, Mercosur or APEC, trade unions need to respond to the new regional modalities of capitalist development that neoliberals like Ohmae (1995) are claiming are emerging. Paradoxically, this may be providing some opportunities. Hence, as Haworth and Hughes (2002, p. 163) have argued, '[t]here is a positive aspect to regional labour activity today. A combination of three factors – internationalization of capital, the Social Clause/ Labour Standards debate and regional integration – has provided labour with a need, a platform and a context for action'. Certainly, the regional transnationalism of the South does not share the same dynamic of the EU, for example, but clearly this domain will gain in importance. The dilemma it poses labour, however, is whether it displaces the national terrain and whether it in some way lessens the importance of global labour solidarity.

There is now a growing tendency to accept that we might think globally but act locally. Herod (2001, p. 118) has argued persuasively that whilst 'workers may think that if they cannot organise globally, there is no point in attempting to organise at other scales', this belief is not only politically paralysing but it also ignores the extent to which TNCs can be effectively challenged locally. This is not presented as a 'small is beautiful' or 'local trumps all' argument, but simply recognises that workers need not (indeed, often cannot) respond to capital's movement at the same scale. Whilst it is clear that concentrating action against local pressure points may be effective in challenging a TNC, there is still the dilemma posed for workers worldwide who might accept that 'another world is possible' in principle but do not see a global vision that is achievable coming from the traditional labour organisations.

Clearly, these different scales of labour activity are not like rungs on a ladder, and in practice they overlap as one would expect, given the uneven and combined development of capitalism itself. The point here is not to rake over these debates, but simply to reinforce the point that labour's contestation of capitalism and its effects will more often than not be multiscalar.

Strategies

In a revealing comment, leading Latin American trade unionist and ICFTU Director and international labour specialist, Kjeld Jakobsen (2001, p. 78), declared that: '[f]or all its 300 million unionized workers, the world trade union movement cannot bring the neoliberal experiment to an end on its own'. We might go further and argue that organised labour, on its own, will not even be able to develop an adequate social and spatial strategy to defend its position in the era of globalisation. Thus, our conclusion will be to call for a new global social movement unionism (popularised by Moody (1997), albeit from a traditional Fordist workers' perspective) which also addresses labour's others, outside the formal structures of the labour movement. Whilst recognising that a rapprochement between organised labour and the global justice movement will not be easy, it is clear to us that the new capitalism requires a new unionism. That movement will need to create new places and spaces and learn to play by new rules from those of the nation-statist era, if it is to empower working people worldwide.

At the end of the twentieth century international trade unionism was confronted by a tragic paradox. There were more wage-earners than ever before, around 3 billion according to Freeman (2006). The ICFTU/GU, with 150 or more million members, covered more countries, unions and workers than ever before. This was due, as suggested, to the incorporation of most of the formerly-Communist or national-populist unions. However, at the same time that these events were taking place, neoliberal globalisation was facilitating the simultaneous weakening of traditional unionism's century-old national-industrial base, the shift of that base to countries of the South (particularly China), the undermining of traditional job security and union rights, and the decline or disappearance of support from social-democratic parties, socially-reformist governments and the most powerful interstate agencies. Moreover, the unions were being confronted with a fact that – in their industrial, national or industrial relations cocoons – they had never previously felt necessary to face: in this globalising world of labour, maybe only one worker in 18 was unionised. Finally, with the disappearance of their competitors in Communist or national-populist unions, the ICFTU/GU found itself not only in an alien and hostile world but ideologically disorientated. Previously it had been able to see itself not only as representing the most advanced union model but as part of the 'free West', opposed to both Communist and national-populist unionism. Now it found itself left behind by the globalisation of capital and by the decreasing political interest of the international hegemons.

If the union internationals initially responded in equal measure with disorientation and retreat, they are now increasingly raising the old notion of 'social partnership' with capital and state from the national to the global level. This has implied a series of specific campaigns, addressed sometimes directly to multinational corporations, sometimes to the international financial institutions and other promoters of globalisation (the World Trade Organisation, the World Economic Forum, and so forth). Hence, as Justice (2002, p. 96) puts it: '[o]ver the years, the global union federations have established an ongoing social dialogue with a number of multinational enterprises in their sectors or industries'. The three major areas of this union work are international labour standards, codes of conduct and corporate social responsibility policies (Jenkins et al., 2002). Meanwhile, the five Core Labour Rights set out below are currently represented by a set of those already issued by the ILO, of which only one is actually less than 30 years old (it should be noted that none of the ILO's approximately 175 member states has endorsed all of them):

- the right to form trade unions ('freedom of association');
- the right to effective collective bargaining between workers and management;
- freedom from forced or compulsory labour;
- an end to child labour;
- freedom from discrimination in the workplace.

What is significant, though, is that this list notably does not include an explicit right to the international solidarity strike, as called for by the International Centre for Trade

Union Rights (Ewing and Sibley, 2000). This is important, because directly or indirectly related to this declaration was the 15-year-plus campaign for a 'social clause' under which the World Trade Organisation (initially the General Agreement of Tariffs and Trade) would discriminate against states that did not respect international labour rights. This attempt to get labour rights institutionalised by the very organisation that is promoting 'free trade' at the cost of labour has not only failed but has provoked much disagreement, as well as forceful criticism, within the union movement in the South and among labour specialists (John and Chenoy, 1996; *WorkingUSA*, 2001).

For their part, 'Global Framework Agreements' between particular GUFs and multinational corporations are described as:

> agreement[s] negotiated between a multinational company and a global union federation concerning the international activities of that company. The main purpose of a framework agreement is to establish a formal ongoing relationship . . . which can solve problems and work in the interests of both parties. (ICFTU, 2004)

Such agreements, though, do not require internationally enforceable legislation and are not backed by the force of law. This is a major problem with such voluntary 'codes of conduct', for they can be difficult to monitor and are often left to under-funded and unaccountable NGOs (Jenkins et al., 2002; for samples of such framework agreements, see ICFTU, 2004).

Such voluntary global social contracts have been presented on a slightly more public stage by union endorsement of the UN's Global Compact. This latter is another voluntary initiative, aiming to 'mainstream' socially responsible business activities through policy dialogues, learning and local projects. Union support for the Global Compact, even though the initiative lacks the power of enforcement or even monitoring, was revealed in a joint UN-ICFTU/GU declaration in 2000:

> [i]t was agreed that global markets required global rules. The aim should be to enable the benefits of globalization increasingly to spread to all people by building an effective framework of multilateral rules for a world economy that is being transformed by the globalization of markets . . . the Global Compact should contribute to this process by helping to build social partnerships of business and labour. (ICFTU, 2000)

More recently, we have also seen union co-sponsorship of the ILO's World Commission on the Social Dimension of Globalisation (also dominated by statespeople, corporate figures and academics), which has published a report entitled *A Fair Globalisation: Creating Opportunities for All* (ILO, 2004).

Together these activities suggest the international union movement is shifting focus from states and interstate bodies, previously seen as the major spatial locus of regulation, toward the multinational corporations, seen as the major powers in the global economy. Whilst the social-democratic international unions broadly welcome such projects (Justice, 2002), others see in these accords an embrace by UN institutions of the multinationals at the expense of civil society (Judge, 2001). Whilst such efforts do suggest a reorientation in reaction to globalisation, international trade unions are nevertheless continuing their traditional efforts at union building, in defence of labour rights and in support of workers and unions internationally (for a review see Fairbrother and Hammer, 2005). This seems to involve new and more assertive language. An exemplar might be the International Transport Workers' Federation, the 2002 Congress of which was devoted to the theme of 'Globalising solidarity'. A turning point in its practical solidarity activity is indicated by, on the one hand, its failure to support the Liverpool dock workers effectively during the major lockout of 1995–1998 (Waterman, 1997) and its more effective support for the Australian dock workers during a related dispute later (see Sadler and Fagan, 2004). However, much national and international union solidarity activity is still carried out under the rubric of 'development cooperation' and financed by the state or interstate organisations. It is, though, notable that most of this solidarity activity appears to be on a North–South axis and in a North–South direction. A more holistic, multifaceted and multidirectional notion of labour solidarity is yet to emerge, and the ICTU website reveals only an implicit recognition of the broader global solidarity movement.

Conclusions

We live in an era of rapid transformation where quick judgements are not wise. On the one hand, there is a tendency towards the formation of a global working-class. For some twenty years now, there has been a tendential process towards the formation of a global labour market, whilst management consultant William Johnston had declared at the start of the 1990s that 'The globalisation of labour is inevitable' (Johnston, 1991, p. 126). Of course, in practice no more than one fifth of the world's workers are directly linked to the global political economy in terms of labour relations. Yet the possibility of global unions is not diminished by this fact when we take into account the much greater impact of what we call globalisation on labour relations worldwide. This leads cautious labour scholars Harrod and O'Brien (2002, p. 14) to conclude that 'a global labour force can be discerned, if it is defined as those workers connected to the global economy'.

There is also, however, a powerful counter-tendency that in Beck's somewhat Eurocentric language has been called 'Brazilianisation' (Beck, 2000, p. 1), by which he means that whilst globalisation brings an ever greater number of workers within its ambit, it is also creating greater diversity, disruption and insecurity to the world of work. The pattern of employment once typical in countries such as Brazil – namely a preponder-ance of 'informal' labour relations and great levels of income disparity – has now become generalised across the affluent North, albeit with particular nuances. So, whilst capitalist globalisation does tend towards the creation of an integrated global market, it also gener-ates a dispersal tendency based on informalisation and flexibilisation. Clearly, labour's organisations cannot respond to this situation as they did in the North Atlantic during the so-called golden era class compromise wherein there was a powerful welfare state.

If global capitalism is characterised by uneven and combined development as much as it was in Marx's day, we are unlikely to see global unions springing up fully formed to confront it. The globalisation of the working-class condition has clearly not worked out in the way that Marxists assumed or hoped for. Instead of generalising and homogenis-ing the condition of the industrial proletariat (of mid-nineteenth-century Britain), we see proletarianisation occurring without the Marxists' internationalist and revolutionary proletariat. Differentiation rather than homogenisation seems to be the rule. The appeals of 'Workers of the World Unite!', 'You Have Nothing to Lose but Your Chains!', 'You Have a World to Win!' or 'Black and White Unite and Fight!' fail to appeal to workers who experience international competition, who have a job or TV or pension to lose, and whose ethnic or local identity is as significant to them as that of class. It is the internationalists who still have a 'working class to win', and this task is as much a matter of winning hearts and minds as is the internationalism of women, of indigenous peoples, of Africans or of slumdwellers. Given, indeed, that the differentiated and dispersed working classes also have these other identities, a new working-class internationalism would seem to be dependent on an intimate articulation of *this* with the internationalism of *those*. The question remains of whether *trade union* internationalism can further, rather than obstruct, such a reinvented internationalism!

By focusing on the spatial as well as social complexity of transnational labour relations and contestation, we move beyond the paradigm of globalisation as subject. We must heed Urry's (2000, p. 40) warning that 'many globalisation analyses treat the emergent global properties as too unified and powerful', producing a static and reductionist picture. In brief, 'many globalisation analyses . . . deal insufficiently with the *complex* character of emerging social relations' (Urry, 2000, p. 39, emphasis in the original). This is less true today, with second or third generation globalisation studies focusing on global networks, communities and fluids that are fully cognisant of global complexity. In the new labour geography, there is also close attention to, and understanding of how, '[b]uilding solidarity across space – especially internationally – is not a straightforward matter, but rather is fraught with complexities' (Herod, 2001, p. 218). Above all, we must bear in mind that transnational labour practice is 'as much about geography as it is about class' (Herod, 2001, p. 218). A general strategy for labour fit for purpose in the era of globalisation must, perforce, be simultaneously local-national-regional-global and open to all, whilst working at one or another spatial scale in practice. The new multiscalar capitalism requires a multiscalar labour response capable of denaturalising space and turning it to labour's advantage. Our conclusion to this article might thus mirror Ramsay's (1999, p. 215), namely, that '[t]his is not a message of hopelessness, but one which emphasises the complexity and difficulty of the international union project'.

References

Beck, U. (2000), *The Brave New World of Work*, Cambridge: Polity Press.

Carew, A. (1996), 'The American labour movement in Fizzland: the free trade union movement and the CIA', *Labor History*, **39**, 25–42.

Castree, N., N. Coe, K. Ward and M. Samers (2004), *Spaces of Work: Global Capitalism and Geographies of Labour*, London: Sage.

Catalano, A.M. (1999), 'The crisis of trade union representation: new forms of social integration and autonomy-construction', in R. Munck and P. Waterman (eds), *Labour Worldwide in the Era of Globalisation: Alternative Union Models in the New World Order*, Houndmills: Macmillan, pp. 27–40.

Clarke, R. (1994), 'US labour "missionaries"' – no blessing for Russian workers', available at: www.nathan-newman.org/EDIN/.labor/.files/.internat/.russia.html.

Ewing, K. and T. Sibley (2000), *International Trade Union Rights for the New Millennium*, London: International Centre for Trade Unions Rights and Institute for Employment Rights.

Fairbrother, P. and N. Hammer (2005), 'Global unions: past efforts and future prospects', *Relations Industrielles/Industrial Relations*, **60** (3), 405–31.

Forman, M. (1998), *Nationalism and the International Labor Movement: The Idea of the Nation in Socialist and Anarchist Theory*, University Park, PA: Pennsylvania State University Press.

Freeman, R. (2006), 'China, India and the doubling of the global labor force: who pays the price of globalization?', available at: www.zmag.org/content/showarticle.cfm?ItemID=8617.

Gorz, A. (1999), 'A new task for the unions: the liberation of time from work', in R. Munck and P. Waterman (eds), *Labour Worldwide in the Era of Globalisation: Alternative Union Strategies in the New World Order*, Houndmills: Macmillan, pp. 41–63.

Greenfield, G. (1999), 'Democratic trade union responses to globalisation: a critique of the ICFTU-APRO's

"Asian Monteray Fund" proposal', paper presented to the Hong Kong Confederation of Trade Unions, September, available at: www.labournet.de/diskussion/gewerkschaft/greenf.html.

Gumbrell-McCormick, R. (2004), 'Putting the labor into labor standards', *Labor History*, **45** (4), 522–9.

Harrod, J. and R. O'Brien (2002), 'Organised labour and the global political economy' in J. Harrod and R. O'Brien (eds), *Global Unions? Theory and Strategies of Organised Labour in the Global Political Economy*, London: Routledge, pp. 3–28.

Harvey, D. (1999), 'Globalization in question', *Rethinking Marxism*, **8** (4), 1–17.

Haworth, N. and S. Hughes (2002), 'International labour and regional integration in the Asia-Pacific', in J. Harrod and R. O'Brien (eds), *Global Unions? Theory and Strategies of Organised Labour in the Global Political Economy*, London: Routledge, pp. 151–64.

Herod, A. (2001), *Labor Geographies, Workers and the Landscapes of Capitalism*, New York: Guilford Press.

Hirsch, F. (2004), 'Build unity and trust among workers worldwide', available at: www.labournet.net/world/0407/hirsch.html.

Hyman, R. (2005), 'Shifting dynamics in international trade unionism: agitation, organisation, bureaucracy, diplomacy', *Labor History*, **46** (2), 137–54.

ICFTU (International Confederation of Free Trade Unions) (1997), *The Global Market: Trade Unionism's Greatest Challenge*, Brussels: ICFTU.

ICFTU (International Confederation of Free Trade Unions) (2000), 'Joint UN-ICFTU statement on the global compact', available at: www.icftu.org/displaydocument.asp?Index=991209381&Language=EN.

ICFTU (International Confederation of Free Trade Unions) (2004), 'Framework agreements with multi-national companies', available at: www.icftu.org/displaydocument.asp?Index=991216332&Language=EN.

ILO (2004), *A Fair Globalization: Creating Opportunities for All*, Geneva: International Labour Office.

Jakobsen, K. (2001), 'Rethinking the International Confederation of Free Trade Unions and its Inter-American Regional Organisation', in P. Waterman and J. Wills (eds), *Place, Space and the New Labour Internationalisms*, Oxford: Blackwell, pp. 59–79.

Jenkins, R., R. Pearson and G. Seyfang (eds) (2002), *Corporate Responsibility and Labour Rights*, London: Earthscan.

John, J. and A. Chenoy (eds) (1996), *Labour, Environment and Globalisation: Social Clause in Multilateral Trade Agreements – A Southern Response*, New Delhi: Centre for Education and Communication.

Johnston, W. (1991), 'Global work force 2000: the new world labor market', *Harvard Business Review*, March–April, 115–27.

Judge, A. (2001), '"Globalization": The UN's "Safe Haven" for the world's marginalised – the Global Compact with Multinational Corporations as the UN's "Final Solution"', available at: http://laetusinprae-sens.org/docs/globcomp.php.

Justice, D. (2002), 'The international trade union movement and the new codes of conduct', in R. Jenkins, R. Pearson and G. Seyfang (eds), *Corporate Responsibility and Labour Rights*, London: Earthscan, pp. 90–100.

Lefebvre, H. (1991), *The Production of Space*, Oxford: Blackwell.

Marx, K. and F. Engels (1848/2008), *The Communist Manifesto*, London: Pluto Press.

Michels, R. ([1915] 1999), *Political Parties: A Sociological Study of the Oligarchical Tendencies of Modern Democracy*, New Brunswick, NJ: Transaction Publishers.

Mills, C.W. ([1948] 2001), *The New Men of Power: America's Labour Leaders*, Champaign, IL: University of Illinois Press.

Moody, K. (1997), *Workers in a Lean World: Unions in the International Economy*, London: Zed Books.

Munck, R. (2001), 'Globalization, regionalism and labour: the case of MERCOSUR', *Labour, Capital and Society*, **34** (1), 8–25.

Munck, R. (2002), *Globalisation and Labour: The New 'Great Transformation'*, London: Zed Books.

Ohmae, K. (1995), *The End of the Nation State: The Rise of Regional Economies*, New York: McKinsey and Company.

Ramsay, P. (1999), 'In search of international union theory', in J. Waddington (ed.), *Globalisation and Patterns of Labour Resistance*, London: Mansell, pp. 192–220.

Ruiz, A. (2004), 'The question remains: what is the AFL-CIO doing in Venezuela?', Znet, available at: www.zmag.org/content/print_article.cfm?itemID=5074&sectionID=45.

Sadler, D. and B. Fagan (2004), 'Australian trade unions and the politics of scale: re-constructing the spatiality of industrial relations', *Economic Geography*, **80** (1), 23–43.

Scipes, K. (2006), 'Worker-to-worker solidarity committee to AFL-CIO: cut all ties with NED', available at: www.zmag.org/content/showarticle.cfm?ItemID=10191.

Silver, B.J. (2003), *Forces of Labor: Workers' Movements and Globalization Since 1870*, Cambridge: Cambridge University Press.

Silverman, V. (2000), *Imagining Internationalism in American and British Labour, 1939–49*, Urbana, IL: University of Illinois Press.

Smith, N. (1993), 'Homeless/global: scaling places', in J. Bird, B. Curtis, T. Putnam, G. Robertson and L. Tickner (eds), *Mapping the Futures: Local Cultures, Global Change*, London: Routledge, pp. 87–119.

Taylor, P. (1982), 'A materialist framework for political geography', *Transactions of the Institute of British Geographers*, New Series, **7**, 15–34.

Urry, J. (2000), *Global Complexity*, Cambridge: Polity Press.

van der Linden, M. (2003a), 'The ICFTU at the crossroads: an historical interpretation', paper presented at conference on 'Labour and New Social Movements in a Globalizing World', Linz, Austria: 11–14 September.

van der Linden, M. (2003b), *Transnational Labour History: Explorations*, Aldershot: Ashgate.

van Holthoon, F. and M. van der Linden, (eds) (1988), *Internationalism in the Labour Movement 1830–1940*, Leiden: Brill.

Wahl, A. (2004), 'European labour: the ideological legacy of the social pact', *Monthly Review*, **55** (8), available at: *www.monthlyreview.org/0104wahl.htm*

Waterman, P. (1997), 'New interest in dockers and transport workers: locally, nationally, comparatively, globally – some real and virtual resources', available at: www.labournet.net/docks2/9712/itf1212.htm.

Waterman, P. (2001), *Globalisation, Social Movements and the New Internationalisms*, London: Continuum.

Waterman, P. (2004), 'Trade unions, NGOs and global social justice: another tale to tell', in C. Phelan (ed.), *The Future of Organised Labour: Global Perspectives*, Oxford: Peter Lang, pp. 161–75.

Webster, E., R. Lambert and A. Bezuidenhout (2008), *Grounding Globalization: Labour in the Era of Insecurity*, London: Blackwell.

Wills, J. (2004), 'Re-scaling trade union organisation: lessons from the European front line', in R. Munck (ed.), *Labour and Globalisation: Results and Prospects*, Liverpool: Liverpool University Press, pp. 85–104.

Worker to Worker Solidarity Committee (2006), 'Touch one touch all', available at: www.workertoworker.net/worker_to_worker_afl_cio_letter.html.

WorkingUSA (2001), 'Labour rights in the global economy', *WorkingUSA*, **5** (1), 3–8.

16 Methodological nationalism and territorial capitalism: mobile labour and the challenges to the 'German Model'

Christian Berndt

Introduction

When the former Chancellor, Helmut Schmidt, introduced the term '*Modell Deutschland*' during a national election campaign in 1976, it reflected the self-confidence of a political economy apparently at the height of its evolution (Esser et al., 1979; Esser and Fach, 1981). Disappearing quickly from the German scene in the wake of economic difficulties, it was in fact foreign academics and journalists who kept the mythical keyword alive (for example, Markovits, 1982). The label gained new popularity during the 1990s, when attention turned to territorial capitalist variants (for example, Albert, 1993; Esping-Andersen, 1994) and again more recently with the 'varieties of capitalism' approach (Hall and Soskice, 2001). Difference in detail notwithstanding, there is broad agreement in the literature that the institutions formatting labour relations constitute a key building stone of the German Model (Bathelt and Gertler, 2005; Berndt, 2001).

In today's global age, where the conditions allowing the production of quasi-natural national economies and societies have ceased to exist, the viability of territorial capitalist models is increasingly put into question. Applying a perspective which privileges mobility over stability, this chapter analyses the dilemmas confronting the contemporary German political economy focusing on industrial and labour relations. I argue that the German Model was founded on a particular geographical compromise: resting mainly on the mobility of goods, the country's economic success crucially depended on an elaborate regime of limited cross-border mobility of production factors (labour, capital). Only through this spatial negotiation of mobility and immobility was the maintenance of the sedentary lifestyles and relatively high living standards of a core of the workforce facilitated. In more recent times, though, the global stretching of production systems beyond national boundaries, and the tremendous pressure on unionised labour in the wake of this, together with the mobility across Germany's borders of so-called 'low-skilled' labour, appear to be contributing to the erosion of the stable postwar territorial compromise. In light of these changes, then, I criticise the 'methodological nationalism' characteristic of the predominantly defensive measures adopted by German economic decision-makers (including trade union officials). Specifically, I argue that, recent changes notwithstanding, these decision-makers have not yet come to terms with the requirements and configurations of an increasingly connected world. Rather, trapped territorially they instead unintentionally create new dilemmas for every problem they seek to solve.

In terms of organisation, the chapter starts with a brief reconstruction of the particular geography of the institutions underpinning *Modell Deutschland*, putting emphasis on how it centred on territorial stability and a sedentary lifestyle for a majority of workers. The second section shifts the focus towards transnational labour geographies and the challenges these imply for more sedentary actors. I close the chapter with a discussion of the dilemmas confronting decision-makers as they attempt to reconcile a dated territorial with a still largely undefined transterritorial order.

Modell Deutschland: the rise and fall of a territorial system of labour regulation

Territorialisation: the production of the 'normal' worker
The institutionalisation of German capital–labour relations cannot be separated from the historical project which, first, transformed a fragmented and loosely connected political mosaic of regional political entities into a territorial nation state and, second, consolidated this relatively young territorial entity as a welfare state (*Wohlfahrtsstaat*). According to Claus Offe (1999, 2003), the labour side of the German welfare state has four key features. The first concerns *regulations designed to protect the worker* at the workplace and in the labour market. Early examples date back to the nineteenth century and include the temporal limitation of working life, the working week and the working day. The overriding concern was to protect the workers at work, apparently justifying certain limitations imposed upon the freedom of contract.

The second feature comprises all measures and programmes that are designed to protect workers and also their dependent family members outside work through the specific German version of social security (*Sozialversicherung*). As time passed, ever wider segments of the workforce were included in the ranks of mandatory contributors to, and beneficiaries of, social security. This meant that the relationship between worker and employer is embedded in an order where a paternalist state imposes duties (to contribute) and rights (to benefits) upon those subjects that perform the economic role of regular employees. Distinguishing this arrangement both from liberal and from socialist variants, Offe (1999, p. 203) argues that this allowed the German state to mediate between the conflicting forces of a class-divided society.

The third key feature of the German welfare state refers to the well-known institutions which safeguard a particular way of determining the workers' income, including collective wage bargaining, strong actors on both sides of the labour market (the so-called social partners, that is labour unions and employers' associations), *Flächentarifverträge* (industry-wide, regional collective agreements), *Tarifautonomie* (the constitutionally enshrined provision banning the state from directly interfering with wage determination) and strict time limits to the organisation of strikes by unions.

Finally, there is the period of consistently high levels of employment from 1955 to 1975, which provided the context in which the regulations governing social security and industrial relations were able to bring about their positive effects. Only with a large and stable base of fully employed workers were labour unions able to negotiate the pay rises and the increase of social protection so characteristic of that era. Together with the continuing economic boom, this made labour a scarce 'commodity', providing incentives to maximise efficiency through technological innovations, to invest in training and skilling and to foster cooperative relations between workers and employers. Economists coined the term '*Produktivitätspeitsche*' (productivity whip), that is a virtuous mechanism almost naturally leading to continuous growth.

By defining a 'standard employment relationship' (*Normalarbeitsverhältnis*), this institutional environment draws sharp borders between the insiders and outsiders of *Modell*

Deutschland. Insider positions are assigned to those who belong to the 'community of the insured', that is those covered by the social security system. Amongst the 'outsiders' are, above all, workers in so-called atypical employment or those who in one way or another work in segments of the labour market deemed 'informal' (that is, illicit work, day labour, 'undocumented' migrants). In so doing, the social security system produced a broad middle segment of the population in stable, full-time and lifelong employment. (I will illustrate below that it is this stable, sedentary segment of the workforce that is strongly affected by the current rearticulation of German capitalism.)

The 'standard' form of labour has an ambivalent meaning for those workers who come to Germany from abroad. On the one hand, it provides migrants with a means with which to participate in social life. Hence, many scholars argue that the labour market has been the primary mechanism of integration into a society which denies political participation (Häußermann and Siebel, 2001). On the other hand, this applies only to those in stable employment, with the important consequence that the right to stay in Germany is jeopardised by job loss and unemployment. Still worse off are those migrants who are either excluded legally from the formal labour market (for example, asylum seekers) or who meet the demand for unregulated, 'informal' work which has always been a prominent feature in the German economy. It is no exaggeration, therefore, to conclude that the specific labour market arrangements of *Modell Deutschland* played a crucial role in the formation of an exclusionary national-territorial project (Markovits, 1982, p. 6; Streeck, 1997, p. 246).

The demarcation of insider and outsider positions in the labour market and the corresponding social boundaries outlined above formed an indispensable part in the organisation of the German variant of capitalism and the consolidation of a society priding itself on its prosperous living conditions and social cohesion. Yet these social normalisation and consolidation processes required a further step, namely the projection of social homogenisation to space via the process of territorialisation. Referred to as 'economic-giant, political-dwarf' by international observers, the motor of postwar West Germany was an internationally open and aggressively export-orientated economy. The German version of (neo)liberal integration into international markets, however, rested solely on the mobility of goods. Underlying tensions between the wider German society and its capitalist economy, and also between labour and capital, were solved by striking a geographical compromise: the West German Model, then, 'was conditional on limited mobility of production factors across borders' (Streeck, 1997, p. 252). On the capital side this included the rise of large, interconnected industrial conglomerates and the famous industrial Mittelstand, international players that still produced predominantly domestically when their US counterparts, for instance, already pursued outsourcing opportunities in Mexico, Haiti, Taiwan or Hong Kong. As regards financial markets, Germany's banks – whether large or small – concentrated their resources on the domestic market, venturing abroad only belatedly. On the labour side this included the – ultimately unsuccessful – attempt to control the inflow of low-skilled work and to see to it that the 'lower' segment of the labour market remained of manageable size.

The competitive performance of German high-wage capitalism therefore depended on the state's capacity to control mobility and to police the boundaries of the social market economy. This in turn required continuous intervention by public and semi-public actors whose legitimisation was coded territorially: the state at various regional levels (Federal,

Länder, regional), the complicated territorial division of labour defining the realms of the 'social partners' (regional collective bargaining districts, multiscalar organisation of labour unions and employers' associations), the regional hierarchy of the institutions administering the social security systems, and so on. With hindsight, economic and political decision-makers were relatively successful in their policies of controlled mobility and the policing of social and spatial borders. However, the architecture of the German Model had an inbuilt weakness: its dependence on international markets and trade, that is on processes which are difficult to control and contain by actors firmly locked into the old territorial order (for earlier warnings, see Esser et al., 1979; Markovits, 1982).

Globalisation: the dissolution of 'normal' work and taken-for-granted certainties
During the past 20 years or so, political and economic decision-makers have had to come to terms with the paradoxical situation that Germany's main economic strength has turned out to be the country's Achilles heel. The well-being of the German political economy continues to depend almost exclusively on the successful performance of the export sector. Whilst the logics of global product and financial markets have changed dramatically compared to the international economy of the 1960s and 1970s, the institutional arrangement underpinning the postwar German economic success has only done so hesitantly. The result is a mismatch, with obvious geographical implications, between a globally integrated network economy and a regulatory regime firmly centred on national territorial institutions.

If one attempts to come to terms with the numerous analyses and studies of Germany's recent economic performance, it is easy to get lost. So contradictory are the interventions that one regularly gets empirical evidence for opposite claims. These debates often resemble attempts to read the coffee grounds, with empirical results and policy recommendations influenced by the normative frames used to access statistical data and other information. It is not my intention to participate in this debate. Rather, I illustrate a wider process which is – different normative interpretations notwithstanding – largely undisputed: the reconfiguration of the institutional arrangements underpinning capital–labour relations in Germany, and, more specifically, the erosion of the power of the German labour union movement in the current global environment.

The increasing porosity of the national economy can be illustrated with reference to two processes involving capital flows: the spatial reconfiguration of production and supply chains (outsourcing and offshoring) and the globalisation of the German capital market, both having direct repercussions on labour relations. To start with the former, the transfer of work and production steps to business units in third countries like Poland and Hungary is a hotly debated phenomenon in the German media. During the 1990s German manufacturing companies appeared to have discovered the advantages of 'contracting out', above all the cost advantages of production sharing with East European economies. Only very belatedly jumping onto the outsourcing bandwagon, transnational supply chain management strategies gained their momentum with the opening of East European economies and the double advantage of low production costs and spatial proximity ('nearshoring').

As regards financial markets, there is ample evidence that the bank-based German financial system is currently undergoing fundamental change, reflected in the increasing influence of foreign institutional investors in large German companies, the turbulences surrounding the country's leading stock exchange in Frankfurt, the presence of Anglo-American decision-makers at German supervisory and executive boards, and the wider shift towards 'value-orientated' corporate governance models (see, for instance, Deeg, 1999; Berndt, 2001; Clark et al., 2002).

How does all this affect labour in Germany? Even if there is evidence for upgrading in East European countries such as Hungary, where simpler tasks are already moving further east or south-east (for example, to Romania, Bulgaria and Serbia), outsourcing decisions to Eastern Europe are mainly driven by cost considerations. The limited evidence available suggests that there is a correlation here with the shrinking demand for so-called 'low-skilled' and increasingly also 'medium-skilled' work in Germany (see, for instance, Geishecker, 2006). Moreover, the pressure exerted by foreign and domestic investors above all on the management of manufacturing firms further intensifies the search for inefficiencies and low-cost alternatives. It is no surprise, therefore, that it is workers with a lack of or the 'wrong' professional skills who are amongst the main losers in the changes, in particular since there are few alternative sources of employment.

As German companies followed the lead of their foreign competitors and built up transnational production, supplier and marketing networks, the territorialised institutions governing labour and industrial relations in Germany were put under tremendous pressure. The balance of power between capital and labour shifted gradually as the state additionally introduced supply-side measures in an attempt to restore competitiveness. Yet international competition made it more and more difficult to finance the continuing increase in German wages and productivity simply by expanding product markets. Companies instead reverted to the 'downsizing' of their workforces, partly with the help of the state which allowed employers to socially externalise the costs of restructuring. These strategies to reduce the quantity of labour (for example, early retirement, reduction of working time) soon overstretched the already-weakened social security system to an extent that these comfortable ways to 'dispose' of excess (low-skill) labour supply had to be closed, further aggravating the problem. The alternative option, the improvement of the employability of workers via skilling (that is, increasing the quality of labour), was only considered a viable option by companies for the shrinking core of their workforces. Core employees were subjected to various flexibilisation strategies designed after managerial models emanating from companies, think tanks and business schools located in the US or in Japan. The wider task of improving the qualifications and skills of the 'losers' of the changes was left to the state, which appears to lack the financial and organisational means to do so. It is hardly surprising, therefore, that marginalised segments of the workforce had to settle with the remaining option, a strategy to lower the price of labour in order to compete with 'human capital' in those countries which profit from the influx of German FDI.

All this had serious consequences for the intermediate actors representing both sides of the collective bargaining process. Both employers' associations as well as labour unions suffered a large-scale decline and a deep fragmentation of their membership base, a process gaining momentum with the collapse of the industrial base in East Germany. During the 1990s, union membership declined to such an extent that in 2000 there were no more union members in united Germany than there had been in West Germany in 1990 (see Figure 16.1). So far, both traditional 'social partners' and, in particular, the labour unions still have not found an adequate organisational response to the decentralisation

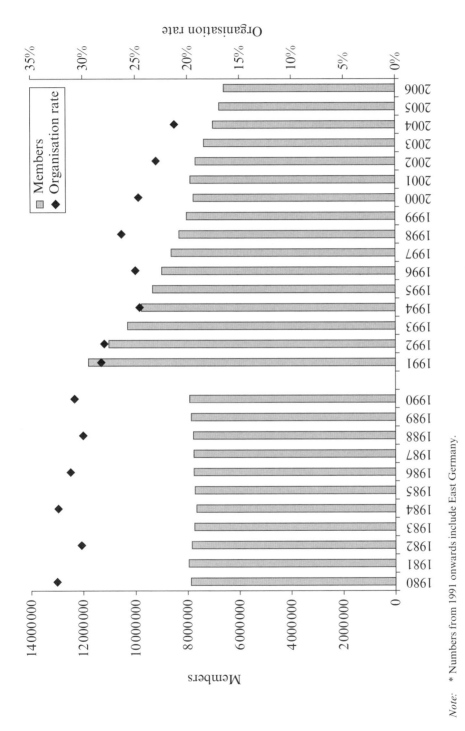

Source: DGB (2007).

Figure 16.1 Deutscher Gewerkschaftsbund (DGB), members and rate of organisation, 1980–2006

and rescaling of collective bargaining. Thus, they have sometimes openly resisted these processes, sometimes proactively accelerated them (for example, allowing differential wage settlements for firms in different economic conditions) but also they have quite often simply looked the other way (Streeck and Hassel, 2004, p. 113; Berndt, 2000).

With German capital increasingly substituting low-road price for high-road quality competition, workers are confronted with downward pressure on wages and a rise of 'abnormal', that is precarious, employment. All this occurs in a context of profound ideological change, a 'new social consensus' providing the basis for the changing balance of power and the reconfiguration of capital–labour relations in Germany. With differences in detail, the main political actors formulate their recipes against a perceived 'German disease' on the basis of often-simplistic arguments. First, there is the free market topos, that is the unquestioned assumption that one only needs to re-establish 'freedom of contract' in the labour market (and to scale back the reassuring promise of employment stability) in order to bring about positive employment effects. Linked to this is the second topos, the normative position of welfare contractualism which provided the ideological fodder for the welfare reforms initiated by the Clinton Administration or by New Labour in the UK. In the case of Germany, such workfare ideology was implemented by the second Schröder administration (2002–2005) with the so-called *Hartz-Gesetze reforms*, which were heralded by the infamous catchphrase '*fordern und fördern*' (literally to 'demand and support').

Transnational labour geographies: ambivalent responses to a mobile world
I now turn to the question of how sedentary stakeholders of the German Model are responding to the challenges outlined above. This will be done in two steps. I start with more recent, proactive measures involving attempts to transnationalise labour relations. Specifically, I argue that, by and large, these measures have not borne the expected fruits, as organised labour and state representatives have fallen back upon tried and tested approaches, namely defending territorially embedded relations and formulating reactive strategies mainly designed to strictly control cross-border mobilities (capital outwards, labour inwards).

Movement over borders: building transnational networks
'In a connexionist world', argue Luc Boltanski and Eve Chiapello (2005, p. 363), 'some people's immobility is the precondition for the profits others derive from their ability to move around'. In this regard, the dominance of global capital is not so much based on its transnational networks per se but, rather, on the mobilisation of resources in these networks vis-à-vis less mobile actors, above all workers and labour unions. It is obvious, therefore, that a true counterweight can only be established if labour rises beyond regional and national containers and attempts to match the transnational networks constructed by capital. This is a realisation that some labour unionists and activists more generally have begun to come to and, as a result, they have started to build cross-border solidarity in cases where workers were being played off against each other.

A good example for this strategy is the instrument of European Works Councils (EWCs), which are heralded by some as new actors participating in *the establishment of a transnational system of industrial relations*. However, observers are very cautious as to the effects of this instrument. Albeit acknowledging that the EWCs constitute a long overdue step towards cross-border networking and coordination, they criticise the limited space for active engagement on the part of labour representatives (see Gohde, 2005; Wills, 2000). German labour representatives in particular are sceptical of EWCs, a scepticism translating into very hesitant implementation of the 1994 EU-directive. Immersed in cross-border European production networks like no other EU member state, Germany accounts for the largest number of multinationals affected by the directive. However, numbers for 2005 illustrate that only 27.3 per cent of those companies in which EWCs could be established actually have them (123 out of 450; see Figure 16.2), a number which places Germany amongst the bottom countries for EWC establishment, compared to the remaining EU-15 member states, Switzerland and Norway (see also Kerckhofs, 2006).

The slow adoption of the EWC as an instrument of cross-border labour organising is easily explained, however, given that there are two optional blueprints for the establishment of a EWC: the German variant, with a council exclusively made up of labour representatives; and the French one, where representatives of labour and capital each make up one half of the members. Significantly, roughly two-thirds of extant EWCs follow the French Model. Given, then, that the majority of EWCs constitute a step backwards for German labour representatives, they prefer to revert to tried and tested routines and coalitions, utilising the EWC predominantly from a national perspective. Two recent examples illustrate this argument.

The first concerns a bitter dispute surrounding an Electrolux plant in Nuremberg which erupted after the management of the Swedish household appliance producer announced the closure of the plant in December 2005. After 83 years of delivering washing machines and dishwashers to German households under the well-established AEG brand, the Electrolux executive board decided to shift production to facilities in Poland (Siewierz and Zarów) and to a plant in Italy. The relocation decision affected 1750 jobs and is part of a corporate restructuring programme designed to regain competitiveness in an extremely tight global market by reducing the number of plants in high-wage countries. This decision pitted workers in Germany against workers in Poland and Italy. However, apart from a Europeanwide action day organised on 21 October 2005 by the European Metalworkers' Federation (EMF), there was little pan-European solidarity in response to this decision; affected workers instead reverted to localised protests embedded in established regional and national support networks. More importantly, though perhaps not surprisingly, labour representatives did not succeed in linking up the 'winners' in Poland and Italy with the 'losers' in Nuremberg. The important thing to take away from this example, then, is that a fragmentation of interests occurred between workers, despite the existence of a EWC which had been agreed upon and signed on 3 February 1995.

The second, more positive, example seems to contradict this assessment. Hence, in the academic literature the EWC at General Motors Europe (GME-EWC) is frequently taken as a role model exhibiting relatively advanced transnational structures. Indeed, by using this works council, labour representatives have been able to minimise the damage of recent restructuring measures and to at least limit the degree with which individual plants have been pitted against each other. Thus, when GM management threatened to close plants in the wake of decisions about the so-called 'epsilon platform' (which will service, for example, the Opel Vectra) in 2004, a situation of plants being played against each other almost erupted after an Opel plant in Rüsselsheim (Germany) and a Saab

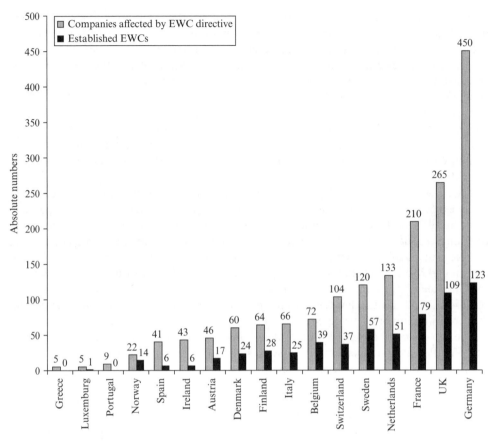

Source: ETUI-REHS (2005).

Figure 16.2   European Works Councils (EWCs), 2005

plant in Trollhättan (Sweden) were singled out as possible candidates. However, using the communication lines offered by the EWC, local works councils reached an informal agreement not to engage in competitive undercutting. The conflict ended with a framework agreement negotiated by the EMF and the GME-EWC, with the GME management laying down obligatory rules of conduct for the restructuring process that have to be honoured by all European production locations. In addition to this, the agreement included a medium-term renunciation of plant closures and the fair distribution of the costs of restructuring between all plants. Whatever one might think about the outcome, then, GM was not able to break the ranks of the works councillors and union representatives, and so was largely unable to play one plant against the other. In similar vein, when GM recently announced that various plants would have to compete for the production of the new Astra generation (using the 'delta platform'; Scherrer and Weinert, 2005), works council members in Germany, Belgium, Great Britain, Poland and Sweden signed an agreement that commits them to negotiate according to a common strategy and to refrain from solo efforts.

The relative positive effect of the GME-EWC for German high-wage locations can be explained by the composition of the institution. Although it is implemented alongside the French model, German representatives enjoy a comfortable position. The majority of the council members are delegates from German plants and the EWC head therefore routinely has a German passport. This balance of power sees to it that the interests of potential 'losers' of restructuring are better taken into account, minimising the potential gains of potential 'winners'.

Both of the examples outlined above, then, demonstrate that regional and national interests play a crucial role when organised labour attempts to catch up with the trans-nationalisation strategies implemented by capital. They also reveal, though, important spatial tensions and conundrums which German workers must confront. Thus, on the one hand, the conflicts accompanying these attempts are logical consequences of strategies to harmonise institutions which have very different historical roots. On the other hand, and this is most obvious in the Electrolux case, they are testimony to the huge dilemmas with which German organised labour is confronted. In particular, because they enjoy a relatively comfortable position in Germany, it makes more sense, at least at first sight, for workers and their representatives to stick with the fragmented status quo of national systems of labour regulation. At the same time, however, it is difficult to imagine anything other than some sort of renunciation of coveted achievements (codetermination, wages and so on) if transnationalism is to be effectively built in the future.

Borders over movement: labour vagabonds, sedentary workers and the territorial state
The argument so far has dealt with the increasing ability of mobile capital to take advantage of a pan-European labour market by moving production activities abroad. The situation for more place-dependent production, above all certain service activities, however, is quite a different one. Specifically, for these activities transnationalisation means that it is labour that moves towards the site of production, thereby allowing sedentary capital also to enjoy the advantages of a flexible workforce segment. Here the dilemmas of the two relatively immobile stakeholders of the German Model, the state and labour, become particularly visible. Notwithstanding internal fragmentation and conflicts of interest, both unions and governments at different spatial scales routinely respond with contradictory and 'conservative' measures one-sidedly informed by methodological nationalism. The phrase 'borders over movement' illustrates this.

Contradictions are particularly evident in the context of low-paid labour migration, above all from East Central European (ECE) countries. This has been particularly so in the wake of the recent EU enlargements. Thus, citizens from new EU member states are allowed to travel to Germany without restrictions and are legally entitled to stay there for a period of up to three months. Whilst countries such as the UK, Ireland and Sweden agreed simultaneously to open their labour markets, Germany adopted a more restrictive policy, making use of provisions which allow the closure of the labour market for a maximum period of seven years. With regard to the A8 states (the countries entering the EU in 2004), this is managed in line with the so-called 2+3+2 model, according to which Germany has the right to apply for three periods of grace as long as certain conditions are fulfilled (for example, high domestic unemployment). The German parliament has recently voted to seek the final two-year period (ending in April 2011).

Given that German businesses and private households appear to be as dependent on the employment of low-paid East European workers as their counterparts in other EU-15 countries, local authorities have to individually scrutinise each individual case. Even if responsible officials are instructed to grant exemptions only very restrictively, it is possible, at least in principle, for individual migrants to enter the country and apply for a work permit, provided they are able to prove they have three months of continuous residence and have a potential employer. However, the vast majority of ECE labour migrants legally working in Germany do so under the auspices of bilateral agreements (above all seasonal work, contract work, sectoral exemptions). German law provides various legal codes with a veritable maze of stipulations and exemptions, to an extent that reliable statistical information is impossible to get. The current national migration report (BAMF, 2006), for instance, lists 63 exceptions, ranging from seasonal work in agriculture and contract work in construction to exotic cases such as 'specialty chefs' or 'models, dress men and mannequins'. For A8 workers alone, local and national authorities issued a total of almost 1.2 million work permits from 2004 to 2007 (ZAV, n.d.). Given these astonishing figures, one might speculate that the non-transparent nature of the measures serves two purposes: first, to hide from view the true scale of the phenomenon and the extent to which the German economy depends on low-wage migrants at a time of a difficult labour market situation; second, to control labour mobility, flexibly adjusting quotas in line with economic necessities. In order to achieve these goals, state authorities put up with considerable bureaucratic costs.

A further example concerns ongoing discussions about the introduction of sectoral minimum wages with the so-called *Arbeitnehmer-Entsendegesetze* ('law over the sending of workers'). The first sectoral minimum wage was put into effect within the construction sector in 1996, requiring any foreign company that sends employees to Germany to pay the wage set by the respective collective agreement. This measure has recently been extended towards commercial cleaning. This is an important intervention in the labour market, for once declared mandatory for the whole industry, the lowest wage band in the collective agreement negotiated by employers and unions effectively defines a legally binding minimum wage.

Finally, there is the phenomenon of so-called 'illegal' employment of migrants. Many of these are workers who enter the country without the necessary documents. Unfortunately, though, with the exception of a few case studies (see Alt, 1999; Cyrus, 2000), the empirical picture is still extremely patchy. Nevertheless, the lack of reliable data notwithstanding, there is evidence that efforts by the authorities to control this type of undocumented migration have been intensifying recently, a development which some observers (for example, Bommes, 2006) have connected to regressive national migration policies. The majority of cases, however, concern labour migrants who hold residence titles but who are being employed in Germany in breach of the labour law or collective wage agreements (*Tarifverträge*). In the respective industries and sectors, such as commercial cleaning, construction, or hotel and restaurants, many employers illegally deviate from the agreements with local labour offices, either by paying well below the wage set in the respective collective wage agreement and/or the so-called 'local average' or by reducing the hourly wage by demanding longer hours of work. It is non-EU citizens who are predominantly affected by these exploitative practices, given that their right to stay in Germany is dependent on a regular job.

Geographically, larger cities and urban agglomerations constitute the focuses of these labour flows (with the obvious exception of agriculture). In a recent study focusing on the Frankfurt region, Krieger et al. (2006) give three reasons for this. The first concerns the local labour market. Frankfurt's business sector provides a sizeable number of jobs in various sectors, ranging from construction, commercial cleaning, transport, gardening, care and entertainment/prostitution. To this, one has to add the similarly high demand from the sizeable share of relatively wealthy private households for support in cleaning, private care, gardening and so on. The second reason is linked to Frankfurt's cosmopolitan demography, providing the family and ethnic networks which alleviate the job search for migrants without legal residency. Finally, there is the role of Frankfurt as a major transport hub, with the airport in particular making the city a natural destination for incoming migrants. On the one hand, then, Frankfurt serves as a 'city on the way', as a stopover en route to other European and German metropoles. On the other hand, transit migrants often stay longer than intended, literally getting stuck in Frankfurt.

In light of these developments, critics take issue with the protectionist nature of the policy responses, either being uneasy with thinly veiled nationalist attempts to protect German workers by keeping foreigners out or the unions' efforts to protect the well-paid stable jobs of a declining core workforce by demanding an end to social dumping (Offe, 1999, p. 214). Advocates point to the less mobile losers in this competition: German workers with little or no skills, companies which cannot easily follow the offshoring and outsourcing routes taken by their competitors, or the state at different levels having to forfeit taxes and social security dues. This is a debate which does not have easy answers and solutions. However, at a second glance, it is possible to identify two reasons for the gap between government rhetoric and concrete political practice. The first is that the labour migrants are simply indispensable. Hence, although large parts of the German population themselves expect to lead relatively stable, sedentary lifestyles, these are lifestyles that presuppose global connections and cross-border mobility. Second, if one looks behind the rhetorical façade it becomes obvious that all-encompassing control is impossible. Border security measures are simply evaded in daily migratory practices, for instance in cases where labour migrants routinely renew their three-months' residence title at the border without applying for formal work permits. A Polish migrant working in a private Frankfurt household describes a widespread practice:

> At that moment we were no longer required to have a visa. I was allowed to stay in Germany for three months. This is why I went back to Poland roughly every three months, to get a new stamp at the border. I simply was a tourist in Germany. (Interview, 30 December 2006)

Reacting to the restrictions applying to waged labour migrants after EU enlargement, another widespread way to undermine the sovereignty of the state available to ECE migrants is their registration of a business and their engagement in self-employment. A Lithuanian construction worker explains how he registered two quite disparate businesses:

> When they admitted Lithuania to the EU, my employer, I have been working for him from the beginning, suggested that I registered my own business. This because I was caught working illegally once. . . . Normally I am working as an electrician, but I registered two businesses, one as electrician, another as translator – Russian, Lithuanian and German. (Interview, 10 March 2007)

In another interview, Frankfurt representatives of the *Finanzkontrolle Schwarzarbeit*, the organisation responsible for policing illegal work practices, refer to 'bogus self-employment' (*'Scheinselbstständigkeit'*) and mention cases where migrants registered up to 20 different businesses or – at the other extreme – extremely specialised activities, such as the cleaning of glasses in the food processing industry (Interview, 22 February 2006). These practices result in a marked increase in the overall share of self-employment and in the numbers of East European 'businesses'. In Frankfurt, for instance, a recent study identified Polish firms as the largest group within the international business community (Behrend et al., 2007). A look at business registration data confirms this picture at the national level. Counting only 2366 cases in 2002, the number of Polish businesses increased to 16 704 in 2004 and 38 477 in 2007 (Statistisches Bundesamt, 2007).

Overall, government responses to labour migration have not changed much over the last decades. The sovereignty of the state is legitimised above all through the capacity to define criteria for inclusion and exclusion. In so doing, the state can decide the degree of access 'foreigners' will have to the state territory. Migration, in its manifold disguises, therefore constitutes a structural challenge for the territorial nation state (Bommes, 2000; Wimmer, 1999). This is why migration continues to be represented as a temporary process in official statements, the product of simple pull and push factors, individual decisions and criminal activities. This is the traditional sedentary perspective on migration, a temporary state of mobility interrupting a normal sedentary life. Migration studies, however, have shown that in a global world this classical migration pattern is increasingly becoming supplemented by new migration realities. It is at least as 'normal' for a growing number of people to live a mobile life, with regular periods 'on the move' framing temporary periods of stability. Another Polish labour migrant, working in domestic services in the Frankfurt region, explains how she regularly takes turns with her mother, commuting between Poland and Germany every two months:

> Whenever you take on a job it is normally the case that you stay for a period of two months or so. It depends on the details of the agreement. . . . As I said, we take turns every two months. My mother leaves Aschaffenburg [a city located close to Frankfurt] and I arrive, she goes to Poland. Then it is she who comes back and I go back, as long as it works for the both of us. (Interview, 29 June 2006)

This example is supported by empirical studies that clearly demonstrate the extent to which current migratory practices deviate from the traditional picture. 'Legal' and 'illegal' migration projects both produce and utilise transnational social networks, in the process creating new social realities which stretch beyond the territorial border of one or two nation states (Alt, 2003).

Paradoxical b/orderings

In this section I seek to make sense of the empirical examples given above, connecting the transnational labour geographies of a fledgling global order with the national regulatory compromises of a crumbling territorial order. Although continuing to use Germany as the main reference point, I believe that there are lessons to be drawn for the analyses of labour geographies in other contexts.

The focus of this section is on the political borders which frame national economies. Debates over economic globalisation still often inadequately take into account that the movements of capital, goods and people occur in the context of an ambivalent double play of debordering and rebordering processes. Territorial borders, though, are not just eliminated and eroded, but they are reproduced and sharpened at the same time. Hence, it is more appropriate to assume that borders are made contingent. Thus, as Beck (2002, p. 143; my translation) puts it: 'Globalisation goes hand in hand with an accentuation of borders, an intensification of border controls: these new borders, however, do not work like the old ones. They resemble Swiss Cheese, holes and uncertainties being systematically built in to simultaneously safeguard the flow of information, capital and people'. This quote, then, highlights the asymmetric nature of globalisation processes and underscores the fact that the realities of our global age are to a large extent being negotiated around the axis of mobility/immobility. Within this context, diverging interests between relatively mobile and relatively sedentary actors are fracturing the ranks of all stakeholders of the German variant of capitalism, resulting in ambivalence and uncertainty. This can be illustrated through examining the activities of the three main social actors of German corporatism.

Capital

Businesses are normally regarded as the winners of the ongoing globalisation of relations of production, exchange and circulation. Seen from the perspective of capital, the new power geometry results from the ability to exploit locational differences, actively pushing national and regional actors to compete against each other. An indispensable precondition for geographical arbitrage is a technoscape of uniform standards and norms which provides the global frame of reference allowing corporate decision-makers to compare, classify and benchmark individual production sites. In order for this finely tuned regime of global standardisation (for example, quality norms) and territorial differentiation (for example, wages, taxes, regulations) to work and to maintain its organisational flexibility, it is crucial for capital to be more mobile than other actors, such as the state or labour. In this context, it is obvious that it is to the advantage of capital that the state and labour continue to base their decisions largely on the established territorial order.

However, despite the preponderance of the neoliberal rhetoric of capital mobility, this logic holds only for those businesses which have a certain size and more than one plant and are capable of arranging internal competition for lucrative orders. The conflicts at Electrolux and GM Europe discussed earlier are a good example of this. The situation for less mobile, more place-bound businesses, though, is different, as sedentary capital has quite different interests. The conflicts within the employers' camp during recent wage bargaining rounds, for instance, can to a large degree be explained by mobility mismatches. This holds above all for industries which find it difficult to make use of the opportunity to relocate production activities (for example, construction, agriculture, consumer-orientated services). These businesses utilise an emerging transnational European labour market in a different way, namely the recruitment of workers from the growing pool of East European labour migrants.

It is obvious that both sides within the capital camp pursue different strategies with regard to migration policy. While the former are above all interested in unfettered cross-border mobility of capital and high-skilled employees, the latter's focus is on securing as unbureaucratic an access to the German labour market for predominantly low-paid labour migrants as possible.

Labour

Whether institutionalised in unions and works councils or as individual workers, labour has been forced on the defensive in the global age. All the more important, then, are measures of belated transnationalisation, such as that implemented by individual labour unions bilaterally or by labour representatives in the context of the EWC instrument. However, whereas successful organisational upscaling by labour can be interpreted as a threat to the competitive advantage of mobile capital, on the labour side measures like these necessarily depend on a sizeable, homogeneous group with common interests. In Germany this is provided by the personalised core of *Modell Deutschland*, the normal worker embedded in the 'standard' work relation (that is full-time, unionised, industrial employment, male). It is hardly surprising, therefore, that the relatively successful examples of transnational union activism all involve this segment of the German economy, mainly large companies often dominating oligopolistic domestic markets. Equally, though, it is also hardly surprising that the results of concerted, transnational action often 'only' remain defensive, providing – as important as it may be – a frame for controlled downsizing or for spreading the costs of restructuring less unevenly across production sites in different countries.

From the perspective of organised labour, the erosion of the standard form of employment constitutes a dilemma which is almost impossible to solve, making it a lot more difficult to successfully transnationalise organised labour practices for two reasons. First, to a large extent it is the 'normal worker' who holds membership and keeps unions alive. Given that this shrinking segment of the workforce enjoys relatively high labour standards and wages, the legitimacy of unions crucially depends on the defence of these achievements. This is why German unionists and works councillors regard instruments such as the EWC predominantly as a means to export the benefits of the German system of labour regulation to other countries. This is a noble cause, but not necessarily in the interests of labour elsewhere, a fact which explains the frictions and limits to truly transnational coordination whenever global players announce restructuring programmes. As the Electrolux and GM cases aptly illustrate, the odds are still relatively good as long as German workers play a strong role in the companies involved. However, in the wake of the belated but nonetheless dramatic financial transnationalisation of what has traditionally been termed *Deutschland AG* (Germany Inc.), this position is eroding. In an environment like this it is difficult to imagine how transnationalism might be constructed in the future unless German workers would be willing to give up some of the coveted achievements that are so specific to the German Model.

The second reason concerns relations to workers in the south or east. On the one hand there are those segments of the workforce that perform tasks within production and value chains through which other regions are able to upgrade their production processes (perhaps through the introduction of new technologies which come with the production chain). The closer the labour productivity gap becomes between such workers, though, the stronger is the competition between domestic and foreign workers, and appeals for transnational solidarity increasingly fall on deaf ears. On the other hand, however, there are those remaining segments of the workforce who continue to enjoy a productivity premium over foreign workers. The problem for these workers is that they appear to profit less and less from the wealth generated from this advantage, being confronted instead with stagnating or falling real incomes and a general environment of insecurity.

Again, this provides little incentive for transnational solidarity with workers elsewhere (see Scherrer, 2006).

It is little wonder, therefore, that unions are caught in contradictions. Union migration policy was predominantly directed towards the classical, longer-term migrant, that is guest-workers and their emancipation and integration. These policies are largely ineffective with regard to more flexible and increasingly circular migration patterns. As a consequence of this, labour unions are faced with particularly stark dilemmas regarding their treatment of these migrants. Too positive an attitude may result in lower wages and costs for the domestic workforce. An overtly restrictive attitude, though, does not chime well with the tradition of international solidarity and also neglects that there are always sectors that suffer from a lack of labour supply or that labour migrants often occupy niches vacated by domestic workers (Schmidt and Schwenken, 2006).

In the face of these problems German unions have tended to retreat into restrictive positions, attempting to defend the national-territorial system of labour regulation with demands for controls and sanctions. By representing low-wage labour migration predominantly as a labour supply phenomenon, underlying contradictions are easily disguised. Yet if the increasing demand for the services of low-wage migrants is taken into consideration, it is obvious that comfortable sedentary lifestyles greatly depend on the mobility of both relatively cheap goods and labour. A quite paradoxical situation hence emerges: put in jeopardy by an increasingly mobile world, a once-successful territorial economic system increasingly has to rely on these very movements – movements, however, that in turn put its longevity further into question.

State

Compared to the actors on the capital side, the state is also portrayed as losing out in the wake of globalisation. Being 'about fixity rather than motion' (Harvey, 2006, p. 106), the state appears to have lost much of its power, through, for instance, the – self-inflicted – loss in importance of national monetary or industrial policy. However, a more differentiated analysis is warranted here as well (see Zeller, 2003). Thus, it has largely been the state itself that has been responsible for the contingentisation of its borders. This has been done in the name of sedentary actors both on the capital and the labour side, and is shot through with contradictions. On the one hand, there is a need to grant sedentary actors access to inexpensive labour migrants. This is in the interest of place-dependent service businesses, which are confronted with increasing competition in the wake of liberalisation measures implemented by the EU, as well as private households which safeguard their still relatively comfortable lifestyles with the help of labour migrants. On the other hand, the state is under considerable pressure to protect those domestic workers and businesses that are in direct competition with labour migrants or foreign firms sending workers to Germany. Labour unions, business associations and political decision-makers alike supported decisions such as the full use of the seven-year transition period for legal entry to the German labour market for workers from new EU member states or the gradual introduction of legal minimum wages for sectors deemed sensitive (construction and industrial cleaning).

Policy responses to the current round of EU enlargement are a good example for these dilemmas. On the one hand, German authorities pursue restrictive policies, making full use of the possibilities to delay full liberalisation. On the other, there is a huge interest in the presence of low-paid ECE labour migrants in the German labour market, for the overstretched German social security system is best served by migrants who only stay in the country during their productive age and who incur only limited costs (healthcare, education and so on). Employers, whether corporate or private, are often able to pay low wages because social reproduction largely takes place elsewhere (for example, when the rest of the family remains in the country of origin). Equally, although they may adopt an anti-immigration rhetoric and implement strategies against 'illegal' migration, nation states at the same time frequently actively contribute to short-term labour flows by introducing cross-border mobility programmes and temporary quotas exclusively tailored towards the flexible labour needs of employers in their countries.

It is these contradictions that appear to be partly responsible for the array of exceptions, special cases, bilateral agreements and procedural instructions which gave rise to a non-transparent regime of labour market access, for which Beck's graphic comparison with Swiss cheese appears to be an understatement. However, it is also possible to interpret these contradictory and complicated regulations as a clever measure to hide from view the true scale of cross-border labour migration, with the collection of ever more detailed statistical data helping the state to maintain the illusion that the phenomenon is kept under control. This is how the conceptualisation of borders as being made contingent has to be understood: a finely tuned, highly flexible b/ordering regime which is constantly adjusted to the needs of sedentary actors (businesses, unions, workers, private households and so on).

Conclusion

I started this chapter with a stylised juxtaposition of the German Model in the territorial and the global age. The main argument was that increasing mobility and transnational availability of labour and capital contributed to the erosion of an established territorial economic order. To this, one has to add an important reservation: the national/territorial age only successfully created the illusion of quasi-natural territorial containment, for the production of the national 'has always occurred *across* borders, by *violating* borders, that is it has always been *trans*-national' (Beck, 2002, p. 82; my translation, emphasis in original). The meta-narrative of the territorial model economy, still resurrected regularly today in Germany and abroad, has only been plausible as long as the underlying contradictions remain invisible. In this regard, for instance, we might think of the crucial role of mobile labour from Mediterranean countries during the immediate postwar decades. These transnational conditions for success were made invisible by continuing reference to the labour migrants as 'guests' long after it became clear that many of them were in Germany for good.

In a similar vein, the geographies of the transformation processes outlined above are far more complex than is permitted by the still widespread simplistic globalisation debate. Thus, the unwanted truths of our global age are veiled and disguised, as with the state's deeply contradictory approach towards 'undocumented' migrants or the contradiction that the German government reacts negatively to EU enlargement whilst simultaneously allowing numerous tightly regulated breaches in its border fortifications. Political and economic decision-makers have not yet found forward-looking, constructive responses to the challenges of an increasingly interwoven and mobile world. Rather than pursuing new ways of 'governance in de-bordered spaces' (Habermas, 2007; my translation), they conservatively retreat behind territorial walls. The nation state, however, has changed dramatically. Or, as Claus Offe (1999, p. 218) has put it: the stakeholders of the German Model have not yet fully realised that the 'congruence of the scopes of interdependency and regulation, which is what used to define a "national" economy, has ceased to exist'.

References

Albert, M. (1993), *Capitalism against Capitalism*, London: Whurr.

Alt, J. (1999), *Illegal in Deutschland* [Illegal in Germany], Karlsruhe: von Loeper Literaturverlag.

Alt, J. (2003), 'Problemkomplex illegale Migration' [The problematic issue of illegal migration], *ZAR*, **11/12**, 406–11.

Bathelt, H. and M.S. Gertler (2005), 'The German variety of capitalism: forces and dynamics of evolutionary change', *Economic Geography*, **81** (1), 1–9.

Beck, U. (2002), *Macht und Gegenmacht im Globalen Zeitalter* [Power and countervailing power in the global age], Frankfurt am Main: Suhrkamp.

Behrend, R., G. Gutberlet, D. Herbold, U. Hiltmann, A. Obermann and A. Stücker (2007), 'Wirtschaft International 2007 – Ausländische Unternehmen im IHK-Bezirk Frankfurt am Main' [Economy international 2007 – Foreign companies in the IHK-district Frankfurt], *Frankfurter Statistische Berichte*, **1**, 38–57.

Berndt, C. (2000), 'The rescaling of labour regulation in Germany – from national and regional corporatism to intra-firm welfare?' *Environment and Planning A*, **32** (9), 1569–92.

Berndt, C. (2001), *Corporate Germany between Globalization and Regional Place Dependence: Business Restructuring in the Ruhr Area*, Houndsmills: Palgrave.

Boltanski, L. and E. Chiapello (2005), *The New Spirit of Capitalism*, London: Verso.

Bommes, M. (2000), 'National welfare state, biography and migration: labour migrants, ethnic Germans and the re-ascription of welfare state membership', in M. Bommes and A. Geddes (eds), *Immigration and Welfare: Challenging the Borders of the Welfare State*, London: Routledge, pp. 90–108.

Bommes, M. (2006), 'Migration und gesellschaftlicher Strukturwandel', in Bundeskriminalamt (Federal Criminal Police Office) (ed.), *Illegale Migration – Gesellschaften und Polizeiliche Handlungsfelder im Wandel* [Illegal migration – social change and challenges for policing strategies], documentation from the BKA Autumn Conference 14–16 November, pp. 24–37.

Bundesamt für Migration und Flüchtlinge (BAMF) (2006), *Migrationsbericht 2006* [Migration Report 2006], Nürnberg.

Clark, G.L., D. Mansfield and A. Tickell (2002), 'Global finance and the German model: German corporations, market incentives, and the management of employer-sponsored pension institutions', *Transactions of the Institute of British Geographers*, New Series, **27** (1), 91–110.

Cyrus, N. (2000), 'Komplementäre formen grenzüberschreitender Migration: Einwanderung und Mobilität' [Converging forms of cross-border migration: immigration and mobility], in K.M. Schmals (ed.), *Migration und Stadt* [Migration and the City], Opladen: Leske und Budrich, pp. 115–37.

Deeg, R. (1999), *Finance Capitalism Unveiled*, Ann Arbor, MI: University of Michigan Press.

Deutscher Gewerkschaftsbund (DGB) (2007), Membership statistics, available at: www.dgb.de/dgb/mitglied-erzahlen/mitglieder.htm, accessed 28 September 2007.

Esping-Andersen, G. (1994), 'Welfare states and the economy', in N.J. Smelser and R. Swedberg (eds), *The Handbook of Economic Sociology*, Princeton, NJ: Princeton University Press, pp. 711–32.

Esser, J. and W. Fach (1981), 'Korporatistische Krisenregulierung im "Modell Deutschland"' [Corporatist crisis regulation in the German Model], in U. von Alemann (ed.), *Neo-Korporatismus*, Frankfurt: Campus.

Esser, J., W. Fach, G. Junne, F. Schlupp and G. Simonis (1979), 'Das "Modell Deutschland" und seine Konstruktionsschwächen' [Model Germany and its structural weaknesses], *Leviathan*, **7** (1), 1–11.

ETUI-REHS (2005), European Works Councils database, June 2005, available at: www.ewcdb.org/graphics.php, accessed 1 August 2006.

Geishecker, I. (2006), 'Does outsourcing to central and eastern Europe really threaten manual workers' jobs in Germany?', *The World Economy*, **29** (5), 559–83.

Gohde, H. (2005), *European Works Councils: Analysis and Recommendations*, Frankfurt am Main: Bund-Verlag.

Habermas, J. (2007), 'Europapolitik in der Sackgasse' [European policy at a dead end], paper presented at the IX Philosophiekongress 'Philosophy meets politics' conference, Berlin, 23 November.

Hall, P.A. and D. Soskice (2001), 'An introduction to varieties of capitalism', in P.A. Hall and D. Soskice (eds), *Varieties of Capitalism: The Institutional Foundations of Comparative Advantage*, Oxford: Oxford University Press, pp. 1–68.

Harvey, D. (2006), *Spaces of Global Capitalism: Towards a Theory of Uneven Geographical Development*, London: Verso.

Häußermann, H. and W. Siebel (2001), 'Integration und Segregation – Überlegungen zu einer alten Debatte' [Integration and segration – thoughts on an old debate], *Zeitschrift für Kommunalwissenschaften*, **1**, 68–79.

Kerckhofs, P. (2006), *European Works Councils Database*, Brussels: European Trade Institute for Research, Education and Health and Safety (ETUI-REHS).

Krieger, W., M. Ludwig, P. Schupp and A. Will (2006), *Lebenslage 'Illegal': Menschen ohne Aufenthaltsstatus in Frankfurt am Main* [Living 'illegally': people without official residency status in Frankfurt], Karlsruhe: von Loeper Literaturverlag.

Markovits, A.S. (1982), 'Introduction: Model Germany – a cursory overview of a complex construct', in A.S. Markovits (ed.), *The Political Economy of West Germany: Modell Deutschland*, New York: Praeger, pp. 1–11.

Offe, C. (1999), 'The German welfare state: principles, performance, prospects', in J.S. Brady, B. Crawford and S.E. Wiliarty (eds), *The Postwar Transformation of Germany – Democracy, Prosperity, and Nationhood*, Ann Arbor, MI: University of Michigan Press, pp. 202–24.

Offe, C. (2003), 'Freiheit, Sicherheit, Effizienz. Spannungen zwischen Gerechtigkeitsnormen für Arbeitsmarkt und Wohlfahrtsstaat' [Liberty, security, efficiency. Tensions between the norms of justice in the labor market and the welfare state], in J. Allmendinger (ed.), *Entstaatlichung und soziale Sicherheit. Verhandlungen des 31. Kongresses der Deutschen Gesellschaft für Soziologie in Leipzig 2002*, Opladen: Leske + Budrich, pp. 15–32.

Scherrer, C. (2006), 'Weltmarkt und Gewerkschaftsarbeit' [The global market and union organising], *WSI-Mitteilungen*, **1**, 2–4.

Scherrer, P. and R. Weinert (2005), 'Auf dem Weg zur europäischen Tarifpolitik' [Towards a European wage bargaining policy], *Frankfurter Rundschau*, 10 August, p. 13.

Schmidt, V. and H. Schwenken (2006), 'Irreguläre Migration und Gewerkschaften im internationalen Vergleich' [Irregular migration and unions: an international comparison], *WSI-Mitteilungen*, **1**, 41–6.

Statistisches Bundesamt (2007), 'Gewerbeanzeigestatistik [Business notification statistics] (selected years)', available from: www.destatis.de.

Streeck, W. (1997), 'German capitalism – does it exist? Can it survive?', *New Political Economy*, **2**, 237–56.

Streeck, W. and A. Hassel (2004), 'The crumbling pillars of social partnership', in W. Streeck and H. Kitschelt (eds), *Germany: Beyond the Stable State*, London: Frank Cass, pp. 101–24.

Wills, J. (2000), 'Great expectations: three years in the life of a European Works Council', *European Journal of Industrial Relations*, **6** (1), S. 85–107.

Wimmer, A. (1999), 'Territoriale Schließung und die Politisierung des Ethnischen' [Territorial closure and the politicization of ethnicity], in C. Honegger, S. Hradil and F. Traxler (eds), *Grenzenlose Gesellschaft?* Opladen: Leske + Budrich, pp. 510–18.

Zeller, C. (2003), 'Bausteine zu einer Geographie des Kapitalismus' [Building stones for a geography of capitalism], *Zeitschrift für Wirtschaftsgeographie*, **47** (3/4), 215–30.

Zentrale Auslands- und Fachvermittlung (ZAV) (unpublished), Work Permit Data 2004–2007.

17 European Works Councils: from the local to the global?

Ian Fitzgerald and John Stirling

Introduction

European Works Councils (EWCs) are unique entities established by a supra-state institution, the European Union, to counterbalance the power of multinational capital by enabling workers to develop cross-border solidarities. Such a grandiose claim is quickly tempered by the reality of the operation of EWCs and any realistic assessment of 'countervailing' power. Nevertheless, EWCs offer a different dimension in the flat landscape of industrial relations structures that rarely stretch beyond national horizons. In this regard, they may challenge entrenched national systems or be merely subservient to the industrial relations cultures and laws of the host country of 'their' multinational corporation. Administratively, they sit inside a global infrastructure of trade union organisation, with its conglomerations of European and international sector-based bodies and structures of national confederations (with their arcane relationships and circumscribed representational functions). In a few cases, European works councils have become global works councils. EWCs comprise workers directly employed in their companies, and not at one remove, and thus have at least the opportunity for facilitating a direct engagement between the cross-border role of the EWC and those they represent in their own countries and workplaces.

Our goal in this chapter, then, is to explore how EWCs map on to the extant geography of trade union representation, with its embedded national and local roots and its global branches. How do they relate to the multilayered organisational structures that have been developed historically by unions when trade unions are not even mentioned in the Directive that established EWCs and which saw works councils, rather than the unions, as the representative organisations of a company's workers? In considering such questions, it is certainly important to recognise that EWCs are not all of a kind, for they have the opportunity to work along a very long continuum of engagement and influence on workers' lives. At one end of this continuum, they may be little more than an 'add on' to a largely nationally based multinational whose workers have little inclination to be engaged with workers in other countries, let alone involve themselves in the complexities of multinational trade unionism. At the opposite end of this continuum, we might expect to find EWCs where engagement with European or even global trade union organisations is seen as central to effective cross-border organising and where links with other EWCs can be powerfully built. Although this continuum offers EWCs numerous possibilities, then, research suggests that in practice the former position is considerably more likely than the latter for three key reasons. First, although MNC decisions may be made in a European or global context, they will be delivered locally. Moreover, many key corporate employment and industrial relations decisions may actually be the prerogative of local managers, such that workers will need to challenge this power at its locus. Therefore, workers may see little reason for looking much beyond their local circumstances. Second, put simply, cross-border solidarity is complex because countries are different. Different levels of union density, fractured or centralised union structures, different union 'cultures' in relation to industrial action and a whole range of differences in industrial relations frameworks, which are likely to include significant variations in legal frameworks, all hamper the Europeanising of European works councils. Third, and deriving in part from the foregoing, EWCs have limited legislative power to operate on a multinational level. Thus, the Directive itself is a narrow document that refers only to information and consultation on a restricted range of issues that are solely cross-national. The interpretation of this latter point, though, can be the source of significant conflict, as workers argue, for example, that a workplace closure in one country has inevitable cross-national repercussions, whilst managers try to exclude discussion of an issue affecting more than one country.

In terms of their establishment, employers were generally hostile to setting up EWCs – 60 per cent of companies covered by the Directive had no EWCs by 2008. What is more, employers are easily able to constrain EWC power through restricting the number and length of meetings, controlling agendas and not allowing adequate time or training for worker representatives to carry out their duties whilst remaining within the Directive's strictures. Finally, EWCs' structures mirror those of the companies with which they are associated, with the result that a company's differentiated organisational structure with its delegated decision-making across a range of locations in different economic sectors may give workers little scope to see 'their company' as a relevant locus of power. So the question arises: why invest energy in engaging in an EWC?

Turning now to matters spatial, it is the case, of course, that locating EWCs organisationally locates them geographically too. Internally, EWCs are dynamic clusters of individuals representing locations from within separate countries. This might lead to dominant and subordinate country groupings or relationships that are closer to parity. It will also enhance or inhibit cross-country solidarities within the EWC which can be geographically determined, as with, for example, Nordic or southern European groupings. Structurally, EWCs are located within two dimensions. First, there is that dimension which is occupied by their company, which may have a simple or a complex geographical structure that may be, say, restricted to Europe or may have a global reach (such that, in this latter case, the EWC may also be global). Second, the EWC will be located, through its trade union members, in a potentially complex web of national, European and global union structures, given that historical factors mean that the members from various countries will be differentially connected to an assortment of regional and international labour organisations (Global Union Federations, national confederations, European-wide entities, and so forth). The interaction of this complex set of organisational and geographical relationships, then, will shape the activities of each individual EWC, offering outcomes that might range from the signing of International Framework Agreements at one level to the extension of national bargaining at another.

Bearing all this in mind, in what follows we begin with a short account of the development of EWCs to set their context and then use data from two surveys in the North East of England as the basis for exploring the complex set of power and place interrelationships we identified above. We examine several geographical issues associated with the spread of EWCs into North East England, specifically how the particularities of place in the region are shaping how these EWCs are developing, what role the EWCs' organisational structures are playing in linking workers in different parts of Europe together transnationally and how decisions made at the European level are impacting local labour regimes and organising opportunities. In other words, we contemplate the linkages that have developed between the local scale and the supranational European Union scale as a result of the creation of EWCs.

European Works Councils

Directive 94/45/EC (1994) is the basis of the transposition of national legislation establishing European-wide procedures for informing and consulting employees, commonly known as European Works Councils (see Fitzgerald, 2004 for a discussion of the background). The Directive applied to the then 15 member states of the European Union, with a further three additional countries from the European Economic Area (Iceland, Norway and Liechtenstein). The 2004 EU enlargement has extended the Directive's coverage to a total of 28 countries. The most reliable estimates (Kerckhofs and Pas, 2004) suggest that following enlargement there were 2169 EWCs and that the number continued to grow by some 15 per cent between 2002 and 2004 (European Industrial Relations Observatory, 2004). Estimates of the number of participants are difficult to assess (see Kerckhofs, 2002) but on a conservative estimate of an average of 20 delegates on each EWC there would be in excess of 40 000 European Works Councillors. However, this is a constituency characterised by fluidity as representatives enter and leave EWCs or move on to other EWCs as companies grow, diminish, close and restructure.

The rapid growth of EWCs as a new and transnational institution has led to the development of a considerable descriptive and critical literature[1] drawing on different traditions but commonly adopting the perspective of organised labour. The continued and rising interest of geographers in EWCs as institutions in the academic space formerly solely occupied by industrial relations specialists is particularly notable. Sadler (2000, p. 146), for example, in his review of three dimensions in the geographical literature on trade unions, stressed the significance of EWCs and their 'potential [for] re-scaling labour relations in Europe'. Wills (1998 and 2001, for instance) has made a number of notable contributions to the study of EWCs from the same perspective. Meanwhile, more traditional industrial relations studies have emerged from Lecher's three volumes (Lecher et al., 1999, 2001, 2003) and a range of discussion can be found in Fitzgerald and Stirling (2004). In addition, there are regular policy documents that draw on research as the basis for seeking to influence EU decision-making (for example Jagodzinski et al., 2008). Whatever the academic perspective, though, there has been an underlying orientation in much of the analysis towards how EWCs might support the interests of workers and trade unions.

Equally evident from this literature has been a debate between what have commonly been suggested as 'optimistic' and 'pessimistic' arguments. In reality, the debate centres on the key issue of power and whether, in any real sense, EWCs offer an opportunity to influence cross-border management decision-making. In this context, the EWC is often conceptualised as representing an undifferentiated 'worker'. In other words, the EWC is presupposed to act as an organisation with a single interest (that of 'labour') as against the interest of capital in the multinational company. The reality, however, is that EWCs are highly differentiated organisations and that issues of space and location are critical to understanding the utilisation (or absence) of power in EWCs. To suggest a unity of purpose is to ignore the divisions between workers implicit in geographical location and extended through the variety of coalitions and occupational interest groups suggested by Stirling and Tully (2004). Power is not only exercised between capital and labour but also between labour and labour from different locations in circumstances where national labour/management coalitions have the potential to prove stronger than international labour solidarity – in other words, in cases where workers show greater loyalty to place by aligning themselves with various national capitals than they do to (transnational) class. In effect, before we can discuss the question of the power of EWCs as entities in themselves we must analyse their locational composition and the divisions this may bring. Thus, national and local trade unions may use EWCs to develop their own power strategies as against the interests of others with whom they might be presumed to share a common class identity and orientation, especially as the mobility of capital and 'regime shopping' are expressed directly in the transactions of the EWC.

Despite the evident importance of such geographical questions, they have to date nevertheless largely not been taken on board and much of the argument about EWCs still presumes that they have a unity of purpose, such that the 'optimistic'/'pessimistic' debate continues. This binary can be most clearly understood by subdividing the argument. At one extreme we can suggest an analysis that sees EWCs as bearers of a worker-based international solidarity. Drawing on the work of others, Castree et al. (2004, pp. 114–15) thus suggest that 'new forms of less-formalized international connections between workplaces and unions are emerging – such as so-called "social movement unionism" or European Works Councils – often stimulated by the restrictively hierarchical nature of the international labour organisations'. EWCs are certainly uneasy bedfellows with 'social movement unionism' but the implication of the argument is that solidaristic cross-national union organisation can be focused through an EWC that has its roots in workplace representation. This is a straightforward 'united we stand, divided we fall' analogy.

A second level of approach might be to suggest that EWCs offer an opportunity to actually 'unite' workplace representatives with the 'hierarchical' trade union organisations from which, it is suggested, they are alienated. There can be little doubt that the active agents in formulating EWC agreements and providing the most positive and practical support for European Works Councillors have been the European Industry Federations (EIFs) in general, and the European Metalworkers' Federation in particular. It is certainly arguable that interventions from transnational trade union organisations like the EIFs would help to transcend locational divisions and generate cross-national solidarities. An optimistic picture might, then, focus on the integration of workplace and European-level trade union organisations as mutually strengthening.

A third strand of the argument would sharpen the emerging differences within an optimistic tradition. This argument would ask whether EWCs offer the opportunity for workers and trade unions to gain power and influence through developing partnerships with management, for in this scenario it is partnership rather than confrontation that has the potential to bring influence and power. The significance of such influence is contentious and the evidence cannot simply be drawn from surveys of EWC participants but must be strongly contextualised by the limits and possibilities of the EWCs themselves. Nevertheless, it is clear that we have moved from the optimistic to the pessimistic in terms of this brief review, given that there is little evidence of any real significance of

EWCs exerting major influence over corporate decision-making. Waddington (2003, p. 321) concludes from an extensive survey that 'most EWCs do not meet the initial expectations of the European Commission regarding information and consultation' and this expectation itself must be regarded as strictly limited.

Finally, the focus on EWCs, with the institutional opportunities they offer and supported by funding from the corporations themselves, as well as from the EU, clouds discussion of alternative perspectives. Indeed, it is arguable that the existence of EWCs inhibits alternative forms of worker-to-worker organisation and institutionalises conflicts within the safe boundaries of a 'talking shop', rather than through direct industrial action. By becoming the only game in town, EWCs can be argued to have overtaken nascent cross-border solidarities emerging organically and transmitted via, for instance, electronic networking (on electronic union organising, see Lee, Chapter 23 in this volume) that built independent action more akin to the social movement unionism that Castree et al. (2004) have packaged with EWCs.

In whatever way the model of EWCs as institutions is developed, though, it is clear that they provide a unique opportunity to bring together workplace-based trade unionists at least once a year face-to-face and to allow them to establish networking well beyond those meetings (see, for example, Tully, 2004). These meetings and networks challenge nationally based locational solidarities through developing some, often limited, transparency about the geographical strategies of multinational companies. Put bluntly, EWC members are confronted with responding to management investment decisions. In such circumstances, the relationship of the local and the cross-national is critical. To date, analyses of cross-national solidarities have largely focused upon how EWCs have dealt with issues of competing countries and cultures but have neglected the issue of the relationship between EWCs and the 'place' from which their representatives come. By way of contrast, in this chapter we use evidence from the North East of England, regional data first discussed at an earlier stage in Fitzgerald et al. (1999) and Stirling and Fitzgerald (2001) and now supplemented by a second survey (Fitzgerald and Stirling, 2005), to begin to explore the complex picture of how geographical tensions shape how EWCs operate and how they, in turn, can help structure the ways in which the economic landscape unfolds as a result of the geographical connections between workers in different places/countries that they help inaugurate/expand.

The North East of England and EWCs
The North East of England provides a context from which we can analyse important characteristics of EWCs and their potential for intervening in a European (or global) industrial relations framework. As we suggested at the outset, EWCs are dynamic organisations engaged in a complex network of internal and external relationships. We also argued that their power to act at a European level is predicated on an ability to act locally. Local power may be uneven because of factors external to the EWC, such as national union densities or industrial relations legal frameworks, but these factors play out internally. Equally, partners in an EWC will have perceptions of their fellow delegates that are shaped by the reality/perceived reality of the power that their colleagues have locally, perceptions that may or may not be accurate. This is important, for German, French or Danish delegates' different views and perceptions will have implications both for academic analysis and, more importantly, for the internal interactions of

an EWC. Given this, in terms of our analysis here, before proceeding further to explore issues related to how EWCs function and some of the spatial issues associated with this, it is important first to outline a little about the region we are studying, for this locational context can provide potentially powerful insights into the actual operation of some of the area's EWCs.

The North East of England, then, might be described as a 'global outpost'. Few MNCs are headquartered there, leaving decision-making to be seen as coming 'from elsewhere' and imposed on local workplaces. The region is one in which the economic decline of its traditional industrial base has been responded to through regional regeneration focused on cultural investment (Byrne and Wharton, 2004; Miles, 2004). Global restructuring has seriously undermined the regional manufacturing base in industries such as shipbuilding and steel making, which have all but disappeared, whilst the last deep coal mine closed in 2006. This historical economic profile facilitated the development of an industrial-based trade union movement that remains stereotypically characteristic of the region and strongly influential in a region that retains the highest union density in England. This economic and political restructuring provides a major constraint on the ability of regional trade unionists to become engaged in influencing change and underpins an embedded defensiveness (Fitzgerald and O'Brien, 2005; Pike et al., 2004). Thus, whilst EWCs offer a potential opportunity for North East trade unionists to develop proactive strategies across borders, the more likely reality is that representatives will carry with them a cultural legacy of decline that trade unions have failed to significantly arrest and a desire to defend what remains.

This regional context is reinforced by a national context in which there is a general perception of UK union decline amongst EWC delegates. The demographic of European EWC members as senior union representatives with many years' experience means that they are likely to be aware of 'the Thatcher years' in the UK and the substantial impact this had on union membership density and power. This is often balanced by an aware-ness of, and respect for, Britain's 'shop steward system', which may have been a model for their own workplace union organisation. Awareness may well also extend to the failure of the miners' strike (1984–85), some understanding of the repressive legislative framework for unions in the UK and a generalised perception that much of this was left unchanged under the years of the Blair government. The North East's trade unionists, and British trade unionists in general, are unlikely to bring even the vaguest understand-ing of trade unionism in other countries (for example, Portugal or Sweden) to their EWC. Such differences in perception, whether informed or misinformed, bring cultural differ-ences and cross-border tensions to the EWC with some immediacy, and it is no surprise that awareness of difference is invariably one of the first training demands of EWCs.

In sum, the perception of European trade unionists of North East UK EWC delegates is wrapped around perceptions of national union difficulties, reinforced by a regional 'defensiveness' and underpinned by the fact that the EWC company headquarters are most unlikely to be in the region. Evidently, it is necessary to develop similar geographi-cal profiles of the regions from which come members of any particular EWC if we are to understand the complex cultural relationships that shape power relationships and alli-ances between workers, and between workers and management. In our case, given that we have provided something of the geographical context within which are located the EWCs we are to discuss, we can now look through the lens of our North East data at the key issues that EWCs face in building alliances that cross borders and cultures, fit or fail to fit internal and external structures of both MNCs and trade unions and, ultimately, are able to act on a European basis to influence corporate power.

The survey analysis

Our analysis derives from studies of regional EWC activity in the North East of England over a seven-year period (1998–2005) and the ongoing delivery of EWC training programmes. It offers a view of developments at the sub-national level where the opportunity exists to evaluate how company restructuring and change impacts on the success of EWCs and also if relationships are developing between representatives of differing EWCs based in the same geographical locations. The first study (Fitzgerald et al., 1999; Stirling and Fitzgerald, 2001) identified companies in the North East of England covered by the EWC Directive and their worker participants. Subsequent research (Fitzgerald and Stirling, 2005) added to the database. A total of 89 EWC representatives, on 49 EWCs, were identified in the region and data obtained, from either questionnaires or interviews, from nearly three-quarters of these. Twelve (28 per cent) of the EWC representatives identified in 2005 were present in the earlier study.

The 2005 study (Fitzgerald and Stirling, 2005), the main focus of analysis here, used a semi-structured questionnaire, which had a 58 per cent response rate and involved interviews with eight representatives. In total, data were received from 26 EWC representatives on 20 EWCs. The manufacturing structure of the region is clearly evident from the responses, and the union composition of respondents is entirely to be predicted from this. However, this is not out of line with the European development of EWCs, as the metalworking sector has been dominant in the formation of EWCs, and the European metalworkers' federation has been most active in instigating and supporting action.

We use this data analysis in three key ways in what follows. First, we explore some of the spatial specificity of the region and the UK. Second, we examine how the resources of place have shaped cross-border activity. Third, we consider some of the complex, internally negotiated relationships that seek to transcend space and build what Miller (1999) describes as the 'European in European Works Councils'. Specifically, we investigate what kinds of capacities for shaping company policies and practices the EWCs to which the trade unionists in the North East belong may have, and how representatives to them have sought to influence corporate decisions that, whilst made in countries like the Netherlands and Germany, nevertheless have impacts upon the region.

Impacting on the region

A key element in building a national, internal solidarity is the representativeness of delegates and some level of stability in maintaining a role on an EWC which may meet only once or twice a year. Our survey data suggested strongly, and as we might expect, that EWC representatives are active trade union representatives.

Perhaps not surprisingly, all but one of the respondents held a representative position with their union other than their EWC, with the vast majority undertaking the role of a trade union workplace representative, although some held national positions. Given this engagement in the union, it is again not surprising that they had been elected to their EWC role through the union or directly by the workforce. More significantly for the analysis here, a third represented their own site and 11 per cent represented their own and more than one other site in the region, leaving a majority representing sites beyond the region as well as their own. In effect, EWCs are creating local structures in the UK that rarely existed previously on any formal basis and which have the potential to bind together different workplaces across space. Such structures might be developed within the companies themselves – some form of company-wide representation structures – or as part of trade union organisational structures. Here, though, we see diverging trends. In the case of trade unions, the vitality of cross-plant union organisation, characteristic of some companies in the 1970s, has been severely disrupted as workplace organisation in the UK has simply declined. Equally, union organisation that has a geographical base rather than a workplace base has also been in decline, as these structures did not fit with workplace-based union branches and they were potentially costly. In effect, the opportunities for workplace representatives to meet others through institutional structures have been in a process of continual decline for some time. However, the emergence of information and consultation systems, stimulated by further European Union Directives, has provided a different possibility for institutional forms of contact that unions might populate, although clearly there are contrasting views – as these two delegates show:

> I don't believe that national works councils will help the EWC become more relevant.

> The other [European] members of the EWC have works councils and we have been arguing for these. . . . A UK works council will make the EWC stronger, as it will become much more relevant for our members.

EWC members, then, are representing workplaces and union members where they have no day-to-day contact but we found some significant evidence of the development of site visits, which are being undertaken by over a quarter of the representatives:

> I represented a site in the North West but management would not allow the representatives from this site to meet me and discuss EWC issues so we negotiated a seat for the site on the EWC.

Hence, the evidence from our north-eastern perspective is that trade union-based institutions at the European level are having an unintended impact of encouraging the development of geographical structures in local union organisations that had been in decline, with the focus being on the workplace as the centre of organisation.

Our second point in relation to the importance of representation concerned continuity of membership. Table 17.1 illustrates the changes in our sample. Of the 65 EWCs contacted in 1999 and 2004, 49 differed between the two survey periods, leaving only 16 the same. In 11 of these 16, at least one 2004 representative was the same as in 1999. There is no reason to believe that this fluidity is not commonplace, given that it is largely a response to restructuring. Much of this fluidity was accounted for by either companies leaving the region, as in the case of De La Rue and Courtaulds, or downsizing, as in the case of BT and, particularly dramatically, ICI, the chemical industry giant based in Teesside. Restructuring as fundamental as this is not necessarily a feature of EWCs but it does highlight the problems that they have with continuity of membership. This is significant in terms of building long-term solidarity and increasing the power of EWCs, as turnover inevitably undermines effective communication and organisation.

Table 17.1   North East EWCs: comparison of representation, 1999–2004

European Works Councils	EWC reps 1999	EWC reps 2004
3M European Employee Forum	1	1 (same rep)
ABP/Flooring Consultative Board	3	3 (2x same)
Akzo Nobel European Forum	–	1
Alcan European Works Council	1	1 (same rep)
Barclays Group European Forum	1	–
BT European Consultative Council	2	–
Bunzl Fine Paper Information and Consultation Forum	1	2 (1x same rep)
Cardo European Works Council	–	1
Caterpillar European Works Council	3	1 (same rep)
Coats Viyella European Works Council	1	–
Compass Group European Council	1	3 (1x same rep)
Cooper Industries EU Information and Consultation Forum	1	–
Corus European Works Council	3	3 (1x same rep)
Courtaulds European Works Council	1	–
De La Rue European Employee Forum	1	–
Deutsche Post World Net Forum	–	1
Draka European Works Council	–	1
Dynamit Nobel European Works Council	1	–
EDF European Works Council	–	1
Electrolux Works Council	1	–
Formica	–	4
Freudenberg Euro Forum	1	1
Goodyear European Information and Communication Forum	1	1 (same rep)
Grove European Forum	3	–
Heckett Multiserv Consultative Council	1	–
ICI European Consultative Forum	6	1
Komatsu European Forum	–	1
Kværner European Consultative Committee	3	–
LG Philips Displays European Works Council	1	1 (same rep)
MD Foods European Works Council	–	2
Metro Euro Forum	–	1
Nestlé European Council for Information and Consultation	2	1
Nike European Works Council	1	–
Nissan European Communication Forum	3	1
Norsk Hydro European Works Council	1	–
Pepsico European Employee Forum	1	–
Perstorp European Works Council	1	–
Rothmans International Tobacco Products Council for Information and Consultation	2	–
Saint Gobain Convention for European Dialogue	1	1
Samsung European New Management Committee	1	–
Sanofi-Synthelabo European Works Council Agreement	–	1
SCA European Works Council	2	2 (1x same rep)
Scottish & Newcastle Company Forum	1	1 (same rep)

Table 17.1   (continued)

European Works Councils	EWC reps 1999	EWC reps 2004
SE Group European Works Council	1	–
Solvay European Works Council	–	1
Suez Lyonnaise des Eaux European Social-Dialogue Committee	2	–
United Biscuits European Consultative Council	–	1
Uponor European Works Council	1	–
Zumtobel European Forum	–	3
36 EWCs in 1999 29 EWCs in 2004 49 differing EWCs 1999–2004	58	43

It is clear that representativeness and how it is managed can be catalytic not simply in communicating EWC meeting outcomes but also in adding an extra dimension to existing union structures and opening up new channels of communications. If the EWC itself is to develop effectively, then it is critical that effective local workplace organisation is (re)built, both to support representativeness and to underpin cross-national action. The importance of this, as well as the difficulties, was highlighted by the following respondent:

> [i]t's difficult for members because we now have local bargaining consultation, so all the issues that apply to us are dealt with locally. It's hard for them to appreciate wider issues; it's hard for them to understand what we are going there [the EWC] to talk about. You know, it's hard for me sometimes to know what I'm going to talk about.

In sum, our analysis suggests that a cross-border institution is having significant effects on local trade union organisational structures. This may be partly due to the fractured structure of collective bargaining in the UK and the lack of a legal framework encouraging company-wide consultation, but the effect is, nevertheless, significant.

Building across boundaries
Turning from an inward to an outward focus, we need to ask how have cross-border solidarities been built? Given the restrictions in the Directive on travel and meetings, the establishment of communications networks is crucial. In the first phase of the research we found that 'effective systems of communication both between UK and European EWC delegates were developing rapidly' (Stirling and Fitzgerald, 2001, p. 19) and these systems were clearly in place for representatives in the 2004 study. At least one of the EWCs with representatives in the region for both studies was developing a sophisticated system of communication:

> [w]e have developed a database containing information on the company and matters relevant to the EWC, which can be accessed outside of meetings. We also recently sent out a questionnaire about the EWC to keep people involved.

Significantly, in the first study we found that a third of representatives were isolated outside of EWC meetings, undertaking no communication at all. By contrast, in the later study we found that only one representative was in this position and that 96 per cent of representatives were communicating at either UK, European or both levels. There are limited data on the reasons for communication but in the semi-structured interviews we undertook, delegates noted company restructuring and the introduction of new working practices as important. As one representative commented:

> [l]ocal management wanted to bring in a new level of workplace supervision, so I contacted one of the Dutch representatives, who informed us that this had happened in their plant. He gave me an idea of the important issues around this and we were able to negotiate a successful implementation of the system locally.

Representatives in both the questionnaire and interview data consistently pointed out the importance of social connections outside of EWC meetings:

> [t]o make an EWC really work you need to communicate socially and meet and leave as friends.

These data suggest that company identities and solidarities might be developing and improving across national boundaries where there are clear outcomes in terms of power and influence. Hence, as one delegate put it:

> I never feel that we are outnumbered. There's been real integration, people have really put nationalities to the side.

We can also conclude that cultural differences can be overcome through personal relationships. This latter point is an important one and often neglected when dealing with analysis at the geographical or organisational level. However, personal solidarities provide the basis for class actions and when faced with the challenges of geographical distance and cultural diversity, the personal is indeed political. Given this, it is interesting to note that around two-thirds of representatives in both studies stated that they had personal challenges (most commonly language) in undertaking their EWC role.

This brief review of the indicative regional survey data suggests a growing European influence that is enabling EWCs to develop effectively and is impacting on trade union organisational structures. However, EWCs will be judged by their levels of influence over management.

The question of power
The argument about power and EWCs is necessarily a complex one that particularly relates to the stage of EWC development (see the typologies of EWCs in the series by Lecher et al., 1999, 2001, 2003; and Waddington, 2003) and the views of management that might be nationally and culturally determined. It is not just unions who are dealing with the problems of space and place. Both Waddington's quantitative data (2003 and 2005) and Marginson et al.'s (2004, p. 231) more qualitative research suggest that country of origin might be a significant factor on how EWCs operate and that 'it might be inferred that the impact of EWCs is correspondingly less in MNCs based in the Anglo-Saxon countries than those headquartered in the "co-ordinated market" economies of continental Europe'. Our respondents have a strong Anglo-Saxon base both in terms of their companies and their own culture, so we might anticipate a pessimistic

view of influence. However, one respondent in different circumstances recorded the contrasting view:

> Dutch management locally had very little to do with the UK workforce, which was clearly not a good thing. So I brought this up at the EWC and the Dutch senior management there were shocked and they have installed bi-annual meetings where the whole workforce receive presentations from sales, senior management etc.

The self-assessment of EWC members is also critical to whether they view participation as important or simply the 'annual jaunt', and the first issue to assess is that of the agenda for EWC meetings, as control of the issues discussed controls (and reflects) power and influence:

> [e]very meeting has two labour lawyers and one EWC consultant making sure that discussion stays within the scope of the EWC Directive, not moving from consultation to negotiation. I'm sick to death of hearing that this discussion is outside the scope of our agreement.

Workers in different countries can also work with management to control agendas:

> [a] lot relates to informal influence before meetings in Germany, as the company is German. If the head of the German representatives says 'that doesn't go on the agenda', it doesn't go on. They are very quiet at formal EWC meetings and I get the impression that deals have already been done.

As this last quote indicates, power over the EWC itself might be exercised in a number of ways which may be nationally based and it might also be expressed informally as well as formally. Indeed, the 'optimistic' view of EWCs places particular emphasis on the informal cross-national opportunities that EWCs offer:

> I have found that in our UK and EWC meetings the informal talks to managers at lunch or over coffee have been very effective in getting local problems sorted out.

This can lead to relationships being transferred from Europe to the local workplace:

> [r]ecently the managing director of the company came to our plant. He asked for me by name, then asked me to accompany him on a tour of the plant, explaining what was happening.

Our respondents, though, still indicated a strong vein of pessimism, as the following three sets of comments highlight:

> [m]anagement don't change decisions, they tell you what they are going to do.

> There's no real influence, they just want to tell us what's going to happen.

> It's a waste of time. The EWC has no power. It covers too many sites and workplaces. Issues raised had to cover all areas, not single ones.

Indeed, in one case the importance of EWCs for management influence on local decisions was illustrated:

[t]he company has been having competitive problems and wanted a pay freeze and it was only that I was able to talk directly to the MD at the EWC and question him about this that members voted in favour of this. Otherwise they would have seen it in the typical British way of management trying to get one over us.

Where we have recorded influence, it generally conforms to other research which is summarised by Marginson et al.'s (2004, p. 230) comment that 'where EWCs have an impact on the outcome of management decision-making, this tends to be limited to the implementation of decisions rather than to changing their substance'. This was evident also in our research:

[w]ith the recent long period of divestment we were only informed after decisions were made. We got the company to agree a social policy on employment rights on transfer; on every transfer they will try to guarantee terms and conditions, redundancy package, pensions, etc. So we now have an agreed social package.

Even though this factory is now closing, I was able to use a number of tools at the EWC to not only stall the pace of change but also gain an advantage in negotiation.

However, some respondents were able to use their EWCs more effectively as vehicles for influencing company policy and translating that in ways that influence what happens in local workplaces:

[i]f they're going to shut a factory now, at least they have to look people in the eyes and we can put our case to them. The EWC is certainly not an academic exercise.

We have had a strong influence on projects such as a current one on IT systems. Recently they were also proposing to outsource distribution and the EWC was able to successfully argue that this would not be cost effective, so they relented.

A more substantial approach has been developed in one of our respondent EWCs which is exploring a global dimension to its work. In doing so it took the initiative in establishing a sub-committee of the EWC on corporate social responsibility and a global code of conduct was issued to every employee and will be reviewed each year by the EWC.

Whilst such codes and their negotiation within EWCs is controversial (Miller, 2004), their development in some of the EWCs we studied suggests a significant increase in influence for some workers as a result of the EWC. In this regard, Wills (2004) and others have suggested that international agreements, including those agreed or monitored by EWCs, can also have an influence upon union organising in a locality. This was dramatically illustrated by one of our respondents.

The influence of the EWC was critical in attaining UNISON recognition at the Doxford call centre in Sunderland. Without their wholehearted support UNISON recognition would have never come about. Nationally we could do little; internationally we achieved everything.

Conclusion

Since Streeck's (1997) (in)famous categorisation of EWCs as 'neither European nor works councils', analysts have set out to explore the opposite – that is to say, to explore how they are European and how they function as works councils. However, it seems to us that in some regards this approach is missing some important issues about what the terms 'European' and 'works councils' might mean and how they might be stretched. Thus, in discussions of EWCs, a narrow concept of Europe as the European Union is typically deployed. Even leaving aside the fact that multinational capital is global, this is a constraining factor in itself. Equally, trade unionists are more interested in negotiating bodies than they are in the constraining strictures of information and consultation offered by works councils. Thus, contrary to Streek's point in his polemical argument, we may want more EWCs and for them to be both global and powerful bargaining agencies. If we understand 'European' to mean an organisation capable of acting at that level, then EWCs offer some opportunities but only if the constituent national groupings are strong in themselves and prepared to work collectively. What power might they then exert? First, they may generate local activity and enhance workers' organising capabilities through sharing information, placing pressure on management in other countries and engaging in acts of solidarity, all of which feature in our regional focus and the wider literature (for examples, see Fitzgerald and Stirling, 2004). Second, they might seek to influence their own management, although here the evidence is much less confident about the power to do so in the face of often fierce opposition and the ability of companies to instigate investment strategies that are nationally divisive. Third, EWCs may have a part to play in developing a 'European' industrial relations framework. Our evidence and the wider literature suggests this is an unlikely scenario as, in essence, EWCs have little to gain from this. A common framework of European industrial relations legislation would certainly support their activities and level out national differences but the EU is unlikely to move much further forward in this area in the near future and EWCs are not a cohesive and coherent pressure group. The inability to influence the Commission into revising the Directive in anything like the agreed time frame is illustrative of the level of resistance and the lack of institutional power at this level.

To become more than a 'works council' is also highly problematic, given the embeddedness of industrial relations systems at the national level that we have described and the differences between national union movements (Hyman, 2001). Following directly from this is the necessity of empowering the European works council at the expense of national decision-making structures. However, geographical divisions and tensions make this difficult. Hence, strong trade unions in the north of Europe may see little gain in passing decision-making power to a body that would be required to reach a consensus that was inclusive of weaker and more fragmented national union organisations. In effect, the differing geography of national industrial relations systems undermines the organisational potential for a more powerful, trans-European solidaristic body.

The restructuring of global capital has brought into sharp focus this relationship between locally based trade unionism and internationally based corporations. Despite our reservations, we have suggested that EWCs do offer an opportunity for influence, in spite of the severe constraints likely to be imposed by employers and organisational structures, and that this opportunity is shaped by the relationship between the EWC and local representatives. This is a shift in focus from previous analyses that have been concerned with the emergence of cross-national union relationships and the barriers to successful dialogue and action. Our analysis is twofold, in that it is concerned with the impact that local trade unionists might have on the EWC itself and, equally importantly, how EWC participation might impact on the local workplace.

It might be argued that this is a return to parochialism when EWCs offer trade unions the opportunity for internationalism at precisely the historical point when that dimension is critical to their futures. However, whilst the evidence of influence remains limited and there are clear examples of the view that EWCs are a 'talking shop', there are equally strong alternative arguments. In the first place, a perceived weakness of local delegates in participating in and influencing their EWCs is attributed to a need to 'catch up' with continental counterparts. Given the contrasting Anglo-Saxon and continental European industrial relations cultures, the perception of the need to catch up is based on many years of British exclusion from information and consultation systems. Equally important is that the EWC presence and its impact is communicated effectively through trade union structures to members. In this case we have suggested that EWCs can reinvigorate such structures and provide new opportunities, for example in terms of site visits or other contacts with trade unionists in the UK beyond the locality. This may be reinforced by new, nationally based systems of information and consultation, although there was wariness in our respondents about the use of such systems to bypass union structures.

In terms of the reality of the impact of EWCs on local workplace organisation there is evidence that supports a pessimistic interpretation of factory closures continuing and union influence being restricted to the management of that process. However, that, in itself, should not be neglected, as it may be a significant improvement on past practice. More significantly, we have evidence from respondents of positive engagement through EWCs as a mechanism for supporting trade union objectives. The two clearest cases can hardly be characterised as swallows heralding a warm summer, but the prevention of the introduction of outsourcing and the use of the EWC to invigorate a successful organising campaign are important achievements that will underscore the relevance of the EWC to the local workplace.

Note

1. An early review is in Muller and Hoffmann (2001) and the most significant case study analysis has come from Lecher and his colleagues (1999, 2001, 2003). A comprehensive coverage of key debates can be found in Fitzgerald and Stirling (2004).

References

Byrne, D. and C. Wharton (2004), 'Loft living – Bombay calling: culture, work and everyday life on post-industrial Tyneside', *Capital and Class*, **84**, 191–9.

Castree, N., N. Coe, K. Ward and M. Samers (2004), *Spaces of Work: Global Capitalism and Geographies of Labour*, London: Sage.

European Industrial Relations Observatory (2004), 'Developments in European Works Councils', available at: www.eiro.eurofound.eu.int/2004/11/study/tn0411101s.

Fitzgerald, I. (2004), 'Introduction: employee participation in Europe', in I. Fitzgerald and J. Stirling (eds), *European Works Councils: Pessimism of the Intellect, Optimism of the Will?*, London: Routledge, pp. 1–11.

Fitzgerald, I. and P. O'Brien (2005), 'Like taking coal to Newcastle: a new era for trade unionism in the North East of England', *Capital and Class*, **87**, 17–27.

Fitzgerald, I. and J. Stirling (eds) (2004), *European Works Councils: Pessimism of the Intellect, Optimism of the Will?*, London: Routledge.

Fitzgerald, I. and J. Stirling (2005), *European Works Councils: Building the Regional Dimension*, Newcastle: Northern Region TUC.

Fitzgerald, I., D. Miller and J. Stirling (1999), 'Representing the global outpost: European Works Councils in the North East', *Northern Economic Review*, **29**, 46–62.

Hyman, R. (2001), *Understanding European Trade Unionism*, London: Sage.

Jagodzinski, R., N. Kluge and J. Waddington (2008), *Memorandum: European Works Councils*, Brussels: ETUI-REHS.

Kerckhofs, P. (2002), *European Works Councils in Facts and Figures,* Brussels: ETUI.

Kerckhofs, P. and I. Pas (2004), *European Works Council Database*, Brussels: ETUI.

Lecher, W., B. Nagel and H-W. Platzer (1999), *The Establishment of European Works Councils: From Information Committee to Social Actor*, Aldershot: Ashgate.

Lecher, W., H-W. Platzer, S. Rub and K-P. Weiner (2001), *European Works Councils: Developments Types and Networking*, Aldershot: Gower.

Lecher, W., H-W. Platzer, S. Rub and K-P. Weiner (2003), *European Works Councils: Negotiated Europeanisation – Between Statutory Framework and Social Dynamic*, Aldershot: Ashgate.

Marginson, M., M. Hall, A. Hoffmann and T. Müller (2004), 'The impact of European Works Councils on management decision-making in UK and US-based multinationals: a case study comparison', *British Journal of Industrial Relations*, **42** (2), 209–33.

Miles, S. (2004), 'Newcastle Gateshead quayside: cultural investment and identities of resistance', *Capital and Class*, **84**, 183–91.

Miller, D. (1999), 'Towards a "European" Works Council', *Transfer: The European Review of Labour and Research*, **5** (3), 344–65.

Miller, D. (2004), 'The limits and possibilities of European Works Councils in the context of globalisation: experience in the textile, clothing and footwear sector', in I. Fitzgerald and J. Stirling (eds), *European Works Councils: Pessimism of the Intellect, Optimism of the Will?*, London: Routledge, pp. 198–210.

Muller, T. and A. Hoffman (2001), 'EWC research: a review of the literature', Warwick Papers in Industrial Relations, No. 65, Warwick University.

Pike, A., P. O'Brien and J. Tomaney (2004), 'Trade unions in local and regional development and governance: the Northern Trades Union Congress in North East England', *Local Economy*, **19** (2), 102–16.

Sadler, D. (2000), 'Organizing European labour: governance, production, trade unions and the question of scale', *Transactions of the Institute of British Geographers*, New Series, **25** (2), 135–52.

Stirling, J. and I. Fitzgerald (2001), 'European Works Councils: representing workers on the periphery', *Employee Relations*, **23** (1&2), 13–25.

Stirling, J. and B. Tully (2004), 'Power, process and practice: communications in European Works Councils', *European Journal of Industrial Relations*, **10** (1), 73–89.

Streeck, W. (1997), 'Neither European nor Works Councils: a reply to Paul Knutsen', *Economic and Industrial Democracy*, **18** (2), 325–37.

Tully, B. (2004), 'Organising across borders', in I. Fitzgerald and J. Stirling (eds), *European Works Councils: Pessimism of the Intellect, Optimism of the Will?*, London: Routledge, pp. 165–78.

Waddington, J. (2003), 'What do representatives think of the practices of European Works councils? Views from six countries', *European Journal of Industrial Relations*, **9** (3), 303–25.

Waddington, J. (2005), 'The views of European Works Council representatives', paper presented to the 'What's the Problem?' Project seminar, 4 November, Brussels.

Wills, J. (1998), 'Taking on the CosmoCorps? Experiments in transnational labor organization', *Economic Geography*, **74** (2), 111–30.

Wills, J. (2001), 'Uneven geographies of capital and labour: the lessons of European Works Councils', *Antipode*, **33**, 484–509.

Wills, J. (2004), 'Organising in the global economy: the Accor – IUF trade union rights agreement', in I. Fitzgerald and J. Stirling (eds), *European Works Councils: Pessimism of the Intellect, Optimism of the Will?*, London: Routledge, pp. 211–24.

18 The new economic model and spatial changes in labour relations in post-NAFTA Mexico

Enrique de la Garza Toledo

From 1940 until 1982 the Mexican economy was dominated by a policy of import-substitution industrialisation (ISI) characterised by significant state intervention and regulation of the economy, with the state playing two principal roles: direct producer of goods and services, and driver of aggregate demand via public spending. At the same time, economic policies protected national industry through various tax and credit pro-grammes and favourable treatment on prices of raw materials. In spatial terms, three major manufacturing poles were developed – Mexico City, Monterrey and Guadalajara – which were focused mainly on producing for the domestic market. During this period the economy experienced high growth rates. However, in response to the state's fiscal crisis in the early 1980s – a fiscal crisis which took the form of a default on the coun-try's ballooning foreign debt and a subsequent currency devaluation – a new, neoliberal economic model was established. This new model involved the state's withdrawal from production-orientated investment and its giving priority to controlling inflation rather than directly stimulating economic growth through Keynsian macroeconomic policies. In addition, it involved seeking to attract greater levels of foreign direct investment (FDI). Although movements towards establishing this neoliberal policy began soon after Mexico's 1982 default on its foreign debt, the economy really began opening up to foreign capital in 1986, when Mexico joined GATT, and was given a fundamental boost when the North American Free Trade Agreement (NAFTA) went into effect in 1994. Since 1994, the economy has experienced years marked by profound crisis (1995), fol-lowed by recuperation (1996–2000), and then, once again, economic deceleration. Under this new economic model, the manufacturing export sector has become the principal engine of the economy (De la Garza, 1993a).

With the implementation of this new economic model, conflicts arose between com-panies, the state, and corporatist and independent labour union organisations over how a new system of labour relations would take shape. As we will see, the emergence of this new system has several notable territorial elements to it. In order to understand them, though, it is first necessary to be familiar with the system of work relations in Mexico that was constituted during the 1920s and 1930s and which involved a corporatist pact between the state, private enterprise, and the new labour organisations emerging at that time. The most significant aspects of this pact were that the state guaranteed unions a representational monopoly through various legal and extra-legal mechanisms, extended the closed shop and state control over collective bargaining and strikes, and facilitated the removal of non-corporatist-minded labour leaders. The pact also established a mechanism for consulting with labour unions regarding economic, wage and social security policies, and established labour union representation in labour courts, in social security institutions and in the commission that defined minimum wages. In return, the unions essentially agreed to guarantee labour peace, to support the state's economic policies and to assure that workers voted for the Institutional Revolutionary Party (Partido Revolucionario Institucional – PRI). Union leaders participated in this pact both as union officials and through their positions as elected representatives on various municipal and/or state-level governments and as public functionaries (De la Garza, 1990).

Under this model, then, the state was involved in labour relations on a day-to-day basis, a fact which resulted in their overt politicisation. In exchange for unions' support, the state offered wage and job protections, together with increased job benefits and social security for those members of the working class who were union members. Consequently, industrial workers enjoyed significant protective rules with regard to working conditions and hiring, together with considerable limitations on firing, being involuntarily moved within a firm to another job, being forced to engage in multi-skilling and having their positions undercut by temporary workers and/or subcontractors hired from employment agencies. The formalisation of work rules via legislation was complemented by the clientelistic orientation of labour union leaderships, which, with the support of labour courts, handed out rewards and punishments, depending upon workers' loyalty (or not) to them.

It is important to clarify, however, that this model of labour relations did not function equally for all workers during the import substitution period. Thus, whereas workers in large private and state-owned companies generally enjoyed such conditions and protections, those who worked in small- and medium-sized companies typically had fewer protections, whilst the enormous informal labour sector at the bottom of the employment pyramid had virtually no safeguards. Whereas organisationally the labour relations system that emerged out of the Mexican Revolution reached its zenith during the period of ISI within the state-owned and private sector manufacturers orientated toward the domestic market (which was itself protected by the state), geographically speaking it was most evident in the three key industrial heartland areas of Mexico City, Guadalajara and Monterrey, together with the electricity- and petroleum-producing regions of south-eastern Mexico (see Figure 18.1 for locations). Crucially, however, Mexico's northern border area remained largely excluded from this system, since until fairly recently the region had not been heavily industrialised (De la Garza and Bouzas, 1998). This geographical exclusion has had important implications for the labour relations' regime that has emerged under the country's new, neoliberal economic model. In particular, as it has industrialised as a result of the growth largely of *maquila* industries, northern Mexico has served as an important laboratory for experimenting with new forms of labour relations, with such forms involving not so much a questioning of traditional corporatist relationships but, rather, a reworking of them to produce a lower level of protections for almost all workers (Carrillo, 1990).[1]

In this chapter, then, I will analyse the key aspects of the export manufacturing model and the new labour relations model associated with it. Specifically, I will explore how the move towards labour flexibility and managerial unilateralism which has been part and parcel of the economic transformation initiated in the 1980s has reshaped Mexico's economic landscape not only by facilitating the institutionalisation of a new labour relations model in the nascent industrial zones of the north but, perhaps more importantly, by encouraging its geographical extension throughout the entire country. However, despite such spatial diffusion, it is important to recognise that this new economic and

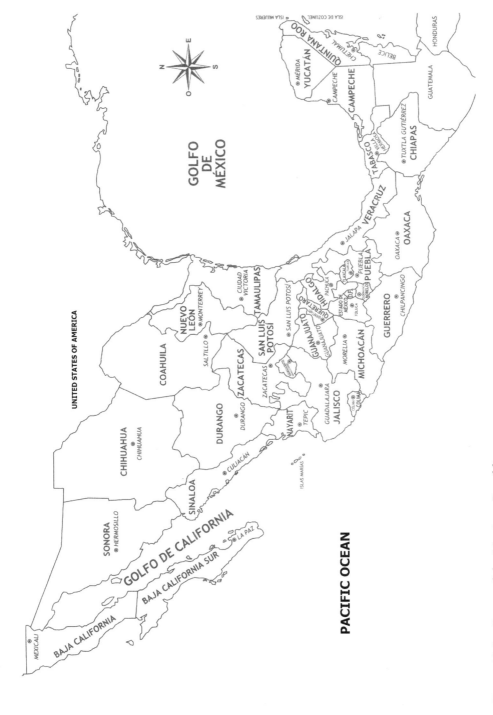

Figure 18.1 States of the Mexican Republic

327

labour relations model – one characterised by low wages, high voluntary turnover of workers, minimal worker identity with the company and labour unions that exist as little more than paper tigers – itself seemed to have reached its limit in the early part of the twenty-first century, as productivity increases began to diminish.[2] In turn, this current crisis of 'precarious Toyotaism' (De la Garza, 2006) will itself be likely to occasion a new restructuring of the economic landscape in the not-too-distant future.

The export manufacturing model and the territorial restructuring of Mexican manufacturing

The initial moves towards transforming the industrial model established during the ISI period began in the mid-1960s when large manufacturing corporations, especially those in the United States, started to develop the US–Mexico border region as a platform for *maquila* production to take advantage of low-waged labour to assemble goods for reimportation back into the US (De la Garza, 1990). However, it was not until the 1982 economic crisis and growing pressure from organisations like the International Monetary Fund that Mexico really embarked upon the export-orientated neoliberal development model that would greatly exacerbate such a transformation. There are several aspects of this model which are important, but perhaps the most significant is that under it the contribution of manufacturing to Mexico's Gross Domestic Product (GDP) has grown tremendously, with the value of manufacturing production increasing 43 per cent (in 1993 prices) between 1995 and 2004, such that by 2000 manufacturing was generating 22 per cent of the country's GDP. Much of this growth has been because of the expansion of the *maquila* sector, the value of whose production increased 308 per cent between 1993 and 2000. Moreover, whilst manufacturing did not come anywhere close to matching the service sector's GDP contribution, it has, however, been by far the largest element in Mexico's exports, accounting for 88.7 per cent of total exports (by value) in 2001. Importantly, most such manufacturing exports come from the *maquila* sector (55 per cent in 2005), which has seen a substantial increase in FDI in recent years (311 per cent between 1993 and 2000) (see Figure 18.2). However, despite the growth in the value of manufacturing, labour productivity between 1988 and 2002 increased by an annual average rate of only 0.3 per cent, and overall productivity actually declined by 1.7 per cent. Equally, although levels of capital intensity (fixed capital/total employees) increased in the 1990s relative to the previous decade, they were still below what they had been during the ISI period. Finally, despite significant early growth, beginning in about 2000 the manufacturing boom began to decelerate (see Table 18.1).

With regard to the *maquila* sector, although *maquila* manufacturing played a leading role in Mexico's export-led development in the 1980s, by the early 1990s this sector had begun to experience problems and, since then, its productivity growth rates have been much lower than for manufacturing overall. The *maquila* sector's importance for manufacturing, though, means that these problems have contributed greatly to the recent downward trend in manufacturing's overall gross profitability (De la Garza, 2006) and, given manufacturing's importance to GDP, in declining profit rates across the economy more generally (Ortiz, 2006). Equally, in both the *maquila* and non-*maquila* manufacturing sectors, employment, which grew prior to 1994, has recently begun to drop off – total employed personnel in manufacturing decreased 14 per cent between 1994 and 2005 (Hernández Laos, 2006). Moreover, working and living conditions for most waged

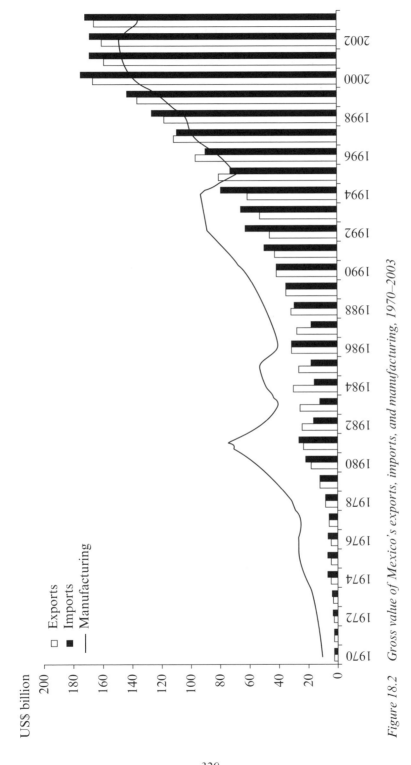

Figure 18.2 Gross value of Mexico's exports, imports, and manufacturing, 1970–2003

Table 18.1   *Index of minimum wage, wages in labour contracts and average real*
remuneration in manufacturing sector (1993 = 100)

Year	Minimum wage	Wages in labour contracts	Average remuneration for person in manufacturing sector
1990	116.0	99.3	94.1
1993	100.0	100.0	100.0
2000	74.9	76.1	90.4
2001	76.9	78.0	96.2
2002	76.1	78.6	98.1
2003	76.3	78.7	99.4
2004	74.7	78.3	99.5
2005	78.1	79.2	95.8

Source: STPS (2005).

workers have not improved during the NAFTA period: 45 per cent of workers do not have a written labour contract; the number of workers who have no labour benefits at all has increased; the percentage of waged workers without health services remains at just below 60 per cent; and the proportion of waged workers in micro-businesses with fewer than five workers (jobs that are generally precarious) has also remained the same. At the same time, the minimum wage in Mexico has declined in real terms (by 22 per cent between 1993 and 2005), as have wages covered by labour contracts (a 21 per cent decrease), and total remunerations for manufacturing personnel (a 4 per cent fall) (see Table 18.1). Unionisation rates have also declined since the emergence of the new economic model, decreasing nationally from 15 per cent in 1992 to 10 per cent in 2002. This has been especially so in the manufacturing sector, wherein coverage dropped from 22 per cent to 15 per cent (see Table 18.2). Meanwhile, Mexican workers appear to have become more quiescent, as the number of strikes decreased from 629 in 1993 to 243 in 2003 and the number of collective conflicts without strikes decreased from 3150 in 1993 to 1693 in 2003.

Part of the explanation for these changes in work and working conditions lies in the fact that the early 1980s heralded the beginning of substantial automation of productive processes, the introduction of new forms of work organisation, a flexibilisation of labour relations, and the formation of clusters amongst clients and suppliers, together with the creation of strategic alliances between large corporations, growing subcontracting and the territorial restructuring of industrial production. Nevertheless, whilst part of the manufacturing sector was modernised and new plants (*maquila* and non-*maquila*) established, it is important to recognise that much industry was not, such that manufacturing became increasingly polarised between a majority of companies that have been unable to make changes – often those located in the traditional manufacturing centres, with their older plant and equipment – and those that have become more productive and more competitive – often located in new industrial regions (De la Garza, 1998). Putting all of this together, then, by the end of nearly three decades of neoliberal-inspired restructuring, it was possible to characterise Mexican manufacturing as follows:

Table 18.2   Unionised workers/EAP* in different industries

	Percent unionised	
	1992	2002
Agriculture	0.57	0.29
Mines, electricity, water and natural gas supply	42.17	52.95
Manufacturing	21.57	15.02
Building	4.36	1.42
Trade	4.24	1.37
Transport, communication and storage	25.34	8.73
Restaurants and hotels	7.54	3.00
Finances and administration	18.46	9.96
Communal and social services	28.23	22.47
National average	14.54	10.00

Note: * EAP: Economically Active Population.

Source: Esquinca (2006).

1. Only a relatively few companies have focused much on developing and introducing new technologies (in 2000 only 0.7 per cent of income generated in the manufacturing sector was dedicated to research and development);
2. Most companies have made relatively simple changes in work organisation;
3. Although most large companies (primarily export companies) remain unionised (66 per cent of large manufacturing establishments had labour unions in 2001) and workers have certain protections through labour contracts concerning working time and full-time employment (94.9 per cent of the workers had regular, full-time employment), they receive low wages (in 1999 average remuneration per hour, including benefits, for workers in manufacturing was just US$2.00) (De la Garza, 2007);
4. Most of the labour force is unskilled (63 per cent of workers in manufacturing in 2001), has little seniority in the company, and has a low level of schooling.

Whatever increases have been made in Mexican manufacturing's productivity, then, especially in the 1990s, appear to have been the result not so much of technological change nor of the payment of productivity bonuses, which represented only a small proportion of total remunerations (De la Garza, 2006), nor of the introduction of numerical flexibility through the use of temporary workers who can readily be hired and fired, depending upon employer need. Rather, they have come from growing functional flexibility in collective bargaining agreements, which have increasingly allowed for greater internal labour mobility, multi-skilling of labour, and promotion based upon skills as opposed to seniority.

Clearly, the new economic model has inaugurated a momentous organisational restructuring of Mexican industry in the past two decades. However, it has also instigated a dramatic spatial restructuring as well. Of the six Mexican states that border the US, prior to the 1980s only two (Coahuila and Nuevo León) had already been fairly heavily industrialised and the region as a whole was dominated by low-value-adding services and agriculture, with a very minimal presence of labour unions (with the exception of agricultural unions in the northern Gulf area and a small number of mining enclaves). Since the 1980s, though, there has been a tremendous growth in the number of *maquila* and other (for instance, automotive) plants in northern Mexico, with virtually all such plants' output being exported – a locational and production strategy that contrasted with the longstanding ISI patterns in which manufacturing plants were located in the central region and orientated toward the domestic market (De la Garza, 1992). Equally, some of the older facilities built during the ISI period have refocused their production towards manufacturing for export.

Certainly, it is not hard to understand why this northern region has grown in terms of industrial production – proximity to the US market and local state governments' promotion of FDI (through tax exemption, donation of land, free infrastructure) have been key. However, a central consideration has also been a desire on the part of many manufacturers to find production sites without a tradition of unionisation in which they can experiment with new ways of organising production. Consequently, in the years prior to NAFTA's passage *maquilas* were established in those cities along Mexico's northern border which did not have much of an industrial or labour union history (Matamoros in the Gulf region was an exception). Likewise, the most complex automotive plants were established in medium-sized cities such as Hermosillo, Chihuahua and Saltillo, although they avoided Monterrey, a city with a long industrial tradition. As time went by, though, this new pattern of industrialisation was further expanded geographically. Thus, toward the mid-1990s, in the second stage of the neoliberal model's adoption, a new manufacturing zone began emerging in central Mexico, focused upon states such as Michoacan, Aguascalientes, Puebla, Tlaxcala, Morelos, and Querétaro, together with Yucatán (see Figure 18.3). Although both *maquila* and non-*maquila* manufacturing establishments were installed in these states, in both sectors manufacturing for export prevailed. The primary factor shaping this locational strategy was the search for low wages and labour tranquility.

Industrial restructuring in the post-ISI era, then, has been decidedly spatial in nature. Certainly, older industrial areas have continued to be important – Monterrey retains numerous non-*maquila* plants established during the ISI period, Guadalajara has experienced some new *maquila* development, and the Mexico City region continues to be home to many small and medium-sized manufacturing establishments which remain focused on the domestic market and are rather traditional in terms of their use of technology and organisation (Ruiz Durán and Dussel, 1999). However, the central characteristic of this post-ISI restructuring has been the formation of the highly industrialised and largely new export region in the states bordering the US, together with the emergence of zones of *maquila* production in central Mexico and the Yucatán peninsula (see Figure 18.4). Furthermore, not only has Mexico's economic geography been transformed in terms of the location of manufacturing facilities but it has also been transformed in terms of the geography of capital intensity. Hence, between 1992 and 2002 such intensity diminished in the northern states as a result of the expansion of the *maquilas* (which are very labour-intensive) and increased only in Nuevo León and Coahuila, where industry is more diversified. (Interestingly, these two states were the only ones in the north to see an increase in labour productivity.)

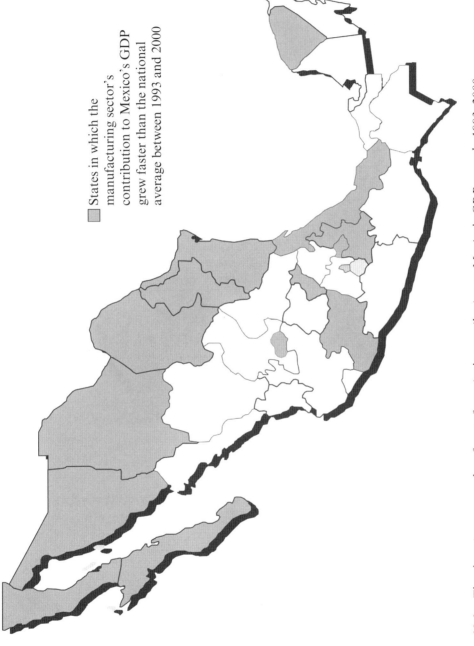

States in which the manufacturing sector's contribution to Mexico's GDP grew faster than the national average between 1993 and 2000

Figure 18.3   The changing geography of manufacturing's contribution to Mexico's GDP growth, 1993–2000

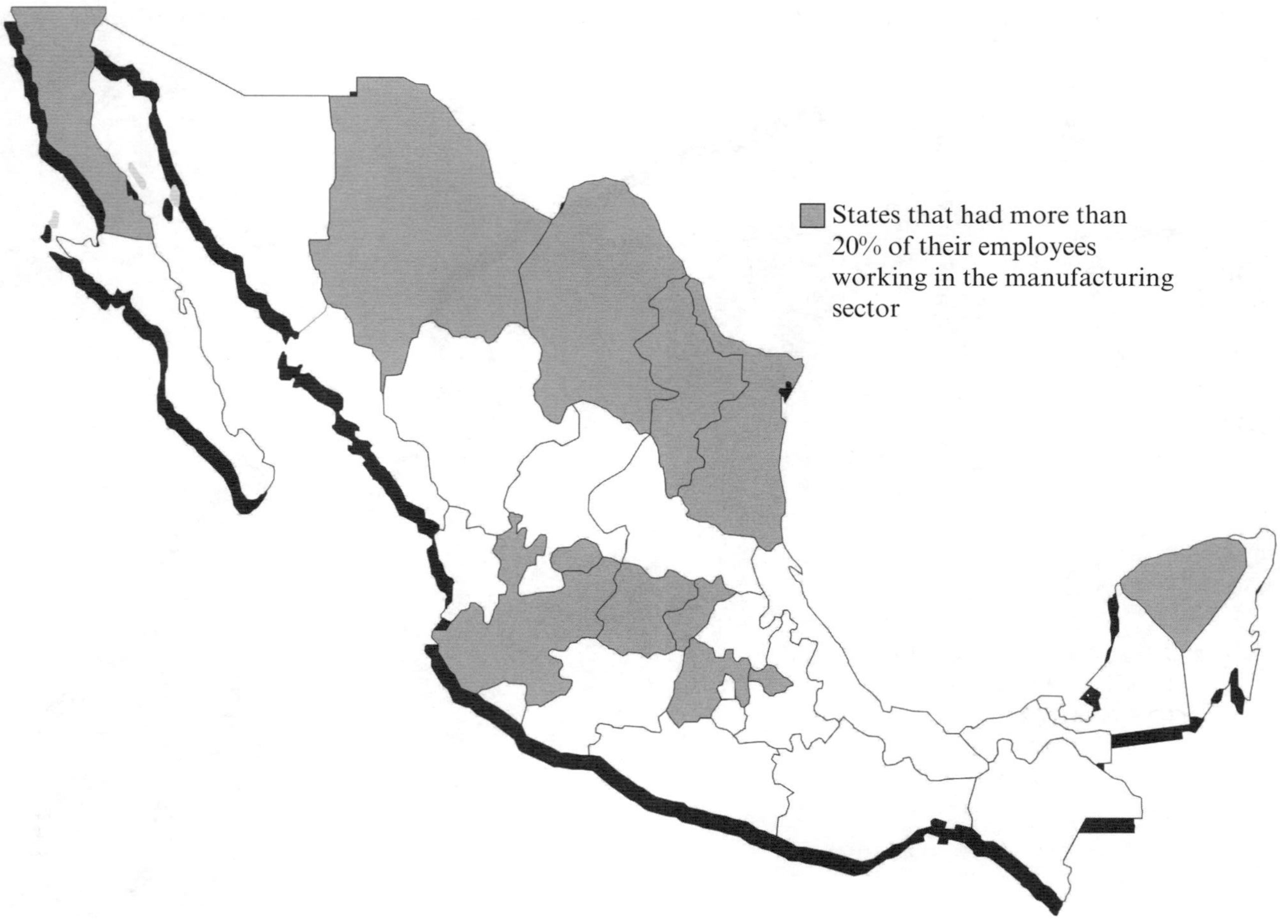

States that had more than
20% of their employees
working in the manufacturing
sector

Figure 18.4 The geography of manufacturing employment, 2002

Significantly, then, it is possible to identify at least two phases in the development of this new geography of Mexican manufacturing in the neoliberal era: whereas in the 1980s *maquilas* tended to locate in the north and in Jalisco, since the early 1990s a growing number have located in the second emerging zone in central Mexico, as well as in Puebla and the Yucatán. This two-part geographical spread of *maquila* manufacturing is important because the new industrial sector in the north has served as the laboratory for the country's nascent flexible labour relations, providing a space for employers both to avoid the 'corporatist protections' granted to workers in the major industries of the import substitution era and to experiment with new systems of work organisation before extending them to other parts of the country. Nevertheless, it is important to recognise that the growth of the *maquila* and final-assembly automotive industry in the north and the establishment of the new flexible model of labour relations that later expanded to the rest of the country took place within, rather than in confrontation with, the corporatist system. Hence, the emergence of the neoliberal economic model has not signified so much an end to the pact between the state and corporatist labour unions as it has a reworking of it (resulting in what some authors have referred to as neoliberal corporatism). Therefore, the old corporatist PRI-affiliated labour unions continue to have nearly unlimited prerogative in the unionisation of new plants in the north because they have been largely willing to accept new flexible labour relations (if with a radical change in the contractual model) in exchange for a continued monopoly over representation of the new labour force, an agreement supported by both the state and the companies involved.[3] As a result, any collective resistance by workers to the new labour regime, though having received significant attention abroad, has been virtually ineffective in practice (De la Garza, 1993b); complaints filed with the NAFTA labour office (NALCA) regarding violations of union freedoms, as well as the struggles waged by the Authentic Labour Front (Frente Auténtico del Trabajo), for instance, have had practically no impact on the nearly absolute control still enjoyed by the PRI unions.

For its part, the new contractual model for labour relations that was introduced in the *maquila* industry in the north (and in the automotive industry that had been installed in the same region) in the 1980s is characterised by: flexibility in internal mobility and multiskilling; the hiring of temporary workers and of subcontracting; a change in the criteria for moving up the job scale (now it is workers' capabilities rather than seniority that is key); the elimination of obstacles for management to hire and fire personnel; decreased benefits relative to those received at the old plants in central Mexico; the acceptance of managerial unilateralism in determining technological changes and work organisation; the extension of workdays relative to traditional industrial zones in central Mexico; and the lowering of wages (generally *maquilas* pay 40 per cent of what is paid in non-*maquila* manufacturing). Overall, then, key elements of the labour relations model that began in the north but which has now been extended to central Mexico are the greater flexibility and unilateralism in decisions regarding the labour force enjoyed by management and the much lower costs per worker (De la Garza, 1993a). Undertaken by subsidiaries of major multinational corporations, as well as by establishments with reorganised or new Mexican capital, the adoption of this new model was heavily supported by the state and by corporatist labour union leaders – the former not only promoted the policy but also pressured labour unions to maintain low wages and flexibility in labour relations, whereas the latter helped keep strikes and collective demands to a minimum (De la Garza, 1990).

Table 18.3   Unionised workers/EAP* in manufacturing by region

	1992		2002	
	Percent unionised	Distribution of all unionised	Percent unionised	Distribution of all unionised
North-west	14.00	3.74	9.64	5.61
North	22.02	6.83	14.54	9.07
North-east	42.47	16.58	35.97	23.30
Central north	12.26	6.36	14.86	10.32
West	22.16	10.77	7.90	5.61
Central	16.14	5.98	12.12	7.28
Central Gulf	36.14	15.85	17.53	8.56
Pacific South	3.63	0.72	3.51	1.04
Yuacatán	15.50	2.11	13.82	2.78
Capital	25.22	31.05	14.72	26.43
National average	23.00	100.00	15.06	100.00

Note: * EAP: Economically Active Population.

Source: Esquinca (2006).

What is important, though, is that this new model not only was adopted in much of the new industry in the country's central and southern regions, but it also exerted pressure for change in how labour relations were conducted and structured in those companies that had been established during the ISI period – companies which were at the very core of labour union corporatism. However, unlike in the new industrialisation zones, in the older zones efforts to impose the new model of labour relations have been met with much greater collective resistance, resistance sometimes led by independent labour union leaders but also, at times, even by corporatist union leaders. Perhaps as a result of this resistance, then, the growth in flexibility and unilateralism in collective bargaining contracts has not been as extreme in the areas dominated by industries established during the ISI period as it has been in the new industrialisation zones (De la Garza, 2006).

In assessing the overall transformation of Mexico's contemporary space-economy, though, it is important to recognise that whereas the recent crisis in *maquila* employment has affected all regions, it has not done so equally. Thus, the emerging region in central Mexico has been the most affected in relative terms by the recent losses of jobs, nearly 42 per cent (165 000) between mid-2000 and the end of 2003. Equally, the geography of deunionisation has been quite uneven. Hence, the regions least affected by deunionisation have been the central, southern Pacific, and Yucatán peninsular regions, together with Mexico City. In contrast, the regions most affected by a decrease in unionisation rates have been the north-eastern, north-western, western, central Gulf, and northern regions – with the exception of Veracruz, all new industrial zones (see Table 18.3). The crisis of unionisation, then, appears to be mostly one affecting the new industries and the new zones of industrialisation (De la Garza, 2006).

As mentioned, in terms of worker resistance to the new flexible, unilateralist model of labour relations, the most important examples have tended to occur in regions with a preponderance of companies established during the ISI period (see Figure 18.5), though the number of strikes and collective conflicts has generally diminished since NAFTA went into effect (De la Garza, 1993a). Typically, worker resistance has not involved striking because of the degree of corporatist control over unions in both old and new industries (by and large, the new, independent unions are to be found in public services – telephone, electricity in the central zone, social security, universities – whilst they are nearly non-existent in the areas of new, private-sector industrialisation, particularly in the *maquila* industry). Rather, instead of collective actions worker resistance has tended to take the form of voluntary individual decisions to leave jobs considered to have poor working conditions and low wages, a voluntary external turnover that has especially affected new industry in the northern and central regions of the country (Carrillo and Santibáñez, 1993). At the same time, a second common form of worker resistance has been the growing number of individual complaints initiated by workers through labour tribunals against companies, though usually without any intervention on their behalf by labour unions (De la Garza, 2005) (see Figure 18.6).

In sum, we can see three significant changes in how the Mexican space-economy is being restructured in the post-NAFTA era. First, a number of new industrial zones have been established *de novo* or have been superimposed over older industrial zones (as with the states of Coahuila and Nuevo León). Second, the productivity crisis which has impacted Mexican industry in the past decade or so has been especially felt in the *maquila* zones in the northern region, with the exception of Nuevo León and Coahuila, where industrial development is more diversified. Finally, it shows that 'maquilaisation' does not bring with it an increase in capital intensity – in fact, quite the opposite.

New work forms – a north–south comparison

Initially, then, *maquilas* were located only in Mexico's northern border states, though changes in the law in the late 1980s allowing them to locate further from the US border subsequently meant that they have now been established in nearly all of the country's states – a geographical expansion that has been called the '*marcha al sur*' ('march to the south'). This expansion appears largely due to *maquilas*' search for lower wages and other regional advantages in other parts of Mexico, and the difficulty in finding workers in the northern border region, as many have preferred either to emigrate to the US or to join the informal sector, where they can earn more money (*maquila* wages have increased since the 1990s, but are now still only 50 or 60 per cent of those in the manufacturing sector (De la Garza, 2005)). Although the growth of *maquilas* has certainly transformed Mexico's overall space-economy, it is important, however, to recognise that there are significant differences within the export *maquila* sector, depending on the branch (the main branches are autoparts, metalworking, garments and electronics), the region, type of capital, and the size of establishment. At the same time, though, as I have argued above, the northern border zone has served as a laboratory for the development of a new production model, and this can clearly be seen in the similarities between *maquilas* in this area and those being established in other parts of Mexico. In order to move beyond the mere assertion that the older *maquila* zone in the north has served as the incubator for the mode of labour regulation that is spreading across the country, then, here I will briefly draw upon two studies to flesh out empirically claims for such a geographical diffusion. These studies are one by Carrillo and Gomis (2004) on the northern border zone

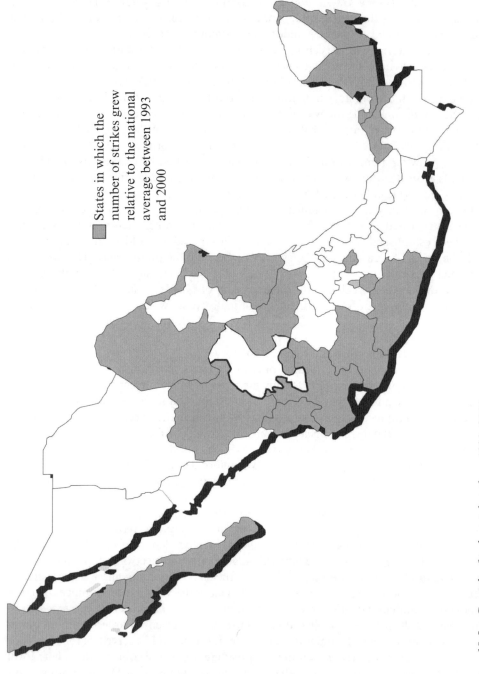

States in which the number of strikes grew relative to the national average between 1993 and 2000

Figure 18.5   Growth of industrial strikes, 1993–2000

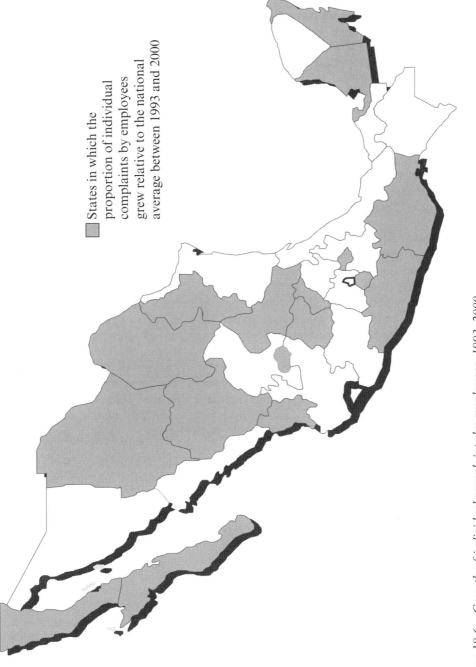

States in which the proportion of individual complaints by employees grew relative to the national average between 1993 and 2000

Figure 18.6   Growth of individual complaints by employees, 1993–2000

and a study of the *maquila* sector in central Mexico (including Puebla) and Yucatán in which I was involved and in which data were collected as part of the Maquila Production Models Survey/Encuesta Modelos de Producción en la Maquila (EMIM).[4]

For their part, in the early 2000s Carrillo and Gomis (2004) surveyed approximately 200 plants in the northern border cities of Tijuana, Mexicali and Ciudad Juarez to catalogue the types of work organisation and labour relations that have developed in the oldest and allegedly most developed zone of *maquila* production. Their research showed that 65 per cent of the plants do not have a technical centre for research and development, 75 per cent do not carry out research and development, and 82 per cent do not design new products. Furthermore, the majority reported that the most important production changes made in the two years prior to being surveyed were related to final assembly and process engineering, and that in 89 per cent of the plants technology was transferred from their corporate networks located in other countries. On average, they considered 40 per cent of their productive processes to be automated, while 70 per cent of their purchases were imported. With regard to the labour force, 50 per cent of workers were women, 75 per cent were line-workers and 12 per cent technicians. *Maquila* workers in this region had worked in an average of 3.1 *maquilas* during their lifetimes and 69 per cent had other labour experience. Their average length of tenure was 3.6 years, whilst their average age was 26. Average monthly turnover was 9 per cent and the primary labour problem identified by management was workers' lack of responsibility.

The research carried out by Carrillo and Gomis (2004), then, provides a good overview of the production methods and worker characteristics that have developed in the oldest *maquila* zones. As *maquilas* have spread to other parts of the country, though, these types of production methods and worker characteristics have spread with them. Thus, the EMIM, which contains a sample of 200 *maquila* establishments in non-border regions, shows that most of the *maquila* manufacturing operations (60 per cent) in these regions are similarly carried out using non-automated equipment and machinery, whilst operations carried out with automated/computerised devices, some integrated in networks and others not, are clearly a minority (15 per cent). This finding reaffirms that *maquilas* generally do not use the highest level of technology available in the manufacturing process but, instead, use labour-intensive forms of production. At the same time, though, most *maquilas* viewed themselves as having outdated technology, and reported that visual – rather than automated – quality control predominates. Equally, just-in-time inventory control is rarely used and they generally do not carry out their own research and development, acquiring technology instead either from their corporate network or purchasing it from other companies. In total, some 77 per cent of *maquila* establishments operate according to a Taylorist–Fordist model (non-automated technology and routine, standardised work), a form of organisation consistent with the intensive use of unskilled labour and with low and medium levels of (non-automated) technology.

Whilst the EMIM catalogued a number of characteristics concerning the *maquilas* in non-border regions of Mexico, it also allowed the development of an index that considers different types of flexibility: numeric (covering companies' capacity to hire or fire workers in accordance with production needs); functional (covering companies' capacity to move and/or use multi-skilled workers within the productive process); and flexibility based upon providing bonuses for productivity and performance. Based on a weighting developed through factorial analysis (for more details see De la Garza, 2005), it is evident that the vast majority (85 per cent) of *maquilas* utilise at least medium levels of work flexibility. Although high levels of flexibility can often be associated with new forms of work organisation (Rankin, 1990), the Taylorist forms of organisation that predominate in *maquilas* and in which each job position has a specialised operator who, preferably, is not moved, however, do not favour the employment of multi-skilled labour. Finally, given the predominance of regular, full-time employees in *maquilas*, the use of bonuses is relatively uncommon. In terms of the profile of the labour force employed in *maquilas* in the south-eastern and central zone, there is nearly an equal number of male and female workers (43 per cent of general workers are male); workers are young (most general workers are between 18 and 26 years of age); workers have little length of time in the job (most general workers have worked in their plant for less than one year); they have a low level of schooling (most general workers have not continued beyond elementary school, and some have not finished elementary school); personnel turnover is high (81 per cent of workers who left the companies did so voluntarily); and there is a common perception among these workers that their wages are low.

In terms of the connections between *maquilas* and other companies within Mexico, the data collected from the EMIM survey indicate that the great majority of *maquilas* do not conduct market and sales research, personnel hiring, training, research and development, publicity, purchase of raw materials and acquisition of machinery and equipment, nor do they share machinery and equipment or engage in any other activity in collaboration with other national establishments. Of these activities, *maquilas* are more likely to share the purchase of machinery, equipment and raw materials than to engage in any of the other activities identified, but even here a very small proportion actually do so (far fewer than 50 per cent). These data are consistent with those concerning the older *maquila* zones regarding the frequency with which raw materials, machinery and equipment are imported from abroad; most raw materials, machinery, and equipment are imported for use in *maquilas* because of tax advantages, so there is little incentive to coordinate and cooperate with other local *maquilas*. Nevertheless, fiscal considerations do not seem to explain the limited occurrence of other types of networking and cooperation between *maquilas* and other companies located within Mexico – the percentage of production value that these *maquilas* subcontract with other companies in Mexico was only 3.7 per cent in 2003, whilst the percentage of income that *maquilas* obtain from being subcontracted by other establishments was only 15.6 per cent in that same year. Rather, it appears that corporations' desire to segment the production process in the international arena may be key in explaining this pattern.

To summarise, on the basis of the micro-data on establishments collected in the EMIM survey it is clear that *maquilas* in the non-border region are organisationally much like those found by Carrillo and Gomis (2004) in the northern border area and are characterised by a combination of Fordist organisation, low or medium-level technology, low or medium flexibility, and low or medium-skilled labour (47.2 per cent of establishments). However, they also exhibit a somewhat greater degree of 'precarious Toyotaism', which involves a combination of Toyotaist organisation (team work, multi-skilled labour, internal mobility) and low or medium-skilled labour, though without extensive delegation of decision-making to workers and with low or medium levels of technology and flexibility. This is, perhaps, due to the fact that they are newer facilities and so were constructed after Toyotaist principles began to shape industrial production – a fact which highlights how the economic landscape crystallises in material form the organisational and productive systems extant at the time of its being put in place.

Discussion

In the 1980s and 1990s, many management gurus, academics (Piore and Sabel, 1984; Pollert, 1989; Pruijt, 1997; Novick and Gallart, 1997; Ozaki, 1999), governments and international organisations suggested that the way to resolve the productivitiy crisis of the 1970s was to implement Toyotaism. They advocated principles of task reintegration (in contrast to the segmentation characteristic of Taylorism); multi-skilled labour versus simplified, routine work; internal mobility among job positions, categories and departments versus fixed jobs for each person; the participation and involvement of workers in placing their tacit, accumulated know-how at the company's disposal versus workers who simply obey the rules; the creation of a specific organisational culture shared by both managers and workers; and the need for workers to identify with the company and their work rather than their adopting a confrontational attitude towards management (Boyer, 1988, 1989). Nevertheless, as one perhaps finds with all abstract formulas, this proposed model had the defect of having ignored the fact that management doctrines are always based on specific territories and local actors, which have their own histories and geographical concerns – such that the actual forms and results of these doctrines' attempted application may differ from the ideal-types of work organisation proposed in the abstract (Anfossi, 1968). Whereas, then, Toyotaism had largely been theorised as a way to reinvigorate the old manufacturing regions of advanced industrial nations like Japan, the US and the Western European economies, its application to manufacturing in a Newly Industrialising Country such as Mexico encouraged the emergence of a particular variety of Toyotaism. Thus, several national and regional particularities have distinctively shaped Toyotaism's adoption in Mexico in much the same way that they had Taylorism's, including:

1. an abundant labour force that has low educational levels, is young, and lacks industrial job experience yet is in search of employment, however unskilled;
2. a labour force that is willing to accept low wages;
3. corporatist labour unions that have largely been willing to accept poor labour conditions;
4. a government that, together with labour unions, has been willing to limit labour dissent through various means;
5. the existence of areas of the country without traditions of unionisation or collective bargaining (Castillo, 1988).

This 'grounding' of Toyotaism (Kochan et al., 1997) in which universal organisational principles have come face-to-face with Mexico's particular conditions of industrialisation have given shape to what I am here calling a 'precarious Toyotaism', particularly in the newly emergent industrial zones. Thus, production in these zones has been characterised by: the partial application of just-in-time and Total Quality Control, which in most companies was reduced to their simplest aspects, such as quality control circles; the continued segmentation between, on the one hand, workers and, on the other, technicians, engineers, and managers, with a predominance of unskilled workers; the flattening of wage scales for workers; extensive wage productivity agreements that mostly reward punctuality and attendance, though with such bonuses being fairly minimal; the persistence of rigidity in employment in the formal sector (the result of the continuance of corporatist labour unions' control over representation – a control endorsed by the state – and the fact that general rules on how to dismiss workers have not changed but remain contained in the Federal Labour Law); functional flexibility that is broader than numerical flexibility; and low wages resulting in a majority of workers living on the edge of poverty (De la Garza, 1990, 1993b). Combined with the greater flexibility seen in collective bargaining agreements negotiated in the second half of the 1980s in *maquila* and new automobile plants in the north (ACLAN, 1997, 1998), 'precarious Toyotaism' has been characterised by high voluntary external turnover and numerous worker claims filed (individually rather than through labour unions) before Labour Relations Boards alleging violations of labour rights (Middlebrook and Quintero, 1998).

Although 'precarious Toyotaism' undergirded Mexico's neoliberal economic expansion in the 1990s and became geographically more widespread as manufacturing, the 'star' sector of the neoliberal model in Mexico, spread beyond the northern border region, its potential for continuing to do so has increasingly come into question at the beginning of the current century, just as Taylorism-Fordism did in the second half of the 1970s. In particular, the combination of economic recession in the United States in the early 2000s, which has lowered the demand for Mexican manufactured products, and competition in overseas markets from countries like China have plunged Mexico into its own recession. This crisis has been exacerbated by domestic factors, including the expansion of the dominant productive models in the *maquila* sector to other sectors; the persistent deficit in the manufacturing balance of payments which has resulted from Mexico choosing to pursue a largely low-value, export-orientated manufacturing model; the almost complete lack of research and development in the country's companies and an increasing trend toward importing machinery and equipment; the problems of access to credit faced by manufacturers as a result of the privatisation of the banks; and, finally, the lack of an industrial promotion policy that might compensate for a time for the disadvantages affecting those subjected to international competition both within and outside the country (Dombois and Pries, 1998). In short, unlike in the early 1980s, when Mexico defaulted on its foreign debts, in the present period it has not been the financial sector which has been at the core of the economic crisis but, instead, it has been manufacturing, particularly manufacturing that adopted the organisational model that emerged in the 1980s. As a result, the crisis has been especially felt in the emerging northern zones (excluding Monterrey), in central Mexico, and in places like Puebla, Guadalajara and Yucatán.

Toyotaism, then, just like Taylorism, is a labour system based on the intensification of work, though this intensification has not come through the adoption of high levels of automation of productive processes. As a result, it can have dramatic physical and social impacts on workers within the workplace, impacts that are formally acknowledged in Japan, where death from excess work is legally recognised (Boyer and Yamada, 2000). However, the crisis of Toyotaism can also be viewed as generating crises outside the workplace – workers' families, for instance, are often forgotten in the face of the long work hours that are necessary to comply with productivity goals (Maurice and Nohara, 1991). Crises in the spaces of paid employment, then, quickly bleed over into the spaces of social reproduction as workers are increasingly forced to make a choice between living and working (Berggren, 1994). Interestingly, though, Mexican workers' responses to such intensification have not generally come through strikes, which have been heavily restricted by the corporatist labour unions that predominate in the emerging zones. Instead, worker resistance has most commonly taken the form of voluntary turnover, which is frequent in Mexico's export *maquila* sector.

As we contemplate changes in the Mexican space-economy and the state's response to this, though, it is important to recognise that not only has corporatism long been part of the Mexican state's *modus operandi* (Cook, 1999) but that this has not ended simply because of the change in government that took place in 2000 when the PRI candidate was defeated in the Presidential elections by the National Action Party's (Partido Acción Nacional) Vicente Fox. Although corporatism has been linked for decades with the PRI, the 2000 election that occurred in the midst of economic crisis demonstrated that its roots run deep in the labour arena as corporatist unions remain connected to the state, even if the party to which they historically owed allegiance (the PRI) is not in power. Thus, although labour unions may be increasingly less important in electoral terms, they remain significant players within the labour relations system. This has been built up over a long period of time and involves the Labour Department and Labour Relations Boards, institutions in which employers and labour union leaders continue to come together and in which corporatism is reproduced primarily as a relationship in which labour peace through labour union control is offered in exchange for labour union leaders maintaining a degree of political power (Bronstein, 1997).

Although corporatism is still alive and well in Mexico, then, there is, however, an important geography to its unfolding politics in the early twenty-first century. In spatial terms, the type of corporatism that is coming to dominate in the newer industrial zones is a type that has lost its capacity to mediate exchanges among workers, companies and the state and is being revealed to be simply an instrument of control for the benefit of companies and labour union leaders (Carrillo and Ramírez, 1990). For instance, in response to the conditions found in these areas, resistance by the new working class in the north generally has not found expression through support for labour unions but, instead, has been seen in individual struggles and dissatisfaction with work, which have led to high labour turnover and/or migration to the United States. This is perhaps related to the fact that the new working class that has emerged in the nascent industrialisation zones in the northern and central regions of the country is different from the old working class – primarily, it is younger and there are more women than has been the case with industrial workers in the past.

Moreover, although this working class is affiliated with corporatist labour unions, as most in the old working class were, its members have never enjoyed the corporatist protections that workers in large companies in the ISI period did, with the result that their loyalty to union leaders is nominal at best, they are largely free from clientelistic ties and corporatist traditions and their working and living conditions are more precarious than were those enjoyed by manufacturing workers employed under the old ISI regime. Consequently, to date members of this new working class have tended not to develop collectivist responses but have, instead, opted for individual or family solutions to the precarious conditions experienced. As a result, arguably the greatest difference between the old and new working classes is that the new working class has a high degree of employment and spatial mobility – it is, in other words, nomadic and is so by its own 'choice'. Hence, unlike what is often theorised to be the case in developed countries, this working class is generally not fired from employment, except in years of crisis. Rather, the workers in this class leave employment due to an accelerated wearing down process, a lack of identity with their employer and poor working conditions. The escape valves for this class of worker, then, typically consist not of unionisation but of movement into the informal sector and international migration, with all of the geographical implications for the tying together of the US and Mexican space-economies and the depopulating of the new industrial zones in Mexico that this brings with it.

Notes

1. The *maquila* sector is a manufacturing sector focused on the final assembly of products for export, especially to the United States. It imports most of its inputs and is subject to a legal system wherein its products are exempted from import, export and value added taxes.
2. For a comparison with China, another rapidly industrialising economy, see Pun and Smith's Chapter 13 in this volume.
3. In the Mexican neoliberal model, 82 per cent of labour unions belong to traditional corporatist organisations. Although the pact with the state has not been broken, labour unions nevertheless do have less influence in designing economic and labour policies, and they are increasingly less able to maintain real wages, to assure job stability and to control working conditions. In addition, the political force of corporatist leaders in the PRI is constantly diminishing, with fewer legislative representatives, senators and governors from this faction.
4. The primary instrument was a survey of *maquila* establishments divided by size, in the states of Zacatecas, Aguascalientes, Michoacan, Guanajuato, Queretaro, the Federal District (Mexico City), Tlaxcala, Puebla and Yucatán. In each state a minimum of 20 per cent of the registered establishments were used (in states with only a few *maquilas*, a census was taken) and they were distributed proportionately according to three sizes: large (with more than 250 workers), medium (with between 100 and 250 workers) and small (with from 15 to 99 workers) (De la Garza, 2005).

References

ACLAN (1997), *Los Mercados de Trabajo en América del Norte* (*Labour Markets in North America*), Dallas: ACLAN.
ACLAN (1998), *Los Mercados de Trabajo en América del Norte: Un Análisis Comparativo* (*Labour Markets in North America: A Comparative Analysis*), Dallas: ACLAN.
Anfossi, A. (1968), 'Principi impliciti nella teoria classica del scientific management' [Implicit principles of the classic theory of scientific management], *Quaderni di Sociologia* (*Sociology Notebook*), **1** (2), 85–120.
Berggren, Ch. (1994), 'Lean production – the end of history?', *Work, Employment and Society*, **7** (2), 163–88.
Boyer, R. (1988), *La Flexibilización del Trabajo en Europa* (*The Flexibilisation of Work in Europe*), Madrid: Ministerio del Trabajo y la Seguridad Social.
Boyer, R. (1989), 'Alla ricerca di alternative al Fordismo: gli anni ottanta' [Looking for alternatives to Fordism: the eighties], *Stato e Mercato* (*State and Market*), **24** (December), 387–423.
Boyer, R. and T. Yamada (2000), *Japanese Capitalism in Crisis*, London: Routledge.
Bronstein, A. (1997), 'Reforma laboral en América Latina: entre garantismo y flexibilidad' ('Labour reform in Latin America: between guarantee and flexibility'), *Revista Internacional del Trabajo* (*International Labour Review*), **116** (1), 5–27.
Carrillo, J. (1990), 'Maquilización de la industria automotriz en México: de la industria terminal a la industria de ensamble' ('Maquilaisation of the automotive industry in Mexico: from manufacturing industry to assembly industry'), in J. Carrillo (ed.), *La Nueva Era de la Industria Automotriz en México* (*The Mexican Automotive Industry's New Era*), Tijuana: El Colegio de la Frontera Norte, pp. 67–114.
Carrillo, J. and J. Gomis (2004), *Encuesta: Aprendizaje Tecnológico y Escalamiento Industrial en las Plantas Maquiladoras* (*Survey: Technological Learning and Industrial Scaling-up in Maquila Plants*), Tijuana: El Colegio de la Frontera Norte.
Carrillo, J. and M.A. Ramírez (1990), 'Maquiladoras de la frontera norte, opinión sobre los sindicatos' ('Maquilas of the northern border region, an opinion about the unions'), *Frontera Norte* (*Northern Frontier*), **2** (4), 121–52.
Carrillo, J. and J.J. Santibáñez (1993), *Rotación de Personal en las Maquiladoras de Exportación de Tijuana* (*Personnel Turnover in the Tijuana Export Maquilas*), Tijuana: Secretaria del Trabajo y Previsión Social, El Colegio de la Frontera Norte.

Castillo, J.J. (ed.) (1988), *Las Nuevas Formas de Organización del Trabajo* (*New Forms of Work Organisation*), Madrid: Ministerio del Trabajo y la Seguridad Social.

Cook, M.L. (1999), 'Trends in research on Latin American labor and industrial relations', *Latin American Research Review*, **34** (1), 237–54.

De la Garza, E. (1990), 'Reconversión industrial y cambios en el patrón de relaciones laborales en México' ('Industrial restructuring and change in the labour relations' model in Mexico'), in A. Anguiano (ed.), *La Modernización de México* (*The Modernisation of Mexico*), Mexico City: UAM-X, pp. 150–200.

De la Garza, E. (1992), 'La polarización del aparato productivo en México' ('The polarisation of the productive sector in Mexico'), *El Cotidiano*, **46** (March–April), 15–25.

De la Garza, E. (1993a), *Reestructuración Productiva y Respuesta Sindical en México* (*Productivity Restructuring and Union Response in Mexico*), Mexico City: Instituto de Investigaciones Económicas, Universidad Nacional Autónoma de México.

De la Garza, E. (1993b), 'La reestructuración del corporativismo en México' ('The restructuring of corporatism in Mexico'), in M.L. Cook, K. Middlebrook and J.M. Horcasitas (eds), *The Politics of Economic Restructuring in Mexico: State–Society Relations and Regime Change in Mexico*, La Jolla, CA: Center for US–Mexican Studies, University of California, San Diego, pp. 60–75.

De la Garza, E. (1998), *Modelos de Industrialización en México* (*Models of Industrialisation in Mexico*), Mexico City: UAM-I.

De la Garza, E. (coord.) (2005), *Modelos de Producción en la Maquila de Exportación* (*Production Models in Export Maquilas*), Mexico City: UAM-Plaza y Valdés.

De la Garza, E. (2006), *Empresas y Trabajadores en México al Inicios del Siglo XXI* (*Businesses and Workers in Mexico at the Beginning of the 21st Century*), Mexico City: Fondo de Cultura Económica.

De la Garza, E. (ed.) (2007), *Los Bonos de Productividad en México* (*Productivity Bonuses in Mexico*), Mexico City: Secretaria del Trabajo y Previsión Social.

De la Garza, E. and A. Bouzas (1998), *Contratación Colectiva y Flexibilidad del Trabajo en México* (*Collective Bargaining and Work Flexibility in Mexico*), Mexico City: IIEc-Universidad Nacional Autónoma de México.

Dombois, R. and L. Pries (1998), '¿Un huracán devastador o un choque catalizador? Globalización y relaciones industriales en Brasil, Colombia y México' ('A devastating hurricane or a catalyzing shock? Globalisation and industrial relations in Brazil, Colombia and Mexico'), *Revista Latinoamericana de Estudios del Trabajo* (*Latin American Review of Studies of Work*), **4** (8), 59–87.

Esquinca, M.T. (2006), 'Afiliación sindical y premio salarial en México' ('Union affiliation and salary compensation in Mexico'), in E. De la Garza and C. Salas (eds), *La Situación del Trabajo en México* (*The Work Situation in Mexico*), Mexico City: UAM-Plaza y Valdés, pp. 459–85.

Hernández Laos, E. (2006), 'La productividad en México: origen y distribución (1960–2002)' ('Productivity in Mexico: origin and distribution (1960–2002)'), in E. De la Garza and C. Salas (eds), *La Situación del Trabajo en México* (*The Work Situation in Mexico*), Mexico City: UAM-Plaza y Valdés, pp. 151–70.

Kochan, T., R. Lansburry and J.P. Duffie (1997), *After Lean Production*, Ithaca: ILR Press.

Maurice, M. and H. Nohara (1991), *Les Mutations du Modèle Japonais de l'Entreprise*, (*Mutations of the Japanese Business Model*), Paris: La Documentation Française.

Middlebrook, K. and C. Quintero (1998), 'Las juntas de conciliación y arbitraje en México: Registro sindical y solución de conflictos en los noventa' ('Conciliation and arbitration courts in Mexico: Union registry and conflict resolution in the nineties'), *Estudios Sociológicos* (*Sociological Studies*), **47** (May–August), 1–40.

Novick, M. and M.A. Gallart (1997), *Competitividad, Redes Productivas y Competencias Laborales* (*Competitiveness, Production Networks and Skills*), Montevideo: International Labour Organisation.

Ortiz, E. (2006), 'La macroeconomía durante el gobierno de Fox' ('The macroeconomy under the Fox government'), paper presented at the Mexican-Brazilian meeting 'Balance of two governments', Mexico City, 26 April.

Ozaki, M. (1999), *Negotiating Flexibility*, Geneva: International Labour Organisation.

Piore, M. and C.F. Sabel (1984), *The Second Industrial Divide: Possibilities for Prosperity*, New York: Basic Books.

Pollert, A. (1989), 'L'entreprise flexible: réalité ou obsession?' ('The flexible enterprise: reality or obsession?'), *Sociologie du Travail* (*Sociology of Work*), **31** (1), 75–106.

Pruijt, H.D. (1997), *Job Design and Technology: Taylorism vs. Anti-Taylorism*, London: Routledge.

Rankin, T.D. (1990), *New Forms of Work Organization: The Challenge for North American Unions*, Toronto: University of Toronto Press.

Ruiz Durán, C. and E. Dussel (1999), *Dinámica Regional y Competitividad Industrial* (*Regional Dynamism and Industrial Competitiveness*), Mexico City: Universidad Nacional Autónoma de México.

Secretaría del Trabajo y Previsión Social (Secretary of Labour and Social Welfare (STPS)) (2005), Estadísticas laborales (Labour statistics), on-line statistics available through STPS website at www.stps.gob.mx.

Section 3.2

Organising in Space and Place

19 Contested space: union organising in the old economy[1]

Bradon Ellem

Much has been written to explain union membership decline and the adoption and impact of various strategies of renewal. Australia is no exception to this, for it is a country in which unionism seemed to be thoroughly embedded in numerical, institutional and even cultural terms. At the height of the postwar boom, the proportion of the workforce belonging to a union was, on some counts, 60 per cent. In 1976, when the current statistical set began, it was still 51 per cent but in every year since then 'union density' has fallen. More alarmingly still, the total number of union members began to fall in 1992. With a growing labour force, this meant that the fall in union density was cataclysmic. It fell from just under 40 per cent in 1992 to less than 19 per cent in 2007. In the same period private sector union density fell from 29 to under 14 per cent (ABS, 1992–2005; ABS, 2006–2008; Bain and Price, 1980; Peetz, 1998).[2] Amid this crisis, the peak body of Australian unions, the Australian Council of Trade Unions (ACTU), adopted 'organising' as its response, a strategy which represented a conscious mimicking of activity in the USA where unions have long faced state and employer hostility.

In the rich body of literature examining these massive disruptions to social and industrial relations, and organised labour's response thereto, there has been no detailed consideration of the geography of the crisis. We know little about the fine grain of unionism in the States[3] or of local patterns; we know little, then, about the central concern of this chapter, namely, how space and union organising constitute each other. Unionism, this chapter argues, is constructed and challenged not at national scales alone but at many scales, including the local.

In this regard, the chapter opens by showing how and why 'geography matters' in union decline and renewal. It goes on to focus on one vital industry, iron ore mining, in one place, the Pilbara region of Western Australia. This union stronghold faced an assault as early as 1986. By 1999 the Pilbara's mining unions were facing eradication. Since then, complex local struggles have dominated this industry, its product markets driven by global steel demand. The chapter concludes by showing how these struggles are geographically distinct, but not unique. Based upon the situations outlined herein, geography, I suggest, matters in all makings and unmakings of unionism.

How geography matters
Apart from insisting that all relationships are spatial, with space being made, not given (Massey, 1994, p. 22, 1995, pp. 3–4), and that 'labor's self-reproduction must take place in particular geographical locations' (Herod, 1997, p. 16), how can we begin to explore the spatiality of unionism?

The most thorough empirical inquiry into the geography of union decline is a British study, by Martin et al., *Union Retreat and the Regions: The Shrinking Landscape of*

Organized Labour (1996; see also Martin et al., 1993, 1994a, 1994b). This account argues that focusing on the overall national scale of union decline means that 'relatively little is known . . . about how far and in what ways the spatial contours of British trade unionism are being restructured' regionally and locally (Martin et al., 1993, p. 37). By focusing upon the sub-national scale, *Union Retreat and the Regions*, then, sought to show that the traditional 'union heartlands' in Britain had proven to be very 'resilient' through the crisis of the 1980s, even as union membership overall declined. In contrast, the growth regions (chiefly the south of England) provided a much harsher terrain.

The core of the argument is that these regional differences are not purely an industry effect. As Martin et al. (1993, p. 55) put it:

> Regionally specific factors and the products of local context are at work in determining unionisation rates over and above any simple correlation with the distribution of industry. Different traditions of unionisation have been established in different geographical areas at different periods, and once established those traditions would appear to have locally emergent effects.

The authors also argue that 'these differences remain after geographical variations in industrial structure, firm size and firm ownership, and so on have been taken into account' (Martin et al., 1994b, pp. 457–8). Significantly, they point out, in places where unions emerged early, newer sectors of the economy and workforce have been successfully organised, even when those sectors are poorly unionised in other places.

Unfortunately, no studies of Australian unionism match the scope of *Union Retreat and the Regions*. However, there is some evidence of variation in unionisation across the landscape, between and within the States. This evidence comes from a number of major longitudinal analyses which consider the geography of union growth and decline disaggregated to the scale of the six States and two Territories which make up the Commonwealth of Australia. These variations are striking. For example, when union density was at its national peak of about 60 per cent in the mid-1950s, Queensland's rate was over 70 per cent (with State legislation delivering absolute preference in employment to unionists), the rate in New South Wales was about the national average, whilst all other States were below the national average. Furthermore, there are quite different historical patterns between the States. Union density peaked in the early 1950s in South Australia and Western Australia but as late as the 1970s in New South Wales. These aggregate statistics also reveal significant differences in gender densities between the States (Bain and Price, 1980, p. 128; see also Peetz, 1998, 2005).

There are also indications of variations within the States. Labour historians have explored the specificity of industrial relations in particular localities (see especially *Labour History*, 2000) and a small number of geographers have also turned their attention to local changes in industrial relations in the light of economic restructuring and regulatory change (Sadler and Fagan, 2004) and to variations within one State, New South Wales (Forrest, 1995). Some industrial relations scholars have addressed the issue of union presence in particular localities but these local studies were, for the most part, industry studies, to which geography was merely incidental; particular places were, more or less, just where these industries happened to be (Walker, 1970; for a critique, Ellem and Shields, 1999).

More recent studies suggest that 'geography matters' within States as well as between them. For Australia's most populous State, New South Wales, several case studies and surveys of mining and steelmaking regions demonstrate the maintenance of above-average levels of union density, even as deindustrialisation occurs. Hence, in the Hunter Valley and Illawarra region, immediately to the north and south of Sydney respectively, several studies reveal the persistence of above-average levels of union density overall (Alexander et al., 1995, pp. 116–17; Macdonald and Burgess 1998; Markey et al., 2001; Markey, 2004). Significantly, in the more extensive Illawarra study, measures of union propensity among employees and of union sympathy among managers appear to be more favourable than the national figures (Markey et al., 2001; Markey, 2004). On the other hand, in the far western city of Broken Hill, the collapse of the local mining industry has gutted employment and sharply reduced the power of the mining union, the local unions' peak body, and all local unions. Here, then, the unions have fared much worse than elsewhere (Ellem, 2005).

If these studies of the State and local scales in Australia suggest that 'geography matters', and that industry itself is not the explanatory factor, then it is necessary to reflect upon why geography affects union fortunes and how, indeed, unions themselves may make geographies.

Why geography matters
Four interrelated elements of spatiality underpin this study: the nature of uneven development, how labour markets are locally structured, social actors' place consciousness and the geographical scales at which they operate. Thus, variations in the geography of unionism arise because of the uneven development of capitalism and because labour markets themselves are spatially-specific, shaped in turn by other spatially-specific structures and processes. Equally, when labour and capital meet in particular places, their orientation to those places and their power within them are shaped by their own geographical mobility and the persuasiveness of the place consciousness which they promote. Furthermore, the scale at which labour is regulated is equally imbricated in geography, be it national regimes or individual workers. Hence, although particular industries and labour processes certainly shape union membership, density and power, they never do so 'non-spatially'. Below, I explore these contentions in a little more detail.

Drawing on Harvey's studies of the geographies of capitalism, and attempting to set up a study of labour geographies, Herod (1997, 1998) argues that places are likely to vary from one another because of the 'uneven development' of capitalism itself. Investment, disinvestment and the creation of different sites of accumulation mean that capital continues to sustain itself despite apparent crises (Harvey, 1982). Because capital necessarily occupies and transforms particular spaces, the distinction between the social and the spatial is an 'impossible dichotomy' (Massey, [1984] 1995, p. 49). More particularly, not only does industry alone fail to explain processes like union decline, there is no such thing as 'industry alone'.

Likewise, 'industry', understood more broadly as the processes of production and paid work, must be located in the actual labour markets in which workers find themselves. In this regard, Peck (1996, p. 13) points to the importance of 'the local', suggesting that 'as capital seeks the local conditions most conducive to profitable production', particular geographies, and particular labour markets, are created. He claims that the local is significant because it 'is the scale at which labor is mobilized and reproduced' (Peck, 1996, p. 11). This privileging of the local scale needs some qualification, as we shall see, but for now two important claims can be drawn from Peck's work. First, '[g]eographies of labor are formed at this intersection, where flows of capital accumulation collide with the structures of community' (Peck, 1996, p. 15). Second, this means that the supply of labour is shaped not simply by price mechanisms but by family, education, social structures and institutional presences (Peck, 1996, p. 38). Union organising is one process which must be understood at these local scales – not solely at these scales but not without them either.

Many scholars have recognised that when capital and labour 'collide' in labour markets they do not do so on an equal footing. In a market economy, workers necessarily sell their labour power in order to 'earn a living'. Taken as a whole, their employers have discretion over whether, how and when to buy this labour power. The structure of the relationship is, therefore, unequal. So is its geography – because capital's mobility is a source of power, immobility is often seen as a weakness for labour. However, the 'rootedness' of labour can, under some circumstances, become a source of power, when working people and their families create distinctive local communities, cultures and organisations. Importantly for the argument here, particular forms of 'place consciousness' and local politics may emerge as part of this process (Storper and Walker, 1989; Beynon and Hudson, 1993).

Capital and labour, then, may create different varieties of place consciousness. Beynon and Hudson capture this dichotomy nicely: capital seeks 'a (temporary) space for profitable production' whereas for workers spaces are different from and more than this – they are 'places in which to live, places in which they have considerable individual and collective cultural investment' (Beynon and Hudson, 1993, p. 182). Beynon and Hudson suggest that 'space [is] the domain of capital' whilst places are 'the meaningful situations established by labour' (Beynon and Hudson, 1993, p. 182), a formulation which, in analysing the mining industry, is particularly striking.

How, then, does this emphasis on the local, mobility and specific forms of place consciousness sit with the demonstrated historical significance of building union power across space, from the local to national and even global scales? Historically, of course, unions sought to standardise wages and conditions between different locations, to create a 'common rule'. However, carrying out this task differed in urgency according to the nature of product and labour markets, as industrial relations scholars from Sidney and Beatrice Webb (1897, 1920) onwards have shown. Thinking spatially, though, adds to this, not by making a fetish of the local but by showing more closely how union traditions are transferred or disrupted over time and space, how 'locales' interrelate. Given that '[w]hat workers do, or fail to do in one place, makes a difference to wider processes of uneven development' (Wills, 1998a, p. 371), a '*geo*historical' analysis of unionism is therefore necessary (Wills, 1998b, p. 132, original emphasis). Consequently, she points to three aspects of this spatial 'translation of trade-union traditions': workers' physical location and relocation, 'demonstration effects' and the search for solidarity in other places (Wills, 1998b, p. 133). By drawing upon these ideas, we can locate the *multiple* sites, types and sources of power (following Allen, 1999), through which union power is made and challenged.

What, then, of the places in which union renewal might happen? A number of scholars, most notably perhaps Green and Tilly (1987), Savage (1998), Walsh (2000) and Wills and Simms (2002), have shown how new forms of work require new spatial strategies for union organising. Interestingly, their work is just as important in re-examining an 'old economy' sector such as iron ore mining as it is in seeking to develop strategies for organising in new economic sectors and locations, for as the next section demonstrates, there are spatial peculiarities in this industry which pose problems for union organising and of which mining managers are only too well aware.

Finally, we turn to the scale of regulation. Industrial relations scholarship has no difficulty in recognising the importance of regulation. Understood as 'rule-making', regulation has long been central to the discipline (notably Flanders, [1969] 1975, pp. 85–6). However, few scholars have read contemporary changes in labour law and bargaining structures in geographical terms (McGrath-Champ, 2005 is an exception; see Herod and Wright 2002; Castree et al., 2004, pp. 96–8 for more on the concept of scale). Yet, these are clearly geographical processes: unions have been confronted by demands at different scales – *global* restructuring and *local* membership loss – and by scale-specific arguments about these processes – the inevitability of *global* competition and the desirability of *individual* representation at work (Sadler and Fagan, 2004).

In sum, four vital points emerge from this discussion. First, capital and labour have different mobilities not just from each other but among themselves. This is important, because mobility affects management strategy, as firms or operations which are less mobile than others are likely to have greater motivation to create conditions conducive to accumulation within particular localities: if they cannot relocate to escape, say, expensive or unruly workforces, then 'capitalists [will] need to develop *place-based* labour control practices' (Jonas, 1996, p. 325, emphasis added). Second, different social actors are likely to have competing senses of locality, contrasting forms of 'place consciousness'. Equally, ideas about social practices in particular places are implicitly or explicitly contextual, comparing one place with others, material or imagined. Third, the scale of labour market regulation is neither self-evident nor given. Fourth, drawing this together, union organising is a geographic process. There are invariably 'scalar tensions' in union campaigns, not least in the unions' 'organising model' which can be characterised as a strategy for grassroots renewal driven by national peak bodies. Having laid out some conceptual issues, I now explore how space and spatiality have been central to the practices of unionisation in the Pilbara region of Western Australia.

A geohistory of the Pilbara

The Pilbara is a vast space shaped by its physical and social geographies and by the tensions between them. It occupies over half a million square kilometres but has a population of only about 39 000 people (ABS, 2003). It is in many ways archetypal 'outback' Australia: hot, arid and physically isolated. The nearest big city is the State capital, Perth, 1600 km to the south. However, the Pilbara's very existence as a site of accumulation is predicated not on its isolation but its integration, its integration with global flows of capital and the ores that the region produces.

Despite much talk over the past twenty years of re-gearing the Australian economy to focus on value-added manufacturing or various forms of information technology and services work, the resources sector, established soon after colonisation, remains critical to the generation of profits and export earnings. There has certainly been massive job growth in the 'new economy' but the significance of mining has not diminished. On the contrary: coal is the single biggest export earner, and in Western Australia's iron ore industry earnings were a record A\$16.1 billion in 2007 (DoIR, 2008). Export volumes have risen to unrivalled levels and export earnings have increased exponentially, driven by huge price rises imposed by the mining companies on the Chinese steel industry. Partly for this reason, mining companies have been reporting record profits with only small turndowns with the onset of economic crisis in 2008.

The industry is thus of tremendous importance. It is also a fascinating industry in socio-spatial terms. Almost all the iron ore mining in Australia takes place in the Pilbara region of the State of Western Australia. In turn, almost all of the Pilbara's mining is undertaken by just two massive global corporations, Rio Tinto and BHP-Billiton (BHP),[4] the latter formed only in 2001 when the Broken Hill Proprietary Company (which had mined the Pilbara since the 1960s) merged with the South African company Billiton to form the world's largest mining company.

The history of the industry, and therefore the Pilbara, has long been vital to the political economy of Australian industrial relations. From the early 1970s, as iron ore mining developed, a pattern of industrial relations emerged which, whilst locally specific, nonetheless encapsulated the militant, male traditions of Australian blue-collar unionism. By the 1980s, there was little doubt that the Pilbara was a 'union space'. However, two of the mining companies working in the Pilbara subsequently de-unionised in landmark industrial disputes. The first took place at the Robe River company over many months from August 1986; the second was at the Hamersley Iron company in 1992–93 (Dufty, 1984; Thompson and Smith, 1987; Swain, 1995; Hearn Mackinnon, 2003; Tracey, 2003; Ellem, 2004, pp. 12–20). Both of these union defeats were emblematic of wider problems; the former is still regarded in Australian industrial relations with the same feelings as the Wapping printers' dispute in Britain or the air traffic controllers' dispute in the USA. The result is that today, the mining employers' lobby group, the Australian Mines and Metals Association (AMMA), is one of the most influential bodies shaping national labour law and has managed to argue, using a highly spatially-aware language of geographical scale, that because of the economic importance of mining to the Australian economy, the local control exercised by these global companies is essential to national well-being (AMMA, 2006; Knott, 2006). In short, the Pilbara plays a significant role in Australian labour relations that stretches far beyond the local scale.

How, then, do we explain how the Pilbara has been structured, and what this means for union organising? The Pilbara, even considered simply in terms of mining, is not a homogeneous space. Rio Tinto, through Hamersley Iron (now a wholly-owned sub-sidiary) and Robe River (in which Rio Tinto has the major share), and BHP operate in quite distinct parts of the Pilbara. There are no physical sites in which workers from different companies mingle. For example, the Hamersley mines are 300 km by road from the main BHP mine and about 400 km from the Robe River site. Mine operations are fragmented within the one company. BHP's mining town, Newman, is 450 km away from its port and treatment facilities at Port Hedland. Hamersley's mines at Paraburdoo and Tom Price are 500 kilometres by road from the port of Dampier (see Figure 19.1). This fragmented geography poses problems for union organising, and the impact of the defeats at Robe River and Hamersley Iron has been only too obvious: the emergence of diverse social geographies. Thus, given that iron ore was the *raison d'être* of the inland towns, these spaces have now become, as one union organiser himself put it, 'Rio Tinto

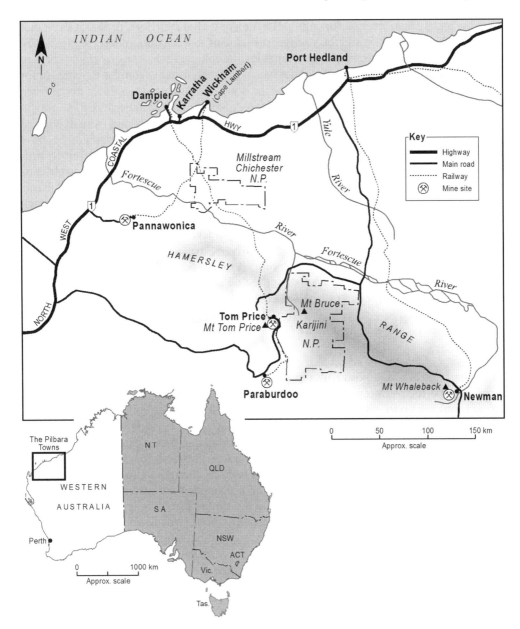

Figure 19.1   The Pilbara towns

territory' (*Rock Solid*, no. 33), for after 1993 only BHP was left running a unionised operation in the Pilbara's iron ore industry.

There are, however, still more socio-spatial tensions which shape union organising. In physically isolated sites such as these, work and non-work, workplace and community issues overlap. These sites are ones in which space is, as Beynon and Hudson argue more broadly, merely instrumental for capital (Beynon and Hudson, 1993, p. 182). Given that the richer the social fabric and the stronger the sense of shared community, the greater the local demands are likely to be on the companies, the companies have increasingly come to favour fly-in/fly-out arrangements (under which workers, usually from Perth, come in for set periods, are accommodated on or near the mine sites and are then flown home when off roster) and the use of contractors. This strategy has been pursued because it is a way to limit the ability of workers to develop the sense of community that comes from living next to one another for, often, years. The resultant 'privatised' social life to which others have referred as being problematical for unions (Hyman, 1999, p. 3) is therefore extremely pronounced in this case – many workers think of 'home' and 'community' as being neighbourhoods in and around cities such as Perth, and not the mining communities of the Pilbara.

Space, however, is also fragmented on the territory of the mines themselves. Although the mines are massive sites, with the open cut operations several kilometres long and hundreds of metres deep, there are typically only a few workers engaged in the pit at any one time: shovel operators, dump truck drivers, drillers and blasters. Workers, in other words, are often isolated geographically at the worksite. Complex shift and roster systems further add to these divisions imposed on labour. In short, geography demonstrably shapes management strategy (see Ellem, 2003 for more detail).

Union crisis and renewal in the Pilbara

Geographies of labour and regulation
The year 1999 saw two powerful and prominent players in Australian industrial relations reshape their strategies. The Australian peak union body, the ACTU, adopted 'organising' as its core response to declining membership. In November, BHP unleashed its strategy for the Pilbara – the removal of any effective union voice from its operations. Both strategies were, quite rightly, seen in terms of leadership change, with a new leadership at the ACTU (Cooper, 2003) and, at BHP, a new president for the steel and energy division who decided that the company needed to effect changes quickly to compete with Hamersley Iron (Ellem, 2004, pp. 27–9). These changes were also thoroughly locked into, and aimed to reshape, geographies of labour and power.

In August 1999, the ACTU published *unions@work*, which set out the aims and methods of the new strategy. The proponents of 'organising unionism' contrasted it with traditional 'servicing', which was based on a 'transactional' relationship where union officials delivered a service and, in exchange, union members paid their dues. Servicing unionism, which was described as the dominant form of unionism throughout the postwar period, was criticised for its reliance on bureaucratic organisation, legal strategies and the state. Unions, it was argued, needed to give the organisations back to the members and, most importantly, shift resources to make membership growth the central priority (ACTU, 1999a). The arguments for change set out in *unions@work* drew upon data from national workplace surveys (Callus et al., 1991; Morehead et al., 1997; Peetz, 1998, pp. 114–34; Crosby, 2005, pp. 75–86), which had demonstrated the critical role that *workplace* structures play in maintaining union membership. They also recommended that unions engage with local communities. There was, then, a new geography of unionism designed to be created at every step of the organising model, though one with an internal tension because it amounts to a *nationally*-driven *local* strategy.

For its part, the company chose to articulate local concerns from the beginning. BHP's senior management had become increasingly alarmed at the efficiencies of its local rival, Hamersley Iron. After considering a merger with Hamersley, managers came to the view that BHP would continue as a stand-alone operation but that to match Hamersley, union influence would have to go. Throughout 1999, the management of BHP prepared the ground for a shift to individual contracts for its workforce of 1100 people. Managers initiated many standard measures of union avoidance. They stalled negotiations for a new collective agreement, reduced the levels of employment, offered attractive redundancy packages to high-profile activists, and ran a series of 'one-on-one' meetings with workers (Interviews: Tracey, Asplin; *Rock Solid*; for more detail, see Ellem, 2003, 2006a). Furthermore, rescaling labour regulation, through implementing Western Australian Workplace Agreements (WPAs), would override collective agreements, allowing BHP to achieve its stated goal of 'the removal of the need to negotiate change with union representatives' (FCA, 2001, para. 187, see also para. 98, pp. 102–3).[5]

Sites of resistance: Unions at BHP
On 11 November 1999, BHP began to offer WPAs to its workers. The agreements themselves were skeletal because the detailed terms and conditions of employment were set out in a separate 'Staff Contract of Employment' and in the *Staff Handbook* (containing details of employees' duties, hours of work, remuneration, leave entitlements and other conditions). The contracts promoted managerial prerogative in several ways: requiring employees to 'work outside . . . normal hours' or change from night to day work or from one shift to another as directed; salaries would be 'adjusted at the company's discretion'; and employees could be required to move between Newman and Port Hedland. Any disputes were to be handled by an 'Issue Resolution Process'. Only after a complainant had met with the President of the Company could the matter be shifted outside the company and referred to the State's Industrial Commission (BHP Iron Ore, 1999, clause 9.1; copies of rejected contracts; Interviews: Asplin, Davis, Tracey, Schapper).

For union leaders and members, within this new system representation was the principal problem: they argued that this was a process intended to thwart the complainant and remove any effective collective representation. For many workers, though, the contract offers seemed attractive enough, with significant wage increases and access to accrued sick leave (FCA, 2001, paras 84–110). However, the money did not tempt those most loyal to the union, mainly because of concerns about the scope of managerial prerogative. According to one of the train drivers, 'you didn't need to be a rocket scientist' to work out that, in return for the immediate gain, employees were giving away any control on the job (Interview: 'John'; Observation of delegates' meetings, Newman and Port Hedland, June 2001).

The unions' response to the BHP offer was threefold, and multi-scalar. First, they undertook a national-scale legal strategy. This national court strategy attempted to emulate the successful 1998 claim of maritime workers, who argued they had been unlawfully sacked by an anti-union employer. Although the BHP workers' attempt ultimately failed, the year-long case did successfully impose a freeze on the contract offer after January 2000 and so bought vital time for union regrouping. Hence, the unions argued in Federal Court that BHP had contravened the Workplace Relations Act by 'injuring' workers in their employment and offering 'inducements' to resign from a union. Initially, on 31 January 2000, the Court delivered an interlocutory decision in the unions' favour, instructing the company to offer no further individual contracts pending a final decision (FCA, 2000). However, in its final decision, handed down on 10 January 2001, the Court ruled that the company was within its rights to offer WPAs and had not specifically interfered with workers' rights to belong to a union (FCA, 2001; see also Dabscheck, 2001; Interview: Burton).

Second, at the State scale union leaders sought a new 'Award' to cover union loyalists.[6] Hence, they pursued a collective arbitrated Award for their members, one which would deliver wage parity with the individual agreements. This wage claim was shaped by the need to organise around locally-identified issues as part of the drive to rebuild unionism. On 2 November 2001, the Western Australian Industrial Relations Commission handed down the new Award. Significantly, this granted a wage rise of 14 per cent during the length of the Award (with 6 per cent to be paid in the first 12 months), thereby matching the increases which WPA workers had been given (WAIRC, 2001; see also WAIRC, 2002).

Third, and perhaps most importantly, national unionism and local activism were intermeshed through ACTU, community and workplace interventions around the organising strategy. As a result, it was at the local scale, through the organising strategy, where the struggle played out most viscerally. The Pilbara was a difficult site at which to apply this strategy, given the socio-spatial divisions outlined above and management's growing command of these places. Furthermore, the company had seized the initiative with its contract offer. Moreover, although local readings of the Pilbara's labour history offered some solace, they also suggested problems for the unions. Thus, many experienced workers had deep reservations about national union leaderships and the ACTU after earlier union defeats. On the other hand, there remained powerful traditions of workplace activism upon which the strategy might draw. (For a more complete discussion, see Ellem (2002). These paragraphs are drawn from: ACTU 1999b; Interviews: Tracey, Kumeroa, Newman and Port Hedland delegates).

Ultimately, though, local union structures and organisation were transformed. The ACTU's 'lead organiser', Troy Burton, spent two weeks in the Pilbara before returning half a dozen times over the next 12 months to oversee the unions' campaign. In December 1999, a series of ACTU-sponsored planning meetings analysed the strengths and weakness of both the unions and management, as well as specific worker concerns. Within a few months, a delegate structure had been established with activist-to-member ratios of between one-to-five and one-to-ten. Fortnightly meetings of the combined Mining Unions Association became the main forum to plan campaign strategy. Members of the five mining unions – the Australian Workers' Union (AWU), the Construction, Forestry, Mining and Energy Union (CFMEU), the Transport Workers' Union, the Australian Manufacturing Workers' Union, and the Communications, Electrical and Plumbing Union – worked for the most part in harmony. This was a major change occasioned by the threat of de-unionisation. Only six weeks before the contract offer, the two biggest unions, the AWU and the CFMEU, had been in court arguing with each other over membership coverage of the Pilbara. However, throughout the year 2000, their delegate structures were re-worked, based on worksite mapping and effective networking across occupational and union lines.

It is important here to emphasise the role of responses at the individual scale in this collective renewal. Workers began public resistance to de-unionisation, for instance by wearing union stickers and union shirts. Morale grew as these tactics were deployed. At the worksites, as confidence grew, they copied the card system of football referees. There was the warning card – yellow, of course – and then the red card shown to overly persistent supervisors who tried to talk them into signing contracts. Union loyalists made bonfires with the letters offering them contracts and raffled others to raise funds. They quickly dubbed both the WPAs and those who signed them 'woppas'. This term, drawn from the acronym and also a slang term for lies and exaggeration (as in 'He told a woppa'), quickly became standard idiom.

The workplace and the unions were not the only sites of workers' resistance, however. For instance, a women's network was established in January 2000. Within a week, the Port Hedland women had gathered 80 partners for a meeting and barbecue in the town and had established their own group, Action in Support of Partners (ASP). Newman soon followed. ASP established its own website and newsletter, ran speaking tours, sent delegates to Perth and had delegates attend the combined union meetings (Interviews: Palmer, Boyington). The unions also ran candidates in local government elections. Despite the many setbacks suffered by unions from Robe River through to November 1999, the Pilbara was, for many, still a union space. And we really cannot explain the nature of union responses without thinking of space – in terms of the many scales of resistance, the multiple sites of action and the constant insistence by union men and women of the naming of these towns as local union spaces, with a physical union presence – amid these national and global campaigns.

There was, then, a significant turnaround in the time afforded the unions by the Federal Court hearings. In late 2000, the ACTU and the mining unions appointed a full-time organiser, Will Tracey, who was based in Port Hedland but travelled regularly to Newman (and later into the Rio Tinto towns). Fifty-five per cent of the workforce stayed loyal to the unions. The best measure of success came after the Federal Court's final decision. In April 2001, the company made a further round of WPA offers but there was almost no uptake. After the first management moves, it was unionists who had taken the initiative in scaling the dispute, forcing the management into courts and tribunals where it did not want to be. They had also drawn on local traditions and resources to more than match the company's attention to the local scale. The Pilbara was still, they said, union space. Or at least their part was. But what of 'Rio Tinto territory'?

Unions, place and Rio territory

By late 2000, small groups of workers at Hamersley Iron were meeting in their homes with union officials and activists from BHP, including Tracey. They had many complaints about working under individualised work systems, especially annual performance reviews and unilateral changes to rosters and shifts. Grievances over social life in the towns – falling population, low numbers of locals employed, declining social life and infrastructure, fly-in/fly-out labour – were no less important. Looking at events at BHP, they also saw a specific alternative both to management power and 'traditional' unions (Focus groups; Interviews: Hamersley employees, Edward, Small business owners). As in seeking to understand the BHP struggle, then, so here excluding geography from our account would be to miss much of the texture of possibilities and threats and of how union activists themselves understood their campaign.

The first physical indication that unions might be able to reclaim a place in the towns around the Rio Tinto sites had come in August 2001, when the mining unions set up a stall at the 'Nameless Festival', a fair in the mining town of Tom Price. State Parliamentarian Jon Ford (2001) reported that many of those at the festival had told him that 'it was good to see a union presence *in town*' (emphasis added). Within the towns, though, the unions maintained a low-key approach, explicable in terms of their own readings of space. For instance, there were no public rallies or mass meetings – the methods so central to union tradition. Rather, the campaign began in homes, not public places. For the unions, however, problems remained, especially as the majority of workers were sceptical about the legacies of, and prospects for, unionism and many were wary or even fearful of associating with unions if they did return.

Nevertheless, an opportunity to re-unionise the Rio Tinto operations arose in 2002. In that year, a new State Labor government phased out the WPAs upon which Rio Tinto had been relying for a decade and which BHP had introduced in 1999. Both companies would now have to find new ways to regulate their Pilbara workforces. They decided to shift from this State scale – at which the industry had been regulated since its inception – to the national scale. They were able to do so because the Liberal Party and National Party (conservative) coalition government, in power nationally since 1996, had introduced legislation to encourage non-union agreements and reduce union power. Specifically, the Workplace Relations Act (1996) had introduced two instruments which aimed to exclude unions from any effective role in workplace representation: individual contracts, called Australian Workplace Agreements (AWAs), and non-union collective agreements, known as LKs (after the relevant section of the Act).

Seeking to use the new law to its advantage, Rio Tinto offered its 3000-strong Pilbara workforce a national 170LK non-union collective agreement. The company put the agreement to a ballot of employees, as required under the Workplace Relations Act. Given the physically isolated and fragmented nature of the Pilbara, there was little time and capacity for unions to prepare a campaign. In this context, on the first Tuesday in March 2002, the company hand-delivered the agreements to all its workers' homes across the Pilbara, keeping things quiet until then. The ballot itself was to be held a month later. In response, union meetings were hastily arranged and pamphlets printed. Over two hundred people turned out at meetings in Paraburdoo and Tom Price, nearly as many in the coastal towns. Such showings of support for the unions soon changed the tone of the company's campaign, from emphasising the benefits of 'working together' to the threat posed to the company and workers by voting 'no' (Ellem, 2004, pp. 46–8).

The ballot result, announced on 5 April 2002, shocked the company (Bachelard, 2002). At Hamersley Iron, nearly 60 per cent had voted 'no'. But, what next? How would a union campaign proceed? Importantly, after some negotiations the four unions with claims on these workers agreed to work together. Meanwhile, the ACTU would fund an organiser, Stewart Edward, for a 12-month term, based in the Hamersley mining town of Paraburdoo. From these State, national and local initiatives emerged the Pilbara Mineworkers' Union (PMU), an unregistered body which would act as a 'shopfront' for re-unionisation. Union officials favoured this structure because they recognised that the union structure at BHP had become popular among sympathisers at Hamersley Iron (Focus groups; PMU, n.d.; *Anvil*, no. 1).

Although, then, the LK agreement governed conditions at Robe River, at Hamersley

Iron the company would need an alternative. It decided to turn to the other national option of union avoidance, AWAs. From time to time it also held out the prospect of an agreement with the unions, in one specific form: an Award in the national jurisdiction. This suggestion was rejected by the PMU, however, largely because under that legislation there was less scope than under Western Australia's State industrial tribunal to force a recalcitrant employer to bargain. The PMU argued that the company should not decide for itself which particular regulatory instrument would govern employment conditions (Edward, 2003; Interview: Burton).

Until November 2002, the PMU had a low profile but in that month the ACTU coordinated an 'organising blitz' in the Hamersley mining towns of Paraburdoo and Tom Price. Delegates and officials from a range of unions across the country took part. This national intervention in the towns was a huge success. As a result, about 70 per cent of those who were contacted said that they were willing to support the PMU. Preliminary committees emulated the BHP model of building communication structures and using discussions over Award claims to engage existing members and attract new ones. It was agreed that all mineworkers, including those who had signed AWAs, were eligible for membership. This was a critical decision because, over the summer of 2002–03, over 70 per cent of workers signed AWAs, in many cases because the future was so unclear (Observation of blitz; Interviews: Burton, Edward). Whilst the outcomes at this stage were certainly hard to predict, it seemed that, in part because of a geographically-specific strategy, unions had begun to make a place for themselves in what had long been a very hostile space.

The union space undone
Trying to secure a toehold in 'Rio territory' was but one challenge. The unions also faced a new threat at BHP as the company regrouped. In particular, the company responded to the changed State legislation by offering national AWAs from September 2002. This decision was hardly surprising, with nearly half the workforce still unionised and the LK ballot at Hamersley having failed. Local change emphatically aimed to reassert company control over its workplaces: changes to rosters appeared to isolate union activists and, on application from BHP, the Western Australian Industrial Relations Commission revoked Will Tracey's inspection permit for six weeks after a confrontation with a manager (*Workforce*, 30 August, 6 September, 15 November 2002).

Once again, neither unions nor the workplace constituted the only site of resistance. In February 2003, a new local organisation, drawn from across sections of the town of Newman, was created. The Pilbara Sustainability Taskforce was established after a community meeting on the fly-in/fly-out issue. Labor and Green members of the State Parliament attended the initial meeting, but they and others were of the view that local people needed to take the lead in building the taskforce. Showing an appreciation of how the company sought to use geography as part of its strategy of labour control, many of the speakers at that first meeting – from the mine, small business and families – argued that fly-in/fly-out was a company strategy that reconfigured the spatiality of work to reduce both union and community power by limiting the ability of workers to create community in the Pilbara (PST, 2003a, 2003b, 2003c; Interview: Thiel).

The unions also sought relief at the global scale. Largely through the work of the CFMEU, which had already agitated against Rio Tinto in coal mining, they attempted to hold BHP to account. Using the United Nations Global Compact, to which BHP is a signatory, the union argued that BHP was breaching freedom of association clauses. The union claimed that the company's requirement that new employees sign individual contracts breached its stated commitment to collective bargaining – a commitment necessary for approval under the Compact (Waring, 2004). Interviewed on national radio in November 2003, the Compact's Co-ordinator urged the company to talk with unions about the issue (ABC – AM website; *Rock Solid*, no. 88). On the ground, there was a demonstrably positive impact on unionists' morale and activities (Interview: Tracey; Observation: BHP Convenors Meeting). The result was that even this kind of seemingly obvious example of global intervention is geographically more complex than simply being an intercession by 'global' actors – it is, in fact, multi-scaled, certainly in terms of its impact.

If the unions' struggles with the companies were being shaped across and by spatial and scalar politics, then they were also shaped, as they long had been, by labour's fragmentation. This was evident in the fact that the strategy for organising Hamersley Iron with a united *local* front collapsed under the weight of *national* tensions. In particular, national officials of the AWU struck a secret deal with the parent company, Rio Tinto, to impose the very instrument the locals had rejected, a national Award, without reference to the new union form they had built, the PMU. Activists were incensed at this 'backstabbing' (quoted in Balogh, 2003a) which, they believed, had done nothing more than give the company a way out of bargaining with the PMU in the State jurisdiction (AWU, 2003; Observation: PMU Committee). The PMU's bulletin, *Anvil*, had consistently argued that the company could not decide for workers how their wages and conditions would be determined. This position, though, now seemed fatally compromised. In response, the ACTU leadership urged unity, and committed itself to working with the other mining unions at BHP. However, such a breakdown in unity had already driven all sides back into legal claims against each other (Balogh, 2003a, 2003b, 2003c, 2003d). Following this, in June 2004 the national Industrial Relations Commission ruled that, although other parties could well feel that the AWU's conduct had been 'duplicitous', there was no lawful obstacle to the new national agreement going ahead and, therefore, to the destruction of the PMU (AIRC, 2004, para. 50).

Despite this legal ruling, some national and State union officials were taken aback by the vehemence of the local activists' response to the defeat of the PMU. By the end of 2003 they had agreed to local demands for the establishment of a new body for BHP, the BHP Pilbara Mineworkers' Union. This joint-union structure was eventually launched in mid-2004. Despite struggling against employer opposition and union sectionalism at Hamersley, then, the community-focused, single union structure that had characterised the PMU was ultimately formalised at BHP, where it had emerged in a shadowy form after November 1999 (Observation: BHP Convenors' Meeting).

Despite the PMU coming to BHP, the unions struggled to survive there and to rebuild at Hamersley Iron. This was partly so because the companies had so effectively regrouped, splintering their workforces, ignoring or dividing unions and working adroitly through the courts, and partly because of inter-union rivalry. In 2007, as a result of the fact that new employees had no choice but to sign AWAs, the booming industry had but a core of committed union members. Even after a national electoral victory for the Labor Party based in large part on promises to restore the scope for collective bargaining, the geographies of work and regulation overseen by global companies had, it seemed, all but unmade, for now, this local union space.

Conclusions

This chapter argues for a 'spatialised' understanding of union decline and renewal. Traditional scholarship in industrial relations argues that industry itself explains local variations whilst, perhaps, regulatory frameworks explain variations between nations or within federal nation states. Some geographers would say that it is space itself which is pre-eminent. This chapter argues that all of these phenomena are necessarily inter-related. Neither industry (more broadly, production) nor labour laws (more broadly, regulation) operate free of space.

The spatiality of the mining industry's social relations in the Pilbara is at once obvious and contradictory: multinational corporations, financed and selling internationally, are locked into specific localities because of the fixity of ore bodies; they are constrained to various degrees by competing national and state labour laws; and they are confronted with communities around the mines' sites which often challenge their power. Additionally, in this complex space there are workers and unions, often fractured across space. Moreover, as I have outlined, the social forces seeking to enhance their power have at times constructed strategies and visions that are explicitly spatial – thus, changes in unionism after 1999, and success and failure, were shaped by specific intersections of national and local strategies, whilst place consciousness was complex and, at times, decisive.

Some readers may concede that, in the case studied here – in this isolated and massive landscape with its vital ores and fragmented sites of production – geography obviously shapes union fortunes, but that space is still merely a contextual factor. To this argument for a 'non-spatial industrial relations', there are both general and particular answers. First, to say that a place like the Pilbara is somehow different is in itself a claim about socio-spatial relationships and how they vary across the landscape, even as we must recognise that the Pilbara is no more or less made by its physical geography than is any other place. Second, this chapter shows that trying to remake and reclaim space is central to the contestation over where unions fit into the real and imagined landscapes of contemporary production and social life. Third, and more generally, the spatial and the social cannot be separated from each other: the processes shaping unionism do literally 'take place', and the meanings of, and power over, space change in mutually constitutive ways.

These debates are not purely theoretical. Looking beyond the Pilbara, capital, the state and unions argue over, use and define space to secure and maintain power. How workers, their employers and the state make space is as important as how they make history – but thus far, this fact is less recognised. A spatially-informed analysis of all aspects of the social relations of work, then, yields not only a different but a richer understanding of those relationships in *all* settings, from mines to office blocks, from deserts to suburbs. The intellectual challenge is not, of course, to repeat case study after case study but to try, as this chapter speculatively does, to theorise more broadly about the making and unmaking of union spaces. The chapter began by noting that, for all the detailed and important scholarship we have on Australian unionism, we know little about the local scale in either theoretical or empirical ways. Now we are in a position to say something more: if we see the localised rise and fall of unions as not merely locally-determined, but as the combination of struggles and accommodations at many scales and in many places, then we have a much richer contextualisation of any one situation. We can also 'spatialise' our understanding of union decline and renewal and build a richer, theoretically informed picture which does more than posit one example beside another. Perhaps, too, in recognising the importance and fluidity of space, we might better appreciate how power is mobilised at many scales, in differing places and in diverse ways.

Notes

1. The first half of this chapter has been presented at several conferences, and most recently published as Ellem (2006b). The second half, examining the Pilbara, substantially reworks a previously published article: Ellem (2006a). I am grateful to the editors of *Work, Employment and Society*, BSA Publications Ltd and SAGE for allowing reproduction of parts of this material.
2. In 2006, the recorded membership was 1 786 000. There appear, however, to have been some erratic numbers returned over the last few years (ABS, 2006–08; see Peetz, 2005).
3. I use 'State', the sub-national scale of government in the Commonwealth of Australia, capitalised in this manner, to distinguish it from the 'state', the institutions that exert public authority over citizens in a given place.
4. The mining iron ore division was formally known as BHP Iron Ore; after 2001 this became BHP-Billiton Iron Ore. I have referred to the company throughout by the more convenient, and more commonly used, abbreviation, BHP. At the time of writing, the Fortescue Mining Group had just shipped its first ores to China and other smaller operators were beginning development work and construction for new mines.
5. WPAs were individualised agreements covering terms and conditions of employment agreed to between an employer and employee. They were introduced as part of the 'reform' of Australian labour relations in the 1990s. Significantly, in most cases they could override State or Territory laws with regard to labour law (exceptions include laws related to occupational health and safety and workers' compensation).
6. 'Awards' are agreements concerning minimum wage rates and other conditions of employment under which workers work. They are typically established by government-backed arbitration courts when differences of opinion over such matters between employers and their workers cannot be worked out.

A note on sources and research methods

The research was carried out over a number of visits to the Pilbara between June 2001 and November 2005. On all of these visits, as well as in the ACTU Organising Centre in Sydney, I conducted semi-structured interviews with the people listed below. In most cases, the interviews and discussions began with personal and work details followed by more open questions about perceptions of union and management practices in the past, changes in recent years, and assessments then and subsequently of the likelihood of union success and the efficacy of particular strategies. In June 2002, I ran a series of focus groups with Hamersley Iron employees designed primarily to inquire into the result of the LK ballot. On all these research trips, there has been some degree of participant-observation: I was given access to delegate meetings across all the sites discussed in the chapter and I observed parts of the November 2002 organising 'blitz'. Full details are listed below.

Author's focus groups

Held at the towns of Paraburdoo, Tom Price, Dampier, Karratha, 24–29 June 2002.

Author's interviews

Anonymous BHP delegates, Newman and Port Hedland, 26–29 June, 17, 20 September 2001.
Anonymous Hamersley employees, Tom Price, 18 September 2001.
Anonymous small business owners, Paraburdoo, 16 November 2002.
Asplin, Paul, AWU organiser, Port Hedland, 28 June 2001.
Boyington, Maria, Action in Support of Partners, Port Hedland, 29 June 2001.
Burton, Troy, ACTU organiser, Paraburdoo, 15 November 2002.
Davis, Brett, AMWU organiser, Newman, 26 June 2001.

Edward, Stewart, ACTU organiser, Paraburdoo, 16 November 2002.
'John', train driver, Port Hedland, 29 June 2001.
Kumeroa, Ross, TWU convenor, Newman, 26 June 2001.
Palmer, Colleen, Action in Support of Partners, Port Hedland, 28 June 2001.
Schapper, Derek, union counsel, Perth, 18 October 2001.
Thiel, Sharon, PST chair, Newman, 3 December 2003.
Tracey, Will, ACTU organiser, Port Hedland/Newman, interviewed in Newman, 19 September 2001, 4 December 2003, and in Dampier, 27 June 2002.

Author's observations

Combined unions' delegates' meetings, Newman 27 June 2001; Port Hedland 28 June 2001.
BHP Convenors' Meeting, Newman, 3 December 2003.
PMU Committee, Paraburdoo, 4 December 2003.
PMU meetings, Paraburdoo, Karratha, June 2004.
Union blitz, Paraburdoo, 13–15 November 2002.

References

ABC–AM website, www.abc.net.au/am/, accessed 13 November 2003.
ABS (Australian Bureau of Statistics) (1992–2005), '6325.0: Trade Union Members, Australia', various years, Canberra, Australia: ABS.
ABS (Australian Bureau of Statistics) (2003), '1379.0.55.001: National Regional Profile, Pilbara, 2003', www.abs.gov.au/ausstats, Canberra, ABS, accessed July 2006.
ABS (Australian Bureau of Statistics) (2006–08), '6310.0: Employee Earnings, Benefits and Trade Union Membership, Australia', various years, Canberra, Australia: ABS.
ACTU (Australian Council of Trade Unions) (1999a), *Unions@work*, Melbourne, Australia: ACTU.
ACTU (Australian Council of Trade Unions) (1999b), 'BHPIO – Port Hedland campaign planning sessions', internal notes, 10–12 December, mimeo.
AIRC (Australian Industrial Relations Commission) (2004), 'PR947647, Australian Workers Union and Hamersley Iron; Construction, Forestry, Mining and Energy Union and others, Decision', Sydney, Australia: AIRC.
Alexander, M., J. Burgess, R. Green, D. MacDonald and S. Ryan (1995), 'Regional workplace bargaining: evidence from the Hunter Workplace Change Survey', *Labour and Industry*, **6** (3), 113–26.
Allen, J. (1999), *Lost Geographies of Power*, Oxford: Blackwell.
AMMA (Australian Mines and Metals Association) (2006), 'The changing face of employment relations', AMMA Annual Conference, Launceston, paper by CEO Steve Knott, 16–17 March, available at www.amma.org.au/home/publications/sk_natconf06_address.pdf, accessed July 2006.
Anvil (Pilbara Mineworkers' Union, PMU, Bulletin), PMU.
AWU (Australian Workers' Union) (2003), 'Information and documents concerning the Federal Award developments at Hamersley Iron and Robe River', Melbourne, Australia: AWU.
Bachelard, M. (2002), 'The day a myth called happiness died', *Weekend Australian*, 6–7 April, p. 31.
Bain, G.S. and R. Price (1980), *Profiles of Union Growth: A Comparative Statistical Portrait of Eight Countries*, Oxford: Blackwell.
Balogh, S. (2003a), 'Unions face off over mine coverage', *Australian*, 1 July, p. 6.
Balogh, S. (2003b), 'Union in deal with mine titan', *Australian*, 22 July, p. 6.
Balogh, S. (2003c), 'ACTU faces crisis over Pilbara funding threat', *Australian*, 23 July, p. 6.
Balogh, S. (2003d), 'Back in business', *Weekend Australian*, 26–27 July, pp. 29, 32.
Beynon, H. and R. Hudson (1993), 'Place and space in contemporary Europe: some lessons and reflections', *Antipode*, **25** (3), 177–90.
BHP Iron Ore (1999), *Staff Handbook*, company document, Perth, BHP Iron Ore.
Callus, R., A. Morehead, M. Cully and J. Buchanan (1991), *Industrial Relations at Work: The Australian Workplace Industrial Relations Survey*, Commonwealth Department of Industrial Relations, Canberra, Australia: Australian Government Publishing Service.
Castree, N., N. Coe, K. Ward and M. Samers (2004), *Spaces of Work: Global Capitalism and Geographies of Labour*, Thousand Oaks, CA: Sage.
Cooper, R. (2003), 'Peak council organising at work: ACTU strategy 1994–2000', *Labour and Industry*, **14** (1), 1–21.
Crosby, M. (2005), *Power at Work: Rebuilding the Australian Union Movement*, Leichhardt, Australia: The Federation Press.

Dabscheck, B. (2001), '"A felt need for increased efficiency": industrial relations at the end of the millennium', *Asia Pacific Journal of Human Resources*, **39** (2), 4–30.

DoIR (Department of Industry and Resources) (2008), 'Statistics digest', DoIR, Government of Western Australia, Perth, www.doir.wa.gov.au/, accessed 5 September 2008.

Dufty, N. (1984), *Industrial Relations in the Pilbara Iron Ore Industry*, Perth, Australia: Western Australian Institute of Technology.

Edward, S. (2003), (Stewart Edward, ACTU organiser), personal communication with author, 17 April.

Ellem, B. (2002), '"We're solid": union renewal at BHP Iron Ore, 1999–2002', *International Journal of Employment Studies*, **10** (2), 23–46.

Ellem, B. (2003), 'Re-placing the Pilbara's mining unions', *Australian Geographer*, **34** (3), 281–96.

Ellem, B. (2004), *Hard Ground: Unions in the Pilbara*, Port Hedland, Australia: Pilbara Mineworkers' Union (PMU).

Ellem, B. (2005), 'What about the workers? Labour and the making of regions', in A. Rainnie and M. Grobbelaar (eds), *New Regionalism in Australia*, London: Ashgate, pp. 217–35.

Ellem, B. (2006a), 'Scaling labour: Australian unions and global mining', *Work, Employment and Society*, **20** (2), 369–87.

Ellem, B. (2006b), 'Exploring the geography of union decline and renewal', in B. Pocock, C. Provis and E. Willis (eds), *21st Century Work: High Road or Low Road?*, Proceedings of the 20th Association of Industrial Relations Academics of Australia and New Zealand Conference, Vol. 1, Adelaide, Australia: Association of Industrial Relations Academics of Australia and New Zealand, pp. 159–68.

Ellem, B. and J. Shields (1999), 'Rethinking "regional industrial relations": space, place and the social relations of work', *Journal of Industrial Relations*, **41** (4), 536–60.

FCA (Federal Court of Australia) (2000), Australian Workers' Union v BHP Iron Ore Limited, FCA, Melbourne, Australia, p. 430.

FCA (Federal Court of Australia) (2001), Australian Workers' Union v BHP Iron Ore Limited, FCA, Melbourne, Australia, p. 3.

Flanders, A. ([1969] 1975), *Management and Unions: The Theory and Reform of Industrial Relations*, new edn, London: Faber.

Ford, J. (2001), 'Unions in the Pilbara', Parliament of Western Australia, Legislative Council, 22 August. Copy kindly made available by Jon Ford.

Forrest, J. (1995), 'Spatial segmentation of trade union densities in New South Wales', Lloyd Ross Forum, Occasional Papers, No. 3, Sydney, Australia: Labor Council of New South Wales.

Green, J. and C. Tilly (1987), 'Service unionism: directions for organizing', *Labor Law Journal*, **38** (8), 486–95.

Harvey, D. (1982), *The Limits to Capital*, Oxford: Blackwell.

Hearn Mackinnon, B. (2003), 'How the West was lost? Hamersley Iron, the birthplace of a decade of de-unionisation', in *Reflections and New Directions*, Proceedings of the 17th Conference of the Association of Industrial Relations Academics of Australia and New Zealand, Melbourne, Australia: Association of Industrial Relations Academics of Australia and New Zealand.

Herod, A. (1997), 'From a geography of labor to a labor geography: labor's spatial fix and the geography of capitalism', *Antipode*, **29** (1), 1–31.

Herod, A. (1998), 'The spatiality of labor unionism: a review essay', in A. Herod (ed.), *Organizing the Landscape: Geographical Perspectives on Labor Unionism*, Minneapolis, MN: University of Minnesota Press, pp. 1–36.

Herod, A. and M.W. Wright (2002), 'Placing scale: an introduction', in A. Herod and M.W. Wright (eds), *Geographies of Power: Placing Scale*, Oxford: Blackwell, pp. 1–15.

Hyman, R. (1999), 'An emerging agenda for trade unions?', discussion paper, Labour and Society Programme, International Labour Organisation (ILO), Geneva: ILO.

Jonas, A. (1996) 'Local labour control regimes: uneven development and the social regulation of production', *Regional Studies*, **30** (4), 323–38.

Knott, S. (2006), 'Why workers are voting with their feet', *Australian*, 31 July, p. 14.

Labour History (2000), 78, special section on local history.

Macdonald, D. and J. Burgess (1998), 'Globalisation and industrial relations in the Hunter region', *Journal of Industrial Relations*, **40** (1), 3–24.

Markey, R. (2004), 'The Labor Council of New South Wales, 1871–2001', in B. Ellem, R. Markey and J. Shields (eds), *Peak Unions in Australia: Origins, Purpose, Power, Agency*, Annandale, NSW, Australia: The Federation Press, pp. 152–81.

Markey, R., A. Hodgkinson, T. Mylett and S. Pomfret (2001), *Regional Employment Relations at Work: The Illawarra Regional Workplace Industrial Relations Survey*, Wollongong, Australia: University of Wollongong Press.

Martin, R., P. Sunley and J. Wills (1993), 'The geography of trade union decline: spatial dispersal or regional resilience?', *Transactions of the Institute of British Geographers*, New Series, **18**, 36–62.

Martin, R., P. Sunley and J. Wills (1994a), 'Labouring differences: method, measurement and purpose in geographical research on trade unions', in 'Exchange: Geographies of Trade Unions', *Transactions of the Institute of British Geographers*, New Series, **19** (1), 102–18.

Martin, R., P. Sunley and J. Wills (1994b), 'The decentralization of industrial relations', *Transactions of the Institute of British Geographers*, New Series, **19** (1), 457–81.

Martin, R., P. Sunley and J. Wills (1996), *Union Retreat and the Regions: The Shrinking Landscape of Organized Labour*, London: Jessica Kingsley Publishers and the Regional Studies Association.

Massey, D. (1994), *Space, Place and Gender*, Cambridge: Polity Press.

Massey, D. ([1984] 1995), *Spatial Divisions of Labour: Social Structures and the Geography of Production*, 2nd edn, London: Macmillan.

McGrath-Champ, S. (2005), 'Enterprise bargaining and regional prospects: the effects of rescaling wage regulation in Australia', *Economic and Industrial Democracy*, **26** (3), 413–42.

Morehead, A., M. Steele, M. Alexander, K. Stephen and L. Duffin (1997), *Changes at Work: The 1995 Australian Workplace Industrial Relations Survey*, South Melbourne: Longman.

Peck, J. (1996), *Work-Place: The Social Regulation of Labor Markets*, New York: Guilford Press.

Peetz, D. (1998), *Unions in a Contrary World: The Future of the Australian Trade Union Movement*, Cambridge: Cambridge University Press.

Peetz, D. (2005), 'Trend analysis of union membership', *Australian Journal of Labour Economics*, **8** (1), 1–24.

PMU (Pilbara Mineworkers' Union) (n.d.), Membership form, copy kindly made available by Stewart Edward.

PST (Pilbara Sustainability Taskforce) (2003a), Minutes of Community Meeting, 26 February.

PST (Pilbara Sustainability Taskforce) (2003b), Media Release, 1 August.

PST (Pilbara Sustainability Taskforce) (2003c), Media Release, 29 October.

Rock Solid (BHP Combined Unions Bulletin).

Sadler, D. and B. Fagan (2004), 'Australian trade unions and the politics of scale: re-constructing the spatiality of industrial relations', *Economic Geography*, **80** (1), 23–43.

Savage, L. (1998), 'Geographies of organizing: justice for janitors in Los Angeles', in A. Herod (ed.), *Organizing the Landscape: Geographical Perspectives on Labor Unionism*, Minneapolis, MN: University of Minnesota Press, pp. 225–52.

Storper, M. and R. Walker (1989), *The Capitalist Imperative: Territory, Technology and Industrial Growth*, Oxford: Blackwell.

Swain, P. (1995), *Strategic Choices: A Study of the Interaction of Industrial Relations and Corporate Strategy in the Pilbara Iron Ore Industry*, Perth: Curtin University of Technology.

Thompson, H. and H. Smith (1987), 'Conflict at Robe River', *Arena*, **79**, June, 76–91.

Tracey, J. (2003), 'Individual agreements at Hamersley Iron', in *Reflections and New Directions*, Proceedings of the 17th Conference of the Association of Industrial Relations Academics of Australia and New Zealand, Melbourne: Association of Industrial Relations Academics of Australia and New Zealand.

WAIRC (Western Australian Industrial Relations Commission) (2001), '04082 BHP Iron Ore Award, Western Australian Industrial Relations Commission', Perth, Australia: WAIRC.

WAIRC (Western Australian Industrial Relations Commission) (2002), '05810 AFMEPKIUA vs BHPIO and others', Perth, Australia: WAIRC.

Walker, K.F. (1970), *Australian Industrial Relations Systems*, Cambridge, MA: Harvard University Press.

Walsh, J. (2000), 'Organizing the scale of labour regulation in the United States: service-sector activism in the city', *Environment and Planning A*, **32** (9), 1593–610.

Waring, P. (2004), 'The global compact and socially responsible investment: opportunities for unions?', in M. Barry and P. Brosnan (eds), *New Economies: New Industrial Relations*, Proceedings of the 18th Conference of the Association of Industrial Relations Academics of Australia and New Zealand, Noosa, Australia: Association of Industrial Relations Academics of Australia and New Zealand.

Webb, S. and B. Webb (1897), *Industrial Democracy*, London: Longman.

Webb, S. and B. Webb (1920), *The History of Trade Unionism, 1666–1920*, published by the authors.

Wills, J. (1998a), 'Geographies of trade unionism: translating traditions across space and time', *Antipode*, **28** (4), 352–78.

Wills, J. (1998b), 'Space, place, and tradition in working-class organizations', in A. Herod (ed.), *Organizing the Landscape: Geographical Perspectives on Labor Unionism*, Minneapolis, MN: University of Minnesota Press, pp. 129–58.

Wills, J. and M. Simms (2002) 'Building reciprocal community unionism in the UK: geographies of organised labour', Working Paper 4, Queen Mary College, University of London.

Workforce (subscriber news bulletin).

20 Contesting the new politics of space: labour and capital in the white goods industry in southern Africa

Andries Bezuidenhout and Edward Webster

Mapping the new politics of space

Beverly Silver's path-breaking account of workers' movements since 1870 draws on the work of Karl Polanyi to argue that there is a constant flux between a crisis of legitimacy and a crisis of profitability in capitalism (for more on Polanyi, see Munck and Waterman and Lambert and Gillan, Chapters 15 and 22 in this volume). Since labour is a pseudo-commodity – that is, unlike other commodities, its reproduction is relatively autonomous of capital – the system will constantly be in a state of tension between attempts to treat labour as a true commodity, one reproduced solely under the dictates of capital (which leads to a crisis of legitimacy as capital attempts to turn workers into surplus value-producing automatons), and pressures from workers to decommodify their own labour power (which leads to a crisis of profitability as workers seek to claim more of their own labour time) (Silver, 2003, pp. 16–20; see also Peck, 1996).

If it is to accumulate successfully, capital constantly has to find new ways of solving this tension between legitimacy and profitability. In her analysis, Silver introduces the concept of 'boundary drawing' to show how temporary solutions to the tension may be developed. For Silver, boundary drawing refers to who is 'cut in' and who is 'cut out' when compromises are made over the partial decommodification of labour. Put differently, her analysis is about where the categorical boundaries will be placed around various groupings of workers, according some certain 'rights' whilst denying those rights to others. Silver argues that there are three 'interconnecting forms' that have historically characterised boundary-drawing strategies. Schematically, the first is through segmenting labour markets, a 'strategy pursued mainly by capital' in which some workers are categorised as, for example, 'permanent' or 'core' workers and others are designated 'temporary' or 'peripheral' workers. The second is through the bounding of citizenship, which is pursued mainly by states and guarantees some workers access to particular rights whilst denying it to other, non-citizen workers (as with foreign 'guest-workers'). Finally, workers themselves often construct exclusionary identities on the basis of class or non-class identities (for example, decrying some workers as 'non-locals', giving them an implicitly inferior status relative to their own 'localness'). Through boundary drawing, certain workers – those who are core/permanent/domestic/local – can secure a degree of privilege in the system and, therefore, may exhibit a level of loyalty to it whilst others – those who are peripheral/temporary/foreign/non-local – end up very much as second class economic citizens. Although their exclusion means this latter group may actually develop increased feelings of alienation from the system, such boundary drawing serves as a classic example of dividing-and-conquering workers. This understanding of boundary drawing is particularly useful in the South African context, and Silver draws on Mamdani (1996) and Cooper's (1996) analyses of South Africa to illustrate her case.

What is important for our purposes here – and what is not, in our view, sufficiently explicit in Silver's work – is that such boundaries are not just social boundaries but they are also frequently spatial ones whose extent is subject to significant social contest and negotiation. Hence, concepts of citizenship take as their referent the nation state, which is a spatial unit whose boundaries delimit the geographical extent of specific 'imagined communities' (Anderson, 1983) as well as the territorial limits to particular systems of law and institutions. Equally, the notions of 'local' and 'non-local' that are often used to determine which workers are considered legitimate political actors in certain places are geographical concepts. In the case of labour market segmentation, such boundaries are also often geographical in nature – core workers may be provided access to company housing or earn wages which are high enough to enable them to live in particular communities or may live closer to their place of work than do peripheral workers, who may be denied access to company housing, earn wages which are too low to live in the same neighbourhoods as their core confrères, or may have to be imported from distant locations for short periods of time (as in the case of migrant farm workers).

Whereas boundary drawing, then, may serve to bind certain groups of workers to the extant economic system and so secure their loyalty to it (that is, it serves to create a group of workers who see the system as legitimate), attempts to decommodify labour will invariably lead to crises of profitability. In response, Silver argues, capital has historically sought to develop a number of 'fixes' to address this crisis. The first is a spatial fix, which implies capital relocating production elsewhere, where labour is cheaper or less militant. She illustrates how this is a temporary solution, since spatial fixes create new working classes in the places to which capital flees, thereby merely postponing the crisis of profitability. The second way in which capital has historically addressed crises of profitability is through technological fixes, which imply processes of organisational restructuring to weaken labour's power. The third is a product fix, where capital moves into the production of a different commodity or service in a market that is less crowded. Finally, capital often withdraws from production altogether and engages in speculative financial activity instead – a financial fix (Harvey, 1978, 2001; Silver, 2003). Significantly, here, too, space is implicated, and not just when capital flees a new location. Thus, even when engaging in *in situ* technological fixes, the adoption of new technologies will be likely to have impacts upon the particular locale within which a plant is located – labour-saving technologies may lead to higher local unemployment, which serves to discipline local or regional labour markets within and beyond the community. Equally, developing new product lines will often tie a plant to a different set of locales within the broader regional, national, or global space-economy as raw materials are sourced from new parts of the globe and goods are sent to new market locations. Likewise, engaging in speculative financial activity usually has geographical implications, as investing money in real estate or in other manufacturing companies' shares impacts the built environment in various other parts of the globe.

Silver, then, provides a number of new concepts to describe broad historical processes and, in doing so, she has succeeded in putting geographical concerns at the centre of current approaches to studying labour in the global economy, even if she herself does not couch her analysis in the explicitly geographical terms we have done above. Nevertheless, there are a number of important issues that require further interrogation.

First, whilst the role of the state is analysed and discussed in her analysis,[1] when it comes to spatial fixes, capital seems excessively footloose and, indeed, almost omnipotent. In particular, an area of contestation that is underdeveloped in her account is the role of the state in shaping capital's (geographic) options and fixes. As a way to counterbalance such a capital-centric analysis, in this chapter we use the changing nature of trade union organisation in the South African white goods (household appliance) industry to show how the apartheid state played a key part in establishing the landscape for the politics of boundary drawing, and shaped the spatial fixes that were available to manufacturing capital. These fixes were not based on a search merely for cheap and docile labour, but were also a response to apartheid spatial and racial engineering that gave subsidies and low infrastructural costs to investors in certain areas (the nominally independent 'homelands').

Second, what is missing from Silver's somewhat structuralist conceptualisation of the way capital produces economic landscapes is how labour, too, draws on its sources of power to challenge boundaries, capital's spatial fixes and its scales of organisation. This moves us from accounts of how the geography of capitalism is made which see labour incorporated into explanations largely in terms of how capital chooses between different groups of workers when creating particular economic geographies (an approach referred to as providing accounts which are merely 'geographies of labour') to those wherein labour is seen as an active agent in the politics of space (an approach termed 'labour geography') (Herod, 2001; Waterman and Wills, 2001; Herod and Wright, 2002; see also Keck and Sikkink, 1998; Tarrow, 2005). In arguing for an approach which views workers as active spatial agents, it is important, however, to remember that accounts of agency which do not recognise the realities of power degenerate into a naive voluntarism. Certainly, in the case of the apartheid South African state, which engaged in extra-judicial killings and the legal capital punishment of opponents, 'bannings', proscription of trade unions, and a host of other practices, the power of the state to engage around the highly visible categories of 'race' and gender in deliberative spatial engineering to reconfigure the capital–labour relationship – such as creating various 'black homelands' to serve as labour reserves that would be disarticulated from 'white South Africa' – cannot be underestimated. Nevertheless, as we show, despite this, labour has actively engaged in the politics of producing space and geographical scale to challenge the boundaries drawn and the landscapes envisioned by the apartheid state and employers. As we shall show, central to labour's power were strong shop stewards' committees in factories, committees that were able to build linkages from the local to the national level and, from there, were able to draw on international solidarity to support their struggles. In effect, such committees and the workers they represented were able to 'jump' spatial scales of organisation, to expand their struggles and lines of support from the very local to the truly global.

Colour and craft in white goods manufacturing

The South African white goods industry emerged out of early colonial foundries. Most of these were originally located in the major ports, although the discovery of gold led many subsequently to move inland to be closer to growing population centres. Durban Falkirk, later to become Defy, was one of the country's first white goods producers (Webster, 1985). The company, which is the dominant southern African producer of white goods, operates one of South Africa's oldest factories, in Jacobs, an industrial suburb in the south of Durban. Initially, skilled workers in these foundries were represented by a typical craft union, the Iron Moulders Society, which engaged in a politics of boundary drawing by excluding African workers and by insisting that coloured and Indian workers belong to a separate branch (Webster, 1985, pp. 267–70). In 1919 Durban Falkirk experienced its first major strike, by a small unrecognised union supported by the Amalgamated Society of Engineers (ASE). Management refused to negotiate with the union and only after workers cut the electricity to the works did the strike end (Bezuidenhout, 2004, pp. 102–5). During this time, however, craft unions came under considerable pressure from employers to dilute their control over the major trades in the engineering industry as foundries slowly introduced moulding machines and the like. Because these machines could be worked by less-skilled operatives, the length of apprenticeships and craft unions' control over positions became hotly contested issues. For its part, Durban Falkirk introduced the first mass production of metal in 1936 (Webster, 1985, pp. 32–6, 53). This event threatened the tight control over the job held by white workers and enabled management to undercut them by hiring coloured production moulders (Webster, 1985, pp. 267–70).

The result of such transformations in the workplace was a constant struggle over the 'colour of craft' as white workers used their 'colour' to defend their deskilled 'craft' (Webster, 1985, p. 27). Durban emerged as a crucial battleground over the colour of craft and was where white workers first succeeded in reversing management trends in boundary drawing by effecting greater racial exclusivity in defining craft lines. 'White' tradesmen had been organising themselves into craft unions since 1882, but the trades were not as sharply defined as in Britain. Thus, whilst 'coloured' tradesmen were often incorporated into the craft unions,[2] Africans and Indians were excluded as a rule. Right from the start, then, 'race' had operated as a barrier to craft. However, when competition for jobs increased due to urbanisation in the 1920s and 1930s, craft unions began tightening their definitions of skill (Freund, 1995, p. 47).

In 1937, after a strike by 'white' and 'coloured' workers, the company fired a number of Indian and African workers. In response, other Indian and African workers went out on strike, led by the Natal Iron and Steel Workers' Industrial Union. Several attempts at mediation failed, including one by the High Commissioner of India. Significantly, the firm's management was supported by the craft union and, despite threats by Indian merchants to boycott the company's products, the strike was defeated (Bezuidenhout, 2004, pp. 108–15). As Freund (1995, p. 54) comments:

> The policy of the company was essentially to dismantle a trade union, organised by Indian Communists, but including numerous Africans . . . [M]anagement depended on being able to divide the labour force into racial categories as a normal means of maintaining control in the workplace and found the principle of non-racialism deeply disturbing. Coloured and white workers had struck work earlier, engendering the conflict initially, but they did not participate in the main part of the strike and were not locked out. In fact, the white dominated engineering union, whose own strike initiated the conflict, saw the aroused and organised Indian organisers with their new ideas as potentially dangerous rivals.

A general wave of militancy among the Indian working class subsided after these events. Like many 'white' workers, Indian workers began to see their interests in opposition to those of African industrial workers. Still, they were 'caught between white racism and African attempts to secure jobs and space' (Freund, 1995, p. 53). By 1944 the Iron Moulders' Society (IMS) opened its membership to all production moulders, and by the end of the decade 25 per cent of its members could be classified as 'semi-skilled'. This proportion doubled by the early 1970s. The old craft unions could no longer pretend that their membership and power in the workplace was based on 'craft skill' and the transition from 'craft' to 'colour' as a basis for exclusivity became more pronounced. As a result of the Industrial Conciliation Act of 1956, which prohibited 'mixed' unions (though not unions with separate 'branches' for different population groups), in 1957 the 'coloured' members of the AEU (Amalgamated Engineering Union) at Durban Falkirk joined the No. 5 branch. Four years later these former members formed the first 'coloured' union in the engineering industry – a parallel union called the Engineering Industrial Workers' Union (Webster, 1985, pp. 54, 59, 113 and Chapter 5).[3]

Scales of organising

By the 1970s the craft tradition in production was eroded to a large extent and the transition to mass production had already taken place (see Webster, 1985, pp. 59–66). For its part, the area around Durban and Pinetown formed the bedrock for a new independent trade union movement of 'semi-skilled' and 'unskilled' African workers that emerged after the strike wave of 1973 (see Maree, 1987). The transformation of the division of labour caused by the rise of mass assembly-line production is familiar to students of manufacturing around the world. But the racial division of labour in South Africa created peculiar conditions, which provided additional sources of grievance for black workers and possible bases for collective action. Racially discriminatory practices affected every aspect of the employment relationship. The intersection of brutal industrial conditions and direct racial oppression served as a source of deep discontent among workers and increased their sense that the political and economic systems were fundamentally unjust (Von Holdt, 2003).

It is these conditions that created the space out of which workers could build industrial unions. At the centre of the strategy of this new movement was a shift in emphasis from mass mobilisation against the apartheid state to the strategic use of power at the point of production. With the strong backing of their members, shop stewards had the power to push for concessions from management, which not only created space for further advances but also won concrete improvements in workers' conditions, thereby highlighting the efficacy of direct action. There were two important components to the unions' approach to the strategic use of power: 1) democratic processes to win voluntary consent from members for mobilisation and for restraint when necessary; and 2) tactical flexibility, which included a capacity to distinguish principles from tactics and to choose those tactics most likely to succeed, including negotiation and compromise.

The negotiation of plant-level recognition agreements setting out the rights and duties of shop stewards and trade unions in the workplace was an important step in establishing the 'rule of law' on the shop floor. Trade unions, however, did not win these rights without struggle and during the late 1970s and early 1980s there were hundreds of strikes in support of demands for union recognition. In the case of Defy's Jacobs plant, African and Indian workers went on strike in 1973. This provided the opportunity to organise workers into unions. By 1975 about half the African workforce in the assembly plant were members of the Metal and Allied Workers' Union (MAWU) whilst most of the

Indian workers were organised into the Engineering Workers' Industrial Union (Natal Branch), a registered union (Kirkwood, 1975, p. 56; Webster, 1985, p. 144).[4]

The company's response was again an attempt to prevent independent plant-level organisation by setting up alternative mechanisms for communication, in the form of a liaison committee (as provided for by the Bantu Labour Relations Regulation Amendment Act of 1973). Nominations for six worker representatives from different departments were solicited by management. Management then appointed the chairman and secretary, as well as an *Induna* (a traditional leader, often used as a form of decentralised despotism in the workplace) to interpret. Unsurprisingly, this committee was intended to do only what the name suggested – it was not intended to question managerial prerogative, but merely to communicate management policy back to workers.

In 1975 workers at the plant went out on strike to protest a new bonus system. As in 1937, they lost the strike. But unlike 1937, the approach of the emerging independent unions meant that workers were building a cadre of worker leaders within the factory who could take their struggle forward. In the context of the defeat, the liaison committee continued to operate, but workers were not satisfied with this arrangement. In September 1975 MAWU shop stewards in Defy started to hold regular meetings on the premises, although they never attracted enough support to challenge the liaison committee.

The next year, in February, the union secretary approached management on the matter of union recognition. Pointing to the fact that the company's majority ownership resided in Britain, he argued: '[I]t is in Britain where it can be expected of management to seriously consider the question of union recognition . . . [W]e may consult with the British unions to put pressure on the company for recognition of MAWU' (Webster, 1985, pp. 145–6). This 'up-scaling' of conflict was a strategy followed by a number of independent unions in South Africa, especially in the automobile industry (see Southall, 1995). However, the Defy MAWU branch was unable to follow through because a shop steward tasked with collecting signatures for a recognition petition did not want to continue, the result of difficulties he encountered in getting people to sign.

Subsequently the shop stewards' committee ceased meeting and by mid-1976 members at the branch stopped paying their subscriptions. Workers at the company were generally frightened of getting involved in union activities, and there was talk of 'spies'. Shop stewards sometimes held secret meetings in the toilets, whilst two union representatives who were liaison committee members secretly communicated with workers about union activities. Some workers did not even want other workers to know they were union members. Workers who lived in the company's compound were especially scared to join, for they did not have permits to stay in the township and so losing their job also meant losing their accommodation (for a comparison with worker compounds in China, see Pun and Smith, Chapter 13 in this volume). One worker, who told other workers that the only help they would get was from the union, was told by them that 'I must forget about the union if I want to go on working at Defy' (Webster, 1985, p. 146).

The union's strategic decision to concentrate on building its leadership at the local, factory-level would, though, eventually pay off. Throughout the late 1970s and early 1980s, workers and their trade unions used their increasing strength on the shop floor to fight for better wages and working conditions, as leave, hours of work, safety and pensions became matters for negotiation. But workers were not only becoming a formidable force on the shop floor. They were also seeking to extend the scalar boundaries of their political organisation, by jumping from the local to the national level of activity. Consequently, in November 1974 MAWU's secretary went to Johannesburg and made contact with the Industrial Aid Society, which had been set up by the Wages Commission of students at the University of the Witwatersrand. In the mid-1970s MAWU also set up offices in Johannesburg and Cape Town. These actions were preludes to developing a national bargaining system. Through such efforts, by 1981 MAWU had doubled its membership on the East Rand – another node of white goods manufacturing (Webster, 1985, pp. 139, 150).

A key element in the union's thinking, then, was to transform the geographical context within which decisions at the Jacobs plant were made. Specifically, MAWU sought to engage in centralised, national bargaining as a way to pressure local Defy management. A sizeable issue to face, though, was that there already existed nationwide National Industrial Councils (NICs), which had been established under the Labour Relations Act. Of all such councils, the metal NIC was the largest (Webster, 1983). It had operated since 1944 as a highly centralised body that served the interests of employers and, to a lesser extent, the industry's 14 white-dominated unions. However, the limited, but significant, material benefits gained by the unions' participation in the NIC had often been at the expense of less-skilled, usually African, workers. For MAWU, the unrepresentative and bureaucratic nature of the NIC came to symbolise the worst features of established industrial relations in South Africa. By creating an alternative national system and so bypassing the NIC, MAWU hoped to challenge the extant racial boundaries of bargaining in the industry.

Within this context, four organisational principles underlay MAWU's efforts to develop a new geography of bargaining. We have discussed how the first principle – the building of shop steward structures – emerged in the early stage of MAWU's history when it focused in Durban on selected factories. This localised focus on building shop steward structures fed the second principle – an initial emphasis on factory-level bargaining. A third principle – worker control – became firmly established in the union through the practice of accountability to the rank and file through the system of mandates and report-backs. Finally, MAWU would build out from such local strongholds to the national level.

Significantly, MAWU's approach was in direct opposition to that of the employers, who wished to marginalise the shop floor by locating power at the central industrial level. As a result, employers refused to negotiate at plant level and actively encouraged the establishment of parallel unions 'from above' (Webster, 1983, p. 15). Nevertheless, some employers did break ranks in 1980 and began to negotiate recognition agreements at plant level. Under the pressure of ongoing strike action they did agree to give a greater role to shop stewards but still insisted the union join the NIC. April 1982 would be the highpoint in the 'challenge from below' as workers struck across the industry over wages. Employers, though, refused to negotiate, insisting that MAWU join the NIC. Effective opposition to the NIC was broken when workers at Scaw Metals, the largest organised factory on the East Rand, were dismissed and police intervened. Employer resistance, then, had defeated MAWU's first efforts to transform a geographically localised system of factory-by-factory bargaining into an industrywide arrangement, and the union soon began to lose support in some areas (see Herod, 1997 for an example of a similar effort to move from a spatially localised to a national, industrywide system of bargaining in the US docking industry).

It was in the context of successful employer resistance to bargaining outside the NIC and the failure to coordinate workers on an industrywide basis that discussions on the need for some form of industrywide bargaining took place inside MAWU in the second half of 1982. The need to 'jump-scale' had arrived. Entry into the NIC, it was argued, was a tactical question. Provided certain conditions could be met, MAWU's principles could be retained inside the NIC. MAWU could still fight for the right of workers to negotiate at factory level and insist the democratic and factory-based structures upon which the union was built be involved in the bargaining process.

In the following year MAWU entered the NIC and was to become a powerful force within it. It had 'jumped scale' from factory-level bargaining to national industrial bargaining. The next phase of jumping scale was the involvement of MAWU in the South African branch of the International Metalworkers' Federation (Webster, 1984, pp. 77–94). For its part, a branch of the IMF had been established in South Africa in 1974 to coordinate the activities of all metal unions in the country. Scepticism of the IMF, and their reasons for establishing a local branch, had existed inside MAWU from its formation (Webster, 1984, p. 85). However, little could be gained from staying out of it, so in its first three years MAWU was concerned simply to test the limits of IMF support for shop floor struggle. In October 1977 MAWU went one step further by challenging the representivity of Africans drawn from liaison committees sitting as observers on the South African branch of the IMF. This challenge escalated over the next few years as the balance of power between MAWU and the NIC began to shift and the lines of representation were redrawn inside the IMF with the black trade unions now in the driving seat.

This process of jumping scale from the local factory level in Durban to Johannesburg and then onto the national level soon generated an employer counter-strategy, one explicitly geographical in nature. Specifically, instead of expanding its manufacturing operation in Durban, Defy chose to open two additional plants outside the union stronghold of Jacobs. In 1984 it opened a factory outside East London, just within the border of Ciskei. A second factory was opened in 1986 in Ezakheni, in KwaZulu, 200 km north of Durban. Not only were such plants located outside Jacobs but, importantly, because they were in 'homelands' they were also outside the national space of South Africa, as defined by the apartheid state. Consequently, South African labour laws did not apply to them.

Defy's spatial fix
Whereas workers at the Defy factory in Jacobs were able to organise in a less repressive legislative environment after trade union rights were extended to black workers in 1979, workers in places such as Ezakheni 'still toiled without rights and protection in the "homelands" . . . [,] places Wiehahn[5] never touched . . . [They were] the workers the eighties forgot' (Friedman, 1987, p. 475). The lack of such rights resulted from the fact that in 1970 the government had exempted these areas from most labour laws in the hope that this would help 'homeland' industry grow and provide jobs to stem the flow of Africans to the 'white' cities. What is important here is that because such homelands were exempted they provided a spatial safety valve for capital. Capital could relocate there to avoid more demanding South African laws but could continue to supply the South African market, using much cheaper labour than that available in urban areas (Hart, 2002, pp. 134–5).

Although industrial decentralisation to such homelands only really gathered pace after the labour movement started to challenge the apartheid labour regime from the 1970s onwards, the idea predates formal apartheid, having begun in the 1940s as part of the Smuts government's import substitution industrialisation programme. At this time the state was confronted by increased militancy among African workers in urban areas who had begun to move into skilled operative jobs reserved for whites. In 1942 a functionary of the Industrial Development Corporation (IDC) proposed that, in order to evade colour bar restrictions, 'native reserves' could be used as production locations. In 1944 the IDC followed through on the idea by establishing a textiles factory on land leased from the Native Trust near King Williams Town in the Eastern Cape. Soon after that, in 1948, Frame Textiles followed a similar strategy in Ladysmith when it set up a factory with the support of the local council.

By the 1960s the foundations had been laid for the decentralisation policy to become formalised. Initially, factories were to be located not in 'reserves' themselves but on the end of the 'reserves', as so-called 'border industries'. To facilitate the process, the government put in place tax concessions, loans at low interest rates, transport subsidies, and tariffs to protect from foreign competitors. Importantly, factories located in these areas were also exempted from Industrial Council minimum wage agreements. The IDC also constructed factories, leased premises and bought shares in such firms (Hart, 2002, p. 136).

Towards the end of the 1960s, however, there was a change in policy. In 1967 the further expansion of industrial activity in urban areas was controlled more strictly when the Physical Planning and Utilisation of Resources Act was promulgated. In 1968 the location of firms within the borders of 'homelands' was encouraged directly when the Promotion of the Economic Development of Bantu Homelands Act was passed. During the 1970s incentives were increased to support the further expansion of manufacturing activities in 'homelands' and border areas (Hart, 2002, p. 139).

In the 1980s the state shifted its approach to subsidising industrial decentralisation – instead of tax concessions it now gave direct cash subsidies. Still, extended tax holidays were introduced for some areas, such as the Ciskei. In 1982 the Regional Industrial Development Programme was introduced, which allowed Industrial Development Points to be established. The bulk of these resources were spent in three areas in the then-Natal – Ezakheni, Newcastle-Madadeni and Isithebe. In these areas, the KwaZulu Finance Corporation played a central role (Hart, 2002, pp. 144–6).

Throughout the 1970s and 1980s, the emerging independent trade unions were generally unable to organise factories located in Isithebe and other industrial decentralisation zones. Hence, in addition to exemptions from minimum wage requirements and generous government subsidies, companies that relocated or that were located in places like Isithebe had the added 'advantage' of a repressive regime that violently opposed attempts to organise workers into independent unions.

In order to better understand the landscape for the introduction of a new spatial fix for firms such as Defy in response to rising worker militancy in the 1970s, though, we have to trace the history of another southern African white goods manufacturer which was established in Isithebe in 1975. The name of the entrepreneur involved was Charlie Palmer. In the context of the apartheid state's attempts to foster 'independent homelands', Isithebe was located within the borders of KwaZulu. The company was initially set up under the name 'Palfridge'. Palmer's history in the white goods industry tells an interesting story, since he was directly responsible for setting up no fewer than three of the remaining white goods plants in southern Africa. In the late 1950s he set up a factory in Harare, which now operates under the name Imperial Refrigeration. Because of an apparent falling out with one of the directors at this firm, Palmer moved on to Mozambique, where he set up a factory with Colin Foster. During the war for liberation in Mozambique, Palmer fled the country (Interview: Palmer, 2002) and then moved on to set up shop in Isithebe. He stayed there for a long time, only to move to Swaziland in 1990 to set up 'Swaziland Refrigeration', which later became 'Masterfridge', and then, after liquidation, 'Palfridge'. Hence, the Imperial plant in Harare, the Whirlpool plant in Isithebe, and the Palfridge plant in Manzini were all originally set up beyond the national boundaries of the apartheid South African state – either in the 'independent homelands' or in Swaziland and Zimbabwe. As a result of Palmer's actions, then, 'homelands' had become centres of white goods production and so, for Defy, moving to such a location was not unusual.

An idea of the despotism in the workplace in such pseudo-independent 'homelands' can be gained through the following illustration. Inkatha, the tribal authority over KwaZulu, had established its own 'union', the United Workers' Union of South Africa (UWUSA), mainly to prevent workers in the decentralisation zones from joining independent unions. A worker at the factory remembered an incident from the 1980s, where officials from UWUSA wanted the employees to work on a Saturday without pay to make up for lost production time. Upon resisting this, the worker was shot, presumably by vigilantes linked to UWUSA and the Zulu nationalist movement. Showing the marks left by bullet wounds, he explained: 'Sunday, quarter to eight I got shot . . . At my house' (Interview: Buthelezi, 2001).

Up until the early 1990s, the National Union of Metalworkers of South Africa (NUMSA – MAWU's successor) was prevented by UWUSA's influence from setting up an office in Isithebe. Instead, the union established its presence in Mandini, 11 km away. Whereas the union was not able to organise openly in Isithebe, Ezakheni was a different matter altogether. An anti-apartheid alliance had emerged in Ladysmith and its environs in the 1980s which wove together 'Zulu patriarchal sentiments and practices associated with an agrarian past with those that were startlingly new' (Hart, 2002, p. 125). This alliance would lead to strong support for the ANC when the first local government elections took place in 1996, with the ANC winning 62 per cent of the seats and roundly defeating the Inkatha Freedom Party, which emerged with only one seat (Hart, 2002, p. 241). When the newly elected ANC councillors took over, they immediately convened 'large and extremely lively open budget meetings at which residents were explicitly invited to educate the councillors about their priorities' (Hart, 2002, p. 254).

The result of raising the expectations of their constituents was the anticipation that the 'disabling' impact of globalisation would be confronted. Consequently, in late 1996 the newly elected ANC mayor visited India and China as part of a delegation organised by the KwaZulu Marketing Initiative (KMI) to solicit foreign investment. A year later a local economic development forum was formed with representatives from capital, labour, the local state and NGOs, although this initiative came to a standstill when the unions made it clear they strongly opposed the foreign investment strategy pursued by the council (Hart, 2002, pp. 273–4). Nevertheless, these visits to solicit investment from

East Asia continued, even as they circumvented the involvement of the community and the local NUMSA branch (Interviews: Qwabe, 2005, Mchunu, 2005). Whilst the ANC in Ezakheni managed to attract nearly 70 per cent of the vote in the next local elections in 2000, the open budget meetings they had initiated had led residents to develop a 'sense of themselves as political actors in relationship to elected officials as well as local bureaucrats'. Consequently, township dwellers increasingly pressed their demands for urban services, 'invoking histories of forced removals to drive home their claims . . . to address much broader issues of dispossession' (Hart, 2002, pp. 285–6).

In the late 1990s unions had spoken about developing a new spatial strategy around the social wage by forging connections between townships and surrounding rural areas. However, ongoing job losses with large numbers of retrenched workers had begun to impact these communities, making it difficult for the ANC to win local support. This situation is captured succinctly by Hart (2002, p. 7):

> In the name of both democracy and efficiency, local councillors and bureaucrats have been called upon to confront massive redistributive pressures with minimal resources. Simultaneously they have been assigned major responsibility for securing the conditions of accumulation under the aegis of 'local economic development'. The local state, in short, has become a key site of contradictions in the neoliberal post-apartheid order.

The result of this was a growing realisation of the limitations of political parties and a search for security within the community, rather than in political parties. Although grassroots networks have emerged, providing crucial support in the neighbourhood, they are not seen as having the capacity to solve community problems.

For the unions, though, things have changed in the post-apartheid era. Hence, NUMSA now has a local office in Isithebe, and UWUSA no longer has a presence in the area. The Chemical, Energy, Paper, Printing, Wood and Allied Workers' Union and the Southern African Clothing and Textiles Workers' Union also have offices in the same complex. A list of companies who operate from the area shows that most of the factories are involved in the clothing and textile industries. However, whilst these areas are now being systematically brought back into the national labour regime, wages are still lower than in urban areas. Moreover, unions find it very hard to organise, especially many of the clothing companies, where workers are sometimes paid as little as R300 a month. Nevertheless, now that the 'independent homelands' have been reincorporated into the national space of South Africa and so are subject to South African labour laws – in other words, now that the spatial safety valve for capital has largely been shut off – a new spatial fix is being sought by capital, as many firms seek out other industrial districts in countries where workers have fewer rights. Such a location is the Matsapha Industrial Area, just outside Manzini in Swaziland. Indeed, this is where Charlie Palmer went in 1990. As the sites that served as capital's spatial fix in the 1980s become integrated into the national regime and NUMSA has consolidated its national presence, capital, then, has begun to seek a new spatial fix, and countries like Swaziland and Lesotho are becoming the new arenas for the practices of boundary drawing.

New boundaries of exclusion
As South Africa emerged from apartheid in the 1990s, the country also rapidly liberalised trade. The end of international sanctions allowed South African firms to expand abroad,

and many of the conglomerates unbundled their less-profitable manufacturing operations. Several of the white goods manufacturers were hit hard by this double shock – rising imports as a result of trade liberalisation, as well as capital restructuring (Bezuidenhout, 2005). The labour movement faced three significant challenges to its power in the industry.

The first of these was a general sense of crisis, as several factories closed down. This, coupled with rising rates of structural unemployment, led to a decline in their marketplace bargaining power. For instance, Kelvinator SA, one of the oldest white goods manufacturers, was closed down after failed attempts by NUMSA to negotiate with a foreign investor to buy the plant. Its equipment was bought by Defy in 1999, who moved it to their Ezakheni operation in 2000. Following Defy's decision to relocate the Kelvinator equipment to Ezakheni, where industry sources estimated it was about a third cheaper to employ workers, the media speculated that it was 'convenient for Defy to pull out of Johannesburg, having ensured that no fresh competitor would resurrect the Kelvinator plant' (Anon. 2000).

The second challenge to labour's power was the reworking of the spatial fix mentioned above. Charlie Palmer's new operation in Swaziland became a significant player in the South African market. When Kelvinator was liquidated, this was blamed on Masterfridge's access to low wages. As Peter Bruce (1999, p. 4), editor of the *Financial Mail*, bemoaned:

> [W]hite goods is a brutal business. Over in Swaziland, Masterfridge has been able to pay its labour about a fifth of what Kelvinator was paying here. And how are you supposed to grow a business in SA's interest rate climate? . . . It's a damn[ed] shame, though I hope we don't hear any calls for tighter curbs on imports.

But, of course, such calls were made. As Sipho Ngcobo (1999) lamented in the *Business Report,* '[i]f this is not a lesson to South Africa, nothing ever will be. The fact of the matter is, cheap imports from low-wage economies destroy South Africa's manufacturing base. The end result is massive job losses, which we are already experiencing'. Thus, he argued:

> Kelvinator saw this coming. But repeated appeals to the department of trade and industry for tariff protection against competitors with lower labour costs in neighbouring countries went unheeded. A similar appeal to the department for anti-dumping legislation, following the opening up of South Africa, against overseas producer Whirlpool also went unheeded.

A third and final challenge to the workplace bargaining power of labour was the segmentation of the white goods internal labour market into permanent and fixed-term contract workers. The use of fixed-term contract workers was introduced in the mid-1990s to deal with seasonal fluctuations in demand. Its effect has been, though, that there is now a segment of workers with access to the gains made by the labour movement since the 1970s, whilst another sector does not have such access. Indeed, a third of the workers employed in the industry in practice have very few of the benefits and rights enjoyed by their colleagues on permanent contracts of employment (Bezuidenhout, 2005; Fakier, 2006).

The developments since the formal end of apartheid, then, have witnessed a new politics of space emerging. With the opening of South Africa's domestic space-economy to imports, the geography of manufacturing has again begun to change. Equally, new boundaries are being drawn within the labour force, between core and peripheral workers. Given the legacy of apartheid, these boundaries are highly racialised. These developments are having impacts upon the unions and workers. Hence, whilst MAWU, and later NUMSA, were successful in constructing a national union and drew on international solidarity in order to do so, the new macroeconomic and labour regimes of post-apartheid South Africa have led to new challenges – and the need for a new spatial politics to respond to this.

Conclusion

In this chapter we have focused on one sector, the white goods sector, and showed how workers engaged with capital's use of space and, in response, jumped scale from the local, to the national and then to the global. We also showed how employers responded through spatial fixes to relocate production to low-wage rural areas where union organisation is more difficult. It is obvious from such developments, then, that the contested nature of space has been a central part of the capital-labour relationship in South Africa.

Significantly, a similar politics of space can be identified in the textile industry. Thus, a global production chain has been created in the southern African region through the creation of 50000 jobs in Lesotho to export garments to the industry's major buyer, Gap Clothing in the United States (Webster and Bezuidenhout, 2003, p. 284) (see Pickles and Smith, Chapter 6 in this volume, for more on the textile industry in Eastern Europe). The creation of this chain is noteworthy because textile workers were at the core of the Durban strikes in 1973 and the unions that formed in the wake of these strikes (such as the National Textile Workers' Union) followed the same factory-based strategy as did MAWU. Hence, NTWU also jumped scales to the national level. More recently, textile unions, with the assistance of the International Textile, Garment and Leather Workers' Federation, a Global Union Federation (GUF), have sought to jump beyond the confines of the South African space-economy by organising across southern Africa, a development reflected in the fact that the South African Clothing and Textiles Workers' Union has now amended its name to the *Southern* African Clothing and Textiles Workers' Union. SACTWU has also expanded its boundaries geographically beyond the factory by organising homeworkers (Bennett, 2003; Van der Westhuizen, 2005).

Whilst it is clear that NUMSA has successfully engaged with the politics of space to build up a national union, capital's ability to create a new spatial fix by relocating to rural areas within and beyond South Africa has challenged this strategy. Furthermore, initial attempts to organise in places such as Ezakheni have been greatly constrained by the whip of international competition, growing unemployment, and casualisation of the employment relationship through fixed-term contracts of employment at Defy. This has weakened the workplace and marketplace bargaining power of the union (Fakier, 2006) and many workers have retreated into their households and turned to forms of informal employment as a survival strategy. The result of this latter practice is that any attempt to rebuild trade union organisation will have to focus on local organisation, as it is at the local scale that the new politics of space can be built as unions seek to make linkages between those workers who have become increasingly spatially isolated in the economic landscape. As capital has fled urban spaces and as space has been fragmented as production has moved from the factory to the space of individual homes (Herod, 1991), the new spatialisation of manufacturing which this is auguring will require unions to rethink the geographies of their organising.

Notes

1. We refer here to Silver's analysis of labour and the politics of war and her consideration of claims that states have lost power under globalisation.
2. Webster (1985, p. 67, note 38) notes that the Durban branch of the Iron Moulders' Society made union history in 1920 when they became the first branch to allow 'coloureds' to join.
3. See also Webster's (1985, pp. 267–70) discussion of the case of Morris, a 'coloured' production moulder at Durban Falkirk who, after years of struggle against racial discrimination in the company and the union (the IMS), decided to leave both. This union featured again in 1975 in a dispute about bonuses at Defy – see discussion below.
4. MAWU later merged with the National Automobile and Allied Workers' Union (NAAWU) and a number of other unions to form the present-day National Union of Metalworkers of South Africa (NUMSA).
5. The Wiehahn Commission was set up by the government to investigate labour legislation and recommended the incorporation of black workers into the formal industrial relations system.

Interviews

Buthelezi, Jabu (pseudonym): Employee of Whirlpool, Isithebe, South Africa, May 2001.
Mchunu, Mbuso: National Union of Metalworkers of South Africa (NUMSA) Ladysmith Local Organiser, June 2005.
Palmer, Charlie: President of Palfridge Refrigeration, Manzini, Swaziland, November 2002.
Qwabe, Themba: Ladysmith Municipal Manager, Ladysmith, South Africa, April 2005.

References

Anderson, B.R. (1983), *Imagined Communities: Reflections on the Origin and Spread of Nationalism*, London: Verso.
Anonymous (2000), 'Defy freezes Kelvinator factory (and 650 Gauteng jobs)', *Business Report*, 8 June, available at www.busrep.co.za/index.php?fSectionId=650&fArticleId=79273, accessed 27 April 2009.
Bennett, M. (2003), 'Organising in the informal economy: a case study of the clothing industry in South Africa', *SEED Working Paper*, No. 37, Geneva: International Labour Organisation.
Bezuidenhout, A. (2004), 'Post-colonial workplace regimes in the white goods manufacturing industries of South Africa, Swaziland and Zimbabwe', thesis submitted to the Faculty of Humanities, University of the Witwatersrand, Johannesburg, South Africa, for the degree of Doctor of Philosophy.
Bezuidenhout, A. (2005), 'South Africa, Swaziland and Zimbabwe – white goods in post-colonial societies: markets, the state and production', in T. Nichols and S. Cam (eds), *Labour in a Global World: Case Studies from the White Goods Industry in Africa, South America, East Asia and Europe*, Basingstoke: Palgrave Macmillan, pp. 57–91.
Bruce, P. (1999), 'Editor's note', *Financial Mail*, 10 September, p. 4.
Cooper, F. (1996), *Decolonization and African Society: The Labor Question in French and British Africa*, Cambridge: Cambridge University Press.
Fakier, K. (2006), 'Contract workers on a quest for security', *South African Labour Bulletin*, **30** (2), 34–7.
Freund, B. (1995), *Insiders and Outsiders: The Indian Working Class of Durban 1910–1990*, Pietermaritzburg: University of Natal Press.
Friedman, S. (1987), *Building Tomorrow Today: African Workers in Trade Unions 1970–1984*, Johannesburg: Ravan Press.
Hart, G.P. (2002), *Disabling Globalization: Places of Power in Post-Apartheid South Africa*, Pietermaritzburg: University of Natal Press.
Harvey, D. (1978), 'The urban process under capitalism: a framework for analysis', *International Journal of Urban and Regional Research*, **2**, 101–31.
Harvey, D. (2001), *Spaces of Capital: Towards a Critical Geography*, Edinburgh: Edinburgh University Press.
Herod, A. (1991), 'Homework and the fragmentation of space: challenges for the labor movement', *Geoforum*, **22** (2), 173–83.
Herod, A. (1997), 'Labor's spatial praxis and the geography of contract bargaining in the US east coast longshore industry, 1953–89', *Political Geography*, **16** (2), 145–69.

Herod, A. (2001), *Labor Geographies: Workers and the Landscapes of Capitalism*, New York: Guilford Press.
Herod, A. and M.W. Wright (eds) (2002), *Geographies of Power: Placing Scale*, Oxford: Blackwell.
Keck, M.E. and K. Sikkink (1998), *Activists Beyond Borders: Advocacy Networks in International Politics*, Ithaca, NY: Cornell University Press.
Kirkwood, M. (1975), 'The Defy dispute: questions of solidarity', *South African Labour Bulletin*, **2** (1), 55–63.
Mamdani, M. (1996), *Citizen and Subject: Contemporary Africa and the Legacy of Late Colonialism*, Princeton, NJ: Princeton University Press.
Maree, J. (ed.) (1987), *The Independent Trade Unions 1974–1984: Ten Years of the South African Labour Bulletin*, Johannesburg: Ravan Press.
Ngcobo, S. (1999), 'Free trade is not free or fair', *Business Report*, 11 September, available at www.busrep.co.za/index.php?fSectionId=650&fArticleId=68636, accessed 27 April 2009.
Peck, J. (1996), *Work-Place: The Social Regulation of Labor Markets*, New York: Guilford Press.
Silver, B.J. (2003), *Forces of Labor: Workers' Movements and Globalization since 1870*, Cambridge: Cambridge University Press.
Southall, R. (1995), *Imperialism or Solidarity? International Labour and South African Trade Unions*, Cape Town: University of Cape Town Press.
Tarrow, S.G. (2005), *The New Transnational Activism*, Cambridge: Cambridge University Press.
Van der Westhuizen, C. (2005), 'Women and work restructuring in the Cape Town clothing industry', in E. Webster and K. von Holdt (eds), *Beyond the Apartheid Workplace: Studies in Transition*, Scottsville, South Africa: University of KwaZulu-Natal Press, pp. 335–55.
Von Holdt, K. (2003), *Transition from Below: Forging Trade Unionism and Workplace Change in South Africa*, Durban: University of Natal Press.
Waterman, P. and J. Wills (eds) (2001), *Place, Space and the New Labour Internationalisms*, Oxford: Blackwell.
Webster, E. (1983), 'MAWU and the Industrial Council – a comment', *South African Labour Bulletin*, **8** (5), 14–19.
Webster, E. (1984), 'The IMF in South Africa', *South African Labour Bulletin*, **9** (6), 77–94.
Webster, E. (1985), *Cast in a Racial Mould: Labour Process and Trade Unionism in the Foundries*, Johannesburg: Ravan Press.
Webster, E. and A. Bezuidenhout (2003), 'Fair globalization in Southern Africa: a response to the ILO's World Commission on the Social Dimension of Globalization', *Labour, Capital and Society*, **36** (2), 262–96.

21 The multi-scalarity of trade union practice

Jeremy Anderson, Paula Hamilton and Jane Wills

Introduction

Globalisation has dramatically altered the scalar architecture of capitalism, with wide-reaching implications for trade unions. This chapter highlights elements of this changed architecture, such as the emergence of transnational corporations (TNCs), global cities, and new transportation nodes, which, together with the increasing fragmentation of employment relationships, present distinct geographical challenges to efforts of trade unions to organise workers.

The chapter begins by exploring the limitations of contemporary forms of trade union organisation in countries like the UK, where the primary focus is on workplace organisation backed up by national union structures. We argue that although the workplace remains critical to the labour movement and its future, in itself it is an insufficient basis for trade union power. Rather, the growth of TNCs and other transnational economic practices demands that we locate the workplace in this wider spatial architecture of capital. In this context, a key imperative is developing new spatial relationships amongst unions themselves. Hence, whereas traditionally the principal focus of the trade union movement has been the relationship of workplace and national union structures, trade unions now need to develop deeper and qualitatively different relationships across national borders that boomerang (reverse) attempts by capital to gain spatial leverage over workers. In addition, the expansion of subcontracting highlights the importance of locating the 'real' employers at the centres of corporate power. With both of these developments, unions need to develop the capacity to affect employer profiles negatively, something which can be achieved most decisively when trade unions engage non-union allies. In the case of the private sector, such efforts can use the media to tarnish a corporate image, mobilise consumers, communicate with regulatory authorities and spread doubt among investors. In the public sector, campaigners can question the use of public money to stimulate poor quality employment and services. Significantly, though, these strategies are quite geographically contingent. Thus, as these arguments are made most effectively by connecting workplace trade union organisation to a wider set of networks at the local, urban/regional and transnational scales, they rely for their success on the specific relationships that unions are able to form 'in place' with religious organisations, shareholders and lenders, and political figures, as well as interactions with other vectors of mobilisation.

More specifically, the chapter illustrates the spatial possibilities for trade unions by exploring a number of examples drawn from current research into changing patterns of employment and labour organising. Such examples are used to highlight the complexity of the situation facing labour today. Hence, in some industries, where TNCs directly employ their staff, it might be possible to target these companies in two or more countries simultaneously. In the case of subcontracted labour, however, locating strategic influence within the industry becomes particularly important. Consequently, where manufacturing employers have international or global supply chains, this might require a globally scaled response, networking workers' organisations on the ground with activists in the key markets and home countries of the major TNCs. By way of contrast, in those sectors where it is difficult to map the supply chain of any one firm, it might be better to organise across employers within a strategic node like a global city or major port. Moreover, in such key nodes of the global economy, the juxtaposition of leading corporations, political authorities and media institutions with low-paid workers performing essential jobs provides fertile ground for living wage campaigns to take root in the public imagination.

After highlighting the limitations of the prevailing model of workplace trade union organisation, the chapter looks at the way in which the US Service Employees' International Union (SEIU) has led efforts to develop global capacity to target TNCs in the contract cleaning, catering and security sectors. The union has identified global cities as key sites to remake labour markets in the property services sector. We then move on to explore the strategic significance of the global logistics sector, whose workers move components to production and goods from production to market via complicated subcontracting arrangements. Whilst these workers are potentially powerful, there is less clarity in their employment relationships and less consumer engagement with the leading corporations involved than in many other, more direct, employment relationships. In this instance, the research highlights the importance of organising at key nodes in the industry, such as ports, airports, road and rail terminals, nodes where workers and goods from a host of different logistics companies are concentrated at any one time.

The chapter then moves on to explore the development of low-waged urban labour markets and the success of living wage campaigns. By moving beyond the workplace and building broad-based coalitions that incorporate a range of community organisations, living wage campaigns have been able to improve the wages and conditions of some of the most vulnerable and worst paid workers in the US and the UK, and the example of London is briefly addressed.

These examples highlight not only the need to organise workers, but also to develop a multi-scalar approach that includes strategic targeting of corporate power centres, strategies that target geographical zones, not just single workplaces, and the development of extra-workplace networks that incorporate actors from a variety of locations. As such, we understand the challenges facing unions not only as political and economic, but also as fundamentally spatial in character. We substantiate this argument in more detail below.

Workplace trade union organisation: results and prospects
Historically, trade unions in countries like the UK[1] have been focused on workplace organisation. Trade union representatives emerged early in the print, metals, engineering, textiles, docks and coal industries in the late nineteenth century. As the state and employers became more willing to recognise the legitimate role of trade union organisation in the management of capitalism, particularly during and after the Second World War, shop steward structures spread to manufacturing, the public sector and private service organisations. By the late 1970s and early 1980s, there were as many as 300000 union representatives in workplaces across the UK, with 10000 of them on full-time release (Terry, 1995). In the wake of legislative support given to workplace trade unionism by the 1974–79 Labour Government, employers were encouraged to give union

representatives facility time so that they could engage in union training, recruitment, collective bargaining, health and safety and individual representation.

For over a hundred years, workplace trade union representatives have played a central role in recruiting, retaining and representing union members at work. These activists have been the life-blood of the British trade union movement, keeping local organisation alive. They have formed the social infrastructure of union branch organisation, representing the members, distributing information, upholding union democracy and mobilising for action. In the years since the 1970s, however, the economic, political and cultural factors that sustained this model of trade union organisation have changed almost beyond recognition. It is well known that Margaret Thatcher came to power determined to undermine trade union power, and she succeeded with devastating effect. Through public hostility, direct legislation and the impact of privatisation it became much harder to maintain strong trade union organisation with the power to effect workplace change.

But in addition to the changes wrought by Thatcherism, the development of economic globalisation has further augmented rates of decline. With the integration of the global economy, particularly since the fall of the Berlin Wall in 1989, trade unions in the manufacturing sector have been engulfed by a sharp upturn in competitive pressure, often backed up by the threat or reality of relocation and/or investment elsewhere. For transnational corporations, the ability to operate at the global scale has meant ever more profitable opportunities for investment, production and market development. Moreover, the subcontracting of production has made it more difficult for workers to organise, wherever they are (see Hale and Wills, 2005).

In a country such as Britain, globalisation has accelerated the loss of heavy industrial and manufacturing jobs and more than three-quarters of workers are now employed in service work. The old engines of employment in coal, steel, textiles, engineering, manufacturing and the docks, sectors which sustained trade union organisation, have long been exported or automated. Although some of the small-scale manufacturing activity, and much of the private sector service employment that remains, is much less vulnerable to global competition, these workplaces have often historically been union-free. Growing numbers of workplaces in the business and personal services, retail and distribution, hospitality and leisure sectors are small, with high labour turnover, and employ large numbers of part-time and agency staff and workers who often have very little experience of trade unionism. Just as in manufacturing, there is also a growing tendency to contract-out public and private services, undermining the potential to establish effective collective bargaining over the terms and conditions of work. Given this, it is clear that workplace trade unionism does not have the effectivity it did in the past.

Trends in union membership and commitment illustrate this decline in the influence and effectiveness of workplace trade union organisation in the UK. At a national level, trade union membership has declined very rapidly from its historic peak of just over 50 per cent density in 1979 to just under 30 per cent of all workers today. The 7 million trade unionists that remain are now heavily concentrated in the public and ex-public sector and in large, long-established manufacturing plants and private services firms. In those establishments that have opened since 1979, rates of union recognition are dramatically lower than they are in much older firms. In 1998, 50 per cent of private sector manufacturing workplaces that had opened in or before 1980 recognised unions, in contrast to only 14 per cent of those opened after this date (Cully et al., 1999).

Moreover, workplace trade unionism was never strongly implanted in the private services sector, or amongst women workers, and it is these parts of the economy and workforce that have grown most since 1979. Even though only a rather desultory 25 per cent of private sector service establishments that opened in or before 1980 recognised unions, for those that opened during the 1980s and 1990s a mere 18 per cent did so. This is significant, for without union recognition in these younger firms, there is no opportunity to appoint local union representatives who can then recruit, retain and represent staff. Moreover, even if they did secure recognition, data collected for the Workplace Employee Relations Survey in 1998 (Cully et al., 1999) indicated that as many as one in four union-recognised workplaces and as many as one in two workplaces in the private services sector did not have any union representative appointed on site.

In a dramatic demonstration of the growing weakness of workplace trade unionism, the 1998 survey also found that the number of workplaces with high union density and a wide and well established collective bargaining agenda had fallen from 47 per cent of recognised establishments in 1980 to only 17 per cent in 1998 (Millward et al., 2000). Thus, whilst the incidence of union recognition has fallen across the economy, so too has the voracity of the trade unionism that remains. In many cases, union organisation in the workplace has subsided almost beyond the point of no return, as 50 per cent of workplaces with union representation did not have any local negotiations over key issues such as pay, conditions, staff recruitment, training, equal opportunities, health and safety, performance management and grievance handling.

In this context, it is perhaps not surprising that when non-union members were asked about the difference that a union would make to their workplace in the British Social Attitudes Survey in 1998, only 18 per cent said they thought it would make it better (and the majority of these were manual rather than non-manual staff) and as many as 65 per cent said they thought it would not make any difference at all (Charlwood, 2002). Most alarmingly for the trade unions, however, this scepticism was also common amongst those who were already signed up. Only about half of the thousands of union members sampled for the 1998 Workplace Employee Relations Survey said that their union was taken seriously by management and that it made a difference at work (Cully et al., 1999). Similar figures were generated by the 1998 British Social Attitudes Survey: 43 per cent of those employed in workplaces with a trade union or staff association present said that the workplace would be no different without the trade union (Charlwood, 2002).

These figures suggest that there is a crisis in workplace trade union organisation in countries like the UK. Not only is prevailing organisation weak, but it is found in an ever-smaller number of workplaces, and those that are most prone to closure (in manufacturing) or contracting out (in the public sector). In this sense the debate over organising and partnership which polarised the British union movement during the 1990s does not address the core challenges that trade unions face. Consequently, trying to establish workplace trade union organisation in newer workplaces, even if it proves possible, is not in itself likely to be sufficient to reinvigorate trade union organisation. This is because the changing geo-politics of the global economy has undermined traditional workplace-level trade union organisation. Thus, if labour organisers are going to have the power to tackle the structure of the new economy in order to improve wages and conditions at work, they will need a new geographical imagination, one that allows workers to influence the power-brokers at the top of supply chains in both the private and the public sectors. A growing body of union experience suggests that this can be done only by building alliances between trade unions and non-union actors such as development and anti-poverty activists, feminists, anti-racists, faith organisations, environmental groups and/ or community groups. In many cases, these initiatives have involved the establishment of new organisations or hybrids of the old, with the new being typified by, for instance, living wage coalitions and global justice networks (see Rowbothom and Mitter, 1994; Gordon, 2001; Pastor, 2001; Waterman and Wills, 2001; Fine, 2005; Hale and Wills, 2005). In what follows, then, we explore some current examples of new geographical thinking and practice in the international trade union movement.

The global ambitions of the SEIU

The Service Employees' International Union (SEIU), the largest union in the US, is rapidly developing a new geographical imagination. Since 2004, 'Building Global Strength' has become a key pillar of the union's strategic outlook and the union has committed unprecedented levels of resources to this work. The SEIU used to think globalisation was something that happened in the manufacturing sector. However, the entry of TNCs into the cleaning, security, catering and public transport sectors during the 1990s forced the union to rethink its relation to global economic processes and to imagine organising transnationally. For Andy Stern, the union's president, a long-standing campaign to organise school bus drivers in Minnesota proved to be the trigger for this shift in scalar thinking. Stern recalls wondering: 'Why was this so hard?' 'Normally, our in-state political leverage and the workers' solidarity would have been enough to overcome employer resistance. But the company was owned by this British employer who was immune to local politics and local conditions' (cited in Meyerson, 2005, p. 1).

To respond to such non-local employers, the SEIU has systematically incorporated a global perspective into its strategic outlook. The union has reopened its international department, this time under the moniker of Global Partnerships, to build global capacity through partnerships with foreign unions, strengthen links with the Global Union Federations (GUFs), and disseminate international experience (Tattersall, 2006). The union has recognised the advantages that come from the geographical rootedness of jobs in the sectors in which they organise. The non-mobility of jobs in cleaning, catering, care and public transport renders global cooperation between workers less problematic than in sectors like manufacturing, where workers compete on the basis of labour costs. In this context, the SEIU leadership has shifted from viewing multinational capital as an uncontrollable threat to an arena of political possibility. According to Emily Stewart, the head of the union's Public Services division:

> Whereas a year ago we were still in that . . . 'we can't do certain things because the company is global' [mindset], now we are actually saying 'Oh, we will make a list of what are the companies in our industry that have global connects', because we see that as an opportunity of how to campaign. (Interview, 2006)

In contrast to much international union activity in which unions seek solidarity when they are already in a dispute, the SEIU's global strategy is a concerted and wide-ranging attempt to develop a proactive and anticipatory disposition towards global capital. Moreover, the union understands that the possibilities for action at the current juncture are both spatially and temporally contingent. Grant Williams, an SEIU strategist posted to London, comments:

> We said, you know the company Wal-Mart? Years ago Wal-Mart had 50 000 employees, mainly in the South and the Mid-West. And [it] was a small company that could have been beat back then. Had the union there jumped on . . . [them] at that time, we might be looking at a whole different issue in the food service [sector]. (Interview, 2006)

In emergent sectors such as property services, however, the union sees an opportunity to construct a more worker-friendly power-geometry:

> What we are saying is that these companies worldwide are the future. ISS, Rentokil, Compass, they are maybe a couple of million workers now but some day they will be 10 million workers. So we need to jump on them right now worldwide, get them all to do what ISS did. Which is . . . [to say they will] recognise . . . unions in every country. . . . So right now when they still are vulnerable, before they have billions of dollars to lobby politicians and everything else, is when we need to move. (Interview, Grant Williams, 2006)

The SEIU seeks to map TNCs and identify their weaknesses with a view to creatively using the geography of trade union organisation to resist. The public transport sector was the test site for this new brand of transnational comprehensive campaigning and the strategy has been most developed in relation to property services, as is outlined briefly below.[2]

In the case of the bus industry, the SEIU developed the capacity to confront the First Student company, a leading US transporter of children to schools with whom it had been having a protracted battle in Minnesota, on completely different spatial terms than would a traditional union-organising campaign orientated against a local school district's transportation provider (Anderson, 2009). Thus, in 2004 the SEIU learnt that the company's parent, First Group, was based in the United Kingdom, where 80 per cent of its employees were members of the Transport and General Workers' Union (T&G), a British trade union that was similarly looking to develop its organising capacity.[3] Working together, the unions launched the Driving Up Standards campaign. They sought to use the T&G's relationship with First Group in the UK to leverage additional support for organising efforts at First Student in the US. This transnationalisation of the SEIU's comprehensive campaigning model, then, involved an attempt to project the regulatory practice of the British state and the norms of the British industrial relations environment into the US labour market. Noticing First Group's financial dependence on public sector contracts in the UK, the unions alerted UK policy-makers and elected officials to the company's poor record in safety and key performance indicators, as well as its aggressive labour relations and poor staff retention in the US. Moreover, the unions implied that creeping Americanisation was infecting First Group's operations in the UK. In addition, the unions targeted and mobilised shareholding T&G members who, together with an institutional shareholder, put up a resolution about union recognition at the company's AGM.

At the time of writing, the campaign is still underway, with both the SEIU and T&G anticipating an extended fight. But this brief summary illustrates the potential for multifaceted comprehensive campaigns in transnational space. The campaign also illustrates the importance of transnational union partnerships. Indeed, the SEIU's relationship with the T&G seems to have developed particularly deep roots, born from a profound sense of common purpose, as this SEIU official explains:

Well, the time we started working with the T&G was almost magical really, because when Tony Woodley was elected General Secretary it was on, everyone who ran . . . ran with an organising agenda. . . . There was a point a couple of years ago when Tony had a powerpoint of his vision where he wanted to see the T&G go . . . [and] it was almost conceptually interchangeable with some of what Andy Stern from SEIU had been talking about (Interview: Emily Stewart, 2006)

Whereas international union cooperation has often been hobbled by lingering suspicion, the SEIU–T&G relationship has been fuelled by the affective disposition of the two sets of leaders, which has afforded a commitment not premised on particular campaigns but on a broad, long-term strategic outlook. As such, the relationship has proved able to absorb tensions arising within particular campaigns and it has served as a platform for a variety of global initiatives, such as the SEIU's even more ambitious plans for the property services industry.

Whereas in public transport the SEIU and the T&G are currently learning the ropes of transnational comprehensive campaigns, in property services the former is seeking to marshal a much larger number of allies in order to shape the terms of the global industry. Specifically, the SEIU's strategy for property services is targeted at the big four property services providers: ISS, Group 4 Securicor, Securitas and Rentokil Initial. Collectively, these companies have nearly one million employees, a combined turnover of US$27 billion and operations in over 100 countries. Three of these companies are headquartered in the relatively benign industrial relations environs of Western Europe whilst all have a significant presence in SEIU heartlands in the US. In a move that echoes the public transport campaign, the first key plank of the SEIU's property services strategy has been to consolidate union power in these markets and then project it outwards through agreements that guarantee global union neutrality and other union-friendly measures.

In addition, the property services strategy has been specifically targeted at the global city, for it is here that there are the largest concentrations of property services workers and also where the employers are best equipped to finance their proper remuneration. For Stephen Lerner, the SEIU's Director of the Property Services Division, organising in global cities, then, involves confronting capitalist exploitation at its sharpest edge. Moreover, given the fractions of capital present (in many cases, large financial institutions), there is also greater opportunity to influence the powerful:

[C]leaners bring home the contradictions most because they are cleaning up after and personally taking care of the richest persons in the richest corporations. So I think our campaigns cut this issue incredibly sharply in terms of what is going on in the world . . . in the big cities around the world, whether that be New York, London, Johannesburg or Dubai . . . [and] unlike the factory worker who is producing a good for a boss who is far away, we are in the boss's office. (Interview: Stephen Lerner, 2006)

Interestingly, Lerner argues that the possibilities for global union organisation in global cities is often reinforced by the presence of migrant workers, who are already involved in an array of daily transnational practices. Moreover, it is also significant that the SEIU is looking inwards at the same time as it looks outwards. Thus, the property services strategy is also designed to change the structures of trade unions themselves. In this regard, according to Lerner and others in the SEIU leadership, the centre of gravity of the international trade union movement will need to shift from national headquarters to structures that transcend national boundaries. As Lerner argues:

> We believe the future of workers is in building global unions that do not have an allegiance to any country. It should just have an allegiance to the workers . . . For me, the glue is common employers and a common strategy. (Interview, 2006)

The SEIU is thus working with the GUF in this sector, Union Network International (UNI), to establish a new global organising fund to which 20 per cent of the dues of members recruited as part of any campaign will be remitted. This represents the most significant development in transnational trade unionism since the creation of the GUFs in the late nineteenth and early twentieth centuries. It is fair to say, then, that the SEIU has a global vision that is taking its geography seriously. It understands that the existing spatial formations of trade unionism are ill-equipped for tackling capital in contemporary conditions.[4] Moreover, the SEIU perceives that globalisation has not rendered capital omnipotent but, rather, that its reconstituted geographical basis has resulted in new strategic targets, such as global cities and, as we shall see in the next section, the key nodes in the infrastructure of global logistics.

Lubricating globalisation: contract logistics and the challenges for organisation
Contract logistics companies, or third-party logistics providers (3PL), have grown exponentially since the 1990s. Driven in part by deregulation and liberalisation across multiple modes of transport, the harnessing of new technologies, mergers and acquisitions and the increasing complexity of supply chains, these companies have grown in both number and scale to run logistics contracts for corporations in almost all industries across the globe. As examples, companies like Kuehne and Nagel have grown 21.5 per cent in terms of turnover, and their number of employees has increased from 19 000 to 45 000 (236 per cent) since 2003 (Kuehne and Nagel, 2006). In 2003, approximately 6.51 per cent of the global workforce was employed in the transport, storage and communications sectors and there were at least 20 leading logistics companies involved with strengths in different regions and particular industrial markets. Indeed, in the US alone, the top 50 3PLs employed over 250 000 workers and had over 3800 facilities (WEF, 2004).

As a result of these developments, employment in the sector has been transformed. Jobs that were once associated with specialist logistics companies (many of them in the public sector) in particular transport sectors (road, rail, air and sea), or with large TNCs that controlled their own distribution divisions, are now part of complex mosaics of supply chains made up of a large number of different employers. In this system large TNCs subcontract their distribution requirements to 3PL companies who, in turn, often manage the supply chain through contracts with locally based transport companies. Any one TNC may have a supply chain that is managed by several 3PLs that contract different logistics companies in different places, using different modes of transport, to move goods from one place to another. Workers in this sector make globalisation possible and yet they remain hidden from view in a complex pattern of differentiated subcontracted employment relationships. Furthermore, trade union structures in this sector remain focused on national structures that organise workers according to their mode of transport such as road, rail, air and sea, with further divisions between the public and private sectors. Not surprisingly, union structures have failed to keep up with dramatic change in the sector and now look woefully out of date.

As an example of this growing complexity, the UK Department of Health recently announced that it was outsourcing the National Health Service's (NHS) national logistics division, NHS Logistics, and the consumables purchasing function of the NHS Purchasing and Supply Agency (PASA) to the German-owned company DHL Exel Supply Chain. On 1 October 2006, around 1650 NHS workers were effectively transferred to DHL Exel Supply Chain, thereby joining the 150 000 workforce in the Deutsche Post World Net (DPWN) Logistics Division, a company that operates across 41 different countries offering contract logistics services to manufacturers, retailers and public entities.[5] As a result, former NHS logistics workers have not only been moved from the public to private sector but their occupation has been reclassified as well – they are now classified as logistics workers, alongside other road transport drivers, warehouse staff, train drivers and merchant seafarers. Despite doing the same jobs as before, these workers have become part of a global TNC, which is itself dependent upon a network of other contract logistics providers working for other TNCs. However, whilst this has been seen as a threat by UNISON, the British public sector union, from another point of view, these trade union members now have the potential to develop relations with logistics workers in other parts of the globe. The key challenge in such efforts, then, is to re-align trade union structures and strategy to allow this to happen and to ensure that labour organisations find new points of leverage in this changing world of employment.

Unions' efforts to organise in this sector, however, are complicated by the fact that in some cases 3PL companies are being relied upon to secure competitive advantage through their activities in particular parts of supply chains but in others they are being used to manage whole chains, wherein they move components and goods from one place to another as fast and as cheaply as possible but also track the movement of goods, add value through their activities and find savings in the reorganisation of the supply chain itself. Given this latter, it is, perhaps, unsurprising that logistics has been referred to by some (such as Hum, 2000) as the last frontier for the development of strategic competitive advantage. Notably, though, logistics could also be a key new frontier in the reconfiguration of the international trade union movement, for the importance of global logistics in securing competitive advantage, and the role of logistics workers in making globalisation possible, gives trade unions some substantial potential leverage in the sector. Indeed, if trade unions were able to organise successfully, they could have a major impact on logistics companies and the supply chains of leading TNCs. However, organising does pose some major challenges. For instance, the jobs in this sector are necessarily mobile as workers are employed to move goods within individual supply chains. Equally, as we have seen, the workers in any one network will span different employers and different modalities of transportation (road, rail, air and sea). Moreover, logistics companies are also increasingly involved in basic packaging, assemblage and warehousing work at major transport nodes, further widening the characteristics of the workers involved. Due to historical jurisdictional boundaries between trade unions, however, different unions are likely to focus on each of these different bodies of staff.

The industry is also dependent on intermodal transportation zones where goods are moved from one form of transport to another. These nodes include seaports, airports, rail and road depots and they are found in every region of the global economy. Such nodes have similar strategic significance to global cities in the day-to-day functioning of global capitalism – they are, in fact, the heart of the global logistics industry, as it is from here that logistics are operationalised and coordinated. Whilst these nodes are important economically, they are also recognised as being important for national economic development, and governments are heavily invested and interested in their success. As such, just as the SEIU has focused on global cities in its campaign to unionise the property services sector, the same could be done for key distribution and transport nodes in the global logistics industry. For the unions, then, it would make sense to focus organising efforts at these key nodes in global logistics.

In this regard, the International Transport Workers' Federation (ITF), the GUF for workers in the transportation sector, has supported a number of initiatives to explore these organising possibilities, including the research on which this chapter is based. Research has been conducted in Germany, Hong Kong, the UK and the US, and although there is a long-standing union presence in the transportation sector in Europe and the US, it is also clear that unions have failed to keep up with developments in the sector. In Hong Kong, for example, research has identified that there is no union presence in any of the 12 different 3PLs where interviews were conducted. Moreover, even in areas of strong unionisation, such as the UK, the way in which the industry is ultimately controlled by the TNCs at the top of the supply chain has been found to erode union strength. However, unlike jobs such as cleaning, catering and security, where subcontracted workers are employed for one major client on one site, often with the client on site, workers in the logistics sector are potentially employed for a large number of clients and travel between a large number of sites, out of sight of the client. This makes it harder to tackle the 'real employer' and reinforces the need to focus on the strategic spaces of the industry, whereby organising logistics workers across employers and transport modes and fostering new alliances at one site may allow unions to apply pressure to a very large number of clients.

Any such union campaign will be faced with the difficulty of identifying which companies are involved in any 3PL logistics operation, not to mention the challenges of unpacking the corporate supply chains involved (for similar examples in the garment sector, see Hale and Wills, 2005). The complexity of corporate relationships in networked supply chains, then, makes it difficult to trace connections and even more problematic to find organising strategies before the networks have changed. In addition, unions are hampered by internal fragmentation. This is largely because the contract logistics sector has emerged out of a mixture of manufacturing, retail and public sector outsourcing (and liberalisation), alongside restructuring within the transport sector itself. This evolution has resulted in a plethora of unions with membership and organisation from within and beyond the transport sector itself, such that in the UK, for example, pilots, retail workers, warehousing staff, car manufacturing workers, railway staff, communication workers and truck drivers are all in different unions. Consequently, there is confusion at the regional and global union federation levels, as trade unions with membership and/ or organisation within 3PLs cannot be assumed to be transport-related trade unions. As a result, just determining existing trade union density within 3PLs is a challenge, never mind detailing organising strategies.

Nevertheless, despite such difficulties, at the time of writing a number of transnational union-organising initiatives are in development. For instance, at the ITF's 40th

Congress, held in Vancouver in 2002, Resolution 5 concerned the ITF's work on logistics, and specifically referred to the promotion of 'international trade union coordination within logistics companies, including working together with other global union federations concerned with logistics, such as UNI' (ITF, 2002). Additionally, the ITF and UNI trade union affiliates have identified four key global companies which hold substantial market share within the wider express and logistics sector and which they plan to target: DHL, TNT, UPS and Federal Express. In this regard they have established a joint 'integrators project' to meet and discuss their work in these companies, have agreed to an International Day of Action (in November 2006) and have held two separate organising training/planning meetings. There are now ongoing efforts to develop more geographically sophisticated international organising campaigns.

Spatial agglomerations of possibility

As outlined above, the SEIU and the unions in the global logistics sector are thus beginning to focus their efforts on particular nodes of the global economy where trade unions might have leverage and therefore the potential to disrupt distribution and/or target key global corporations. In this context, transport nodes and global cities are particularly important sites for organising workers. As is illustrated by the work of the SEIU, global cities have been targeted as sites where TNCs are concentrated, where politicians are located, where the contrast between rich and poor is often most stark and where there is a transnational workforce employed. In addition, large cities often have their own identity, culture and media. They are the places that exercise policy-makers who seek to ameliorate the damage caused by widening inequality, poverty, ethnic divisions and unsustainable lifestyles. In this context, trade unions are well placed to argue that the labour market is important in the reproduction of social and economic divisions and so should be an arena for government intervention. Consequently, there is scope for labour organisations to champion an anti-poverty and ethnic integration agenda and build common cause with other social movements and organisations.

Large cities in the global North are now characterised by polarising labour markets with strong demand for labour at the top and bottom of the occupational hierarchy. Armies of low-paid workers literally make the city work, in retail, leisure, hospitality, cleaning and caring. These jobs are largely unorganised and characterised by low pay and very poor conditions of work. Workers move regularly between such jobs, trying to increase their pay and improve their conditions by mobility rather than by organisation. In global cities like London there is also a marked 'migrant division of labour', whereby disproportionate numbers of foreign-born workers are found doing these jobs (see May et al., 2007; Wills et al., 2010). At a time when all major public and private sector organisations have tendered out their cleaning, catering and security jobs, most of these jobs involve working for subcontractors, often the very large multinational companies identified by the SEIU.

In such an environment, traditional workplace trade union organisation makes little sense. It is the clients that pay for services, determine the level of service delivery and the employment environment. If they are to organise successfully, then, trade unions thus need to develop zonal strategies and reconfigure the local labour market. This may require a scalar strategy within the space of the city itself. Large clients and contractors have to be forced to meet new standards of pay and conditions within particular areas.

This might be defined in terms of a relatively broad canvas, such as a city, which will require strong political support from urban administrations, or the construction of sub-urban labour markets, such as a fashionable office block or hotel district. In either case, the participation of actors beyond the workplace, such as community organisations, is critical.

Some of the most exciting new examples of trade union organising strategy and tactics are evident at this pan-urban scale. Taking an example from the UK, London Citizens is a broad-based organisation that includes about 150 faith, education, community and trade union organisations (Jamoul and Wills, 2008). The organisation launched a living wage campaign in 2001 in order to improve the wages and conditions of low-paid, sub-contracted workers in hospitals, financial institutions, hotels, universities, the transport sector and the planned Olympic development site. The campaign has worked with the Mayor and the Greater London Authority to establish a living wage rate for London, along with fair employment conditions that include improved holiday entitlement, sick pay and access to a trade union. The campaign has sought to make large public and private sector organisations responsible for the poor quality jobs provided by contrac-tors, asking them to put more money into their contracts to support living wage jobs. In the public sector, campaigners have argued that taxation should not be used to support poor quality jobs, with all that it implies for service standards and community welfare. In the private sector, campaigners have used the media to threaten the reputation of brand name companies to demand that they improve the conditions of work (see Wills, 2004; Holgate and Wills, 2007).

Wherever possible, the relevant trade union, UNISON in the public sector and the T&G in the private sector, has organised in the workplace whilst London Citizens has targeted the employers, media and politicians. The campaign has turned trade union issues into community concerns, arguing that low pay is an issue for the whole community. Thousands of workers have won living wages and improved conditions of work, and many have been brought into trade union membership. Perhaps just as importantly, however, the broad-based coalition has gone on to other campaigns, such as housing, public safety, youth education and the rights of irregular migrant workers. Through working with London Citizens at pan-urban and extra-workplace dimensions, then, trade unions have been able to act on a wider range of concerns than would have been possible had they adopted more traditional workplace-focused organising strategies.

Conclusions

This chapter has outlined the array of geographical challenges that trade unions currently face. Not only has capital spread across national boundaries, but vertical disintegration has greatly complicated traditional lines of authority and accountability, a process which is observable in both the private and public sector. These arrangements not only obscure the 'real' employers but also protect them from union-organising efforts. In order to navigate the increasingly complex catacombs of employer power, unions need creative new strategies that fundamentally reconstitute the geography of their practices.

As we have seen throughout this chapter, the process of geographical reconstitution is well under way. The material presented here suggests that there are four impor-tant dimensions of the new geographical strategies being developed by trade union organisations. First, many unions have engaged in a strategic emphasis on power analysis to identify the key trends and geographical patterns of each sector of capital. Second, they have developed zonal strategies that seek to intervene and regulate capital in particular areas, and also at key political-economic nodes such as global cities and transportation hubs. Third, they have explored efforts to develop leveraging strategies that project trade union power from stronger to weaker spheres of union organisation. Finally, they have engaged in constructing alliances with non-union groups.

The complexity of contemporary employment relationships, then, requires careful analysis of where power lies. As we have seen in this chapter, in conditions of sub-contracted employment the workers' direct employer rarely has the most influence over his or her terms of employment. Thus, as subcontracting becomes increasingly paradigmatic, trade unions need to rethink the geography of their organisation. Living wage campaigns, for example, have focused on the clients of contract cleaners as well as the key contracting companies, and the same needs to be done in other services and the manufacturing sector. However, a strategic power analysis would also need to look at the global extent of a company or economic activity, the relationships involved, and other important groups of workers involved in any supply chain. This latter is important for, as intimated here, logistics workers are particularly significant in moving goods around within supply chains, making them critical to the lubrication of the global economy itself.

Trade unions are beginning to recognise that one way of tackling these new global networks of subcontracted employment relationships is to organise for zonal agreements at particularly strategic political and economic nodes, such as urban districts, urban conurbations or transportation hubs. By first constructing and then regulating particular labour markets, say, for contract cleaners in London, a union can realise the traditional union goal of taking wages out of competition across the majority of key employers. As unions increasingly confront transnational employers in this manner, their ability to project their influence from stronger to weaker spheres of organisation will be of much greater significance. Inasmuch as new urban strategies are important, not all cities are created equal, and workers in strategic cities for particular industries such as New York (finance) or Stockholm (property services) may be able to mobilise their power to support workers elsewhere whereas workers in other cities may not. Trade unions thus need international union structures that are able to transmit a sense of common interest across a terrain that is currently very fragmented. However, as we saw in the case of logistics, the multiplicity of unions that currently have a stake in the sector is slowing down the formulation of a coherent global strategy. In response, the SEIU's vision for, for instance, property services involves ceding unprecedented levels of authority to the GUF which operates in this industry (the UNI) so that it might avoid some of this fractionalisation by operating at a higher, pan-union scale and providing it with an independent source of income for such campaigning.

Lastly, unions need to build a broad base of support for their aims at whatever scale they are operating. As we saw in the case of living wage campaigns, cities provide fertile territory for alliances between unions and other civil society groups, particularly faith groups, around issues that cast a wide moral appeal. The same is true at a transnational scale over alliances around fair trade and corporate social responsibility. In this regard, trade unions are at the early stages of developing new geographical imaginaries, strategies and the capacity to match the changing spatial architecture of capitalism. The next few years will be critical as such developments begin to take hold.

Acknowledgement

This research is based on a number of different research projects. Jeremy Anderson was funded by TEC New Zealand to undertake Ph.D. research into new forms of transnational union organising. Paula Hamilton is an ESRC CASE student working with the International Transport Workers' Federation. Jane Wills had ESRC funding as part of the ESRC Identities and Social Action programme for a project entitled 'Work, identity and new forms of political mobilisation: an assessment of broad-based organising and London's living wage campaign'.

Notes

1. This section concentrates on the UK context. However, it broadly resonates with the rise and decline of union movements elsewhere, particularly in the anglophone world.
2. The SEIU was not the first union to use transnational leveraging strategies. For example, Juravich and Bronfenbrenner (1999) and Herod (2001) outline the highly sophisticated campaign run by the United Steelworkers of America against the shadowy international financier Marc Rich to secure the reinstatement of locked-out workers in West Virginia. However, what is notable here is that the SEIU is now extending strategies from its own experience in proactive, as opposed to primarily defensive, campaigns.
3. The T&G has now merged to form Unite the Union. However, in this chapter it is still referred to as the T&G, as the dynamics relate specifically to this element of the merged union.
4. Over the next decade, the period 2004–2008 may come to represent the high watermark of the SEIU's internationalism. Although the strategy bequeathed the union some major industrial successes and a much boosted profile in the global union movement, the election of Barack Obama in 2008 was a potential landmark of its own and suffused the national outlook with new hope.
5. In some cases, DHL directly employs workers in logistics, but in others it relies on contractors.

Interviews

Lerner, Stephen: Director, Property Services Division, Service Employees' International Union, interviewed June, 2006, Washington DC, US.
Stewart, Emily: Director, Public Services Division, Service Employees' International Union, interviewed June, 2006, Washington DC, US.
Williams, Grant: Global Partnerships Strategist, Service Employees' International Union, interviewed January, 2006, London, UK.

References

Anderson, J. (2009), 'Labour's lines of flight: rethinking the vulnerabilities of transnational capital', *Geoforum*, **40** (6), 959–68.
Charlwood, A. (2002), 'Why do non-union employees want to unionize?', *British Journal of Industrial Relations*, **40** (3), 463–91.
Cully, M., S. Woodland, A. O'Reilly and G. Dix (1999), *Britain at Work: As Depicted by the 1998 Workplace Employee Relations Survey*, London: Routledge.
Fine, J. (2005), 'Community unions and the revival of the American labor movement', *Politics and Society*, **33** (1), 153–99.
Gordon, J. (2001), 'Organizing low wage immigrants – the workplace project, Interview with Jennifer Gordon', *Working USA*, **5** (1), 87–102.
Hale, A. and J. Wills (eds) (2005), *Threads of Labour: Garment Industry Supply Chains from the Workers' Perspective*, Oxford: Blackwell.
Herod, A. (2001), 'Labor internationalism and the contradictions of globalization: or, why the local is still important in the global economy', in P. Waterman and J. Wills (eds), *Place, Space, and the New Labour Internationalisms*, Oxford: Blackwell, pp. 103–22.
Holgate, J. and J. Wills (2007), 'Organizing labour in London: lessons from the campaign for a living wage',

in L. Turner and D.B. Cornfield (eds), *Labor in the New Urban Battlegrounds: Local Solidarity in a Global Economy*, Ithaca, NY: Cornell University Press, pp. 211–33.

Hum, S.H. (2000), 'A Hayes-Wheelwright framework approach for strategic management of third party logistics services', *Integrated Manufacturing Systems*, **11** (2), 132–7.

ITF (International Transport Workers' Federation) (2002), 'Resolutions of the 40th Congress of the ITF', London: ITF, available at http://www.itfglobal.org/about-us/40thcongress-res.cfm#5.

Jamoul, L. and J. Wills (2008), 'Faith in politics', *Urban Studies,* **45** (10), 2035–56.

Juravich, T. and K. Bronfenbrenner (1999), *Ravenswood: The Steelworkers' Victory and the Revival of American Labor*, Ithaca, NY: Cornell University Press.

Kuehne and Nagel (2006), *Annual Report 2005*, Schindellegi, Switzerland: Kuehne and Nagel International.

May, J., J.Wills, K. Datta, Y. Evans, J. Herbert and C. McIlwaine (2007), 'Keeping London working: global cities, the British state, and London's new migrant division of labour', *Transactions of the Institute of British Geographers*, New Series, **32** (2), 151–67.

Meyerson, H. (2005), 'Globalism for the rest of us', *The American Prospect*, 30 August, available at http://www.prospect.org (last accessed April 2008).

Millward, N., A. Bryson and J. Forth (2000), *All Change at Work? British Employment Relations 1980–1998 as Portrayed by the Workplace Industrial Relations Survey Series*, London: Routledge.

Pastor, M. (2001), 'Common ground and ground zero? The new economy and the new organising in Los Angeles', *Antipode*, **33** (2), 259–88.

Rowbothom, S. and S. Mitter (eds) (1994), *Dignity and Daily Bread: New Forms of Economic Organising Among Poor Women in the Third World and the First*, London: Routledge.

Tattersall, A. (2006), 'What union–community coalitions tell us about effective global union collaboration. Exploring the potential of the SEIU Global Partnerships Unit', paper presented to 'Global Companies, Global Campaigns, Global Unions, Global Research' Conference, Cornell University, New York, 9–11 February.

Terry, M. (1995), 'Trade unions: shop stewards and the workplace', in P. Edwards (ed.), *Industrial Relations: Theory and Practice in Britain*, Oxford: Blackwell Business, pp. 203–28.

Waterman, P. and J. Wills (eds) (2001), *Place, Space and the New Labour Internationalisms*, Oxford: Blackwell.

WEF (World Economic Forum) (2004), 'Logistics and transportation corporate citizenship initiative draft working document', 30 August, Geneva, Switzerland.

Wills, J. (2004), 'Organizing the low paid: East London's living wage campaign as a vehicle for change', in G. Healy, E. Heery, P. Taylor and W. Brown (eds), *The Future of Worker Representation*, Basingstoke: Palgrave Macmillan, pp. 264–82.

Wills, J., K. Datta, Y. Evans, J. Herbert, J. May and C. McIlwaine (2010), *Global Cities at Work: New Migrant Divisions of Labour*, London: Pluto Press.

22 Working space and the New Labour Internationalism

Rob Lambert and Michael Gillan

Introduction: defining space

> The problem of the proper conceptualization of space is resolved through human practice. . . .
> (Harvey, 2006, p. 275)

Our focus in this chapter is the challenge of constructing a New Labour Internationalism (NLI), one which aims at empowering workers to assert social needs over market logic. Such a type of internationalism, we would suggest, contrasts markedly with tendencies in the widely practised and long-standing model of Existing Labour Internationalism (ELI), whose essence Dan Gallin (2006, p. 4) has summarised thus:

> We do have an international trade union movement, such as it is. It has no vision, and it does not inspire anyone. Its principal organization, the ICFTU [International Confederation of Free Trade Unions, now the International Trade Union Confederation (ITUC)], has been mired for decades in lobbying activities in international institutions controlled by transnational capital. Despite the obvious failure of such activities to make any significant impact on the ground, there is no sign of a change in perspective. What we have here is an ideology of global 'social partnership'.

The NLI, then, is distinguished from this extant model through its leadership style, politics, global networked movement orientation, the framing of action and its self-conscious efforts to actively produce the global geography of capitalism in new and different ways than heretofore.

For their part, the terms NLI and ELI can be understood as providing an evaluative conceptual framework for positioning international labour movements and organisational practices according to a series of binary oppositions (hierarchy/bureaucracy versus democracy/participation; social partnership and accommodation to neoliberal restructuring versus struggle for an alternative political vision of society; career-orientated and institutionalised leadership versus political activism; workplace focus versus broader civil society movement orientation). Although such ideal-type opposites are clearly an example of dualistic thinking, their presentation as antithetical forms nevertheless does allow, we feel, for critical reflection on existing forms and practices of internationalism, even accepting that trade union internationalism is, in fact, positioned along a spectrum, and the lines between new and old forms are sometimes porous and often blurred, especially in situations where the old established patterns are currently being contested.

What we are focusing upon, then, is a process of organisational becoming and the spatialities that are implicated in such a process. Hence, rather than being fully in existence today, the NLI is currently in the process of being realised, with the result that its contested character is being shaped by intense and ongoing dialogue between labour movement scholars and activists as to its conceptualisation, embodiment and potential (Waterman, 2004, pp. 217–53). Conversely, the ELI with which we engage in this chapter refers to labour internationalism in its historically evolved institutional form and as represented in the shape of, for instance, the ITUC and various international union organisations like the Global Union Federations (GUFs), which have brought together unions operating in different economic sectors (transportation, metalworking, chemicals, and so forth) in numerous countries around the world. Given their historically central roles in efforts to develop international labour solidarity, the ITUC and GUFs have been important elements in the ELI because they aim to represent and support national union federations and/or local unions in specific sectors, have very well-defined organisational structures and have long-standing links to the formal trade union structures operating in various countries. Significantly, however, although they represent the more traditional approach to developing international solidarity, certain of them are also serving as arenas in which a degree of experimentation with the NLI is taking place (see Munck and Waterman, Chapter 15 in this volume).

The aspect of the NLI which we scrutinise here is its engagement in the deliberative production of new spatial relations and forms of spatial organisation as a source of power. As we have already articulated, such struggle and organisation grows out of an alternative vision of society. Given the centrality of space in shaping the character of the NLI, though, this key concept ('space') needs some clarification. Indeed, the multiple meanings of the term 'space' render it one of the most complicated words in the English language (Harvey, 2006, p. 270). In this vein, we want to take on board and engage with the double meaning of 'working space' that the editors of this *Handbook* have suggested with their subtitle. Thus, in the first sense the term 'working space' can be taken to mean the spaces within which work and employment relations literally take place – the spaces within which work is conducted and how these are shaped by various social actors. In the second sense, though, and the one in which we are really most interested here, the concept can be developed to theorise resistance by focusing upon how unions and other civil society movements attempt to (re)work space, that is to say how they seek to produce and actively structure space to re-empower labour. In this process the vital role of agency is evident, for these efforts generate a new consciousness and the opportunity to imagine and construct different sets of global spatial relations. Significantly, though, these actions also spawn internal struggles in which efforts to develop new models of organisation are pitted against the institutional inertia of national unionism and ELI.

In short, 'working space' is about securing a new strategic direction and form of unionism, which is social movement and global in character, extending beyond the workplace and nation. These transformations, however, do not occur spontaneously but are the product of an intense, imaginative, collective labour, requiring commitment and resources. Filling out the detail of this organisational struggle to produce space, then, is our contribution to the labour geography literature, which, in our view, needs to further deepen its understanding of the new forms of labour organisation which are emerging and how these movements work space *in practice*. In exploring the constraints and the potential of this new direction, though, we feel it is important to keep in mind Lefebvre's ([1974] 1991) threefold formulation of space, for this exemplifies the complexity of the concept of 'space' and its production: i) 'spatial practices' (the practices through which specific places and spatial arrangements of social objects are produced materially); ii) 'representations of space' (the various images of space as presented, for instance, in the theories and depictions of space put forward by spatial planners – in other words, how space is conceived of in social thought); and iii) 'spaces of representation' (the spaces in which social actors live, shaped by symbols and associated spatial images – in other words, the world as it is experienced spatially and geographically signified by social actors).[1]

Before proceeding, however, it is appropriate to observe that this tripartite division identified by Lefebvre is rendered exceedingly complex by the class conflicts through which space is produced to consolidate power and realise material interests. Thus, not only might different social groups – capitalists and workers – seek to make the material spaces of capitalism differently, but they may also have quite different ideas about the appropriate representation of space. Hence, those articulating a neoliberal set of interests for capital invariably lay out 'powerful imaginations of space . . . a vision of total unfettered mobility, of free unbounded space' (Massey, [2005] 2007, pp. 81, 87) wherein manufacturing and finance capital are spatially liberated from state regulation. This ideology, which asserts the right to corporate geographic freedom/mobility, claims to generate comparative advantage and economies of scale efficiencies through unimpeded ability to relocate to take advantage of investment opportunities and product markets anywhere across the globe. Harvey (2000, p. 24) characterises this process as the creation of a particular type of 'spatial fix', which he defines as the attempt to resolve the internal contradictions of capital accumulation spatially through the relocation of investment. In related fashion, Silver (2003, p. 39) argues that this neoliberal spatial vision sees the landscape as one in which there should be a 'successive geographical relocation of capital' as capital should always be free to leave for regions of the highest possible return, regardless of the social consequences thereof. Neoliberal theorists, then, contend that such a policy of facilitating unfettered spatial mobility is a potent force to realise the general interests of society, as this corporate spatial dynamic, represented as facilitating 'global competition' as capital seeks out locations of higher return, they claim, creates jobs, generates income and promotes individual freedom.[2]

Others, though, see such geographical mobility in quite different terms, a fact which produces an alternative analysis of these changes and their power geometries (Lambert, 1999, 2004; Lambert and Gillan, 2007; Webster et al., 2008). For such analysts, corporate power within these unbounded spatial configurations has consolidated to such a degree that restructuring (factory closures and geographic shifts) appears irreversible, and not for the better. Furthermore, the human impacts of these changes are compounded by work restructuring in the form of intensification (longer hours and faster pace), outsourcing and casualisation (Moody, 1997; Webster et al., 2008). Much of the work on these issues in this latter vein – and certainly our own – has been informed by Polanyi's ([1944] 2001) *Great Transformation*, which critiques the idea of the self-regulating market and analyses movement responses to it. Within this theoretical frame, then, we pose the following questions: how can workers challenge the new corporate spatial fixes that are emerging as corporations increasingly criss-cross the globe with their investments? What role might space play in constructing such opposition? And what are the problems of organising internationally so as to realise these goals, that is to say to produce new material geographies of the global economy? These questions cannot be answered, we would aver, outside of an engagement with the contested meanings of what an appropriate economic landscape is – is it one of immense deregulation in which capital is free to flow pretty much anywhere almost at the drop of a hat or is it one in which capital's geographical mobility and ability to play workers in different places against each other are/should be limited?

The issue of the uneven growth of a NLI is at the centre of our response to these questions. The argument is developed thus. First, we explore some of capital's efforts to develop a spatial fix appropriate to its condition at the present given time, as the ability to impose this spatial fix provides the framework within which workers' movements must struggle. In particular, through briefly analysing the changing relationship between finance capital and the dynamics of manufacturing, we sketch the context driving NLI initiatives detailed later in the chapter. Second, we situate the NLI within Polanyi's conception of the counter movement, whilst also critiquing his undifferentiated conception of society and the absence of agency or a consideration of spatialised thinking in his movement theory. The third section of this chapter focuses on the realm of the spatial imagination as we present a model demonstrating how a NLI could relate to the existing structures of labour internationalism and perhaps even transform these practices. Here we draw on labour geography's notions of agency (Herod, 2001) and show how an activist leadership style is critical to the emergence of a NLI. In this section we show also how a fairly sophisticated theorisation of space – as with regard, for instance, to the spatial hierarchies of organisation – is crucial to building a NLI. This exercise in exploring the spatial imagination is meant to stimulate debate rather than to assert the superiority of any singular organisational pathway, for unless such a debate enters the organising worlds of national unions, their powerlessness before the forces we identify will remain. The fourth part presents an insight into the real world of organisational struggle through analysing an experiment in the NLI, which works space as a new source of power. Finally, we contemplate what the efforts to structure the geography of the global economy in new and different ways may mean for workers in the future.

Capital's spatial fix

> Global space, as space more generally, is a product of material practices of power. . . . What is at issue are the constantly-being-produced new geometries of power, the shifting geographies of power relations. . . . (Massey, [2005] 2007, p. 85)

In proclaiming the removal of barriers to competition on a global scale as being the pathway to efficiency, lower prices and economic growth, neoliberal policy obscures how changes to market regulation accelerate acquisitions and mergers, resulting in a high concentration of corporate power, the erosion of competition, democracy and state sovereignty (Leys, 2003). This restructuring is the outcome of capital accumulation propelled by intense competition between private corporations where 'one capitalist always strikes down many others' (Marx, [1867] 1976a, p. 929). Such a competitive war between private companies is the 'driving fire' of the rationalisation of production (Marx, [1894] 1976b, p. 254), which results in the expropriation of the many by the few.

A historical geographical overview reveals a spatial competitive dynamic to this process, which creates and destroys productive forces. The accumulation of capital is indeed a 'profoundly geographic affair' where spatial reorganisation, which exploits uneven geographic development, is the defining feature of competition (Harvey, 2000,

p. 57). In this a clear geographic pattern emerges, one marked by factory closures and relocations. For instance, in North America, substantial sections of manufacturing have moved southward to Mexico and across the Pacific to China; in Europe, there has been an eastward drive into Central Europe (see Pickles and Smith, Chapter 6 in this volume); in Asia, a movement from Korea and Japan to China (see Pun and Smith, Chapter 13 in this volume); and in Australia, a movement to China and Thailand. The magnet in each of these restructurings is the absence of effective independent unionism and the uneven geographical strength of labourers.

In analysing these global dynamics there is certainly a need for a more integrated view of the relationship between financial capital and manufacturing capital (Harvey, [1982] 1999, p. 326). This is especially so because efforts to resolve the internal contradictions of capital accumulation through the creation of new spatial fixes seem to be proceeding with ever greater intensity as a consequence of transformations in this relationship and the apparent speeding up of capital mobility and restructuring. Indeed, particular forms of finance capital – hedge funds and private equity – are accelerating corporate manufacturing restructuring for short-term financial gain to such a degree that even leading conservative market analysts conclude that these institutions are bringing the legitimacy of capitalism into question.[3] Part of the reason that these developments are occurring, though, relates to the fact that even though advocates of neoliberal globalisation seek to minimize rules pertaining to publicly listed corporations, it always seems that there is yet another round of 'deregulation' that can take place, such that any regulations on capital mobility are deemed unacceptable.[4] In this context, private equity companies have been established 'to conduct their business outside of the rules' that apply to publicly listed corporations (Stevens, 2006, p. 1), a fact that is important because these entities now play a pivotal role in globalisation, becoming 'the lubricants of global capitalism', with their core strategy being to acquire corporations, restructure through 'savage cost cutting to boost returns' and then sell them at a profit (Toohey, 2006, p. 17) – to give but one example, in Australia alone, between June and December 2006, private equity firms bought out A$30 billion worth of Australian companies (Stevens, 2006, p. 1).

Whilst hedge and private equity funds claim to be innovators in today's global economy, driven by a philosophy of 'buy it, strip it and flip it', even free market analysts fear their destabilising potential. In 2006 there were nearly 7000 international acquisition and merger transactions worth an estimated US$880 billion. Of these, 172 so-called 'mega' international acquisition and merger deals accounted for an astonishing estimated two-thirds of the value of all such transactions (UNCTAD, 2007, p. xv). Private equity firms, which accounted for some US$158 billion of acquisition and merger deals in 2006 (UNCTAD, 2007, p. xvi), have been at the forefront of accelerating corporate concentration. These forces continue to drive the prominence of TNCs in the global economy, with some 78 000 corporations expanding their production and sales to account for one-third of global exports and 10 per cent of global GDP (UNCTAD, 2007, p. xvi). Notably, with regard to aggregate employment, China has the largest number of workers in TNCs (24 million), whereas in the United States TNC affiliate employment reduced by 500 000 jobs between 2001 and 2004 (to a total of 5.1 million).

Growth in the size and power of these corporations gives them the capacity to transform politics and the state (Leys, 2003, pp. 15–19). This power arises out of their considerable financial leverage, which provides them with negotiating resources that frequently outstrip those of nation states. These companies invest enormous resources in information technology, giving them a marked communications advantage over many states. As a result, they are powerful lobbyists with often-instant access to government leaders. This corporate dominance of the state and political parties (conservative and social democrat) has led 'to a remarkably rapid erosion of democratically-determined collective values and institutions . . . what is happening is incompatible with democracy – and in the long run, with civilised life' (Leys, 2003, pp. 4–5). The result, Leys (p. 6) observes, is that 'party politics and state-policy making are themselves now more power-fully market-driven and less and less likely to defend, let alone renew and revitalise, the prerequisites of democracy [and w]e need to understand this in order to develop an effective alternative politics'.

This concentration of corporate power, erosion of democracy and the creation of new globally orientated corporate spatial fixes in which firms are establishing branches in numerous places across the planet – in other words, in which they are spreading their geographical wings by becoming increasingly transnational – are the objective condi-tions determining the organisational character and spatial engagement of the NLI. From a labour movement perspective, though, the restructuring is contradictory. On the one hand, every enterprise closure and downsizing disorganises the local power base of unionism, as workers are spun out of production, with unions seldom moving beyond simply seeking redundancy packages. On the other hand, the changes are indicative of a dire need for unions to discover a NLI and new spatial strategies to challenge this logic. This is important, for failure to imagine and then to organise alternative responses will accelerate the demise of nation state-centred unionism. A crucial step in building a NLI, then, is stimulating a new discourse on markets and what the economic geography of the global economy should look like, a discourse which challenges the neoliberal paradigm's claims.

Creating a discourse that effectively challenges that of the neoliberal spatial imagina-tion is imperative, we would argue, for the discursive moment is 'a form of power, . . . a mode of formation of ideas and beliefs' (Harvey, 1996, p. 83). Ideas and beliefs that are alternative to the market discourse are thus essential to construct a labour movement response. Such a response is the defining characteristic of the NLI, for movements only arise when there is a clear alternative vision (Touraine et al., 1987). Hence, as Sassoon (1996, p. 7) has argued,

> [t]hose who define, create. 'Democratic' politics, that is, modern mass politics, is a battlefield in which the most important move is that which decides what the battle is about, what the issue is. To be able to define the contending parties, name them and thus establish where the barricades should go up, or where the trenches should be dug, gives one a powerful and at times decisive advantage. This is what all the major movements for social change have had to do.

Having briefly empirically explored how corporations are wiring the global economy together in new and different ways within a discourse that seems to laud the power and righteousness of the market, we now analyse Polanyi's conceptualisation of the rela-tionship between markets and society and suggest that his work on counter movements has some bearing upon understanding the issues which trigger a NLI response to such economic (and geographical) restructuring.

Markets and society

Neoliberal proponents' representation of space centres on widening economic opportunity in the 'general interest' through the ability to freely seek new vistas of investment, regardless of the social costs felt by those in communities and labour forces that are suddenly abandoned by relocating capital. Continuous spatial restructuring, so the argument goes, maintains a competitive edge to secure wealth production, jobs and social progress. Responding to free market ideology on its own terms, then, is self-limiting, for the terms of the debate are set up in such a way that the logic of allowing capital ultimate spatial freedom of movement is really the only rational outcome achievable once the initial premises have been accepted. In contrast, Polanyi ([1944] 2001) does not accept the arguments of the logic of the free marketeers, and seeks, instead, to understand markets within a discursive frame that explores the dynamic between markets, society and nature. He concludes that the market project is utopian and cannot 'exist for any length of time without annihilating the human and natural substance of society' ([1944] 2001, pp. 3–4). This occurs because the idea of the self-regulating market is a 'system of crude fictions', regarding persons and the Earth as commodities, even though they are 'obviously *not* commodities' ([1944] 2001, pp. 75, 76, emphasis in the original).

For Polanyi ([1944] 2001, pp. 75, 76), then, the market mechanism should not be 'the sole director of the fate of human beings', for this has the potential to 'demolish society' through treating persons as though they were simply a commodity to be 'disposed of' by the market, in accordance with its needs and without proper recognition of 'the physical, psychological and moral' dimensions of being a person. Such a position had been articulated a century earlier by Marx ([1961] 1966, p. 93), in his 'Economic and philosophical manuscripts', when he stated that: 'the worker sinks to the level of the commodity, and to a most miserable commodity . . . the misery of the worker increases with the power and the volume of his production' and this is 'a necessary result of competition . . . the accumulation of capital in a few hands'. According to Marx, then, the devaluation of the human world increases in direct relation to the increase in the value of the world of things, for labour not only creates goods but it also produces itself as a commodity (Marx, [1961] 1966, p. 95), such that 'definite social relations between persons' assume 'the fantastic form of a relation between things' (Marx, [1867] 1976a, p. 165). This fetishism of the commodity identified by Marx, in which the social relations between persons are seen to be relations between things, is something also explored by Polanyi. Indeed, Polanyi argues that the history of the nineteenth and twentieth centuries reveals that a pendulum-like movement arises in response to the thing-like status imposed on persons. Hence, in nineteenth-century Britain an active society arose, taking the form of trade unions, cooperatives, the organisation of the factory movement to curtail the length of the working day, the Chartist movement to extend political rights and the rudimentary development of political parties (Burawoy, 2003, p. 198). The paramount challenge of the twenty-first century, then, is to imagine and construct a global counter-movement with the power to challenge the resurgence of market relations.

Although we accept Polanyi's critique of the ideology of the 'free market', there are, however, several problems inherent in his theorisation of the rise of counter-movements (see Webster et al., 2008, pp. 5–17). These include his failure to adequately define society, his implicit notion that movements arise spontaneously, the absence of a concept of power in his work and, finally, the need to consider the question of space and scale. These latter lacunae are addressed in the following section, where we contend that the NLI is a vital component of a counter-movement, for given the global reach of corporations and markets, the predicaments faced by localities (for example, factory closures and relocations) can only be challenged through globalising local resistance. The unique characteristics of the NLI, however, grounded as it is in a movement-orientated local unionism, can transform, we suggest, commodification through the movement-building process, thereby empowering the local as a springboard to the production of new spatial relations, which deepen and extend the power of networked places. As the following sections will show, there is no phoenix-like spontaneity or inevitability to the emergence of such a movement, only political will, vision, imagination, commitment and intense struggle – a long battle against enormous odds.

Spatial imagination

> What I am interested in is how we might imagine spaces for these times; how we might pursue an alternative imagination. . . . How easy it is to slip into ways of thinking that repress the challenge of space; and how politically significant spatial imaginaries can be. (Massey, [2005] 2007, p. 13)

Neoliberal theorists' imagination of global space defines the battleground. Challenging this model is a Herculean task, given the hegemony of these ideas, the consolidation of power and the popularised notion that there is no viable alternative. Gallin (2006) is right – there is scant hope of a serious challenge from the representatives of ELI, given their eschewal of organised resistance in favour of lobbying in the corridors of power, except where the ideas of the NLI are penetrating these structures through intense contestation and internal struggle.[5] An activist NLI with the political will and geographic imagination to confront neoliberalism's geometry of power, then, is a crucial development.

Examples of the emergence of the NLI as a force are the formation of The Southern Initiative on Globalisation and Trade Union Rights (SIGTUR) in 1991 and the creation of the Mining and Maritime Global Initiative (MAMGI) in 2005. SIGTUR is a networked social movement of democratic unions in 20 countries in the global South, spanning Latin America, Africa, Asia and Australasia. The spatial connection across the South is innovative because it links movements with a common history of resistance, in contrast to the passive, bureaucratised North–South model of the ITUC. This history of confrontation with anti-democratic, authoritarian states produced an imaginative engagement with space as unions searched for empowerment through civil society (Seidman, 1994). Another feature is their adoption of an organisational model of radical internal democracy and worker control through leadership mandates and systems of accountability.[6] This creates participation, which further empowers through transforming the commodity status of workers within the movement.

SIGTUR and MAMGI reinforce this thrust through replicating the democratic model in the construction of a NLI. The biannual Congresses of SIGTUR are open, participatory, week-long, live-in events based on workshop commissions and plenary discussions leading to realisable action statements rather than the standard format of ELI, which are, apart from some notable exceptions, structured around speeches and pre-ordained resolutions, which inevitably lead to thin participation. The NLI style further consolidates the de-commodification of workers, for they are taken seriously within these structures as persons with capacities and valuable experiences to share. They are given voice and they come to realise that they are indeed the architects of a new future. In contrast to ELI, the non-hierarchical, flat, open form of a networked NLI maximizes grassroots participation, which leads to the discovery of a full humanity.[7] Such a discovery is never a finally achieved outcome, since union activists experience commodification daily in their workplaces. However, the counter-experience of recognition, of a different sense of self, has potential to reinforce movement engagement as the individual struggles to overcome these interior tensions. MAMGI has created a similar style and culture.

Massey ([2005] 2007, p. 7) observes just how little space is thought about explicitly in organising. By way of contrast, the NLI explicitly imagines spatial relations as a new source of power and is grappling with the organisational issues surrounding the production of space. Consequently, SIGTUR has unequivocally formulated a conception of space as an opportunity for developing new forms of solidarity action grounded in local place, whilst simultaneously transcending the local through globally networked spatial connections with other local places within the same global corporation. Whilst space is generally not thought about explicitly, meaning that a consciousness of space does not arise spontaneously, movements have a pivotal role in developing such awareness. In contrast to institutionally patterned organisations, movements are, in essence, fluid upsurges of persons united in collective action to challenge specific issues and roles imposed on them by social institutions (Castells 1978, 1983; Touraine et al., 1983, Touraine et al., 1987; McAdam et al., 1996; Tarrow, 1998). Since collective action creates a movement, movements therefore are the form through which space can be produced. Lefebvre's threefold conception (material space/representation of space/spaces of representation) provides an insight into this potential.

Material or absolute space is the space of experience and is fixed and bounded. This is the space of private property or other bounded territorial designations. Movements are constructed within these material spaces. Prior to being formally organised, though, workers are connected with each other through a myriad of informal group relationships (Baritz, 1960). However, within this space, market forces strive to produce individualised and commoditised social relations and the fundamental aim of movement building within corporations is to ground organisation in existing informal networks as a base for collective action, which produces a new spatial dynamic through representing (framing) space as a medium for solidarity relations and organising to produce space in this way. As an independent and democratic force within the corporation, unions create spaces of representation where workers collectively express their emotions, their imagination and aspirations for security, material well-being and human dignity as 'repertoires of contention', which create a new sense of social identity (Tarrow, 1998, pp. 20, 21).

Historically, the dynamic of unionism is to link the bounded spaces of workplaces, creating a movement within the nation state. Such a process aims to pressure the state into recognising and institutionalising organising and bargaining rights at a national level. Within this model, international unionism has evolved as a bureaucratic connection of these national entities in which the notion of working space is absent. However, neoliberalism's geometry of power has led to a new spatial imagination as unions search for empowerment, firstly through constructing local and national relations with civil society movements and, secondly, through the attempts to link workers globally within the same corporation. Before proceeding to the final section, which will consider the practical opportunities and constraints in the shift towards working space, a strategic issue needs to be addressed.

From the movement's formation in 1991, SIGTUR never defined itself as an *alternative* to established labour internationalism, even though some within the ITUC viewed the initiative as a surrogate of the World Federation of Trade Unions (WFTU) in the global South.[8] As a networked movement, SIGTUR's sole purpose is to engage ELI through spatial experiments connecting workers across the global South and linking north–south within global corporations. Foregrounding such a strategic commitment might seem at variance with the critique of the orientation of ELI articulated throughout this chapter. However, at this point in the argument, we wish to add a layer of complexity to the relationship between the old and the new by contending that there are struggles for renewal within established structures. Through SIGTUR's engagement with certain GUFs in the fight against the restructuring of specific global corporations, these internal contradictions of ELI are likely to be exacerbated. This is reflected in ongoing internal struggles within certain GUFs for and against working space – that is to say, for and against creating new spatial relationships between various parts of the globe. The most creative leaders in these battles to transform labour internationalism do not envisage impregnable barricades between the established and the new but, rather, a transformation of the old by the new. Hence, as Paddy Crumlin (2008), Vice President of the International Transport Workers' Federation GUF and General Secretary of the Maritime Union of Australia (MUA), has argued:

> [t]his is our time, not a time of the past but a time of the future, a time of reaching out in practical action. Labour internationalism has to learn – don't say the words but do the deeds. GUFs have to discover how to act, how to build and organise, how to nurture and engage on the ground, they have to move beyond their bureaucratic and Euro-centric past.
> We have to move to a point where the different facets of labour internationalism are indistinguishable. We have to develop a holistic approach.[9]

The established labour movement at national and international levels, then, faces a moment of critical choice in which key contradictions need to be confronted and resolved if the concentration of corporate power is to be challenged. We now map these choices.

As can be seen from the summary in Table 22.1, the distinctions in orientation between ELI and the NLI have the potential to dissolve most tellingly on the question of new forms of action, although most of the established formations have, to date, remained fairly conservative in their choice of action, eschewing the more radical pathway. However, as indicated, there are notable exceptions within certain GUFs, where some are ready to test new boundaries, thereby displaying characteristics of the NLI as they struggle against corporate power. For example, going back several decades, the International Union of Food Workers (IUF), under the leadership of Dan Gallin and now Ron Oswald, has always been committed to an action-orientated internationalism, the promotion of genuine democratic unions, and a socialist politics that is at once deeply democratic. Through the IUF Gallin led a remarkable global action campaign against Coca Cola in Guatemala. Similarly, the International Metalworkers' Federation (IMF), with the involvement of exceptional leaders such as Julius Rowe and others, and the Union Network International (UNI) have also developed new style campaigning, not to mention the bold endeavours of the Service Employees' International Union (SEIU).

Table 22.1   Strategic choice for space

	ELI	NLI
Political Orientation	Social Democratic: acceptance of market economy + social programmes; Social partnerships with corporations; Negotiating Global Framework Agreements (GFA)	Social regulation & democratic control of corporations; global unionism; challenging the character of corporations; the logic of finance capital, captive states, global governance. A society against market-driven politics through democratic control. Supportive of GFAs.
Organisational form/ Leadership style	Traditional national trade unionism; hierarchical, centralised control systems; career bureaucrats in leadership positions; leadership institutionally groomed & constrained by past historical practice; risk averse; present at the World Social Forum (WSF), but not engaged in formulating a new movement style	Social movement orientation; horizontal linkages into the community; global in orientation, working space within corporations; engaged with WSF to a degree; networked, flat, non-bureaucratic orientation; activist, deeply committed leadership; experimental; risk takers.
Collective Spatial Action Grounded in Local Place	Forms of action constrained and shaped by social partnership model and a degree of integration into the management structure of corporations; influenced by postwar European social compacts. Negotiations on Global Framework Agreements to secure union rights in corporations; promoting global unionism and initiating capital committees; at this point, has not yet considered working space in new ways. However, the IUF and the ITF, in particular, are actively searching for ways to work space. Service Employees' International Union (SEIU) is another instance of a more radical and experimental engagement with working space	Searching for new sources of power; testing the boundaries of logistical power – examining the arteries of the global economy to testing new forms of action; establishing capital committees to pressure corporations; committed to building global unionism, working space through networking scale.

Crumlin is working intensely within the ITF to shift the federation towards a NLI. These leaders are at the forefront of a struggle to re-invent labour internationalism, thereby creating new strategic possibilities.

The purpose of the distinctions made in the above classification is to open an important debate on the politics, organisational form and mode of action which will consolidate a counter-power to global corporations through movement action. However, there are significant constraints in ELI, which need to be reviewed if progress towards an effective global counter-movement is to be realised, for such a movement will only be empowered through synergies and consequent transformation as ELI and NLI interact in a common endeavour. The architecture of such a counter-movement, though, needs to be inclusive, bringing together a range of ideas and experiences into the project to transform the essential character of corporations, the state and politics.

However, this interface is not an exercise in trade union diplomacy nor should it be constrained by those sections of the movement seeking to protect narrow self-interest. The interface will only prosper if fundamental choices are considered and strategic decisions made. There are three basic choices that need to be confronted:

1. Is the leadership willing to commit to resisting the global corporations through working space, or are they integrated into corporate governance structures to such a degree that they are compromised, negotiating deals that fail to challenge the character of corporate restructuring, environmental degradation and the war machine?

2. Is the leadership looking to transform organisations into movements, which are fighting machines (coordinators of spatial resistance) with a real capacity to act, or is the political will absent, with the production of space dissolving into paper resolutions leaving no trace of action?

3. Is the leadership about imagining and committing to an alternative to neoliberal globalisation, or do they remain confined within the Social Democratic compromise of the developed North, which embraces market fundamentalism and the primacy of corporations over society, contending that this commitment provides the material base to sustain a social agenda?

These are not rhetorical questions. They are an exploration of the character of agency, so they are critical to the issue of whether or not space will be successfully fashioned in new ways by labour internationalism. As part of our imagining new spatial relations of resistance within corporations, we present diagrams (Figures 22.1 and 22.2) of a possible confluence between established ELI and a potential NLI. The first representation (Figure 22.1) captures ELI in its purest form, with its spatially hierarchical structure and its foundation in existing national trade union federations. The second, flatter, networked structure is grounded in the struggle to transform national into global unionism and to construct a counter-movement. The latter is based on the premise of a notable transformation of ELI along the lines indicated in Figure 22.2. This is a necessary struggle within these structures, the outcome of which will determine whether or not trade unions make the transition to a new form of global empowerment, the failure of which may signal the continued decline of unionism across the globe.

Compared to Figure 22.1, then, Figure 22.2 represents a vision of a new kind of movement with a fundamentally different geographical structure to it, one developed in the spirit of Harvey's (2000, p. 201) concept of 'thought experiments', which are our capacity to imagine what does not yet exist. Whilst those considering the constraints in shifting existing institutional patterns and the absence of imagination might view such a transition as utopian, there are indeed experiments and initiatives that could become the pressure points for a breakthrough in the spatial architecture of labour internationalism, which is a critical component of counter-movement power.

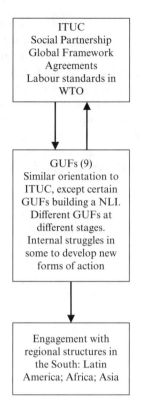

Figure 22.1   Existing Labour Internationalism (ELI): limited working of space

We now turn, then, to an analysis of one such initiative, which highlights both the opportunities and the constraints in the transition from these established patterns of organisation to new networked forms of movement and new forms of empowering action. We capture this through an analysis of the networking aspect of the global campaign against the Rio Tinto Corporation, revealing the extraordinary resource commitment required. In particular, we seek to ponder whether unions can sustain working space in this manner and what implications this resource allocation has for sustaining the local.

Geographies of resistance

> What is always at issue is the content, not the spatial form, of the relations through which space is constructed. (Massey, 2005 [2007], p. 101)

There is a chasm between spatial imagination and resistance, one which can only be bridged through human agency, through 'thinking outside of the box' and then committing to organisationally construct what does not exist.[10] In this final section, we analyse an initiative which strove to overcome the gulf between vision (imagination) and the production of a new geography of resistance (working space). Such resistance is a response to the spatial fix of corporations, which reveals the *content* of the production of new spatial relations by movements. These initiatives demonstrate the daunting nature of the task

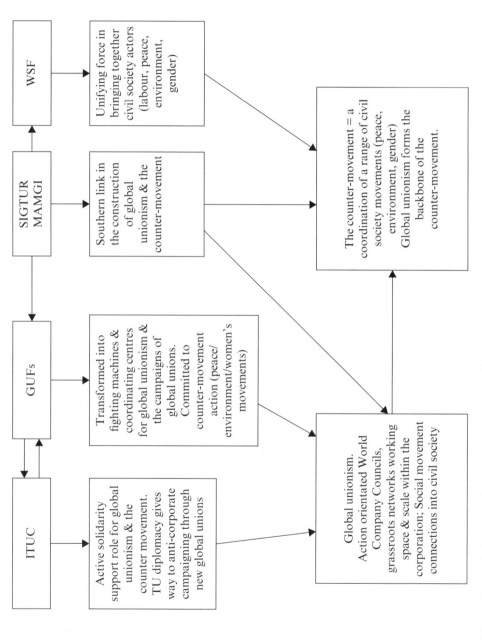

Figure 22.2 Networked New Labour Internationalism (NLI) producing spatial resistance

for it requires an intense organisational commitment that involves contradictory human and financial resource choices between local place, national and global engagements.

Addressing these organisational dilemmas is our contribution to labour geography as a field of study, one which needs to consider the content of these new spatial relations. In this we draw on Herod's conception of networking scale where the metaphor of spatial scale as a hierarchical ladder is challenged (Gibson-Graham, 2002; Latham, 2002; Herod and Wright, 2002; Herod, 2003a and 2003b; Sadler and Fagan, 2004). Thus, in the long-standing image of scale as a vertical ladder there is a notion of moving up or down the hierarchy of spatial scales, where the global is the highest rung and where each scale is seen to be a distinct rung (Herod, 2003b, p. 238), an image which implies empowerment when moving up the ladder (to the global scale) and disempowerment when moving down it (to the local scale). In contrast, a network metaphor suggests that the world of places is not conceived as bounded spaces, but as intertwined, networked together, connected in a single whole, 'simultaneously global and local (and regional and national) without being wholly one or the other' (Herod and Wright, 2002, p. 8).

We explore the organisational challenges of realising this model, which need to be further developed in the labour geography literature, through an analysis of a significant attempt to challenge the spatial fix of a global corporation. The global campaign against Rio Tinto, one of the world's largest mining corporations, is scrutinised because this union-led action is a fine illustration of the opportunities and organisational constraints in Herod's model of networking space.

Networking space

The campaign against the global mining corporation Rio Tinto illustrates the inherent contradictions in working space. Rio Tinto, with 60 operations in 40 countries, has attacked union rights and downsized continuously, creating workload and health and safety problems (Global Union Research Network, 2008).[11] In Australia, the Construction, Forestry, Mining and Energy Union (CFMEU) organised intense local struggles at Rio Tinto's mine sites to counter restructuring. Despite an extraordinary year-long strike in Northern Queensland, the company refused to negotiate, which led the CFMEU to conclude that local struggle alone was doomed. Hence, as Ric Fowler, the International Secretary of the CFMEU at the time, observed:

> [w]e had one site out on strike for one week short of a year, but Rio didn't budge. In fact they became more aggressive. Another site was on strike for six months, but Rio refused to negotiate. We had tried everything at a local site level and at a national level but we could no longer defeat the company. We had to look at other methods.[12]

The leadership then committed to networking scale, forming the Rio Tinto Global Union Network (RGUN), with the International Chemical, Energy and Mining Federation (ICEM) global union federation playing an important coordinating role. CFMEU and ICEM President John Maitland had worked intensely to transform the global entity from a passive bureaucratic structure into a 'fighting machine'.[13] ICEM demanded the corporation abide by core ILO Conventions, which protect worker rights through negotiating global agreements with effective monitoring mechanisms. The initiative is one of the most sophisticated engagements with scale the union movement has ever attempted and the following analysis, drawn from Fowler's reflections, reveals the content of working space and the demands such a project makes on organisational resources. The Rio Tinto experience also highlights the organisational stages in the process of constructing new spatial relations.

As we noted earlier, Massey ([2005] 2007, p. 7) observes that space is seldom thought about explicitly in union campaigns. Therefore, the first step in networking scale is to heighten the awareness of space and power. Hence, as Fowler put it:

> [i]f you are going to establish a global network, the union membership has to know what you are doing and why you are doing it. You cannot build and sustain a network without their support and without their knowledge. If they are not properly informed and engaged in the process, they immediately become skeptical and will question the whole initiative.

This is an educational process on the nature of corporate strategies (spatial fixes), which reveals why working space is critical. In this the union leadership had to:

> [l]earn from the membership. We had to learn not what they wanted, but what they were pre-pared to *fight* for. Given the power of these corporations, we needed to discover new methods of struggle, new pressure points – we needed to consider what weapons we had at our disposal. And so education was a two-way process – we put forward ideas as to the methods we thought might be effective and then we listened, we learned from them as to whether they were willing to take on the fight against the corporation in this form.

Research was a key component in this dialectic. The leadership deepened their knowl-edge of the corporation to share new ideas with the membership. Research focused on the following dimensions of corporate strategy: future investment plans (the geography of investment); the structure of its financing and shareholdings; movements in product market and the nature of competition in the sector; labour relations strategy in differ-ent sites across the globe; relationship with governments; the health and safety record at these different sites; and environmental impacts. Knowledge is indeed power, for it enables a definition of the terrain of struggle, exposing how corporations such as Rio Tinto exploit geographical difference in the evaluation of labour; for example, conced-ing health and safety standards at one geographic location and denying them at others. Fowler contended that geographical knowledge is 'the ammunition' at the disposal of the network, for such an initiative is created for resistance. Hence, he averred:

> [a]s the global network was patiently constructed through cyberspace linkage of local mine sites and as the consciousness-raising process progressed, a second phase was introduced when the leadership extended the network beyond the union and the workplace, linking with environ-mental and human rights organisations. The union framed Rio's attack on workers as a justice and human rights issue and they highlighted the corporation's degradation of the environment. RGUN constructed a broad-based, multi-faceted civil society movement where workers take solidarity action on issues beyond production, involving Amnesty International and various environmental groups.

Fowler continued:

> [w]e were able to show that a corporation that cares little about the damage it does to the envi-ronment is also one that is indifferent when they hurt the lives of workers and their families. Through this they become aware and committed to worker issues and they recognised the need for alliances to challenge Rio on each of these fronts. All of a sudden we had a very broad, a very wide network.

This broader social movement strategy proved more effective in pressuring Rio Tinto than strike action, which aimed at coercing Rio Tinto to come to the bargaining table by 'hurting the company financially'. Moreover, research revealed the company achieved between US$1.5 and $2 billion in profit annually, hence it could withstand strikes. Furthermore, in the case of the year-long coal strike in Australia, Rio Tinto simply exploited its geographical reach by producing more coal from its Indonesian, Canadian or Chilean mines. Research revealed that Rio Tinto is a 'cashed up company with little debt to banks or other lending institutions'. The union therefore sought to test stock market responses to challenges to Rio Tinto's public image. RGUN homed in on Rio Tinto's human rights abuses in their Brazilian mines, where company security agents shot and killed a peasant scavenging for gold in the tailings. The union succeeded in getting SBS, an Australian public television broadcaster, to produce a documentary on the incident. The global network also made an issue of the company's negative environmental impacts. At this point the RGUN opened another front to intensify the pressure when they created a global network of politicians linking the United Kingdom, the European Union and the US. This resulted in sympathetic politicians (for example an ex-miner in the UK parliament) speaking out against Rio Tinto's practices. These interventions hurt the company's public image, which was further corroded through the network's strategic participation in shareholder meetings, which widened the discourse from financial reporting to these justice and environmental questions.

A key feature of the network was a continuous mobilisation of the grassroots into action. This was important, as efforts to create new configurations of the capitalist space economy are doomed if they fail to activate union and other civil society movements at the local level, for members then become passive observers of the activities of a small leadership group. A number of opportunities for engagement were therefore created. Fowler observed:

> [c]ontinuous campaigning lay at the heart of our strategy. So, for example, our world meeting of leaders led to us organising a sticker day, with the slogans translated into different languages. We encouraged all the unionised workers in Rio Tinto mines, processing plants and wharves across the globe to wear the same sticker on the same day. This led to discussion at the local level and raised consciousness. We then upped the ante and had a week of action across the globe. We had to keep up the pressure; we had to keep moving forward, even when there was a lull in the conflict with the company. Even though there were periods when there were no disputes, you had to keep the network alive; you had to sustain it through action. We sustained this intensity over a five-year period.

The model of networking used was fundamental to involving the grassroots. As it turned out, RGUN experimented with two models – a centralised and a de-centralised network, represented in Figures 22.3 and 22.4 respectively. The Rio Tinto campaign utilised both models and viewed them as complementary. Fowler made the following assessment of the strengths of the more centralised form of networking: '[t]he strength of the centralised network is that you have a person controlling what is going out and so there is verification of what's going out. There are no wild exaggerations, no misleading information – the information has to be accurate'. Fundamental to this centralised dynamic was the production of a quarterly newsletter, which was distributed through the network and posted on the website. The newsletter identified where the corporation honoured collective agreements and where they denied rights, thereby creating a global social consciousness that transcended the limits of localism.

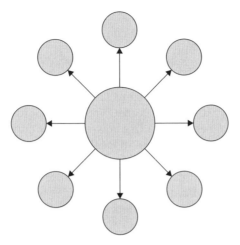

Figure 22.3   Centralised networking

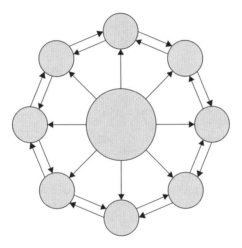

Figure 22.4   De-centralised networking

The second model stressed grassroots interaction between work sites, with the role of the centre defined as to stimulate debate and create global consciousness. As Fowler observed, '[t]he information goes around the network, there is no coordination. You send a message, they add to it, and as it goes around it develops beyond the original communication'. This model, however, made the union officials and organisers feel insecure, for:

> [t]here is no moderator in this process and its strength is that information circulates swiftly. A weakness of that is that quite a few union officials felt that they were not in the system. We have to build trust with workers to talk to workers, about anything, about general issues.

Another challenge to seeking to rework the geography of the global economy is to securely ground the network in each country. A global network does not spring to life spontaneously, nor can it simply be generated solely through the Internet (see Lee, Chapter 23 in this volume regarding the contribution of the Internet to international union organising). Such an initiative is the product, rather, of an intense organising drive, country by country, where local leaderships are won over to the idea of a resistance-based network. The Rio Tinto network, then, was built and grounded in the local through a series of country-based launches.

This creation of a new spatiality to international union coordinating required intensive organisation where global network leaders moved from country to country to promote and then assist local organisers in creating a local network, which could then be globally linked to local networks in other countries. This organising drive developed a social consciousness of Rio Tinto's global strategy, which expressed itself in precisely the same form at every local place, the key features of which were aggressive cost-cutting, intimidating local unions, threatening not to re-negotiate collective agreements and accusations of the union undermining profitability. In this they aimed at retrenching union members and then bringing in non-union contractors who were employed at less than union rates. These meetings with key union leaders from each country focused on these issues during the local launches of the network, thereby creating the building blocks of one, interactive, global network.

Sustaining such a network is resource intensive and requires a long-term commitment. Fowler observes:

> [a]fter two years we began to see some results. This is a slow process. A global network just doesn't spring into being in an instant. Some believed this could be easily achieved within a short time span. Consequently, there was a lot of frustration at the slowness of the process. People felt there was nothing happening.
>
> The problem is you are spanning a lot of countries and you are trying to get a lot of work sites activated. When you are on the job you know how difficult it is to activate the workforce in a single factory, or mine site. We were trying to activate workers on a world stage. It's going to be slow; it's going to be frustrating!
>
> But our experiment has shown what is possible to achieve. We eventually reached a situation where workers were prepared to walk off the job to support workers being victimized in a far distant country. That is the kind of activism that we have built through the network.

Brazil is one example of how the painstaking construction of these new spatial relations created the possibility of global solidarity action. One Monday the Brazilian Miners Union communicated through the network that Rio Tinto had refused to negotiate a new collective agreement. The company was flooded with protest messages from around the globe, demanding the company negotiate. By Wednesday, the mining giant had returned to the table. Fowler argued that this demonstrated the potential power of a global response:

> [t]he turnaround was remarkable. The action occurred within five days, yet it took five years to get to there – five years of intense organising work. I doubt if that could've happened in year one, but it happened in year five. These experiences taught us the power of global networking. You really can get workers and their unions within a global corporation responding to local pressures in a swift, cohesive manner. So this is the sort of system we are operating now.

The Rio Tinto network is a fine illustration of a working space dynamic *led* by the organised union movement, one where key institutions of ELI are transformed by this engagement. There are, however, other instances where attempts to work space have been undermined by the ELI, hence the need for an ongoing effort to engage and transform the ELI.

Prospects

At the outset we defined working space as the way movements actively structure space to re-empower society over markets/corporations. Given the astonishing concentration of corporate power and the role of finance capital in accelerating this transformation, re-empowering society is a daunting challenge. This chapter has considered the prospects of resisting corporate spatial fixes through a NLI, which empowers the local through restructuring the spatial relationships within which workers live and toil. In this we have tried to capture the complexity and dynamic of the spatial imagination of sections of the labour movement as they attempt to engage new spatial strategies. In this process of struggle, ELI and NLI are viewed not as a binary divide but, rather, as processes of contestation. In the current phase there are examples of spatial experimentation. We have provided a narrative of one such endeavour, which had elements of both success and failure. For instance, whilst Rio Tinto made concessions, there was a backlash from the ELI leadership within the ICEM, who assured the corporate executives that the campaign would be 'controlled' at the moment of Rio Tinto's greatest vulnerability. As a result of this John Maitland was so marginalised that he eventually chose to resign from the Presidency of ICEM. Firm predictions cannot be made. Lines are drawn between leaderships committed to working space and those bureaucrats who articulate a mode of 'challenging' global corporations through quiet lobbying over a glass of iced Chardonnay. Others are testing the boundaries through imagining the potential of new spatial relations.

As we outlined in the chapter, ELI is a site of struggle between the politics of partnership and the politics of socially regulating corporations, between an organisational style of bureaucratic control and a participatory democracy which energises and transforms workers, between lobbying activities and new forms of action, between a scant consciousness of space and recognition of the power of creating new spatial relations, between bureaucratic connections and networking scale as a mode of power. Human agency is the critical force in this contestation, bringing to bear the power of imagination and the will to work space through organising and producing global relations to resist corporate restructuring. This has the potential to inspire a counter-culture, one which challenges the individualistic model of market relations. As International Transport Workers' Federation Vice President Paddy Crumlin (2008) puts it:

> We are dealing with people who think they own us. Of course they don't. We own each other; we own the love, the affection and the humanity, the ability to construct and integrate, the ability to have empathy and sympathy, and the most wonderful thing is our ability to share. We say in the knock around world, good people share. If we are able to work together and unleash the tremendous human creativity and potential inherent in our own humanity, we are a political and economic and industrial force in which almost anything is possible..

Working space extends this culture of solidarity beyond the local and national to the global in a project of creative imagination, propelled by political will, commitment and a determination to overcome the obstacles we have identified. As Kenny Riley (2008),

President of the International Longshoreman's Association (ILA) Local Union 1422 on the east coast of the US and a unionist involved in the global initiative underway to network mining and maritime unions, has argued:

> I grew up in the South during the civil rights movement. I thought growing up black in the South was tough, but now being a unionist in the South is much more difficult. We are building a new model. We have established our objectives, identified our targets and we have developed strategies necessary to hit those targets. We have built a new kind of movement in South Carolina – a permanent network of civil society organizations – some sixty five groups. When issues hit the network, we all respond. We have now magnified this local movement through networking globally. We have used our power in the global economy to fight the issues – threatening to shut down ports until disputes are settled. You learn how to network through struggle.

The role of labour geography within this transition, then, is not only to conceptualise space through these human practices but also to explore the content of the practices to deepen and advance the struggle of society against markets.

Notes

1. Schmid (2008, pp. 39–40) puts this triad slightly differently, referring to them as 'perceived space', 'conceived space' and 'lived space'.
2. Of course, this ignores the fact that for surplus value to be extracted capital must come to rest somewhere, even if ephemerally (see Chapter 1 in this volume). Nevertheless, the image of an almost infinitely footloose capital is, we would aver, a powerful one within the neoliberal spatial imagination.
3. In a review article entitled 'Going for broke', Ian Macfarlane (2008), previously Governor of the Australian Reserve Bank, argued that 'the soundness of the dominant economic model is being questioned'. Similar arguments can be found in books by Morris (2008) and Soros (2008). The current global financial crisis, triggered by sub-prime mortgage lending in the US, reveals the costly and catastrophic consequences of the absence of regulation and accountability.
4. 'The publicly held corporation, the main engine of economic progress in the US for more than a century, has outlived its usefulness in many sectors of the economy and is being eclipsed'. Private equity acquisitions are viewed as reflecting a 'structural shift away from listed companies' (Guerrera and Hoyos, 2006).
5. Gallin, of the International Union of Foodworkers (IUF), was advanced in his thinking, developing ideas and forms of action which anticipated the NLI. John Maitland fought hard within the International Chemical, Energy and Mining Federation (ICEM) when he won the presidency of that organisation, only to be undermined and defeated later in his term. Paddy Crumlin, General Secretary of the Maritime Union of Australia (MUA) and Vice President of the International Transport Workers' Federation (ITF), is an exemplary internationalist with a profound understanding of what needs to be done. He is a key figure in the creation of MAMGI, perhaps the most important of all NLI developments, given its capacity to operationalise logistical power. Adriana Von Rosenvaig, of Union Network International (UNI), is another exceptional leader and visionary, and is committed to new forms of mobilisation and action.
6. Such a model is unevenly developed in the global South. However, the larger, better established formations such as the Congress of South African Trade Unions (COSATU), Brazil's Central Unica dos Trabalhadores (CUT) and the Korean Confederation of Trade Unions (KCTU) are leaders in this regard, exposing the newer formations in South-east Asia to these organisational ideas.
7. Over the past decade Lambert, Webster and a team of researchers have conducted regular surveys and qualitative interviews with SIGTUR activists (Lambert and Webster, 2001). These highlight this psychological transformation, where the experience of commodity status is changed through movement engagement (Lambert, 2007).
8. The WFTU was an international labour organisation in the post-WW2 era made up largely of the Communist unions associated with the Eastern bloc countries and unions in some of the Arab countries, though it had other members too.
9. Paddy Crumlin, speaking as Vice President of the ITF and General Secretary of MUA, 'Keynote Address' at the Sydney Conference of MAMGI – Mining and Maritime Global Initiative, 14 April 2008.
10. 'Thinking outside of the box' was a 1999 comment by John Maitland, then President of ICEM. Maitland played a key role in imagining a new global response to the repressive strategies of the global mining corporation, Rio Tinto.

11. The company focuses on large, long-term, low-cost mining and minerals processing operations in aluminium, copper, coal, uranium, gold, industrial minerals and iron ore. For an analysis of the Rio Tinto campaign, see Sadler and Fagan (2004).
12. The analysis that follows is based on a transcript of a presentation by Ric Fowler, the International Secretary of the CFMEU to the AMWU global workshop of white goods union leaders, held in Sydney, Australia, in November 2004. It was Fowler's presentation that so upset the Swedish union leaders, who viewed networking scale as a move to undermine the corporation's profitability. All the quotes that follow are from Fowler's presentation.
13. Interview, April 2008.

References

Baritz, L. (1960), *Servants of Power: A History of the Use of Social Science in American Industry*, Middletown, CT: Wesleyan University Press.
Burawoy, M. (2003), 'For a sociological Marxism: the complementary convergence of Antonio Gramsci and Karl Polanyi', *Politics and Society*, **31** (2), 193–261.
Castells, M. (1978), *City, Class and Power*, New York: Macmillan.
Castells, M. (1983), *The City and the Grassroots: A Cross-Cultural Theory of Urban Social Movements*, London: Edward Arnold.
Crumlin, P. (2008), 'Keynote address', the Sydney Conference of MAMGI – Mining and Maritime Global Initiative, Sydney, 13–15 April.
Gallin, D. (2006), 'Organizing: means and ends', paper presented to the 'Global Unions, Global Justice' Conference, Cornell Global Labor Institute, New York, 9 February.
Gibson-Graham, J.K. (2002), 'Beyond global vs. local: economic politics outside the binary frame', in A. Herod and M.W. Wright (eds), *Geographies of Power: Placing Scale*, Oxford: Blackwell, pp. 25–60.
Global Union Research Network (2008), Strategic Position Paper.
Guerrera, F. and C. Hoyos (2006), 'Hidden value: how unlisted companies are eclipsing the public equity market corporate government', *The Financial Times*, 15 December.
Harvey, D. (1996), *Justice, Nature and the Geography of Difference*, Oxford: Blackwell.
Harvey, D. ([1982] 1999), *The Limits to Capital*, London: Verso.
Harvey, D. (2000), *Spaces of Hope*, Edinburgh: Edinburgh University Press.
Harvey, D. (2006), 'Space as a keyword', in N. Castree and D. Gregory (eds), *David Harvey: A Critical Reader*, Oxford: Blackwell Publishing, pp. 270–93.
Herod, A. (2001), *Labor Geographies: Workers and the Landscapes of Capitalism*, New York: Guilford Press.
Herod, A. (2003a), 'The geographies of labor internationalism', *Social Science History*, **27** (4), 501–23.
Herod, A. (2003b), 'Scale: the local and the global', in S. Holloway, S. Rice and G. Valentine (eds), *Key Concepts in Geography*, London: Sage, pp. 229–47.
Herod, A. and M.W. Wright (2002), *Geographies of Power: Placing Scale*, Oxford: Blackwell Publishing.
Lambert, R. (1999), 'Global dance: factory regimes, Asian labour standards and corporate restructuring', in J. Waddington (ed.), *Globalisation and Patterns of Labour Resistance*, London: Mansell, pp. 72–105.
Lambert, R. (2004), 'Death of a factory: an ethnography of market rationalism's hidden abode', *Anthropological Forum*, **14** (3), 297–313.
Lambert, R. (2007), 'Self regulating markets, restructuring and the New Labour internationalism', in A. Gamble, S. Ludlam, A. Taylor and S.J. Wood (eds), *Labour, the State, Social Movements and the Challenge of Neo-Liberal Globalisation*, Manchester: Manchester University Press, pp. 147–70.
Lambert, R. and M. Gillan (2007), '"Spaces of hope?" Fatalism, trade unionism and the uneven geography of capital in white goods manufacturing', *Economic Geography*, **83** (1), 75–95.
Lambert, R. and E. Webster (2001), 'Southern unionism and the new labour internationalism', *Antipode*, **33** (3), 337–62.
Latham, A. (2002), 'Retheorizing the scale of globalization: topologies, actor-networks, and cosmopolitanism', in A. Herod and M.W. Wright (eds), *Geographies of Power: Placing Scale*, Oxford: Blackwell, pp. 115–44.
Lefebvre, H. ([1974] 1991), *The Production of Space*, Oxford: Blackwell.
Leys, C. (2003), *Market Driven Politics: Neoliberal Democracy and the Public Interest*, London: Verso.
Macfarlane, I. (2008), 'Going for broke', *The Australian Literary Review*, 3 (7), August.
Marx, K. ([1961] 1966), 'Alienated labor: economic and philosophical manuscripts', in E. Fromm (ed.), *Marx's Concept of Man*, New York: Frederick Ungar.
Marx, K. ([1867] 1976a), *Capital*, Vol. 1, London: Penguin.
Marx, K. ([1894] 1976b), *Capital*, Vol. 3, London: Penguin.
McAdam, D., J. McCarthy and Z. Mayer (1996), *Comparative Perspectives on Social Movements*, Cambridge: Cambridge University Press.
Massey, D. ([2005] 2007), *For Space*, London: Sage.

Moody, K. (1997), *Workers in a Lean World: Unions in the International Economy*, London: Verso.

Morris, C.R. (2008), *The Trillion Dollar Meltdown: Easy Money, High Rollers, and the Great Credit Crash*, New York: Public Affairs.

Polanyi, K. ([1944] 2001), *The Great Transformation: The Political and Economic Origins of Our Time*, Boston, MA: Beacon Press.

Riley, K. (2008), Address by Kenny Riley, President of International Longshoreman's Association Local Union 1422 (USA) to the Mining and Maritime Global Initiative (MAMGI), Sydney, Australia, 15 April.

Sadler, D. and B. Fagan (2004), 'Australian trade unions and the politics of scale: reconstructing the spatiality of industrial relations', *Economic Geography*, **80** (1), 23–43.

Sassoon, D. (1996), *One Hundred Years of Socialism: The West European Left in the Twentieth Century*, London: I.B. Tauris Publishers.

Schmid, C. (2008), 'Henri Lefebvre's theory of the production of space: towards a three-dimensional dialectic', in K. Goonewardena, S. Kipfer, R. Milgram and C. Schmid (eds), *Space, Difference, Everyday Life: Reading Henri Lefebvre*, New York: Routledge, pp. 27–45.

Seidman, G. (1994), *Manufacturing Militancy: Workers' Movements in Brazil and South Africa, 1970–1985*, Berkeley, CA: University of California Press.

Silver, B. (2003), *Forces of Labor: Workers' Movements and Globalization since 1870*, Cambridge: Cambridge University Press.

Soros, G. (2008), *The New Paradigm for Financial Markets: The Credit Crisis of 2008 and What It Means*, New York: Public Affairs.

Stevens, M. (2006), 'Evangelists of debt rewrite the rulebooks', *The Australian*, 16 December, p. 1.

Tarrow, S. (1998), *Power in Movement: Social Movements and Contentious Politics*, Cambridge: Cambridge University Press.

Toohey, B. (2006), 'Private equities, public pain?' *The West Australian*, 18 December, p. 17.

Touraine, A., M. Wieviorka and F. Dubet (1987), *The Workers' Movement*, Cambridge and New York: Cambridge University Press (translated by Ian Patterson).

Touraine, A., F. Dubet, M. Wieviorka and J. Strezelecki (1983), *Solidarity: Poland 1980–81*, Cambridge: Cambridge University Press.

United Nations Conference on Trade and Development (UNCTAD) (2007), *World Investment Report*, New York and Geneva: United Nations.

Waterman, P. (2004), 'Adventures of emancipatory labour strategy as the new global movement challenges international unionism', *Journal of World-Systems Research*, **10** (1), 217–53.

Webster, E., R. Lambert and A. Bezuidenhout (2008), *Grounding Globalization: Labour in the Age of Insecurity*, Oxford: Blackwell.

23 Online union campaigns and the shrinking globe: the LabourStart experience

Eric Lee

More than a decade ago, I published what was the first book-length discussion of trade unions and the Internet (Lee, 1997). The penultimate page included the following passage:

> When Marc Belanger in Ottawa and Vassily Balog in Moscow are discussing an international labour university online, where are they? One answer Internet users will usually give is 'cyberspace'. That's true, but it's not enough. Because the discussion about Belanger's proposal took place not so much in cyberspace as in a particular part of it which I have been calling the emerging global labournet (Lee, 1997, p.185).

In raising the question of 'place' back in 1996/7, I was touching on issues which I address more fully in this chapter. The published book included a link to a website which had been set up to include updates listing, for example, new websites set up by trade unions. Within a few months, that website had become much more than its author had intended. First, it began including a 'labour website of the week' feature – not a simple task considering how few labour websites there were back in 1996–7. Then it included an annual competition for the Labour Website of the Year, which was won, in the first year, by a site which achieved just one vote more than the competition.[1] By the end of 1997, it began to include links every day to labour news stories about South Korea.

In March 1998 that site was re-launched as 'LabourStart', specifically designed as a portal for trade union members around the world.[2] It featured daily labour news, links to union campaigns and a directory of union websites. LabourStart quickly evolved and grew into a massive project, with hundreds of volunteer correspondents adding news links to its database. By May 2008, it had over 550 such correspondents.[3] LabourStart then launched a system for syndicating labour news, picked up by over 700 union websites.[4] It went multilingual, eventually appearing in more than 20 languages, including Chinese, Russian, English, French, Spanish, Indonesian, Creole, Norwegian, Finnish, Arabic, Hebrew, German, Danish, Swedish, Turkish, Portuguese and the international auxiliary language Esperanto. LabourStart gradually acquired a campaigning capacity of its own, launched in 2002 as 'ActNOW'. (The initial links to campaigns were to existing union campaigns on union websites.)

This chapter focuses on both the news and campaigning aspects of the vast LabourStart project and how they have contributed to the reshaping of space for the trade union movement. In terms of the chapter's layout, the next section outlines the challenge which organising across space presents to unions. The third section explains the initial use of the Internet for union purpose, as a news-providing mechanism. The fourth section provides coverage of online campaigning, and the fifth discusses campaigns connected specifically with the LabourStart website. Whilst the Internet constitutes a huge new union resource, not every initiative has been successful. The sixth section outlines some of the campaign successes and failures, as well as survey-based insights concerning language and Internet campaigning, whilst the next section outlines non-LabourStart Internet campaigns. A further two sections of the chapter provide a sobering consideration of new impediments to online campaigning and how these may be addressed, followed by a conclusion assessing both the challenges and the opportunities awaiting unions who seek to use the Internet when organising.

Space and distance as problems for trade unions

Space has been a 'problem' for unions and for working people – and much more of a problem for them than it has been for corporations. In the early 1970s the process we now call globalisation was well under way. Most trade unionists knew little or nothing about it, but some – those operating already at global level in the European-based International Trade Secretariats (ITSs) – started to show concern. One of them, Charles ('Chip') Levinson, general secretary of the chemical workers' ITS now known as the International Federation of Chemical, Energy, Mine and General Workers' Unions (ICEM), wrote about the subject (Levinson, 1972, 1974).[5] Levinson predicted that the rise of powerful global corporations – institutions not limited by place and space in the ways that local and national employers had been – posed a new challenge for unions. Unions would need to create, at the global level, what Levinson called a 'countervailing power'. The main mechanism they would use to do this, he argued, was global 'company councils'. These company councils were created on the basis of the belief that if an auto company such as Ford had gone global, then unions representing Ford workers around the world should globalise themselves. Levinson pointed to many examples of this process beginning to take place, and even to examples of cross-border strikes, such as one at St Gobain glass in the late 1960s (see Weinberg, 1978, pp. 56–7 for details).

Two decades later, Levinson's 'countervailing power' had clearly not yet emerged. Company councils proved to be a largely unrealisable ideal because no unions could afford the costs of gathering large numbers of union representatives together in meetings. Even though the price of air travel had plummeted over the years, it was still prohibitively expensive to call together representatives of, say, Ford workers around the globe. This, of course, was far less of an issue for corporations for a number of reasons. First, corporations have greater resources than unions, and could afford the air travel and hotel costs that global meetings incur. Second, corporations had the resources even early on to use advanced telecommunications, including videoconferencing, long before unions had that capacity. Finally, whilst unions need to hold meetings as part of the democratic process of decision-making, corporations are much less constrained. Hence, in Wal-Mart and McDonald's, managers from around the world do not have to meet and vote in order to take decisions; decisions are made from on high. With unions, on the other hand, democracy is an essential part of the decision-making process.

Despite the hopes of the 1960s, by the early 1990s, with the Soviet empire having collapsed and some intellectuals (for example, Fukuyama, 1992) declaring the triumph of the free market model, unions were in retreat almost everywhere. They desperately needed a way to realise Charles Levinson's vision of company councils, of cross-border strikes and of the creation of a countervailing power to the global corporate elite. What they needed was something to overcome the tyranny of distance, a way to communicate, to spread news, to campaign together with colleagues around the globe. Holding international conferences was still expensive. If only a revolution would happen in the field of telecommunications, something to make it possible to communicate instantly and at almost no cost around the world. Otherwise, unions faced growing irrelevance and possible extinction in the age of globalisation. As it turned out, such tools were just around the corner.

When Tim Berners-Lee invented the World Wide Web back in 1991, he was not dreaming about uniting the workers of the world. He was thinking of a good way for his fellow scientists at the European Organization for Nuclear Research (CERN) and elsewhere to share scientific research. In the late 1960s, when the US Department of Defense funded the creation of the original Internet – known as Arpanet – they were creating it as part of an attempt to secure computerised information in the event of nuclear war. No one had any real idea what these tools were going to be used for. As early as 1992 and 1993, however, at international conferences held in Manchester, trade unionists and other social change activists gathered to discuss ways in which new communications technologies (including some which have now disappeared, such as Gopher and electronic bulletin board systems, known as BBSs) could help unions. My book was written at a time when unions were still grappling with these technologies, sometimes understanding that they could be really useful but without any real idea what they would actually be used for. The next section outlines the initial usage of the Internet by unions – for news-spreading purposes.

Online labour news in a shrinking world
It became evident that one of the things those technologies could be used for was to 'shrink the world' by spreading information from everywhere to everywhere, in all languages, at very high speed. For its part, LabourStart's news works in the following way. Individual trade union activists sign up to be volunteer correspondents. Each correspondent is given a unique username and password, and sent instructions on how to add news links to LabourStart's database. Those correspondents then visit union and mainstream news websites, find news stories of interest, and add the web addresses (URLs) of those stories, plus a title, to the LabourStart database. Those stories appear on LabourStart's front page, as well as on individual pages by country, by company and by region. They are sorted by language and shown on each of the more than 20 separate language sites. Every day, LabourStart senior correspondents (of which there are about a dozen) select one or two of these stories and make them headlines on the main LabourStart global news page in English. The aim is to have about 10 top priority news stories per week.

Presently, there are more than 550 such volunteer correspondents, based on every continent and in all the major industrialised countries. At any given time, only a minority of them are active. Some of them post only one news link per month, often news from their own union or city. But others post dozens of such links every time, often by visiting websites from around the world. The core group of correspondents have met together only twice. The first time was at a London conference organised by the London School of Economics and the Harvard Trade Union Program in late 2002.[6] The second event took place in London in May 2008. Otherwise, they communicate entirely by email, over the telephone (increasingly, by using Skype) and through an online Wiki, a password-protected area of the LabourStart website that anyone who can read can also edit. To a large degree, this core group and some of the more active correspondents have begun to function in a world that is effectively much smaller than the world in which most trade unionists live. For example, many of them are acutely aware of time differences and cultural differences, in a way that is not typical of trade unionists active only at a local or national level. They talk amongst themselves, by email, as members of a community with a shared purpose and, increasingly, a shared language and traditions. Most of them collaborate every year, as they have now done for four years, and teach an online class on global labour movements at an American university.[7] Those who are part of the core group meet up in twos and threes at various conferences, and through the Global Union Federations (GUFs) and the International Labour Organisation.

Very early on, it became clear that the vast majority of trade union members would never become regular visitors to the LabourStart website, so a means was found to syndicate its content to any website which wanted to use it. By May 2008 some 740 trade union websites, including many local and branch unions, were using LabourStart news feeds on their pages. In many cases, local unions were running automated lists of links to LabourStart's global news or global campaigns, introducing rank-and-file members for the first time to the international trade union movement which, until then, had been rather remote. For example, members of Airline Lodge 714 of the International Association of Machinists, a Canadian union, see links to the latest LabourStart campaigns around the world automatically displayed on the front page of their Lodge's website. In Oslo, Norway, the first thing members of the Transport Workers union see on their local website is the latest five Norwegian-language news stories from LabourStart's news database. The same is true for members of the Russian nuclear power workers union, who see on the very top of their union's website the latest LabourStart news headlines in Russian. The instant syndication of news via LabourStart to union websites in 36 different countries is providing workers with common information in real-time in a manner that had never previously been feasible. The amount of information being collected and distributed is enormous: on average, some 250 news links are added every day to LabourStart's database, for a total of over 90 000 such links every year.

What I have outlined here, then, is a process that includes not only LabourStart's correspondents and not only the tens of thousands of regular visitors to the website, but many thousands more who are ordinary rank-and-file union members visiting their own local or national union website. Workers who belong to a union are now being exposed every day to massive amounts of labour news in a way that was unthinkable a decade ago. That news is not limited by borders or distance. However, the news is only part of the story and not even the most dramatic part. Rather, it is the new technology's capacity for facilitating organising that perhaps is its most significant characteristic.

Online campaigning

Online campaigning is not new in the labour movement. In fact, we are today at the beginning of the third decade of online campaigning. This is not some experimental technology, then, but a proven and mature one. In fact, the earliest examples of online campaigns by unions were probably some rudimentary efforts made by Global Union Federations – then known as International Trade Secretariats – back in the 1980s, when they were among the first trade union organisations to experiment with computer communications. In terms of form, then, an online campaign conducted in the 1980s was not that radically different from one today – a union would collect information about an issue or dispute, send that out by email to its affiliates, and this would in turn trigger messages of protest or solidarity to be sent to an employer, or government, or directly to a union on the front line. What is different between then and now, though, is the question of the scale of the campaign, as by even the early 1990s there were enough trade unionists online to justify the holding of international conferences to discuss the use of computer communications, even if the creation of a single, comprehensive list of email addresses of all trade unionists online was still being attempted.

There were already some success stories, even in the early days. A notable one involved trade unionists and other activists spreading the word (by email) of the jailing of some Russian comrades, passing on the phone number of the police station at which they were being held. The result of this was a large number of phone calls to bewildered local police, and the release of the prisoners. By the mid-1990s, though, a full decade after the technology had become available, online campaigning began to take on its now familiar form. Unions and other campaigning organisations began to embrace web-based campaigning, with software specifically designed to allow the rapid launch of large-scale, and often highly effective, online campaigns.

What, then, were the advantages of online campaigning? Why did the new technology take off? In order to answer such questions we have to remember how campaigns were previously done – and, particularly, how global campaigns were waged. In an earlier era, prior to the 1980s, many unions had international secretaries or international departments which were put in charge of global solidarity issues. Those individuals or departments would receive appeals for international solidarity from the ITSs, or the International Confederation of Free Trade Unions (ICFTU), or the individual union concerned. They could decide to ignore such appeals, or they could arrange for the union president or general secretary to send off a message to an appropriate figurehead. On rare occasions, they might pass on the information to others in the union, and there were even some cases where actual rank-and-file members of the union, in the workplace, would be asked to be involved. But those examples were extremely rare. So, if a trade unionist were to be jailed somewhere in the world, the best that was likely to happen would be that a few dozen trade union general secretaries in developed countries would, within a few days or weeks, send off fax messages of protest or solidarity, either directly to the offending government or to the union which had made the appeal. And that was a best-case scenario.

One result of all of this was that international work was given a relatively low profile in nearly all unions and was marginalised. The irony was that a previously vigorous trade union internationalism had been marginalised at precisely the moment in which globalisation had taken hold. Just when unions needed to be thinking globally and acting globally, they had relegated international solidarity work to the back burner. The first advantage of online campaigning, therefore, was that it could potentially involve far more people than could the more traditional methods. Instead of the union president or general secretary being the only one to know about specific cases, or even generally about the broader issues of workers' rights and solidarity, now that involvement and that consciousness could seep down through all levels of the union. A successful campaign would now no longer involve counting how many unions had sent fax messages but, instead, would count how many individual members of those unions, regardless of their title or office held, had sent off email messages. Instead of aiming to get, say, a hundred unions to send one message apiece, the aim would be to get 5000 members involved.

A second advantage of online campaigning was its immediacy. The traditional global trade union campaign was paper-based, certainly up until the 1980s. The international trade secretariats based in Geneva, Brussels and London would produce newsletters and bulletins and could send out urgent appeals by airmail. Back in the days before fax machines, it would take days or even weeks following the arrest of a trade union leader before messages of protest would reach a government. Even the really successful organisations campaigning offline back then, such as those of Amnesty International, relied upon paper-based campaigns using the global postal network – meaning that there was always a significant gap in time between the cause of a campaign (an arrest, for example) and the beginning of a public outcry. Fax machines changed that to a considerable extent, and should be seen as what we now know them to have been: a transitional technology bridging the gap between paper- and postal-based campaigns and truly online campaigns.

The involvement of much larger numbers of individuals, and the much greater speed of reaction, were huge changes, but a third advantage should be noted as well. Online campaigns were not only less expensive than their paper predecessors – they were in many cases absolutely free of charge. Once a union had email and, later on, a website, the costs of doing an online campaign, be it national or global, had dropped not by half or a third, but all the way down to virtually zero. This was particularly important when we are considering global campaigning. Traditionally, international solidarity work was expensive. To send a couple of union representatives to an international meeting could cost thousands of dollars. To bring over a speaker from overseas was a considerable investment. Even making international phone calls or sending faxes abroad was not cheap. Computer-based technology, on the other hand, suddenly made international solidarity work accessible to large numbers of rank-and-file union members, at almost no cost, and with an immediacy never previously experienced.

However, there was also a downside to online campaigning. The Internet is not, and cannot be, a substitute for a face-to-face meeting, a picket line or a mass demonstration. It had to be understood as a new tool, and no more than that, in labour's toolbox. Some over-enthusiastic activists saw this differently, believing that Internet-based campaigns could somehow be a substitute for the real work of building strong organisations. Some campaigners saw online efforts as alternatives to the traditional institutions such as the ITSs, rather than understanding the more complex role that the ITSs had in both inventing online campaigns and, later on, running some of the more effective ones. Loose and informal networks based on groups of net activists never grew into anything much larger than that. Meanwhile, the traditional institutions of the labour movement embraced the new technology and used it with growing effectiveness. As unions increasingly campaigned online, then, the question of what is and what is not an online campaign frequently came up. It is vital to be clear about what a campaign is: campaigns are efforts to mobilise people to put pressure on governments or employers. They are not articles or editorials on a website.[8] In addition to putting pressure on targets (employers, governments), campaigns often have the intended or unintended consequence of raising morale among those workers on the front lines. In many cases, the really important thing about a specific campaign is not that it convinced an employer or government to change its practice, but that it raised the spirits of the men and women on the picket line or in jail.

If a campaign raises the morale of striking workers enough to encourage them to outlast the employer by just one day, then that could make the difference between winning and losing a strike.

LabourStart's campaigns

Having discussed campaigns up until now in a general sense, this section focuses on a number of global online campaigns with which I have been involved for nearly a decade. These are the campaigns connected to the LabourStart website.

To put recent developments into perspective, in 1998 LabourStart had a mailing list which initially pulled together some 500 email addresses of trade union activists who were using the net. The growth of that mailing list, and its relationship to the online campaigns, is central to this story. From the very beginning, LabourStart gave publicity on its front page to union campaigns online. But, increasingly, unions would ask for help getting a campaign up and running. Most unions did not have – and still do not have, even today – the technical capacity to develop software tools for online campaigning. In response, in August 2002 LabourStart launched its own system to allow the rapid creation of online campaigns. To test-drive the system, we asked the ICFTU if there was a current campaign with which we could help. We were given the case of some sugar union leaders in Congo who had been arrested. At the time, the LabourStart mailing list consisted of some 3000 names and addresses of trade unionists. We were not sure what percentage of them would respond to a campaign, and were very surprised when, instead of getting 300 responses (which would have been impressive enough), our campaign actually generated over 3000 messages. It was a response rate of 100 per cent. How was this possible? Well, it became clear that a mailing sent out to the 3000 email addresses of union activists on LabourStart's list would reach a multiple of that number. People sent on the messages to additional mailing lists – to other activists concerned with human rights, to members of their union local and so on.

In the April of 2003 I witnessed this myself. Invited by the Canadian Association of Labour Media (CALM) to do a live demonstration in a Toronto hotel to a group of communications people from a wide range of unions, we launched an online campaign using LabourStart's system, including a mailing to our list. The following morning, I was shown by a trade union friend the half dozen versions of my email message he had received from the various lists to which he subscribed. In military terms this is known as a 'force multiplier' – a factor that dramatically increases (hence 'multiplies') the combat effectiveness of a military force. Based on the experience of the 2002 Congo campaign, that multiplier may be 10 or more. Mailings sent to 3000 activists might be reaching 30000 – or even more. This meant that expanding the size of LabourStart's mailing list became vital for the success of all future campaigns. Hence, the online campaigning system was set up to allow people who were sending off a message to join LabourStart's mailing list. The default was to tick the box subscribing them to the list. One could easily un-tick the box and, of course, every message sent to the list gave a link to unsubscribe. But, as a campaigning group, we felt it was right to make the process of joining the mailing list as effortless as possible.

As a result, the mailing list grew and grew from year to year. By May 2008 it had grown to over 53000 addresses. At this rate, it is only a matter of time before the list has 100000 addresses and, later, a million. The growth of the mailing list ensured that campaigns would not only attract more and more support, but that the speed at which people signed up to campaigns would increase. I call this the 'velocity' of a campaign. In 2003, when we launched a campaign to put pressure on the right-wing government of the Canadian province of British Columbia, we were able to grow from 0 to 1000 messages in about 40 hours – a rate of 25 per hour. At the time, we considered this quite impressive. But little more than two years later, in the August 2005 campaign launched in support of striking catering workers at London's Heathrow Airport, we were able to deliver the first 1000 messages of protest to the employer in four hours. The velocity of the campaign had accelerated tenfold in two years. We were now delivering 250 messages per hour. It is not just the numbers that change, but the whole impact of a campaign. With the ability to deliver a thousand messages four hours after a campaign's launch, we were now beginning to move into the realm of real-time responses to the violations of workers' rights. This was international solidarity at the speed of light.

The growing mailing list was by far the most effective means of promoting a campaign – but it was not the only one. Two other methods were pioneered by LabourStart from an early stage. The first was the use of Google's keyword-based advertising, which we began using in March 2002 – even before launching our campaigning software.[9] Since then, LabourStart has shown over 61.1 million advertisements on Google – at a cost of around $18 000. This is a remarkably small amount of money to reach tens of millions of people, nearly a quarter of a million of whom have clicked on the links in the advertisements and visited LabourStart's site. In 2003, when we launched the British Columbia campaign, we asked the Canadian trade unionists which Google keywords we should target. They came up with 'Winter Olympics', as the province was at that time bidding to host the games. We felt it would be very embarrassing to the provincial government if every time someone searched Google for the phrase 'Winter Olympics' they would see on top of the page, to the right of the regular search results, a small ad reading 'Olympic bidder guilty: British Columbia violates workers' rights says UN body – find out more'. The most successful online advertisement ever run, however, was not actually in support of a specific campaign. In 2002, when New York City's transit workers threatened a strike, and again in 2005, when they walked out for three days, we ran a Google campaign in which our advertisement read 'NYC transit strike: Which side are you on? We support the TWU and the right to strike'. The advertisement was shown over 100 000 times, and some 3.5 per cent of those who saw it clicked through to learn more. The cost was a paltry $159.32, an amount affordable even with limited resources.

The second innovative way we spread the news of online campaigns was through syndication. Just as trade union websites could run the last five labour news links from our database, we also created a tool to allow them to run links to our last five online campaigns. A large number of unions adopted this newswire and, as a result, when LabourStart launches a new online campaign, within 15 minutes a link to it appears on the front page of union websites around the world.

Another way we have drawn attention to LabourStart's campaigns is by integrating the campaigns and the news – thereby blurring the distinction between reading about a violation of workers' rights and doing something about it. When we run a news story that is related to an ongoing campaign, there will be a link next to the title of the story which reads 'Act NOW'. By clicking on that link, you are drawn to the specific campaign page. The same integration means that, on the campaign page, in addition to the static content (the text about the campaign itself), there is also a dynamic display of the latest news relating to the campaign. As an example, in January 2006 LabourStart was supporting the workers at the Bauen hotel workers' cooperative in Buenos Aires with a new campaign. The top news story on our front page read 'Bauen hotel co-op meets Buenos Aires officials'. Next to this there was an Act NOW link. Clicking on this took you to a page headlined 'Argentina: Solidarity with Bauen hotel workers'. In the upper right corner of that page it read 'Latest news about this campaign' with a list of six links. The first one is the news story which initially brought the reader to the page ('Bauen hotel co-op meets Buenos Aires officials'), along with five others.

All LabourStart campaigns originate with, and are authorised by, trade unions. We are often approached by individuals or groups, but insist on the approval of the union in order to undertake a campaign. It is not only the approval of the union we are seeking, but also its active involvement. Unions use LabourStart's campaigning system to mobilise their own members – many of whom then join LabourStart's mailing list and get involved in other campaigns affecting other unions in other countries. A union member might sign up to a particular campaign because it is their union, or their company or country, but then find that they are then on a mailing list about other, similar campaigns affecting countries about which they may know very little. Commonly, they get involved in those campaigns too. As a result, over time an online community is created of trade unionists who sign up for campaign after campaign, giving their support to workers anywhere who ask for it. In other words, workers who might have participated in a global online campaign for local reasons (supporting their own union in their own country) are drawn into a global network campaigning for workers' rights. They are educated and informed by the weekly mailings they receive, and they become active in a worldwide movement about which they may previously have been unaware.

Success (and failure) stories

There is absolutely no point in doing any of this if these campaigns do not succeed, at least occasionally. From the summer of 2002 through to today, LabourStart has launched scores of campaigns. Some of them – a significant minority – have been resounding successes. For instance, in November 2003 we were able to report a big victory following the launch of a LabourStart campaign. Our campaign was part of a much broader international effort, spearheaded by the International Union of Food, Agricultural, Hotel, Restaurant, Catering, Tobacco and Allied Workers' Associations (IUF) in support of the demand that British American Tobacco end its involvement with the Burmese dictatorship. Likewise, in March 2004 we reported that our campaign in support of six imprisoned construction union leaders in South Korea had contributed to their release from jail. (One of the officials, who had lost both legs and an arm in an industrial accident, was denied bail – ostensibly because of the authorities' fear that he would 'flee prosecution'.) Later that month, an appeal made by the IUF – and publicised by LabourStart – contributed to another big victory in Colombia, this time for striking banana workers. As noted on LabourStart at the time, 'This is especially important as Colombia is the most dangerous place on earth to be a trade unionist. More trade unionists are killed every year in Colombia than anywhere else'.

In July 2004, LabourStart appealed to its readers to come to the defence of Andrew Bolesworth, a delegate (shop steward) for the Service and Food Workers' Union

(SFWU) in New Zealand. Bolesworth had been sacked by his employer – a casino in Dunedin – for his union activity. Some 1200 messages were sent and, in only a few days, Bolesworth had his job back. In September 2004, we announced that, following the sending of some 3000 messages through an online campaign, workers at the Raffles Hotel chain in Cambodia had won a big victory. This campaign – again, spearheaded by the IUF – was further evidence of the particular vulnerability of certain sectors, such as hotels, to online campaigning. Finally, at the end of 2005 we were able to report victories in three disputes, all of which involved online campaigns and LabourStart.

First, in Haiti, we reported an end to the long-running, bitter dispute in the Codevi Free Trade Zone, which had been the focus of not one but several online campaigns. The union (Batay Ouvriye) announced that a final agreement was signed between management and the union ending the dispute. The base salary more than doubled, and salaries would rise by an agreed 45 per cent over three years. Union recognition was agreed, work conditions were improved and health and safety, maternity leave and sexual harassment issues resolved. Second, in the Philippines, the year-old strike at Hacienda Luisita – scene of a massacre of strikers earlier in 2005 and a very big online campaign – ended. According to one of the two unions on strike (the United Luisita Workers' Union), the dispute was ended based on its seven-point proposal, including the payment of wages and benefits due to all workers, permanent or casual, the rehiring of 52 sacked workers and retirement packages for 15 terminated permanent workers. Third, in Canada, following a 51-day strike (and an online campaign launched by LabourStart) cleaning employees employed at British Columbia hospitals forced their employer, Sodexho, to sign a first contract with their union, the Hotel Employees' Union. The deal included a 25 per cent pay hike for the workers.

Other victories followed in 2006, including a big win for Indonesian security guards following an unprecedented three online campaigns launched by LabourStart. Significantly, these are only a selection of the victories over a two-year period. In many of the cases, the union involved was explicit about the key role played by the global online campaign. That campaign was often initiated by a GUF, and publicised by it and also by LabourStart, although in some cases it was a LabourStart campaign done at the behest of a union with minimal involvement from a GUF.

Whilst it is good to read about victories, we do, however, also need to talk about defeats. Sometimes our campaigns are abysmal failures – and sometimes we know they are going to be failures even before we launch them. And yet, we do them anyway. Why? Frequently, the main reason is that certain campaigns can have tremendous didactic importance, even if they do not result in a union victory on the specific issues at hand. Thus, several years ago, LabourStart was asked by the IUF to provide assistance on an international campaign to put pressure on the dictator of Belarus, Alexander Lukashenko, who was crushing the last remaining free and independent trade unions in his country. We had only two weeks in which to conduct the campaign, as Lukashenko was about to wrest control over a major union, replacing its leaders with his own stooges. The campaign was not a success. Only a few hundred people sent off messages and, of course, the dictator in Minsk was not moved. The union was crushed. This did not come as a big surprise. After all, very few trade unionists knew very much about Belarus, making it hard to mobilise large numbers around this issue. Nevertheless, the campaign was worth doing because it had enormous educational value. For most of those hearing about it, it was the first time they had come across the existence of Europe's last dictatorship. When there is a further opportunity, it will be easier to mobilise more people as a result.

As a way to assess our successes and failures, in 2006 LabourStart conducted its first online survey, on the subject of online campaigning.[10] The total number of respondents to the survey was 1441. These were overwhelmingly people who participate in LabourStart's online campaigns (95.9 per cent said they did so). Geographically it was a reasonably balanced group, with 41 per cent from North America, 30.5 per cent from Europe (mostly Britain) and 26.2 per cent from Australia and New Zealand. However, very few respondents were from the developing countries, a fact that should remind us that distance can be measured not just in Euclidean terms of miles or kilometres but also by levels of social and economic development, given that trade unionists in the global North often feel closer to those in countries with similar advanced capitalist economies than they do to those in poor countries for whom capitalism is a distant goal rather than a daily reality. Of those responding to the survey, over 40 per cent were women. This provides grounds to question the observation by Haworth and Ramsay (1984, cited in Herod 2003, p. 129) about 'international union solidarity to date having largely remained a male preserve'. This does not appear to be entirely so. However, the survey revealed that, whilst international union solidarity may no longer be the exclusive domain of men, there does remain a strong generational divide. The largest group of participants in those campaigns fell in the age group 51–60 (28.8 per cent), with the second largest group aged 41–50 (28 per cent). In other words, the people using online campaigns to support international union solidarity are overwhelmingly middle-aged and older. Perhaps surprisingly, this is not the Facebook generation.

When asked what changes they want made to LabourStart's online campaigning, the most popular response was to add additional languages. The languages that were most requested were Spanish, French, Chinese, German and Italian. We did so, and our campaigns now work in English, French, Spanish, German, Norwegian, Indonesian, Russian, Polish, Italian, Turkish and Malay, with even more languages soon to be included. This has been an important development, for our experience has been that the number of respondents to a campaign within a particular language group is a nearly exact correlation of the number of people on a mailing list in that language. In other words, we have 20 times as many people on the English language mailing list as on our Norwegian language list. Not surprisingly, we get about 20 times as many messages sent off in English as in Norwegian in our campaigns.

I want here to elaborate briefly on the question of language because it relates to the issue of space and distance. People are not only separated by distance but by language, and some languages create greater distances than others. For example, people who speak Norwegian and Danish can understand one another. Spanish speakers can often understand written or sometimes spoken Portuguese. In general, people whose languages belong to the same broader families (for example, Romance languages) feel 'closer' to one another than do peoples divided by languages that have little or nothing in common. This is significant, for long before there was an Internet, visionaries dreamed of a world shrinking not because of new technologies but through the means of a shared international language. The most intriguing of those ideas was Esperanto, which steadily grew in popularity from its creation in the 1880s up until its bloody suppression by Stalin and Hitler in the 1930s. (The German and Soviet Esperanto movements were the largest and most powerful in the world until they were crushed.) Esperanto made great progress in the labour movement, and at one point left-wing Esperantists were routinely taking texts from their countries in their languages and translating them into Esperanto. These texts were then translated back into native languages in other countries. This way, someone who could read only English and Esperanto could have access to materials published in many different languages. Whilst Esperanto has essentially died off, the idea of an international language has not, and English is now (imperfectly) filling that role. Because of its widespread (though not universal) use in the international trade union movement, global solidarity actions have become possible and distances have shrunk.

Other online campaigns
So far this chapter has focused attention on LabourStart's experience with global online campaigning, but other online campaigning systems – of unions and non-government organisations (NGOs) – also merit attention. One of the most important and effective online campaigning systems is the one used by a number of US trade unions – Get Active.[11] This system offers everything LabourStart's campaigning software does, plus much more. The method of operation is the same: you go to the web page of one of the Get Active campaigns and, by filling in an online form, you send off a message of protest or solidarity. The Get Active system features a much more powerful back-end, however, allowing unions to target supporters of particular campaigns as well as to engage in geographic filtering.

For its part, the IUF has been using an online campaigning system closely modelled on LabourStart's. One distinguishing feature of the IUF's campaigns is that they, like the LabourStart website, are available in a large number of languages.[12] LabourStart, then, is not the only labour support group which carries out online campaigns and certainly was not the first. A real pioneer of this activity has been the Washington, DC-based Campaign for Labor Rights (CLR).[13] CLR's website does not feature a single campaign system as one would find on LabourStart, the IUF or any union website using Get Active. Rather, its approach seems more improvised, with some campaigns consisting of texts, others being PDF files and so on. Nevertheless, one feature the CLR campaigns share with all the others is a reliance on a large email address database to make sure that participation in the campaigns is maximised.

Although here I have focused upon examples of unions and labour support groups using the Internet for campaigning, it would be remiss to neglect the experience of other NGOs with online campaigning, particularly human rights groups. Organisations like Amnesty International practically invented modern campaigning, and it, together with Oxfam, Greenpeace, Friends of the Earth and others, has mastered the art of online campaigning. A couple of years ago, a number of those groups met in Oxford to review their experience with online campaigns. It was a fascinating day as different models and experiences were discussed, and a highlight was a session with a representative 'from the other side' – a public relations officer from Nestlé, the global food giant which has been the target of several successful campaigns. Unfortunately, despite having been invited, not a single union participated in the event.[14]

Beyond the traditional email campaign
So far, I have painted a picture of online campaigns as being potent tools for unions, and have highlighted some success stories. However, it is important to include a cautionary

note. Whilst the past five years has been a great time to be doing online campaigning, it is not going to last. There is a window of opportunity, but it is about to close. There are problems at both ends of online campaigns, involving both the participants and the targets.

In regard to participants, there was a time, several years ago, when one would be delighted to receive email. Email messages were few, and each new one would be a pleasant surprise. That era is long gone; we now all get far more emails than we can handle, and those of us who are online activists are frequently overwhelmed by our messages. Appeals for help will increasingly fall on deaf ears, even among those people who have in the past been the most involved. Even if one wants to continue to be involved and to send off 10 messages a day to 10 different campaigns, increasingly email campaigners are finding it harder to break through anti-spam barriers and filters. Simply put, spam is killing off the traditional email campaign. If you send a message off to your list with a phrase like 'Urgent!' in the subject line, it is likely to be reported as spam and blocked. Some powerful anti-spam filters may even decide that your email server is sending out spam all the time, and will add it to a blacklist so that nothing you send will be received. At the same time that spam is making it harder and harder for campaigning organisations to reach their audiences by email, participants in campaigns are also showing signs of 'campaign fatigue'.

At the other end of the equation, targets of email campaigns are becoming less and less vulnerable. Thus, in 2002 LabourStart was asked by an Australian union (the Liquor, Hospitality and Miscellaneous Union, LHMU) representing hotel workers in Sydney to send off messages to the general manager of the Sydney Hilton. At the end of the first day of campaigning, with a few hundred messages sent off, that manager contacted the union and offered to open negotiations – if the online campaign would be called off. All it took was a few hundred messages to bring pressure. Today, with anti-spam filters and email campaigns becoming increasingly common, the volume of emails needed for equivalent impact is much greater. Where once a few hundred messages would have sufficed, today it takes several thousand messages to have the same impact.

Companies, then, are more aware of the ease with which email campaigns are organised. Consequently, it takes much more effort than before to get a company's attention, and it will take far more than the traditional email campaigns of today to change the behaviour of companies in the future.

A way forward?

If the traditional email campaign is declining in effectiveness – even if there are still many cases of it being successful – what can replace it? Here we have to return to some of the early, pre-Internet days of the labour movement to look for inspiration. After all, unions in the past did not limit themselves to simple corporate campaigns, asking supporters to send off postcards. We had – and have – a vast toolbox of campaigning practices and techniques.

One good example of this is solidarity fund-raising. Often, the key to winning a dispute is keeping the workers on the picket line, hanging on just one day longer than the boss in order to win. An example of this was in 2002 when I visited striking workers at the Azteca tortilla company in Chicago. These workers had joined up with a union which, whilst well-intentioned, was not well funded and did not have a proper strike fund at its disposal. The strikers were facing the hardships of a Chicago winter on the picket line with dwindling resources and declining morale. At the request of the union, we organised a global online campaign through LabourStart. However, whilst we delivered several thousand messages to the employer, this had no effect. We asked the union how else we could help and came up with the idea of raising money online for the strikers using a secure payment system (PayPal). We did not raise as much as we hoped. But when the union organiser showed up on the picket line one freezing day and began handing out the money, telling the workers that these were donations from workers around the world, workers who may never have heard of Azteca tortillas, this simple gesture of solidarity greatly raised morale. The workers stayed on the picket line for several more months, eventually reaching a compromise with their boss and returning to work.

Three years later, a similar effort mounted by LabourStart in support of striking Gate Gourmet catering workers at London's Heathrow Airport produced a far larger amount of money which was transferred to the union's special 'hardship fund' set up for the strikers. In this case, the union was well enough organised to have a fund, but did not yet have the experience of using secure online payment facilities like PayPal. In place of this, the website of the Transport and General Workers' Union (TGWU) pointed visitors to LabourStart if they wished to make a donation online. Similarly, in 2006, at the peak of the fighting in Lebanon, LabourStart raised funds at the request of the Education International in support of two teachers' unions in that beleaguered country. This was an example of a campaign that consisted solely of fund-raising, with no email component. Nevertheless, our experience so far with fund-raising online has not been an unmitigated success, as a small minority of those who are prepared to send off a solidarity message are also willing to make a donation, even a small one.

Another possible use of the net for campaigning, taking online campaigning beyond the simple message of protest and solidarity, is to conduct web- and email-based boycott and 'buy union' campaigns which encourage consumers to buy goods/services produced using union labour. For decades unions have used the twin tools of boycotts and buy union campaigns to punish some employers and reward others, and to build the strength of the labour movement. The net allows us to take this much further. Unions have had lists of products and companies from which we should buy or not buy on their websites for some time, though these are often buried deep in the sites. There are some easy ways to raise the prominence of these lists, such as using Google advertisements. This could be strengthened if every search on Google for every company being boycotted by unions resulted in a small advertisement being shown with a link to a union web page with more information about the company and why we should not buy from it.

One of the more successful uses of the net by the Dean (and Kerry) US Presidential campaigns in 2004 was the use of 'Meetup', an online tool that allowed supporters of these candidates to meet up in the real world.[15] Meetup has two million registered users and has allowed many grassroots movements to rapidly get off the ground as people find co-thinkers in their own local communities. Unions could use existing communities like Meetup or they could create their own. In either event, the purpose would be to get computer users up and out of their chairs, out of their homes, and into the real world where union members and supporters can use more traditional campaigning tactics. Such activities have particularly important implications for furthering the practice of 'community organising'.

Conclusion

This chapter has reviewed the introduction of the Internet as a distance-crossing union campaigning and information solidarity and organising tool, and has considered the successes, as well as the emerging limitations, of Internet campaigning. Although email fatigue and anti-spam filters pose problems, they do not mean that the traditional email protest campaign described in this chapter is ready for the dustbin of history. These campaigns are often still quite potent and we have barely tapped their potential.

Nevertheless, as campaign fatigue sets in amongst participants, and as targets become harder to reach due to anti-spam measures, unions will need to be imaginative in finding new tactics which maximise the new technology. Their inspiration should come from tried-and-true tactics such as solidarity fund-raising, boycotts and traditional real-world mobilisations – all amplified through the strategic use of the new communications technologies, which allow workers to communicate across space more easily than ever before.

Notes

1. The Labour Website of the Year continues to this day. See: www.labourstart.org/lwsoty/.
2. LabourStart is located at: www.labourstart.org.
3. A full list of the currently active ones is at: www.labourstart.org/correspondents.shtml.
4. A full list of the 700 union websites using the syndicated news service is at: www.labourstart.org/cgi-bin/show_lnwgn.pl.
5. Levinson's friend and colleague Dan Gallin wrote a short obituary available at: www.globallabour.info/en/2006/10/funeral_speech_for_charles_lev.html.
6. There is a full report on this conference available online at: www.labourstart.org/conference.doc.
7. The course is entitled Comparative Labour Movements and is a part of the Division of Labor Studies at Indiana University. It is taught entirely online by Eric Lee, with the support of about 15 trade union activists from different countries, mainly LabourStart correspondents.
8. For an example of this, see the 'offshoring campaign' on the website of Amicus, which consists of a single page of text: http://web.archive.org/web/20060105102442/http://www.amicustheunion.org/Default.aspx?page=219.
9. For more on the subject, see 'Google and online campaigning', published in *Industrial Worker* in May 2003 and available at: www.ericlee.info/2003/05/google_and_online_campaigning.html.
10. The full survey is available online at: www.surveymonkey.com/Report.asp?U=215935788547.
11. See Get Active in action on the AFL-CIO's Working Families e-Activist Network, at: www.unionvoice.org/wfn/main.html.
12. The IUF campaigns are integrated into their news stories, available at: www.iuf.org/.
13. The CLR website is at: www.clrlabor.org/.
14. The work of this forum continues online and offline. The website is at: www.ecampaigningforum.com/.
15. Meetup's website is at www.meetup.com/.

References

Fukuyama, F. (1992), *The End of History and the Last Man*, New York: Free Press.
Haworth, N. and H. Ramsay (1984), 'Grasping the nettle: problems in the theory of international labour solidarity', in P. Waterman (ed.), *For a New Labour Internationalism: A Set of Reprints and Working Papers*, The Hague: International Labour Education, Research and Information Foundation, pp. 59–85.
Herod, A. (2003), 'Workers, space and labor geography', *International Labor and Working-Class History*, **64** (Fall), 112–38.
Lee, E. (1997), *The Labour Movement and the Internet: The New Internationalism*, London: Pluto Press.
Levinson, C. (1972), *International Trade Unionism*, London: Allen and Unwin.
Levinson, C. (1974), *A Concrete Trade Union Response to the Multinational Company: ICF's Emerging Countervailing Power*, Geneva: ICF.
Weinberg, P.J. (1978), *European Labor and Multinationals*, London: Praeger.

24 'Across the great divide': local and global trade union responses to call centre offshoring to India
Phil Taylor and Peter Bain

Introduction

The last decade has seen a massive expansion in the offshoring of business services from the so-called developed nations of the global North to low-cost, developing countries of the global South, with such offshoring facilitated by the use of Information and Communication Technologies (ICTs). Despite the increasing importance of diverse back-office processes within these migratory flows, the principal focus has been the much-publicised relocation of call centre services from English-speaking countries to India. There is no denying India's significance in the emerging global market for Business Process Outsourcing (BPO) and in contributing to a new international division of service labour. Consultant reports (for example, Nasscom-McKinsey, 2005) suggest that India accounts for almost half of all offshored BPO. Further, the industry body Nasscom – National Association of Software and Service Companies – (2007, p. 63) calculated that India employed 545000 in BPO by early 2007, with more than 50 per cent engaged on voice services. The impact on the UK is evidenced by the fact that in 2006 an estimated 40000 agents 'faced' UK customers (Taylor and Bain, 2006a, p. 24).

It is necessary to acknowledge the transformative role played by TNCs in extending the reach of capital accumulation and in reconfiguring service delivery chains. The formation of Indian BPO is associated with the decisions taken in the mid-1990s by US corporations GE Capital and American Express to situate back-office (and, later, 'voice') facilities in India (Taylor and Bain, 2003). Of the 26000 employed globally in 2007 by GE (now Genpact), more than 20000 are based in seven locations in India. Prominent UK-based companies have also shaped the sector; Aviva Global Services employed over 7000 by late 2007, whilst HSBC totalled 18000 and Barclays 5000. Evidently, business process offshoring has moved far beyond its exploratory phases to constitute a key component in many corporate strategies. However, the role played by economic actors should not diminish our appreciation of neoliberal 'globalisation' as a political process (Callinicos, 2001), facilitated and sustained by the institutions and rules of global governance (for example, the WTO and the G8), and by the actions of specific states themselves. The overarching 'political-economic' context has proved hugely influential for call centre relocation. For example, the Indian government's turn to attract inward investment following the 1991 economic crisis, its commitment to deregulation (particularly telecommunications) and its willingness to liberalise labour markets have made the country attractive as a destination for TNCs and encouraged indigenous suppliers (Das, 2002). Concomitantly, the UK government has actively promoted the virtues of 'globalisation', encouraging reciprocal flows of capital between India and the UK (DTI, 2004a).[1]

In the UK it seems that, as victims of an all-encompassing 'race to the bottom', workers have no choice but to resign themselves to massive redundancies. The union

Amicus (2003, p. 2), now part of UNITE, forecast the loss of '200 000 finance sector jobs . . . in the biggest industrial collapse since manufacturing was decimated in the early 1980s'. Other predicted consequences are work intensification, 'whipsawing' and the degradation of pay, conditions and employment rights. Since many companies migrating to India (notably in financial services) have historically granted unions recognition, off-shoring poses a tangible threat to trade unions in respect of membership and their ability to exert wider influence on employers.[2] Faced with accelerating offshoring the prospects for UK unions appear bleak. This sense of powerlessness is reinforced by the prescriptions of government (DTI, 2004a). The clear message is that to seek alternatives to the free market is futile and anachronistic. This futility applies as much to the state, which, it is argued, should not intervene to protect jobs, as it does to unions and workers, should the latter consider resisting 'inexorable' global economic forces.

In contrast, it is assumed that the English-speaking graduates who comprise the call centre/BPO workforce in India embrace their employment opportunity so eagerly that they uncritically identify with their company's success and subordinate themselves completely to managerial demands. Even critical analysts pessimistically conclude that factors such as high salaries, professional identity and sophisticated HR practices 'impede the development of any kind of collective' (Noronha and d'Cruz, 2006a, p. 2120). Strategies of 'corporate culturalism' aimed at winning employees' 'hearts and minds' effectively contribute to keeping unions at bay (Noronha and d'Cruz, 2006b). Employer attempts to sustain unitarist cultures are bolstered through a broader ideological project, by which the government strives to unite the nation in a mission of economic growth based upon attracting FDI and promoting indigenous companies. Accordingly, union formation in BPO would discourage FDI and serve only to destabilise the industry and jeopardise the careers of the new Indian professionals who 'buy in' to this 'hegemonic discourse' (Noronha and d'Cruz, 2006a, p. 2118).

As this dichotomisation suggests, 'globalisation' means different things to different groups of workers in different places. It is held that the loss of call centre jobs in the UK is simultaneously an employment opportunity in India. What is common to both places, though, is the sense of union impotence. Unions appear incapable either of defending jobs in the UK or of organising the virgin workforce in India, let alone developing internationally coordinated responses to combat TNCs as they foster inter-place competition.[3] Capital appears to have succeeded in driving permanent wedges between the geographically dispersed call centre workforce.

Scope of chapter

This chapter challenges the conventional wisdom of union impotence and argues, instead, that passivity in the face of offshoring is unjustifiable. It argues that the uneven development of global servicing brings parallel and intertwined, although contrasting and asymmetrical, challenges for trade unions in the UK and India. In the UK, the immediate tasks are to prevent redundancies, defend conditions and maintain organisation, whilst in India the more modest but no less challenging objective is to establish a presence in the union-free BPO industry. Of course, there are distinctive 'national' dimensions, given that labour is spatially differentiated and embedded in contrasting ways in local communities and labour markets. Yet from the broader perspective of the interests of the international working class and the short- and long-term needs to counter the power of TNCs, the fortunes of unions in one place are strongly influenced by, if not dependent on, the actions and power repertoires of unions in the other. They are dialectically related.

Consequently, 'organising globally' should not be counterposed to, or privileged over, 'organising locally'. We agree with the important arguments developed by labour geographers, that there is 'no set scalar formula by which workers and their organisations should go about challenging TNCs' (Herod, 2001, p. 424) and that 'organizing at both scales simultaneously may best serve their goals' (Herod, 2002, p. 83). Multi-scalar organising, as we hope to demonstrate, is particularly apposite when considering how call centre employers may be most effectively combated.

These debates foreground the chapter's central focus, namely union responses to off-shoring within, and across, both sides of the seemingly unbridgeable geographical divide between the UK and India. First, we evaluate the nature and effectiveness of UK union initiatives to prevent or mitigate redundancy at company level. Given the enormity of the challenge, union successes have been partial and contingent, but positive lessons can be learned from campaigns at the Prudential, Reality and Siemens Business Services.[4] Secondly, we analyse the potential for collective organisation in Indian BPO. We acknowledge the considerable obstacles facing unionisation but identify emerging issues of employee concern that might enable trade unionism to establish a meaningful presence. The most significant development is undeniably the formation in September 2005 of UNITES (Union of Information Technology-Enabled Services Professionals).

Analysis of union responses is prefaced by necessary conceptualisation and contextualisation. The chapter is informed by theoretical developments in, and empirical evidence from, economic and labour geography (for example, Wills, 1998, 2002; Herod, 2001, 2002; Kelly, 2002; Castree et al., 2004), studies themselves influenced by earlier seminal contributions (Harvey, 1982; Massey, 1984). Employment relations researchers, including the authors, have striven to integrate the fundamental geographical concepts of 'place, space and scale' (McGrath-Champ, 2005) in order to make sense of the contemporary world of work. Thus, geographical factors are not merely colourful 'background scenery' (Herod et al., 2003, p. 176) to relations between capital and labour and to understanding the processes and potentialities of union organisation. These observations are particularly true in the case of the call centre, for its offshoring was always an intrinsically spatial project. Thus, the call centre provides a particularly apposite example of the requirement for social scientists to think in explicitly geographical terms (see Herod et al., 2007; Rainnie et al., 2007). We therefore explain some of the call centre's defining characteristics and then provide summaries of the scale and nature of offshoring, and of market dynamics in India. We begin by summarising the sources utilised in the successive research projects that generated the empirical data presented below.

Data sources
Since 2002 the authors have continuously researched call centre and back-office offshoring, combining investigations of the intentions and practices of UK/Scottish companies with detailed examinations of the Indian BPO industry. Parallel research has documented UK trade union responses to offshoring and tracked union emergence in India.

Primary data consists of mostly qualitative data sets. In India, during eight separate periods of fieldwork, we made visits to 27 call centre/BPO facilities, representative of the 'captive', TNC and Indian third-party segments of the industry. In-depth semi-structured interviews with senior management, lasting on average one and a half hours, were taped and transcribed. Our attendance at seven Nasscom conferences afforded many opportunities for informal interviews with senior industry personnel, and transcribed proceedings provided an invaluable source. Supplementing these sources is extensive documentation: reports, briefings, industry and company data, newspaper archives. More than 50 employee interviews, conducted either individually or in groups and organised both through, and independently of, UNITES, explored workers' perceptions and experiences. More focused interviews with union officers responsible for establishing UNITES enabled us to chart the union's early development. Participation at UNITES's founding conference and subsequent seminars proved equally helpful.

In the UK an audit of Scottish call centres (Taylor and Bain, 2003) was supplemented by a study of offshoring involving 25 semi-structured interviews with senior management of UK/Scottish financial sector companies (2005–06). In total, 43 interviews with full-time officers and representatives of unions and staff associations helped map union responses. Much research activity focused on financial sector unions; Amicus and its pre-merger organisations (MSF and UNIFI), plus staff associations/unions (LTU, ANGU, UFS). Interviews were also conducted with officers and representatives of other unions affected by offshoring: CWU, TSSA, USDAW, PCS and UNISON.[5] Additional data was gathered from 25 union conferences and seminars and a range of documentary material. Altogether, these datasets provide comprehensive evidence of employer strategies, managerial practices, union responses and worker experiences.

Understanding the call centre
As critics have observed (Ellis and Taylor, 2006), there is a tendency to treat call centres as disembodied entities. The inability to answer the central questions of how and why the call centre became an organisational imperative for companies as they reconfigured their servicing and sales activities is a critical analytical weakness of much of the call centre literature, leaving it incapable of explaining the offshoring phenomenon.

The call centre's genesis and evolution are inexplicable without taking full account of the revolution in ICTs from the late 1980s, which included increases in information storability and transmission through networked databases, digitalisation in telecommunications, and the (later) widespread application of optical fibre technologies (Miozzo and Ramirez, 2003), all of which produced considerable cost reductions in computing and telephony. The key innovation was Automatic Call Distribution (ACD) switching (Taylor and Bain, 1999), which enables calls to be routed in succession through headsets to available operators either within or, significantly for offshoring, between networked centres. Without succumbing to technological determinism, it is important to acknowledge that innovation and application in ICTs have profoundly shaped work organisation and facilitated its geographical diffusion (Taylor and Bain, 2007).

The vital point is that with the arrival of the call centre it was no longer necessary to locate servicing sites in geographical proximity to customers. The 'distance shrinking' technologies enabled remote delivery and generated economies of scale through the centralisation of previously dispersed facilities. Cost reduction was achieved concurrently through novel forms of labour utilisation, in which Tayloristic developments (control, monitoring, statistical measurement) were integrated with the performance of emotional labour. The restructuring of work organisation was inseparable from a thorough transformation in the spatial division of labour, an observation that recalls Massey's (1984) earlier insight about how these two are interrelated. Thus, the reconfiguration of the process of service delivery was intimately connected with a transformation in their geographical loci. Hence, in the UK distinctive clusters emerged in particular cities and (peripheral) regions as companies capitalised on supplies of skilled but relatively cheap labour (related to job losses in manufacturing industry in the 1970s and 1980s), the availability and low cost of property, advanced telecommunications connectivity and regional development incentives (Richardson and Marshall, 1996).

From one perspective the drive to offshore should be regarded as an extension, albeit dramatically and at a transnational scale, of the same cost-saving, profit-enhancing, spatial dynamic inherent in the call centre from inception at the national scale. Adapting Harvey's (1982) idea of a 'spatial fix' to encompass its potential meaning as a 'solution' might help us understand offshoring. Thus, the spatial reorganisation of business services has been driven by the accumulation strategies of corporations operating within fiercely competitive markets, as they have sought to exploit the unevenness of global capitalist development, in a similar (if exaggerated) manner to the ways that regional unevenness had earlier been exploited within national boundaries. Here, then, the term 'fix' is employed to signify a resolution, or attempted resolution, to the perpetual 'problem' of capitalist profitability. Hence, the first major migratory wave was stimulated by recessionary pressures following the collapse of the dot.com bubble. It has been sustained by the 'devil take the hindmost' imperative of capitalist competition as corporate management, often under powerful shareholder pressure, has attempted to emulate the gains made by fellow offshorers.

Capitalist competition also helps explain why the work system of the call centre, particularly in its most common 'mass production' type, has come to be used more intensively (Taylor et al., 2005). This intensity is most manifest in escalation of targets, tightened call-handling times and continuous technological innovation (DTI, 2004b).[6] ACD switches were adapted to re-route calls between sites creating 'virtual' call centres. Since calls could be directed either to different UK centres or to India – wherever there were non-engaged agents – costly 'idle time' could be further reduced and staffing levels 'optimised' (that is, minimised). Thus, what was offshored was not the 'first generation' call centre but an intensified variant accompanied by process re-engineering. This development might be termed 'Taylorism through export'. The call centre, then, should be regarded not as a fixed organisational form, but as one in which its 'inner workings' are articulated with the dynamics of capitalist political economy (Taylor and Bain, 2007).

Several implications follow that raise important questions regarding labour's power repertoires and trade union potential. The fact that most companies 'virtually' connect their UK and Indian centres (whether in-house or outsourced) binds call handlers together in processual terms, even though they are separated geographically. For example, Prudential's centre in Stirling is networked with operations in Mumbai, Aviva's in Norwich and York with Noida, Bangalore and Pune, and HSBC's UK sites with 'Global Servicing Centres' in Hyderabad and Bangalore. When serving the so-called mass market, Indian agents handle the same calls 'alongside' their UK counterparts. Since call centres, as lean servicing regimes, bear certain similarities to lean manufacturing systems (like low staffing levels) (Moody, 1997), virtualisation means that disturbance of service delivery at any of a company's sites, wherever located in the transnational chain, could have profound organisation-wide consequences. However, the potential for disruption is arguably even greater in servicing networks than in just-in-time production systems, given that call centres demand an immediacy of response to customer demand. Significant interruption in service delivery would instantly create call queues and customer dissatisfaction.

Finally, the fact that many call handlers experience work as highly pressurised (Baldry et al., 2007) suggests that similar conditions in India and the UK might become articulated into sets of common interests. Nevertheless, conditions of work alone do not lead deterministically to the growth of collective organisation, nor does the experience of similar conditions necessarily create a sense of commonality amongst workers in different places. In sum, there is a contradiction. The fact that call centre workers are united across space and yet divided by place is simultaneously a source of potential solidarity and of competition and underscores the importance of adopting an explicitly geographical perspective to understanding the phenomenon of worker organising associated with such centres.

Globalisation, offshoring dynamics and the Indian market
Prima facie, the call centre is an exemplar of contemporary seamless global relocation; its distinctive technologies enable customers to be served in real time from remote locations and the massive cost differential between the UK and India makes the case for offshoring unassailable. The call centre's spatial and temporal elasticity seems to confirm the popular view that the world is truly flat (Friedman, 2005). However, concrete analysis of the nature and extent of offshoring reveals a contradictory situation and supports those sceptics who argue that capital's relocational ability has been exaggerated and that TNCs are only relatively footloose (McGrath-Champ, 2005). Arguably, 'globalisation' actually heightens the importance of the characteristics of those places in which companies choose to situate facilities (Harvey, 1989, p. 294). In the specific case of call centre offshoring the existence of appropriate linguistic resources is one of the key distinguishing attributes of labour in its place that profoundly shapes firms' locational decisions.

Here we can do little more than sketch an outline of the complex and nuanced dynamics of firm migration (see Taylor and Bain, 2003, 2004, 2005, 2006a, for detailed analyses). Undeniably, the overriding factor driving migration has been the promise of overall cost savings of 40–50 per cent (Nasscom, 2004, 2005a, 2005b, 2006) whilst more conservative estimates suggest 30–40 per cent savings (Nasscom-McKinsey, 2005). The most significant contribution to these economies is India's outstanding country advantage, the low cost of its English-speaking graduate workforce. However, the wage differential of '70–80% for offshorable processes' (Nasscom, 2003, p. 65) has been reduced, as average labour costs have risen by 10–15 per cent per annum over the last three years (Nasscom, 2006, p. 74) due to wage inflation in tight labour markets. Phenomenal expansion is responsible for difficulties which demonstrate that relocation has not proved unproblematic and that labour is not automatically substitutable between places (Taylor and Bain, 2004, 2005). Foremost are the related issues of labour supply and attrition. There is not an inexhaustible supply of skilled graduates. Nasscom-McKinsey (2005) believe that only 10–15 per cent of graduates have the necessary skills for direct employment, and Nasscom estimates that only 3–5 per cent of applicants are employed. Excessive labour demand, which was predicted to cause a shortfall of 500 000 BPO employees by 2008, is manifest most in staggering levels of attrition, averaging perhaps 65–75 per cent for the industry overall.[7] 'Push' factors of difficult working conditions, particularly those associated with night-time voice work, contribute additionally to labour turnover (Taylor and Bain, 2005). Nor has the recent attempt at creating a new spatial fix by relocating facilities beyond the established cities (Bangalore, Hyderabad, Mumbai, greater Delhi and Chennai) to 'Tier 2' and 'Tier 3' cities solved the problems of overheating, rising labour costs and 'talent' shortages.

Prominent amongst the other inhibiting factors are linguistic and cultural difficulties (Taylor and Bain, 2004, 2005). It cannot be assumed that 15 years of education in the English language and extensive accent 'neutralisation' and acculturation programmes ensure that Indians are necessarily able to communicate with customers to quality standards deemed acceptable by Indian suppliers, their Western clients and TNCs. Researchers have discussed more fully (Mirchandani, 2004; Taylor and Bain, 2005, 2006b) the implications of 'locational masking', whereby companies construct the illusion that remote services are being delivered onshore whilst being sourced from remote low-cost offshore locations. Practices include the managerial obligation (or encouragement) of Indian agents to adopt Anglicised pseudonyms, to deliberately conceal location and/or to emulate the national or even the regional accents of the customers they serve. The fact that these attempts at 'making Americans', to use Mirchandani's term, have not succeeded has caused many firms to withdraw from the most extreme practices in the face of customer opposition. Nor are agents always willing to subordinate themselves to these managerial prescriptions (Poster, 2007). In sum, labour is not automatically and unproblematically substitutable across space and between places.

Companies make decisions to relocate services on the basis of their evaluation of the locational, economic, political and cultural factors driving, facilitating and inhibiting offshoring. Some companies (Royal Bank of Scotland, HBOS, Alliance and Leicester) have declared against offshoring and others (LloydsTSB, Esure, Powergen) have repatriated voice services following customer resistance. In sum, call centre offshoring represents a qualified 'race to the bottom'. If low cost was the sole factor determining location then China and countries with lower costs than India would be the preferred destinations. It is the ensemble of factors, including infrastructure and 'soft' skills, that provide the basis of comparison between places and which ensures that many call centre services will remain in the UK.

The implication is that unions should understand that offshoring is more contradictory for companies than is often acknowledged.[8] Identifying weaknesses in corporate strategy and service delivery does create opportunities. Nevertheless, variation in company policy means that the magnitude of the challenge facing unions differs. Evidently, differences in scale, in the size of proposed job loss, the timescale of redundancies, the likelihood of further offshoring and the nature of jobs (skill, complexity, back-office/call centre mix) to be migrated, all impact upon the power resources available to unions and the strategies and tactics adopted. Hence, a genuine TNC like HCBC, which can readily transfer operations within its global service delivery network, poses a more significant threat than do companies which pursue offshoring to a more limited scale.

Trade union responses in the UK

Nationalism and internationalism
The diverse approaches identified reflect not just the varied economic, political and sectoral contexts within which unions operate (Cumbers, 2004), but also their contrasting

traditions, structures, power resources and orientations. Both nationalist and competitive tendencies on the one hand, and internationalist and solidaristic behaviours on the other, are evident (Wills, 1998). At the extreme protectionist end of the spectrum is Lloyds Trade Union (LTU), a staff association unaffiliated to the TUC. In petitioning customers it cultivated nationalistic sentiments. Leaflets and stickers, emblazoned with Union Jacks, bore the slogan 'Keep Lloyds TSB jobs in Britain' and asked customers 'Happy to have your account managed in India?'. Its campaign against offshoring took the form of a roadshow with 'days of action' outside company premises where signatures were gathered for a mass petition.

Less overtly nationalistic was the Communication Workers' Union's (CWU) opposition to British Telecom's 'remote sourcing'. Their campaign centred on a large inflatable pink elephant which, the National Executive hoped, would become a widely recognised symbol of resistance to offshoring. Rejecting industrial action, the CWU prioritised media coverage, parading the inflatable outside major BT sites. Although officers from other unions insisted that this initiative flirted with nationalist protectionism, redolent of a 'British jobs for British workers' stance, the CWU retorted by re-affirming its opposition to racism, stating that its argument was with BT and not with Indian workers. To date, the CWU has refused to reach agreement with BT, arguing for the full repatriation of the jobs offshored. This stance effectively prevents initiatives being taken which could focus on BT's Indian service providers (HCL and Progeon). For the CWU, focusing on Indian workers would be tantamount to endorsing BT's offshoring project. What makes this response more questionable is HCL's purchase in 2003 of BT's Belfast call centres in the first instance of 'reverse offshoring'. The recent de-recognition of the CWU by HCL shows the company's willingness to exploit the union's failure to have formulated a strategic approach that included taking organising initiatives in both places.

In contrast, the most common position has been a formal internationalism, evident in the policies of the main finance sector unions (Amicus/Unifi). Whilst this has not always meant the dominance of 'progressive' over 'regressive localisms' (Castree et al., 2004), unions do acknowledge they must develop strategic responses, rather than making simplistic promises to members that offshoring can be completely halted or reversed. Unifi's 'globalisation charter' (2003) displays a pragmatism which seeks to work within the migration process, negotiating minimum guarantees on consultation and job security and the longer-term importance of union organisation in India.

Examples of union success

In three notable instances (at Prudential, Reality and Siemens) in contrasting sectors, campaigns by Amicus, USDAW and PCS respectively succeeded in wringing significant concessions from employers. From these cases it is possible to draw certain general lessons regarding union effectiveness which challenge the conventional wisdom that resistance to offshoring is futile.

In the Prudential, Amicus prevented the proposed closure of the Reading call centre, forcing the company to sign a 14-point agreement which included 'no compulsory redundancies' and a three-year job security package (Amicus-Prudential, 2002). The union's ability to draw upon several related power resources was central to success. A campaign led by workplace representatives fully involved the membership.

We set up a 'war cabinet' within our [Prudential] section, three or four lay reps, seconded reps, to decide what we wanted to do. We organised regular mass meetings, where we would report back. [At the first, attended by 700–800,] the general feeling was one of confrontation, 'Let's get on with this, why don't we walk out now?'. Certainly 60–70 per cent of the room were quite happy or prepared to walk out. (Interview, rep, 15 January 2004)

The 'bottom-up' campaign prepared the ground for industrial action by challenging the company's business case for offshoring and articulating employees' sense of injustice. Prudential's profitability and the Chief Executive's excessive pay award were contrasted with the dismissive treatment of the workforce. Since Prudential's negotiators knew that strike action was 'a serious, and not a hollow threat', the company retreated. Significantly, the leadership resolved the tension between protectionism and internationalism. They adamantly rejected racism and xenophobia, insisting that Indians had a right to employment on good conditions. Directing their campaign at the company rather than the competitive 'threat' from Indian workers, they developed the important argument that there is no necessary contradiction between fighting to defend jobs and communities in the UK and adopting an internationalist stance. The Prudential came to be widely regarded as a 'model campaign' against offshoring.

Equally important, but less well known, was union activity at the home shopping firm Reality, where impending strike action forced a confident employer to concede union demands for guarantees of job security at its call centres in the north-west of England. Having secretly established operations in Bangalore, Reality had refused to negotiate with USDAW. Following intense campaigning, USDAW balloted its members on strike action not just in the call centres but also in the warehouses which formed part of the bargaining unit. The overwhelming endorsement of the strike proposal (84 per cent) forced Reality to sign the 'Bangalore Agreement', by which the level of Indian employment was capped, no centre was to be closed and no one made compulsorily redundant. The union's lead negotiator was clear that it was the 'from the ground up approach' that delivered success. Throughout, USDAW repudiated attempts to portray the campaign in racist terms and denounced the attempted intervention of the fascist British National Party.

The third case is that of Siemens Business Services (SBS). Following its acquisition of the privatised National Savings Bank in 1999, the German multinational sought to cut costs and raise profitability by offshoring 250 jobs to Chennai in 2004. As a result of intense campaigning, PCS secured guarantees over compulsory redundancies and terms and conditions. Similar to the Prudential, the tenor and direction of the campaign were determined by principled leadership: 'We didn't want to see the government exploiting cheap labour at home and abroad, that was the key campaign message. But from the start we made sure it must not be a narrow British campaign and we did not divide workers.' (Interview, PCS-SBS Group President, 6 October 2006)

Alongside the defence of UK jobs, the union sought to establish workers' rights in India. After detailed negotiations, a comprehensive 'Framework agreement on global sourcing' was signed (PCS-SBS 2004), which included assurances over consultation, negotiation and redeployment. Schedule 8 ('Freedom of association and collective bargaining') was framed specifically with the intention of assisting in the extension of union recognition to the offshored activities. In 2006 SBS then demanded further offshoring. A lengthy campaign successfully exploited political sensitivities, due to the UK government's involvement in the decision-making process, and led to agreement with PCS (SBS-PCS, 2007). Although 240 posts were to be migrated, the terms of transfer make this the high-water mark of offshoring agreements to date. The Secretary to the Treasury imposed conditions on SBS, including a 'no compulsory redundancy' guarantee until 2014, no forced relocation, meaningful discussions over pay progression and reaffirmation of the Global Agreement. These improvements in job security and conditions were 'no mean achievement in these days of Globalisation' (PCS, 2007). Success was attributable largely to the enduring strength of workplace trade unionism, reflected in high levels of density (Glasgow 92 per cent, Durham 86 per cent, Blackpool 75 per cent), member participation, and government and management's understanding, on the basis of the union's record, that it could deliver industrial action.

Evaluating union responses

Unsurprisingly, unions have faced major difficulties when challenging offshoring programmes and resisting job loss. The profound asymmetry of power distribution in capitalist employment relations has always left unions weakened when confronted with redundancies and closures (Hyman, 1975, pp. 103–4). Arguably, 'globalisation' exacerbates vulnerability by removing whatever insulation had been gained from operating within national markets, and by adding layers of complexity through the widespread practice of outsourcing. To these factors must be added the longer-term consequences of the decline in union influence and the corroding ideological effects of globalisation. Consequently, the best that union campaigns have achieved have been 'no compulsory redundancy' agreements, such as between AXA and Amicus. Some, as between LloydsTSB and Unifi/Amicus, have fallen short of this minimum. In the worst cases, such as HSBC, global relocation has led to sizable involuntary redundancy.

However, the three cases demonstrate the importance of 'workers' willingness to act as one of the key power resources for unions' (Kelly, 1998, p. 52). They reinforce Martin's (1992, p. 1) observation that power is the 'ghost at the bargaining table'. At both Prudential and Reality the threat of industrial action helped produce favourable outcomes, and at SBS it was awareness of the union's preparedness to mobilise its members that proved influential. Of course, unions cannot automatically replicate these successful actions in every instance. Weak workplace organisation and low union density are serious problems. However, even though union activity has proved unable to prevent offshoring *in toto*, certain lessons from these cases have general applicability.

The evidence suggests that unions can draw upon diverse material and ideological resources and build multi-faceted campaigns. For the 'long haul', it is important to develop critiques of the business cases that accompany companies' offshoring proposals. Independent analysis of company accounts can help overcome passive acceptance of relocation strategies and embolden members as they contest corporate justifications for offshoring. Highlighting corporate greed remains a powerful 'counter-hegemonic' weapon. Unions can contest managerially-defined Corporate Social Responsibility (CSR) agendas, arguing for the inclusion of issues such as the social consequences of redundancy in regions of high unemployment in the UK and the nature of employment conditions in India. Even rhetorically, unions can capitalise on the refusal to extend to India the health and safety standards and worker and union rights that apply in the UK. Customer campaigns can also be utilised, although dangers exist that these might spill over into unacceptable protectionism. However, carefully formulated initiatives highlighting concerns over service quality and data security can be sources of strength, particularly in cases where companies criticise the performance of UK workers in order to justify offshoring (Amicus, 2005). Ultimately, though, media campaigns, political lobbying and canvassing customers are less likely to impact on corporate strategy. Whilst they can contribute to informing and activating union membership, they cannot substitute for it. Mobilised members are the unions' key 'local' resource. As the Prudential and Reality cases illustrate, employers made concessions only when disruption to their profitable phone-based business was imminent.

Union formation in India

Recent geographically-inspired work has correctly reasserted a sense of workers' international potential, but the cases highlighted have been largely from unionised TNCs (for example, Ravenswood, General Motors (Herod, 2001, 2002)), or involve international union solidarity (for example, Merseyside dockers (Castree 2000)). Of equal importance is the relative absence of collective organisation in sectors in the global South where offshoring has impacted (Kelly, 2002, p. 396; Castree et al., 2004, p. 210). In India, there is only the merest union presence in BPO. The central task is to organise the unorganised in conditions where unions face formidable difficulties.

Employers do pursue both 'exclusivist' and 'inclusivist' strategies, and evidence exists of companies 'excluding' employees identified as union members or troublesome in other ways. For instance, Remesh (2005, p. 17) recounts firms 'nipping out any sprouts of organisation' by forcing agents 'who are vocal against management decisions to quit . . . through carefully planned retrenchment mechanisms'. Several employees interviewed believed that if they were to 'come out' then they were likely to be disadvantaged in respect of promotion, appraisals and pay and would be allocated undesirable tasks or more demanding shifts. A smaller number thought they might be 'terminated' (dismissed). Employer opposition to unions is widespread, both amongst Indian third-party suppliers and the many TNCs with industrial relations histories of antipathy towards collective organisation. In addition, Nasscom publicly rejects trade unionism on grounds summarised by its President: 'In the BPO industry the grievances of the workers are addressed promptly and the wages are good so there is no need for unions . . .' (Rediff – India Abroad, 2005).

There is also truth in the view that because employees come from educated, middle class backgrounds and see themselves as professionals in a high status occupation, they will be indifferent to unions. In this regard, many employees certainly do express a desire to work for prestigious companies, particularly TNCs.

> They have spent a great deal on building the brand. Take IBM. There are youngsters in schools and colleges who say to themselves, 'I have to work for IBM'. They also want to work for Accenture or HCL. They have a dream destination and are already sold to that dream. To sell UNITES to them against that resource is difficult. (Interview, union officer, 20 November 2006)

Interviews confirm that many perceive unions to be inappropriate for the BPO industry. Powerful professional identities and the possibility of career advancement (for some) to team leader and middle management levels are further disincentives. We should also mention specifically the opportunities that BPO is providing for a layer of young women, for despite variation according to place, process and location, salaries are attractive in comparison to the alternatives available to these young graduates. Self-evidently, strong labour market conditions have implications for union organising. Whilst high demand places labour potentially in a strong bargaining position, contradictorily, attrition encourages employees to pursue individualised solutions to improving their position (better pay and conditions, promotion) at the expense of seeing the importance of engaging in a collective undertaking (Taylor et al., 2007). Such rapid industry growth rates and dramatic levels of 'churn' militate against attempts to establish clusters of union members in particular workplaces and companies.

Clearly, organising initiatives must take account of the salience of employer hostility and the powerful sense of professional identity. One UNITES officer emphasised: 'If we talk only about unionism, it's going to be a waste of time . . . we need to talk about a knowledge professionals' forum' (Interview, 11 September 2005). However, recognition of these difficulties does not make recruitment impossible, and arguments that companies have captured employees' 'hearts and minds' through cultural control strategies are overdrawn (Noronha and d'Cruz, 2006a). Many employees interviewed conveyed a sense of disillusionment that the stimulating, prestigious career promised is contradicted by the mundane realities of task performance and thwarted ambition. This gap between expectation and experience creates opportunities for UNITES in its attempts to give employees a voice. Tactically, it may be advantageous for UNITES to advance proposals that coincide with employer interests. In advocating for the fuller utilisation of employee capabilities, in suggesting career paths that mean not being stuck indefinitely on the phone, and in proposing skills development agendas, UNITES may engage with a wider constituency and gain legitimacy with employers who are concerned to reduce attrition. No matter how employer-friendly in tenor, the intention of such overtures, though, would be as much to persuade workers of the need for independent employee representation as the imperatives of work organisation will inevitably constrain opportunities for job enrichment, skill enhancement and career development. Significantly, however, in this regard certain employers have actually conceded that 'unions might help them control attrition' (Bhargava, 2005, pp. 12–13). Hence, in an unprecedented meeting with UNITES in November 2006, Nasscom's president suggested that unions might help reduce turnover and regulate the labour market (Interview, union officer, 19 November 2006).

Nevertheless, an aspiring union cannot avoid engagement with 'harder' employee concerns engendered by the experience of work and the employment relationship. Since offshored workflows tend to be an exaggerated form of the 'mass production model', quantitative and qualitative targets are imposed rigorously on Indian agents as firms strive to remove uncertainty from customer encounters and to minimise costs. In one study 76 per cent of managers believed that their employees had little or no discretion over work procedures (Batt et al., 2006, p. 16). One worker recounted: 'If you fail to meet your targets, you get put on a Personal Improvement Plan, fail again and you are on a second PIP, fail again and it's "Hasta la vista baby!"' (Interview, 11 September 2005). Significantly, Nasscom (2002, p. 52) itself has recognised this, referencing the problems of 'high-volume induced burnout'.

Distinctive characteristics of the particular place that India occupies in transnational servicing chains exacerbate the generic problems associated with high intensity call centre work. The synchronisation of work times with overseas customers' hours necessitates evening and night-working and is most pronounced for agents serving US customers. This should be seen as an exemplar of 'colonisation with time' to use Adam's (2002) phrase. It has enormous significance for employees, as evidenced by the fact that a majority of employees interviewed reported this as the most disliked aspect of their job. Nor should the discontents caused by lengthy travel-to-work times and company-organised transport arrangements be minimised, as illustrated by this complaint by a Bangalore agent: 'We actually log off at 10.30 a.m., but our cabs leave at 11.15 a.m., and we do not get home until 12.30–1.00 p.m. The Qualis (type of minibus) picks us up again at 1.15 a.m. The main reason people leave is the timings' (Interview, 20 February 2005). Work-time complaints are exacerbated by understaffing, the expectation that agents will work unpaid 'extra time', shift changes at short notice, and work schedules of 9–10 hours and 48-hour weeks, which are far from uncommon. This reminds us that the politics of production are also constituted in social contexts that extend beyond the workplace. Predictably, the consequences for family and social life are damaging, particularly for many women who are most affected by the conflicting demands of unsocial working hours, domestic responsibilities and the pressure of social mores.

Psychological tensions resulting from relentless call-flow are intensified by agents having to negotiate the contradictions between their culture, identity and aspirations, and the requirements of service provision for Western customers, symbolised in the conventions of 'locational masking', speaking with neutral accents (or emulating customers' dialects) and the use of Anglicised pseudonyms. In varied ways, then, customer encounters can add to work pressures. There are 'dignity at work' issues. Workers interviewed recounted instances where to have fallen out with team leaders was sufficient grounds for 'termination'.

Of growing importance are the restrictions imposed on employees' free movement. Employers are adopting multi-layered strategies to curb attrition and wage inflation, including 'non-poaching' pacts at city level (Nasscom, 2006). Employees can secure employment elsewhere only if they possess a 'leaving' or 'relieving' certificate, which employers may actually sometimes withhold. Top-down methods dominate companies' communication systems and no genuine procedures exist for processing employee grievances, other than cosmetic 'shock absorbing mechanisms' (Remesh, 2005, p. 18). There is thus a profound democratic deficit in Indian BPO and a powerful case can be made on ethical, moral and democratic grounds for employee representation.

In endeavouring to provide a voice for BPO employees UNITES has applied a key organising principle, namely understanding the importance of immersion in the experiences of those it is proposing to represent and then identifying and articulating the issues of most concern to them. Many matters of import for Indian workers cannot be anticipated by reference to UK experience. Hence, the issue which provided UNITES with its first tranche of recruits arose from the distinctive industry practice of providing transportation. Employees had long identified concerns over night-time safety, which tragically anticipated the December 2005 rape and murder of Prathibha Srikanth Murthy, a young woman employed by Hewlett Packard (HP) in Bangalore. She had been collected from home on the pretext of being driven to HP for her 2.30 a.m. shift. This horrific crime galvanised public opinion and brought to prominence issues such as corporate responsibility for the safety of, mainly women, employees. HP's CEO, Som Mittal, a member of Nasscom's Executive Council, insisted that it was an 'unfortunate incident' which had 'nothing to do with the company' (Johnson, 2005). The indifference exposed by these remarks provoked protests in which UNITES was prominent, participating in demonstrations, building meetings, organising condolences for Prathiba's family and contributing to debates on improving transportation safety, debates which detailed employers' responsibilities.

The record of UNITES's first year indicates genuine progress (UNITES, 2006). In organisational terms, it secured legal status through the Labour Commission in Karnataka, and has been granted 'Provisional Affiliation' to the Indian National TUC. It now has a structure and presence in six cities and claims 6000–7000 recruits, although paid membership is closer to 600–700 (Interview, officer, 19 November 2006). By early 2007 it had signed two collective agreements, although these were with small third-party operations. Perhaps more significantly, UNITES has recruited clusters of members in major Indian third-party companies and TNCs. The following example from the company GBK (pseudonym) based on interviews (17 November 2006) with two members provides excellent insight into the process of union formation.

I made contact with UNITES through an uncle who worked for a trade union. I went to a meeting and was really impressed about workers' rights and the problems the younger generation have and about how we can form a union for our own industry. I then went to the Mumbai conference and when I came back I started my one-to-one meetings with people, but when I was trying to talk to them about unions nobody was really interested because of the word 'union'. So I would say, this is not unions, this is an organisation, our organisation, 'Let's have some group meetings' but we never called them union meetings. I would take people to meetings and some joined, but then I left my company and joined GBK on the 3rd February. I was in a training batch of 50. (Member 1)

On the last day of February, or the first day of March, when we were supposed to get paid, we did not receive our salaries. It became a very big issue because there are many boys who come from different states and they are staying in rented accommodation or as paying guests. (Member 2)

And they had to pay their rent on the 1st or within a week. A few of the boys had been badly treated by their house owners and were forced to vacate. Management said they should borrow money from others, but because they were new to the city they didn't know anybody. Then we decided to go and speak to the management and the reason they gave was that cheques were lost, which is not a good reason for such a big company. So I spoke to my friend and he said we do not have to worry about anything because there is a union for IT professionals and we can all be one together and we can go together to management. So we all went back to the training manager who got very angry because he thought this was a kind of union formation and said, 'No point in talking to me, you won't be getting your salaries so you can all go back'. So the boys got even more angry and said 'Let's call the media'. I came in between them and tried to find someone from senior management to speak to. I told the boys we have an organisation, UNITES, which is working for us. They started asking, 'What is UNITES?', which is how we started spreading the news about UNITES. We then contacted the UNITES director who advised, 'Don't call the media people because we should sort this out ourselves. Let's be positive, not negative' and we said 'OK, let's all go together and have one voice'. So we all went to the HR Manager, but he was stalling. Then he saw we were all together and he said, 'I will talk to you now'. Then he said, 'Tomorrow you will be getting your cheques'. And the next day they did. This was the first win for UNITES. So a bit later I got the membership forms printed and people joined. We now have 110 GBK people in UNITES because they are knowing about the work we are doing and what our motive is. (Member 1)

Discussions at UNITES conferences and seminars, and interviews with officers and members, reveal that it is striving to become a forum that reflects the professional aspirations of its constituency. To this end, it understands that to declare itself prematurely as a full-blown trade union might leave it isolated from potential supporters and exposed to employer counter-mobilisation. Nevertheless, prevailing conditions of work and employment compel it to address questions of justice, fairness and rights over a range of issues. In all likelihood, future success will depend on UNITES's ability to straddle the contradictions between providing a network for BPO professionals, acting like a conventional trade union in the making and embracing elements of community unionism.

Conclusions

Even accounts ostensibly sympathetic to trade unionism suggest that 'the labour movement has been historically superseded' in the globalised networks of the information age (Castells, 1997, p. 360). This chapter has attempted to show that call centre 'globalisation' and the new international division of service labour should produce neither resignation nor compliance on the part of labour in the contrasting geographies.

In the UK, unions should be encouraged that, although facing real threats to members' jobs and under considerable pressure to make concessions, since relocation is not inevitable and labour not automatically substitutable, their position is often stronger than commonly believed. Notwithstanding the powerful cost reduction dynamic and the distance-shrinking technologies driving offshoring, call centre capital is only relatively footloose. The overall conclusion from the positive cases highlighted is that unions, where sufficiently organised, have certain power resources upon which they can draw. Key here is an ability to mobilise members and a capacity to act in ways that threaten to disrupt customer servicing in these lean and internationally-networked systems. Of course, not every union in every set of circumstances can mount an effective defence of jobs, and even in cases where unions have been able to secure concessions, these are temporary and contingent. In this regard, Prudential's renewed offshoring of 2006 is instructive (Seib, 2006). Nonetheless, certain generalisable lessons can be learned from successful campaigns.

Whilst the success of developments in India should not be exaggerated, the emergence of UNITES demonstrates that Indian BPO professionals are not simply more intensively exploited units of capital and the objects of corporate relocation strategies, but are active social and cultural participants who are constructing their own meanings of work. Overt opposition to managerial authority may be limited, but there is sufficient evidence of the workplace (and beyond) as contested terrain to challenge the 'totalising discourses' of cultural control (Noronha and d'Cruz, 2006b). Admittedly, the professionally-orientated graduate workforce may not be the most fertile soil for trade unionism, but the conditions of work and employment will continue to generate issues which will enable UNITES to engage with them. Some employee concerns are familiar to UK trade unions and are associated with the labour process of 'mass production', quantitative-driven call centres. Other concerns are the product of unique national (and more localised) characteristics and the profound 'democratic deficit' in Indian BPO. Essentially, the task facing UNITES is, to paraphrase Marx, the primitive accumulation of members.

Actions taken by UK unions can impact positively on UNITES's ability to establish an organised presence. For example, the PCS and UNITES could jointly pursue with SBS the extension of recognition to include employees on the offshored processes based in Chennai, as implied by the global agreement. Equally, the CWU could reverse its abstentionist stance and develop a strategy to organise the HCL workforce in Belfast, Noida and Chennai. The emergence of UNITES as a credible organisation is potentially an important development for UK unions attempting to extend union organisation to India, since they now have a focal point for organising initiatives. The mere existence of UNITES gestures towards union potential to mould geographical scale.

At HSBC, where UNITES claims members in its Bangalore and Hyderabad sites, support from Unite in the UK could encourage organising. This could involve financial and material assistance but should necessarily involve direct communications, the sharing of information, articulating common interests and exploring the possibilities of joint approaches to the company. Inviting UNITES to UK union conferences, and developing international awareness campaigns amongst members, are additional elementary steps. Some of the principles regarding direct worker contact and solidarity are pertinent (Waterman, 2001). Reciprocal delegations, where face-to-face meetings take place between employees of the same company or those who are part of the same supply chain, could be hugely significant. HSBC provides a fine example of Herod's (2001) insistence on multi-scalar organising. If the company grants union recognition in India it will undoubtedly be the outcome of union activities in different places and at different scales, membership growth in global sites, increased union influence in the UK, the development of international collaboration, and initiatives taken by Unite and other unions in myriad geographical locations coordinated through UNI (Union Network International) that are aimed at securing a global framework agreement.

It is encouraging that UNI, the Global Union Federation (GUF) responsible for business services and which initiated UNITES, has developed through its Offshoring Charter (UNI, 2006) an internationalist perspective which explicitly rejects 'arguments that could be construed as racist, xenophobic or protectionist'. Its principal objective is the achievement of Global Framework Agreements (GFAs) with TNCs, which simultaneously defend workers in the global North whilst advancing labour standards and workers' rights in the global South. However, effective international solidarity remains relatively limited and ITS members have tended to 'think and act in national terms' (Gallin, 2002, p.240). Yet the offshoring of interactive customer services is still in its infancy. Solidaristic actions taken at this early stage can have a major influence on future patterns of organisation and the geographies of resistance as unions seek to counter the global movements of capital. To paraphrase Marx, geographers have only interpreted the world, but the point is to change it.

Notes

1. India is now the second largest overseas investor in the UK. Increasingly, this includes 'reverse' call centre/business process migration as Indian companies operate facilities in the UK, such as First Source and HCL in Northern Ireland and Diligenta (a subsidiary of Tata Consultancy Services) in Peterborough.
2. Finance companies recognising unions/staff associations include Prudential, Barclays, Lloyds/TSB, Royal and Sun Alliance, Abbey, Zurich, HSBC, Aviva (partial recognition). Beyond financial services, companies that have offshored and which recognise unions include British Telecom, National Rail Enquiries, Thomas Cook, Reality (retail), Vertex, Capita and Siemens Business Services (outsourcers).
3. The Chief Executive of HSBC's unfavourable comparison of UK workers with Indian counterparts (see Taylor and Bain, 2005, p. 262) is only the most notorious example.
4. The Siemens case involved 'back-office' processes but is included here because of its salience for wider campaigns against offshoring, which most often embrace both voice and non-voice elements.

5. UNITES: the UK's largest manufacturing, technical and skilled employees' union; MSF: Manufacturing Science and Finance Union; UNIFI: a union for the finance industry; LTU: Lloyds TSB Group Union; ANGU: Abbey National Group Union; UFS: Union of Finance Staff; CWU: Communication Workers' Union; TSSA: Transport Salaried Staffs' Association; USDAW: Union of Shop, Distributive and Allied Workers; PCS: Public and Commercial Services Union; and UNISON: public service trade union.

6. The DTI's overview contains the frank admission that the industry 'witnessed a massive increase in the use of efficiency-enhancing technology in the mid-to-late 1990s, aimed at pushing through as many calls as possible' (2004b, p. 140). The report details the principal Computer Telephony Applications, such as caller-line identity, skills-based routing, touchtone IVR, call-blending and screen popping. CRM (Customer Relationship Management) software involving multi-screen navigation is also significant.

7. Turnover and attrition is likely to have moderated to some extent with the global financial crisis, as is common during periods of economic adversity.

8. The cultural and linguistic factors inhibiting the offshoring of 'voice' services apply far less to back-office processes, to the extent that in the longer term the call centre might represent a special case.

References

Adam, B. (2002), 'The gendered time politics of globalization: of shadowlands and elusive justice', *Feminist Review*, **70**, 3–29.

Amicus (2003), 'Finance update', mimeo, London: Amicus, September.

Amicus (2005), 'AXA ABS quality questionnaire report', mimeo, London: Amicus, October.

Amicus-Prudential (2002), 'Amicus-MSF and Prudential UK and Europe operations 14-point plan', London: Amicus, 4 November.

Baldry, C., P. Bain, P. Taylor, J. Hyman, D. Scholarios, A. Marks, A. Watson, K. Gilbert, G. Gall and D. Bunzel (2007), *The Meaning of Work in the New Economy*, Basingstoke: Palgrave Macmillan.

Batt, R., V. Doellgast, H. Kwon, M. Nopany, P. Nopany, and A. da Costa (2006), *The Indian Call Center Industry: National Benchmarking Report,* Ithaca, NY: Cornell University Press.

Bhargava, A. (2005), 'Exploited? No Empowered!', *Economic Times*, 17 January, pp. 12–13.

Callinicos, A. (2001), *Against the Third Way: An Anti-Capitalist Critique*, Oxford and Malden, MA: Polity Press and Blackwell.

Castells, M. (1997), *The Power of Identity*, Oxford: Basil Blackwell.

Castree, N. (2000), 'Geographic scale and grass-roots internationalism: the Liverpool Dock dispute, 1995–98', *Economic Geography*, **76** (3), 272–92.

Castree, N., N.M. Coe, K. Ward and M. Samers (2004), *Spaces of Work: Global Capitalism and Geographies of Labour*, Thousand Oaks, CA: Sage.

Cumbers, A. (2004), 'Embedded internationalisms: building transnational solidarity in the British and Norwegian trade union movements', *Antipode,* **36** (5), 829–50.

Das, G. (2002), *India Unbound: From Independence to the Global Information Age*, Delhi: Viking.

DTI (2004a), 'Trade and Investment White Paper, 2004: making globalisation a force for good', London: DTI, Cm 6278.

DTI (2004b), *The UK Contact Centre Industry: A Study*, London: Department of Trade and Industry.

Ellis, V. and P. Taylor (2006), '"You don't know what you've got till it's gone": re-contextualising the origins, development and impact of the call centre', *New Technology, Work and Employment*, **21** (2), 107–22.

Friedman, T.L. (2005), *The World is Flat: The Globalized World in the 21st Century*, London: Allen Lane.

Gallin, D. (2002), 'Labour as a global social force: past divisions and new tasks', in J. Harrod and R. O'Brien (eds), *Global Unions? Theory and Strategies of Organized Labour in the Global Political Economy*, London: Routledge, 235–50.

Harvey, D. (1982), *The Limits to Capital*, Oxford: Basil Blackwell.

Harvey, D. (1989), *The Condition of Postmodernity: An Enquiry into the Origins of Cultural Change*, Oxford: Basil Blackwell.

Herod, A. (2001), 'Labour internationalism and the contradictions of globalization: or, why the local is sometimes still important in a global economy', *Antipode*, **33** (3), 407–26.

Herod, A. (2002), 'Organizing globally, organizing locally: union spatial strategy in a global economy', in J. Harrod and R. O'Brien (eds), *Global Unions? Theory and Strategies of Organized Labour in the Global Political Economy*, London: Routledge, pp. 83–99.

Herod, A., J. Peck and J. Wills (2003), 'Geography and industrial relations', in P. Ackers and A. Wilkinson (eds), *Understanding Work and Employment: Industrial Relations in Transition*, Oxford: Oxford University Press, pp. 176–92.

Herod, A., A. Rainnie and S. McGrath-Champ (2007), 'Working space: why incorporating the geographical is central to theorizing work and employment practices', *Work, Employment and Society*, **21** (2), 247–64.

Hyman, R. (1975), *Industrial Relations: A Marxist Introduction*, London: Macmillan.

Johnson, T.A. (2005), 'BPO rape, murder clouds Bangalore', *The India Express*, 17 December, available at www.indianexpress.com/res/web/pIe/full_story.php?content_id=84118

Kelly, J. (1998), *Rethinking Industrial Relations: Mobilisation, Collectivism and Long Waves*, London: Routledge.

Kelly, P.F. (2002), 'Space of labour control: comparative perspectives from Southeast Asia', *Transactions of the Institute of British Geographers*, New Series **27** (4), 395–411.

Massey, D.B. (1984), *Spatial Divisions of Labour: Social Structures and the Geography of Production*, London: Macmillan.

McGrath-Champ, S. (2005), 'Globalization's challenge to labour: rescaling work and employment', *Economic and Industrial Democracy*, **26** (3), 323–34.

Martin, R. (1992), *Bargaining Power*, Oxford: Clarendon Press.

Miozzo, M. and M. Ramirez (2003), 'Services innovation and the transformation of work: the case of UK telecommunications', *New Technology, Work and Employment*, **17** (1), 62–79.

Mirchandani, K. (2004), 'Practices of global capital: gaps, cracks and ironies in transnational call centres in India', *Global Networks*, **4** (4), 355–73.

Moody, K. (1997), *Workers in a Lean World: Unions and the International Economy*, London: Verso.

Nasscom (2002), *IT Enabled Services: Background and Reference Resource*, New Delhi: Nasscom.

Nasscom (2003), *Strategic Review 2003: The IT Industry in India*, New Delhi: Nasscom.

Nasscom (2004), *Nasscom's Handbook for Indian ITES-BPO Industry: Background and Reference Resource – 2004*, New Delhi: Nasscom.

Nasscom (2005a), *Strategic Review 2005: The IT Industry in India*, New Delhi: Nasscom.

Nasscom (2005b), *Nasscom's Handbook for Indian ITES-BPO Industry: Background and Reference Resource – 2005*, New Delhi: Nasscom.

Nasscom (2006), *Strategic Review 2006: The IT Industry in India*, New Delhi: Nasscom.

Nasscom (2007), *Strategic Review 2007: The IT Industry in India*, New Delhi: Nasscom.

Nasscom-McKinsey (2005), *Nasscom-McKinsey 2005 Report: Extending India's Leadership of the Global IT and BPO Industries*, New Delhi: Nasscom-McKinsey.

Noronha, E. and P. d'Cruz (2006a), 'Organising call centre agents: emerging issues', *Economic and Political Weekly*, **41** (26), 2115–21.

Noronha, E. and P. d'Cruz (2006b) 'Being professional: organizational control in Indian call centres', *Social Science Computer Review*, **24** (3), 342–61.

PCS (2007), 'PCS-Siemens Update', no.140, London: Public and Commercial Services Union, 30 January.

Poster, W.R. (2007), 'Who's on the line? Indian call centre agents pose as Americans for US outsourced firms', *Industrial Relations*, **46** (2), 271–304.

Rainnie, A., A. Herod, and S. McGrath-Champ (2007), 'Spatialising industrial relations', *Industrial Relations Journal*, **38** (2), 102–18.

Rediff – India Abroad (2005), 'BPOs don't need unions: Karnik', *Rediff – India Abroad* 17 October, available at www.rediff.com/money/2005/oct/17bpo.htm.

Remesh, B.P. (2005), *Labour in Business Process Outsourcing: A Case Study of Call Centre Agents*, Noida: VV Giri National Labour Institute.

Richardson, R. and J.N. Marshall (1996), 'The growth of telephone call centres in peripheral areas of Britain: evidence from Tyne and Wear', *Area*, **28** (3), 308–17.

SBS-PCS (2007), 'Framework agreement on global sourcing', London: Public and Commercial Services Union, 9 November.

Seib, C. (2006), 'Pru prompts threat of strike vote with plan to move jobs to India', *The Times* [London], 27 April, p. 55.

Taylor, P. and P. Bain (1999), '"An assembly line in the head": work and employee relations in the call centre', *Industrial Relations Journal*, **30** (2), 101–17.

Taylor, P. and P. Bain (2003), *Call Centres in Scotland and Outsourced Competition from India*, Stirling: Scotecon.net.

Taylor, P. and P. Bain (2004), 'Call centre offshoring to India: the revenge of history?', *Labour and Industry*, **14** (3), 15–38.

Taylor, P. and P. Bain (2005), '"India calling to the far away towns": the call centre labour process and globalization', *Work, Employment and Society*, **19** (2), 261–82.

Taylor, P. and P. Bain (2006a), *An Investigation into the Offshoring of Financial Services Business Processes from Scotland to India*, Glasgow: Scottish Development International (SDI).

Taylor, P. and P. Bain (2006b), 'Work organisation and employee relations in Indian call centres', in J. Burgess and J. Connell (eds), *Developments in the Call Centre Industry: Analysis, Changes and Challenges*, Abingdon: Routledge, pp. 36–57.

Taylor, P. and P. Bain (2007), 'Reflections on the call centre: a reply to Glucksmann', *Work, Employment and Society*, **21** (2), 349–62.

Taylor, P., G. Gall, C. Baldry and P. Bain (2005), 'Striving under chaos: the effects of market turbulence and organizational flux on call centre work', in P. Stewart (ed.), *Employment, Trade Union Renewal and the Future of Work: The Experience of Work and Organizational Change*, Basingstoke: Macmillan, pp. 20–40.

Taylor, P., D. Scholarios, E. Noronha, and P. d'Cruz (2007), *Union Formation in Indian Call Centres/BPO: The Attitudes and Experiences of UNITES Members*, Bangalore: UNI/UNITES.

UNI (2006), *UNI's Offshoring Charter*, Nyon, Switzerland: UNI.

Unifi (2003), *Globalisation Charter: Unifi@work in HSBC*, August, Haywards Heath: Unifi.

UNITES (2006), *Review of UNITES @ One*, Bangalore: UNITES.

Waterman, P. (2001), *Globalization, Social Movements and the New Internationalisms*, London: Continuum.

Wills, J. (1998), 'Taking on the CosmoCorps? Experiments in transnational labor organization', *Economic Geography*, **74** (2), 111–30.

Wills, J. (2002), 'Bargaining for the space to organize in the global economy: a review of the Accor-IUF trade union rights agreement', *Review of International Political Economy*, **9** (4), 675–700.

PART 4

AFTERWORD

25 Workers, economies, geographies
Noel Castree

Introduction

In his magisterial book *Geographical Imaginations* Derek Gregory (1995) usefully distinguished between the discipline and the discourse of geography. He argued that whilst the two had more or less mapped onto each other for over a century, this was no longer the case. The so-called 'spatial turn' taken by several social sciences from the mid-1980s meant that the discourse of geography was now extending beyond the discipline of that name. Moreover, it was extending, most notably, into fields where questions of identity and difference were central preoccupations – such as cultural studies, political theory and large parts of sociology.

When Gregory was writing, labour geography was entering adolescence after a healthy infancy. It was still far too young a field to contribute meaningfully to any wider 'turn' towards questions geographical. But that is no longer the case. Today this now mature sub-discipline has engendered the kind of broader discourse that is a condition of possibility for this *Handbook* – a discourse that its editors and contributors seek to extend and enrich. In short, labour geography is no longer the preserve of professional geographers interested in issues of work and employment. However, unlike the discourse of geography to which Gregory referred in the mid-1990s, the discourse of labour geography involves fields where the economy is a central preoccupation (such as industrial relations and the sociology of work and employment). As such, it is part of a wider move in parts of both critical and mainstream social science to refocus analytical energies away from 'cultural issues' broadly defined – or at least to re-embed analysis of 'the cultural' firmly in 'the economic'.

It's worth noting that, far from lamenting the 'loss' of their field to fellow travellers in other disciplines, geographers who research labour issues celebrate the fact – and in some cases are chief architects of the field's spreading influence. The reason why is not hard to fathom. Labour geographers, myself included, want non-geographers to take the geographies of labour seriously. So, the greater the cross-disciplinary appeal of labour geography becomes, the more that issues of place, location, scale and the like will enjoy overdue salience in analyses of one of the most elemental acts of living: the act of work, whatever specific forms that act takes. Today, then, the sub-discipline of labour geography is happily relinquishing ownership of its objects of analysis and enjoining many others to deepen and broaden the discourse of labour geography.

I narrate the rise-and-rise of labour geography in terms of discipline and discourse for good reason. In this chapter I want to address those who have made the field what it is today and those new to it. In other words, if the sub-discipline of labour geography constitutes the 'heartland' of the wider discourse, then I want to say something to members of that sub-discipline as well as those outside it who, as relative newcomers, want to enrich the discourse. The contributors to this *Handbook* are from both these domains, as are its audience – the readers. My task, however, will be no mean feat. Seasoned labour geographers will expect more than a potted summary of their field's achievements to date. The less seasoned, meanwhile, will expect a lucid account of the field that does not presume too much lest it remain *terra incognita*. I have, I hope, struck an appropriate balance in what follows.

My argument in this Afterword is organised into three sections. I begin by doing what others before me have done (including the editors of this *Handbook*). In fairly simple terms, I explain how and why 'geography matters' to the study of labour issues. This recap done, the subsequent section is less celebratory in tone. It points to several areas where labour geography as currently constituted requires further development. This leads to a third and final main section where I try, in brief, to show the value of systematic thinking about the geographies of labour. A short conclusion then rounds off the chapter.

Workers and geographies that matter
This section covers some well-trodden ground. There are now several incisive surveys of labour geography available, authored by leading figures such as Andrew Herod, Don Mitchell, Jamie Peck and Jane Wills. However, I hope to summarise what's distinctive about labour geography in a way that's a little different from existing review essays. Accordingly, this section – intended for those curious to know more about labour geography – is complementary to the editors' contributions to this volume. I begin with some general observations about the field before offering more detail about how and why geography matters to workers (and why it should therefore matter to labour researchers at large). Those who consider themselves familiar with labour geography may want to skip ahead to the next section. But, then again, they may appreciate a bare-bones reminder of what the field is all about.

Origins, axioms, foci, theory and politics
'Labour geography' has its origins in the well-established sub-discipline of economic geography. The term is perhaps most closely associated with the already-mentioned Andy Herod, a geographer at the University of Georgia and co-editor of this book. In a programmatic mid-1990s essay in *Antipode: A Radical Journal of Geography*, Herod distinguished between 'labour geography' and a 'geography of labour'. Unlike the latter, where workers were regarded by both mainstream and radical economic geographers as just one aspect of firms' locational decision-making, for Herod labour geography was 'an effort to see the making of the economic geography of capitalism through the eyes of labour' (Herod, 1997, p. 3). Since he wrote these words, labour geography has become a significant sub-discipline within its parent subject. Its impressive rise to prominence has been achieved through fairly conventional but evidently effective means. Agenda-setting books – notably Peck's *Work*-Place (1995), Mitchell's (1996) *The Lie of the Land: Migrant Workers and the California Landscape*, Herod's (as editor) *Organizing the Landscape* (1998) and his single-authored *Labor Geographies* (2001) – began to codify the field and inspired others to sign up to the cause, not least the graduate students of these and other pioneering authors. The post-millennial publication of an advanced textbook – which I co-authored – testified to the field's maturity more than a decade after its inception (Castree et al., 2004). More recently still, as this *Handbook* attests, labour geography has caught the eye of labour researchers in fields such as industrial sociology, labour

and working class history, 'new working class studies' and the sociology of institutions (like trade unions and NGOs). Once again, Herod has been important here. He is argu- ably the most accomplished proselytiser for a wider discourse of labour geography in the Anglophone world. His lucid renditions of labour geography in the journals *Labour and Industry*, *International Labor and Working-Class History* and *Social Science History* (Herod, 2002, 2003a and 2003b) have undoubtedly helped to 'spread the word'. But non-geographers, including two of the editors of this volume, have played no small part in giving labour geography credibility outside its discipline of origin. And, from the per- spective of someone like myself, it always helps when such non-geographers invite labour geographers to write for their edited collections – examples being *New Working-Class Studies* (Russo and Linkon, 2005) and *Understanding Work and Employment* (Ackers and Wilkinson, 2001). Such invitations, after all, have exposed labour geography to a wider audience whilst challenging the persistent stereotype that geography is all about maps, capes or bays.

So much for the history of labour geography. What is its essential insight? Put simply, labour geographers take it as axiomatic that geography matters to workers whilst workers, conversely, matter to geography. I will unpack this seemingly simple statement in the next two sub-sections. For now, though, I can do no better than cite the words of Herod who, in *Labor Geographies*, offered the following observation:

> The production of space in particular ways is not only important for capital's ability to survive by enabling accumulation and the reproduction of capitalism itself, but it is also crucial for workers' abilities to survive and reproduce themselves. Just as capital does not exist in an aspatial world, neither does labor. The process of labor's self-reproduction (both biological and social) . . . must take place in particular geographical locations. Given this fact, it becomes clear that workers are likely to want to shape the economic landscape in ways that facilitate this self-reproduction. (Herod, 2001, p. 8)

For those unfamiliar with academic geography, there are some seemingly strange terms in here (such as 'the production of space', an apparent oxymoron). But Herod's key point is, I think, clear enough. Non-geographical approaches to understanding work and employment, he was arguing, miss some essential, rather than merely incidental, ele- ments of the story. As Herod et al. put it, the geography is more than simply 'background scenery' (2001, p. 176). Instead, it has a constitutive role to play in the drama of what happens to workers and what workers can do to alter the terms and conditions of their employment.

This insistence that 'the geographical factor' matters connects to a second signature feature of labour geography: namely, its focus on worker agency. In this it has a great deal in common with some of the already-mentioned fields where labour issues are central objects of analysis. Geography, as I will explain below, is made rather than given. In their research labour geographers have shown that, whilst workers are not the only actors who constitute the material landscapes of human existence, they play a very significant role. This is because they are fundamental to the functioning of the economies – capitalist and otherwise – that deliver life's essentials and luxuries to all of us. Only in situations where workers are subject to coercion do they have little or no agency. Accordingly, labour geographers have had little difficulty in showing that workers, adopting a range of tactics and strategies, are significant geographical actors. Workers have the capacity

– often stymied in practice to be sure – to realise their own geographical visions at home and abroad. When actualised, this capacity can have significant consequences not only for workers themselves but for other actors also, such as firms, states, families and communities. Because labour geographers see workers as active and capable agents, it is clear that they have had little truck with the analytical excesses of 1970s structuralism or the similar privileging (in spirit if not letter) of 'blind' social forces to be found in some uses of post-structural theory from the mid-1980s onwards.

My next summary comment about labour geography is this: it is a field with few, if any, analytical boundaries. This has become apparent over time and will become more apparent still as the discourse of labour geography expands further. In the early days, labour geographers had their eyes fixed firmly on paid employment and production issues. But it was inevitable that things could not remain this way. I say inevitable because the geographies of labour are potentially as many and varied as are workers themselves. Only an arbitrary fixation on one sort of work could place limits on the research agenda. For instance, even if one remains focused on capitalist economies – in which workers are fictitious commodities obliged to sell their labour power to those who own the means of production – it is clear that the geography does not begin and end at the sites of commodity production. One must also consider (for all economic sectors) the geographical structure of labour organising (union and non-union), the locally variable constitution of labour markets, the effects that journey-to-work options have on who gets what job where, and so on. The development of labour geography since the early 1990s confirms this insight. As Herod et al. (2001, p. 177) put it,

> [i]n recent years this stream of geographical research has evolved from an initial focus on the role of labour in industrial (re)location to embrace issues as diverse as the organization of domestic work, the social constitution of workplace identities, the governance of local labour markets and labour control regimes, and emergent forms of labour activism from the very local to the truly global.

Whether this expanding research agenda is a blessing or a curse is a matter of perspective.

Even though the research agenda of labour geographers has been expanding year-on-year, this is not true of the theoretical armoury these geographers deploy in their analyses. Most labour geographers do not subscribe to orthodox theories of economics, and nor (as I have already intimated) do they subscribe strongly (or exclusively) to 'cultural' approaches like post-modernism and post-structuralism – which is not to say that they ignore questions of discourse and representation. Instead, it is no exaggeration to say that most labour geographers operate with some version (often a mixture) of Marxian, feminist, anti-racist or institutionalist approaches to work and employment wherein power and social relations get central attention. Though the labour movement in the West suffered historic defeats through the 1970s and 1980s, Western academics (myself included) have not given up on analyses that challenge the supposed neoliberal orthodoxy of our times in its classed, gendered and racialised forms of expression. Labour geography illustrates well this enduring commitment to critical theory in which issues of systemic inequality loom large.

My final, related observation about labour geography concerns the politics of the field. By 'politics' I mean the values written into the research as well as labour geographers' understanding of what their research is for, practically speaking. Let me take each aspect in turn. Though there is by no means a party-line evident in either the sub-discipline or the discourse, I think it is fair to say (and have already intimated) that labour geography is dominated by figures of the Left. Within my own discipline this is certainly true: so-called 'critical human geographers' are the key players, without exception. For instance, Herod and Mitchell are both students of the Marxist geographer Neil Smith and in their work it is clear that a broadly 'pro-worker' stance is taken from the outset. This does not make them and like-minded labour analysts uncritical of any and all worker actions. Indeed, a key insight of Herod's publications is that workers often resort to geographically exclusionary activities that disadvantage fellow workers elsewhere (see Herod, 2001, chapter 6 for instance). This raises the interesting question of how one, as a 'critical' researcher, judges the propriety of such actions. But such important complications aside, a broad sympathy for the plight of working-class people distinguishes labour geography from the values written into many a human resource management text or business school analysis of corporate strategy. Labour geography, in short, is not simply about working people (and certainly not about managing them better), but is in some sense for them too.

It is, however, one thing to be 'for' workers epistemically: that is, to represent their actions and perspectives in print, in the seminar room or in the lecture theatre. But it is quite another to mobilise one's professional capacities and outputs as a researcher to enter the rough and tumble world of worker politics in activist mode. To my knowledge, and with a few exceptions (such as Jane Wills in her campaign research for low-paid workers in east London), labour geographers within and without the discipline of geography remain resolutely academic. That is to say, these analysts typically study labour issues without getting involved in them: their hands are 'clean' rather than 'dirty'. I present this as an observation rather than necessarily a problem. There are advantages to maintaining a separation between the researcher and the researched. But, equally, one can only change the world if one actively puts one's understanding of it to work in real situations. Herein lies a difficult choice for labour geographers, given their general sympathy for working-class people: to be a relatively 'objective analyst' or an activist-scholar? It is a choice to which I will return later. Nevertheless, in the meantime it is fair to say, I think, that in broad terms exceptions to the 'analyst only' mode of scholarship are more common amongst those who deploy the conceptual tools of labour geography and are situated in, for example, the academic discipline of industrial relations than it is amongst labour geographers who work within departments of geography. However, given that fields like industrial relations are much older and larger, this may be more a matter of geographers' shorter history of working with workers and thus their having fewer institutional connections with, say, labour unions than it is a lack of desire to do so.

Making space for geography

Having identified what I regard as the essentials of labour geography, let me now explore the 'geography' of the field in a bit more detail. In preparation for this chapter I re-read carefully the review essays on labour geography authored by Andy Herod and others. They are very good indeed. However, from the perspective of readers unfamiliar with human geographers' discourse, they are not always as helpful as they could be. Part of the problem is terminology. For instance, my colleague Kevin Ward (2007) recently published a programmatic piece on labour geography in the journal *Work, Employment and Society*. For him, the importance of geography to workers (and vice versa) is captured in the trio of concepts place, space and scale. Compare this with Herod et al. (2001), who focus on space, place and uneven geographical development in their review, or Mitchell (2005) who utilises the master concept of landscape. This use of varied geographical concepts (or varied meanings thereof) would be no problem if all these authors were talking about the same things, albeit using different names. But untutored or unwary readers might not be able to detect the signals in the noise. For this reason it is useful, I think, to go back to geographical basics. This sub-section does just that, as a prelude to the next one, in which I spell out in simple terms how and why geography matters to wage workers (though not only wage workers).

A useful starting point is the one that professional geographers began from a few decades ago. They asked themselves (and others): what forms does the 'denial of geography' take? This is a salient question because even today many social sciences – pre-eminently economics, notwithstanding the recent rise of 'geographical economics' – study the world as if geography is something that can be abstracted from unproblematically. Even in analyses of 'globalisation' – an eminently geographical phenomenon if ever there was one – one all too often finds a profound understanding of the geographical dimension eclipsed by hyperbolic reference to a 'borderless world', 'time-space compression' or the 'annihilation of space by time'.

To my mind, the denial of geography takes at least three forms in contemporary analyses of society, economy, politics and culture. The first, which has a very long pedigree, is the view that geography is all about 'context' but never substance. It is this view that allows social scientists to use concepts like 'economics', 'society' and the like as if their geographic integument can be bracketed out because it is deemed to be non-constitutive. The second mode of denying geography operates in a less ontological register. Reaching its apogee in Thomas Friedman's (2005) best-seller *The World is Flat*, this view suggests that neoliberal policy has been a global leveller, equalising previous peaks and troughs of development by removing barriers to investment, innovation and trade. Finally, the denial of geography operates even in research seemingly teeming with geographical ideas. The 'spatial turn' in parts of social science to which Gregory referred has proceeded apace since he published *Geographical Imaginations*. Today, many a post-colonial theorist or media studies researcher (for example) can be found using concepts such as 'location', 'site', 'region', 'locality' and 'spatiality', to name but a few. However, as Neil Smith and Cindi Katz (1993) observed presciently, much of this 'geography talk' is purely metaphorical. The literal referents that make the metaphors intelligible are not, they argued, at all self-evident, meaning that the real significance of geography is here being obscured even as it is apparently acknowledged.

So how can we begin to register that significance? The notion of space provides an answer, in part because it perhaps remains the signifier of choice among geographers keen to persuade others that what they study matters. However, 'space' has become a portmanteau term freighted with multiple meanings. It has also bred a family of what even some professional geographers regard as clumsy and pretentious-sounding collateral terms, such as 'spatialisation' and 'spatiality'. For these reasons I will deliberately cut a direct path through the semantic minefield. For me (and many geographers) space is not some metaphysical realm, nor is it simply the antonym of place (as in 'global versus local'). Instead, I use the term in a very simple, overarching sense to mean the territorial arrangement of things: that is, where they are and how their relative positioning influences how they relate (or not). So I am using the term 'space' in an abstract sense to summarise myriad concrete geographies; that is, as a way of saying that pretty much everything must – ontologically – have a foothold somewhere as a condition of existence and of being which is connected with other things (noting, too, that the connections themselves have concrete geographies).

Lest this seem banal, let me take things a bit further. Ontologically, there are at least two approaches to space. The lingering presence of the first of these explains why – regrettably – the three 'denials of geography' to which I have referred still have currency today. This first approach – going back to Kant, Descartes and Newton – sees space as *absolute*: as an empty container within which processes and events unfold. Against this view of space as an 'empty matrix' waiting to be filled there is a *relational* view dating back to Spinoza, Leibnitz and, in the twentieth century, A.N. Whitehead. Here space is seen as the product of social, economic, political and cultural processes, a product which, in turn, may modify those processes. So, in this relational view, space is regarded as a constitutive element of the world. This is not the same as saying that space has effects 'in and of itself'. This would be to flip from seeing space as the outcome of supposedly aspatial processes to an equally one-sided position called 'spatial fetishism' (Anderson, 1973). Against such antinomian thinking, the relational view asks us to see space as both medium and outcome, both consequence and cause. Space is – to use Foucault's (1998, p. 177) evocative phrase – 'laden with qualities' precisely because it is the expression and modifier of the myriad human practices that constitute life as we know it. Space, then, is part of human practice, not simply a God-given static arena or some equally inert social construct. It occupies a plane of immanence along with all the other elements of the world – it is coeval, not secondary.

From geography to geographies

I realise that these claims about space will be too abstract and insufficiently grounded for some readers. So let me conclude this first section of the essay by illustrating how and why space matters to workers by drawing upon some additional geographical concepts. Given the way I have defined space, these additional concepts exist at a lower level of abstraction and can readily be fleshed out empirically – as the concrete research of many labour geographers shows. For the sake of clarity (rather than comprehensiveness) I focus on just two concepts – namely place and scale. What connects both is their role in what Herod (1997) usefully termed labour's 'spatial fix'. Playing on David Harvey's (1982) key insight that capital restlessly seeks spatial fixes for latent problems of over-accumulation, Herod (1997, p. 3) argued that 'workers' abilities to produce and manipulate geographic space in particular ways is a potent form of social power'. This means that we have to understand geography to fully comprehend what happens to workers, as well as what potential and actual options workers have to respond to their situation. Workers do not simply use the existing landscapes in which they are embedded; they may also be able to make new ones that facilitate their future self-reproduction.

The first geographical aspect of workers' existence worth highlighting is place (or what is often called 'locality'). Place, in simple terms, is the material arena within which workers' everyday lives unfold. Places are socially produced and reproduced, not only by events endogenous to them but also by exogenous forces; as Doreen Massey (1995) has persistently argued, these days the global is in the local (and vice versa). This means that place residents have only partial control of the fortunes of their locality, though they are obliged to feel the full benefits or costs of changes not entirely of their making. Even if this historically specific argument did not apply, place has an ontological importance for workers because of the finite, fleshy and grounded nature of human existence. As Herod (2003a, p. 118) puts it,

> All workers . . . are spatially embedded, whether by kinship or familial ties, by residence, by work ties or by some other social [glue]. . . . Even migrant workers are dependent, no matter how ephemerally, upon the . . . relationships that tie them into the local labor markets of wherever they happen to be working. . . . Thus, whilst workers may escape particular geographical relationships . . ., they can never escape [place] . . . per se.

It is, however, one thing to assert that place matters to workers. It is another to show how. Two examples will suffice. First, because workers are place-based (ontologically speaking) and because (historically speaking) inter-place competition and uneven geographical development are endemic to capitalism, wage workers routinely structure their thoughts and actions around resolutely *local* goals. For instance, in an excellent study of a cross-class alliance in the town of Clarksburg, West Virginia, Herod (1991) shows why a workforce in an economically vulnerable locality chose to cooperate with local capitalists and the local state. This case study is one of many by labour geographers that explains why workers are not guilty of 'false consciousness' when they choose to think and act locally in competition with workforces elsewhere. Instead, workers' embeddedness in place is partly constitutive of their thought and practice.

Secondly, lest we fall into the trap of thinking that places are unified and homogeneous nodes within wider networks of global connectivity, geography also has constitutive effects on workers at the *intra-local* level. For instance, it has been observed that even in places with high unemployment rates, many jobs go unfilled. Non-geographical analyses have typically attributed this, variously, to a skills mismatch, disincentives built into the welfare system and so on. However, many labour geographers have shown that 'spatial mismatch' is often a key factor. This occurs where potential workers are unable to access 'local jobs' because those jobs are not spatially accessible for reasons of transport availability, transport cost, and associated lack of time or money to travel to and from work. Indeed, such is the importance of geography in these cases that worker campaigns have been organised around getting suitable transportation provided.

So much for place. What about geographical scale? Place (or the local) is, of course, itself a geographical scale. But this observation does not tell us much about the nature of scale. For many non-geographers, scale is assumed to be a mental device which we use to carve up the world into territorial pieces. Similarly, the notion of cartographic scale (as used in maps) refers to a relationship between a simplified representation and definite parcels of geographical space being re-presented. However, the problem with these purely epistemic approaches to scale is that they duck the ontological and historical question: at what real geographical scales are human affairs organised, why and with what effects? In this regard, as the Marxist geographers Neil Smith and Peter Taylor argued from the 1980s, geographical scales are those definite, but historically variable, territorial parcels within which certain events, processes and relations are organised. For instance, the 'national scale' is not given in nature, nor is it a mere mental convenience for delimiting global geography. Instead, it is a real and very consequential human construct that has emerged during the long post-Westphalian period of modern history. Likewise, in the realm of trade relations, the World Trade Organisation is a global-scale institution which enforces equally global rules that govern the cross-border traffic in commodities. So, then, geographical scales are made, unmade and remade: they are material, they are constructed and there is a politics to them.

Labour geographers have, in their research, focused a great deal on geographical scale, and not just the local scale. Since there is far too much research on this theme to summarise, I will once again make brief reference to a germinal study by Herod (reprinted in Herod, 2001, chapter 5). Herod explores the re-scaling of labour relations in the US docking industry during the 1960s in response to technological innovations (specifically containerisation) in that industry. As he outlines, from the 1950s containerisation had a profound effect on dockers and the geography of dock work worldwide. It not only destroyed tens of thousands of jobs but it also decoupled ship loading/unloading from the filling/unfilling of individual containers. In the US, this decoupling was influenced by the construction of the new interstate highway system which allowed long-haul trucks to serve major urban markets from far-distant ports. In this context, Herod's study examines the strategies of the New York-based east coast dockers' union (the International Longshoreman's Association). Initially opposed to a national wage agreement stretching from Maine to Texas, the ILA changed its tune when it realised that its highly paid members could fend off competition from distant southern ports by pushing for a national wage rate set at the New York level. The result, by the early 1970s, was a new geography of remuneration in the dock industry and a rescaling of employment relations intended to prevent employers playing off local dock workforces against one another in a 'race to the bottom'. Here, as Herod shows, new scales of solidarity were made and certain local differences erased as part of the politics of struggle with employers. In short, Herod demonstrates that geographical scale is malleable, a focus of struggle and manifestly consequential for the relevant parties.

Before I move on, just a final point about place and geographical scale. In both cases it is worth noting that discourse and representation have an important role to play. Though I have emphasised the ontological and material importance of place and scale, this does not mean that 'representation' is relegated to a position of secondary importance. A good deal of labour geographers' research illustrates this, focused as it is on how discourses about place and geographical scale can have real effects on workers, employers and regulatory actors. After all, if place and scale are the conditions and outcomes of various forms of human practice, then it becomes difficult to separate out the discursive and non-discursive aspects of that practice. They are two sides of the same coin.

Labour geography: a work in progress
Having summarised labour geography and saluted its achievements, I want now to offer some rather more critical comments on the field as currently constituted. If the previous section was aimed at those new to labour geography, this one will (I hope) interest seasoned practitioners. To return to the distinction I made in the introduction, if the sub-discipline of labour geography constitutes the heartland of the wider discourse then

I now want to argue that those outside the heartland should not mimic it too slavishly. Labour geography is now at the point when systematic questions about its content and aims need to be asked and answered. Having undergone a 'building phase' for well over a decade, the house of labour geography now needs to inspect all its rooms and consider whether there's foundation or merely extension work to be undertaken. If, as I've suggested, it is now a 'mature' field, then part of that maturity must surely be a capacity for auto-critique without rancour, recrimination or defensiveness.

I am not, I hasten to add, saying that labour geography has been resting on its laurels. Practitioners are certainly aware of new research frontiers. Herod's authoritative review essays indicate as much. For instance, in his *International Labour and Working-Class History* (2003a) piece, he devotes a whole section to considering how the fast-changing geography of capitalism is posing new analytical challenges to the field of labour geography. From my perspective, these analytical challenges include: understanding new transnational scales of labour organising, be they union-led or not; understanding the connections between trade union organising and new social movements at a variety of scales; understanding how the micro-geography of employment affects the use of and capacity to organise 'contingent workers', given the relative decline of 'core' jobs world-wide; comprehending how employers use geography – both materially and discursively – to control workforces in zones where capitalism has recently 'arrived'; understanding how geography factors into the so-called 'new slavery' prevalent in parts of the global South, as well the displacement of peasant populations; and figuring out how labour migrants' identities affect how and with whom they choose to represent their interests institutionally, and at what geographical scales. Given the fact that the global workforce (paid and unpaid) is larger than at any previous point in human history, given the diversity of this workforce, given that trade unions are no longer the principal institutions by which worker interests get represented, and given near-record numbers of transnational labour migrants, it is clear that the research focuses above (and doubtless others not listed) are in need of close attention.

However, I do not want to confine my comments about 'work still to be done' to the predictable claim that reality – in a capitalist world where change is the only constant – is always inevitably out-running the capacity of labour geographers to keep up with it. To my mind, the existing reviews of labour geography tend to limit their (gentle) criticisms of the field to precisely this claim, as if the field's intellectual capital is, in essence, still paying dividends. But there's another kind of critique that is both possible and desirable. If it is to progress beyond its long building phase and its recent related phase of 'outreach' to other fields of labour analysis, then labour geography arguably needs to do a stock-take of its assumptions, aims, normative values and similar fundamentals. It needs, in other words, to look not simply 'out there' at new real world developments but also internally at its own fixed capital of concepts and precepts to see if they are fit for purpose. Don Mitchell (2005), in his otherwise celebratory overview chapter on labour geography in *New Working-class Studies*, recognised this fact. 'Surprisingly,' he observes (2005, p. 95), 'and the merits of the new labor geography notwithstanding, geographers have shied away from developing a robust working-class geography . . . in all its . . . complexity'. In the same spirit as Mitchell I want now to suggest that the house of labour geography may require some structural attention before more newcomers within and beyond academic geography come to inhabit it. I have seven points to make in no particular order, all of them delivered rather telegraphically and crudely given the space constraints under which I am operating. I do not expect all readers will agree that my criticisms are valid.

The first relates to worker 'agency'. As I said earlier, the focus on agency – be the agency reactive or proactive – is a signature feature of both the discipline and discourse of labour geography. However, and paradoxically, agency is both under-theorised and under-specified in most labour geographers' analyses of it. The term 'agency', to my mind, has become a catch-all for any instance in which some group of workers undertake any sort of action on behalf of themselves or others. All too often labour geographers resort to reporting on the 'facts' of what some worker group has done as if reference to the empirical domain in-and-of-itself tells us all we need to know about 'agency'. What is missing is a discriminating grasp of worker agency that both informs and arises from a variety of empirical studies. Instead, one typically finds 'case studies' of working group X, Y or Z undertaking this or that action with varying degrees of success. Surely we need to set these case studies in context, both theoretically and comparatively, so that their full import can be registered. The current inability to satisfy this need has political as well as analytical consequences, since a failure to distinguish kinds of agency and their enabling/disabling conditions leads to an inability among analysts to say much sensible about worker strategy, normatively speaking. For all the talk by leading labour geographers that worker visions and actions are necessarily geographical, their failure to be systematic about forms of agency and how geography permits or proscribes them must be counted as a strategic weakness. The fact that this weakness exists is all the more peculiar given the rich theoretical resources for understanding agency bequeathed us by the likes of Giddens, Bourdieu and other social scientists.

My second point of criticism relates to labour migration. I am not talking about contemporary migration but, rather, migration as a topic of analysis in itself. The overwhelming majority of labour geographers focus on workers acting either in place (locally-cum-regionally) or in tandem with others at the national or international scales. The study of labour migrants, for all sorts of historical reasons, has tended to be undertaken by others – for instance, 'population geographers' or researchers in development studies. This has produced an unfortunate imbalance in labour geography, wherein questions of worker migration – such as, who goes where?, for what jobs?, for how long?, with what effects on source and destination zones?, and how, if at all, do labour migrants organise themselves collectively? – are not addressed with the vigour that questions relating to geographically 'fixed' workforces are. To be sure, there are some talented labour geographers working on migration issues (such as Vinay Gidwani). But they are in a minority. For both substantive and empirical reasons, the geographies of labour migration need to become a more integral aspect of the labour geographer's trade. If one looks at existing exemplar texts in labour geography – Mitchell's aside – migration barely warrants a mention, a state of affairs that ought to be rectified. The challenge is not only to understand labour migrations in their own right but also to integrate their analysis into those of other labour geographies, given that migration is never about migrants alone.

Third, it seems to me that the state constitutes a similar blind-spot in many labour geographers' analyses. Be it the capitalist state or otherwise, all too often this enormously important regulatory actor (and employer) is weakly thematised and theorised – appearing more often than not at the level of empirical reporting on this or that labour dispute, this or that strike, this or that worker defeat/victory. Given that labour geography has emerged from the critical wing of economic geography, this is ironic: geographical political economists like Neil Brenner, Kevin Ward, Martin Jones, Joe Painter, Mark Goodwin and Gordon Macleod (among several others) have done much to advance our theoretical understanding of how the state and its geographies are interconnected. Perhaps the supposed 'withdrawal' of the state in many Western countries has duped some labour geographers into thinking that the focus should now be on firms, communities and workers above all else. As always there are exceptions: for instance, Jamie Peck's research typically pays close attention to the dynamics of the capitalist state and Bob Jessop's contribution (as a non-geographer) to this book, likewise. But it seems to me that if we are to fully understand the agency of workers – apropos my first point – a full-blooded engagement with the state is a *sine qua non* of all analysis.

In the fourth place I would argue that labour geographers need to make greater efforts to synthesise the geographical concepts they deploy. I earlier made use of the trio of concepts of space, place and scale (as others before me have done) to illustrate the constitutive role of 'the geographic factor'. But I also observed that a panoply of geographic concepts is now in play, including notions of 'landscape', 'territory', and 'borderlands'. Whilst I recognise that there will never be complete unanimity as to the meaning and significance of these meta-terms, I nonetheless believe that more could be done to use them with precision, consistency and in a 'joined-up' way. Read as a whole, the published literature of labour geographers is almost bewildering when you consider the fact that different geographic terms are used differently by different authors and often in isolation. Given that we live in a world of interconnections, not discrete parts, a conceptually parsimonious labour geography should aim for clarity and connectivity of analysis. For instance, imagine an investigation of the biogeography of a southern Mexican peasant: embedded in one locality (or place), s/he then leaves to negotiate the US–Mexico border (a quite different geography) to then arrive in a quite other place (small town New Mexico) for illegal, low-paid employment so that remittances can be sent home. Ideally, an investigation of this case would be able to deploy notions of place and borderland (and no doubt scale) with precision and in relation as part of one person's real geographical itinerary.

In the fifth place, I agree with Mitchell (2005, p. 96) that too much labour geography fails to put '*working people* at the center of analysis'. What he means is that labour geography typically focuses on the employment aspect of a person's or group's life, as if this can be separated analytically and ontologically from their wider existence. Yet, as some labour geographers show in their work, the richest forms of analysis are holistic: they connect work and the reproductive sphere, class and non-class identities, local affairs and global forces and so on. In other words, the 'best' kind of labour geography analyses the geographies of employment and labour struggle not in and of themselves but as windows onto the wider question of how people live and seek to live. Such analyses are, admittedly, hard won. They demand of researchers extraordinarily close attention to the social and geographical tapestry (I use the metaphor advisedly) of workers' lives so they are represented as what they really are: lives of people who are far more than just 'workers'.

My sixth programmatic comment relates to what are called 'moral geographies'. All workers, knowingly or not, operate with moral geographies. These are sets of values relating to modes of conduct – potential and actual – towards other people, near and far. These values become articulated in the kinds of activities that labour geographers typically study – say a local campaign to save jobs or the formation of a new 'community union' to advance living-wage issues in a specific locality. However, these moral geographies are not, typically, the focus of labour geographers' analyses. This is unfortunate. Moral geographies matter because they are the ethical basis for all worker solidarity and division, at whatever geographical scale happens to interest us. Whether workers acknowledge the fact or not, these geographies of concern (or indifference) involve lay use of key ideas like 'justice', 'rights', 'responsibilities' and 'entitlements'. Individual workers, labour activists or groups thereof may have contradictory and complex moral geographies, different aspects of which do (or do not) come to the fore in particular situations. These deserve analysis in their own right, as do the critical issues of how these moral geographies are fashioned, how they might be changed, and to what ends. Currently, labour geographers tend to take moral geographies for granted: they underpin and animate campaigns and activities that are the focus of empirical research, but rarely become foci in their own right.

This brings me to my final point, which relates to the normative side of labour geography. In the previous section I noted both that labour geographers are typically figures of the Left and that they routinely face the dilemma of 'analysis versus intervention' in respect of the real world they study. I have no particular brief for labour geographers 'getting their hands dirty', though I certainly respect those who wish to do so. To my mind, there are advantages to maintaining critical distance between the researcher and the researched, and it is perfectly possible to be a Left academic without wishing to directly alter that which one studies. However, where I do think the politics of labour geography is weak is in relation to the areas of evaluation and policy. Evaluation entails passing justified judgements on some or all aspects of what particular workers do and do not do socially, geographically or temporally. Policy prescription, though formally separate from acts of evaluation, is potentially connected because critical evaluations may feed into definite suggestions for how things should or could be done differently. Though again I probably overgeneralise, it seems to me that labour geography is surprisingly uncritical of its objects of real world analysis and very light on policy prescription. Typically, case studies adopt a putatively 'neutral' stance on what a given group of workers have done/not done, or else an implicitly celebratory one. This is a way of saying that most published studies by labour geographers are long on analysis and very short on normative issues at the level of both principle and policy. One can be a 'friend' of labour by way of constructive or even withering critique. Labour geographers need to focus less on what workers actually do and spend at least as much time examining what they could or ought to do.

Joined-up geographies: identifying signals in the noise
In this final section I want to look ahead to the future of labour geography: to consider briefly 'what next?'. Over the next few years where might seasoned labour geographers go with their research, and what further 'value added' might newcomers derive from close inspection of, and engagement with, the field? As I suggested in the previous section, there are many possible answers to such a question, relating both to immediate real-world challenges and the intellectual architecture of the field. I choose here to follow

up two of the criticisms made of labour geography in the previous section: namely, those concerning the need for more holistic geographical analysis and the need for more normative theorising. This choice reflects my own interests and does not disbar other ways of taking labour geography forward. The reason I consider the two issues together is simple. A considered argument about what wage workers should do to improve their terms and conditions can only emerge from a systematic attempt to understand the geographies that actually affect them and which they may, in turn, influence.

Many non-geographers might find this a peculiar claim. Such is the enduring caricature of geography as an atheoretical 'fact-based' discipline that being 'systematic' about geography will strike many non-geographers as a contradiction in terms. As David Harvey (2001, p. 4) has put it, looking back at how geographers themselves once thought about geographical knowledge: 'The established doctrine was that the knowledge yielded by geographical inquiry was different from any other kind. You can't generalize about it, you can't be systematic about it. There are no geographical laws..[or] principles to which you can appeal'. Even though human geographers have clearly moved on from this so-called 'idiographic' position – labour geographers included – it is still abroad within the wider social science community. In order to challenge this position it is essential that efforts are made to be systematic about 'the geographical factor'. Otherwise, this factor gets reduced to an endless list of concrete phenomena, the nature and influence of which becomes a purely empirical case-by-case issue.

However, as I noted in the previous section, even labour geographers have not done all they might to be systematic about the nature and importance of geography. For instance, Herod's otherwise excellent reviews can, in my view, easily be (mis)read as challenging the idiographic position only by resorting to a highly formalised 'list' of how and why geography matters to workers. For instance, his *Labour and Industry* (2002) piece goes for the trio of uneven development, embeddedness and the remaking of scale. Whilst insightful as far as it goes, this trio appears almost as a set of generic categories with little or no necessary connection as part of a connected and differentiated reality. Much the same can be said of my reference to place and scale earlier in this chapter – they can easily be seen as meta-categories of a descriptive, almost ahistorical nature rather than substantive explanatory ones. To my mind the British labour geographer Jamie Gough is among the few to avoid formalism and genericism by default in identifying 'the geographical factor'. Yet his Marxist-inspired theoretical work (1991, 1992) does not loom large in most discussions of labour geography's achievements to date.[1]

In thinking systematically about workers and geography, my own starting point is the germinal (but decidedly non-geographical) debate about the 'post-socialist' Left between the philosophers Nancy Fraser, Iris Marion Young, Seyla Benhabib and Judith Butler. In a series of incisive publications in which they acted as interlocuters, all four sought to understand the constituencies and agendas of *fin-de-millénaire* Left politics, given the world-historic collapse of Communism from the late 1980s, the new dominance of 'free market capitalism', and the rise of identity politics worldwide (secular and otherwise). This quartet of authors, writing through the 1990s, took it as a given that we live in a 'more-than-capitalist world': that is, one that exceeds the logics and effects of capitalism but which nonetheless cannot be understood in abstraction from them either. Where they disagreed was on the salient issues, points of solidarity and markers of difference for a 'properly' Left political programme aimed at addressing myriad contemporary injustices.

Table 25.1 Positions in contemporary Left politics

	Affirmation	Transformation
Redistribution	*the liberal welfare state* surface reallocations of existing goods to existing groups; supports group differentiation; can generate misrecognition	*socialism* deep restructuring of relations of production; blurs group differentiation; can help remedy some forms of misrecognition
Recognition	*mainstream multiculturalism* Surface reallocations with respect to existing identities of existing groups; supports group different-iations	*deconstruction* deep restructuring of relations of recognition; destabilises group differentiation

Source: Fraser (1997, p. 27).

Since I do not have the space to rehearse the fine detail of the Fraser–Young–Benhabib–Butler debate, let me just point to the value of their attempt to think systematically about the post-socialist Left. Fraser's (1997) book *Justice Interruptus* is illustrative in an exemplary way because it is so relentlessly programmatic in its arguments. Following Max Horkheimer's famous lecture, Fraser distinguishes between 'symptomatic' and 'critical' thinking. For her, the former merely reflects the 'common sense' of the times, whilst the latter seeks to challenge it. Her critical interrogation of the 'post-socialist condition' involves challenging the putative divide between the social Left – preoccupied with class and wealth redistribution – and the cultural Left – preoccupied with identity and recognition. This does not involve assimilating economic justice issues into those of cultural justice (or vice versa). Instead, Fraser aims to think the problematics of class and non-class identity together.

Starting from an ideal-typical scenario in which both forms of injustice can be redressed alone, she shows how 'bivalent collectivities' – such as female workers – confound such neat separations. She then sets herself the task of 'developing a *critical theory of recognition . . . that defends only those versions of the cultural politics of dif-ference that can be coherently combined with the social politics of equality*' (1997, p. 12, emphasis added). This task is important because a seemingly intractable 'redistribution-recognition dilemma' can arise where achieving justice in one register creates or perpetu-ates injustice in another. Ameliorating this dilemma involves identifying those groups and situations in which the pursuit of cultural justice – for her, the proper recognition of 'despised' or denigrated identities – is relatively consistent with economic justice – for her, the redistribution of wealth to those relatively lacking in it. Fraser further distin-guishes between 'affirmative' (or reformist) measures and more 'transformative' ones in relation to both kinds of justice. This leads her to map out a matrix of political positions as shown in Table 25.1. On this basis Fraser concludes that a combination of socialism and deconstruction offers bivalent groups and individuals the best hope for justice. This means that either strategy alone is inadequate, as is the combination of liberal welfarism and multiculturalism.

I summarise Fraser not because she offers the last word on the aims and consitituencies of Left politics today. Instead, her work – along with that of Young, Benhabib and Butler – illustrates that in a more-than-capitalist world we need to understand Left politics synthetically: in a joined-up way where synergies and contradictions are identified and efforts made to connect potentially rival constituencies. The relevance of all this to labour geography is simultaneously strong and underdeveloped. It is strong because Fraser, Young, Benhabib and Butler recognise that workers' multiple subject-positions mean that class politics alone will never be enough to secure justice for them or their dependents. But it is also underdeveloped because, as I noted above, there is no geography in their debate. Systematicity about points of social similarity and difference is not matched with a systematicity about geographical connection and division. This renders the debate radically incomplete.

Ideally such systematic geographical thinking would be built into the kind of project that Fraser and others undertake from the very start (which is to say organically). It could occur both at the level of pure philosophy-cum-theory (not, in truth, most labour geographers' stock-in-trade) but also by learning from analysis and synthesis of actual worker actions (the former being a strength of labour geography). A glimpse of what this combined project might look like – in all its complexity – has been offered by Nancy Ettlinger and David Harvey in separate programmatic contributions.[2] Ettlinger's (2002) unjustly overlooked essay 'The difference that difference makes in the mobilization of workers' takes to heart Mitchell's plea that workers be seen as whole persons, not simply class subjects. It is ostensibly about labour internationalism, but on closer inspection it is really about worker organising at any geographical scale in conditions where 'difference' of one kind or another is a perennial organisational challenge. Ettlinger is concerned to understand the social and geographical circumstances in which certain workers decide (or not) to act alone (or in concert with others) in certain places at certain times. As she puts it:

> Any one individual has multiple allegiances, and these . . . may conflict . . . [P]eople defined along particular axes of difference, such as gender, age, ethnicity and so forth, have different circumstances in different contexts. . . . There are no necessary unifying themes along specific axes of difference because contexts and perspectives are diverse. . . . The main point is not to presume anything but to raise questions about [the] needs and goals of different people and groups. (Ettlinger, 2002, pp. 838–9).

This is very much a non-essentialist approach to worker identities and interests. Geography features here in an interesting way. Ettlinger goes beyond the idea that what she calls 'the friction of difference' is a function of distance – that is, the presumption that local worker identities and bonds will generally outweigh (always be 'thicker' than) attachments to distant strangers. She argues that in our restless world, in which long-distance migration is so evident, the friction of distance can be local too: workers may not engage in solidarity with erstwhile allies on their doorstep and may equally (as so-called 'transnational communities' reveal) feel strong bonds with distant others far away (expressed, for instance, through remittances). This has a number of normative implications for worker organising. First, the friction of difference has local and translocal geographies that are constitutive of it and which may compound the sort of social divisions and dilemmas that Fraser highlights. These divisive geographies need to be understood relationally as feeding off, and into, social divisions of gender, ethnicity, religion and so on. Second, to the extent that such divisions and dilemmas can be overcome, workers' geographical imaginations and practices may need to be challenged. Though competition and enmity between workforces within and between places can be highly functional to firms, it can also be challenged if workers are obliged to alter their sense of self, place and other. A topical example is the situation of a white, working-class male worker in a Western country – someone who might be disposed to see migrants as a 'threat' to their job and the cultural integrity of their homeplace. The question then is this: what sorts of local geographical practices and what sorts of new geographical knowledges might break down at least some boundaries and connect migrant and domestic workers in a common cause without losing sight of the socio-geographic differences that both groups might value? Because workers' sense of self, other and solidarity is at least partly constituted by geographies of fixity (place) and connection (via migration or long-distance labour organising), then this question becomes very important indeed for labour organising.

David Harvey's book *Justice, Nature and the Geography of Difference* (1996, chapters 1, 11 and 12) seeks, like Ettlinger's much briefer contribution, to integrate questions of geography into those regarding solidarity and difference. Though perhaps guilty of overlooking frictions of difference within places, his book nonetheless offers some useful resources for thinking systematically about the role of geography in worker identity, interests and organising. Following Raymond Williams, Harvey argues that the labour movement as a whole must always confront the challenge of connecting particular local identities, agendas and forms of struggle into wider fields of worker belonging and action. As Williams (1989, pp. 245, 115) put it, '[t]he unique and extraordinary character of working class self-organization has been . . . to make real what is at first sight the extraordinary claim that the defense and advancement of certain particular interests, properly brought together, are in fact the general interest'. This claim is 'at first sight extraordinary' because the barriers to worker cooperation can be quite formidable – not just those formally 'external' to the economic sphere, like the 'cultural' differences Nancy Fraser connects to class issues, but those 'internal' to the economic domain too. Among these, as a Marxist geographer, Harvey counts the ineluctable place-based aspects of all identities and politics, the latter's historically specific scaling (for example, national identities overlaying local ones, national trade unions overlaying local ones), and the capitalist logics of territorial competition and uneven geographical development. The challenge, then, is to strategise for ways to connect in non-antagonistic fashion what Williams called 'militant particularisms'. Failure to so strategise, Harvey argues, can play into the hands of a capitalist system where spatial divide-and-rule is a structural tendency.

In both organisational and normative terms Harvey is, therefore, against place-*bound* forms of worker politics. But for good reasons (ontological, logistical and moral) he is not against place-*based* worker politics. Indeed, he goes beyond the recognition that pretty much all worker politics is connected to what Kevin Cox (1998) has called people's 'space of dependence' – those on-the-doorstep zones where much of daily life is necessarily played out. Harvey proceeds from the fact that these spaces of dependence matter to people both materially and emotionally to argue for people's 'right to geographical difference'. Accordingly, Harvey's development of Williams's ideas defines a rich and complex problematic for analysis and politics overall. Geographical difference, he argues, must somehow be transcended and yet defended. This apparently contradictory formulation leads to the fundamental question: what sorts of geographical differences are worth protecting or nurturing, and how might forms of translocal solidarity relate to the amelioration or even elimination of certain existing geographical differences in identities, loyalties and interests?

I have no ready answer to this question. Like Fraser's non-geographical attempt to think through a Left politics where the dilemmas of economic and cultural justice are minimised, Harvey's work (like Ettlinger's) usefully prods us in important analytical and normative directions. Harvey asks us to examine how and why specific, territorially embedded working groups think and act in the ways they do, to what ends, and with what consequences for others near and far. But he also asks us to reflect critically on this. We should be prepared, he suggests, to argue against certain worker identities, interests and related forms of geographical politics because they actively ignore and even disadvantage working populations elsewhere. To play on Fraser's terms, Harvey asks us to consider how 'economic-geographical' and 'cultural-geographical' justice can best be combined – where the 'geography' in both cases may involve the elimination of certain territorial differences in identity, interests and material resources by workers acting transnationally as a class in order to create new, or protect certain other existing, forms of place-based difference.

In light of this brief discussion of Fraser's, Ettlinger's and Harvey's arguments it is, I hope, possible to discern an important set of research agendas of great political consequence for labour geographers. I have elsewhere termed these agendas the quest to understand 'contrapuntal geographies': that is, real and potential efforts to conjoin local place-based actors with distant others in order to serve common interests, yet doing so without sacrificing local commitments (Castree et al., 2007). I am not suggesting that these agendas have been entirely overlooked so far (for instance, Herod's already-mentioned reviews and his book *Labor Geographies* hint at them strongly). But I think few labour geographers have grappled with the complex and normatively dilemmatic issues that workers face even in apparently simple local-level campaigns or actions (or would face if they were more aware of the socio-geographic relations near and far that structure their thoughts and actions). A combination of more joined-up, holistic theorising with equally synthetic empirical research of actual worker imaginings and doings could yield substantial rewards for labour geographers. Not least, it would offer a genuinely realistic understanding of what workers do to improve their lot in life, as well as an informed basis for normative arguments about what workers should do in any given instance.

Conclusion

This chapter has tried to speak to two audiences. It has both summarised the nature and achievements of labour geography to date, and suggested some hitherto un- or under-researched issues in need of future attention. The great strength of – and also challenge for – labour geography is its large and encompassing research agenda. Though a seemingly 'specialist' field because it is about 'labour', the reality is that labour geography seeks to embed all sorts of workers and all sorts of employment in their geographical conditions of constraint and opportunity. Labour geography is thus never about labour alone (or, if it is, then only arbitrarily by analytical fiat). Properly speaking, it is about working people in a more-than-capitalist world that demands joined-up analysis of how economies, forms of work and their geographies co-constitute one another. Because meeting this demand is formidable, it is, alas, much more likely that labour geographers will settle for 'adding geography' to the analysis of this or that labour dispute, this or that programme of job restructuring, this or that campaign of transnational labour solidarity. We may, perhaps, have to accept the possibility that the socio-geographic complexities of workers' lives may ultimately outrun our capacities to make sense of them in more than a partial sense. It will be far easier to proliferate separate empirical case studies of worker actions in one or other dimension than to capture the totality of workers' lived geographies. The challenge for a robust labour geography – at the levels of description, explanation and normative judgement – is to set the bar high and think holistically about a world of connectivity and difference. After all, workers (like all of us) live joined-up lives (however disjointed they may look and feel). Analysis and politics needs to represent the tapestry of existence with its local/global, economic/non-economic threads, loops and stitches. To my mind, the discourse of labour geography will mature further only if its practitioners rise to this formidable challenge.

Notes

1. I am not sure why this is the case. Gough is a rigorous theorist but few labour geographers draw upon his conceptual work.
2. I would also mention much of Linda McDowell's (McDowell, 2003; Perrons et al., 2006) work here, with its acute sensibility to how class, gender and geography interweave.

References

Ackers, P. and A. Wilkinson (eds) (2001), *Understanding Work and Employment*, Oxford: Oxford University Press.

Anderson, J. (1973), 'Ideology in geography: an introduction', *Antipode*, **5** (3), 1–6.

Castree, N., N. Coe, K. Ward and M. Samers (2004), *Spaces of Work: Global Capitalism and Geographies of Labour*, London: Sage.

Castree, N., D. Featherstone and A. Herod (2007), 'Contrapuntal geographies: the politics of organising across difference', in K. Cox, M. Low and J. Robinson (eds), *Handbook of Political Geography*, London: Sage, pp. 305–21.

Cox, K. (1998), 'Spaces of dependence, spaces of engagement and the politics of scale, or: looking for local politics', *Political Geography*, **17** (1), 1–23.

Ettlinger, N. (2002), 'The difference that difference makes in the mobilization of workers', *International Journal of Urban and Regional Research*, **26** (4), 834–43.

Foucault, M. (1998), 'Different spaces', in M. Foucault, *Aesthetics: The Essential Works*, Vol. 2, London: Penguin, pp. 175–85.

Fraser, N. (1997), *Justice Interruptus*, New York: Routledge.

Friedman, T. (2005), *The World is Flat*, New York: Farrar, Straus and Giroux.

Gough, J. (1991), 'Structure, system and contradiction in the capitalist space economy', *Environment and Planning D: Society and Space*, **9**, 433–49.

Gough, J. (1992), 'Workers' competition, class relations and space', *Environment and Planning D: Society and Space*, **10**, 265–86.

Gregory, D. (1995), *Geographical Imaginations*, Oxford: Blackwell.

Harvey, D. (1982), *The Limits to Capital*, Oxford: Blackwell.

Harvey, D. (1996), *Justice, Nature and the Geography of Difference*, Oxford: Blackwell.

Harvey, D. (2001), *Spaces of Capital*, Edinburgh: Edinburgh University Press.

Herod, A. (1991), 'Local political practice in response to a manufacturing plant closure: how geography complicates class analysis', *Antipode*, **23** (4), 385–402.

Herod, A. (1997), 'From a geography of labor to a labor geography: labor's spatial fix and the geography of capitalism', *Antipode*, **29** (1), 1–31.

Herod, A. (ed.) (1998), *Organizing the Landscape: Geographical Perspectives on Labor Unionism*, Minneapolis, MN: University of Minnesota Press.

Herod, A. (2001), *Labor Geographies: Workers and the Landscapes of Capitalism*, New York: Guilford Press.

Herod, A. (2002), 'Towards a more productive engagement: industrial relations and economic geography meet', *Labour and Industry: A Journal of the Social and Economic Relations of Work*, **13** (2), 1–17.

Herod, A. (2003a), 'Workers, space, and labor geography', *International Labor and Working-Class History*, **64** (Fall), 112–38.

Herod, A. (2003b), 'Geographies of labor internationalism', *Social Science History*, **27** (4), 501–23.

Herod, A., J. Peck and J. Wills (2001), 'Geography and industrial relations', in P. Ackers and A. Wilkinson (eds), *Understanding Work and Employment*, Oxford: Oxford University Press, pp. 176–92.

Massey, D. (1995), 'The conceptualization of place', in D. Massey and P. Jess (eds), *A Place in the World?*, Oxford: Oxford University Press, pp. 46–79.

McDowell, L. (2003), *Redundant Masculinities: Employment Change and White Working Class Youth*, Oxford: Blackwell.

Mitchell, D. (1996), *The Lie of the Land: Migrant Workers and the California Landscape*, Minneapolis, MN: University of Minnesota Press.

Mitchell, D. (2005), 'Working-class geographies', in J. Russo and S.L. Linkon (eds), *New Working-Class Studies*, Ithaca, NY: Cornell University Press, pp. 78–97.

Peck, J. (1995), *Work-Place: The Social Regulation of Labor Markets*, New York: Guilford Press.

Perrons, D., C. Fagan, L. McDowell, K. Ray and K. Ward (eds) (2006), *Gender Divisions and Working Time in the New Economy*, Cheltenham, UK and Northampton, MA, USA: Edward Elgar.

Russo, J. and S.L. Linkon (eds) (2005), *New Working-Class Studies*, Ithaca, NY: Cornell University Press.

Smith, N. and C. Katz (1993), 'Grounding metaphor: towards a spatialized politics', in M. Keith and S. Pile (eds), *Place and the Politics of Identity*, London: Routledge, pp. 66–81.

Ward, K. (2007), 'Thinking geographically about work, employment and society', *Work, Employment and Society*, **21** (2), 265–76.

Williams, R. (1989), *Resources of Hope: Culture, Democracy, Socialism*, London: Verso.

Index